Major Problems in
Asian American History

MAJOR PROBLEMS IN AMERICAN HISTORY SERIES

GENERAL EDITOR
THOMAS G. PATERSON

Major Problems in
Asian American History

DOCUMENTS AND ESSAYS

EDITED BY
LON KURASHIGE
UNIVERSITY OF SOUTHERN CALIFORNIA

ALICE YANG MURRAY
UNIVERSITY OF CALIFORNIA, SANTA CRUZ

HOUGHTON MIFFLIN COMPANY
Boston   New York

Editor in Chief: Jean L. Woy
Senior Associate Editor: Frances Gay
Associate Project Editor: Reba Libby
Editorial Assistant: Kendra Johnson
Associate Production/Design Coordinator: Christine Gervais
Manufacturing Manager: Florence Cadran
Senior Marketing Manager: Sandra McGuire

Cover image: "Chinatown, San Francisco" by artist Jade Fon Woo (1911–1983) from the Michael D. Brown Collection.

Printed in the U.S.A.

Library of Congress Control Number: 2001131519

ISBN: 0-618-07734-0

123456789-CRS-06 05 04 03 02

Contents

C H A P T E R   5
Imperialism and Anti-Imperialism in the Early Twentieth Century
Page 138

CHAPTER 6

Orientalism and Popular Culture, 1904–1930s

Page 180

CHAPTER 7

Interethnic Tensions and Alliances in the 1920s and 1930s

Page 215

C H A P T E R   8
Americanization and the Second Generation, 1920–1942
Page 249

C H A P T E R   9
War, Race, and the Meaning of Citizenship, 1941–1988
Page 285

CHAPTER 10
Asian Americans and the Cold War, 1945–1965
Page 319

DOCUMENTS

C H A P T E R   1 3
Panethnicity, Asian American Activism, and Identity, 1965–2000
Page 419

Preface

The 2000 United States Census identified Asian Americans as the fastest growing racial population within the United States. The classification "Asian American," however, did not exist before the 1960s. During the social movements of the late 1960s and 1970s, students, activists, and scholars began using the term to promote solidarity among people of Asian ancestry. Programs in Asian American Studies, the first of which was founded in 1968, as well as early scholarship, often emphasized a common history of struggle by primarily Chinese and Japanese immigrants and their descendants. Beginning in the 1980s, research began to uncover the histories of Korean Americans, Filipino Americans, Southeast Asians, South Asians, Hawaiians, and mixed race individuals. More recent studies have analyzed the diversity within ethnic groups and sources of conflict and cooperation among Asian American groups and between them and other racialized peoples. Now Asian American history is a burgeoning field that includes studies on ethnicity, migration, politics, economy, work, class, legal issues, community, families, education, religion, gender, sexuality, and culture.

Major Problems in Asian American History invites readers to explore this dramatic growth in excellent scholarship through primary and secondary sources on the rich and diverse history of Asian Americans. Our main goal in this volume is to join the recent wave of new perspectives and scholarship about Asians in American history with the enduring insights of earlier studies. We are not simply showcasing new interpretations or preserving classic ones. Rather, we seek to bring old and new points of view into dialogue with each other to encourage a more comprehensive understanding of the past. And so it is that the reader will find essays written by Ronald Takaki, Sucheng Chan, Roger Daniels, and other prominent historians in the same volume as those of younger scholars such as Mae Ngai, Lili Kim, Rhacel Salazar Parrenas, and Sandhya Shukla. Likewise, essential documents, including the original Chinese Exclusion Act (1882) and General John L. DeWitt's rationale for Japanese American internment (1942), are put alongside less conventional primary sources, such as ethnic press articles and unpublished oral histories that offer intimate views of Asian American agency. And perhaps most important, we have stretched this diversity of documents and essays across the entire chronology of U.S. history, from the eighteenth to the twenty-first centuries.

In addition to expanding the boundaries of what is considered Asian American history, we took great pains to encourage the comparative analysis of ethnic groups and individual experiences, paying particular attention to the significance of gender, geographical region, and economic, political, and cultural conditions. In each chapter we have made it a point to include documents and essays that focus on a wide variety of Asian American experiences, while at the same time making sure that the leading groups and issues in the designated period remain central. We performed this same balancing act to ensure that the voices and experiences of women and Asian Americans outside the West Coast were validated and included in the understanding and analysis of the Asian American past. The book is also organized so that comparisons can be made across different time periods. For example, the post-1965 migrations highlighted in chapter 11 can be compared with the nineteenth century labor migrations addressed in chapter 2, while the examination of Asian American culture in chapter 14 can be read fruitfully against the earlier formations of "Orientalism" that are the subject of chapter 6. In a similar way, the recent Asian American political activism presented in chapter 13 can be compared with the early twentieth century political struggles for and against immigration exclusion at home and imperialism abroad, which are taken up by chapters 4 and 5, respectively.

The first half of the book (chapters 1–8), prepared by Lon Kurashige, covers the period from the late 1700s to America's entry into World War II in 1942. Early chapters explore the impact of U.S.–China trade relations and Japan's world status on perceptions of Asian immigrants. Students can compare the independence campaigns of Hawaiian, Filipino, Indian, and Korean nationalists. We examine the experiences of nineteenth century plantation workers, agricultural laborers, miners, prostitutes, and debates about the causes and consequences of the Chinese Exclusion Act of 1882. A chapter on early twentieth century popular culture includes a discussion of "yellow peril" imagery, representations of sexuality, and the tremendous influence of popular author Pearl S. Buck. Another chapter analyzes the cooperation manifested in interethnic and interracial marriages and the confrontations between Japanese immigrant farmers and Filipino immigrant laborers in the California Delta. We end the first half of the book with a chapter on the different memories of childhood and views of Americanization for second generation Asian Americans who came to age before the 1940s.

The second half of the book (chapters 9–15), prepared by Alice Yang Murray, examines the period during and after America's participation in World War II. Selections address debates about Japanese American cooperation or resistance with World War II internment policies and the impact of the "red scare" on Asian American labor movements and ethnic communities. We look at how Asian American communities have been transformed by the influx of new immigrants following the Immigration Act of 1965, the arrival of refugees from Southeast Asia and China, and changing relations with other racial groups, including conflict between African Americans and Korean immigrants during the Los Angeles riot of 1992. A chapter on pan-ethnic coalitions includes a celebration of 1960s "yellow power," a satire of sexism in the Asian American movement, a report on anti-Asian violence in the 1980s, criticism of Asian "settler privilege" by Hawaiian sovereignty activists, and the mobilization to defend Los Alamos scientist and "accused spy" Wen Ho Lee. A chapter on contemporary culture explores charges that Asian American authors have misrepresented Asian American culture and communities, the rise of Asian American hip-hop artists, and the influence of Hong Kong Cinema. We end the book with a discussion of globalization, the changing demography of Asian America, assaults on South Asian Americans after the attack on the World Trade Center on September 11, 2001, and the relationship between the growing multiracial population and traditional ethnic and racial communities.

This book follows the same general format as other volumes in the *Major Problems in American History* series. Each chapter includes a short introduction that provides general historical context, a selection of primary documents, and two to three essays. Headnotes to the document and essay sections explain the historical themes and interpretive issues in the selections. We provide a "Further Reading" list at the end of each chapter for students interested in additional research.

Many people have helped in the preparation of this volume. We are grateful to the colleagues who gave us thematic and bibliographic suggestions: Lili M. Kim, Hampshire College; Sandhya Shukla, Columbia University; Judy Yung, University of California at Santa Cruz; Xiaojian Zhao, University of California at Santa Barbara; Lori Pierce, Wabash University; Yong Chen, University of California at Irvine; Karen Leong, Arizona State University; Paul Spickard, University of California at Santa Barbara; K. Scott Wong, Williams College; Moon-Ho Jung, University of Washington; and Emily Lawsin, University of Michigan at Ann Arbor.

Alice Yang Murray thanks the Committee on Research at the University of California at Santa Cruz for funding research assistance by Hiroyuki Matsubara and Joel Wilson. The talented staff at Houghton Mifflin deserves special mention. We could never have completed this book without the editorial support of Jean Woy, Frances Gay, Martha Rogers, Reba Libby, Kendra Johnson, and Marcy Lunetta. We also received helpful advice from Thomas G. Paterson, editor of the Major Problems series. Finally, we express our deep gratitude to our families for their encouragement and understanding as we completed this book. Lon Kurashige thanks Anne Cherian Kurashige for her unfailing support and Cole and Reid Kurashige, who along with their mother, have made all the hard work put into this book worthwhile. Alice Yang Murray thanks Steve Murray and David Yang-Murray for inspiring and sustaining her throughout this project.

We welcome comments, suggestions, and criticisms from students and instructors so that we can continue to improve this book.

L.K
A.Y.M.

Major Problems in
Asian American History

Framing Asian American History

Studying Asians in American history is both an old and a new endeavor. It is old in that early in the twentieth century, social scientists began to document the experiences of Asian immigrants in seeking to explain their tumultuous impact on American society. Sociologists, who by profession were concerned with the negative effects of the nation's rapid urbanization, were especially interested in figuring out how such small numbers of these newcomers could provoke intense and widespread racial fears fueling anti-Asian massacres, immigration exclusions, prohibitions against Asians becoming American citizens, and other legal and extralegal actions designed to discourage Asian American settlement. Sociological works challenged the popular racism that viewed Asian immigrants as genetically unable to assimilate into a white culture and society. Instead of looking at the immigrants' racial characteristics, the sociologists examined the more malleable social and cultural conditions that had encouraged Asians to isolate themselves from the broader society. In this framework, anti-Asian racism was seen as resulting from the immigrants' refusal, for whatever reason, to become American.

A later generation of scholars dismissed the early sociological works, arguing that these were themselves racist because they placed the blame for anti-Asian racism on the victims rather than on the victimizers. This was an understandable critique from those who experienced the revolutionary changes in racial attitudes in the two decades after World War II. During this period, the "Oriental problem" in American history became reenvisioned as a problem of white supremacy. The shift in perspective influenced, and was influenced by, a handful of historians who became the first cohort in their profession to see Asian American issues as a significant part of the nation's past. But it was not until the civil rights movement transformed into black nationalist struggles in the late 1960s that the field of "Asian American history" became possible. Inspired by black radicals and intellectuals, Asian American activists, mostly college students from the second and third generations, created a new historical awareness that they believed was crucial for the liberation of Asian Americans as subjugated racial minorities. This new historical awareness underscored the centrality of anti-Asian racism and highlighted the struggles of Asian immigrants, and their descendants, to overcome their racial predicament. To Asian

American activists, the study of history, as well as the creation of ethnic identity, culture, and Asian American studies programs at colleges and universities, was an inextricably political act.

The growth of Asian American history as a field of scholarship was seeded by the political winds of the late 1960s and early 1970s. Activists became professional scholars, and their Ph.D. dissertations, books, journal articles, and teaching would produce the most robust scholarly attention that Asian Americans had ever received. By the 1990s Asian American studies had all the features of an academic discipline: researchers of Asian American history could publish findings in two scholarly jour-nals dedicated to their subject, join a professional organization complete with an annual conference, and teach in one of a sizable network of degree-granting pro-grams and departments through the nation.

Another sign of the professionalization of Asian American history was the expansion of new and competing perspectives. Such perspectives stem in part from focusing on different Asian American groups, but, in a more fundamental sense, they are rooted in different ways of framing the past and different understandings of how history works.

E S S A Y S

In the first essay, Roger Daniels, professor of history at the University of Cincinnati and an early and prominent historian of Asian American history, stresses the importance of race for understanding the neglect of Asian Americans in over a century of scholar-ship on American history. Daniels's contention that Asian Americans have been treated as "perpetual foreigners" is shared by the author of the second essay, Ronald Takaki, professor of ethnic studies at the University of California at Berkeley and a well-regarded expert on American race relations. Takaki maintains that racism is central to the experience of the many and diverse groups that have immigrated from Asia. To him, an "Asian American" is someone who has been, and will continue to have the potential to be, subjected to racial discrimination and abuse. In the third essay, Stanford University anthropologist Sylvia Yanagisako critiques Takaki's racial centrality thesis by focusing on the significance of gender, nationality, and class. While acknowledging the salience of race, she draws attention to key processes of social mobility, transnational kinship, and women's subordination that have been minimized, if not ignored, by the focus on racial domination.

In the fourth essay a team of University of California sociologists—Paul Ong, Edna Bonacich, and Lucie Cheng—add another layer of complexity to the racial cen-trality thesis. Their view of the historical context of Asian migration since 1965 looks beyond the effects of race and racism, focusing instead on the vast changes, or "restruc-turing," of global capitalism in the latter half of the twentieth century. Finally, in the fifth essay, legal scholar Bill Ong Hing, of the University of California at Davis, underscores the wide and meaningful diversity within contemporary Asian America. His view of Asian American identities as subjective and flexible, while not necessarily incompatible with the racial centrality thesis, makes it difficult to speak of a singular Asian American identity. The question thus becomes one of layers of identification. In what historical settings does an Asian American identity make sense? In what specific contexts do more local identities rooted in generation, occupation, national allegiance, language, gender, sexuality, region, or some other social distinction within the group take precedent over racial allegiance? What is the relationship between these two layers?

Neglect and Distortion of Asian Americans by American Historians

ROGER DANIELS

Two tiny, adjacent islands in New York harbor, Ellis Island and Liberty Island, are home to the twin icons of American immigration. Although the Statue of Liberty, erected on what was then called Bedloe's Island in 1886, was intended by its French donors to be a monument to republican liberty, its imposing presence in the harbor and Emma Lazarus's poem added to its American-designed pedestal, quickly transformed it. The creation, in 1892, of the immigrant reception center on nearby Ellis Island, merely underlined the statue's association with immigrants. The refurbishment of the Statue for its centennial and the creation of a magnificent museum of immigration on Ellis have made the association inescapable, even at a time of increasing nativism. There is, however, another island, which is an immigration icon of a different sort. If the statue—"The Lady" as many call her—and Ellis Island are primarily icons of welcome, of acceptance, that other island, three thousand miles to the west, is an icon of suspicion, of rejection.

Angel Island, whose 740 acres make it the largest island in San Francisco Bay, was associated with immigration for only thirty years, 1910–1940. During those years it was the site of the Angel Island Immigration Station, which was primarily a detention facility for Asian immigrants, mostly Chinese men and Japanese women. . . .

. . . The need for an immigration facility in San Francisco—and for a national immigration bureaucracy—was a direct result of anti-Chinese legislation, the Page Act of 1875 and the Chinese Exclusion Act of 1882. These were the first effective pieces of American restrictive immigration legislation; the latter was the hinge on which the legal history of immigration turned. With the passage of the exclusion act, the immigration of Chinese laborers was outlawed for ten years; this was renewed for another ten years in 1892, and the law was made "permanent" early in Theodore Roosevelt's administration. . . .

It is not possible, at this time, to be precise about the number of people who passed through Angel Island. Some workers connected with the state park have estimated it at 500,000 persons, but this figure is much too high. My own current guess is that perhaps 100,000 persons, mostly Asians, spent some time on the island. I assume that most of the nearly 60,000 Chinese who are recorded as entering the United States between 1910 and 1940 passed through Angel Island, as did most of the nearly 10,000 Chinese who were deported in those years. Although one sometimes gets the impression from the literature that most Chinese who attempted to enter were denied admission, this was not the case, but the rate of rejection was very high. Some 50,000 came in, while perhaps 9,000 were barred, a rejection rate of about one in six, many times larger than the rate for Ellis Island. To put these numbers into perspective, during the Angel Island years, Chinese who never constituted as much as 1 percent of the nation's foreign born, were more than 4 percent of those deported.

From Roger Daniels, "No Lamps Were Lit for Them: Angel Island and the Historiography of Asian American Immigration," *Journal of American Ethnic History,* 17: 1 (1997) pp. 10–17. Copyright © 1997 by Transaction Publishers. Used with permission.

Although the bulk of the literature about the island speaks chiefly if not exclusively about Chinese, many other nationalities, Asian and European, also passed through. The meal arrangements testify to this. There were two mess halls: one was used by Asian men, who ate from bare wooden tables. The other—called the "oil cloth dining room" because its tables were covered—was used, in separate seatings, by Europeans and Asian women. The separate seatings testified not only to the racist notions of the time but also to the different menus provided. The Asian food, served without bread and with less meat and potatoes, was prepared by Chinese American cooks.

Perhaps 6,000 of the Asians were Japanese women, most of them the so-called picture brides, who came to the United States as a result of the Gentlemen's Agreement of 1907–1908 until the immigration act of 1924 cut off all Japanese immigration. These were women who had been married by proxy, often to men they had never seen, although some were rejoining husbands. In addition, a significant number of Japanese Americans returning from schooling in Japan were held on the island, until their status could be verified. Added to these were some Koreans, people from India, other Asians, a relatively small number of European immigrants, and a few from the Caribbean. The photographic archives of the immigrant station include pictures of Turkish, Serbian, Russian, and Jamaican immigrants. Most of the non-Chinese immigrants spent relatively little time on the island. The Japanese women, the largest single non-Chinese group, were usually cleared in a matter of days: only when a husband failed to appear, or when there were medical problems, were these women kept for any appreciable length of time or sent back. . . .

Most of the Chinese women who were held on the island were attempting to enter as wives of merchants or American citizens. From 1906 through 1924 a yearly average of 150 alien Chinese wives were admitted; for six years after the 1924 immigration act—which barred all "aliens ineligible to citizenship"—no alien Chinese wives were admitted. A 1930 statue relaxed the ban by allowing the entrance of such wives as long as the marriage had taken place before 26 May 1924. From then until Pearl Harbor about 60 such women were admitted annually.

In 1970, thirty years after Angel Island had been abandoned by the INS, a California park ranger, Alexander Weiss noticed a large number of Chinese characters carved into the walls of what had been the detention barracks, and, although he could not read Chinese, he realized that they were of historical significance. Failing to interest his superiors, he got in touch with Professor George Araki of San Francisco State University, who helped generate interest among the local Asian Americans. Community pressure resulted, five years later, in a quarter of a million dollar appropriation from the California legislature for the preservation of the buildings.

The calligraphy on the walls, of course, were the now famous Angel Island poems. Their rediscovery—there had been some Chinese language versions published by former inmates but they had attracted little attention—sparked a flurry of interest and publication. The most important work to emerge was a book called *Island,* first published in 1980 by the doyen of the historians of Chinese America, Him Mark Lai, and two younger scholars, Genny Lim and Judy Yung. In addition to the English and Chinese texts of the 135 extant poems, with English annotations, the volume contains excerpts from a number of oral histories and a wonderful collection of pictures. These poems are all by men. There were apparently some by women, but if so, they were destroyed in the 1940 fire. All of the poems are sad, and some are also angry. An angry poem reads:

> . . . I hastened to cross the American ocean.
> How was I to know that the western barbarians had lost their hearts, and reason?
> With a hundred kinds of oppressive laws, they mistreat us Chinese.
> It is still not enough after being interrogated and investigated several times;
> We also have to have our chests examined while naked.
> Our countrymen suffer this treatment
> All because our country's power cannot yet expand.
> If there comes a day when China will be united,
> I will surely cut out the heart and bowels of the western barbarian.

The foregoing should explode any notion that Angel Island was, as is often stated, the Ellis Island of the West. It is, however, a useful symbol of the invidious ways in which the American government treated Asian immigrants between 1875 and 1965. Similar invidious treatment can be seen in the ways in which historians have written—and not written—about immigrants from Asia. That historiography has different rhythms than those which govern American history generally. Instead of paradigms about federalists and whigs, progressives and proponents of consensus, the historiography of Asian America may be divided into four phases or periods: a period of scorn, lasting into the 1920s; a period of benign neglect, lasting into the 1950s; and two contemporary and overlapping phases, one of increasing but limited awareness, and one of Asian American history, which have characterized the histori-ography in recent decades. I will people these periods with some representative his-torians and comment upon the current state and status of Asian American history.

For the era of scorn the chief exemplar must be Hubert Howe Bancroft (1832–1918), the premier historian of California. In the seventh volume of his *History of California* (1890) he wrote that the Chinese were "alien in every sense":

> The color of their skins, the repulsiveness of their features, their undersize of figure, their incomprehensible language, strange customs and heathen religion . . . conspired to set them apart.

In his memoirs, published in 1912, Bancroft laid out his notion of the proper place of Asians in American life: they should be what post-war Germans called *gastarbeiter,* guest workers.

"We want the Asiatic," he insisted, speaking about both Chinese and Japanese, "for our low-grade work, and when it is finished we want him to go home and stay there until we want him again." As long as they stayed in that role, Bancroft felt that Asian workers were superior to any of the alternatives. They were not "lazy and licentious" like the Negro in whom "the animal overbalances the mental." As for those from "the cesspools of Europe" the Chinese were not "anarchistic dirty and revengeful like the Italian, [nor] thieving and vermiparous like the Slav, or im-pudent and intermeddling like the Celt and Teuton," and, he was sure, they would not make love to American women or "breed a few million yellow piccaninnies for American citizenship."

Bancroft, of course, was a political reactionary, but the progressives of the early twentieth century were not significantly different when it came to Chinese and other Asians. Professor Woodrow Wilson, in his popular five-volume *History of the American People,* insisted that "Caucasian laborers could not compete with the Chinese . . . who, with their yellow skin and debasing habits of life, seemed to them hardly fellow men at all, but evil spirits rather." The progressive era socialist, Morris Hillquit, echoing Samuel Gompers, denounced Chinese and Japanese immigrants as "an inflowing horde of alien scabs." In 1922, a more sophisticated scholar, the Wisconsin-school labor economist Selig Perlman, could write that:

> The anti-Chinese agitation in California, culminating as it did in the Exclusion Law passed by Congress in 1882, was doubtless the most important single factor in the history of American labor, for without it the entire country might have been overrun by Mongolian labor and the labor movement might have become a conflict of races instead of one of classes.

To be sure, there were, even in the era of scorn, some "pro-Asian writers," most often those with an axe to grind, be it mercantile or business interests, religious conversion, or sometimes even what seemed to be a good Gilded Age solution to the servant problem. But there were also a few friendly scholars, the most important of whom was Mary Roberts Coolidge, whose *Chinese Immigration* (1909) was the first historical treatment of Chinese in America. Coolidge (1860–1945) was an establishment reform intellectual who espoused a multitude of causes. The daughter of a college professor—her second husband was related to the thirtieth president—she earned two degrees from Cornell and an 1896 Ph.D. from Stanford. She taught history in private schools and at Wellesley, and sociology at Stanford and Mills College. She was a Unitarian, a Republican, and a member of the American Indian Defense Association; her public service included terms on the California State Board of Education and as a trustee of the Pacific Colony for the Feeble-minded. In addition to *Chinese Immigration,* she wrote or co-authored nine other books on Indians, the woman question, and social work. Her work was as much an attack on the immigrant leaders of the anti-Chinese movement as it was a defense of the Chinese, whom she saw as hewers of wood and drawers of water essential to middle-class America.

The rise of immigration history as a professional discipline did little to change the picture. For the two founding fathers of professional immigration history, George Stephenson and Marcus Lee Hansen, that history was the story of European immigrants. Edith Abbott, in a book of documents compiled in 1924, expressed the prevailing professional attitude nicely, asserting that "the study of European immigration should not be complicated for the student by confusing it with the very different problems of Chinese and Japanese immigration." She thus failed to include in her "select documents" any of the fifteen statutes by which Chinese exclusion was effected. (Even today it is a rare textbook which describes, accurately, the 1882 Exclusion Act.)

Carl Wittke, in his 1940 survey, *We Who Built America,* did devote space to Asian immigration, but insisted that it was "but a brief and strange interlude in the general account of the great migrations to America." Similarly, Oscar Handlin, writing in an optimistic, consensual mode in 1957 about "American Minorities Today," recognized that "the Japanese and the Indians . . . had their share of grievances" and that "the postwar period brought no confidence that a remedy was within sight." And, seven years later, his student, Gunther Barth discovered that the

Chinese were not immigrants at all, but sojourners who, in essence, brought their troubles on themselves.

To be sure, some historians had already begun to probe the long history of anti-Asian discrimination, but they did so by focusing on the excluders rather than on the excluded. This line of inquiry was pioneered by Elmer C. Sandmeyer's painstaking 1939 monograph on the anti-Chinese movement; later laborers in this vineyard included Roger Daniels, Stuart Creighton Miller, Alexander Saxton, and Peter Irons, to name only a few. In fact, of the Euro-American scholars writing books about Asian Americans through the 1960s, only the sociologist Stanford M. Lyman paid much attention to the Asian Americans themselves.

Only a very few Asian Americans were in the professoriate prior to the 1980s, but there had been a few pioneer authors. Earliest was the immigrant, Yamoto Ichihashi, who had a chair at Stanford because the Japanese government subsidized it. His 1932 work, *Japanese in the United States,* was a work of both scholarship and apologetics, as Ichihashi was at great pains to conceal not only the subsidy which created his position but also the manipulative nature of the Japanese government's intervention in the lives of its subjects living in America. The first major scholarly work created by a native-born Asian American was the sociologist Rose Hum Lee's, *The Chinese in the United States of America* (1960), which, although marred by many factual errors, was an important and insightful advance. In 1967, Betty Lee Sung, who would not earn her doctorate in sociology for another sixteen years, published a popular history, *Mountain of Gold: The Story of the Chinese in America,* which gave, for the first time, an accurate picture of the breadth of the Chinese American experience.

The development of Asian American studies programs in the 1970s and 1980s has been accompanied by a growing preponderance of Asian Americans among the leading authorities in the still relatively new field. The prominence and authority of such scholars as Sucheng Chan, Gary Okihiro, and Ronald Takaki, all trained in traditional disciplines, provided role-models for younger academics. Symptomatic of the growing acceptance of the field, it is now possible for an American Historical Association member to check off Asian American as a specialization. (Incidently, one can also check African American, Chicano, and Minority, but NOT immigration.) Perhaps of more significance, there are now ongoing Asian American studies series at three university presses—Temple, Illinois, and Stanford—and two other presses, Washington and California, publish Asian American books regularly. The burgeoning Asian American historical literature is being produced, for the most part, by young Asian American scholars, many of them third or fourth generation Americans, although there are also a growing number of scholars who have had their initial training in Asia, primarily the People's Republic of China, and have earned Ph.D.s at American institutions.

And, yet, even a glance at mainstream scholarship demonstrates that the neglect of Asian Americans continues. I will give three examples of what I mean, two from general textbooks, and one from our own journal. In a 1991 textbook covering United States history for the period since 1945, William H. Chafe emphasizes that "gender, class and race constitute fundamental reference points for understanding," but he does not mention even one Asian American individual in some 500 pages of text. A footnote supposedly justifies this by noting that "while the category of race covers a wide range of ethnic backgrounds, this book focuses specifically on

Afro-Americans in highlighting the importance of race in American society." He also fails to discuss immigration or changes in immigration law.

Similarly, in the preface to their 1995 text, *Liberty, Equality, Power: A History of the American People,* six historians write: "We have tried not to ghettoize [sic] the concerns and achievements of women, Indians, African Americans, Hispanics, Asians, and other minorities." These are good intentions, but rarely fulfilled. For example, in James M. McPherson's chapter on "Reconstruction, 1863–1877," there is no discussion of a crucial episode in Asian American history, the deliberate exclusion of "Asians" from the eligible classes in the expanded version of the naturalization statute whose revision the 14th Amendment made necessary. This made Asians the only racial group who were "aliens ineligible to citizenship."

And, for my final example, in a paper first presented at the 17th International Congress of Historical Sciences in Madrid and then published in an Italian journal and in the *Journal of American Ethnic History,* five distinguished scholars of American immigration, writing an otherwise quite perceptive essay under the rubric of "The Invention of Ethnicity," managed not only to ignore Asian Americans in their text, but also did not cite even one work that focused on Asian Americans in their seventy-six footnotes, almost all of which were of a bibliographical nature. Each of these distinguished scholars is, of course, well aware of the presence of Asians in American society. How then can one account for such a glaring and seemingly deliberate omission? The answer is, I think, at least two-fold.

In the first place, the entire historiographical tradition of American immigration—a tradition which is less than eighty years old—has, until very recently, concentrated almost exclusively on Europeans. The first two generations of immigration historians, as we have seen, generally excluded Asians from the immigrant canon. Most contemporary immigration historians explicitly reject both nativism and racism, but tend, almost reflexively, to assume that, for most of the American past, the term "immigrant" and "European" were interchangeable.

In the second place, until quite recently Asians and their American-born descendants were but a minuscule portion of the total population. As late as 1940 there were only about a quarter million Asian Americans, or less than two-tenths of 1 percent (.0019) of the mainland population, and Asian immigration seemed permanently halted by restrictive immigration laws. Thus, historians and other students of our immigrant past became used to writing off Asian immigration as an aberration. In addition, many, perhaps most, of the historians of immigration wrote about their own ethnic groups, and, even today, all but a handful of historians of immigration are Euro-Americans with a propensity to identify the immigrant past with Europe.

Perhaps the literary scholar Lisa Lowe puts it best when she identifies a persistent motif in American culture, the notion that Asian Americans are "perpetual immigrants" or "foreigners within."

According to the 1990 census, close to two-thirds of the nearly seven million Asian Americans were immigrants and more than half of the immigrants had arrived in the previous decade. Almost none of these immigrants had come through Angel Island. Yet, for millions of Asian Americans, Angel Island is a symbol of what their predecessors and they have experienced, just as Ellis Island has been a symbol for descendants of German and Irish immigrants who came before Ellis existed, and it continues to be a symbol for immigrants, including Asian Americans, who have arrived since it closed as an immigrant reception center. Angel Island will never replace Ellis Island as the universal symbol of immigration, nor should it. But surely somewhere in the vast iconography of the American experience a place must be found for Angel Island.

The Centrality of Racism in Asian American History

RONALD TAKAKI

In Palolo Valley on the island of Oahu, Hawaii, where I lived as a child, my neighbors had names like Hamamoto, Kauhane, Wong, and Camara. Nearby, across the stream where we caught crayfish and roasted them over an open fire, there were Filipino and Puerto Rican families. Behind my house, Mrs. Alice Liu and her friends played mah-jongg late into the night, the clicking of the tiles lulling me to sleep. Next door to us the Miuras flew billowing and colorful carp kites on Japanese boys' day. I heard voices with different accents, different languages, and saw children of different colors. Together we went barefoot to school and played games like baseball and *jan ken po*. We spoke pidgin English. "Hey, da kind tako ono, you know," we would say, combining English, Japanese, and Hawaiian: "This octopus is delicious." As I grew up, I did not know why families representing such an array of nationalities from different shores were living together and sharing their cultures and a common language. My teachers and textbooks did not explain the diversity of our community or the sources of our unity. After graduation from high school, I attended a college in a midwestern town where I found myself invited to "dinners for foreign students" sponsored by local churches and clubs like the Rotary. I politely tried to explain to my kind hosts that I was not a "foreign student." My fellow students and even my professors would ask me how long I had been in America and where I had learned to speak English. "In this country," I would reply. And sometimes I would add: "I was born in America, and my family has been here for three generations."

Indeed, Asian Americans have been here for over 150 years. Resting on benches in Portsmouth Square in San Francisco's Chinatown, old men know their presence in America reaches far into the past. Wearing fedora hats, they wait for the chilly morning fog to lift; asked how long they have been in this country, they say: "Me longtime Californ'." Nearby, elderly Filipinos—*manongs*—point to the vacant lot where the aging International Hotel had once offered these retired farm workers a place to live out the rest of their lives. They remember the night the police came to evict them and the morning the bulldozers obliterated a part of their history. In the California desert town of El Centro, bearded and gray-haired men wearing turbans sit among the fallen leaves on the grounds of the Sikh temple. One of them describes what life was like in California decades ago: "In the early days it was hard. We had a hell of a time. We had a hell of a time. We had to face a lot of narrow mindedness."

Asian Americans are diverse, their roots reaching back to China, Japan Korea, the Philippines, India, Vietnam, Laos, and Cambodia. Many of them live in China-towns, the colorful streets filled with sidewalk vegetable stands and crowds of people carrying shopping bags; their communities are also called Little Tokyo, Koreatown, and Little Saigon. Asian Americans work in hot kitchens and bus tables in restaurants with elegant names like Jade Pagoda and Bombay Spice. In garment factories, Chinese and Korean women hunch over whirling sewing machines, their babies sleeping nearby on blankets. In the silicon Valley of California, rows and rows of Vietnamese and Laotian women serve as the eyes and hands of production assembly lines for computer chips. Tough Chinese gang members strut on Grant Avenue in San Francisco and Canal Street in New York's Chinatown. In La Crosse, Wisconsin, welfare-dependent Hmong sit and stare at the snowdrifts outside their windows. Holders of Ph.D.'s, Asian-American engineers do complex research in the laboratories of the high-technology industries along Route 128 in Massachusetts. Asian Americans seem to be ubiquitous on university campuses: they represent 11 percent of the students at Harvard, 10 percent at Princeton, 16 percent at Stanford, 21 percent at MIT, and 25 percent at the University of California at Berkeley. From Scarsdale to the Pacific Palisades, "Yappies"—"young Asian professionals"—drive BMWs, wear designer clothes, and congregate at continental restaurants; they read slick magazines like *AsiAm* and *Rice.* "I am Chinese," remarks Chester in David Hwang's play *Family Devotions.* "I live in Bel Air. I drive a Mercedes. I go to a private prep school. I must be Chinese." . . .

Yet very little is known about Asian Americans and their history. In fact, stereotypes and myths of Asians as aliens and foreigners are pervasive, in American society. During Lieutenant Colonel Oliver North's testimony before the joint House-Senate committee investigating the Iran-Contra scandal in 1987, co-chair Senator Daniel Inouye became the target of racial slurs: some of the telegrams and phone calls received by the committee told the senator he should "go home to Japan where he belonged." But Senator Inouye was born in the United States and had been awarded a Distinguished Service Cross for his valor as an American soldier during World War II. The belief that Americans do not include people with Asian ancestries is usually expressed more innocently, more casually. A white woman from New Jersey, for example, once raved to William Wong of the *Oakland Tribune* about a wonderful new Vietnamese restaurant in her town: "We were there the other night and we were the only Americans there." Wong noted with regret: "She probably meant the only white people."

But her remark reveals a widely shared assumption in American culture—one that reflects and is reinforced by a narrow view of American history. Many existing history books give Asian Americans only passing notice or overlook them altogether. "When one hears Americans tell of the immigrants who built this nation," Congressman Norman Mineta of California recently observed, "one is often led to believe that all our forebearers came from Europe. When one hears stories about the pioneers going West to shape the land, the Asian immigrant is rarely mentioned." . . .

We need to "re-vision" history to include Asians in the history of America. . . . Their stories belong to our country's history and need to be recorded in our history books, for they reflect the making of America as a nation of immigrants, as a place where men and women came to find a new beginning. . . . But, coming here from

Asia, many of America's immigrants found they were not allowed to feel at home in the United States, and even their grandchildren and great-grandchildren still find they are not viewed and accepted as Americans. "We feel that we're a guest in someone else's house," said third-generation Ron Wakabayashi, National Director of the Japanese American Citizens League, "that we can never really relax and put our feet on the table."

Behind Wakabayashi's complaint is the question, Why have Asian Americans been viewed and treated as outsiders? In his essay "The Stranger," sociologist Georg Simmel develops a theory, based on the experiences of Jews, to explain the discrimination and estrangement experienced by a group entering another society. Not belonging in the new place initially, the intruders bring qualities that are not indigenous. Not bound by roots to the new place, they are in a state of detachment, viewed as clannish, rigidly attached to their old country and their old culture. Their "strangeness" stands out more sharply as they settle down in the new land and become traders and merchants, for they still lack organic and established ties of kinship and locality. What is stressed in the host society is not the individuality of the newcomers but their alien origin, the qualities they share with one another as "strangers."

While Simmel's theory is heuristic and insightful for the study of Asian Americans, it needs to be grounded in history—the particularities of time and place. What transformed Asians into "strangers" in America was not simply their migration to a foreign land and their lack of indigenous and organic ties to American society, but also their point of origin and their specific reception. Their experiences here, as they turned out in historical reality, were profoundly different from the experiences of European immigrants. To be sure, the immigrants who crossed the Atlantic Ocean suffered hardships and anguish. As historian John Higham has described so powerfully in *Strangers in the Land,* the Italians, Jews, Irish, and other European-immigrant groups were victims of labor exploitation, social ostracism, and the sharp barbs of intolerant American nativism. Nevertheless, immigrants of European ancestry had certain advantages in America. The promise of this new world for them, as F. Scott Fitzgerald portrayed it, was mythic: here an individual could remake himself— Gatz could become Gatsby. They could give themselves new identities by changing their names as did Doris Kapplehoff to Doris Day, Bernie Schwartz to Tony Curtis, Issur Danielovitch to Kirk Douglas, and Edmund Marcizewski to Ed Muskie. "America represented a new life, new hope, new perspective," observed J. N. Hook in his book *Family Names.* "Why not enter it with a new name, an 'American' name that would have no association with the life forever left behind." A new "American" name also opened the way for economic opportunities. "Some immigrants believed, rightly in some instances, that their chances for material success would be improved if their name did not betray their origins." Others became "Americans" mainly by shedding their past, their ethnicity—the language, customs, dress, and culture of the old country. Physically indistinguishable from old-stock whites in America, they were able to blend into the society of their adopted country.

Asian immigrants could not transform themselves as felicitously, for they had come "from a different shore." In the present study, the term "shore" has multiple meanings. These men and women came from Asia across the Pacific rather than from Europe across the Atlantic. They brought Asian cultures rather than the traditions and ideas originating in the Greco-Roman world. Moreover, they had qualities they could not change or hide—the shape of their eyes, the color of their hair, the complexion of their skin. They were subjected not only to cultural prejudice, or ethnocentrism, but also racism. They wore what University of Chicago sociologist Robert E. Park termed a "racial uniform." Unlike the Irish and other groups from Europe, Asian immigrants could not become "mere individuals, indistinguishable in the cosmopolitan mass of the population." Regardless of their personal merits, they sadly discovered, they could not gain acceptance in the larger society. They were judged not by the content of their character but by their complexion. "The trouble is not with the Japanese mind but with the Japanese skin," wrote Park as he observed American-white attitudes in 1913. "The Jap is not the right color."

"Color" in America operated within an economic context. Asian immigrants came here to meet demands for labor—plantation workers, railroad crews, miners, factory operatives, cannery workers, and farm laborers. Employers developed a dual-wage system to pay Asian laborers less than white workers and pitted the groups against each other in order to depress wages for both. "Ethnic antagonism"—to use Edna Bonacich's phrase—led white laborers to demand the restriction of Asian workers already here in a segregated labor market of low-wage jobs and the exclusion of future Asian immigrants. Thus the class interests of white capital as well as white labor needed Asians as "strangers."

Pushed out of competition for employment by racial discrimination and white working-class hostility, many Asian immigrants became shopkeepers, merchants, and small businessmen. "There wasn't any other opportunity open to the Chinese," explained the son of a Chinese storekeeper. "Probably opening a store was one of the few things that they could do other than opening a laundry." Self-employment was not an Asian "cultural trait" or an occupation peculiar to "strangers" but a means of survival, a response to racial discrimination and exclusion in the labor market. The early Chinese and Japanese immigrants had been peasants in their home countries. Excluded from employment in the general economy, they *became* shopkeepers and ethnic enterprisers. They also developed their own separate commercial enclaves, which served as an economic basis for ethnic solidarity, and their business and cultural separateness in turn reinforced both their image and condition as "strangers."

Unlike European immigrants, Asians were also victimized by the institutionalized racial discrimination of public policies. The Chinese Exclusion Act of 1882 singled out the Chinese on a racial basis, and the National Origins Act of 1924 totally prohibited Japanese immigration while permitting the annual entry of 17,853 from Ireland, 5,802 from Italy, and 6,524 from Poland. Furthermore, the 1924 law supported the formation of families in European-immigrant communities, allowing European-immigrant men to return to their homelands and bring wives back to the United States. Their wives were accorded nonquota status, that is, there were no limits to the number of European women who could come here as wives. The law had the very opposite effect on Asian-immigrant communities. Seeking to prevent the development of Asian families here, it barred the entry of women from China, Japan, Korea, and India. Even U.S. citizens could not bring Asian wives into the country, for the latter were classified as "aliens ineligible to citizenship" and hence inadmissible. While the 1924 law did not apply to Filipino immigration (because the Philippines was a territory of the United States), the Tydings-McDuffie Act of

1934 provided for the independence of the Philippines and limited Filipino immigration to fifty persons a year.

The laws not only determined who could come to the United States but also who could become citizens. Decades before Asian immigration had even begun, this country had already defined by law the complexion of its citizens. The Naturalization Law of 1790 had specified that naturalized citizenship was to be reserved for "whites." This law remained in effect until 1952. Though immigrants from countries like Ireland and Italy experienced discrimination and nativist reactions, they nonetheless could become citizens of the United States. Citizenship is a prerequisite for suffrage—political power essential for groups to defend and advance their rights and interests. Unlike their European counterparts, Asian immigrants were not permitted to exercise power through the ballot and their own Tammany Halls. As "aliens ineligible to citizenship," they were also prohibited by the laws of many states from land ownership—the condition Frederick Jackson Turner celebrated as the foundation of democracy in America. One of the laws went even further. The 1922 Cable Act provided that any American woman who married "an alien ineligible to citizenship shall cease to be a citizen of the United States." . . .

But the most terrible and tragic insurance of this difference occurred during World War II. Setting aside the Constitution of the United States, President Franklin. D. Roosevelt issued Executive Order 9066, which targeted Japanese Americans for special persecution and deprived them of their rights of due process and equal protection of the law. Unlike German Americans and Italian Americans, Japanese Americans were incarcerated in internment camps by the federal government. Even possession of U.S. citizenship did not protect rights and liberties guaranteed by the Constitution: two thirds of the 120,000 internees were American citizens by birth.

Behind state policy lay a powerful traditional vision of America as a "homogeneous" nation. In a sermon given aboard the *Arbella,* John Winthrop told his fellow Puritans as they sailed to America in 1630 that they would be establishing a "city upon a hill," with the "eyes of the world" upon them. Their colony was to be a "new" England. This conception of the character and purpose of the English "errand" to the New World embraced a racial identity. "In the settlement of this country," historian Winthrop Jordan noted, "the red and black peoples served white men as aids to navigation by which they would find their safe positions as they ventured into America." The question of the relationship between race and nationality became immensely important as the colonies struggled for independence and transformed themselves into a new nation. In 1751 Benjamin Franklin offered his thoughts on the future complexion of American society in his essay *Observations Concerning the Increase of Mankind.* All Africa was black or "tawney," he noted, and Asia was chiefly "tawney." The English were the "principle Body of white People," and Franklin wished there were more of them in America. Why should we, he asked, "darken" the people of America: "Why increase the Sons of Africa, by Planting them in America, where we have so fair an opportunity, by excluding all Blacks and Tawneys, of increasing the lovely White?" After independence, one of the *Federalist Papers* announced: "Providence [had] been pleased to give this one connected country to one united people—a people descended from the same ancestors, speaking the same language, professing the same religion, attached to the same principles of government, very similar in their manners and customs." In a letter to James Monroe,

President Thomas Jefferson wrote that he looked forward to distant times when the American continent would be covered with such a people. Earlier, in his *Notes on the State of Virginia,* Jefferson had identified the particular people who should occupy the new continent, saying he recoiled with horror from the possibility of "either blot or mixture on that surface" and advocating the removal of blacks from the United States. America, for Jefferson, was to be a "sanctuary" where immigrants from Europe would establish a new society for themselves and their progeny. Jefferson's hope for America was articulated over a hundred years later by the United States Supreme Court in the 1923 decision of *U.S. v. Bhagat Singh Thind.* Denying naturalized citizenship to Asian Indians because they were not "white," the Court noted the assimilability of European immigrants: "The children of English, French, German, Italian, Scandinavian, and other European parentage, quickly merge into the mass of our population and lose the distinctive hallmarks of their European origin."

But America also had a counter tradition and vision, springing from the reality of racial and cultural diversity. It had been, as Walt Whitman celebrated so lyrically, "a teeming Nation of nations" composed of a "vast, surging, hopeful army of workers," a new society where all should be welcomed, "Chinese, Irish, German— all, all, without exceptions."

> Passage O soul to India! . . .
> Tying the Eastern to the Western sea,
> The road between Europe and Asia. . . .
> Lands found and nations born, thou born America,
> For purpose vast, man's long probation fill'd,
> Thou rondure of the world at last accomplish'd. . . .
> Europe to Asia, Africa join'd, and they to the New World.

The new society's diversity was portrayed by Herman Melville in his novel about the chase for the great white whale. The crew of the *Pequod* is composed of whites, blacks, Indians, Pacific Islanders, and Asians. As they work together, they are integrated in the labor process and united in a relationship of dependency, mutual survival, and cooperation. Nowhere is this connectedness more graphically illustrated than in the "monkey-rope," which is fastened to both Ishmael and Queequeg. Lowered down to the water to secure the blubber hook onto the dead whale, with vicious sharks swirling around it, Queequeg is held by a rope tied to Ishmael. The process is perilous for both men. "We two, for the time," Ishmael tells us, "were wedded; and should poor Queequeg sink to rise no more, then both usage and honor demanded, that instead of cutting the cord, it should drag me down in his wake." There is a noble class unit among the crew, and the working class aboard the *Pequod* is saluted. An "ethereal light" shines on the "workman's arm," and the laborers are ascribed "high qualities" and "democratic dignity." In the early twentieth century, a Japanese immigrant described in poetry a lesson that had been learned by farm laborers of different nationalities—Japanese, Filipino, Mexican, and Asian Indian:

> People harvesting
> Work together unaware
> Of racial problems.

A Filipino-immigrant laborer in California expressed a similar hope and understanding. America was, Macario Bulosan told his brother Carlos, "not a land of one race or one class of men" but "a new world" of respect and unconditional opportunities for all who toiled and suffered from oppression, from "the first Indian that offered peace in Manhattan to the last Filipino pea pickers."

Rethinking the Centrality of Racism in Asian American History

SYLVIA YANAGISAKO

While some variation exists among introductory courses in Asian American History, there is a high degree of uniformity as regards the topics covered, the periodization of time, the linkage between periods and topics and the core required readings. The usual chronological sequence of topics begins with the mid-nineteenth-century Chinese immigration experience. Students are introduced to the international and domestic political economy that shaped Chinese labor migration and the discriminatory laws passed to control Chinese immigration, prohibit naturalized citizenship and racial intermarriage, and restrict the movement and enterprises of immigrant Chinese. The violent racism of the nineteenth-century anti-Chinese riots, which led to the concentration of Chinese into segregated Chinatowns, is described, as is the symbolic violence committed by that era's virulent racial stereotypes of Chinese.

Courses then move on to Japanese immigration at the end of the nineteenth century. Here again the initial experiences of the first-generation immigrants are presented within the context of the political economy of labor immigration and the discriminatory legislation against Japanese. The early labor history of Japanese Americans as agricultural workers is followed by coverage of their uprooting experience during World War II, when all Americans of Japanese descent on the West Coast were imprisoned in concentration camps. Following this, attention in most courses shifts to the Filipino immigrants who arrived during the depression years and, in particular, to their experiences as migrant workers on the West Coast.

During the post–World War II period, the focus is on the new immigrants (in particular the Southeast Asians), their problems of economic and social adjustment, and their need for social services. Courses commonly include a section on the resurgence of anti-Asian racism in the 1980s, often linking it to resentments spawned by the increased flow of Asian immigration and by the expansionist success of Japanese business.

Between the pre–World War II past of the early immigrants and the post-1960s present of the new ones, occasionally there is sandwiched a brief section on the social-class mobility of third- and later-generation Chinese and Japanese Americans. It is notable that a discussion of the "model minority myth"—which casts Asian Americans as the minority whose success affirms the American myth of equality of opportunity—is generally not incorporated into this section on social-class mobility. Instead, the critique of this myth, which is a distinctive feature of all introductory

Asian American history classes, is placed either at the beginning of the course, where it is followed by the harsh history of anti-Chinese racism, or at the end of the course, where it is juxtaposed with the precarious situation of the new immigrants. . . .

. . . In the late 1980s, a small number of books were used so commonly as to qualify as the canonical texts of Asian American history. . . . [T]hese . . . core texts emphasize the working-class past of Asian Americans. The heroic figures of that past are the working-class men who struggled to survive the lean years of hard labor, racist violence, and class exploitation. Although women are not entirely absent, the laboring past has an unmistakably masculine cast to it. I do not mean to claim that materials by and about Asian American women are entirely excluded from courses on Asian American history: All the courses I reviewed included some materials on Asian American women, although there was nothing close to a "gender balance" in them. The readings on women, however, tend to avoid the issue of sexual inequality *among* Asian Americans. Instead, they either present a "woman's version" of the past or they show how Asian American women have been doubly burdened by the racism and sexism of White society. . . .

Acts of Exclusion and Redundancy in Meaning of Asian American History

The pedagogical practice of privileging a masculine working-class past in Asian American History courses molds a uniform ethnic, gender, and social-class consciousness out of more divergent material realities. In one sweep, the experiences of women, farmers (as opposed to farm laborers), and petty bourgeoisie are pushed to the margins of the collective past. That the occupational past of Asian Americans was much more diverse and dynamic than its representation in these courses is documented in a wide range of articles and books, all of which are accessible to college undergraduates.

Lacking, too, is a discussion of the relationship between Asian American social mobility and their economic and political organizations in the post–World War II era. For example, Takaki's book *Pau Hana,* in which Japanese Americans are one of the key groups in the Hawaiian plantation labor force, is not followed by an account of how second-generation Japanese Americans (Nisei) came to dominate the Democratic Party and state government in Hawaii after statehood. Nor does it discuss the key role they have played in linking U.S. mainland and overseas capital to local real estate development. Likewise, studies of Japanese American agricultural workers in California do not evolve into studies of Japanese American farms and agribusiness, their ethnic business organizations (such as the Nisei Flower Growers Association), and their labor practices (for example, the latter's conflicts with the United Farm Workers Union).

The privileging of each successive immigrant group's earliest social and class experience produces a redundant ethnic history that drowns out different stories and lessons that might be gleaned from other experiences in other periods. Just as an immigrant group or its children begins to experience significant social mobility, Asian American History courses shift their gaze to more recent immigrants. This practice is mirrored in some of the comprehensive volumes on Asian American History recently published. Takaki's *Strangers from a Different Shore: A History of*

Asian Americans best exemplifies this narrative strategy. Not only are the first 400 of the 491 pages of his book devoted to the period up until the end of World War II, but the two chapters concerned with the post-war period are devoted primarily to the second wave of recent Asian immigration—those who Takaki labels the new "Strangers at the Gates Again." . . .

My point is not simply that Asian American Studies courses suppress the histories of social-class mobility and economic success of Asian Americans, but rather that they deny the constitutive character of these experiences. In other words, the past that constitutes Asian American subjectivity—the collective conscience and sense of being and acting in the world—is deemed a working-class one.

The acts of exclusion and redundancy in meaning of Asian American History courses reflect the issues and dilemmas, at once political and pedagogical, that the instructors of these courses feel compelled to address. Not surprisingly, they move to correct the erroneous but prevalent assumption that all Asian Americans arrived at these shores with slide rulers in hand and surplus capital to invest in business enterprises. Most Americans, including some Asian Americans, after all, are ignorant of the working-class history of many Asian Americans and their struggles against class-exploitation and racial discrimination.

The redundant narrative and exclusions of these courses, however, signal the social gaps instructors feel they must bridge to construct a unifying and politically mobilizing ethnic identity. One such gap is that between the early and the recent waves of immigrants. The weight given to the working-class past is an attempt by the descendants of the early immigrants, who comprise the predominantly Japanese American and Chinese American instructors of these courses, to bridge the economic and cultural distance between themselves and the recent immigrants from Vietnam, Cambodia, China, Korea, and the Philippines. It is this latter group, after all, that constitutes the contemporary Asian American working-class. In celebrating the laboring past of their ancestors, the college instructors and students link their ancestral past with the present of the new immigrants and thereby construct a shared and seemingly stable Asian American working-class identity.

The second gap Asian American History courses attempt to bridge is both wider and of greater political significance: it is the gap between Asian Americans and other people of color in the United States. Both in terms of their assigned place in the racist hierarchy of essential, biogenetic difference and on the basis of social class, Asian Americans are precariously perched at the margins of this category. Certainly, ample evidence can be marshalled to debunk any claims of uniformity in Asian American economic success. At the same time, however, it cannot be denied that, as a whole, Asian Americans enjoy significantly higher levels of income, education, and occupational status than do African Americans, Chicanos, and American Indians. Two telling indicators of the economic gap between Asian Americans and African Americans, for example, are rates of infant mortality and college attendance. While the former are comparatively high and the latter are low among African Americans, the reverse is true of Asian Americans. Facts like these make strikingly clear the comparatively favorable socioeconomic position of Asian Americans among people of color in the United States.

The emphasis on the working-class past of hardship, struggle, and resistance is an attempt by instructors, many of whose commitment to Asian American Studies was forged in the Asian American student movement of the late 1960s, to challenge the stereotype of Asian Americans as an accommodating model minority striving for acceptance by White society. What is offered in its place is a collective identity of an oppressed but resistant minority that has more in common with other people of color than with White Americans.

One of the dominant themes guiding Asian American student activism a well as other student movements in the 1960s and 1970s was a critique of U.S. imperialism. Asian American immigration and labor history were located within the context of American imperialism and labor exploitation of third-world peoples, both at home and abroad. According to Nee and Nee, the student activists in the San Francisco community in the early 1970s

> feel that as victims of racism and economic exploitation, American Chinese share a similar experience with blacks and other minority groups in the U.S. as well as third world people in Asia, Africa, and Latin America. They see themselves as standing in solidarity with these people and the international workers' movement in a broadly based political struggle against a common oppressor which they have identified as American imperialism.

Emerging as they did out of this student movement, Asian American History courses became the pedagogical practice through which this analysis was inscribed in the collective historical consciousness of students for whom that past had been lost in more ways than one.

The tension between the desire of the founders of Asian American Studies to stand in solidarity with other people of color and the fact that in socioeconomic terms Asian Americans are more like White Americans than African Americans, Chicanos, and American Indians, helps to explain why the attack on the "model minority myth" is a core theme of Asian American History courses. There are, of course, several good reasons for challenging this myth, the most obvious being to refute the claim embedded in the myth that the success of Asian Americans is proof that equal opportunity exists in the United States for all races and, consequently, that those groups which have not been successful are responsible for their own failure. After all, thinly disguised behind the celebration of Asian American achievement in the myth is both the legitimization of White privilege and the reinforcement of racist beliefs about African American failure.

Above all, however, the critique of the "model minority myth" has become an integral practice of Asian American Studies because the myth calls into question the solidarity of Asian Americans with other people of color in the United States. By casting Asian Americans in the category of the successful and, consequently, the advantaged, the myth raises doubts about whether Asian Americans share the same experience and interests with other people of color and—in the context of the academy—makes for the uneasy coexistence of Asian American Studies with other ethnic studies programs.

Asian American Studies has responded to the challenge of the anomalous status of Asian Americans in both "advantaged" and "oppressed minority" categories by displaying Asian Americans' historical credentials as members of the working class. They have done this most effectively through Asian American History courses and their metanarrative of struggle and survival.

The *masculine* character of that working-class past calls for a different explanation. It might be explained in part by the sexism of instructors and by their tendency to privilege male actors. Certainly, one of the histories submerged by the dominant narrative of Asian American Studies is the history of Asian American sexism. Such a history would undoubtedly compromise the heroic stature of Asian American men by casting them as both oppressed and oppressor. This appears to have been the main reason why Maxine Hong Kingston's book *The Woman Warrior* was so strongly criticized by many Asian American Studies scholars when it was first published. Kingston's epic-mythical tale of the liberation of a young Chinese American girl, who is struggling to throw off the binds of a "tradition" that devalues women, hangs out the "dirty laundry" of Chinese American sexism.The almost exclusive focus on working-class *men,* it should be noted, cannot be explained by the absence of working-class women in the Asian American past. Asian American women, after all, have labored as farm workers, factory workers, domestic workers, and prostitutes. No doubt it might be somewhat controversial to identify as the founding "ancestresses" the first working-class Asian women on U.S. soil—namely, the prostitutes; but it would certainly reduce the redundancy of the masculine heroic narrative.

Yet a blanket charge of sexism and chauvinism is both too simple and too general an explanation of the androcentrism of Asian American History courses. I suggest that it is more illuminating to trace the marginalization of women to some key dilemmas of Asian American identity. In the following section, I argue that the "women problem" of Asian American History is in fact an issue that goes beyond gender and lies at the heart of the dilemmas of Asian American identity.

Dilemmas of Asian American Identity

The first of these dilemmas derives from the fact that the only experience shared by all Asian Americans is that of having been assigned an essential character by what Edward Said has called "Orientalism." Although his concept refers specifically to French and British discourse on the Middle East, it is also applicable to American (and western European) discourse on the Far East—the region that Americans today are most likely to identify as "the Orient." "Orientalism" refers most broadly to a style of thought based upon an ontological and epistemological distinction between "the Orient" and "the Occident," which is the starting point for elaborate theories, epics, social descriptions, and political accounts of the Orient, its people, customs, and destiny. It is the "corporate institution" for making statements about the Orient, authorizing views of it, describing it, teaching about it, and (above all) ruling over it.

Just as earlier British and French discourses on the "Orient" of the Middle East and South Asia erase the cultural differences between societies as diverse as India and Egypt, lumping them together in moral opposition to the "West," so during the nineteenth and twentieth centuries American discourse on the "Orient"—that is, the Far East—asserted a similar dualism. Like French and British discourses, the American one defined the essential characters of East and West in terms that justified the political and cultural hegemony of the West. Whereas the East was portrayed as mired in traditionalism, the West moved boldly ahead in its modernism; where the East respected the authority of fathers and emperors, the West lauded the independence of sons and rational individuals, thus facilitating both the technological inventiveness and the democratic justice of advanced, western industrial society. Finally, whereas the East languished in an unmistakably feminine passivity, the West struck a decisively masculine pose.

Said's critique of "Orientalism" enables us to see that to be labeled an "Oriental" in the United States is to be identified as having origins in a cultural tradition that is supposedly antithetical to that of the West and inferior to it. It was this system of representations and the power relations inscribed in them that student activists in the late 1960s rejected—along with the label "Oriental"—when they redefined themselves "Asian Americans." Naming oneself was an integral part of reappropriating intellectual authority over one's own historical experiences.

The emphasis on the active agency of men in Asian American history is likewise a conscious attempt to challenge the metonymic equation of Asian with the feminine. To celebrate male ancestors characterized by an "indomitable spirit, fiercely hopeful and resilient" is to undermine the symbolic equation that East is to West as female is to male. . . .

The move to restore the masculine dignity of Asian American men unfortunately relies upon, and thus reproduces, one symbolic opposition inscribed with relations of domination for the sake of challenging another. An Orientalist characterization of Asians as "female" and "passive" in opposition to a "male" and "active" West is challenged; but what remains unquestioned is the equation of active agency with men and passivity with women and the logic of male dominance that flows from it. Nor are the disadvantages of this attempt to restore the masculine honor of Asian American men limited to its reproduction of gender hierarchy. As I will show in the next section, it drowns out other accounts that would enhance our understanding of both the past and the present.

The second issue to which I trace the marginalization of women in Asian American History courses is one generated by the demand for exclusive national allegiance from people whose experiences, families, and commitments have often crossed the borders of a single nation-state. The confinement of Japanese Americans in prison camps during World War II was accompanied by the coercive confinement of their allegiance to a single country. First-generation Japanese Americans (who had only Japanese citizenship because they had been barred by U.S. law from becoming naturalized citizens) and their U.S.-born children (most of whom had only U.S. citizenship) were asked to declare exclusive allegiance to the U.S. government and forswear any allegiance to Japan and its Emperor at the risk of deportation. This precipitated both great distress and intense conflict within families. Many second-generation Japanese Americans found themselves in bitter disagreement with parents; siblings chose opposing sides; and the government's segregation of the "loyal" from the "disloyal" Japanese Americans broke up families, some of which never reunited after the war. Following all too quickly upon the heels of this Japanese-American nightmare was the Chinese-American one of the Cold War and the demonization of Communist China.

The demand that Japanese Americans and Chinese Americans confine their political loyalties within the borders of the nation led to a suppression of relations that crosscut national spaces. Not only did World War II and the Cold War cut off the flow of people, goods, and information across national borders but it also stigmatized and silenced talk about relations with people defined as political enemies. This in turn led to the confinement of historical memory to spaces inside the nation. In addition, in the case of Japanese Americans, the government suppression of Japanese-language schools during World War II resulted in the loss of the linguistic means among the third generation of reestablishing those relations and recovering their histories through Japanese texts even after the end of overt political hostilities.

In spite of its emergence as a counter-hegemonic practice, Asian American Studies has born the legacy of this demand for exclusive national allegiance by including only those people, relations, communities, and institutions located on U.S. soil in its field of study. The marginalization of women is part and parcel of the suppression of a history of transnational relations that threatens to disrupt the narrative of an ethnic history neatly encompassed within the borders of the nation and the working class. Women disrupt these seemingly exclusive, natural boundaries of class, nation, and ethnic identity by signalling the boundary crossings that have occurred. . . .

Chinese American Women and Transnational Families

In the Chinese American case, the overwhelming predominance of men in the Chinese immigrant population until the 1960s would appear to justify the centrality of men in any Chinese American historical narrative. Where wives were present, the link between women and entrepreneurship was rather different from the Japanese American case. The few women who were brought in as wives were usually married to merchants. Hence, among Chinese Americans it was not that wives provided labor crucial to entrepreneurship, but rather that men with capital could afford wives and were allowed to bring them from China.

An attempt to recover ancestresses in early Chinese American history might appear to lead only to the prostitutes who were the complement to the "bachelor society." Granting prostitutes a central place in the narration of Chinese American history would surely be a useful corrective to current practices, not only because it would bring women into the early history of that group, but also because it would open up important topics of inquiry regarding sexual exploitation, entrepreneurship, social class, and the links between them in Chinese American communities.

A history of Chinese American prostitution, however, would not uncover all the women hidden by the androcentrism of Asian American History courses. Above all, it would miss the wives and mothers in China whose key role in Chinese American history has been rendered invisible by a nationalist mode of historiography that ignores the contributions of people outside the borders of the United States.

Books such as *Strangers From a Different Shore* draw empathetic attention to the "lonely [immigrant Chinese] bachelors stranded in a foreign land" and lament the fact that "for the overwhelming majority of Chinese men, the future would not include the possibility of a family in their new land." It is well documented, however, that at least half the Chinese "bachelor" population was married and had wives and children in China. Many of these children, especially the sons, came to the United States as the next generation of immigrants. Lyman, for one, claims that it was common for an immigrant Chinese man "to return to China periodically, visit his wife, sire a child, hopefully a son, and then to return to America alone. Later, these China-born sons would be brought to America and asked to help out in and eventually take over the father's business." In some Chinese American communities, family businesses were handed on from one generation to the next despite the geographical dispersal of conjugal families.

Although it is not clear what percent of Chinese immigrant men returned to China and with what frequency, we know enough to conclude that the wives—as well as, most likely, the mothers and sisters "left behind"—played a crucial role in producing the next generation of immigrants and, in many cases, the labor for their overseas husbands' enterprises. They also provided the "homes" to which immigrant men aspired to return, whether or not they eventually did.

For Lyman and O'Brien, as for Takaki, "family groups" did not exist for Chinese immigrants. Yet, I would argue that Chinese male immigrants—whether married or single—did indeed belong to "family groups." These family groups were transnational ones that cut across national boundaries and pursued coordinated economic strategies in spite of immigration exclusion acts. Only a narrow, ethnocentric definition of "family" as the "natural unit" of the conjugal (nuclear) family composed of husband, wife, and unmarried children who live under the same roof blinds us to the existence of families whose members inhabit not only different houses but different countries.

Conclusion

Asian American Studies has responded to dilemmas of national allegiance and class alliance by confining "Asian American experience"—in other words, the collective experiences that constitute Asian American ethnic subjectivity—to locations within the borders of the nation rather than viewing it as a transnational process involving individuals, families, communities, events, and sociopolitical structures that crosscut these borders. Social class, likewise, has been construed as an exclusive, stable position rather than as a historical process often entailing multiple locations. By confining Asian American History within the narrative space of working-class history, the boundaries of social class are stabilized and naturalized along with those of the nation and the ethnic group.

The recognition that national borders do not constitute social borders would open up Asian American History to include a multitude of people, both female and male, who never set foot in the United States but whose lives and labors were integral to the formation and transformation of Asian American communities. Little research has been undertaken on these people, families, and communities, yet such research would prove extremely useful for amplifying our understanding of the transnational context in which Asian American communities have been forged along with modes of entrepreneurship, political organization, and social mobility. It would also offer an opportunity to break out of the restrictive boundaries of a nationalist Asian American historiography. For the exclusion of those people "left behind" is rooted in a model of culture and society that can only reproduce an ideology of the Nation as a fixed, natural unit, even while it challenges its monoracial representation. Setting aside this nationalist ideology would open up a new transnational dimension to Asian American Studies that would enable us to better understand the ways that flows of people, money, labor, obligations, and goods between nations and continents have shaped Asian American experiences.

Capitalist Restructuring and the New Asian Immigration

PAUL ONG, EDNA BONACICH, AND LUCIE CHENG

Since the mid-1960s, immigration from Asia has been renewed on a large scale. The only other period that witnessed a similar influx started with the gold rush in the mid-nineteenth century and extended to 1934; during this time, thousands of Asians immigrated to the United States. Coming primarily from China, Japan, and the Philippines, they were mostly single men from rural villages, seeking to make money to support families in their home countries and in some cases hoping eventually to return in an improved economic position. Many of them worked as unskilled laborers in the mines, railroads, fields, canneries, and service industries of Hawaii and the West. Some were able to bring wives, establish families, and move into business and farm ownership, creating settled Asian American communities.

The early Asian communities faced considerable hostility from the surrounding society. Efforts were quickly made to curtail immigration from each of the Asian countries of origin, so that the scale of immigration was cut to very modest numbers. For those who did manage to come, anti-Asian agitation took the form of segregation, denial of citizenship, restrictions on land-ownership, physical abuse, and even massacre. The height of anti-Asian action was reached during World War II, when more than one hundred thousand Japanese Americans were evacuated from the Pacific Coast and put in concentration camps.

For two decades after the war, the local Asian American communities developed without any significant new immigration. De facto exclusion remained in place, singling out Asia as the sole continent from which immigration to the United States was unacceptable. This exclusion was eliminated in 1965 with the passage of a new immigration act that equalized immigration rights for all nationalities. The change of law prompted a new wave of Asian immigration to the United States.

The new Asian immigrants are different from the old in several important respects. Although they include people from such earlier sources as China and the Philippines, new sending countries have emerged, most notably South Korea, India, and Vietnam. No longer constrained by exclusion laws, the new immigrants are coming in much larger numbers than before. Women constitute a far higher proportion than in the past and now make up the majority of immigrants from some countries. And a substantial number are from urban, educated, middle-class backgrounds. These immigrants come to the United States as professionals, managers, and entrepreneurs.

Some of the shift toward higher-educated, professional immigrants is a product of U.S. immigration law, which gives preference to highly trained people. Still, the law alone cannot explain why the United States is pursuing immigrants with these skills, nor can it account for the fact that so many of them are coming from Asia. These new trends need to be explained.

It is important to note that not all the new Asian immigrants are middle-class professionals and managers. Indeed, Asian communities often reveal a class polarization. At one end are the well-off groups we have mentioned, and at the other are people working in low-skilled, minimum-wage, service-sector and manufacturing jobs, or who are unemployed. Although the median income of several of the Asian communities is relatively high, Asians suffer twice the poverty rate of the dominant society.

Much international migration theory has focused on the movement of unskilled labor from poor, underdeveloped countries to the core countries of Europe and North America. Some of the new Asian immigration reflects these old patterns. But the new professional-managerial stratum does not. Old theories are not very helpful in understanding the new conditions, and we must devise more adequate explanations.

The purpose of this volume is to describe and explain the new Asian immigration. Other authors have examined this subject, providing many useful insights. Our approach tends to differ from theirs in stressing the importance of placing the immigration in the context of the restructuring of global capitalism, particularly in the Pacific Rim area. Other authors, have looked at immigration in this context, but they focus on the movement of labor and do not give much attention to the new professional-managerial immigration. This volume contributes to the expansion of migration theories by including the movement of professionals and managers and examining that movement in terms of global restructuring. . . .

The economic development of Asia is of particular relevance to the studies in this volume. Before the 1960s, industrial production was dominated by the developed countries of Europe and North America. Now some previously underdeveloped countries, many of them in Asia, are engaging in manufacturing. The rise of Japan as one of the world's leading economic powers is the prime example of this shift, but of increasing importance are the newly industrializing countries (NICs). In most of these countries, several factors—the expanding world economy; a special relationship with the United States, which was seeking alliances in the Pacific region against the Soviet Union and China; a weak civil society with no powerful groups to challenge the state; and a population that has long held values of thrift and hard work—converged to allow a strong, authoritarian state to emerge to guide economic development.

Leading the group is Japan, which was nurtured out of post-war disaster by the United States to stave off Communist threat. With lavish amounts of foreign aid in the late 1940s and 1950s, a generous share of the U.S. domestic market, little expenditure for national defense, and the opportunity to serve as a major supplier for U.S. military operations in Korea and Vietnam, Japan was able to create the first economic miracle in Asia. Its focus on manufacturing for export was to become the magic wand for the NICs in the 1960s.

The Asian NICs are generally seen to be Hong Kong, Singapore, South Korea, and Taiwan. All experienced their great economic growth from the mid-1960s through the 1980s. Although some Latin American countries, especially Mexico and Brazil, have also been referred to as NICs, their growth has not been sustained to the same extent as in the Asian NICs.

Several factors were critical to the success of the Asian NICs, especially South Korea and Taiwan. Coming out of a long period of colonization by Japan after World War II, both countries benefitted from a special relationship with the United States as it struggled for hegemony with the Soviet Union in the Pacific region. The United States provided large amounts of foreign aid to these countries during the 1950s and 1960s, helping stabilize their economies and guaranteeing the survival of their authoritarian governments. South Korea and Taiwan, faced with possible extinction by their Communist counterparts, rallied their populations behind an anti-Communist ideology, accompanied by urgings of austerity. U.S. aid made it possible for the states to develop autonomously, thus laying the basis for effective state intervention in economy and society, as they pushed for exported industrialization in the 1960s at the insistence of the United States.

The expanding world economy in the 1960s also provided a niche for the other two Asian NICs, the entrepôt city-states of Singapore and Hong Kong. A strong authoritarian state in Singapore supplied the political and social stability necessary to attract foreign private investments. Hong Kong's proximity to China provided a source of cheap labor that gave the colony a comparative advantage in pursuing labor-intensive manufacturing. In addition, a well-developed organizational infrastructure and a close partnership between the colonial government and the banks made Hong Kong the financial and service capital of the region.

Confucianism, a powerful cultural heritage in all these Asian countries, was a significant contributing factor in their rapid economic development in at least two ways. Its praise of thriftiness and self-denial led to a savings rate that is the highest in the world. In addition, the Confucian work ethic has made the labor force willing to endure the world's longest working hours.

Besides the "four little tigers," or "minidragons," as the Asian NICs are sometimes called, other Asian countries, such as Thailand, Indonesia, Malaysia, India, and the Philippines, are trying to pursue the same development course. Primarily, that means entering the global economy by manufacturing for export. Typically, the strategy involves strong state participation in the development process, an effort to attract foreign capital, and enclave development in the form of free trade zones (FTZs). The regimes are often authoritarian and tend to support a "free market" capitalist ideology, despite active state intervention in the economy. Their ideology is consonant with the conservatism espoused by Western restructuring economies.

China is a latecomer in the process of world capitalist incorporation. Although still engaging in a socialist discourse, the Chinese state is following a path of development similar to that pursued by the NICs. The sheer size of the Chinese economy is bound to have a great impact on global restructuring and to pose serious challenges to the world system. . . .

As part of any effort to move up the ladder of technological innovation, many Asian developing countries are promoting higher education. Some students are sent to the developed industrial countries, such as the United States, for advanced training. Others are trained at home, often in schools developed under the aegis of advisers from the advanced capitalist countries. As a result, a highly educated stratum of trained technicians and professionals exists in many Asian countries. These people have become an important element in the new Asian immigration to the United States.

More recently, as the Asian countries have emerged from their peripheral status within the world economy, their focus on scientific and technical innovation is luring back many of their professional expatriates from the United States. This phenomenon has three consequences. For the developing Asian countries, the return of highly educated and experienced people helps relieve a significant shortage of professionals in selected fields. For the United States, the departure of these highly trained professionals with experience in the most advanced areas of research presents a potential threat. Finally, for the world system as a whole, the frequent movement back and forth of professionals contributes to the internationalization of the professional-managerial stratum.

The rise of Asian developing countries acts as an independent force on global restructuring. These nations have been active players, leading rather than merely following the developments in the world capitalist system. Although there are myriad ties between them and the advanced core states, they have the capacity to pursue a course of development somewhat independent of the needs and actions of the developed countries of the West. Restructuring is, to an important extent, being imposed on countries such as the United States by challenges from Asia.

Asian Immigrants and Restructuring

The large-scale immigration from Asia after 1965 not only coincided with economic restructuring, but was affected by and contributed to these structural changes. The immigration of Asians to the United States is both an economic and political phenomenon. In particular, the new Asian immigration has grown in response to the passage of legislation in 1965 that finally removed all vestiges of Asian exclusion in U.S. immigration policy. This shift in policy was at least partially responsive to the changing role of U.S. capital in the region. With a rise in the activities of U.S. TNCs [transnational corporations] in Asia, along with U.S. military activity that supported this expansion, the United States could no longer afford to maintain a blatantly racist immigration policy with respect to the region. . . .

Asian immigrants to the United States play a multitude of roles in the restructuring process. They help supply the labor, skills, and entrepreneurial energy that facilitate economic restructuring. Some are hired, often through direct recruitment, to fill critical shortages brought on by the neoconservative policies. That is especially true for highly skilled occupations requiring advanced education. The lack of adequate funds for advanced training, the tendency of some of the best students to pursue high-salary jobs in the financial and legal sectors, and the inability to alleviate some oppressive working conditions have produced a shortage of personnel in the health, engineering, and scientific fields. Professionally trained Asian immigrants have been employed to offset some of these shortages. These professionals work in the innovative and technically developing aspects of restructuring.

As we have observed, there is a tendency for new Asian immigrants to be heavily drawn from the middle class. Many Asian immigrants are educated, urban individuals who come to the United States as professionals, technicians, managers, and small business owners. The U.S. Immigration Act of 1965 encouraged this stratum to come by giving preference to trained people and to those with capital to invest. The legislators did not anticipate, however, that people from Asia would fill these slots.

Why did the United States encourage professional and managerial immigration, especially in the mid-1960s? And why did Asians in particular, respond to this call? These questions are central to understanding the new Asian immigration.

On the U.S. side, as suggested above, restructuring has two prongs: cheapening labor and pursuing innovation. This duality produces a contradiction in the area of education. On the one hand, the United States wants to cut social spending, including spending on education. On the other, it needs highly trained personnel. This duality leads to efforts to stratify educational system more, by promoting elitism and differentiation between schools. Nevertheless, there is a strong democratic impulse in the nation that defines equality of opportunity in educational terms. If U.S. capitalism is to be open to all equally, then equal schooling must likewise be universally available. Otherwise, the immense inequalities in the society cannot be justified.

The educational system of the United States is thus a major political battlefield. Conservatives push for greater inequality in the schools. Democratic forces push for greater equality. And parents try to get the best for their children to give them an advantage in this competitive system. Such wrenching issues as school desegregation, busing, and public funding for private schools have left the U.S. educational system in a shambles. Meanwhile, there has been an underproduction of certain kinds of trained personnel.

The public schools are not the only locus of this problem. Cutbacks in social spending (as part of the cheapening of labor strategy) affect other spheres, too. The United States has been reluctant to spend money on the training of health personnel, such as nurses, in a general effort at cost containment for health care. The ultimate goal is to reduce health care costs for capitalist employers by lowering the costs of their benefits packages. This policy creates a shortage of nurses in the United States and a demand for immigrant nurses.

In general, the cheap labor approach to restructuring has the impact of curbing the development of local professionals by limiting the opportunities of the local working class. People who work for minimum wage can hardly afford to send their children to college. Attacks on the working class thus have the consequence of undermining the strategy of reorganization and innovation by limiting the growth of the class that can implement it. This contradiction sets the stage for the immigration of professionals and managers.

On the Asian side, as already mentioned, education has been fostered among the NICs and other developing countries. Some of the training (e.g., nurses' education in the Philippines) has been developed for the express purpose of emigration and the remittances it produces. But most educational plans in Asian countries aim at developing their own professional-managerial stratum, in pursuit of development through innovation. . . .

The continuing demand for Asian professionals on the U.S. side does not ensure their continued immigration, as shown by changes in U.S. immigration policy in the 1970s that made this immigration more difficult. Interest groups in the United States are divided about professional immigration, and those who feel the effects of competition exercise what political influence they have to make the arrival of Asian professionals more difficult. Actual immigration policy thus reflects not only the economic needs of capital, but also the political fallout of the conflicts that filling these needs engenders.

The contributions of Asian immigrants to economic restructuring are not limited to those made by professionals. Many Asian immigrants rely on small businesses to establish a foothold in the United States. As in the past, they use familial and other collective resources to start their ventures. In doing so, they help establish the contracting shops that are part of vertical fragmentation, provide services such as restaurants for the growing PMC [professional and managerial class], and run mom-and pop operations in the deteriorating inner city, where fleeing white retailers have left a vacuum of opportunity.

Not all Asian businesspeople fall into the petty capitalist class. Others are owners, executives, and investors of major Asian transnational businesses that are establishing bases in the U.S. economy. In other words, these Asian immigrants are manifestations of a globalizing economy, in which national boundaries no longer confine business activity.

Finally, as mentioned earlier, despite the greater visibility of Asian immigrant members of the middle class and the international business community, a sizable proportion of new Asian immigrants are forced to join Latino immigrants as low-wage workers or to depend on public assistance. Many of these poor immigrants are refugees from Southeast Asia, but substantial numbers of immigrants from other Asian countries also arrive without the educational or financial resources to propel them into professional or business-owning occupations.

Asian immigrants have played a role not only in economic restructuring but also in political restructuring. The cold war has come to an end. The European ex-Communist bloc is making efforts to join the capitalist world economy and its renewed commitment to free markets. Most of the post-1965 Asian immigration to the United States occurred within a cold war context, however. Indeed, U.S. military involvement in Asian countries to try to halt the spread of Communism has been a major theme of the post–World War II period.

Asia has experienced several Communist revolutions, starting with China in 1949. Since then, revolutionary movements in Korea and Vietnam have led to wars in which the United States played the role of defender against the spread of Communism. The United States has also supported anti-insurrectionist governments in such countries as the Philippines.

While these efforts were mainly aimed at curbing Soviet and Chinese influence, they had an economic underpinning. Their purpose was to keep as much of the world open to capitalist investment and markets as possible. Anti-Communist wars were thus a part of the world capitalist political economy.

The new Asian immigration to the United States has obviously been deeply affected by both actual and potential warfare. Many new Asian immigrants have come to the United States as refugees, particularly from Southeast Asia. Others, such as Koreans, and Chinese from Hong Kong and Taiwan, have come from divided countries, where political instability and the threat of war or Communist takeover have made the future uncertain.

Many of the new immigrants have been aligned with the United States and its military in these conflicts, and their political ideology, at least on arrival, is to the right of center. As with Cuban immigration, some of the new Asian immigrants are fiercely anti-Communist and have the potential for pushing the United States to the right. That is especially likely for the refugees from anti-Communist wars. On the other hand, some Asian immigrants from divided countries have lived under right-wing, authoritarian regimes and are more likely to be critical of the ideology of anti-Communism. The internal politics of Asian American communities today can thus be quite complex, with the political struggles of their homelands replicated in their new home. Of course, once these immigrants arrive in the United States, local experiences also come to shape political identification and ideology.

Many Asian immigrants to the United States are helping to renew capitalism, not only through their economic activities, but also by reinforcing its values. In part reflecting developments in their homelands, they embrace capitalism with enthusiasm. This trend poses a challenge to those political forces in the United States that are more critical of capitalism, as well as to older Asian Americans, some of whom have developed a "progressive" politics.

The political leanings of the new Asian immigrants remain to be worked out. The harsh realities of economic inequality and racism fostered by the system may lead some to turn toward the left. And in some cases, such as South Korea, a vibrant leftist movement in their homeland may inspire some new immigrants to question capitalistic values.

As their numbers grow and their influence increases, Asian immigrants are not merely filling the positions that are being created as a result of restructuring. They are actively participating in the restructuring process. They are helping reshape the economic landscape by creating new and alternative ventures. And they have the potential to emerge as an important new political force, influencing legislation and policy on both the local and the international level.

What Does It Mean to Be Asian American?

BILL ONG HING

Throughout this book I have used the term Asian Americans to describe all Asian immigrants to the United States as well as American-born citizens of Asian ancestry. But no one should infer that a singular ethnicity has evolved. In fact, the immigration-generated mosaic of diverse communities calls into question the very use of the term Asian American. Yet the assumption of a single ethnicity might very well be resented even if the broader Asian Pacific American term were used to include those from the Pacific Islands. Clashing personality types and extreme political and socioeconomic polarities suggest that the more plausible picture is one of relative unity only among certain segments of Asian America. We need to ask what that new limited ethnicity means to the rest of Asian America and to the mainstream.

Whether there is, will be, or even should be a single ethnicity is a complicated question. While the various communities share elements of a common history, their individual histories, demographics, and experiences are unique. The current diversity within and between groups—demographically, culturally, socially, politically, and economically—would appear to create too many obstacles to such a single identity. Today as I walk around a predominantly foreign-born neighborhood like Chinatown, it is hard to imagine (although they should be asked) that the people on the street would not first think of themselves as Chinese American, or even Chinese. They are Chinese immigrants who look Chinese, speak Chinese, and spend most of their time in Chinatown. Yet similarities in terms of race, experience, treatment by the mainstream, and political values have drawn some Asian Americans (not only the American-born) together, and not always simply for utilitarian political purposes or because the situation calls for it.

A look through the eyes of Asian Americans would no doubt enlighten our understanding of identity and ethnic formation. My views and experiences might be relevant here.

I generally think of myself as Asian American rather than Chinese American, but that may in part be because I was born in the United States, I have many Japanese, Chinese Korean, and Filipino friends who are also American-born or have lived here most of their lives, I communicate with them in English, and despite our different opinions I share with them many experiences. I work in a university where Asian American is a common label, and the vast majority of my Asian American co-workers and students are American-born Japanese and Chinese Americans. I also have been a member of many political and social groups (formal and informal) that are labeled or regarded as Asian American and have members of varied Asian backgrounds. I do regard myself as Chinese American when specific cultural signals are invoked, such as when I am with relatives (most of whom are Chinese American), in Chinatown, or a Chinese restaurant. I do not recall ever being able to regard myself simply as an American. My racial features inevitably evoke certain reactions, looks, body language, and treatment from the people with whom I interact, so that I am constantly reminded that I am Asian American or Chinese American.

But I cannot serve as the standard. Asian America today is predominantly foreign-born and not of Chinese ancestry. Informal surveys, which I and others have conducted of Asian Americans on how they identify themselves, reveal a range of responses. Many, even some born in the United States, see themselves as Chinese Americans, Japanese Americans, or Vietnamese Americans. Others insist that they are simply Americans, resent any prefix, and claim that because they act and think of themselves as Americans, they are treated as such. Still others respond that their identity depends on the time of day. In a work environment lacking other Asian Americans, some regard themselves as simply Americans, while others are reminded that they are Asian American, and all might regard themselves as Filipino or Chinese American if they volunteer after work at a community center.

Here is a sampling of the varied comments about identity I have heard from a predominantly middle-class cross section of Asian Americans.

> I think of myself primarily as Taiwanese. I think of myself as Asian American when I'm in a political situation, like in voting and supporting candidates, because the Taiwanese community is pretty small. So I think of what candidates would represent the Asian community or if there happens to be a Taiwan-related issue at hand, I'll look at that first. (Taiwan-born women, age 41, immigrated at age 22)

> I think of myself as Vietnamese. Sometimes I think of myself as Vietnamese American. I never think of myself as Asian American. I don't feel more affinity with other Asian groups such as the Japanese or Chinese. Historically, Vietnam has not had a friendly

relationship with these countries because these countries dominated us. I check the box Asian American in all my forms (employment, etc.) but that's because they don't have a Vietnamese American box (Vietnam-born man, age 50, entered as refugee at age 38)

I think of myself as Asian American. I think of myself as Vietnamese when I'm with other Vietnamese, and I think of myself as American when I'm in Europe. (Vietnam-born woman, age 20, immigrated at age 4)

I regard myself as an American. I grew up in a setting with few other Asians, and I was treated as a regular person by my white friends. So I think of myself as simply an American. (American-born woman, Chinese ancestry, age 42)

I think of myself as an American. My parents are Chinese, but I grew up in the United States. A few years ago I went to China where I couldn't relate and I realized I wasn't Chinese. In the United States we have to think of ourselves as American in order to get respect. (American-born man, Chinese ancestry, age 45)

I think of myself as Japanese American. the racism that I and my friends have experienced over the years is a constant reminder that I am different and will never be accepted simply as an American. (American-born man, Japanese ancestry, age 66)

I think of myself as Taiwanese American. I rarely identify myself as anything else, but sometimes if I'm at an Asian dance, I will consider myself as Asian. It depends on the environment. . . . It's hard for me to relate to the Vietnamese. I identify more with Chinese and Taiwanese. (Taiwan-born man, age 25, immigrated at age 3)

I think of myself as Chinese American. I grew up in Chinatown and went to Chinese school after regular school every day. Both my parents were immigrants. I've never been out of the Bay Area, and I continue to work, eat, and shop a lot in Chinatown even though I live in the Richmond district [with many Chinese American neighbors] of San Francisco. (American-born man, age 45)

I'm Filipino. I fought in World War II for the United States in the Philippines and not until recently are they going to give the citizenship I earned. I want to be an American citizen, but I will always be a Filipino. (Philippine-born man, age 75, immigrated at age 63)

Through high school I told people I was Chinese, and if I wanted to refer to all Asians I used the word Orientals. . . . At college I was told that the proper label for me was Asian American, that Oriental was a word to describe furniture, not people. But what is the difference? . . . Minority groups want new labels to give themselves a more positive image. But unless the stereotypes disappear as well, is it really going to help very much? (Chinese American sophomore at Yale)

The complexity of Asian American identity underscores the need for a more sophisticated understanding of it and its continuing evolution. This understanding must account for those many Asian Americans who switch identities from situation to situation and who tell us that Asian American is not an identity for all times and all purposes. And it must respect the unique cultural backgrounds that the foreign-born majority represent.

When we speak of an Asian American identity, are we referring to a new ethnicity with common traits, customs, and cultural characteristics, a political identity for mobilization purposes, or both? Is it proper to use these terms interchangeably as some do? Assuming that a new ethnicity would entail a cultural identity, would that be different from political identity? A new cultural identity or ethnicity could very well be established for collective mobilization for political purposes, but diverse groups can be mobilized without forming a new cultural identity. It's a substantial leap to a new ethnic identity from collective mobilization. Otherwise, the so-called new Asian American ethnic identity must be limited to those like myself—those middle-class, American-born Chinese or Japanese Americans with exposure to an array of community issues and similar educational experience.

To many, then, the concept of Asian American identity may not involve a new cultural identity. Rather, it might properly be viewed as a means of achieving political integration. For some, this may simply be situational political mobilization. But for others it could involve a more permanent process of developing a political identity or platform while maintaining separate ethnic identities for non-political purposes. In that sense, it is a civic identity that transcends single situations and is more lasting in nature. On the other hand, it falls short of a new ethnic or cultural identity since it can be established simply for political reasons. This type of ethnic mobilization is essentially a form of social interaction between culture groups.

Situational mobilization acknowledges a more pliant character than identity formation. Though independent community mobilization may damage prospects for pan–Asian American efforts, given the diversity of Asian immigrants it is too much to expect that intra-community organizing and a turning inward will not occur. The persistence of Chinatowns, Filipino American suburbs, and Vietnamese business pockets promotes intra-community mobilization. The flexibility of the situational model permits more than one mobilization response without foreclosing the possibility of others in different contexts, in light of different issues.

A less flexible view of Asian American identity is dangerous. Rudimentary calls for unity or uninformed claims of an emerging uniform culture involve several interrelated risks. First among them is exclusivity. Those who do not find themselves in the description of Asian America are likely to be turned off or alienated, and that would be counterproductive to unity. Second is the notion of the incorporation, or loss of identity, by smaller groups. Finally, the dominance of middle-class, American-born Chinese and Japanese Americans risks distorting information about Asian America.

The dangers of inflexibility should also give great pause to those who believe in cultural pluralism. At what expense are we willing to assume or call for a new Asian American ethnicity? Are there not elements of cultural sacrifice in that notion that affront us for the same reasons we abhor strict demands of Americanization or assimilation? A single ethnicity smacks of the same cauldron-like approach we have resisted in the Anglo conformity or melting-pot models of Americanization. The formation of Asian American political, social, and cultural identity must be accompanied by the same respect of cultural heritages and democratic development that we have so long sought from the mainstream. Just as most Asian Americans have come to realize that developing and identifying an alternative, pluralistic structure may be a natural (and possibly necessary) response to the barriers erected to exclude them from mainstream institutions, so the retention of ethnic culture, heritage, and values, or a multitiered mobilization is also natural and possibly necessary.

Is it misguided to regard Asian American identity as one might view a coalition of people of color, gays and lesbians, and feminists? The racial identification shared by Asian Americans does distinguish the two. Yet, just as in people of color–gay–feminist coalition work where varied interests are respected and understood, and time to caucus independent from the larger coalition is honored, immigration-generated diversity demands respect and space. We must also remember that identity may be linked less to race than to gender, class, and perhaps even geography. These are worthwhile lessons for those who challenge the feasibility of Asian American mobilization or ethnic formation on diversity grounds. Diversity exists within any mobilized coalition or, for that matter, any ethnicity.

No one can claim to know what Asian American ethnicity is or what it will become. No one can claim that a uniform identity exists. And certainly no one can claim to speak for Asian America.

● *F U R T H E R   R E A D I N G*

Chan, Sucheng. "Asian American Historiography," *Pacific Historical Review* 65 (1996): 363–399.
———. *Asian Americans: An Interpretive History* (1991).
Chang, Gordon H. "Asian Americans and the Writing of Their History," *Radical History Review* 53 (1992): 105–114.
———."History and Postmodernism," *Amerasia Journal* 21 (1995): 89–93.
Chang, Mitchell J. "Expansion and Its Discontents: The Formation of Asian American Studies Program in the 1990s," *Journal of Asian American Studies* 2 (1999): 181–206.
Compomanes, Oscar V. "New Formations of Asian American Studies and the Question of U.S. Imperialism," *Positions: East Asia Cultures Critique* 5 (1997): 523–550.
Daniels, Roger. *Asian America: Chinese and Japanese in the United States Since 1850* (1988).
———. "No Lamps Were Lit for Them: Angel Island and the Historiography of Asian American Immigration," *Journal of American Ethnic History* 17 (1997): 3–18.
Dirlik, Arif. "Asians on the Rim: Transnational Capital and Local Community in the Making of Contemporary Asian America," *Amerasia Journal* 22 (1996): 1–24.
Hing, Bill Ong. *Making and Remaking Asian American Through Immigration Policy, 1850–1990* (1993).
"Histories and Historians in the Making," special issue, *Amerasia Journal* 26 (2000).
Hune, Shirley. "Pacific Migration to the United States: Trends and Themes in Historical and Sociological Literature," Research Institute on Immigration and Ethnic Studies, Smithsonian Institution (1977).
Jensen, Joan M. "Women on the Pacific Rim: Some Thoughts on Border Crossings," *Pacific Historical Review* 67 (1998): 3–38.
Lowe, Lisa. *Immigrant Acts: On Asian American Cultural Politics* (1996).
Nomura, Gail M. "Significant Lives: Asia and Asian Americans in the History of the U.S. West," *Western Historical Quarterly* (1994): 69–88.
Okihiro, Gary Y. *Common Ground: Reimagining American History* (2001).
———. *The Columbia Guide to Asian American History* (2001).
———. *Margins and Mainstreams: Asians in American History and Culture* (1994).
———. *Teaching Asian American History* (1997).
Ong, Paul, et. al. *The New Asian Immigration in Los Angeles and Global Restructuring* (1994).
Nomura, Gail M. "Significant Lives: Asia and Asian Americans in the History of the U.S. West," *Western Historical Quarterly* (1994): 69–88.
Takaki, Ronald. *Strangers from a Different Shore: A History of Asian Americans* (1989).
Wong, Sau-Ling C. "Denationalization Reconsidered: Asian American Cultural Criticism at a Theoretical Crossroads," *Amerasia Journal* 21 (1995): 1–27.
Yanagisako, Sylvia. "Transforming Orientalism: Gender, Nationality, and Class in Asian American Studies," in *Naturalizing Power: Essays in Feminist Cultural Analysis,* ed. Sylvia Yanagisako and Carol Delaney (1995), 275–298.

Colonization, Pacific Markets, and Asian Labor Migration to the United States Before the Civil War

It is common practice to begin the story of Asian Americans with the first wave of Chinese laborers to come to the kingdom of Hawai'i and the California Territory in the 1830s and 1840s. This makes sense given that historians of Asian Americans have been preoccupied with themes of social history, including the migrations, communities, work experiences, and mentalities of everyday people. But in the past decade historians have paid increasing attention to how white Americans perceived Asian immigrants. To understand the origins of this perception, it is claimed, Asian American history needs to begin at least with late eighteenth-century trade relations between the new American nation and China. There is, however, a common denominator to both sides of the origins question: the actual arrival of Asian immigrants and the American image of these immigrants were each rooted in global economic transformations set into motion by the dawn of the modern world of exploration, colonial conquest, and global commerce.

Spain ushered in the modern era in its "discovery" and conquest of the Americas. In colonizing what would be called the "Philippine Islands," Spain created the conditions for the establishment of what may well be the first modern settlement of Asians in North America. This was the Filipino community of Louisiana, created perhaps as early as the 1760s by a small number of ex-seamen from the Manila galleon trade, which circulated between the Spanish colonies of Mexico and the Philippines. But by 1835 a larger and steadier influx of Chinese contract laborers began to arrive in Hawai'i. Known as "coolies,"* these cheap, exportable laborers were

---

*A term originating in India for the lowest class of workers put into global currency by Portuguese traders in Asia.

the nineteenth-century alternative to slavery, which at this time was being aban-
doned throughout the world. Hundreds of thousands of Chinese and East Indian
coolies filled the demand for plantation labor throughout the Caribbean and Latin
America. But Hawai'i was the only place in the New World where Asians (Chinese
would be joined by Japanese, Filipinos, and Koreans) came to constitute the vast
majority of workers. These labor migrations, of course, were made possible by the
colonization of Hawai'i, for Americans would not invest heavily in Hawaiian sugar
plantations unless they, and not a powerful Hawaiian monarch, had command of
the islands' major political and economic institutions.

Perhaps the best known of the early Asian migrations to North America is that
of the Chinese who came with the onset of the California Gold Rush in 1849. Like
their brethren who went to Hawai'i and the many more scattered throughout South-
east Asia, these Chinese forty-niners emigrated from China's southern regions in and
around the Pearl River Delta. By the mid-nineteenth century this area was one of the
country's most prosperous, containing its oldest and best developed market-oriented
economies. Consequently, Chinese immigrants to California had been plugged into a
global network of trade, communication, and cultural understanding that extended
to the United States. Their quest for economic riches was but one element in a circuit
of trade and labor migrations that embraced the entire world.

☙ D O C U M E N T S

Contrary to the popular beliefs of Americans, the early Chinese immigrants in California
had come from a modernizing nation that was vitally linked to global markets. As
Document 1 implies, the market economy was especially vigorous, if not politically
sanctioned, in the southern provinces adjacent to China's main international port at
Canton. And so it was that by the eighteenth century the Chinese emperor chastised the
farmers of Fujian and Guangdong for allegedly selling crops for profit rather than feeding the people of their province. Given the extent of entreprenuerism in the Canton region, it was no coincidence that the vast majority of Chinese migrants to San Francisco,
and throughout the world, came from China's southern provinces. Document 2 reveals
that by 1850 the route from Canton to San Francisco was well mapped and traveled by
American vessels.

If getting to the United States was not a problem for the Chinese, then getting
rich, or even making a decent return for their long journey, was. A serious obstacle to
Chinese immigrant livelihood was American anti-Chinese sentiment. All classes of
Americans—Brahmin or pauper, immigrant or native—were unsympathetic to Chinese
migrants. Document 3 presents the view of one of America's greatest philosophers,
Ralph Waldo Emerson, who sarcastically quipped that the height of Chinese civilization
was making tea. While many Americans, especially China traders, romanticized the
greatness of Chinese civilization in the same way that Marco Polo had done centuries
before, Emerson's image of China was akin to those of contemporary American missionaries who condemned what they saw to be a decadent, corrupt, and heathen society.

The next two documents deal with the American colonization of Hawai'i that took
a great leap forward with the opening up of land ownership to whites in 1850 and culminated with the official annexation of the islands by the United States in 1900. Document 4 reveals an exchange between commoners on the island of Maui and the formal
Hawaiian government about the question of foreign ownership of land. Document 5
provides a glimpse of what would happen in the islands after foreigners could legally
own land, in the form of a request for massive land purchases from an American to

Hawaiian government officials. It was the ability to own land that spurred western investment in Hawaiian sugar plantations, whose increasing numbers, in turn, heightened the demand for Asian labor.

The hunger for global markets at this time led as well to the American mission to open up Japan, which had closed its borders to the world for over 250 years. Document 6 is an excerpt from the official journal of the naval commander charged with the assignment of opening Japan. In it the author captures Commodore Perry's overriding purpose of securing favorable trade relations. The reason for this is elaborated upon in Document 7, a newspaper account tremendously optimistic about the prospects of trade between the United States and Japan.

Finally, Document 8 addresses the long-standing Filipino community of Louisiana by providing a brief genealogy of one of its early families. Interesting here is the unique racial context of the American South, where Filipinos could be considered "white" for purposes of work and intermarriage.

1. Chinese Emperor Decries Market Expansion in South China, 1727

The governors of both Fujian and Guangdong Provinces have often said that this province [Guangdong], produces so little rice that it is not enough to meet the demand of the population. Governor-General Gao Qizhuo has memorialized [the emperor] about this. Similarly, Governor Yang Wenqian has reported that the yield of rice in Guangdong in a year of good harvest is only enough to last for half a year. The emperor thinks that Guangdong's inability to produce sufficient rice to meet its own need for food is understandable if it happens in years of poor harvest. If such insufficiency happens every year, including years of good harvest, then it is rather inconceivable. [This could have been caused by three reasons:] the fields are deserted and farmland has not been productively utilized, or, laziness in cultivation and the failure to use enough labor; or cunning people sold rice illegally oversees at high prices. It is uncertain which one of the three is the true cause. The emperor gave exhortations to the officials of the court yesterday. Governor Han Liangfu of Guangxi Province memorialized that Guangdong is densely populated and depends on Guangxi for rice supplies. Within Guangdong, the natives only desire wealth and care about their economic interest, and they use their land to grow products like logan [a popular fruit in China], sugarcane, tobacco, and indigo. Therefore, people have accumulated wealth but rice production remains insufficient. How could Guangxi Province, where land is barren and population is sparse, supply the neighboring province? . . . This memorial is consistent with the emperor's previous exhortation. Hence, we know the reason why Fujian and Guangdong Provinces cannot produce enough food for [their] population. The governors of the two provinces are hereby ordered to educate people, with concentrated and persistent effort, so that everyone would know foodstuff is the most important. Everyone must be engaged in the proper business and do their best to work the land. They must not abandon agricultural work in order to go after profit. They must not go after the superficial and

---

From "Imperial Edict, the Fifth Year in the Reign of the Emperor Yongzheng [1727]," in *Zengcheng xianzhi,* trans. Yong Chen (1820; reprint, Taiwan: Chengwen Chubanshe, n.d.), vol. 1, p. 8.

insignificant and forget how difficult it is to cultivate the land. They should turn to things like fruit trees only when they have extra land and extra energy. How can they only focus on [achieving] temporal interest and ignore the source of livelihood?

2. An American Trader Recommends a Route from California to China, 1850

The interesting nature of this subject induces us to return to it often, even at the risk of intriguing some of our readers. In a former article, we ventured the opinion, based upon reliable information, that the best route across the Pacific would be the Bonin Island and through the Straits of Matsmai or round Cape Awa, the south-eastern point of the island of Niphon, making a depot at Port Melville and Preble. We also advocated Shanghae as the terminus, in preference to Canton or any other point. A gentleman who has long been connected with the China trade, and whose opinions are entitled to much weight, entertains entirely different views, and as any information on this subject is valuable, we shall proceed to make a sketch of his route.

He recommends the line of travel to be from San Francisco to Macao, China, by the Sandwich Islands, Guam, and Manila. The advantages of this route are as follows: on the outward voyage there is but one season of the year that any difficulty might apprehended from unfavorable winds, and that is during the prevalence of the north-east monsoon in November, December, and January. From Manila to Macao strong gales and heavy seas are to be expected, but the distance is very short—not over 650 miles—and it might be steamed in from three or four days at farthest. During the prevalence of the south-west monsoon, but little if any difficulty is to be apprehended, as that wind is neither so strong nor so regular. The steamers between Singapore and Hongkong do their work faithfully and regularly, although unsuitable in size and steampower for those seas. The letters from New York are delivered at the latter place in from sixty-four to seventy days. No difficulty then is anticipated in making the passage from Manila to Macao during the north-east monsoon, nor in returning from Macao to Manila during the prevalence of that from the south-west. The greatest objection to Macao as a terminus is, that the distance is much greater than to Shanghae; but it is urged that the latter place is not much nearer San Francisco than is Canton, the trade of which is far greater than that of Shanghae.

Our informant regards the trade of the Sandwich Islands and of Manila as far more important than that of Japan—and Manila he regards as much more profitable to American commerce than Shanghae. By a late order of the Spanish government, whaling vessels of all nations are allowed to enter the port of Manila without the payment of the usual duties. The latter place and Hongkong are the depots of the whalers who cruise on the coast of Japan, and at the Sandwich Islands a large fleet of whaling vessels stop every year. He therefore regards the Sandwich Islands and Manila as far most important stopping places on the route; and Canton, from its position and having the balance of trade in its favour—from its being already the depot for the Peninsular & Oriental line of steamers, its accessibility, and its being the principal

From the *San Francisco Daily Herald,* October 17, 1850.

residence of the American merchants, is urged as preferable to Shanghae for the terminus of the line. The distance from San Francisco to the Sandwich Islands is 1890 miles—thence to Guam 3320 miles thence to Manila 1353 miles—thence to Macao 630 miles—and thence to Canton by the river steamers 70 miles—making the total distance 7263 miles from this to Canton. This route is regarded as preferable in case Macao is made the depot for coals, and for the distribution of the mails;—in the event that Shanghae is fixed upon as the terminus, the Bonin Islands are decidedly preferable as a depot. It is urged, however, that the navigation of the Yangtse-kiang [Yantze River] is extremely difficult and dangerous, while the port of Macao presents no difficulties, and the Canton river possesses excellent pilots. Furthermore, the largest amount of the tea trade is said to be still in possession of the Canton merchants, and it is doubtful whether it could be turned into any other channel for a long time to come. The supply of coals could be procured from Sydney, Borureo, and Formosa.

3. Writer Ralph Waldo Emerson Excoriates Chinese Civilization, 1824

[April 6, 1824]   Does a bold eye never grow impatient of the ill-starred monotony of history nor ask *to what end* (cui bono) this everlasting recurrence of the same sin & the same sorrow? Why does the same dull current of ignoble blood creep through a thousand generations in China without any provision for its own purification, without the mixture of one drop from the fountains of goodness & glory? Does the secret Agent who pours the tide of existence hope any new result of this ancient experiment? In our feeble vision, it would seem that the immoveable institutions of the yellow men will disappoint for 50 centuries more all expectations of a change. Or is their cheerless (because hopeless) stupidity thus embalmed for immortality on account of any faith or philosophy or science of which they are depositaries & which they keep for other members of the family of nations? No, they worship crockery Gods which in Europe & America our babies are wise enough to put in baby houses; the summit of their philosophy & science is how to make tea. Indeed, the light of Confucius goes out in translation into the language of Shakespeare & Bacon. The closer contemplation we condescend to bestow the more disgustful is that booby nation. The Chinese Empire enjoys precisely a Mummy's reputation, that of having preserved to a hair for 3 or 4,000 years the ugliest features in the world. I have no gift to see a meaning in the venerable vegetation of this extraordinary people. They are not tools for other nations to use. Even miserable Africa can say I have hewn the wood & drawn the water to promote the wealth & civilization of other lands. But, China, reverend dulness! hoary ideot!, all she can say at the convocation of nations must be—"I made the tea." Egypt, Assyria, Persia, Palestine, polished Greece & haughty Rome have bequeathed us arts & instit[utions], the memory & books of great men, & the least legacy that has been left is the moral & argument deducible from the outlines of a history. These nations have left ruins of

From William H. Gilman et al., eds., *The Journals and Miscellaneous Notebooks of Ralph Waldo Emerson,* vol. 2 *1822–1826* (Cambridge: Harvard University Press, 1961), 378–379.

noble cities as the skeleton & monument of themselves. China is her own monument. For myself if such inexplicable doubts (as this Cui Bono) chance to obtrude themselves, they are entertained as a raree shew a little time & then dismissed from the prodigal Memory. But I know & revere some whose life is th[ei]r thought, who zealously pursue all those inquiries that promise to make a little light in the Cimmerian shade of man's state & relations, who encounter doubts & scowl on Sceptics & whose impatience won't let a cloud lie on the ways of Providence. I very much wonder how the pages of history are viewed by such. . . . Are God's blessings geographically circumscribed? No lesson is taught, no good that we know is done by Asia's miserable immense population. And the kindling of a new star, in the abysses of space to hold for a myriad of years the same unmixed unrighteousness & ignorance would shock all our notions of heaven. "What can we reason but from what we know." Calvinism is one hypothesis to solve the prob[lem] but as bad itself.

4. Hawaiians Petition the Privy Council to Halt Foreign Influence in the Islands, and the Council Replies, 1845

A Petition to your gracious Majesty, Kamehameha III., and to all your Chiefs in the Council assembled.

To His Majesty Kamehameha III., and the Premeir Kehaulaahi, and all the Hawaiian Chiefs in council assembled; on account of our anxiety, we petition you, the father of the Hawaiian kingdom, and the following is our petition.

1. Concerning the independence of your kingdom.
2. That you dismiss the foreign officers whom you have appointed to be Hawaiian officers.
3. We do not wish foreigners to take the oath of allegiance and become Hawaiian subjects.
4. We do not wish you to sell any more land pertaining to your kingdom to foreigners.
5. We do not wish taxes in a confused obscure manner to be imposed in your kingdom.
6. This is the cause of our wishing to dismiss these foreign officers. On account of difficulties and apprehensions of burdens that will come upon us. There are your chiefs, who may be officers under you, like as their fathers were under your father, Kamehameha I., and good and intelligent men, in whom you have confidence; let these be officers.

Therefore we make known unto your most gracious Majesty, and to the Premier Kehaulohi, and to all the chiefs of the Hawaiian kingdom, some of our thoughts relative to the above named articles.

From *The Friend,* August 1845, 18–19; reprinted in Lilikalā Kameʻeleihiwa, *Native Lands and Foreign Desires: Pahoa La E Pono Ai?* (Honolulu: Bishop Museum Press, 1992), 334–337.

1. *Concerning the independence of the Hawaiian kingdom.*

We assure your Majesty, and the Premeir Kekauluohi, and the Chiefs and all your common people that we understand your kingdom to be independent. You and your Chiefs perceived the perilous situation of the Hawaiian kingdom in reference to foreigners. Therefore you sent one of your own men and a foreigner, viz: T. Haalilio and Mr Richards, respectfully to beseech large independent nations that your nation might independent. These large nations, viz: the United States, Great Britain, France and Belgium, have declared your kingdom to be independent. By this distinct expression, that these large nations have declared the independence of the Hawaiian kingdom, therefore it is very clear to us, that it is not proper that any foreigner should come in and be promoted in your kingdom, among your Chiefs, and your people. But that it be according to the petition of the ministers, whom you sent to these large nations, praying that the Hawaiian kingdom might be independent by itself.

This is independence; that your gracious Majesty, Kamehameha III. be King, and the Chiefs of your kingdom be your assistants, and also your own people.

Thus may you and your Chiefs act, that your kingdom and all your people may be blessed.

On account of these our thoughts, we petition and beseech you and your Chiefs.—

We the common people of your kingdom hereby subscribe our names.

[It is said that over 1600 names were subscribed to this petition.]

Reply of the Council assembled to the Petition.

July 3d, 1845.

To His Majesty and to the Nobles of the Council assembled, and to the delegates of the common people.

This is our reply to the petition of the common people of Lahaina, and Wailuku and Kailua, and it is submitted for your approbation or disapprobation.

1. *"Concerning the independence of your kingdom."*

This is the meaning of independence:—that Kamehameha III. be King of the Hawaiian Islands, and there be no other King over him. This is the reason of the independence; Great Britain and France, America and Belgium say that "the Hawaiian government are qualified to transact business with foreigners."

How can they transact business with foreigners! In this way only; let His Majesty select persons skilful like those from other lands to transact business with them.

2. *"That you dismiss the foreign officers whom you have chosen to be Hawaiian officers."*

If these shall be dismissed, where is there a man who is qualified to transact business with foreigners? There is no one to be found at the present time; hereafter perhaps the young chiefs will be qualified, when they have grown up to manhood, and shall have completed their education.

3. *"We do not wish foreigners to take the oath of allegiance and become Hawaiian subjects."*

Shall foreigners who become officers take the oath? If not, then they have a chief in another land, and Kamehameha III. is not their proper sovereign, and they will not act righteously between the King and their own countrymen. But if they take the oath of allegiance to Kamehameha III., will they not be faithful to him. And will they not cease to have regard for the chief they have foresaken?

Shall other foreigners take the oath of allegiance? This is a land which lies where ships in the Pacific ocean often come. Shall not foreigners come on shore? They do come on shore. Can they not be permitted to live on shore?—According to the treaties they can. Who shall be their proper sovereign? Will not difficulties arise between some of them and the Hawaiians? Difficulties will arise, for formerly there were many difficulties, and the land was taken; it was not taken because the government was really in the wrong, but because evil was sought. Here is the difficulty which ruins the government, viz: the complaint of foreign governments followed by the infliction of punishment. Foreigners who take the oath of allegiance can apply to only one sovereign, viz: Kamehameha III.; he will adjust their difficulties in a proper manner, and they will render important services to Hawaii, their land.

Some say, let none but good foreigners take the oath of allegiance. How then shall it be with those who are not good? Shall they not live on shore? How can they be driven off? Shall they be put on board another man's ship! If so, the owners will forsake the ship, and the government must pay the damages. Messrs. Bachelot and Sport were thus treated, and the result was a fine of $20,000.

Let no one have apprehensions concerning those who take the oath of allegiance. If they conduct properly, then the land is blessed by them. If they transgress, here are laws to punish them, and there is no other nation which will interfere in behalf of wicked foreigners, when we punish them. Here is wherein other nations will favour us; they will not take the part of their people, who transgress our laws, neither will they punish us without a cause, as they did formerly.

4. *"We do not wish you to sell any more land pertaining to your kingdom to foreigners."*

This is our opinion; it is by no means proper to sell land to aliens, nor is it proper to give them land, for the land belongs to Kamchameha III.; there is no chief over him. But we think it is proper to sell and to his Majesty's people, that they may have a home. But if these persons wish to sell their lands again, they cannot sell to aliens, for there is only one sovereign over those who hold lands; but if the people wish to sell to those who have taken the oath of allegiance, they can do so, for Kamehameha III. is King over them. If his Majesty thinks it expedient to sell lands to his own people, is it proper for him to refuse another, who has forsaken the land of his birth, and his first chief, and become a Hawaiian subject! By no means, for this would be using partiality. There has not been much land sold, but foreigners have heretofore occupied lands through favor, without purchasing. It is better to sell. The people have not thought much about purchasing lands; but those who have been to the Columbia River see the advantage of purchasing land, and they will hereafter wish to purchase lands.

If the common people had petitioned that land should not be sold to sailors, would not the petition be unjust? It is proper to sell small farms to natives and also to foreign subjects, and let them cultivate alike, that the skilful may instruct the ignorant in the work.

5. *"We do not wish taxes in a confused obscure manner to be imposed in your kingdom."*

That is right, they are not thus imposed. They were so indeed, formerly, to the injury of the common people; but now this matter is regulated by law, and so it will be hereafter should new laws be enacted.

This is our reply to the petition laid before you, with due reverence.

JOHN YOUNG.
JOHN II.

This reply was corrected and approved by the assembly of chiefs and delegates of the common people in the hall of legislation, on the 8th of July, 1845, with no dissenting voice.

KAMEHAMEHA.

5. A Foreigner Speculates on Hawaiian Land Acquisition, 1849

The lands set aside as Gov't lands if put into market now will sell readily, adding both to the immediate revenue of the Gov't and the wealth and prosperity of the Kingdom. I learn that great changes have taken place since I left and hope that among the advances made, you have exploded the foolish prejudice against giving titles in fee simple to aliens. I know you have always coincided with me on this front, and also on the necessity of having the lands put into market at a regular graduated price & will only say that these two points are of the utmost importance. If in the Gov't lands there are any natives the Gov't should buy them out.

There are a great many good men with capital here ready and anxious to purchase lands and settle them, but an idea is *general* that no lands can be procured, and that a thousand humbugs exist. This general impression can only be refuted by the actual & prompt sale of lands in fee simple.

There is an engineer here who will come down and survey the whole group of Islands into sections and plot them; with the maps of this survey in the land office—and a regular established price—the whole unoccupied lands could be sold at once yielding a handsome revenue—securing the improvement of the lands & the settlement of the group by an enterprising and intelligent race. But I will enlarge no more upon the advantages of this course; you and every intelligent man must see its results.

From Andrew W. Lind, *An Island Community: Ecological Succession in Hawaii* (Chicago: University of Chicago Press, 1938), 53.

Now for the business—I wish you to purchase on my account a plot of land applied for Y.—and located in Hilo Bay. It comprises about two thousand acres, and I expect you can get it for $7.00 per acre title in fee simple to which I am entitled, being a denisen.

I wish you would immediately purchase on our joint account 20 good plantations—half of the village of Lahaina & ½ of Hilo Bay and as much land in Honolulu & Nuuanu Valley as you can get hold of all at low rates and on time; send the deeds to me. I could sell them all at a handsome advance here for cash.

You have the funds and credit to make such a grand operation & I know of no one in whose hands such an undertaking would be better managed. If you cannot get hold of a lot of land immediately in your own right, secure plots of land for plantations and house lots from Gov't and send me the plots with power of attorney to sell from the king. You must beware of raising prices too high, if you do, you will check the flood of emigration. I wish you would purchase on your account the lots on the beach east of the Fort with wharf rights. They will soon be valuable.

You will please keep this private, for I intend to make something now & eventually to settle there.

6. American Commodore M. C. Perry Opens Up the Japanese Market, 1856

From the circumstances of the case, there was novelty in the features of the mission on which Commodore Perry was sent. Little or no guidance was to be derived from our past diplomatic experience or action. The nearest approach to such guidance was to be found in our treaty with China, made in 1844. This, therefore, was carefully studied by the Commodore. It purports to be "a treaty or general convention of peace, amity, and commerce," and to settle the rules to "be mutually observed in the intercourse of the respective countries." . . .

It certainly was very desirable to obtain, if possible, similar privileges from Japan. The Commodore resolved that, if the Japanese would negotiate at all, his first efforts should be directed to that end. . . . He was not sanguine enough to hope that he could procure an entire adoption of the Chinese treaty by the Japanese. He was not ignorant of the difference in national characteristics between the inhabitants of China and the more independent, self-reliant, and sturdy natives of the Japanese islands. He knew that the latter held the former in some degree of contempt and treated them in the matter of trade very much as they did the Dutch. He was also aware that the Chinese, when they made their treaty, did know something of the advantages that might result from an intercourse with the rest of the world. As to the Japanese, in their long-continued isolation, either they neither knew nor desired such advantages, or, if they knew them, feared they might be purchased at too high a price in the introduction of foreigners who, as in the case of the Portuguese centuries before, might seek to overturn the empire. It was too much, therefore, to expect that

From Francis L. Hawkes, *Narrative of the Expedition of an American Squadron to the China Seas and Japan, Performed in the Years 1852, 1853, 1854, Under the Command of Commodore M. C. Perry, etc.* (New York: D. Appleton and Company, 1856), 445–447, 452–453.

the Japanese would imitate the Chinese in *all* the particulars of a treaty. Still, they might be disposed to adopt some of its most important features when suggested to them by a knowledge of what other orientals had done. . . .

The Commodore, whose wish it was to do as far as possible everything that might conciliate, of course made no objection to a request [to translate the treaty] so seemingly reasonable, though he knew it to be needless, and was content to wait patiently for their reply. In one week that reply came in writing, and was very explicit: "As to opening a trade, such as is now carried on by China with your country, we certainly cannot *yet* bring it about. The feelings and manners of our people are very unlike those of outer nations, and it will be exceedingly difficult, even if you wish it, to immediately change the old regulations for those of other countries. Moreover, the Chinese have long had intercourse with western nations, while we have had dealings at *Nagasaki* with only the people of Holland and China."

This answer was not entirely unexpected, and put an end to all prospect of negotiating a "commercial treaty," in the European sense of that phrase. It only remained, therefore, to secure, for the present, admission into the kingdom, and so much of trade as Japanese jealousy could be brought to concede. At length, after much and oft-repeated discussion, the point was yielded that certain ports might be opened to our vessels. . . .

. . . [T]he whole treaty shows that the purpose of the Japanese was to try the experiment of intercourse with us before they made it as extensive or as intimate as it is between us and the Chinese. It was all they would do at the time, and much, very much, was obtained on the part of our negotiator in procuring a concession even to this extent.

But, as he knew that our success would be but the forerunner of that of other powers, as he believed that new relations of trade once commenced, not only with ourselves but with England, France, Holland, and Russia, in the progress of events, could not fail effectually and forever not only to break up the old restrictive policy and open Japan to the world, but must also lead gradually to liberal commercial treaties, he wisely, in the ninth article, without "consultation or delay," secured to the United States and their citizens all privileges and advantages which Japan might hereafter "grant to any other nation or nations."

As far we we have yet learned, all other powers have been content to obtain just what we, as pioneers, have obtained. Their treaties are like ours. . . .

We respectfully submit, that all, and indeed more than all, under the circumstances, that could reasonably have been expected, has been accomplished. Japan has been opened to the nations of the west. It is not to be believed, that having once effected an entrance, the enlightened powers that have made treaties with her will *go backward,* and, by any indiscretion, lose what, after so many unavailing efforts for centuries, has at last been happily attained. It belongs to these nations to show Japan that her interests will be promoted by communication with them. As prejudice gradually vanishes, we may hope to see the future negotiation of more and more liberal commercial treaties, for the benefit, not of ourselves only, but of all the maritime powers of Europe, for the advancement of Japan, and for the upward progress of our common humanity. It would be a foul reproach to Christendom now to force Japan to relapse into her cheerless and unprogressive state of unnatural isolation. She is the youngest sister in the circle of commercial nations. Let those who are older kindly take her by the hand, and aid her tottering steps, until she has reached a vigor that will enable her to walk firmly in her own strength. Cautious and kindly treatment now will soon lead to commercial treaties as liberal as can be desired.

7. *New York Times* Heralds New Trade with China and Japan, 1858

Events are conspiring in every part of the world to give great importance to our possessions on the Pacific slope. Hitherto one-third of the entire population of the world have been shut in from intercourse with other nations, in China and Japan. The exclusive and seclusive policy of both these countries has now all at once been abandoned, and the western coasts of the Pacific Ocean are about to become as active with the hum of commerce as the northern coasts of the Atlantic. We doubt if the commercial activity of the United States, England, Holland and Sweden will hereafter at all compare with that of the Chinese and Japanese nations; now that scope has been given to the enterprise of these people, and a freer intercourse with European and American merchants has been legalized. The population of these countries vastly exceeds that of the commercial nations of Europe, and the trade carried on in their waters will probably exceed, in the course of a few years, that of all the American and European ports of the Atlantic, in as great a degree as the number of their people exceeds that of the populations of the commercial nations of Christendom.

It is impossible to over-estimate the magnitude of the trade which, in the course of the next ten years, will have grown up between these two populations on the one side, and the European and American cities on the other. To predict that in the course of time it will *equal in magnitude and value the present entire trade between the nations of the Christian world* would hardly be extravagant. . . . It is natural to suppose that immense marts of commerce will soon grow up on our Pacific coast. The shortest route by many hundred miles from the ports of China and Japan to London, and the shortest by more than a thousand miles from these ports to New-York, lies across the Pacific to California, and thence by the routes over Central America. The most direct routes, still shorter, lie directly across our Continent from our Pacific ports. These circumstances cannot fail to attract an immense population to our Pacific States; and, acting in conjunction with the influence of the gold and silver deposits which lie along the whole coast, and the natural tendency of our agricultural population to emigrate and colonize in that direction, an accumulation of population on those coasts more rapid than has ever before been known in the history of human migration cannot fail to result. . . .

But, after all, there can be no doubt that the cheapest lines of communication with our Pacific settlements and the chief tides of travel will pass over the lower latitudes of the continent. In the course of years this movement will exert an immense influence upon the affairs of Mexico; a region of country which will sooner or later loom up into immense importance under the influence of the trade of China and Japan, and the rapid growth of population upon the Pacific slope. The pestilential

---

From "The Newly-Opened Trade with the East—Its Results upon Our Pacific States and upon Mexico," *New York Times*, December 3, 1858.

vapors of the narrow portions of the continent will always impose more or less dis-advantage upon the transits through Panama and Nicaragua, and Mexico will con-stitute the bridge over which the chief intercourse between the Atlantic and Pacific ports and populations must have their passage. *It is probable that Mexico may lie for several years longer the prey of contending factions, the victim of anarchy and lawlessness;* but sooner or later the necessities of the greatest commerce which the world has yet seen, and the convenience of a mightier migration to and fro than has ever yet been known in international or intercontinental intercourse, will reduce it to the dominion of civilization, government, and law, and convert it, with the aid of its native resources of climate, soil, and mineral wealth, into one of the most flourishing and important regions of the habitable earth.

8. Researcher Traces Early Nineteenth-Century Origins of Filipino American Family, 1988

By far the oldest documented Filipino family that I have come across in my nine years of research is that of Felipe Madrigal, whose arrival in Louisiana some of his descendants estimated to be in the early 1800s. They claimed that Felipe, better known as Philip, hailed from Manila in the Philippines. Since the name Madrigal is rather popular in the island of Negros, it is quite possible that Felipe was a Visayan just as most of the early Filipino settlers in Louisiana. Whatever his exact place of origin, he is still remembered; a fading picture of Felipe Madrigal is kept by Lillian Martinez Burtanog, 74, Felipe's great-granddaughter.

The story goes that Felipe Madrigal came to Louisiana when New Orleans was becoming an important port of call for ships coming from Europe and the New World. As an experienced seaman, Felipe did not encounter any difficulty landing a job on one of the passenger ships that plied between Europe and America. On one of his home-bound trips, Felipe met his future bride, an Irish woman named Bridgett Nugent, who was a passenger on the clipper. Bridgett was with her parents and brother, who were bound for America. During the three-month journey from Ireland, Felipe and Bridgett became well acquainted and were married upon their arrival in New Orleans. Her parents were extremely disappointed for they had hoped their daughter would marry a rich American. Bridgett's parents continued north and were never to contact their daughter again. Felipe quit his job as a seaman in order to be with his bride, and they settled on the Westbank of New Orleans.

Out of this union, three daughters were born: Helen, Mary Ellen and Elizabeth. When the girls were growing up, Felipe proved to be a model husband and father. This set a good example for his children to follow. The daughters emulated their mother by also marrying Filipinos. Helen married Teodoro Victoriano, better known as Doro. Mary Ellen to Daniel Reyes, and Elizabeth to Baltic Borabod. Because there was no son to keep the name of Madrigal alive, it was lost after the second generation.

Felipe tried his hand at business and opened his own restaurant. During the Civil War when the U.S. dollars were changed to Confederate money, he managed to

From Marina E. Espina, *Filipinos in Louisiana* (New Orleans: A. F. Laborde, 1988), 58–59, 61, 63, 65; this essay appeared earlier in *Perspectives on Ethnicity in New Orleans,* ed. John Cooke (New Orleans: Committee on Ethnicity in New Orleans, 1979).

hide some. Somehow Felipe had ambivalent feelings about the Americans fighting among themselves, but he was very confident that the divided states would again be reunited. At the end of the war, Felipe's faith in the American dream was proven when he dug up what he had buried in 1861, a can containing 200 Yankee dollars. He was quite a rich Filipino in a land of Confederate money.

The Madrigal family tree has indeed grown. There are now seven generations, and descendants can be found in the four corners of the United States: from Washington state to Connecticut and from California to Virginia. . . .

At age 13, Elizabeth, the youngest of the Madrigal sisters, was married to Baltic Borabod, a Filipino from Cebu who had come to Louisiana in the 1850s. Baltic was an overseer at the Wilkinson Plantation in Myrtle Grove for many years. As he grew older, his thick mass of white hair made a striking impression as he rode about on his white horse, overseeing the field hands.

As a Filipino's daughter, Elizabeth blended perfectly into French-Spanish Louisiana by being a fluent speaker of French, Spanish, English and Tagalog. Baltic and Elizabeth had five children: Mathilda, Othelia (Lily), Sidonia, Rosalie and Peter. Grandma Beth, as Elizabeth was fondly called by her grandchildren, taught her offspring a sense of togetherness. She would constantly impress upon them that they should keep in touch with each other no matter how far they might be apart and no matter how many years might intervene. To this day, these descendants return regularly for a reunion with their cousins in New Orleans. So close are they that the grandchildren talk familiarity of each other despite the fact some of them have never met. They share a common motto they acquired from their Grandma Beth: no fighting amongst ourselves but together we can whip the outsiders.

E S S A Y S

The first essay, by University of California at Irvine historian Yong Chen, focuses on British colonialism as the engine driving a large wave of Chinese to emigrate from south China. These migrants, who started leaving in the late 1840s, were the first Asians to arrive in the United States's newly conquered territory of California. In the second essay, historian Ronald Takaki of the University of California at Berkeley reveals the origins of Hawai'i's multi-Asian workforce in efforts by Americans to control the Island's political economy.

Origins of Chinese Emigration to California

YONG CHEN

Most studies of Chinese America have focused on the new world that these immigrants entered. This essay attempts to understand the old world (namely, the delta region that was home to all major emigrant communities) that the immigrants had left. It seeks, in particular, to add to and to modify the prevailing interpretation of the internal causes of mid-nineteenth-century Chinese emigration to California. The

From Yong Chen, "The Internal Origins of Chinese Emigration to California Reconsidered," *Western Historical Quarterly* 28 (winter 1997): 520–522, 528–534, 537–541, 545–546. Copyright © 1997 Western Historical Society. Used with permission.

common interpretation has viewed the emigration primarily as a desperate flight from impoverishment. The emigrant communities, this perspective says, were not only plagued by problems such as over-population, but were further devastated by certain new developments, especially the arrival of Western imperialism, marked by the Opium War (1840–1842).

Such an interpretation is not so much wrong as it is incomplete in explaining why Chinese emigration began in the mid-nineteenth century and why almost all emigrants came from the delta region, which remained the main source of U.S.-bound emigration until after World War II. My analysis concerns primarily the early phase of Chinese emigration. It is during the crucial initial phase that the pattern of migration was established by the pioneers, who in various ways facilitated the departure of others from the same villages and areas for the United States in later years.

Real hardships undoubtedly existed in the region around the mid-nineteenth century and played a role in prompting the exodus, but their significance has been overstated. Socioeconomic problems, such as land shortage, did not arise suddenly around the time emigration began; these problems had existed in the delta and beyond for decades. The impact of the Opium War and other events was by no means more keenly felt in the emigrant communities than elsewhere. And, those who simply wanted to flee unbearably harsh situations did not have to cross the vast Pacific Ocean to do it. California, which received a relatively small number of emigrants, could hardly function as a safety valve for China.

To understand the origins of Chinese emigration, we need to scrutinize, more closely than before, the local emigrant communities. Such an examination will enhance our understanding of the specific local circumstances, under which some individual residents decided to journey to California—as a choice rather than a desperate flight. . . .

. . . [L]et us turn to Xinning County, one of the empirical local cases that has been used to prove that emigration was caused by unbearable conditions at home. Overall, this county was the most important source of Chinese emigration to the United States, sending more people there than any of the other counties from the 1860s to the early twentieth century. In the delta area, Xinning was also know for its rough mountainous terrain and its barren soil, as well as for its lack of adequate agricultural land. Undoubtedly, in terms of economic prosperity, it did not rank very high in the area.

But the Xinning case is more complex than it appears at first glance, First, it was still much better-off than many other counties beyond the delta area. More important, it did not become an unrivaled source of emigration until the 1860s. During the 1850s Xiangshan County sent about as many people to America as Xinning. Yet Xiangshan had many more natural and economic resources than Xinning. Its agricultural production, in particular, was better than that of Xinning and remained strong, even at times of political instability. After the Red-Turban Rebellion, for instance, the enterprising Xiangshan agriculturists made "great profit." Second, the case can be made that Xinning's numerical superiority in sending emigrants was attributable to its position as a supplier of labor in the entire region's commercialized economy. As such, the county had many experienced wage-earning laborers ready for new opportunities in new market economies.

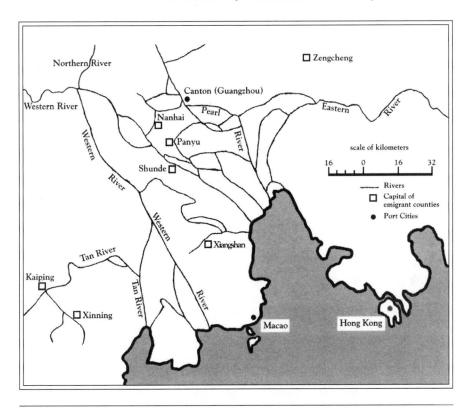

Major emigrant counties and port cities of the Pearl River Delta region.

If the emigrants had simply wanted to escape poverty in Xinning or elsewhere in the delta region, they did not have to go to California. There were other, easier options available to them. Compared to the long, unknown journey across the Pacific Ocean, for example, they could have taken a reasonably well-known voyage down to Southeast Asia on a junk manned, and often owned, by their fellow countrymen. In Southeast Asia, they would have been able to work with, or for, their own countrymen—who had ventured there as merchants or laborers from Guangdong and Fujian since the fifteenth century.

Opportunities in Southeast Asia were widely known in South China. Large numbers of Chinese ships that regularly traveled there, carrying goods as well as emigrants and other passengers, caught the attention of foreigners in the Canton area. In May 1832, *The Chinese Repository,* a Canton-based periodical, declared that "[a]t the present time . . . Chinese ships . . . are frequently seen, and in considerable numbers, at Penang, Bangkok, and in many of the ports of the Eastern Archipelago." . . .

Indeed, no matter how hard life was for various groups in mid-nineteenth century South China, California hardly served as its "safety valve." Of the millions of

Map courtesy of Yong Chen. Reprinted by permission of *The Western Historical Quarterly.*

emigrants who had left mainland China by the 1860s, most had traveled to Southeast
Asia from Guangdong and Fujian provinces. In 1860, according to federal census
figures, the Chinese population in the continental United States (primarily on the
West Coast, especially in California) was about 35,000, which is less than one-
fourth of the Chinese community in Java. Overall, Chinese emigration to America
represents only a trickle of the massive Chinese overseas migration. Between 1849
and 1859, less than 70,000 people chose to go to California. By comparison, in an
indisputable attempt to escape hunger, caused mainly by the failure of the potato
harvest, nearly one and one-quarter million Irish people rushed to America between
1846–1854. The emigration of a much smaller number of people from China
to California over a longer period of time does not appear to be simply a panic-
stricken flight from poverty and hunger at all. Such a flight would have included
far more people.

Not only must we avoid overestimating the significance of socioeconomic
hardships in creating the Chinese exodus to California, but equally importantly, we
must recognize that despite its problems, the pre-emigration delta had been one of
the most prosperous areas in China. . . .

A number of factors account for the vitality and prosperity of the region,
which had been blessed by nature in various ways. Overall, it had the most fertile
and productive land within the province. What is more, it had an ideal natural environment for internal and international trade. Its many inland waterways served to
link different counties within the region, and the long, curved coastline offered fine
harbors, connecting the region to economies overseas. Central to the regional
economy, Canton had been an important port city for centuries. Between 1757 and
the end of the Opium War, it was designated as China's sole port for international
trade. Even for decades after the Opium War, Canton remained a significant international port city. As a result, a dynamic economy emerged in the delta region long
before the mid-nineteenth century, an economy characterized by the production of
agricultural and non-agricultural commodities for domestic as well as international
markets. Such a market-oriented economy constituted the foundation of the region's
prosperity. It also enabled a population growth that exceeded what a subsistence
economy could sustain.

To fully understand the situation in the emigrant communities, we must use local
sources. Students of Chinese emigration do not have documents like the British
Register of Emigration that Bernard Bailyn used in his study of English emigrants,
Voyagers to the West. No systematic statistical data are available about early emigration to California, and the information about individual emigrants is scarce,
particularly for the period before the 1860s. Nonetheless, there are abundant local
sources of varied sorts that reveal a great deal about the world from which the emigrants came. . . .

. . . [N]othing records the conditions of the emigrants' home districts more sys-
tematically and extensively than the local gazetteer. The gazetteer is a special
genre of literature in the centuries-old tradition of Chinese historical writing that
can be traced back to the Han Dynasties (206 BCE–220 CE). The Ming and the
Quing (especially) dynasties marked the genre's most fruitful period. Overall,
more than eight thousand gazetteers have survived the passage of time, and about
five thousand, or 70 percent, of them are from the Qing Dynasty. The gazetteer was

written at various levels, ranging from the province to the village. The most common are those written at the county level, called *xianzhi* (meaning "country gazetteer" or "county records").

The xianzhi compilers relied on different kinds of sources. They used local archives and other published and unpublished documents. They also sent interviewers to different parts of the county to collect first-hand information from local residents orally. Each xianzhi represents an encyclopedic source for the county that it covers, providing rich information about its economy, demography, and natural environment as well as its history, literature, and social customs. It also includes biographies of individual local men and women. . . .

As the xianzhi and other local documents indicate, by the mid-nineteenth century subsistence agriculture had long ceased to be the dominant economic feature in the emigrant communities. They had been incorporated into a longstanding market-oriented economy in the region. . . .

The delta region's market-oriented economy emerged long before the Opium War. It was centered around Canton and extended to nearby Macao and, later on, to Hong Kong. An extensive network of local markets formed a solid foundation for that economy. "Markets are everywhere in Guangdong," noted an eighteenth-century native Cantonese writer. During the eighteenth century and the early nineteenth century, the number of markets significantly increased in many areas across Guangdong, especially in the Pearl River Delta. Many markets in that region were specialized in certain kinds of products, such as *longan* (a popular local fruit), medicine, spices, and pearls.

Those markets were closely connected to Canton, the heart of the regional economy, through the many ocean and inland waterways. By the early nineteenth century, when Americans arrived in increasing numbers, Canton had become a busy metropolitan city of regional and international trade, characterized by bustling economic activities. A young American named W. C. Hunter recalled later what he had seen upon entering this busy port city in February 1825 abroad the *Citizen:* "It was then crowded with native vessels . . . these brought cargoes from Teenpak and places on the coast south-westward of Macao. . . . The number of cargo boats from the interior, of passenger boats, floating residences and up-country craft . . . was prodigious."

. . . [W]hat we find in those counties was no pure traditional agrarian economy. In Xinning County, for instance, there were over 70 local market places in the mid-nineteenth century. What is more, people in Xinning and Enping counties traveled to work in more developed market economies. During the fall and winter seasons and during times of poor harvest, people from these two counties, especially Xinning County, went to other counties, such as Nanhai, to seek employment as artisans and other types of workers. These less developed counties entered the region's commercial network as suppliers of labor.

Such differences between the sanyi counties and those like Xinning reflected the regional economic structure. It is necessary to note that such structural differences were transplanted to the New World. It was common knowledge among the immigrants that while those from Xinning and other less developed counties were likely to be laborers, merchants tended to be from the sanyi counties. As a major supplier of labor in the economy of the Pearl River Delta, Xinning had a ready pool of laborers with experience, and willingness to travel and work elsewhere. That

Xining occupied this position in the regional market economy, helps explain why it became the single most important sending county during the first century of Chinese emigration. By comparison, the rich tradition in commerce in the sanyi counties offered . . . sanyi people various vital resources, making it relatively more likely for them to become merchants. . . .

To enrich our understanding of Chinese emigration, we also need to appreciate the cultural vitality of the Pearl River region. Situated in the forefront of China's maritime frontier, the Pearl River region became the focal point of contact between China and the West, where westerners clustered. In particular, the region had long and significant connections with the United States. Such connections were built by Yankee China traders and missionaries, who first arrived in China in 1784 and 1830 respectively, as well as by numerous local residents who had traveled to the United States. This region maintained close ties to America after the Opium War, thanks to Cantonese merchants' control over such merchandise as tea and to the renowned geographic conditions of the ports of Canton and neighboring Macao and Hong Kong. For local people, the region's American connections constituted important cultural resources.

Because of such connections, these people were among the first in China to learn about the United States. In fact, the Cantonese coined some early Chinese terms for it, such as the "Flowery-flag Country," which was based on their impression of the flag that Americans carried to China. These Americans helped disseminate information about the United States through their varied contact with local residents. In the hospital that he founded in Canton in 1835, for example, the American medical missionary Peter Parker treated tens of thousands of patients, including a great number of people from various emigrant communities. Americans also wrote about the United States for the Chinese audience. . . .

Of particular importance were the direct and longstanding connections between Canton and California. For years, the American Pacific Coast supplied some of the most marketable goods for American China traders, including sea otter skins. California became more important in that trade during the 1830s, when the Pacific Northwest lost its attraction to China traders. Numerous Yankee settlers in California joined the China trade. One of them was Alpheus Basil Thompson, a New England native, who settled in Santa Barbara. We can get a glimpse of California's extensive involvement in that trade from a letter that a Honolulu-based American company named Pierce and Brewer sent to Thompson on 9 August 1837:

> The Griffon on her arrival back here, will proceed immediately to China, and return here with a cargo. —Should you feel disposed to give Capt. Little orders for China goods we shall be willing to import them . . . either to be delivered on California or at this place. We intend to run her as a regular trader between this place, China & California. . . . The otter Skins are still on hand and are in good order—from Capt. Little you will learn the State of [the] China Market as it regards that article.

San Francisco was America's West-Coast center of the China trade, where a wide variety of goods was brought from China, indicating vividly the extensive economic connection across the Pacific Ocean. Around 1850, two visitors to San Francisco took notice of the extensive use of Chinese goods in numerous places. Inside the building of J. L. Riddle and Co., for example, they found that "nearly all the furniture then was of China importation; and very commodious, stylish and comfortable it was, too." In their description of the city in 1852, the authors of *The Annals of San Francisco* mentioned a "large and imposing edifice of granite," occupied by "Adams & Co., express agents, and Page, Bacon & Co., bankers." They reported: "The stone for this building was prepared in China and put up in San Francisco by Chinese workmen."

The old timers in the China trade knew firsthand the best routes to take across the Pacific. By 1850, there existed a well-established and heavily-traveled route from San Francisco to Macao and Canton by way of the Sandwich Islands, Guam, and Manila. This 7,263-mile route was the most ideal of all, because it allowed mariners to avoid unfavorable winds and to have easy access to coal supplies in Sydney and Taiwan.

Traveling on this route, China-bound vessels not only brought goods to the Chinese market but also news about events on the other side of the Pacific Ocean. The English-language newspapers published in South China frequently carried reports of such news, sometimes taken directly from San Francisco-based periodicals, such as the *San Francisco Daily Herald,* the *Alta California,* and the *Daily Journal of Commerce.* Therefore, it did not take long before Americans and other Westerners there learned about gold in California. In a letter to his brother back in the United States, the American, S. Wells Williams, wrote on 26 March 1849 from Canton: "The discovery of gold in California to such an unlimited extent has thrown our community into the same ferment as elsewhere." By early summer of that year, articles appeared in the English-language periodicals in the Canton area, such as *China Mail,* advising people not to believe the inflated stories. Apparently, the discovery of gold was already old news by then.

There is no doubt that local residents in the emigrant communities were among the first Chinese in China to learn about California gold. While it remains unclear exactly how the news first reached them, individual emigrants could have heard about it from a multitude of different sources. While some would have gotten the news when working as seasonal laborers away from home, others would have received it directly from Americans like Peter Parker. Successful merchants from the emigrant communities, who developed close connections with Americans, must have also played an important role in spreading the word. The most famous one among them was Wu Bingjian (also known as Wu Yihe) of Nanhai County, whom Westerners called Houqua (also spelled Howqua). His extensive personal and business relations with Americans and his strong local ties in Nanhai are clearly recorded in both Chinese- and English-language documents. Moreover, there had been a few Cantonese individuals in America before the Gold Rush, including merchants, sailors, and others brought to the United States by veteran Yankee China traders and missionaries. Some of these Chinese would have helped disseminate the news. Legend has it, for example, that a man named Chun Ming, who had come to California as a merchant earlier and became a successful gold miner during the Gold Rush, was among the first to break the news to people back in Canton from overseas.

Based on such news that they learned one way or another, local Chinese formed their image of California: during the very first years of Chinese emigration, they knew California as "Jinshan" (meaning "Gold Mountain" or "the Country of Gold" in Chinese). Indeed, gold was what most early emigrants had in mind when going to California. A Chinese-language article in the San Francisco-based *The Oriental* stated that "most of the Chinese arriving in this city are gold-miners," and few came for other reasons.

In a word, it is the longstanding trans-Pacific connections that offer a key reason why Chinese emigration occurred in the mid-nineteenth century and why an over-whelming majority of Chinese immigrants came from the Canton area. . . .

. . .[I]n order to understand more completely the internal origins of mid-nineteenth century Chinese emigration to California, we need to adopt a new per-spective and examine carefully local conditions in the emigrant communities. That is, we must fully recognize the economic resources and informational advantages available to the delta region's residents, instead of over-emphasizing the socioeco-nomic disadvantages. In its relatively highly developed market economy, while Cantonese merchants accumulated capital and contributed to building an extensive network of trans-Pacific communication, others acquired valuable experience as hired laborers. Because of the historical and geographical position of this region, moreover, local residents were among the first Chinese to hear about the gold mines in California. Such a new perspective will enable us to see emigration not as forced flight, but as a rational decision by the emigrants based on their experience and knowledge gained in their home communities. It will also allow us to understand the hope and aspirations of the emigrants to achieve upward social mobility for themselves and for their families.

Native and Asian Labor in
the Colonization of Hawai'i

RONALD TAKAKI

In Koloa, "a mere hamlet, seldom visited by even a missionary," the Hawaiian natives noticed in 1835 the arrival of William Hooper of Boston, Massachusetts. They had seen white men before: in 1778, some of them had travelled to Waimea, sixteen miles away, to get a glimpse of Captain James Cook, or had heard stories about the English explorer's momentous visit—how he had sailed into the bay in two huge ships with billowing white sheets, how his men had carried awesome weapons of fire and destruction, and how they had left behind them, with the native women, a dreadful disease. Many of the natives still possessed souvenirs of Cook's visit, the iron nails they had ripped from his landing boats and the butcher's cleaver one of them had stolen.

As the natives curiously scrutinized their new visitor, they compared Hooper to the other white men at Waimea: the merchants shipping the fragrant sandalwood to China and supplying whaling vessels with water and provisions, and the missionaries building a new church there and spreading Christianity among the natives. But the people of Koloa did not realize that Hooper, more than the merchants and the mis-sionaries, represented the beginning of a new era in the history of Hawaii. Sent to Koloa by Ladd and Company of Honolulu to establish the first plantation in the

From Ronald Takaki, "*An Entering Wedge:* The Origins of the Sugar Plantation and a Multi-ethnic Working Class in Hawaii," *Labor History* 23, no. 1 (winter 1982); 34–46. Copyright © 1982 Taylor & Francis Ltd. Used with permission. www.tandf.co.uk/journals.

Sandwich Islands and to cultivate sugar cane as a cash crop, he was there to remake Hawaii in his own image: to advance American capitalism and civilization to a new Pacific frontier, undermining in the process the feudal society of Hawaii and the people's traditional relationship with their land.

During the next century, the Hawaiian sugar industry, which Hooper had initiated, transformed both the ethnicity of the people and the economy of the islands. In 1835, nearly the entire population was Hawaiian: foreigners constituted only .55 percent of the total, or only 600 out of a population of 108,000. In 1920, persons of Hawaiian ancestry made up only 16.3 percent of the population, while Caucasians represented 19.2 percent, Chinese 9.2 percent, Japanese 42.7 percent, Koreans 1.9 percent, Puerto Ricans 2.2 percent, and Filipinos 8.2 percent. Eighty years after Hooper had planted his first field of sugar cane, Hawaiian plantations produced 556,871 tons of sugar, representing the leading industry of the islands and providing the basis of five large and powerful corporations—American Factors, Castle and Cooke, C. Brewer and Company, T. H. Davies and Company, and Alexander and Baldwin.

While the relationship between the ethnic diversity of the people of Hawaii and the development of the sugar industry is readily apparent, little is known about the early origins of both of them. Fortunately, we have documents which can help to unshroud much of this history—the handwritten diary of Hooper and the extensive collection of his correspondence with Ladd and Company. Together they can enable us to reconstruct the critical early years of modern plantation Hawaii. . . .

As a young man of twenty-six years, William Hooper keenly understood the significance of his enterprising venture in Koloa. Only two years earlier, he had landed in Honolulu with Peter Brinsmade and William Ladd; together they had opened a mercantile trading house named Ladd and Company. The company had leased from King Kamehameha III a tract of land, 980 acres on the east side of the Waihohonu Stream in Koloa, for 50 years at $300 a year, for the cultivation of sugar cane. The company had also secured permission to hire natives to work on the plantation. It had agreed to pay Kauikeouli, the King of Kauai, and Kaikioewa, the Governor of Kauai, a tax for each man employed, and to pay the workers satisfactory wages. The King and Governor, in return, would exempt the workers from all taxation except the tax paid by their employer.

As Hooper surveyed the newly leased land and the natives to be inducted into his work force, he must have thought Koloa was a fitting place for the beginning of the sugar industry in the islands, for the name itself meant "Great Cane"—"Ko" (cane) and "loa" (great). . . .

Within one year, the young man from Boston had transformed both the land and native society in Koloa. On September 12, 1836, he proudly listed his accomplishments. He had 25 acres of cane under cultivation; in addition, he had erected twenty houses for the natives, a house for the superintendant, a carpenter's shop, a blacksmith's shop, a mill dam, a sugar house, a boiling house, and a sugar mill. Pleased with the progress of his plantation, Hooper recorded in his diary his thoughts on the meaning of the Koloa experience:

> Just one year to day since I commenced work on this plantation, during which I have had more annoyances from the chiefs and difficulty with the natives (from the fact of this land being the first that has ever been cultivated, on the plan of *free* labour, at these islands) than I ever tho't it possible for one white man to bear, nevertheless I have succeeded in

bringing about a place, which if followed up by other foreign residents, will eventually emancipate the natives from the miserable system of "chief labour" which ever has existed at these Islands, and which if not broken up, will be an effectual preventitive to the progress of civilization, industry and national prosperity. . . . The tract of land in Koloa was [developed] after much pain . . . for the purpose of breaking up the system aforesaid or in other words to serve as an entering wedge . . . [to] upset the whole system.

A sense of mission lay behind Hooper's energetic enterprise. More than profits were at stake. In building his plantation, Hooper viewed himself as a "white man," as a pathfinder or an advance guard of "other foreign residents," introducing the system of "*free* labour" in order to "emancipate" the natives from the miserable system of "'chief labour.'" For young Hooper, the Koloa plantation was the "entering wedge" of capitalism, designed to split apart, irrevocably, the ancient system of feudalism in Hawaii.

As they watched Hooper begin his enterprise, the natives of Koloa must have felt a profound ambivalence. They undoubtedly viewed his new operation very apprehensively, fearful of the negative effects the plantation system would have on their culture and way of life. They also saw him as a *haole,* an outsider, and identified him with the destruction of the sandalwood forests, the denuding of the *aina* or land, and with the sailors who were infecting native women with venereal diseases. But the natives also must have hoped Hooper would offer them an escape from the old Hawaiian system of exploitation and fear. Hawaii for the common people, the *makaainana,* was hardly paradise. The king owned all of the lands, and chiefs holding land did so in return for payment of feudal dues. Common people, in order to secure the use of small tracts of land, had to labor for the king or local chiefs, the *alii. Kapus,* or tabus, strictly enforced by the *ilamuku* or police, severely restricted their activities and ambitions. Commoners, reported the Hawaiian historian David Malo who had been educated by missionaries and who was forty-two years old when Hooper founded the Koloa plantation, were subjected to hard labor, heavy taxation, and cruelty. If they were slack in performing labor for their chief, they were expelled from the land, or even put to death. They held the chiefs in "great dread," living in a state of chronic fear." Theirs was a "life of weariness . . . constantly burdened by one exaction after another."

Seeking to improve their lot, twenty three natives went to work for Hooper on September 13, 1835. But two days later, they suddenly stopped working. "The kanakas having discovered the chiefs were to pay and not me," Hooper wrote in his diary, "concluded that 'all work and no pay' was poor business, therefore spent most of the forenoon in idleness." Apparently Hooper's workers thought they were to be paid through their chiefs and refused to work, doubting they would be paid at all. They were quickly offered an "inducement." They were promised to be paid directly "one real" or 12½ cents per day, and "they sprang to it, and at sundown finished their stint." Workers were also given food and shelter, in addition to their wages. . . .

Native families, reported Hooper's neighbor James Jarvis, readily "volunteered" to have their taxes paid for them and to work for the Koloa plantation for wages. "The inducement of regular wages, good houses, and plenty of food, when compared with their usual mode of living," was one few native resisted. Hooper's work force increased from twenty five in September of 1835 to forty in May of 1836. In March of 1838, Hooper noted that one hundred men, women, and children looked to him for their "daily Poe [poi]." By the end of the year, he counted four hundred workers in his employ.

Among Hooper's workers were native women. Employed to strip the cane and assist in grinding and boiling operations, they proved to be such effective workers that Hooper wrote to Ladd and Company on June 12, 1838: "I am in want of no more Sugar Boys, The women on the plantation now make good ones and it is best that I should keep them constantly at work." They were not only worked constantly; they were also paid less than the men, only six cents per day while the men received twelve and one half cents. Hooper justified this dual wage system by saying that it kept the women employed and allowed them to make "more than enough to support their families."

No longer peasants, Hooper's laborers found themselves in a new world of modern industrial agriculture. They no longer worked on their traditionality held small plots of land, sharing their crops with the *alii*. They no longer directed their own labors, making their own decisions regarding what to plant and when to work, rest, or go fishing. As plantation laborers, they found their time controlled by unfamiliar workday sounds, schedules, and rhythms. "At sunrise the laborers are turned out by the ringing of the bell," Jarvis wrote, "and work till sunset, sufficient time being allowed for their meals. At night they are assembled and paid by a sort of bank note, considered as good as money all over the island and redeemable in goods on Saturday." The workers, Hooper reported to Ladd and Company, "meet me in the field at six in the morning, work till 7½—go to breakfast & return to work till 12½—an hour at dinner & then work till sundown at which time I pay them off in paper. . . . Friday is allotted to them to take care of their Tarrow [taro] Patches & Saturday to cook their Grub." Where they had before followed the movements of the sun to space their time and activities, they were now awakened by the ringing of the plantation bell, and a clock determined when they would eat, work, rest, and work again. And their days were organized into weeks, with weekdays for working and weekends for providing themselves with food. . . .

Drawn away from their feudal lands and traditional homes, Hooper's native workers entered a new plantation community. They lived on the plantation, in houses allotted to them by Hooper. Assigned plots of land to cultivate crops for their own food and allowed time on weekends to work their gardens, they also received from Hooper a barrel of fish every third week. This system in which the workers supplemented their own subsistence needs enabled Hooper to minimize both wages and production costs. . . .

Plantation workers not only labored, lived, and shopped on the Koloa plantation; they also received medical care when they became ill. Initially Hooper himself attended the medical needs of his workers. On April 29, 1836, he reported to Ladd and Company: "They are often ailing. . . . They are troubled with sore eyes etc etc which need & ought to have advice & medicine." The next year Hooper sought to contract the services of a Doctor Lafore. Ladd and Company, in a letter to the doctor on October 16, 1837, wrote: "In reference to your inquiry on Sat. last, as to what amt. might be expected from us, for medical attendance on the natives in our employ, we have only to repeat that it would be exceedingly gratifying to us to have you as a neighbor and for all medical attendance on those in our employ, we should expect to pay you, by the year, the price to be decided by yourself, at its commencement or termination." What Hooper was developing on the Koloa plantation was a system of capitalist paternalism which would embrace the total needs of plantation workers and which would set a pattern for planter-worker relationships in Hawaii.

Though they were dependent on Hooper for their "daily Poe" and other needs, native workers refused to give him the control and loyalty he expected. Time and again Hooper found himself in a state of exasperation over his inability to exact from his workers satisfactory obedience and sustained labor. Throughout his Koloa diary, he described his workers with great disgust as undependable, as children, as "dull asses," and as "Indians." His letters to Ladd and Company chronicled the frustrations he felt as the supervisor of recalcitrant laborers. February 23, 1836: "It requires the concentrated patience of an hundred Jobs to get along with these natives," their obedient masks of loyalty" hiding their "dissatisfaction" and repugnance toward plantation labor. September 21, 1836: "Cane grows rapidly, some of it astonishingly—my natives are on their oars." October 3, 1836: "I would write more on this sheet but my men are, as usual, on their oars in my absence." October 26, 1836: "The natives do but little when my back is turned." December 10, 1836: The native laborers need to be "broken in" but "when that will be *I* can not tell." May 12, 1838: "A gang of Sandwich Island men are like a gang of School Boys. When their master is with them they mind their lessons, but when he is absent it is 'hurra boys.' They display so little interest for their employment that it makes my *heart ache.*"

Hooper's laborers required constant surveillance or else they would not work. They became skillful pretenders, and Jarvis often "amusingly" watched them practice their art of deception. While working in the fields, natives were always ready to deceive their employer and escape from work. If an overseer left for a moment, down they would squat and pull out their pipes. Then the "longest-winded fellow" would begin a story, "A sort of improvisation which would entertain everyone with "vulgar" humor and which would often "mimic the haole (foreigner)." As soon as the overseer came back within sight, they would seize their spades and quickly "commence laboring with an assiduity" that baffled description and "perhaps all the while not strain a muscle."

But Hooper did not find their behavior amusing. Irritated and impatient, he castigated his native workers for their inefficiency and doubted they would ever become useful as plantation workers. Their "habits and customs" which had been handed down to them from their forefathers and which they preserved so tenaciously would remain "the great obstacle to their employment" as agricultural wage laborers. Centuries, at least, Hooper lamented, would intervene before they would understand that it was a part of their "duty" to serve "their masters faithfully." He conceded that there were many good men among the natives who would take hold and turn themselves into "white kanakas" for one or two years. But he had no confidence that their patience would hold out. As long as the plantation depended on native labor, the superintendant would have to be a *"Slave Driver."*

To help him supervise his native workers, Hooper employed white overseers, but he discovered that sometimes the overseers themselves needed to be broken in, to be introduced to the system of stern plantation discipline. On one occasion, a recently hired overseer named Titcomb had overheard a conversation among the workers expressing dissatisfaction with their wages. Reporting the incident to Ladd and Company, Hooper wrote:

It seems that he secreted himself long side of his tea stick fence to hear the conversation of some natives in a house nearby—by it, he learned that the natives were on the morrow to demand 25 cts. per day—no mistake—so down he came to find out what was to be done. I very calmly told him that if he would take a whip and undertake to drive off the natives from his land, he would in my opinion have experience enough to last him a month. I have heard nothing more since.

Apparently Hooper heard nothing more from his workers as well as from Titcomb.

Frustrated because he could not convert the natives into docile and efficient modern agricultural workers, Hooper turned to the Chinese as a solution to his labor problem. He had first noticed their presence in Waimea: there a few of them were grinding wild cane, brought to them by natives, in a small sugar mill owned by William French. After visiting this mill in the spring of 1835, Hooper wrote to Ladd and Company:

> I have seen the Chinese sugar works in successful operations; although extremely crude, yet they ware doing well. They have worked 6 days in the week ever since its first establishment, making abt 210 lb sugar per day & molasses by the cord. They could make four times as much by increasing the size of kettles. Mr. F. is much elated with its success and from what I learn from Mr. Whitney you may expect a Host of Chinese. . . . Mr. French's establishment at Waimea is a great eye sore to the natives. They have to work *all* the time—and no regard is paid to their complaints for food, etc., etc. Slavery is nothing to it.

Shortly after the completion of the construction of his own mill, Hooper projected the need for Chinese labor. "We may deem it," he advised Ladd and Company, "at a future day, necessary to locate some halfdozen Chinese on the land, if the establishment grows it will require them. The Supt. cannot feed the mill, boil the juice, make the sugar, etc etc, and to trust it to the natives is worse than nothing—they are alas, children, boys, and always will be."

In a letter to Ladd and Company on December 1, 1838, Hooper insisted that the Koloa plantation needed a source of labor from other countries, and that no other country offered itself but China. "A colony of Chinese would, probably, put the plantation in order, to be perpetuated, sooner and with less trouble than any other class of husbandmen." By this time, several Chinese were already working for Hooper: they had probably been recruited from French's mill which had been put out of business due to competition from the Koloa mill. A pattern of ethnic labor segmentation was already evident, for Hooper tended to assign his Chinese laborers to the mill and Hawaiian laborers to the fields. Unlike the native workers, who lived on the plantation with their families in individual houses, the Chinese workers seemed to be all male and were housed together in a barrack-type structure. In April 1838, Hooper informed Ladd and Company that a "large comfortable building" had been erected for the "Chinamen." "They are highly pleased," he added, "and by their fixtures on doors I should suppose they intend to spend their days in it." Thus, Chinese workers, too, now looked to Hooper for their "daily Poe." Early in 1839, Hooper ordered from Ladd and Company a supply of rice for them.

But the use of Chinese workers did not mean the end of labor difficulties. Hooper's workers, Hawaiian and Chinese, found new ways to resist management and avoid work. Some of the natives simply helped themselves to merchandise in the plantation store without paying for them. On January 28, 1837, Hooper angrily scribbled into his diary: "[Detected] the natives stealing—therefore paid out no goods to day." And three days later, he wrote: "5 natives taken before Hukiko [Hukiku, the headman at Koloa]—convicted of stealing and sentenced to work on the roads." But by this time, some of his workers had devised a more ingenious way to acquire goods from the plantation store: they used counterfeit coupons. As the natives learned how to read and write from a young schoolmaster in the village, some of them utilized their newly acquired knowledge and skills to make artful reproductions of Hooper's medium of exchange. The counterfeit coupons, according to Jarvis, were "so strikingly like the original, imitating the signatures with scrupulous exactness, that it was some time before the fraud was detected."

But the fraud was eventually discovered. On June 11, 1836, Hooper, surprised and dismayed, wrote in his diary: "Some native has attempted to counterfeit the papers which I issued for dollars." Some of the counterfeiters were Chinese. The problem caused Hooper much distress: unless it were checked, the counterfeit conspiracy could undermine his entire enterprise. His laborers would have little incentive to work, for they would have their own source of script. Determined to outwit his workers, Hooper asked Ladd and Company to have paper bills engraved in Boston. In its letter to the printer on November 15, 1837, Ladd and Company gave instructions to have the currency printed from a copper plate in order to be certain it could not be duplicated: "If the ground work is fine waved lines, or a delicate net work, and the border highly wrought, we doubt if we shall be troubled with counterfeits from the Chinese or any other source." But it took time to order the printed currency from Boston and have it sent to Hawaii. Meanwhile, on January 5, 1839, Hooper again found counterfeit coupons in circulation, and urged Ladd and Company to hurry the order for the printed money: "I send you up a specimen of what I suppose to be *native* ingenuity in shape of counterfeit money. I have six reals of it." Acknowledging its genuine appearance, Hooper confessed: "I would not swear it was not mine." Finally three months later, Hooper was relieved to receive the bank bills printed in Boston, which he though were "very nicely executed."

The founding of the Koloa plantation had been a very trying experience for Hooper. The new land did not yield easily. The rainy seasons, with their howling winds and pelting showers, forced him to stay indoors, and the enveloping dampness agitated his rheumatism. Cut off from family and friends and from the security and comfort of Boston, he suffered from intense isolation, finding his new life in Koloa "lonesome" and "dull as death." And the people of the new land had not been as pliant as he had hoped: they were difficult to manage and often drove him to dispair. They seemed to resist him at almost every point. They were also more intelligent than he had assumed, able to avoid work and to extract extra compensation in creative and devious ways. Physically exhausted from his constant struggle with his workers, Hooper vented his frustrations to Ladd and Company in 1838: "No galley slave looks forward to the day when he is to be made free with half so much satisfaction as I do when I shall bid a *final* adieu to intercourse with Hawaiians! Gracious Anticipations!"

A year later, Hooper was granted his wish, but he left behind him, in Koloa, a place transformed. In a sense, Hooper may remind us of William Shakespeare's Prospero and Mark Twain's Connecticut Yankee: Prospero had settled on an island and inducted a native, Caliban, into his service, his work force; and Hank Morgan had travelled to another island, Arthurian England, where he had imposed a modern industrial order. Reflecting the expansionist culture portrayed in Prospero and

Morgan, Hooper had removed himself to an island. There, employing native labor, he had cleared the wild grass from the land in order to plant ordered rows of cane; he had altered the very character of the tiny hamlet of Koloa, bringing to it the dark smoke and the loud and dissonant mechanical sounds of a modern factory. He had integrated economic and moral motives, seeking both to earn corporate profits for Ladd and Company and liberate natives from an oppressive feudalism. Converting them into free laborers, he had removed them from their farms and villages to his plantation where he offered them housing and paternal care. He had opened the way for the development of a corporate dominated sugar economy and a paternalistic racial and class hierarchy of social relations in the islands.

Setting in motion dynamic forces which would transform the ethnicity of Hawaii's population, he had initiated the making of a multiethnic and transnational plantation labor system which would draw into the plantation work force not only people from Hawaii itself but also from China, Japan, Portugal, Norway, Germany, Korea, Puerto Rico, the Philippines, and even Russia. Though he had been at Koloa for only four years, Hooper had proven it was possible to induce the natives to labor as wage earners and to produce sugar as a cash crop. His invoices for 1837–38 showed that he had shipped to Honolulu approximately 30 tons of sugar and 170 barrels of molasses—a small but nonetheless portentous beginning of a new plantation economy which would penetrate Hawaiian society like an "entering wedge."

🕮 *F U R T H E R   R E A D I N G*

Beechert, Edward. *Working in Hawaii: A Labor History* (1985).

Borah, Eloisa Gomez. "Filipinos in Unamuno's California Expedition of 1587," *Amerasia Journal* 21 (1995/1996): 175–183.

Chan, Sucheng. "European and Asian Immigration into the United States in Comparative Perspective, 1820s–1920s," in Virginia Yans-McLaughlin, *Immigration Reconsidered: History, Sociology, and Politics* (1990): 37–74.

Chen, Yong. *Chinese San Francisco, 1850–1943* (2000).

Cordova, Fred. *Filipinos: Forgotten Asian Americans: A Pictorial Essay, 1763–Circa 1963* (1983).

Crouchett, Lorraine Jacobs. *Filipinos in California: From the Days of the Galleons to the Present* (1982).

Duus, Peter. *The Japanese Discovery of America: A Brief History with Documents* (1997).

Espina, Marina E. *Filipinos in Louisiana* (1988).

Hirata, Lucie Cheng, and Edna Bonacich, eds. *Labor Immigration Under Capitalism: Asian Workers in the United States Before World War II* (1984).

Kameʻeleihiwa, Lilikalā. *Native Lands and Foreign Desires: Pahoa La E Pono Ai?* (1992).

Lind, Andrew W. *An Island Community: Ecological Succession in Hawaii* (1938).

Malo, David. *Hawaiian Antiquities* (Moolelo Hawaii) (1898).

Miller, Stuart Creighton. *The Unwelcome Immigrant: The American Image of the Chinese, 1785–1882* (1969).

Neu, Charles E. *The Troubled Encounter: The United States and Japan* (1975).

Okihiro, Gary. *Margins and Mainstreams: Asians in American History and Culture* (1994).

Takaki, Ronald. *Pau Hana: Plantation Life and Labor in Hawaii, 1835–1920* (1983).

Tchen, John Kuo Wei. *New York Before Chinatown: Orientalism and the Shaping of American Culture, 1776–1882* (1999).

Tinker, Hugh. *A New System of Slavery: The Export of Indian Labour Overseas, 1830–1920* (1974).

Yun, Lisa, and Ricardo René Laremont. "Chinese Coolies and African Slaves in Cuba, 1847–74," *Journal of Asian American Studies* 4 (2001): 99–122.

CHAPTER
3

The Work of National
Expansion in
the American West,
1848–1908

*The territorial expansion and industrial development of the United States in the
latter half of the nineteenth century generated a huge demand for workers that was
not totally satisfied by the great migrations from Europe. In the newly conquered
hinterlands of the American West, the Chinese—followed in the late nineteenth
and early twentieth centuries by immigrants from Japan, Korea, India, and the
Philippines—played a vital role in the development of the region. No better symbol
of this was the establishment of the first transcontinental railroad in 1869, a national
landmark that relied significantly on Chinese labor. More than a technological wonder, the railroad linkage between east and west coasts provided the infrastructure for
the economic takeoff of the American West. Such a transformation was spurred by
rapid expansions in the agricultural and mining industries, both of which benefitted
tremendously from Asian immigrant labor.*

*By the turn of the century, the Japanese replaced the Chinese as the nation's
largest Asian group, a position they would retain until the 1980s. Agricultural
expansion in California played an essential role in driving Japanese labor migration.
But Japanese government officials and intellectuals were also crucial to this process.
Many of them championed emigration to the United States as a peaceful colonization,
that is, as a means for advancing Japan's economy and global prestige without
engaging in the military conquest that was usually prerequisite to colonization. In
this sense, the American West served as more than a magnet attracting Asian immigrant labor. The West's open spaces and mythology of economic riches, invited late-
coming nations, like Japan, to imagine that it too could participate in the development
of the New World.*

DOCUMENTS

The first four documents provide a look at working conditions for Chinese immigrants. Document 1 offers a brief observation of a Chinese mining camp by Scottish journalist and artist J. D. Borthwick. Unfortunately, no account written by a Chinese has yet to be found in the United States. But, as Document 2 reveals, Chinese workers did leave a report of the anti-Chinese riot that erupted in the Wyoming Territory town of Rock Springs in 1885. Such violent outbreaks were all too common in the American West, as European immigrants and native-born whites carved out economic advantages for themselves at the expense of Asians, as well as Mexicans, Native Americans, blacks, and other racially marked peoples. Document 3, an exposé of a San Francisco brothel by journalist Helen Grey, reveals that women, especially non-whites like the Chinese, faced a different sort of subordination on the western frontier. Document 4 is a photograph of a Chinese merchant's store in Holyoke, Massachusetts, in 1904.

The final four documents address, either directly or indirectly, the importance of emigration to the United States for the rising world power of Japan. Document 5 is excerpted from the writings of Fukuzawa Yukichi, Japan's leading authority on the West. Although Fukuzawa is critical of the West in this discourse on the process of civilization, in the end it is clear that he regards Europe (and by extension the United States) as having achieved a higher stage of civilization than Japan and the rest of the world. Document 6 is part of an editorial in a Japanese newspaper that appeared in the wake of Japan's military defeat of China in 1895. The editorial told its readers that emigration to the United States was a sign that Japan had become a world leader. But not just any Japanese was qualified to migrate to the West, for the government took pains to ensure the respectability of its emigrant representatives. For example, Document 7 lists the Japanese government's criteria for its citizens to work in Hawai'i. Another aspect to Japan's concern about its image in the world of nations involved the treatment of its citizens abroad. Document 8, a Japanese official's condemnation of working conditions for Japanese plantation laborers, shows the diplomatic importance that the government placed on its immigrants.

1. Writer J. D. Borthwick Observes Chinese Miners in California, 1857

While at this camp, I went down the river two or three miles to see a place called Mississippi Bar, where a company of Chinamen were at work. After an hour's climbing along the rocky banks, and having crossed and recrossed the river some half-dozen times on pine logs, I at last got down among the Celestials.

There were about a hundred and fifty of them here, living in a perfect village of small tents, all clustered together on the rocks. They had a claim in the bed of the river, which they were working by means of a wing dam. A "wing dam," I may

---

From J. D. Borthwick, *Three Years in California* (Edinburgh and London: W. Blackwood and Sons, 1857; reprint, Oakland, Calif.: Biobooks, 1948), 215–219 (page citations are to the original edition).

here mention, is one which first runs half-way across the river, then down the river, and back again to the same side, thus damming off a portion of its bed without the necessity of the more expensive operation of lifting up the whole river bodily in a "flume."

The Chinamen's dam was two or three hundred yards in length, and was built of large pine-trees laid one on the the top of the other. They must have had great difficulty in handling such immense logs in such a place; but they are exceedingly ingenious in applying mechanical power, particularly in concentrating the force of a large number of men upon one point.

There were Chinamen of the better class among them, who no doubt directed the work, and paid the common men very poor wages—poor at least for California. A Chinaman could be hired for two, or at most three dollars a-day by any one who thought their labour worth so much; but those at work here were most likely paid at a still lower rate, for it was well known that whole shiploads of Chinamen came to the country under a species of bondage to some of their wealthy countrymen in San Francisco, who, immediately on their arrival, shipped them off to the mines under charge of an agent, keeping them completely under control by some mysterious celestial influence, quite independent of the laws of the country.

They sent up to the mines for their use supplies of Chinese provisions and clothing, and thus all the gold taken out by them remained in Chinese hands, and benefited the rest of the community but little by passing through the ordinary channels of trade.

In fact, the Chinese formed a distinct class, which enriched itself at the expense of the country, abstracting a large portion of its latent wealth without contributing, in a degree commensurate with their numbers to the prosperity of the community of which they formed a part.

The individuals of any community must exist by supplying the wants of others; and when a man neither does this, nor has any wants of his own but those which he provides for himself, he is of no use to his neighbours; but when, in addition to this, he also diminishes the productiveness of the country, he is a positive disadvantage in proportion to the amount of public wealth which he engrosses, and becomes a public nuisance.

What is true of an individual is true also of a class; and the Chinese, though they were no doubt, as far as China was concerned, both productive and consumptive, were considered by a very large party in California to be merely destructive as far as that country was interested.

They were, of course, not altogether so, for such a numerous body as they were could not possibly be so isolated as to be entirely independent of others; but any advantage which the country derived from their presence was too dearly paid for by the quantity of gold which they took from it; and the propriety of expelling all the Chinese from the State was long discussed, both by the press and in the Legislature; but the principles of the American constitution prevailed; the country was open to all the world, and the Chinese enjoyed equal rights with the most favoured nation. In some parts of the mines, however, the miners had their own ideas on the subject, and would not allow the Chinamen to come among them; but generally they were not interfered with, for they content themselves with working such poor diggings as it was not thought worth while to take from them.

This claim on the Yuba was the greatest undertaking I ever saw attempted by them.

They expended a vast deal of unnecessary labour in their method of working, and their individual labour, in effect, was as nothing compared with that of other miners. A company of fifteen or twenty white men would have wing-dammed this claim, and worked it out in two or three months, while here were about a hundred and fifty Chinamen humbugging round it all the season, and still had not worked one half the ground.

Their mechanical contrivances were not in the usual rough straightforward style of the mines; they were curious, and very elaborately got up, but extremely wasteful of labour, and, moreover, very ineffective.

The pumps which they had at work here were an instance of this. They were on the principle of a chainpump, the chain being formed of pieces of wood about six inches long, hinging on each other, with cross-pieces in the middle for buckets, having about six square inches of surface. The hinges fitted exactly to the spokes of a small wheel, which was turned by a Chinaman at each side of it working a miniature treadmill of four spokes on the same axle. As specimens of joiner-work they were very pretty, but as pumps they were ridiculous; they threw a mere driblet of water: the chain was not even encased in a box—it merely lay in a slanting trough, so that more than one half the capacity of the buckets was lost. An American miner, at the expenditure of one-tenth part of the labour of making such toys, would have set a water-wheel in the river to work an elevating pump, which would have thrown more water in half an hour than four-and-twenty China-men could throw in a day with a dozen of these gim-crack contrivances. Their camp was wonderfully clean: when I passed through it, I found a great many of them at their toilet, getting their heads shaved, or plaiting each other's pigtails; but most of them were at dinner, squatted on the rocks in groups of eight or ten round a number of curious little black pots and dishes, from which they helped themselves with their chopsticks. In the centre was a large bowl of rice. This is their staple article, and they devour it most voraciously. Throwing back their heads, they hold a large cupful to their wide-open mouths, and with a quick motion of the chopsticks in the other hand, they cause the rice to flow down their throats in a continuous stream.

I received several invitations to dinner, but declined the pleasure, preferring to be a spectator. The rice looked well enough, and the rest of their dishes were no doubt very clean, but they had a very dubious appearance, and were far from suggesting the idea of being good to eat. In the store I found the storekeeper lying asleep on a mat. He was a sleek dirty-looking object, like a fat pig with the hair scalded off, his head being all close shaved excepting the pigtail. His opium-pipe lay in his hand, and the lamp still burned beside him, so I supposed he was already in the seventh heavens. The store was like other stores in the mines, inasmuch as it contained a higgledy-piggledy collection of provisions and clothing, but everything was Chinese excepting the boots. These are the only articles of barbarian costume which the Chinaman adopts, and he always wears them of an enormous size, on a scale commensurate with the ample capacity of his other garments.

2. Chinese Laborers Report
on a Race Riot at Rock Springs,
Wyoming Territory, 1885

We, the undersigned, have been in Rock Springs, Wyoming Territory, for periods ranging from one to fifteen years, for the purpose of working on the railroads and in the coal mines.

Up to the time of the recent troubles we had worked along with the white men, and had not had the least ill feeling against them. The officers of the companies employing us treated us and the white man kindly, placing both races on the same footing and paying the same wages.

Several times we had been approached by the white men and requested to join them in asking the companies for an increase in the wages of all, both Chinese and white men. We inquired of them what we should do if the companies refused to grant an increase. They answered that if the companies would not increase our wages we should all strike, then the companies would be obliged to increase our wages. To this we dissented, wherefore we excited their animosity against us.

During the past two years there has been in existence in "Whitemen's Town," Rock Springs, an organization composed of white miners, whose object was to bring about the expulsion of all Chinese from the Territory. To them or to their object we have paid no attention. About the month of August of this year notices were posted up, all the way from Evanston to Rock Springs, demanding the expulsion of the Chinese, &e. On the evening of September 1, 1885, the bell of the building in which said organization meets rang for a meeting. It was rumored on that night that threats had been made against the Chinese.

On the morning of September 2, a little past seven o'clock, more than ten white men, some in ordinary dress and others in mining suits, ran into Coal Pit No. 6, loudly declaring that the Chinese should not be permitted to work there. The Chinese present reasoned with them in a few words, but were attacked with murderous weapons, and three of their number wounded. The white foreman of the coal pit, hearing of the disturbance, ordered all to stop work for the time being.

After the work had stopped, all the white men in and near Coal Pit No. 6 began to assemble by the dozen. They carried firearms, and marched to Rock Springs by way of the railroad from Coal Pit No. 6, and crossing the railroad bridge, went directly to "Whitemen's Town." All this took place before 10:00 A.M. We now heard the bell ringing for a meeting at the white men's organization building. Not long after, all the white men came out of that building, most of them assembling in the barrooms, the crowds meanwhile growing larger and larger.

About two o'clock in the afternoon a mob, divided into two gangs, came toward "Chinatown," one gang coming by way of the plank bridge, and the other by way of the railroad bridge. The gang coming by way of the railroad bridge was the larger, and was subdivided into many squads, some of which did not cross the bridge, but

From "Memorial of Chinese Laborers Resident at Rock Springs, Wyoming Territory, to the Chinese Consul at New York," September 18, 1885; reprinted in *"Chink": A Documentary History of Anti-Chinese Prejudice in America, ed.*, Cheng-Tsu Wu, (New York: World Publishing, Times Mirror, 1972), 152–159.

remained standing on the side opposite to "Chinatown"; others that had already crossed the bridge stood on the right and left at the end of it. Several squads marched up the hill behind Coal Pit No. 3. One squad remained at Coal Shed No. 3 and another at the pump house. The squad that remained at the pump house fired the first shot, and the squad that stood at Coal Shed No. 3 immediately followed their example and fired. The Chinese by name of Lor Sun Kit was the first person shot, and fell to the ground. At that time the Chinese began to realize that the mob were bent on killing. The Chinese, though greatly alarmed, did not yet begin to flee.

Soon after, the mob on the hill behind Coal Pit No. 3 came down from the hill, and joining the different squads of the mob, fired their weapons and pressed on to Chinatown.

The gang that were at the plank bridge also divided into several squads, pressing near and surrounding "Chinatown." One squad of them guarded the plank bridge in order to cut off the retreat of the Chinese.

Not long after, it was everywhere reported that a Chinese named Leo Dye Bah, who lived in the western part of "Chinatown," was killed by a bullet, and that another named Yip Ah Marn, resident in the eastern end of the town, was likewise killed. The Chinese now, to save their lives, fled in confusion in every direction, some going up the hill behind Coal Pit No. 3, others along the foot of the hill where Coal Pit No. 4 is; some from the eastern end of the town fled across Bitter Creek to the opposite hill, and others from the western end by the foot of the hill on the right of Coal Pit No. 5. The mob were now coming in the three directions, namely, the east and west sides of the town and from the wagon road.

Whenever the mob met a Chinese they stopped him and, pointing a weapon at him, asked him if he had any revolver, and then approaching him they searched his person, robbing him of his watch or any gold or silver that he might have about him, before letting him go. Some of the rioters would let a Chinese go after depriving him of all his gold and silver, while another Chinese would be beaten with the butt ends of the weapons before being let go. Some of the rioters, when they could not stop a Chinese, would shoot him dead on the spot, and then search and rob him. Some would overtake a Chinese, throw him down and search and rob him before they would let him go. Some of the rioters would not fire their weapons, but would only use the butt ends to beat the Chinese with. Some would not beat a Chinese, but rob him of whatever he had and let him go, yelling to him to go quickly. Some, who took no part either in beating or robbing the Chinese, stood by, shouting loudly and laughing and clapping their hands.

There was a gang of women that stood at the "Chinatown" end of the plank bridge and cheered; among the women, two of them each fired successive shots at the Chinese. This was done about a little past 3:00 P.M.

Most of the Chinese fled toward the eastern part of "Chinatown." Some of them ran across Bitter Creek, went up directly to the opposite hill, crossing the grassy plain. Some of them went along the foot of the hill where Coal Pit No. 4 stood, to cross the creek, and by a devious route reached the opposite hill. Some of them ran up to the hill of Coal Pit No. 3, and thence winding around the hills went to the opposite hill. A few of them fled to the foot of the hill where Coal Pit No. 5 stood, and ran across the creek, and thence by a winding course to the western end of the "Whitemen's Town." But very few did this.

The Chinese who were the first to flee mostly dispersed themselves at the back hills, on the opposite bank of the creek, and among the opposite hills. They were scattered far and near, high and low, in about one hundred places. Some were standing, or sitting, or lying hid on the grass, or stooping down on the low grounds. Every one of them was praying to Heaven or groaning with pain. They had been eyewitnesses to the shooting in "Chinatown," and had seen the whites, male and female, old and young, searching houses for money, household effects, or gold, which were carried across to "Whitemen's Town."

Some of the rioters went off toward the railroad of Coal Pit No. 6, others set fire to the Chinese houses. Between 4:00 P.M. and a little past 9:00 P.M. all the camp houses belonging to the coal company and the Chinese huts had been burned down completely, only one of the company's camp houses remaining. Several of the camp houses near Coal Pit No. 6 were also burned, and the three Chinese huts there were also burned. All the Chinese houses burned numbered seventy-nine.

Some of the Chinese were killed at the bank of Bitter Creek, some near the railroad bridge, and some in "Chinatown." After having been killed, the dead bodies of some were carried to the burning buildings and thrown into the flames. Some of the Chinese who had hid themselves in the houses were killed and their bodies burned; some, who on account of sickness could not run, were burned alive in the houses. One Chinese was killed in "Whitemen's Town" in a laundry house, and his house demolished. The whole number of Chinese killed was twenty-eight and those wounded fifteen.

The money that the Chinese lost was that which in their hurry they were unable to take with them, and consequently were obliged to leave in their houses, or that which was taken from their persons. The goods, clothing, or household effects remaining in their houses were either plundered or burned.

When the Chinese fled to the different hills they intended to come back to "Chinatown" when the riot was over, to dispose of the dead bodies and to take care of the wounded. But to their disappointment, all the houses were burned to ashes, and there was then no place of shelter for them; they were obliged to run blindly from hill to hill. Taking the railroad as their guide, they walked toward the town of Green River, some of them reaching that place in the morning others at noon, and others not until dark. There were some who did not reach it until the fourth of September. We felt very thankful to the railroad company for having telegraphed to the conductors of all its trains to pick up such of the Chinese as were to be met with along the line of the railroad and carry them to Evanston.

On the fifth of September all the Chinese that had fled assembled at Evanston; the native citizens there threatened day and night to burn and kill the Chinese. Fortunately, United States troops had been ordered to come and protect them, and quiet was restored. On the ninth of September the United States government instructed the troops to escort the Chinese back to Rock Springs. When they arrived there they saw only a burnt tract of ground to mark the sites of their former habitations. Some of the dead bodies had been buried by the company, while others, mangled and decomposed, were strewn on the ground and were being eaten by dogs and hogs. Some of the bodies were not found until they were dug out of the ruins of the buildings. Some had been burned beyond recognition. It was a sad and painful sight to see the son crying for the father, the brother for the brother, the uncle for the nephew, and friend for friend.

By this time most of the Chinese have abandoned the desire of resuming their mining work, but inasmuch as the riot has left them each with only the one or two torn articles of clothing they have on their persons, and as they have not a single cent in their pockets, it is a difficult matter for them to make any change in their location. Fortunately, the company promised to lend them clothing and provisions, and a number of wagons to sleep in. Although protected by government troops, their sleep is disturbed by frightful dreams, and they cannot obtain peaceful rest.

Some of the rioters who killed the Chinese and who set fire to the homes could be identified by the Chinese, and some not. Among them the two women heretofore mentioned, and who killed some Chinese, were specially recognized by many Chinese. Among the rioters who robbed and plundered were men, women, and children. Even the white woman who formerly taught English to the Chinese searched for and took handkerchiefs and other articles.

The Chinese know that the white men who worked in Coal Pit No. 1 did not join the mob, and most of them did not stop work, either. We heard that the coal company's officers had taken a list of the names of the rioters who were particularly brutal and murderous, which list numbered forty or fifty.

From a survey of all the circumstances, several causes may be assigned for the killing and wounding of so many Chinese and the destruction of so much property:

1. The Chinese had been for a long time employed at the same work as the white men. While they knew that the white men entertained ill feelings toward them, the Chinese did not take precautions to guard against this sudden outbreak, inasmuch as at no time in the past had there been any quarrel or fighting between the races.
2. On the second day of September 1885, in Coal Pit No. 6, the white men attacked the Chinese. That place being quite a distance from Rock Springs, very few Chinese were there. As we did not think that the trouble would extend to Rock Springs, we did not warn each other to prepare for fight.
3. Most of the Chinese living in Rock Springs worked during the daytime in the different coal mines, and consequently did not hear of the fight at Coal Pit No. 6, nor did they know of the armed mob that had been assembled in "Whitemen's Town." When twelve o'clock came, everybody returned home from his place of work to lunch. As yet the mob had not come to attack the Chinese; a great number of the latter were returning to work without any apprehension of danger.
4. About two o'clock the mob suddenly made their appearance for the attack. The Chinese thought that they had only assembled to threaten, and that some of the company's officers would come to disperse them. Most of the Chinese, acting upon this view of the matter, did not gather up their money or clothing, and when the mob fired at them they fled precipitately. Those Chinese who were in the workshops, hearing of the riot, stopped work and fled in their working clothes, and did not have time enough to go home to change their clothes or to gather up their money. What they did leave at home was either plundered or burned.

5. None of the Chinese had firearms or any defensive weapons, nor was there any place that afforded an opportunity for the erection of a barricade that might impede the rioters in their attack. The Chinese were all like a herd of frightened deer that let the huntsmen surround and kill them.

6. All the Chinese had, on the first of September, bought from the company a month's supply of provision and the implements necessary for the mining of coal. This loss of property was therefore larger than it would be later in the month.

We never thought that the subjects of a nation entitled by treaty to the rights and privileges of the most favored nation could, in a country so highly civilized like this, so unexpectedly suffer the cruelty and wrong of being unjustly put to death, or of being wounded and left without the means of cure, or being abandoned to poverty, hunger, and cold, and without the means to betake themselves elsewhere.

To the great President of the United States, who, hearing of the riot, sent troops to protect our lives, we are most sincerely thankful.

In behalf of those killed or wounded, or of those deprived of their property, we pray that the examining commission will ask our minister to sympathize, and to endeavor to secure the punishment of the murderers, the relief of the wounded, and compensation for those despoiled of their property, so that the living and the relative of the dead will be grateful, and never forget his kindness for generations.

Hereinabove we have made a brief recital of the facts of this riot, and pray your honor will take them into your kind consideration.

(Here follow the signatures of 559 Chinese laborers, resident at Rock Springs, Wyoming Territory.)

3. Journalist Helen Grey Exposes the Activities of a Chinese Brothel Owner, 1899

Suey Hin, a Chinese slave-owner, who has been importing Chinese girls into San Francisco for years, has just been converted to Christianity. To show her sincerity she has freed the seven girls in her Possession, valued by her at $8,500, and will endeavor to see them safely married. Several of the girls were kidnaped and they will be returned to their parents. In the light of her new faith, Suey Hin uncovers the whole nefarious Chinese girl slave trade in San Francisco, and describes how the girls are sold here among the Chinese for a few hundred dollars. She herself when only five years old was sold into the trade by her own father, and lived out the whole dreadful life to the time when she adopted Christianity.

Suey Hin, importer, seller, keeper of slave girls, has become a Christian. She says her seven girls may go free if they will live a right life. She is the first woman slave-keeper in Chinatown ever known to give up her business for the Christian religion.

From Helen Grey, "Confession of a Chinese Slave-Dealer," *The Call,* April 2, 1899, p. 25; reprinted in *Unbound Voices: A Documentary History of Chinese Women in San Francisco,* ed. Judy Yung (Berkeley: University of California Press, 1999), 145–153.

She did not intend to become a Christian. She wanted the "white teachers" to be friends because sometimes her girls were sick, sometimes they were kidnaped. Then, shrewd Chinese believe that the white teachers are good friends to have in a contest with highbinders. Suey Hin reasoned that way, and she went about gaining their friendship in the usual shrewd Chinese way.

She went to the lassies of the Salvation Army and asked them to come and pray for her. She returned with them to her little sitting-room, with its great carved and canopied bed, with its shrine and burning punk sticks and prayers on scarlet paper pasted at the side of the altar. "May honorable guests constantly visit this house," and the punctured red paper which makes the money god happy. Only two of the seven slave girls were in the room, and they knelt while the lassies prayed. They could not understand English, so their slaveowner thought the prayers could not hurt them, but it was a way to gain the good will of the lassies. Suey Hin did not understand the prayers herself at first, but the more she did understand them the better she remembered her mother and the old home in Shantung, and how life was before she began to buy and sell young girls.

She owned seven girls. There was Ah Lung, she would sell for $1300, and Ah San, she would bring just as much. Hom Get and Man Yet and Wo Sing, they would each bring $1200. Ah Ho and Ah Ching were both sick, but they were each worth $1000. That made $8200. Little Ah San was only 3 years old, but she was worth at least $300. Eighty-five hundred dollars in all, and Suey Hin would have to give it all up if she became a Christian. To be sure she had money put away, but not much. Then she must not leave the highbinders out of her calculations. There was the Hop Sing Tong and their protege tong, the Kwai Hung. They would not forcibly oppose, but they would be very unfriendly.

So Suey Hin took a little room by herself and night and day she considered the problem: "Shall I become a Christian?"

For weeks she lived apart, revolving the whole matter in her mind.

It took Suey Hin five months to "get" so much conversion that she reached the point where she could give up her trade. Then she went back to her home where the seven girls had been under the care of a woman she called her sister.

It was in this home I listened to her story, partly in her own pigeon English and the rest from the lips of an interpreter. And this is the story she told me in her broken pigeon English:

"I am old, very old, too old to be an American. I like Americans, and if I were younger I would be one. Long, long ago I was born in Shantung, where the flowers are more beautiful and the birds sing more sweetly than in any other place. But my people were poor. There was not enough for all our stomachs. Two baby girls had been left exposed—that is, to die, you know. They were born after me and my father said often, 'She is too many.'

"Once there was an old woman came to our house and she looked at me. I was 5 that year, 6 the next. When she looked at me I was afraid and I hid myself behind my mother. My father told the old woman to go away.

"But that night she came back again and talked to my father and mother. She put a piece of gold money in my hand and told me to give it to my father. I did, for I wanted nothing to do with her. I had enough; yes, I had plenty to eat!

"But that night the old woman carried me away, and I kicked and screamed and said I would not go. I do not remember much more about the beginning. I remember the ship, and I remembered playing with other little girls. We were brought to San Francisco, and there were five or ten of us and we all lived with a woman on Ross alley. Every little while some one would come and see us, and as we grew older the girls were sold.

"One day it was my turn. They said I was 14 years old, but I was really 12. I don't know how much I cost, but I know both my hands were filled three times with all the gold they would hold. The money, you know, is always put in a girl's hand when she is sold.

"Well, then I was a slave for ten years. There was a man who loved me, but he was a poor washman, and he worked eight years and saved all, all the time. I saved all I could get, too, but it took eight years before we had saved $3000. Then we bought me from my owner and we were married.

"Then, ah, it's all of my life I like to think about. It wasn't but two next years, three years. My husband got sick and didn't get any better, and then he died. I didn't have anything but must myself, and I had to live, and I could not live on nothing. No, I had to have things, so I got a little house; you know, one with a little window over the door.

"Then pretty soon I went back to China, but I did not go to my own village. No, my parents would not want to see me. I went to Hongkong and I bought three girls. Two of them are dead, but Ah Moy, that's Ah Moy, she was a baby, and I paid her father 50 cents for her. After I had returned here a few months I went back to China again. I wanted to see my village, always I wanted to go back to my home. So I went, but I didn't let anybody know I was there. I went to the place where they put the babies to die. There was a baby there. A little bit of a brown baby, and she didn't look much good anyway. But I wanted some one from my own village, and so I took the baby, and she is Ah Lung. Don't you think she is a pretty girl now? She's not a slave you know. She's a good girl, just the same as white girls. She comes from Shantung, so I say she shall never be like the others. Slave girls most all die soon. It's bad, yes, and only the girls who want to be good and the dear Jesus knows about that. You see she is a girl and her people sold her, so what can she do?

"That trip I brought home four girls besides Ah Lung. You see it was not hard to smuggle the girls into this country then. You can't do it so easy now. Sometimes they come, only sometimes now. You see the Hop Sing tong fix it with the Custom House. They swore to the officers that the children were born here and went to China to visit. Some witnesses come and they say they knew the girl who wants to land was born here, and they tell all about it. Then they say they know she is the same because they saw her when they went back to China. It was not hard to swear them into this country.

"Then I went back once more. That was only a year ago and I brought back six girls. They did not seem to be with me when we got to the landing, but I watched them. I made the girls learn the answers to the questions the highbinders said would be asked by the Custom House. I told the girls if they made any mistakes the white devils would get them. I said white men liked to eat China girls, they like to boil them and then hand them up to dry and then eat them.

"Oh, the girls didn't make any mistakes when the inspector asked them questions and when they were landed they didn't want to run away. I told them that the girls only stayed at the missions till they got very fat and then Miss Cameron and Miss Lake sold them. Oh, I was bad—wasn't I bad? But I love Jesus now.

"One girl I sold to Loo Wing. All the other girls are here now. I will not make them bad any more. They are all free—they may go or they may stay, but I watch where they go. Hom Get, she is going to China. I bought her in Hongkong. You want to talk to her?"

I said I did, and Hom Get smiled her eyes out of sight and came in with a funny little Chinese swing of her trousered legs. She seated herself as all Orientals do, cross-legged.

"Oh, yes indeed, I'm going home," she said, through the interpreter. "I'm going back to my own home. My father didn't sell me; he would not do it. He just wrote a letter to me. You want to see it? My father he loves me and he doesn't forget. I was stolen. You see my father he quarreled with a man. The man wanted to do him harm. So this wicked man he got another man who knew my father and who lived in Hongkong to write me to visit his family. My father didn't know his enemy was doing anything and he let me go. Then the man took me down town and lost me so my father's enemy could find me.

"Then my father's enemy sold me to Suey Hin and she brought me here.

"My father did not know where I was till the white teachers wrote to him in China. The teachers said I was freed because Suey Hin loved Jesus. Then my father wrote this letter and he sent $70. Isn't that such a lot of money? Don't you think my father loves me? And I'm going home and I will see my sister and I'll see my two brothers, but I, oh, I don't know, you see I'm not like all the other girls at home now. I love Jesus, yes, but then—. You want to see the letter my father wrote?"

While we were talking there was the bustle and chatter of some one coming in. Suey Hin called out and Man Get, Ah Ho and Ah Chung came into the room. We shook hands all around and the girls said they had been to a white man's store to do some shopping. They opened their parcels and showed Suey Hin and me what they had purchased and bragged about how cheap they had bought them. Ah Ching gave a piece of blue ribbon and a pair of long blue silk stockings to Man Get. The girl looked pensive and took the blue things and patted them.

"She has just heard her father is dead. You see I bought her in Victoria [British Columbia]. When I wanted to love Jesus I thought I would ask her father to take her home and get her married. I wrote to him, but you see he is a very bad man. He went right to a man, showed my letter and said: 'You are going to San Francisco. That fool woman gone crazy. You but Man Get. I sell her cheap.' So he sell her to Loo Wing for $250. He was sure she was very sick, so he sell her very cheap.

"Loo Chee did buy her and then came here to me. He said, 'I will take Hom Get [Man Get] to her father. He wants her and she can stay at home and be married. He never sell her any more.' You see? He lied.

'I almost let Hom Get [Man Get] go with Loo Chee. He went away, he said, to buy a ticket to take Hom Get [Man Get] to Victoria. But he drop this piece of paper on the floor. Ah San she was playing with Loo Chee and she picked the paper up quick and brought it to me. See, here it is:

BILL OF SALE

Loo Wing to Loo Chee—

April 16—Rice, 6 mats, at $2	$12
April 18—Shrimps, 50 lbs, at 10c	5
April 20—Girl, $250	250
April 21—Salt fish, 60 lbs at 10c	6
	$263

Received payment,

LOO CHEE.

Victoria, B.C., May 1, 1898.

"Then I know Loo Wing had sold Hom Get [Man Get] to Loo Chee, but I said no, oh no, not at all! I would not let Hom Get [Man Get] go. Then Loo Chee went to the Kwai Kung [Hung] tong and made a big complaint about me.

"Fong San came and he said I must give Hom Get [Man Get] to Loo Chee or he would make me trouble. After all the money I have paid Fong San. No! Oh, I have given him plenty money to protect me! Well, he knew Hom Get [Man Get] belonged to me because I only said I would send her to her father if he would keep her and get her married. When he sold her that broke the bargain.

"Well, that was two months ago. Last week Fong Sing came to see me. He told us Loo Wing was dead. So now Hom Get [Man Get] has no home and she must stay here and I'll get her married. I won't let her marry any but a Christian man. The blue ribbon she wears? Oh, that's to show she has some one dead. What you call mourning."

While Suey Hin was telling about Hom Get [Man Get] two of the girls brought us tiny cups of tea and confections of dried cocoanut. A little three-year-old girl in a red sam [shirt] and yellow trousers put a doll in my lap. It was dressed in Chinese style most magnificently.

"Lunt gave me," she said, in English.

"You a boy and like dolls?"

"I not boy, I girl; I Ah San." I looked inquiringly at Suey Hin, for the child wore the dress of a boy.

"Oh, yes, she's a girl. I dress her like a boy so the mission people will not steal her. I very cute [smart]! They see I bring her up for a slave girl and then they come and rescue her. Oh, no, no, not at all! I make her look like a boy."

"Where did you get her?"

"Bought her. Bought her when she was ten days old. She's smart. Ah San, come here. Oh, she understands everything! Now, Ah San, sing 'Jesus Loves Me.'"

The little one repeated the sentence and then she said the whole of "The Lord is My Shepherd," and all in very good English.

"What will you do with her?"

Suey's face saddened. You could see she was very fond of the child. "I don't know; maybe give her to the mission. Do you want to go to the mission, Ah San?"

The little face clouded and the tears began to run over the black eyelashes.

Suey gathered the little one up in her arms. Ah San's were not the only wet eyes as she said: "I goo, I good girl, Suey."

"What will you do with the other girls?" I asked.

"Oh, I suppose they get married. Only they must marry Christians. I Christian now, and I work always now for Jesus. I used to work hard for the devil, him you call, Satan, but now I work harder for Jesus."

4. Chinese Merchant Lee Wong Hing's Store in Holyoke, Massachusetts, 1904

Chinese merchants played a vital role as middlemen between Chinese laborers and the broader white community.

From The National Archives and Records Administration, Pacific Alaska Region, Seattle, Wash., Control Number NRIS-85-RS-RS394 Exhibit; found through NARA's web-based searchable collections database (NAIL).

5. Leading Japanese Intellectual Encourages Westernization, 1875

I argued that such designations as light and heavy and good and bad are relative. Now, the concept "civilization and enlightenment" (*bummei kaika*) is also a relative one. When we are talking about civilization in the world today, the nations of Europe and the United States of America are the most highly civilized, while the Asian countries, such as Turkey, China, and Japan, may be called semi-developed countries, and Africa and Australia are to be counted as still primitive lands. These designations are common currency all over the world. While the citizens of the nations of the West are the only ones to boast of civilization, the citizens of the semi-developed and primitive lands submit to being designated as such. They rest content with being branded semi-developed or primitive, and there is not one who would take pride in his own country or consider it on a par with nations of the West. This attitude is bad enough. What is worse, though, those with some intelligence start to realize, the more they find out what is happening, the true condition of their native lands; the more they come to realize this, the more they awaken to the distance separating them from the nations of the West. They groan, they grieve; some are for learning from the West and imitating it, others are for going it alone and opposing the West. The overriding anxiety of Asian intellectuals today is this one problem to the exclusion of all others.[1] At any rate, the designations "civilized," "semi-developed," and "primitive" have been universally accepted by people all over the globe. Why does everybody accept them? Clearly, because the facts are demonstrable and irrefutable. I shall explain this point further below. For there are stages through which mankind must pass. These may be termed the ages of civilization.

First, there is the stage in which neither dwellings nor supplies of food are stable. Men form communal groups as temporary convenience demands; when that convenience ceases, they pull up stakes and scatter to the four winds. Or even if they settle in a certain region and engage in farming and fishing, they may have enough food and clothing, but they do not yet know how to make tools. And though they are not without writing, they produce no literature. At this stage man is still unable to be master of his own situation; he cowers before the forces of nature and is dependent upon arbitrary human favor or accidental blessings. This is called the stage of primitive man. It is still far from civilization.

Secondly, there is the stage of civilization wherein daily necessities are not lacking, since agriculture has been started on a large scale. Men build houses, form communities, and create the outward semblance of a state. But within this facade there remain very many defects. Though literature flourishes, there are few who devote themselves to practical studies. Though in human relations sentiments of suspicion and jealousy run deep, when it comes to discussing the nature of things men lack the courage to raise doubts and ask questions. Men are adept at imitative

"Leading Japanese Intellectual Encourages Westernization, 1875" from Fukuzawa Yukichi, "An Outline of a Theory of Civilization," trans. David A. Dilworth and G. Cameron Hurst, © 1973 Sophia University, Tokyo. Reprinted by permission of the publisher.

[1]Even the obstinate Chinese have been sending students to the West in recent years. You can see how concerned they are about their country. [Fukuzawa's note]

craftsmanship, but there is a dearth of original production. They know how to cultivate the old, but not how to improve it. There are accepted rules governing human
intercourse, and, slaves of custom that they are, they never alter those rules. This is
called the semi-developed stage. It is not yet civilization in the full sense.

Thirdly, there is the stage in which men subsume the things of the universe
within a general structure, but the structure does not bind them. Their spirits enjoy
free play and do not adhere to old customs blindly. They act autonomously and do
not have to depend upon the arbitrary favors of others. They cultivate their own
virtue and refine their own knowledge. They neither yearn for the old nor become
complacent about the new. Not resting with small gains, they plan great accomplishments for the future and commit themselves wholeheartedly to their realization.
Their path of learning is not vacuous; it has, indeed, invented the principle of invention itself. Their business ventures prosper day by day to increase the sources of
human welfare. Today's wisdom overflows to create the plans of tomorrow. This is
what is meant by modern civilization. It has been a leap far beyond the primitive or
semi-developed stages.

Now, if we make the above threefold distinction, the differences between civilization, semi-development, and the primitive stage should be clear. However, since
these designations are essentially relative, there is nothing to prevent someone who
has not seen civilization from thinking that semi-development is the summit of man's
development. And, while civilization is civilization relative to the semi-developed
stage, the latter, in its turn, can be called civilization relative to the primitive stage.
Thus, for example, present-day China has to be called semi-developed in comparison
with Western countries. But if we compare China with countries of South Africa, or
to take an example more at hand, if we compare the Japanese people with the Ezo,
then both China and Japan can be called civilized. Moreover, although we call the
nations of the West civilized, they can correctly be honored with this designation
only in modern history. And many of them, if we were to be more precise, would
fall well short of this designation.

For example, there is no greater calamity in the world than war, and yet the
nations of the West are always at war. Robbery and murder are the worst of human
crimes; but in the West there are robbers and murderers. There are those who form
cliques to vie for the reins of power and who, when deprived of that power, decry
the injustice of it all. Even worse, international diplomacy is really based on the art of
deception. Surveying the situation as a whole, all we can say is that there is a general
prevalence of good over bad, but we can hardly call the situation perfect. When,
several thousand years hence, the levels of knowledge and virtue of the peoples of
the world will have made great progress (to the point of becoming utopian), the
present condition of the nations of the West will surely seem a pitifully primitive
stage. Seen in this light, civilization is an open-ended process. We cannot be satisfied
with the present level of attainment of the West.

Yes, we cannot be satisfied with the level of civilization attained by the West.
But shall we therefore conclude that Japan should reject it? If we did, what other criterion would we have? We cannot rest content with the stage of semi-development;
even less can the primitive stage suffice. Since these latter alternatives are to be rejected, we must look elsewhere. But to look to some far-off utopian world thousands
of years hence is mere daydreaming. Besides, civilization is not a dead thing; it is

something vital and moving. As such, it must pass through sequences and stages; primitive people advance to semi-developed forms, the semi-developed advance to civilization, and civilization itself is even now in the process of advancing forward. Europe also had to pass through these phases in its evolution to its present level. Hence present-day Europe can only be called the highest level that human intelligence has been able to attain at this juncture in history. Since this is true, in all countries of the world, be they primitive or semi-developed, those who are to give thought to their country's progress in civilization must necessarily take European civilization as the basis of discussion, and must weigh the pros and cons of the problem in the light of it. My own criterion throughout this book will be that of Western civilization, and it will be in terms of it that I describe something as good or bad, in terms of it that I find things beneficial or harmful. Therefore let scholars make no mistake about my orientation.

6. Japanese Newspaper *Jiji Shimpo* Views Emigration as Sign of Japan's Military Power, 1896

The recent victory in war not only demonstrated to the world the military power of Japan but it has convinced the Japanese people that in vitality and spirit, they are outstanding by far among Eastern nations and are among the outstanding races of the world. If the politicians and leaders, as such, give guidance to this deeply held belief of the people and draw up a major plan, they will probably realize that, right before their eyes, there are new homes for the Japanese race, everywhere in the Orient and in the South Seas. The dreams of people in olden times of expanding overseas need no longer end as dreams, but can now be certainly realized. This is indeed the one chance in a thousand years. We can hardly bear the happiness in our heart.

Though it is an incontrovertible fact that the Japanese race is not inferior to the peoples of the West in ability and vitality, the Japanese are unable to free themselves of narrow-minded propensities simply because by accident of nature their country is positioned in a distant corner of the Far East and thus was delayed in riding the currents of modern civilization. They view the civilized nations of the West as the penniless do the extremely rich; outwardly they talk big, saying they are people and we are people, but if their innermost thoughts are probed, they fear Western capability, power and knowledge and are resigned to the thought that they possibly cannot ever win in competition with them. . . .

To urge a weakling who has no confidence in his own strength to cross the boundless seas to set up a new home is like urging a cripple to run. Thus, in spite of the earnest debate to date over emigration, it is no coincidence that it has not succeeded. However, the single fact that Japan has defeated the ancient and great country of China has opened the minds of the conservative, diffident Japanese people and has convinced them that in capability and in vigor, they are not inferior to any race in the world.

From *Jiji Shimpo*, February 3, 1896; reprinted in Yasuo Wakatsuki, "Japanese Emigration to the United States, 1866–1924: A Monograph," *Perspectives in American History* 12 (1979): 443.

7. Japanese Government Criteria for Emigrants to Hawai'i, 1885

(1) The emigrant laborer shall meet the following conditions:

(a) The person shall be a *bona fide* farmer.

(b) The person shall abide by the terms of the agreement on emigrant labor and shall be in a state of health to withstand farm work.

(c) The person shall be between 25 and 30 years of age. However, when a person under 40 years of age qualifies under Article 2, he shall be classified as a substitute and may be accepted by the examiners after due deliberation.

(d) The person(s) shall be a single person or a married couple with no dependents.

(2) A person who falls under any of the under-mentioned categories shall not be eligible for recruitment:

(a) *Shizoku* (person of the *samurai* society class), a merchant, a craftsman, a handyman, or a farmer who at the same time engages in trading, handicrafts or miscellaneous services.

(b) A person who will reach the age of conscription during the contract period and has military service obligation.

(c) A person who is under 20 or older than 40 years in age.

(d) A female who is more than four months pregnant.

(e) Any suffering from chronic or hereditary diseases.

(f) A person who is without a wife but with an infant.

8. Japanese Official Condemns Brutal Working Conditions on Hawaiian Plantations, 1885

My investigations have shown me that in very many instances the complainants were authorized in their manifestations of discontent, while I find that often the ill usage and harsh treatment that accusation has been made of, have arisen from the difficulty that the Japanese on the one side and their employers on the other, have had in understanding each other. . . . A very just cause of complaint . . . is the unwarrantable and frequent acts of violence that have been perpetrated upon Japanese by overseers on many of the plantations. . . . The Japanese Government considers Your Excellency's Government the direct protector of all Japanese subjects during the period of their probation of three years and that it it the safeguard of their liberty to prevent completely and absolutely all arrests for civil breach of contract. . . . Furthermore planters should be notified that hereafter no overseer will be allowed to put his hands in any way on any Japanese for any purpose whatever, and that violation of this order will be considered sufficient cause by Government for removal.

"Japanese Government Criteria for Emigrants to Hawai'i" by Yasuo Wakatsuki, originally published in "Japanese Migration to the United States: A Monograph," *Perspectives in American History*, vol. 12, 1979, pp. 387–516.

Excerpt from *An Island Community: Ecological Succession in Hawaii* by Andrew W. Lind. Copyright 1938 University of Chicago Press. Used with permission.

⊕ E S S A Y S

In the first essay, historian Sucheng Chan, emeritus professor at the University of California at Santa Barbara, documents a pattern of Chinese immigrant employment corresponding to large economic transformations in California and the American West. Confronted with changing economic opportunities, Chinese gold miners shifted to railroad construction and then later to agricultural work. In the meantime, other Chinese immigrants established themselves in urban trades and businesses such as cigar making and laundries. Faced with constraints similar to those of the Chinese, Japanese immigrants were also drawn to agriculture and small business as they began immigrating to the West Coast in the early twentieth century. But as Harvard University professor Akira Iriye notes in the second essay, immigration for the Japanese carried the additional opportunity of strengthening Japan's economy and international standing among the world's leading nations.

Shifting Chinese Immigrant Employment

SUCHENG CHAN

The singular importance of gold to the early immigrants in California is reflected in the folk memory of many Chinese around the world to this day: until quite recently, they called San Francisco Jiujinshan (Gaogamsan, "the Old Gold Mountain") while Australia is known as Xinjinshan (Sungamsan, "the New Gold Mountain"). A few statistics will also illustrate the significance of gold in Chinese American history. The 1860 census takers found that virtually 100 percent of the Chinese in the continental United States were still living in California. The state continued to hold a majority of the nation's Chinese population until the turn of the century: 78, 71, 67, and 51 percent of them lived in California in 1870, 1880, 1890, and 1900, respectively. Within the state itself, 84, 45, 32, 13, and 12 percent of them were found in the mining counties in 1860, 1870, 1880, 1890, and 1990, respectively. Unlike the independent white prospectors, most of whom had left the mining regions by the late 1850s, sizable numbers of Chinese remained there until the 1880s.

In terms of occupational distribution, in 1860, when surface deposits had already been depleted, fully 85 percent of the Chinese in the mining counties were still panning or digging for gold. A decade later, 65 percent of them were doing so, while in 1880, 59 percent persisted in prospecting. Since the manuscript schedules of the 1890 census were lost in a fire, no computation can be made with regard to how many Chinese miners were still at work that year, but census takers counted over 2,000 Chinese miners in California in 1900—a year when the overall Chinese population was 45,753 in the state and 89,863 in the nation.

Three principal methods were used for obtaining the precious metal: placer, hydraulic, and deep-shaft or quartz mining. The vast majority of the Chinese worked only placer claims. In the early years, when surface deposits were abundant, many miners, including Chinese, used nothing more complicated than a pan, into which they placed a small amount of gold-bearing dirt, swirling it to wash the lighter earth

---

off the rim while letting the gold settle at the bottom. A more efficient contraption was the rocker or cradle—a wooden box with cleats (called riffles) nailed across the bottom and mounted on rockers. "Pay dirt" was placed with water into the box, which was then rocked back and forth. Such motion separated the heavier gold dust and nuggets from the rest of the dirt; as water flowed over the mixture, the gold was caught by the cleats at the bottom, while the nonauriferous dirt flowed out the open end. Another device, the long-tom, was a longer rocker that remained stationary. Mounted at an angle with a continuous stream of water flowing through it, it could handle a large volume of dirt with a minimal amount of human labor. Sluices—a series of open troughs with cleats—evolved from long-toms, requiring large volumes of water for their proper functioning.

Chinese miners used all of the above devices and also introduced some implements of their own. The most notable was the waterwheel, similar to those used by farmers in China. Mounted with buckets to scoop water from a stream or river, the wheel, as it turned slowly, emptied the buckets of water into a trough that carried the water to where it was needed. Chinese were also skilled at building wing dams that diverted water either from a small tributary or one section of a river, in order to expose the riverbed for mining. Perhaps they resorted to such ingenious contrivances because, as J. D. Borthwick observed in the early 1850s, they did not seem to like standing in water for long periods. Borthwick thought that the way Chinese mined resembled "scratching": instead of pushing their shovels forcefully into the ground as Euro-American miners did, they scraped its surface to loosen the gravel.

Only a small number of Chinese attempted hydraulic mining. The most likely reason is that this method, which shot powerful jets of water against ore-bearing hillsides to wash down the dirt, required considerable capital. Since Chinese miners were periodically subjected to violence, investing a lot of money in heavy equipment was simply too risky. Those who did engage in hydraulic mining did so in rather remote areas, largely in the Siskiyou and Trinity mountains of northwestern California.

Documentation regarding Chinese participation in quartz mining—digging tunnels into the mountains that contained veins of ore—is conflicting. Some accounts suggest that no Chinese could be hired by the mining companies extracting gold this way because unionized Euro-American miners—particularly imported ones from Cornwall, who were the world's most skillful deep-shaft operators—stopped any attempts by the companies to employ Chinese. Other sources claim that a large number of Chinese miners worked for companies from the late 1860s on, and although their authors do not indicate the mining methods these companies used, they could not have been exploiting placer claims, which had been completely depleted by then.

The presence of so many miners among the Chinese influenced what other Chinese did for a living. Wherever groups of miners congregated, merchants opened stores to provision them and to serve their social and recreational needs. Merchants imported a variety of ingredients needed for Chinese cooking. Invoices of Chinese import-export firms found at San Francisco's Custom House in the early 1850s list rice, noodles, beans, yams, sugar, tea, vinegar, peanut oil, dried vegetables, bamboo shoots, dried mushrooms, ginger, cured eggs, sweetmeats, sausages, salted fish, dried shrimp and oysters, dried bean curd, and dried as well as fresh fruits. The immigrants' diet was supplemented with vegetables grown by local Chinese truck gardeners, with meat from pigs, ducks, and chickens raised by Chinese farmers, and with fish caught by Chinese fishermen. Once in a while, they also ate American canned sardines and ham, as well as fresh beef purchased from Euro-American butchers.

In addition, merchants brought in Chinese textiles and clothing, although the Chinese miners early learned to wear American leather boots. In time, some workers grew to favor durable blue jeans over baggy Chinese cotton pants. As shown in many photographs taken of them, another item of American apparel they seemed to fancy was felt hats, although men working in the countryside continued to depend on imported conical bamboo hats.

Merchants made it possible for Chinese immigrants to be surrounded by all the essential and familiar items of their material culture. Even rice paper and Chinese ink and brushes found their way across the Pacific, as did matches, firecrackers, joss sticks (made from Hawaiian sandalwood), washbasins, pots and pans, Chinese-style weights and measures, and a large array of herbs. Opium entered without restriction during the early years, but it was not the only recreational drug the Chinese used: most Chinese stores, even those in remote mountain areas, also stocked American cigarettes and whiskey.

Merchants played such a critical role that they became the wealthiest members and most important leaders of the community, even though in the rural areas and small towns they usually comprised only about 3 percent of the population. The larger the urban center, however, the more numerous they were. In San Francisco, not counting the gamblers, brothel owners, and other underworld entrepreneurs, merchants hovered around 10 percent of the gainfully employed.

One development that affected both Chinese miners and merchants was the building of the western half of the first transcontinental railroad—a project that employed more than 10,000 Chinese workers at its peak, many of whom were former miners. In fact, the railroad company's effort to recruit Chinese laborers provided the impetus that finally took large numbers of Chinese away from the mines. Meanwhile, Chinese merchants profited from the construction project, since they served as labor contractors who gathered the men into gangs, charged each one a commission for finding him work, and provisioned the whole lot.

Proposals for a transcontinental railroad had been made since the 1840s, but it took the Civil War to spur Congress finally to pass a bill that made the construction possible. To enable private entrepreneurs to finance such a momentous undertaking, the federal government issued bonds on behalf of and granted public land to the railroad companies—land they were supposed to sell to raise the capital needed. The amount of land granted depended on the miles of tracks laid and on the difficulty of the terrain traversed. The Union Pacific Railroad Company got the contract to build westward from the Missouri River, while the Central Pacific Railroad Company, formed by four Sacramento merchants, was to build eastward from that city. Unlike the Union Pacific, which could lay one mile of track a day across open plains using cheap Irish immigrant labor, the Central Pacific had to traverse several ranges of high mountains and had, moreover, to deal with the fact that California had the nation's highest wages.

First hired as an experiment to do grading in 1865, Chinese workers numbered 3,000 by the end of the year. Despite the skepticism that was expressed about their physical strength, Chinese soon became the backbone of the company's construction crews, providing the bulk of the labor not only for unskilled tasks but for highly demanding and dangerous ones as well. Regardless of the nature of the work they did, however, all Chinese were paid the same wage, which was considerably lower than what Euro-American skilled workers received.

The first true test the Chinese faced was a huge rock outcrop called Cape Horn, around which no detour was possible. To carve a ledge on the rim of this granite bulk, Chinese were lowered by rope in wicker baskets from the top of cliffs. While thus dangled, they chiseled holes in the granite into which they stuffed black powder. Fellow workers pulled them up as the powder exploded. Those who did not make it up in time died in the explosions.

As the road ascended into the high Sierras, it often took 300 men a month to clear and grub a bare three miles. Grading the way thus cleared took even more effort. As the crew neared the crest of the mountain range, they began the almost impossible task of drilling a tunnel through solid granite. Before they got very far, winter came and snow fell. Nevertheless, the company decided to press on, conscious that its rival was racing across the plains and getting the larger share of the land grants. Thousands of Chinese worked underground in snow tunnels around the clock through the winter of 1866. It took all summer and fall to grade the route thus created, but before tracks could be laid, winter descended again with even heavier snowfalls. As one of the Central Pacific's engineers admitted years later, "a good many men" (i.e., Chinese) were lost during the terrible winter of 1867. The bodies of those buried by avalanches could not even be dug out until the following spring. Once the tracks descended the eastern slopes of the Sierras, the Chinese crew sped across the hot, dry plateaus of Nevada and Utah until the two ends of the railroad joined at Promontory Point, Utah in 1869. Despite their heroic feat, the Chinese were not invited to the jubilant ceremonies that marked the completion of America's first transcontinental railroad, hailed as one of the most remarkable engineering feats of its time.

But the railroad was more than a technological wonder: it transformed the American West, especially California. Before its completion, California was geographically isolated from the rest of the country. Immigrants had to come by wagon train, while manufactured goods from the eastern United States arrived by ship around the tip of South America. The state's exports—primarily wheat from the 1860s through the 1880s—traveled by the same long route to Atlantic seaboard and British ports. The railroad's full effect was not felt for more than a decade after its completion because high passenger and freight rates limited its usage. In the mid-1880s, after a second transcontinental railroad was built, the two engaged in a cut-throat rate war. The fares they charged became so cheap that hordes of people rode the trains to California—if not to settle, then at least to sightsee.

The manner in which railroad construction was financed also affected California's development. The railroad company was supposed to have sold most of the land the federal government granted it—some 9 to 11 million acres, depending on how one counts—but it never did so, keeping the land, instead, for speculation. Because prices were so high, few settlers in California could afford to buy land. They blamed the railroad, on the one hand, and the Chinese, on the other, for their plight. As Varden Fuller has argued, in their eyes, were it not for the availability of Chinese "cheap labor," owners of large tracts would have been forced to subdivide and sell the plots at affordable prices. But there was little that angry citizens could do to break the railroad company's power: with its enormous economic assets, it controlled state politics for decades.

Ironically for the Chinese, the completion of the railroad affected them negatively. The company retained several hundred of them for maintenance work, but discharged the rest, thereby instantaneously rendering almost 10,000 Chinese jobless. These former employees were not even allowed to ride the trains free of charge back to California. Instead, they straggled on foot westward in small groups, finding work wherever they could, mostly as common laborers and migrant farmworkers. But as more and more Euro-Americans appeared in California, they began to compete with the Chinese for jobs. Their resentment helped to fan the flames of the anti-Chinese movement.

Discharged Chinese railroad workers could find work in agriculture because California in the 1870s was one of the world's leading producers of wheat, a large percentage of which was shipped to Liverpool, headquarters of the world wheat market. The long and rainless California summers proved to be a real advantage: because the wheat could be thoroughly dried before being loaded in the holds of ships, it did not mold during the long voyage down the South American coast, around Cape Horn through the Straits of Magellan, and across the South and North Atlantic Ocean to Liverpool, where it brought premium prices due to its superior quality. Chinese helped to harvest the wheat but also found employment cultivating, harvesting, and packing a wide variety of other crops.

Farm owners welcomed Chinese workers when they discovered that employing them was convenient: instead of having to deal with individual seasonal laborers, they could simply arrange with a Chinese crew leader or labor contractor to have so many men at a given place on a given date, paying the contractor a lump sum for a specified job. Moreover, the Chinese boarded themselves and even provided their own tents or slept under the starts. Each group of men either chose one of their own to do the cooking or jointly paid the wages of a cook. Some of the contractors were local merchants, who charged each man a small commission for finding him a job and earned sizable profits by selling the crews their provisions.

But harvest labor was not the only kind of agricultural work the Chinese performed. In California's great Central Valley as well as smaller coastal valleys and plains, in Washington's Yakima Valley, Oregon's Hood River Valley, and in arable areas in other states west of the Rocky Mountains, Chinese leased land to become tenant farmers. For the most part, they specialized in labor-intensive vegetables, strawberries and other small fruits, deciduous tree fruits, and nuts. In the Sacramento–San Joaquin Delta, a reclaimed marshland that is one of the most fertile agricultural areas of California, Chinese tenant farmers grew potatoes, onions, and asparagus—leasing large plots, many of which they had earlier helped to drain, dike, and put under the plow. Other Chinese became commission merchants, selling the crops that their fellow countrymen as well as Euro-American farmers produced. Yet others worked as farm cooks, feeding the farm owners' families as well as the workers the latter employed.

Life was quite different for the Chinese in San Francisco, the metropolis of the Pacific Coast, where thousands of Chinese artisans and factory workers lived. Manufacturing occupied some two-fifths of the gainfully employed Chinese in the city in the 1870s and early 1880s. In crowded, poorly lit and ventilated sweatshops and factories, they made shoes, boots, slippers, overalls, shirts, underwear, woolen blankets, cigars, gunny sacks, brooms, and many other items. In other towns along the Pacific Coast, Chinese also worked in a few nascent manufacturing industries, but they did so only in very small numbers: before such places as Sacramento, Stockton, Marysville, Portland, or Seattle could develop into industrial centers, Chinese had already been driven out of light manufacturing as a result of anti-Chinese sentiment and activities. Boycotts against Chinese-made goods in the second half of the 1880s effectively eliminated them from the market.

One occupation that acquired a special significance in Chinese American history is laundering. Large numbers of Chinese eventually became laundrymen, not because washing clothes was a traditional male occupation in China, but because there were very few women—and consequently virtually no washerwomen of any ethnic origin—in gold-rush California. The shortage was so acute that shirts were sent all the way from San Francisco to Honolulu to be washed and ironed at exorbitant prices in the early 1850s.

According to one anecdotal account related by Paul C. P. Siu, the first Chinese laundryman to appear in San Francisco was Wah Lee, who hung a sign, "Wash'ng and Iron'ng," over his premises at the corner of Dupont Street (now Grant Avenue) and Washington Street in 1851. By 1860 there were 890 Chinese laundrymen in California, comprising 2.6 percent of the total employed Chinese in the state. By 1870 almost 3,000 Chinese in California (6 percent of the gainfully employed) were washing and ironing clothes for a living. A decade later, the number had increased to more than 5,000, representing 7.3 percent of the working Chinese in the state. There were still almost 4,800 laundrymen (11 percent of the gainfully employed Chinese) in California at the turn of the century, even though the overall Chinese population had declined drastically from the peak it had reached in the early 1880s.

Important as they were in California, laundries were even more significant in other parts of the United States, for laundering was one of four "pioneer" occupations that enabled Chinese to move eastward across the continent. Just as mining drew Chinese to the Pacific Northwest and the northern tier of the states in the Rocky Mountains and Great Plains, and railroad construction introduced Chinese first to Nevada and Utah and then to Arizona, New Mexico, and Texas, so operating laundries and restaurants allowed them to find an economic niche for themselves in towns and cities of the Midwest and along the Atlantic seaboard. By rendering a much needed service, Chinese laundrymen found a way to survive wherever they settled.

Siu's detailed study of laundries in Chicago gives an idea of how they grew. The first Chinese laundry in the city opened in 1872. Eight years later, there were 67; in 1883, 199; and ten years later, 313. The peak was reached in 1918 with 523; after that, the numbers declined. More interesting than the numerical increase was the spatial spread and the kind of people who made use of Chinese laundries. At first, the laundries were confined to the periphery of the central business district, but they soon became established in more outlying residential neighborhoods. Young married couples with both spouses employed in white-collar salaried jobs and single men and women living in rooming houses were the laundries' two main groups of customers. Relatively few laundries existed in neighborhoods with single-family dwellings; an even smaller number was found in industrial areas occupied by recent European immigrants.

Laundries both sustained and entrapped those who relied on them for survival. On the one hand, washing and ironing clothes was one of the few occupations the host society allowed the Chinese to follow after the 1880s. On the other hand, as one person interviewed by Siu observed: "white customers were prepared to patronize him as a laundryman because as such his status was low and constituted no competitive threat. If you stop to think about it, there's a very real difference between the person who washes your soiled clothing and the one who fills your prescription. As a laundryman he occupied a status which was in accordance with the social definition of the place in the economic hierarchy suitable for a member of an 'inferior race.'"

Precisely because laundering was deemed an "inferior" occupation, those who relied on it for a living were isolated from and subservient to the larger community. Though Chinese laundries were located primarily in white neighborhoods, their occupants lived in a self-contained world. A great deal of both their business and social needs were met by people who came to their doors. Agents of laundry supply companies visited them regularly to take and deliver their orders; drivers of "food wagons" brought them cooked food, fresh produce, and staples; tailors came to take their measurements for custom-tailored suits that they could pay for by installment; jewelers tried to sell them gold watches and diamond rings (two of the conspicuous-consumption items that Chinese laundrymen seemed to fancy); and, on occasion, prostitutes dropped by to see if they felt in need of sex. Most laundrymen left their stores only on Sunday afternoons to eat, gamble, or visit friends in Chinatown.

Restaurants likewise enabled Chinese to settle and survive in communities with few of their fellow countrymen, for their business did not depend solely on a Chinese clientele. In gold-rush California, which was filled with men but had few women, men of any nationality willing to cook and feed others found it relatively easy to earn a living. A few observant Chinese quickly realized that cooking could provide a more steady income than many other occupations. In time, thousands of Chinese worked as cooks—in private homes, on farms, in hotels and restaurants—all over the American West. In the late nineteenth century, Chinese started moving to other parts of the country to open restaurants. Establishments in the larger towns and cities generally served only Chinese food and used only fellow Chinese as waiters and busboys, but those in the smaller communities dished up large plates of American-style beef stew, pork chops, or fried chicken as well as Chinese spare ribs, sweet and sour pork, fried rice, or chow mein, and relied on Euro-American waitresses for help.

One feature common to Chinese enterprises—be they mining claims, groceries, laundries, or restaurants—was that a large number of the people who worked in them owned shares in the business, and were thus partners, albeit often unequal ones. This practice, together with the fact that the men were often bound by kinship ties and lived in the same premises, modulated whatever conflicts might have arisen between the "bosses" and the "workers." The ability to get along with each other in close quarters was crucial: given the inhospitability of the larger society in which they found themselves, "ethnic confinement" was an important survival mechanism.

Chinese—and the other Asian immigrant groups who came after them—could find economic niches that sheltered them because of the nature of American capitalism. In the late nineteenth century, as firms became bigger and more oligopolistic through mergers and the growth of new industrial sectors, independent artisans found it more and more difficult to survive. This development was by no means universal, however: there has always been considerable room in the less-developed parts of the economy for small businesses to operate. Chinese laundries persisted until the 1950s and restaurants to this day because they fill needs unmet by the corporate structure.

Japanese Expansionism in California

AKIRA IRIYE

Japan, like the United States, was at once an imperialist and a nonmilitary expansionist. It was engaged in preparation for control over Korea that was clearly imperialistic. The nation's army, with the support of the government, was contemplating the use of force to assert predominance over a neighboring kingdom and to eliminate foreign influence. But this was only a fraction of the expansion being undertaken and planned by the Japanese, and not all of it involved an overt use of force. The areas of more subtle expansion were pregnant with future implications and had direct relevance to Japanese-American relations.

Japanese thinking can perhaps best be seen in three books on imperialism, all published in 1901: Kōtoku Shūsui, *Nijusseiki no kaibutsu teikokushugi* (Imperialism, the monster of the twentieth century); Takimoto Sciichi, *Keizaiteki teikokushugi* (Economic imperialism); and Ukita Kazutami, *Teikokushugi to kyōiku* (Imperialism and education). Of these Kōtoku's book is best known today, but at that time its influence was no more than that of the other two. All three were timely, coming just when the Japanese people debated the course of their empire, formal and informal, and when they were viewing themselves and the Americans as two latecomers to the ranks of imperialists.

Kōtoku's book opens with the famous passage: "The fashion of imperialism is spreading like a prairie fire. . . . Even the United States seems to be copying it. As for Japan, after the great victory in the Sino-Japanese War the people, both high and low, have been fanatically turning toward it like a wild horse trying to throw off his yoke." Imperialists in Japan and elsewhere are like drunken men, intoxicated by patriotism and militarism, which are nothing but expressions of their animal instincts. They bleed people white with taxes, expand armaments, divert productive capital for unproductive ends, cause prices to rise, and invite excessive imports. These are all for the sake of the state. Government, education, commerce, and industry are sacrificed to patriotism, which is the root of militarism and imperialism. Echoing the argument of contemporary British anti-imperialists, Kōtoku asserts that war, armament, and imperialism retard economic progress and destroy civilization. Prosperity cannot be achieved through territorial acquisitions, national greatness does not come from aggression and plundering, and civilization never progresses by means of dictatorial rule. In an important passage, the author says what he objects to is imperialism in the sense of colonialism and territorial aggrandizement, not expansion itself. The economic expansion of a people should be welcomed, but not the extension of the limits of empire which can be achieved only through the use of force and suppression of other peoples.

Like the American anti-imperialists, Kōtoku argues that imperialism does not really bring about the expansion of national life. On the contrary, it only means the expansion of the interests and self-esteem of a handful of military men, capitalists, and politicians, obtained at the expense of the well-being of the majority of the people. From such a viewpoint, the book gives a harsh indictment of the United States:

> The action of the European powers in Asia and Africa, and the territorial expansion of the United States in the South Seas are all carried out through militarism and armed forces. . . . If the United States truly fought for the freedom and independence of Cuba, why does it try to violate the freedom and independence of the Philippines? To use force to suppress another people's desires and plunder their territory and wealth—does such a thing not bring shame to America's glorious history of civilization and liberty?
> . . . If in the future the United States should be faced with a crisis of national existence, it would result not from the narrowness of its territory but from its unlimited territorial expansion, not from the lack of power in external affairs but from corruption and social decay internally. . . . They [i.e., Americans] are competing with one another to enter the evil path simply to satisfy their ambitions, interests, and patriotic zeal. I not only fear for their future troubles but feel sorrow for liberty, justice, and humanism.

If Japan were not to fall into the same error, it must renounce imperialism through the use of force. Instead it should stress, as Britain did before the age of imperialism the expansion of the people through trade, production, and the spread of civilization. A nation's happiness and greatness, Kōtoku concludes, do not lie in the vastness of its territory, but in the high level of its morality, not in the strength of its armament but in the nobility of its ideals, not in the number of ships and soldiers but in the abundance of products.

A second edition of Kōtoku's book was issued within twenty days. By then newspapers and journals had printed their reviews, reflecting tremendous national concern with the book's subject matter. The reviews were either entirely or partially laudatory, but rarely, if at all, unfavorable. Antigovernment and radical organs such as *Yorozu chōhō and Rōdō sekai* (The world of labor) wholly endorsed the author's ideas and heaped high praise, and Nakae Chōmin expressed his complete agreement with Kōtoku's analysis. The so-called imperialism, Nakae wrote, "is militarism pure and simple . . . the most miserable state of affairs in all history." Influential dailies such as the *Mainichi, Yomiuri, Hōchi,* and *Jiji shinpō* praised the book as a sharp and readable account of the imperialism that was spreading all over the earth. The major point of criticism raised by other reviewers went to the heart of the question Kōtoku's definition of imperialism. He saw it as characterized by militarism and territorial aggrandizement, pushed for their own interests by a handful of men who would resort to the rhetoric of patriotism to arouse the animal instinct inherent in all men. This was too narrow a view for some readers, who argued that not all patriotism was evil, and that not all imperialism was practiced by vicious men. Moreover, not all phenomena in the world could be described in terms of the harmful effects of imperialism; cosmopolitanism, pacifism, economic development, and utopianism were apparently growing in strength. According to such critics as Kayahara Kazan and Taoka Ryōun, all were part of the same global development.

Mankind, according to Kayahara, was becoming conscious of unity through the diversity of individual cultures and nations; and imperialism should be viewed not simply as evil militarism but as an instrument through which peoples of the world could develop a cosmopolitan outlook while refining their individual characteristics. Taoka, too, though sharing Kōtoku's hatred of imperialism, asserted that this was but a stage in a man's evolution toward unity and equality. While less sentimental, reviewers for *Asahi* and *Tokyo Nichinichi* criticized the book for failing to see that the imperialistic outlook was not a product of blind impulses but an expression of basic national energy, made manifest through the organization of the nation-state.

These writers were grappling with a worldwide phenomenon that had become all too visible after the decade of the 1890's. They were not simply concerned with the Manchurian crisis, nor were they talking merely of Japanese interests in Korea; they were trying to gain a sense of world movements so that their country could chart a correct course. Kōtoku gave them a book that became a classic in expounding the negative features of imperialism. Takimoto Sciichi's *Keizaiteki teikokushugi,* by contrast, viewed the economic aspects of the phenomenon and sought to justify imperialism as a necessary policy for national expansion. Published just four days before Kōtoku's, Takimoto's book presented the other half of the picture. As he said, "armed commercialism" was the order of the day, and "any nation which intends to maintain its independence and promote its expansion must be ready to wage this [economic] struggle." Imperialism, from this point of view, was not a machination of a few greedy individuals and groups, but a fundamental necessity for national sovereignty and welfare. No wonder, then, that the most imperialistic countries were also those that were internally united and practiced "industrial democracy." Kōtoku's model of imperialism was British and American; Germany provided Takimoto's best example. Here was a nation in which the government sought to harmonize the interests of various segments of the population so that they would be united behind the struggle in the world arena. It was nonsense, according to this author, to talk of economic cosmopolitanism. Rather, in the new mercantilistic age, the economy was at the service of the state, which would expand its territorial limits to create a self-sufficient, protected economic system. Now that Japan had Hokkaido and Taiwan, they should be made the bases for further imperialistic expansion in order to make the nation the great empire of the East. Unless it became one, the whole of Asia would fall into the hands of Western empires. Imperialism, in this sense, was a necessary, defensive policy, not an impulsive militaristic adventure.

Kōtoku's and Takimoto's books dealt with modern imperialism from two diametrically opposed viewpoints. There is little doubt that they reflected a division in Japanese opinion concerning the future of national expansion. Most people, however, would not have sided with either of these extreme positions. What the Japanese government was doing and the people were supporting was a cross between imperialistic expansion and more peaceful, economic expansion. Ukita Kazutami's book *Teikokushugi to kyōiku* represented the middle position. By profession a philosopher, Ukita was active as one of the influential popularizers of ideas and commentators on current affairs. The book reprinted some of the articles he wrote for *Kokumin shinbun,* edited by Tokutomi Sohō, who obviously endorsed many of Ukita's views. He starts out by saying that imperialism is the only way to maintain the nation's independence and participate actively in world civilization and politics.

The new modern imperialism is represented by Britain, Russia, and the United States, and differs from the old imperialism of the Spanish or Dutch type. The latter is aggressive, political, militaristic expansionism, whereas the former is fundamentally economic and propelled by the people's energy rather than by the state. Modern imperialism does often carry out territorial aggrandizement, but this is basically because of the struggle for survival among races. Certain races and countries simply do not have the will to remain independent, but their incorporation into stronger nations will advance world civilization as a whole. There are, in other words, ethical factors in imperialism, and Japan should try to be an ethical imperialist.

Most of the earth's surface, Ukita continues, has already been absorbed by the imperialist powers. If Japan is to adopt a policy of imperialism, it can do so only through lawful expansion of Japanese rights in relation to the West and assistance to Asian countries to carry out reform programs and achieve independence. The Japanese government should be prepared to promote such expansionism so that the people will migrate abroad and plant seeds of future success. He asserts that, since the Japanese variety of imperialism must take an economic and peaceful form, there will be no limits to such expansion save those conditioned by the level of education of the Japanese people.

"The areas for our expansion," according to Ukita, "obviously are confined to the Asian continent, the New World, and the South Seas." While Japan must persist in "peaceful, economic, and commercial" expansion in these parts of the world, it must be prepared to make an exception in the case of Korea, as its "independence" is a fundamental national policy. Even this is not aggressive imperialism, since Japan only desires a preponderant economic and political position in the peninsula. Interests are not comparably extensive in China, and Japan will gain most by encouraging that country's reform and modernization. On the other hand, it is desirable to settle and protect Japanese people in the Pacific and the New World. In this task Japan "is destined to compete with American imperialism." Such competition, however, is "peaceful competition." the Japanese can achieve victory only by inculcation in practical subjects such as commerce and economics. Pragmatism and efficiency ought to be the guiding principles of Japanese public education. Individual students must learn to develop their personal morality integrity, and perseverance so as to equip themselves for the peaceful competition of imperialism. Only if they develop "internalized, spiritual, autonomous, and self-reliant" morality, will they be able to guide Asia's hundreds of millions along the path of modernization and to go out and live in the South Seas and the American continents.

Records of Japanese expansion prior to the Russo-Japanese War show that Ukita correctly predicted the general outline it was going to follow. Apart from Korea, there was no premeditated design to extend the limits of Japan's formal empire to the continent of Asia or to the Pacific Ocean. Japanese imperialism did not take so aggressive a form as that urged by Takimoto. Neither did the nation completely renounce its right to assertive expansion, as Kōtoku insisted. Beyond the clear limits of imperialistic policy in Korea, the Japanese were practicing and rationalizing their expansion much as Ukita suggested. . . .

The Asian continent was not what most Japanese had in mind when they considered expansion. The wider Pacific region was more frequently mentioned as an ideal area for undertaking peaceful expansion. Interest in the Philippines did not wane in the years immediately following the Spanish-American War. In 1902, for instance, there were about 1,500 Japanese laborers in the islands, a threefold increase over 1898. But the Philippines were not as promising as Hawaii as a place of the emigration of Japanese manual laborers, where there was a sufficient supply of Filipino workers. What was needed there was the importation of Japanese capital and skills, which was to increase steadily but at first only slowly. Japan's interest in the Philippines lay in their promise as a market. As Moriyama Nobunori wrote in his *Bei-Sei sensō* (The Spanish-American War), probably the only book-length study of the war by a Japanese at that time, now that the United States had acquired the islands its capital was likely to rush in and contribute to the industrialization of the Philippines. Japan should take advantage of their proximity to Taiwan and "should never give up enormous profits that we could obtain in peacetime." The author admitted that American annexation of the Philippines had in effect frustrated Japanese ambitions southward, but this expansion was a historical fact and Japan could not oppose it. The Philippines and Cuba were to the United States what Taiwan and Korea were to Japan. They fell within the respective empires, and the only competition possible between the two was economic.

Hawaii and the West coast of the United States held the greatest interest for Japanese expansionists. The number of passports issued to Japanese laborers going to Hawaii increased from 5,913 in 1897 to 12,952 in 1898 and 27,155 in 1899, reflecting a relaxation in the anti-Japanese movement in the islands after their annexation. But as they came under territorial rule in 1900, the United States law forbidding contract labor was applied to Hawaii, causing Japanese immigration to drop to 4,760 in 1900. Freed from the contract system, Japanese laborers began moving to the continental United States, bringing about a near doubling of the Japanese population between 1899 and 1900. There were about 24,000 Japanese in the United States in 1900, and the number doubled again in the following four years. Not only laborers from Hawaii, but students, merchants, and farmers began arriving directly from Japan. Immigration companies which hitherto had arranged contract emigration to Hawaii now sent out shiploads of Japanese to the West coast of the United States.

Numerically, the presence of Japanese in Hawaii and North America was impressive: on the eve of the Russo-Japanese War, there were over 65,000 in Hawaii and nearly 40,000 on the West coast. Together they comprised more than two-thirds of the Japanese population abroad. Economically speaking, emigration to China and Korea was considered less important than that to the Pacific American continent. The preference for a warmer climate and richer soil, long expressed by Japanese writers, stayed with them as they pondered the more immediate questions of international politics in Manchuria. The urgent need, as they saw it, was still to enrich the nation, and economic expansion could most easily be visualized in connection with trade with and emigration to the territories bordering the Pacific Ocean. This was particularly the time when interest in emigration to America reached unprecedented intensity.

"Hawaii! The new world of North America! How wonderful it is that our farmers, laborers, and merchants, all vigorous and healthy, have been turning their attention more and more to these islands and the new world." Thus ran a typical passage from one of the numerous guides to work abroad, published at the turn of the century.

Reflecting the growing interest in working in the United States and its possessions, a new genre in Japanese journalistic writings emerged: pamphlets on how to prepare for going abroad and conduct oneself overseas. Titles such as *Kaigai dekasegi annai* (A guide to working abroad) and *Kaigai risshin no tebiki* (How to get ahead abroad) began to appear, and most concentrated on emigration to the United States. The first-named was a booklet published by the Emigrants Protection Association, organized in 1902 to assist prospective emigrants. In it the editor pointed out that in Hawaii a Japanese laborer could easily earn over 30 yen a month, and that in San Francisco a domestic servant could make nearly the same amount, whereas in Japan they would not be able to get half as much through harder work. To prepare for overseas emigration, of course, one would need enough initial capital. According to this booklet, about 20 yen would have to be paid as a fee to an emigration company to help a prospective emigrant move to Hawaii. There were twenty-eight emigration companies in existence in 1902, of which nineteen had been founded after 1898, and as many as eight in the year 1902 alone. They made arrangements for the departure of an emigrant, who then had to pay 60 yen for passage, and, upon arrival in Hawaii, had to show the immigration officials that he had at least 91 yen in his possession. Now that the contract labor system had been abolished, the immigrant would be free to engage in any kind of work, and it should be easy for him to recover the investment of 171 yen for his removal. If he desired to go farther, to the West coast of the United States, it would cost more money, but he would have the opportunity of earning more.

"Going to America," wrote the socialist Katayama Sen in 1903, "has now become the ultimate wish of our people. All men from all classes—students, laborers, gentlemen, businessmen—have joined their voices to repeat the wish and put their brains together to study it. . . . At a time when North America's power is rapidly rising and its influence steadily spreading all over the world, it is extreme foolishness not to go there. It is no exaggeration to say that it is a stupid, uncivilized thing not to consider going to America." Katayama had studied in the United States in the 1880's, and at the turn of the century was a recognized authority on American life, especially in connection with Japanese emigration. He mapped out the basic intellectual and practical guideline for this movement, and remained for a number of years the most influential writer on the subject. His first book on emigration, published in 1901, *To-Bei annai* (How to go the United States), quickly went through several editions, and subsequently he wrote other similar tracts. In *To-Bei annai* Katayama notes that Japan's fundamental concern is the present and future welfare of its increasing population, now approaching 40 million. The obvious solution is to encourage migration overseas, not only to reduce the homeland's population but also, more fundamentally, to promote Japanese industrialization. The Japanese overseas will introduce their country's products to distant lands and make Japan better known to the rest of the world. Unfortunately, he writes, reflecting a prevailing view of that time, the Japanese people are too insular and parochial; even Japanese overseas are not free from provincialism. "If they give up this insular mentality, understand the true meaning of civilization, and engage in business in a spirit of civilization, then their country, Japan, will cease to be a remote island in the Orient and they will be able to expand their influence all over the world." Of all the potential lands for Japanese emigration, Katayama insists that the United states is the most suitable. This is because "the United States is the freest country in the world; it surpasses all other countries in its industrial, commercial, economic and scholastic advancement." Since labor is considered sacred, wages are high; laborers can even afford to spend part of their earnings on education. Moreover, individual Japanese can go there own initiative. All they need is some small initial capital and, more important, determination.

There were two ways of reaching the continental United States. The more popular was first to go to Hawaii as a laboring immigrant and then move to the West coast. This involved less difficulty and less initial capital than the second method, going directly to America. The Japanese government was much more strict in the issuing of passports to the continental United States to avoid causing an anti-Japanese movement on the West coast, and as a rule massive emigration solely for the purpose of manual labor was discouraged. As a result, it was the younger people, especially students, who were most likely to be moved by Katayama's plea to go east and settle in the United States. As students, merchants, or visitors, their departure involved fewer bureaucratic difficulties, and only determination and a small sum of money were needed. The young emigrant was likely to procure a passport from his prefectural government if he provided letters endorsing his personal reliability and financial stability. He would then be ready to pack his suitcases—Katayama suggested that the emigrant take at least one new suit, two to three shirts, six handkerchiefs, six pairs of socks, a pair of shoes, a toothbrush and toothpaste, and an English dictionary—and, without much further ado, board the ship, with a strong body and perseverance as his only capital.

The trip to the West coast of the United States took about two weeks. Immigration proceedings were not difficult, and the new arrivals could live among fellow countrymen in such major centers as Seattle and San Francisco. Through Japanese connections they found menial jobs as waiters, "schoolboys," and gardeners. They assuredly would earn enough money to live and, if they had the will, to study. Many of them enrolled in local high schools and colleges, while working morning and evening hours as domestic servants.

Not all Japanese in the United States fitted Katayama's ideal. By 1901 reports abounded of the poor quality of Japanese in America. *To-Bei annai* contained letters written by Japanese student-immigrants in California. One wrote, "the Japanese here are all mediocre types, unable to breathe the air of civilization even though they are in America. They speak of Americans disparagingly and engage in the least enlightening conversations." Another reported that eight or nine out of ten Japanese in California "are simply idlers with whom it is below my dignity to deal." Such reports revealed that many young Japanese who went to America immersed themselves in daily living and lost whatever higher aspirations they might have had before they left home. From another point of view, however, they were in fact quite successful emigrants. They made a living in the new land and expanded Japanese commerce through their purchases and merchandising of Japanese goods. They built enclaves of Japanese settlement in San Francisco, Seattle, and other cities on the West coast. While their number was hardly sufficient to justify a grandiose vision of Japanese expansion, hope persisted that in time they would prove to be the vanguard of the Japanese thrust abroad. At the very least, by being forced to scramble for a living, they would learn to maximize profit and rationalize life. Economic necessity would breed a new attitude toward life and the world. From such a situation new types of men would emerge, Katayama argued. Another writer, long resident in the United States, expressed the same confidence graphically:

> Picture yourself boarding a huge ship of over 10,000 tons, crossing the Pacific Ocean in fifteen or sixteen days . . . arriving in America, entering the spacious city lined with stone buildings thirteen or fourteen stories high, walking on clean stone pavements, observing the development of machinery which can build tall buildings with only a handful of men . . . going to a college where men and women engage in education cheerfully and sincerely, riding a train at the speed of fifty or sixty miles an hour through the interior of the country where all you see are vast spaces without a trace of man—and compare this with life in Japan where you will be living on a modest income of thirty or forty yen a month, fighting with your neighbors over a foot or two of land, or involved in lawsuits to obtain water for irrigating a small plot of land. Before you know it your mind will be opened up, your horizon broadened, and your narrow provincialism will melt like a block of ice placed under the sun.

Obviously there was an element of idealism about immigrating to the United States. It appeared as the country from which the Japanese were considered likely to draw the greatest benefits, culturally as well as economically. There was an underlying image of a nation receptive to the coming of people from Japan, especially its youths and educated classes, who would cooperate with Americans in enriching the two countries and contributing to the peace and welfare of the Pacific. Perhaps for this reason, a great deal was written about the need to bring the cultural and life style of Japanese in America up to the level of the Americans themselves. The author of *Kaigai risshin no tebiki* exhorted emigrants to the United States not to strip naked, no matter how hot. "If you behave like African savages," he said, "you can't complain if the whites despise you." It was undesirable, wrote Noma Gozō, a member of the Diet, to send too many ignorant farmers and fishermen to North America before educating them in things Western. Katayama Sen repeatedly urged that the prospective emigrants be equipped with determination, perseverance, and, above all, flexibility so as to adapt themselves to a new environment. He echoed other writers in criticizing Japanese in the United States for failing to learn the customs and institutions of the new land. So long as they behaved as if they were still in Japan, they would bring the scorn of the people down on themselves and would never be able to deal with them on equal footing. As an extreme example, Katayama noted that some Japanese going to the United States from Hawaii still wore Japanese clothes, walked in Japanese slippers, covered their chins with washcloths, hung carrots and white radishes from their shoulders, and otherwise gave the impression that they were going to the next village in Japan. No wonder they were despised by Americans! He implied that, once the Japanese immigrants overcame their uncouth provincialism and tried to understand and adapt themselves to American customs, they would be accepted and treated with respect.

As these authors well recognized, incidents throughout the Pacific coast of the United States revealed anti-Japanese prejudice. On occasion Japanese were denied entry; at least once they were quarantined in San Francisco during a pest epidemic; and in California and Nevada a movement was on foot to apply anti-Chinese restrictions to Japanese. But as yet there was no widespread movement specifically directed against Japanese immigrants in the United States. The government and Congress supported revision of laws to put an end to the long-standing policy of nearly un-limited immigration. The rising concern at this time was not with the coming of Japanese but of many other peoples, especially from south and eastern Europe. There was little indication that Japanese expansion toward the United States would meet with determined opposition from the American people—so long as the Japanese were cultured and behaved themselves. The Tokyo government saw to this by curtail-ing the number of passports issued to laborers. Otherwise no control was exercised over individual Japanese as they came into increasing contact with Americans.

Although Japanese and Americans regarded one another as imperialists in cer-tain areas of the world, they also pictured their relations as involving a large sphere beyond the limits of their respective empires. In this sphere relations were by and large peaceful.

FURTHER READING

Barth, Gunther. *Bitter Strength: A History of the Chinese in the United States 1850–1870* (1964).

Chan, Sucheng. *This Bittersweet Soil: Chinese in California Agriculture, 1860–1910* (1986).

Chen, Yong. *Chinese San Francisco, 1850–1943* (2000).

Cheng, Lucy. "Free, Indentured, Enslaved: Chinese Prostitutes in Nineteenth-Century America," *Signs* 5 (1979): 3–29.

Chui, Ping. *Chinese Labor in California, 1850–1880* (1967).

Cohen, Lucy M. *Chinese in the Post–Civil War South: A People Without a History* (1984).

Hsu, Madeline Yuan-yin. *Dreaming of Gold, Dreaming of Home: Transnationalism and Migration Between the United States and South China, 1882–1943* (2000).

Ichioka, Yuji. *The Issei: The World of the First Generation Japanese Immigrants, 1885–1924* (1988).

Iriye, Akira. *Pacific Estrangement: Japanese and American Expansion, 1897–1911* (1972).

Iwata, Masakazu. *Planted in Good Soil: A History of the Issei in United States Agriculture,* 2 vols. (1992).

Kingston, Maxine Hong. *China Men* (1977).

Lyman, Stanford M. *Chinese Americans* (1974).

McKeown, Adam. *Chinese Migrant Networks and Cultural Change: Peru, Chicago, Hawaii, 1900–1936* (2001).

Patterson, Wayne. *The Ilse: First-Generation Korean Immigrants in Hawai'i 1903–1973* (2000).

———. *The Korean Frontier in America: Immigration to Hawaii, 1896–1910,* (1988).

Saxton, Alexander. *The Indispensable Enemy: Labor and the Anti-Chinese Movement in California* (1971).

Miyoshi, Masao. *As We Saw Them: The First Japanese Embassy to the United States (1860)* (1979).

Moriyama, Alan Takeo. *Imingaisha: Japanese Emigration Companies and Hawaii, 1894–1908* (1985).

Wakatsuki, Yasuo. "Japanese Emigration to the United States, 1866–1924: A Monograph," *Perspectives in American History* 12 (1979): 387–516.

Yung, Judy. *Unbound Feet: A Social History of Chinese Women in San Francisco* (1995).

CHAPTER
4

Confronting Immigration
Exclusion, 1860s–1920s

The exclusion of immigrants by the U.S. Congress is usually seen by historians as a dreadful aberration from the nation's remarkable history of open borders. But for Asian immigrants, exclusion was the rule rather than the exception. From 1882 to 1934, every immigrant group from Asia faced immigration restrictions that were more severe than those faced by European groups. The Immigration Act of 1924 offers a notorious example of this anti-Asian discrimination. While setting up national quotas that dramatically decreased the numbers of European immigrants, Congress virtually stopped Asian immigration by refusing to grant even a token quota to Asian nations.

Scholars have long debated the causes of Asian immigration exclusion. Historically, the question has turned on the relative significance of three variables: class, race, and politics. The class argument portrays Asian immigrants as tools of big business used to undermine the rising power of labor unions. Asian exclusion, from this perspective, is seen as a victory for the white American working class. The race argument, on the other hand, underscores the common class position of Asian and white workers and as a result attributes Asian exclusion to the race consciousness, and not the class consciousness, of the American labor movement. Finally, the politics argument recognizes the importance of both class and race but casts exclusion as fundamentally rooted in negotiations among elected officials and the workings of the American political system during moments when the call for Asian exclusion was loudest.

In addition, historians have opened up an entirely new dimension of the exclusion question by focusing on the victims of exclusion. Recent studies have begun to reveal the creativity, and limited success, of Asians in seeking to enter the United States. But more than this, it has become apparent that in resisting exclusion, Asian immigrants created legal precedents, changed administrative policy, and in various other ways affected the larger process of American immigration. This was particularly true for Chinese immigrants, the first national group excluded from immigrating to the United States and the longest to be denied entry within its borders.

96

The first six documents take up the issue of Chinese exclusion. Document 1 presents the views of Henry George, reformer, journalist and future author of *Poverty and Progress* (1879), a widely popular book that championed the notion of ending poverty by taxing rich land owners. A decade earlier, George supported Chinese exclusion because he believed that Chinese immigrants had a deleterious effect on white wages and a common American culture. Document 2 provides a counterpoint to the exclusionists in the form of an illustration depicting the imprisonment of the fiery anti-Chinese movement leader Dennis Kearney. In it Kearney is being taunted by Chinese workers holding the products of the industries in which they worked in San Francisco. Document 3, an excerpt from a speech delivered on the floor of the Senate by a senator who opposed Chinese exclusion, offers another counterpoint to anti-Chinese sentiment. The opposition failed and in 1882 Congress approved the Chinese Exclusion Act. The complete text of the Act is reprinted in Document 4 and reveals the mechanics of exclusion along with additional rationales for its necessity. Document 5 is a response by Chinese merchants, who as a class were free from immigration restrictions, to the renewal of the Chinese Exclusion Act in 1892. Document 6 is a photograph of Wong Kim Ark, whose successful Supreme Court case (*Wong Kim Ark* v. *U.S.*) in 1898 prevented the extension of immigration exclusion to American-born Chinese.

The next three documents focus on the exclusion of Japanese (and Korean) immigrants. Document 7 is taken from the proceedings of one of the most vociferous pressure groups for Japanese exclusion. It lays out the economic, racial, and sexual basis for opposing Japanese immigration and settlement. Document 8 is an editorial in a white workers' periodical opposing the anti-Japanese prejudice that was commonplace within the labor movement. Document 9 reveals the response by the editor of a Japanese newspaper to the 1924 exclusion of Japanese immigrants.

Document 10 is part of a published legal critique of the Supreme Court ruling that upheld the legality of East Indian immigration exclusion and various state laws discriminating against these immigrants.

1. Editor Henry George Supports Chinese Exclusion on Economic and Racial Grounds, 1869

The Wages Question

It is obvious that Chinese competition must reduce wages, and it would seem just as obvious that, to the extent which it does this, its introduction is to the interest of capital and opposed to the interests of labor. But the advocates, upon the Pacific Coast, of the free introduction of these people, hold that this is not so, and, insisting upon the literal acceptance of the half truth that "the interests of labor and capital are identical," argue that a reduction of wages by this means will be a real benefit to the community at large, by attracting capital and stimulating production,

From Henry George, "The Chinese in California," *New York Tribune,* May 1, 1869; reprinted in *Racism, Dissent, and Asian Americans from 1850 to the Present: A Documentary History,* ed. Philip S. Foner and Daniel Rosenberg (Westport, Conn.: Greenwood Press, 1993), 84–87.

while it will do no harm to the working classes, as the lessening of the cost of production will so reduce prices that the laborer will be able to purchase with his lower wages as much as before. According to them, the saving effected by the use of low-priced Chinese labor is precisely the same as that effected by the use of machinery; and as the introduction of machinery has resulted in increased comfort and employment for all classes, so, they argue, will the introduction of Chinese labor result. For, say they, the occupation of the lower branches of industry by the Chinese will open opportunities for the displaced whites in the higher, giving them employment as foremen, superintendents, clerks, etc., when they lose it as journeymen mechanics.

This, I believe, is a fair statement of the opinions held by a large and powerful class, and inasmuch as they are put forward by the most influential portion of the press, and advocated by many who claim the position of public teachers, they are worth an examination in detail. And as in examining them we touch upon questions which are and would be of general interest, even if there was not a single Chinaman in America or any prospect of one coming here (and for the sake of greater clearness), let us eliminate at first the Chinese and local considerations, and treat the general problem. If a general reduction of wages would, as it claimed, work no hardship to the laborer, because prices would fall in the same proportion, then the converse is true that it would work no benefit to his employer—as his receipts would diminish in the same ratio as his expenses, while the power of his capital would not appreciate, and no increase of production could take place.

If this position is correct, then the knotty labor question is indeed solved; the interests of labor and capital are indeed identical. Provided the movement be general, to raise wages as high and as often as asked would be only an act of empty complaisance on the part of the employers; to submit willingly to any reduction, only cheap courtesy on the part of the employed.

This fallacy rests upon the assumption that all profits, rents, etc., would be reduced by and in the same proportion as the reduction in wages, which is manifestly absurd. Nor, when we speak of a "general reduction of wages" in the sense the term is used in this discussion, we do not mean all wages, but only the wages of manual labor. Wages of superintendence, the professions, etc., would be unchanged, and could only be affected indirectly and after some time, by a reduction in the wages of manual labor.

And, as consumers constitute a larger body than laborers, even if consumers get the whole benefit of the reduction in the cost of production consequent on the lowering of wages, it is evident that the laborer's gain as a consumer would be less than his loss as a laborer. It requires no argument to show that to take $5 a day from five men, and to divide it again between them and two more, would be a losing operation to the five.

But consumers would not necessarily get the benefit of any part of the reduction in cost of production. The whole benefit would at first go to employers in increased profits. Whether any would subsequently come to consumers would depend upon the competition which increased profits caused. The more general the reduction of wages, the longer would it take for this competition to be felt; for if wages sank equally and profits rose equally, there would be no inducement for capital to leave one occupation and seek another, and the fresh accessions of capital to produce competition could only come from abroad or from new savings.

Plainly, when we speak of a reduction of wages in any general and permanent sense, we mean this, if we mean anything—that in the division of the joint production of labor and capital, the share of labor is to be smaller, that of capital larger. This is precisely what the reduction of wages consequent upon the introduction of Chinese labor means. . . .

Character of the Chinese

The population of our country has been drawn from many different sources; but hitherto, with but one exception these accessions have been of the same race, and though widely differing in language, customs and national characteristics, have been capable of being welded into a homogeneous people. The Mongolians, who are now coming among us on the other side of the continent, differ from our own race by as strongly marked characteristics as do the negroes, while they will not as readily fall into our ways as the negroes. The difference between the two races in this respect is as the difference between an ignorant but docile child, and a grown man, sharp but narrow-minded, opinionated and set in character. The negro when brought to this country was a simple barbarian with nothing to unlearn: the Chinese have a civilization and history of their own; a vanity which causes them to look down on all other races, habits of thought rendered permanent by being stamped upon countless generations. From present appearances we shall have a permanent Chinese population; but a population whose individual components will be constantly changing, at least for a long time to come. A population born in China, expecting to return to China, living here in a little China of its own, and without the slightest attachment to the country—utter heathens, treacherous, sensual, cowardly and cruel. They will bring no women with them (and probably will not for a little while yet) except those for purposes of prostitution; and the children of these, of whom there are some hundreds in California, will exercise upon the whole mass but little perceptible influence, while they will be in all respects as essentially Chinese as though born and reared in China.

To a certain extent the Chinese become quickly Americanized; but this Americanization is only superficial. They learn to buy and sell, to labor according to American modes, just as they discard the umbrella shaped hat, wide drawers and thick paper shoes, for the felt hat, pantaloons and boots; but they retain all their essential habits and modes of thought just as they retain their cues. The Chinaman running a sewing machine, driving a sand cart, or firing up an engine in California, is just as essentially a Chinaman as his brother, who, on the other side of the Pacific, is working in the same way, and with the same implements, as his fathers worked a thousand years ago.

2. "The Tables Turned: You Sabe Him? Kealney [Kearney] Must Go!," 1877/1878

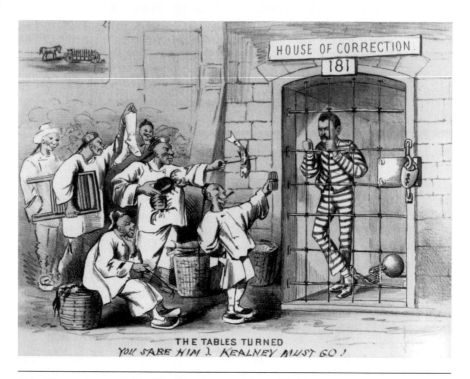

THE TABLES TURNED
YOU SABE HIM ᗡ KEALNEY MUST GO !

This lithograph appeared in San Francisco at a time of heightened anti-Chinese sentiment during the depression of the 1870s. It is a comedic reversal of the conflict between organized labor and Chinese immigrants. Labor leader Dennis Kearney, a working-class hero known for his enmity against the Chinese, is chained behind bars and is being taunted by a group of smiling Chinese workers brandishing symbols of the type of work that Kearney and many others considered ruinous to the living standards of white wage-earners. Implicit in this commentary is a third position in the conflict that seems to neither defend Chinese workers nor support Kearney's frequent convictions for illegally organizing the unemployed workers. Which groups in San Francisco might have identified with this third position? Who might have this illustration been speaking for and to?

Courtesy of The Bancroft Library, University of California, Berkeley, Calif. Photo #BANC PIC 1993.020-AX; reprinted in the California Digital Library, http://www.oac.cdlib.org.

3. Senator George Hoar Declares Chinese Exclusion Un-American, 1882

Nothing is more in conflict with the genius of American institutions than legal distinctions between individuals based upon race or upon occupation. The framers of our Constitution believed in the safety and wisdom of abstract principles. They meant that their laws should make no distinction between men except such as were required by personal conduct and character. The prejudices of race, the last of human delusions to be overcome, has been found until lately in our constitutions and statutes, and has left its hideous and ineradicable stains on our history in crimes committed by every generation. The negro, the Irishman, and the Indian have in turn been its victims here, as the Jew and the Greek and the Hindoo in Europe and Asia. But it is reserved for us at the present day, for the first time, to put into public law of the world and into the national legislation of the foremost of republican nations a distinction inflicting upon a large class of men a degradation by reason of their race and by reason of their occupation.

The bill which passed Congress two years ago and was vetoed by President Hayes, the treaty of 1881, and the bill now before the Senate, have the same origin and are parts of the same measure. Two years ago it was proposed to exclude Chinese laborers from our borders, in express disregard of our solemn treaty obligations. This measure was arrested by President Hayes. The treaty of 1881 extorted from unwilling China her consent that we might regulate, limit, or suspend the coming of Chinese laborers into this country—a consent of which it is proposed by this bill to take advantage. This is entitled "A bill to enforce treaty stipulations with China."

It seems necessary in discussing the statute briefly to review the history of the treaty. First let me say that the title of this bill is deceptive. There is no stipulation of the treaty which the bill enforces. The bill where it is not inconsistent with the compact only avails itself of a privilege which that concedes. China only relaxed the Burlingame treaty so far as to permit us to "regulate, limit, or suspend the coming or residence" of Chinese laborers, "but not absolutely to prohibit it." The treaty expressly declares "such limitation or suspension shall be reasonable." But here is proposed a statute which for twenty years, under the severest penalties, absolutely inhibits the coming of Chinese laborers to this country. The bill is intended absolutely to prohibit it.

. . . Here is a declaration made by a compact between the two greatest nations of the Pacific, and now to be re-enforced by a solemn act of legislation, which places in the public law of the world and in the jurisprudence of America the principle that it is fit that there should hereafter be a distinction in the treatment of men by governments and in the recognition of their rights to the pursuit of happiness by a peaceful change of their homes, based not on conduct, not on character, but upon race and upon occupation. You may justly deny to the Chinese what you may not justly deny to the Irishman. You may deny to the laborer what you may not justly deny to the scholar or to

From *Speech of the Hon. George F. Hoar of Massachusetts Delivered in the Senate of the United States, March 1, 1882* (pamphlet), (Washington, D.C., 1882), 6–7, 9, 13–14; reprinted in *Racism, Dissent, and Asian Americans from 1850 to the Present: A Documentary History,* ed. Philip S. Foner and Daniel Rosenberg (Westport, Conn.: Greenwood Press, 1993), 53–55.

the idler. And this declaration is extorted from unwilling China by the demand of America. With paupers, lazzaroni, harlots, persons afflicted with pestilential diseases, laborers are henceforth to be classed in the enumerations of American public law.

Certainly, Mr. President, this is an interesting and important transaction. It is impossible to overstate or calculate the consequences which are likely to spring from a declaration made by the United States limiting human rights, especially a declaration in a treaty which is to become international law governing these two great nations. As my friend from California [Mr. Miller] well said, it is of the earth, earthy. The United States within twenty years has taken its place as the chief power on the Pacific. Whatever rivalry or whatever superiority we may be compelled to submit to elsewhere, our advantage of position, unless the inferiority be in ourselves, must give us superiority there. Are we to hold out two faces to the world, one to Europe and another to Asia? Or are we to admit that the doctrine we have proclaimed so constantly for the first century of our history is a mere empty phrase or a lie?

For myself and for the State of Massachusetts, so far as it is my privilege to represent her, I refuse consent to this legislation. I will not consent to a denial by the United States of the right of every man who desires to improve his condition by honest labor—his labor being no man's property but his own—to go anywhere on the face of the earth that he pleases. . . .

The number of immigrants of all nations was 720,045 in 1881. Of these 20,711 were Chinese. There is no record in the Bureau of Statistics of the number who departed within the year. But a very high anti-Chinese authority places it above 10,000. Perhaps the expectation that the hostile legislation under the treaty would not affect persons who entered before it took effect stimulated somewhat their coming. But the addition to the Chinese population was less than one seventy-second of the whole immigration. All the Chinese in California hardly surpass the number which is easily governed in Shanghai by a police of one hundred men. There are as many pure blooded Gypsies wandering about the country as there are Chinese in California. What an insult to American intelligence to ask leave of China to keep out her people, because this little handful of almond-eyed Asians threaten to destroy our boasted civilization. We go boasting of our democracy and our superiority, and our strength. The flag bears the stars of hope to all nations. A hundred thousand Chinese land in California and every thing has changed. God has not made of one blood all the nations any longer. The self-evident truth becomes a self-evident lie. The golden rule does not apply to the natives of the continent where it was first uttered.

4. Chinese Exclusion Act Suspends Immigration to the United States for Ten Years, 1882

Whereas, in the opinion of the Government of the United States the coming of Chinese laborers to this country endangers the good order of certain localities within the territory thereof: Therefore,

Be it enacted by the Senate and House of Representatives of the United States of America in Congress assembled, That from and after the expiration of ninety days

From *Congressional Record,* 42d Cong., 1st sess., 1882.

next after the passage of this act, and until the expiration of ten years next after the passage of this act, the coming of Chinese laborers to the United States be, and the same is hereby, suspended; and during such suspension it shall not be lawful for any Chinese laborer to come, or, having so come after the expiration of said ninety days, to remain within the United States.

Section 2

That the master of any vessel who shall knowingly bring within the United States on such vessel, and land or permit to be landed, any Chinese laborer, from any foreign port or place, shall be deemed guilty of a misdemeanor, and on conviction thereof shall be punished by a fine of not more than five hundred dollars for each and every such Chinese laborer so brought, and may be also imprisoned for a term not exceeding one year.

Section 3

That the two foregoing sections shall not apply to Chinese laborers who were in the United States on the seventeenth day of November, eighteen hundred and eighty of ninety days next after the passage of this act, and who shall produce to such master before going on board such vessel, and shall produce to the collector of the port of the United States at which such vessel shall arrive, the evidence hereinafter in this act required of his being one of the laborers in this section mentioned; nor shall the two foregoing sections apply to the case of any master whose vessel, being bound to a port not within the United States, shall come within the jurisdiction of the United States by reason of being in distress or in stress of weather, or touching at any port of the United States on its voyage to any foreign port or place: Provided, That all Chinese laborers brought on such vessel shall depart with the vessel on leaving port.

Section 4

That for the purpose of properly identifying Chinese laborers who were in the United States on the seventeenth day of November, eighteen hundred and eighty, or who shall have come into the same before the expiration of ninety days next after the passage of this act, and in order to furnish them with the proper evidence of their right to go from and come to the United States of their free will and accord, as provided by the treaty between the United States and China dated November seventeenth, eighteen hundred and eighty, the collector of customs of the district from which any such Chinese laborer shall depart from the United States shall, in person or by deputy, go on board each vessel having on board any such Chinese laborer and cleared or about to sail from his district for a foreign port, and on such vessel make a list of all such Chinese laborers, which shall be entered in registry-books to be kept for that purpose, in which shall be stated the name, age, occupation, last place of residence, physical marks or peculiarities, and all facts necessary for the identification of each of such Chinese laborers, which books shall be safely kept in the custom-house; and every such Chinese laborer so departing from the United States shall be entitled to, and shall received, free of any charge or cost upon application therefore, from the collector or his deputy, at the time such list is taken, a certificate, signed by the collector or his depute and attested by his seal of office, in such form as the Secretary of the Treasury shall prescribe, which certificate shall contain a statement of the name, age, occupation, last place of residence, personal description, and facts of identification of the Chinese laborer to whom the certificate is issued, corresponding with the said list and registry in all particulars. In case any Chinese laborer after having received such certificate shall leave such vessel before her departure he shall deliver his certificate to the master of the vessel, and if such Chinese laborer shall fail to return to such vessel before her departure from port the certificate shall be delivered by the master to the collector of customs for cancellation. The certificate herein provided for shall entitle the Chinese laborer to whom the same is issued to return to and re-enter the United States upon producing and delivering the same to the collector of customs of the district at which such Chinese laborer shall seek to re-enter, and upon delivery of such certificate by such Chinese laborer to the collector of customs at the time of re-entry in the United States, said collector shall cause the same to be filed in the custom-house and duly canceled.

Section 5

That any Chinese laborer mentioned in section four of this act being in the United States, and desiring to depart from the United States by land, shall have the right to demand and receive, free of charge or cost, a certificate of identification similar to that provided for in section four of this act to be issued to such Chinese laborers as may desire to leave the United States by water; and it is hereby made the duty of the collector of customs of the district next adjoining the foreign country to which said Chinese laborer desires to go to issue such certificate, free of charge or cost, upon application by such Chinese laborer, and to enter the same upon registry-books to be kept by him for the purpose as provided for in section four of this act.

Section 6

That in order to the faithful execution of articles one and two of the treaty in this act before mentioned, every Chinese person other than a laborer who may be entitled by said treaty and this act to come within the United States, and who shall be about to come to the United States, shall be identified as so entitled by the Chinese Government in each case, such identity to be evidenced by a certificate issued under the authority of said government, which certificate shall be in the English language or (if not in the English language) accompanied by a translation into English, stating such right to come, and which certificate shall state the name, title, or official rank, if any, the age, height, and all physical peculiarities, former and present occupation or profession, and place of residence in China of the person to whom the certificate is issued and that such person is entitled conformably to the treaty in this act mentioned to come within the United States. Such certificate shall be primafacie evidence of the fact set forth therein, and shall be produced to the collector of customs, or his deputy, of the port in the district in the United States at which the person named therein shall arrive.

Section 7

That any person who shall knowingly and falsely alter or substitute any name for the name written in such certificate or forge any such certificate, or knowingly utter any forged or fraudulent certificate, or falsely impersonate any person named in any such certificate, shall be deemed guilty of a misdemeanor, and upon conviction thereof shall be fined in a sum not exceeding one thousand dollars, and imprisoned in a penitentiary for a term of not more than five years.

Section 8

That the master of any vessel arriving in the United States from any foreign port or place shall, at the same time he delivers a manifest of the cargo, and if there be no cargo, then at the time of making a report of the entry of the vessel pursuant to law, in addition to the other matter required to be reported, and before landing, or permitting to landing, any Chinese passengers, deliver and report to the collector of customs of the district in which such vessels shall have arrived a separate list of all Chinese passengers taken on board his vessel at any foreign port or place, and all such passengers on board the vessel at that time. Such list shall show the names of such passengers (and if accredited officers of the Chinese Government traveling on the business of that government, or their servants, with a note of such facts), and the names and other particulars, as shown by their respective certificates; and such list shall be sworn to by the master in the manner required by law in relation to the manifest of the cargo. Any willful refusal or neglect of any such master to comply with the provisions of this section shall incur the same penalties and forfeiture as are provided for a refusal or neglect to report and deliver a manifest of the cargo.

Section 9

That before any Chinese passengers are landed from any such vessel, the collector, or his deputy, shall proceed to examine such passengers, comparing the certificates with the list and with the passengers; and no passenger shall be allowed to land in the United States from such vessel in violation of law.

Section 10

That every vessel whose master shall knowingly violate any of the provisions of this act shall be deemed forfeited to the United States, and shall be liable to seizure and condemnation in any district of the United States into which such vessel may enter or in which she may be found.

Section 11

That any person who shall knowingly bring into or cause to be brought into the United States by land, or who shall knowingly aid or abet the same, or aid or abet the landing in the United States from any vessel of any Chinese person not lawfully entitled to enter the United States, shall be deemed guilty of a misdemeanor, and shall, on conviction thereof, be fined in a sum not exceeding one thousand dollars, and imprisoned for a term not exceeding one year.

Section 12

That no Chinese person shall be permitted to enter the United States by land without producing to the proper officer of customs the certificate in this act required of Chinese persons seeking to land from a vessel. And any Chinese person found unlawfully within the United States shall be caused to be removed there from to the country from whence he came, by direction of the President of the United States, and at the cost of the United States, after being brought before some justice, judge, or commissioner of a court of the United States and found to be one not lawfully entitled to be or remain in the United States.

Section 13

That this act shall apply to diplomatic and other officers of the Chinese Government traveling upon the business of that government, whose credentials shall be taken as equivalent to the certificate in this act mentioned, and shall exempt them and their body and household servants from the provisions of this act as to other Chinese persons.

Section 14

That hereafter no State court or court of the United States shall admit Chinese to citizenship; and all laws in conflict with this act are hereby repealed.

Section 15

That the words "Chinese laborers," wherever used in this act, shall be construed to mean both skilled and unskilled laborers and Chinese employed in mining.
Approved, May 6, 1882.

5. New York Chinese Merchants Oppose Renewal of Chinese Exclusion Act, 1892

To the American People, Friends of Humanity:

We, the members of the Chinese Equal Rights League in the United States, who have adopted this country and its customs in the main, are at this moment engaged in a perilous struggle in which our dearest rights as men and residents are involved. Doubtless the reading public is acquainted with the fact that during the last session of the Fifty-second Congress, a Bill was passed, styled the "Geary Bill" or "Chinese Registration Act," in which the attempt is made to humiliate every Chinaman, regardless of his moral, intellectual and material standing in the community, neither

From *Appeal of the Chinese Equal Rights League to the People of the United States for Equality of Manhood* (pamphlet) (New York: Chinese Equal Rights League, 1892), 2–3; reprinted in *Racism, Dissent, and Asian Americans from 1850 to the Present: A Documentary History,* ed. Philip S. Foner and Daniel Rosenberg (Westport, Conn. Greenwood Press, 1993), 118–120.

his long residence in the country is considered. By this mean and unjust Act discriminating between foreign residents from different countries has traversed and contraversed the fundamental principles of common law.

As residents of the United States we claim a common manhood with all other nationalities, and believe we should have that manhood recognized according to the principles of common humanity and American freedom. This monstrous and inhuman measure is a blot upon the civilization of the Western World, and is destined to retard the progress already made by the good people of this country in the East in art, science, commerce and religion.

We appeal to the humane, liberty-loving sentiment of the American people, who are lovers of equal rights and even-handed justice, a people from who sprung such illustrious characters as Washington, Jefferson, Clay, Sumner, lastly Lincoln, the citizen of the world, the friend of humanity and the champion of freedom: such illustrious warriors as Sherman, Sheridan, Logan and Grant, whose deeds of valor in the cause of freedom are to be seen in the grand march of American development—a development which merits the emulation of the nations of the earth. Must this growth be retarded simply on account of the doings of a misguided element who have suffered their feelings to control reason, encouraging a prejudice fiendish in its nature and purpose against a class of people who are industrious, law-abiding and honest? Can there be found a more inoffensive class in the body politic? not that we are cowards, but because we believe that mildness and simplicity should be the controling element in the character of a great man as well as in a great race of people. We have and are still paying our portion of government taxation, thereby assisting in supporting the Government, and thereby sharing an equal part in the support of the nation.

We love and admire the Government, and look with joy to her instrumentality in promoting every good and just cause among men, to her unwavering love of human rights, to her glorious efforts for the advancement of human happiness.

We, therefore, appeal for an equal chance in the race of life in this our adopted home—a large number of us have spent almost our entire lives in this country and claim no other but this as ours. Our motto is *"Character and fitness should be the requirement of all who are desirous of becoming citizens of the American Republic."*

We feel keenly the disgrace unjustly and maliciously heaped upon us by a cruel Congress. That for the purpose of prohibiting Chinese immigration more than one hundred thousand honest and respectable Chinese residents should be made to wear the badge of disgrace as ticket-of-leave men in your penitentiaries; that they should be tagged and branded as a whole lot of cattle for the slaughter; that they should be seen upon your streets with tearful eyes and heavy hearts, objects of scorn and public ridicule. No! We do not believe it, that so great a people as the Americans would consent to so small a principle toward a mere handful of defenceless men.

Our interest is here, because our homes, our families and our all are here. America is our home through long residence. Why, then, should we not consider your welfare ours? Chinese immigration, as well as Irish, Italian and other immigration, cannot be stopped by the persecution of our law-abiding citizens in the United States.

Treat us as men, and we will do our duty as men, and will aid you to stop this obnoxious evil that threatens the welfare of this Republic. We do not want any more Chinese here than you do. The scarcer the Chinese here, the better would be our conditions among you.

6. Wong Kim Ark, 1904

This is a photograph of Wong Kim Ark, an American-born Chinese who, given the ambiguities of American citizenship law in the late-nineteenth century, was refused entry into the United States after travelling to China. Immigration officials deemed that he was not a citizen and therefore was excluded under the Chinese Exclusion Act. Wong appealed to the courts to overturn the decision, arguing that the fourteenth amendment, which granted citizenship to the newly freed southern blacks, extended to members of the "Mongolian race" born on American soil. In 1898 the US Supreme Court agreed with Wong, enabling him to return to his native country. The decision was a crucial legal victory in a long line of Asian American legal defeats.

From The National Archives and Records Administration, Pacific Region, San Francisco, Calif., Control Number NRHS-85-INSSFDEPCAS-12017 (42223)-1A; found through NARA's web-based searchable collections database (NAIL).

7. Asiatic Exclusion League Argues for Excluding Japanese and Korean Immigration, 1908

The fruits of the various Chinese Restriction Acts were enjoyed by the people of the Pacific Coast for a very short time because, immediately following the decrease in the number of Chinese coolies another evil closely followed upon their retreating footsteps. This evil—the Japanese—crept in so easily, so gradually, so secretly, that its danger was not fully recognized by the people at large until after the year 1890. It is true that in the middle eighties, industrial strife had been precipitated by the employment of large numbers of Japanese in the Coast shipping and mines of British Columbia, and it was hoped that the defeat of the ship owners by the Coast Seamen's Union would cause the elimination of that class of labor from among us. The hope was vain. The daily press, from time to time, would call attention to the arrival of Japanese laborers, but they would quietly move to the farming districts where they attracted but little attention, until the white laborers who had been in the habit of obtaining employment throughout the interior, were confronted with, to them, an appalling condition—seeking employment and being refused the same, while gangs of Japanese were busily engaged performing the work which had formerly, and of right, been performed by the actual and prospective American citizen.

The receipt of information of this character from all parts of the State, coupled with the fact that every trans-Pacific and Victoria steamer arrived at San Francisco with its quota of "little brown men," led to a consideration of the question. No better evidence of the extent of the influx could be presented at that time—as now—than a walk through the residence districts of the City of San Francisco. It seemed that every industry had been invaded, the Japs being found in 64 various occupations, outside of the building industries, and at the present time (April 1, 1907), they are even engaged in construction from cellar to roof.

So early as 1895 it was found, upon inquiry among the hop, beet, fruit growers and packers that the employment of Japanese had become general, almost to the total exclusion of white labor. At the same time, numerous rumors of the wholesale importation of these people, under contract, in violation of the United States Alien Contract Labor Laws, were brought to the attention of the California State Bureau of Labor Statistics. . . .

While the Japanese are engaged in every occupation and almost every line of business, and solicit the patronage of the whites, they trade exclusively with themselves and their earnings and profits, except so much as is spent for absolute necessaries, finds its way to Japan for investment. During November, 1905, the money order business of the San Francisco postoffice with Japan amounted to $190,000, and many other postoffices in California, notably Vacaville, Sacramento, Watsonville, Fresno, Los Angeles and Stockton are doing similar business in proportion to their population. It has been estimated that since 1880 the Japanese have sent over $200,000,000 to Japan for investment.

From *Proceedings of the Asiatic Exclusion League,* 1907–1913 (New York: Arno Press, 1977), 10, 16–19, 22–24.

Definite data respecting the actual number of Japanese engaged in farming in California is not available, but enough is known to convince us that the Chinese, Indians and Mexicans have been almost entirely displaced by them, and the total number must exceed 30,000. Respecting the employment of Japanese, their capacity for work and the desirability of maintaining them on the fruit orchards, we quote from the letters of a few ranch owners who, once ardent admires of the "little brown men," are now awake to the danger confronting them, a danger brought upon themselves by their desire to obtain cheap and docile laborers. Let us hear what these gentlemen have to say: "If we have to pay $1.50 to $1.75 per day for this wretched Jap help, where is the supposed saving in allowing the Orientals to come here? Good white help will not come in and compete with the Japanese."

"I live in dread of the coming season. There is no questioning the fact that the Japanese are thoroughly organized and in complete control of the labor proposition."

"If a people were ever cursed with a class of labor more worthless, more rotten and less to be depended upon than California is with the Japanese, I have yet to find it in my travels from Alpine to the Golden Gate."

"It is my opinion that before another year has passed, the farmers and supporters of the Chinese Exclusion Act will understand what a great mistake was made in not also excluding the Japanese. Of the two evils, the Chinese is by far the least."

"It is a well known fact that in sections where fruit, beets and hops are the principle staple, the Japanese invasion is something astounding. They have almost a monopoly in the industries named. Why? Because they are so constituted that they will live on what the average white man will throw to his dog."

"One self-styled Japanese banker rents twelve ranches through his agents. Another controls no less than twenty through money loaned to the cultivators."

"The Jap spends some of his money, but he does not spend it at a white man's store. There is absolutely no business for the white merchant and the 800 Japs in this town bring nothing at all into the avenue of trade."

These admissions on the part of certain employers of the Japs are very amusing, especially to those who recollect through whose instrumentality the Jap was first induced to come here.

Possibilities and Probabilities

The possibilities of the Jap in agriculture are very great. The farmers of California being already in their clutches, they are seeking new fields to conquer. In a recent Consular report Mr. Gada, a Japanese of great wealth, is reported as saying: "I intend to colonize and cultivate about 49,000 acres of land in Texas. The price of the land is $2.50 per acre. The area of the uncultivated land in Texas, where I have undertaken the farming scheme, is larger than Japan. The soil is very rich and will need no fertilizers for ten years to come. From a wage of $15, a laborer should be able to save $10 per month. I estimate that at the end of four years a profit of $1,000,000 will be realized."

Incidentally, it may be mentioned that a race war between Negroes and Japs has already started in San Antonio, Texas.

A gentleman named Saiki, passing through San Francisco on his way to Florida, said: "I am on my way to Florida, where I expect to take up 6,000 acres of land. I expect thousands of people will come out to settle it."

At a Congregational meeting held in San Francisco two years ago, a Mr. Kozaki boasted that some of his countrymen had made $1,000,000 by farming, and that many others had made over $100,000, each in commercial pursuits. He further stated that he intended to establish a large industrial colony of Japanese on the shores of the Puget Sound.

A Mr. Kawakami, writing in the "Independent" some time since, stated that his countrymen owned and farmed some 98,000 acres of the best land in California.

Are these happenings to be considered trifles? Is it not time that others besides Californians awaken to the gravity of the situation on the Pacific Coast? Or shall California be permitted to fight her own battles while we look supinely on?

Japanese and White Women

It has been declared by an authority on such matters—the State Labor Commissioner—that 5,000 white girls have been robbed of their employment as waitresses and domestic servants by the invasion of the Japanese. If this be so, and from present inquiry and investigation we believe Mr. Stafford's figures fall short of the actual number so engaged, the question naturally arises, what has become of the white girls who have lost their jobs as a result of the employment of these thousands of brown servants? Into what horrible calling have they gone? Investigation fails to discover any occupation which shows a sudden influx of white women. What has become of them?

From employment agencies making a specialty of furnishing female help, it is learned that the situation is nothing short of terrible; that hundreds of girls are out of employment who would be glad of any position by which their needs could be decently provided. The following quotations are from the remarks of agents furnishing domestic help:

"Any woman who will pay decent wages and treat her help like human beings can get all the girls she can possibly want."

"People have become so accustomed to Orientals that they forget an American girl cannot live like an Asiatic. They give the Japanese regular hours and nothing is allowed to interfere with their regular routine. But with a hired girl the entire system is changed; the family will remain at the table as long as they choose, and the girl must make no arrangements that will interfere or conflict with such arrangements."

"Many people hire Japanese for an hour or two at a time from any of the house-cleaning companies scattered throughout the city. Those who work in that manner are the 'Student Class,' and it is surprising how many girls are thus crowded out of employment."

"In most of the apartment houses there is a Jap on each floor besides those in the laundry, in the dining room and those engaged in window cleaning; in every instance, these Japs take the place formerly filled by white girls."

"The foregoing statements may be regarded as absolutely reliable. By many of our economic thinkers the elimination of our young women from domestic service is considered the most dangerous phase of the Japanese question, because, if the white girl is not afforded the opportunity of acquainting herself with the problems of domestic economy, how can she fit herself to become the companion and helpmeet of the American wage-earner?

Men Suffer As Well As Women

The Japanese have been no laggards in breaking into other lines of business in San Francisco, as in other parts of the State. They are cutting into the business of the white steam laundries to a great extent by the use of improved machinery and improved methods, in conjunction with a 40 per cent reduction of prices. Restaurants run by Japanese are scattered throughout the city, chiefly in the districts frequented by the floating population, and their places furnish food at such ridiculously low figures—10 and 15 cents per meal—that it is a constant temptation for a man to forget his manhood and patronize the enemies of his race and civilization. Ninety per cent of the saloons employ Japanese as porters and lunch boys, because they are cheap and obsequious. Bakeries employ them in various capacities, and wholesale dealers, whose sole business is with the retailer who supplies the home of the working man with the necessaries of life, are hiring Japanese in large numbers. The shoe repairing business, once profitable to the white cobbler, has been destroyed so far as the white worker is concerned. The Jap, by undercutting the price, has virtually driven the white man out of business. Restaurants, boarding houses, etc., are feeling the pinch caused by the competition of their people, and in many kinds of business the cry is of frequent occurrence, "No white man need apply"; yet, in the face of such aggravating conditions the workingman of California is self-contained and refuses to employ the boycott against his own countrymen, placing confidence in the promises of his representatives that they will finally obtain an Act of Congress for the exclusion of Japanese and Koreans as well as Chinese.

Japanese and Their Relations With Women

Some years ago one of the ablest English critics, Mr. Clement Scott, came to San Francisco after visiting Japan. Speaking of Japanese social life and the prevailing treatment of women in that country, he said: "There are scenes where the Japanese women are placed in positions that are a disgrace to the human race. Freedom and respect for women must blush at the mere aspect of the Yosh-i-wara of Tokio, the capital city of the Mikado. Every city in the civilized world has its soiled doves, but they are not compelled to sit in cages like wild beasts waiting to be chosen and sold to the passer-by."

Sir Henry Norman, in his "Real Japan," is even more severe in his strictures upon the social life in that country.

Mr. Lindell of Boston, who spent many years in Japan, said: "There is no social evil problem in Japan. Institutions for this heinous traffic are not only legalized, but legitimatized by the State, and each community has its public house or Yosh-i-wara, where the surplus girls of a family are apprenticed when twelve or fourteen years of age for a term of three years, at the end of which time they are permitted to marry. Is it any wonder that when a Japanese young man is accused of sending obscene pictures and insulting propositions to American girls that he pleads the monstrous excuse that 'these things are not considered wrong in Japan.'"

With the status of Japanese women we have no concern. Japan's social customs are no business of ours, but we do voice a strenuous objection against the introduction of such status of American social life. Only those who closely study the problem of Japanese immigration know to what extent this is being done. Every few days we read of "Marriages by Photograph," and of the arrival in San Francisco of women who claim to have been so married. This is, of course, the beginning of her career. Its extension may well be a matter of apprehension. The Police Department of San Francisco is well acquainted with these matters, even if the immigration officers deny knowledge of the same, and it is also well known to the police that in some localities it will soon be necessary for white women to arm themselves for protection against the insults of Japanese. Since the boost given to Japanese aggressiveness by the unwarranted utterances of the President and some of his advisers, conditions in some quarters are becoming unbearable. The question is: Shall we obtain the necessary relief from such conditions or shall we become compelled in defense of our womankind to adopt the measures of the Black Belt of our Southern States?

Asiatic exclusion, then, is a question which concerns the whole country and the Japanese Exclusion League is proceeding upon that understanding. The nations of Asia are nations apart from those of the West, nor do they wish to be otherwise. The Asiatic can never be other than an Asiatic, however much he may imitate the dress of the white man, nor will he ever have the slightest concern for our laws, except to evade them; nor with the Government, except to cajole and deceive it. The Japanese in California is just as intensely and essentially a Japanese as though he had never left the rice fields of his native country.

Industrial America is one and indivisible and the injury that is inflicted upon our State is inflicted upon them all. . . .

Pardee's Message to California Legislature, January, 1907

"It is safe to say that the President, when he penned that portion of his annual message in which he referred to the treatment of the Japanese in the San Francisco schools, was not aware of the conditions on this coast, especially in California. In common with the people of the East, who have had no experience with these unassimilable people of Japan and China, the President does not understand the racial differences between the Japanese and Chinese and people of Caucasian blood. Coming into contact only with a few educated individuals of these two races, the people of the eastern states do not understand that to permit the immigration of only a small fraction of the whole of these people means the monopolizing by them of such pursuits as they may engage in. This monopolization would not militate against the public good, were the monopolizers capable of being absorbed into the body politic and in this generation, or even the next, becoming integral parts of our cosmopolitan people.

Unfortunately, however, neither the Japanese nor the Chinese appear capable of absorption and assimilation into the mass of our people. Neither race has, apparently, any desire to renounce allegiance to its mother country, and become in the true sense of the word citizens of the United States. Our laws and customs regard intermarriage with them miscegenation. All their energies are bent towards acquiring a competency here to enable them to live in comfort and affluence in their own country. They collect in colonies, either in the cities or in the country, do only such business as necessity compels with any but those of their own people, and have no close relations of any kind with our people. Being able to live on a small fraction of what seems necessary to support Caucasian people and being, furthermore clannish in the extreme and evincing neither desire nor ability to mingle with our people, the lower classes of these two nations are not in any sense of the word desirable immigrants to, much less citizens of, this country. There are Chinese and Japanese, especially the former, who have lived in this State many years, some of them a half century, and in no essential particulars have they acquired our manners or our customs. They are, practically speaking, as much foreigners in manners, customs, habits of thought and loyalty to their mother country as they were when they came here. The great mass of them make no investments in this country, have no interest in its institutions and no sympathy even with our civilization or modes of thought; they make no attempt to accommodate themselves, even in dress, modes of living or customs to those surrounding them, and, in fact, desire to gain sufficient to enable them to return to their own countries to live out the rest of their lives.

The Causes in the Races Themselves

It is beside the question to say that they show these peculiarities because of the inhospitableness of our people. Were the racial differences in civilization, thought, manners and customs not inseparable between these Asiatics and Caucasians whatever inhospitableness our people might show toward them would insensibly disappear and there would be, in spite of all attempts to the contrary, signs of Americanization in the best sense of the term among them. The Chinese among us are still Chinese; they wear, for the most part, their national costumes and queues; they live strictly in quarters by themselves, and preserve their national customs inviolate. The Japanese also have made no attempts to dissociate themselves from their fellows and become individuals among us. They, like the Chinese, congregate together, not in quarters as the Chinese do, but still apart by themselves. They wear, it is true, American clothes, but they preserve the Japanese customs. And they, even more than the Chinese, refuse to do business when it is possible to avoid it, with Caucasians. It is useless to expect that people with such different racial characteristics and such different civilization can ever mix with our people and become absorbed into our body politic. They cannot become good American citizens; it is useless to attempt to make them such.

But, while the Caucasian cannot reconcile himself to the Asiatic, it must not be forgotten that the Asiatic cannot reconcile himself with the Caucasian. While the Caucasian looks askance at the Japanese and Chinese, both the latter have an equal or greater contempt for the Caucasian. To the Asiatic, the Caucasian is an inferior with whom it is little short of degrading to closely associate. This condition of affairs exists not only in this country but also in Japan and China. Both Europeans and Americans have lived for many years in both these countries, yet there is no mingling of the races even there, no intermarriage, no assuming our terms of equality, amity and unconscious friendliness, of the dress, manners, customs, mode of living or religion of these countries by Caucasians living there. There, as here, each race looks upon the other as inferior.

Reasons for Separate Schools

Under these circumstances it is not at all strange that there is an aversion to the mingling of the children of the two races. And, therefore, California has decreed that, whenever it is so desired, the local school authorities may provide separate schools for the Chinese and Japanese children, in which they shall be taught as Caucasian children are, and by equally capable teachers. In the case of the Japanese this separation seems to be the more necessary, because many of the Japanese who desire to attend our schools are much older than the Caucasian children with whom, on account of their deficient learning, the Japanese must be enclassed. It is not at all desirable that youths, even Japanese youths, at eight, ten years or more of age, should be associated in the schools with children of tender ages. The reason, therefore, is sufficiently explained by its mere statement."

8. Spokane Labor Union Derides Anti-Japanese Prejudice, 1909

The Spokane division of the porters' union (A.F. of L.) held a meeting April 13 to talk over the invasion of the Japanese. According to the "Labor World," "vigorous efforts will be made to eradicate the brown men from industrial competition"— which efforts will have "the support of organized labor in general." The Industrial Workers of the World have the largest labor organization in Spokane or in any part of the country around. It must be understood that the I.W.W. will turn down any effort at discrimination against our Japanese fellow workers. Are we not correct when we say that the trades unions foster a state of affairs which allows one set of workers to be pitted against another set of workers in the same industry; thereby helping to defeat one another? This is the same old game of "divide and conquer" on the part of employers and those labor unions which are influenced by prejudice on account of race, nation or language. If the workers controlled the U.S. government, or had at present anything to say as to whether the Japanese were "desirable citizens," it might be interesting for workingmen to take up the study of comparative ethnology; but the Japanese are here in the United States by the will of the industrial masters; being here, the matter should be dealt with as is best for the working class. Now it is not supposed that the members of the porters' union, for instance, would exterminate the Japanese by murder outright, but would be more humane(?) by letting the Japanese starve to death—providing the Japanese could be so far educated into the A.F. of L. principles as to be willing tamely to starve to death. The Japanese are here, they will not starve to death, and they will work as long as the boss will hire them. This being the case, what does the A.F. of L. man expect to gain by antagonizing these men, the Japanese, who are, it will be admitted, not lacking in brains? From all appearances, the porters' union is not so strong as to refuse help—even from a Japanese! Will any man explain just why, as long as the Japanese are here, it would not be better to unite with them to fight the common enemy, the master, than to waste time, energy and strength in fighting another group of workers simply on account of their color—to the huge delight of the employer? If the porters' union were but half as class conscious as the average Japanese worker, there would be better wages and better conditions for the porter than the wretched ones they are now forced to submit to. The Labor Commissioner of California says that in his long

From "Silly Race Prejudice," editorial, *Industrial Worker,* April 22, 1909; reprinted in *Racism, Dissent, and Asian Americans from 1850 to the Present: A Documentary History,* ed. Philip S. Foner and Daniel Rosenberg (Westport, Conn.: Greenwood Press, 1993), 193–194.

experience, the Japanese is the "most merciless" with his employer of any of the help in the California ranches, and bewails the mistake the employers of California made in getting Japanese who will exact everything possible, if they have but half a chance. Can as much be said of the porters' union—that they are "merciless" with the Spokane employers? Hardly! American or Japanese, Italian or Austrian, Swede or Irishman, German or Frenchman; do the employers quarrel among themselves on account of nationality? Not much! They are too wise.

Let the porter count his miserable pay on Saturday night; look at the wretched working conditions he puts up with, and then consider his comfortable, well-fed employer, and then turning to his Japanese fellow-worker, ask himself if it would not be wiser for him to unite with the Japanese to wring more wages and shorter hours from their common robber—the employer!

9. Tokyo Government Protests Exclusion of Japanese Immigrants, 1924

"Message from Japan to America"

The Japan Times and Mail, October 1, 1924

Japanese, as a people and as a government, have never resented "restriction" as a general thing, although, naturally, regretting that the opportunities of the United States are not open to some portion of her surplus population.

It is "discrimination" which both the Japanese government and the Japanese people resent.

This ought to be clearly understood.

Through the efforts of those who have so successfully made political capital out of the "anti-Japanese" question, the American people generally have been made to believe that it is the desire of the Japanese to "flood America" with immigrants, largely with some vague and undefined political or military object.

That Japan does not resent restriction is evidence from the fact that there has never been in Japan any showing of resentment against the "White Australia" policy, under which emigrants from Japan are not allowed to enter that land nor help to people its great tracts of, as yet, waste country. The reason is that the Australian policy is not "discriminatory."

That Japan does not resent restriction from the United States was evidenced by the willingness with which this country entered into the Gentlemen's Agreement, which agreement Japan has most scrupulously observed, to such an extent that to-day there are fewer Japanese subjects in the United States, including Hawaii, than fifteen years ago.

That there is today no desire in Japan to send many emigrants to the United States is evidenced by the announcement made in the name of the Japanese government a year ago that if Japan were to be included among the "quota countries" under

From Mears, Eliot Grinnell, *Resident Orientals on the American Pacific Coast* (1928; reprint New York: Arno Press, 1978) 516–517.

the pending American Immigration Law, it would be considered here that the Gentlemen's Agreement would remain in effect, so that to even the fewer than two hundred immigrants eligible for admission to the United States under the quota rule passports would not be issued if of the laboring class.

That Japan has no political designs in America through the citizenship right conferred by the Constitution of the United States upon children of Japanese parents born in the United States is well evidenced in the fact that for years Japan has been the only nation, among the many which consider citizenship as based upon race, that has had a provision in its citizenship law permitting children of its race born abroad to renounce the citizenship of the fathers. This law has recently been extended so that the Japanese government recognizes as citizens of the land of their birth all Japanese children born in the United States, except as expressly demonstrate their desire to be regarded as Japanese subjects. Germany, Italy, Spain, to mention only a few, have no such provisions in their citizenship laws.

All the talk of Japanese desire to encourage the Japanese birth-rate in the United States; all the talk of the subsidizing of brides from Japan for Japanese in America, and such, is spread either by those who knowingly deceive the American people in order to profit politically through the racial antagonism aroused, or by those who speak in ignorance, never having impartially investigated the facts.

Japanese emigrants would settle in the United States eagerly, if permitted. That is beyond question, just as the emigrants of every other country of the globe desire to enter America and have been entering America at such a rate as to necessitate the checks of the Immigration Law of 1921, and of this year. Japanese have the same desire to better themselves as have the Irish, the Italians, the Spanish, and every other race.

But Japan has been the only nation among the many which has met the growing objection in America to extensive immigration: the only nation to enter into an agreement to restrict the emigration of her people to America.

Japan has always recognized the right of the United States to determine her own immigration policy, as all other nations determine their immigration policies.

It is not restriction, therefore, but discrimination that is objected to, and Japan believes that in such objection she has right on her side, the right of treaty, law, and humanity.

Particularly does she resent the discrimination in recent American legislation because she believes it has been foisted upon her and upon the great majority of the American people themselves through a campaign of fact distortion, and manufactured evidence, and an appeal to racial sentiment by those to whom the truth, fairness, and all that is included in the term "Americanism" have been subordinated to political ambition.

Japan is frequently held up before the American people as the "traditional enemy," this being particularly so during the past twenty years. On the contrary, America has been held up before the Japanese people as the "traditional friend," the great Power to which Japan has turned in her emergencies, the nation to whom Japan owes so much in the way of modern culture and trade.

Japan, during all the years of anti-Japanese agitation on the Pacific slope, continued to regard America as her best friend, accepting unquestioningly the explanation that the anti-Japanese persecution came from the unthinking minority of the country.

The enactment of the "Exclusion Clause" of the Immigration Law of 1924 came as a wholly unexpected and totally undeserved blow to Japan; a blow from a friend toward whom Japan had during the past three decades done everything possible to show appreciation of what America had done and to whom Japan had given every possible demonstration of the fact of Japanese friendship and regard.

If that Immigration Law had excluded all immigration, Japan would not have resented it, and could not have.

If that Immigration Law had placed Japan on the same basis as other lands, permitting the entry into America of a mere 154 annually, Japan would not have resented it, but would have willingly and gladly taken precautions to see that even that few would not have gone to America.

But Japan does resent a clause that, while not mentioning Japanese specifically, affects Japanese alone of all the races heretofore eligible to enter the United States and which, in an Act of Congress, stamps Japanese as of an inferior race.

Japan has no discriminatory legislation. Her laws regarding land ownership by aliens apply to all aliens. Her laws respecting the right of immigrants of the laboring classes to enter the country apply to the laborers of every land alike. No right or privilege is withheld from American citizens in Japan that is not withheld from all aliens, and the citizens of no land have any privileges whatever in Japan that are not shared in equally by the citizens of the United States.

America has a law that extends a limited right of entry to the emigrants of Europe, Australia, Africa, but excludes Japanese and was enacted specifically to exclude Japanese.

This is the discrimination against which Japan protests and this alone.

This is what Japan hopes the American people will appreciate. To impress this upon all fair-minded Americans is what this edition of *The Japan Times* hopes to help in some degree to accomplish.

10. Ray E. Chase and S. G. Pandit Critique Supreme Court Ruling Excluding East Indians from Citizenship, 1926

With All Due Deference to the Supreme Court of the United States, We Suggest That Its Decision in the Case of United States v. Thind (261 U. S. 204, 43 Supt. Ct. 338, 67 L. Ed. 616), Which Was a Case Determined on Demurrer, Was Erroneous. . . .

The court holds that the test of eligibility for naturalization is that the applicant must be a "white person" . . . ; and that these words have the meaning which they had in the speech of the common man at the time of their enactment. What was that meaning?

The most generally accepted classification of mankind in the Eighteenth Century was that of Linnaeus (1707–1778), who divided men into the European white, Asiatic yellow, American red and African black varieties. Linnaeus, however, was not writing of geographical limits; for he made his European race inhabit *Europe,*

From Chase, Ray E., and S. G. Pandit, *An Examination of the Opinion of the Supreme Court of the United States Deciding Against the Eligibility of Hindus for Citizenship* (pamphlet), (copyright, S. G. Pandit, 1926).

Western Asia and Northern Africa; his Asiatic race peopled Eastern and Northern Asia only; while his African race was absent from the Mediterranean seaboard of *Africa.* . . .

Some indication as to the accepted meaning of the term "white person" (homo albus) about the time of the first enactment of the statute in 1790 and of the general Western attitude toward Asia and Asiatics may be gathered from appended excerpts from the third edition of the Encyclopedia Britannica, published in 1797:

> *Encyclopedia Britannica.* Edinburgh—Published in 1797—3rd Edition, Vol. X. p. 508:
>
> MAN: . . . The following arrangement of varieties in the human species is offered by Dr. Gmelin as more convenient than that of Linnaeus:
>
> (a). White (Homo Albus) formed by the rules of symmetry, elegance and beauty; or at least what we consider as such. This division includes almost all the inhabitants of Europe; *those of Asia on this side of the Oby, the Caspian, Mount Imans, and the Ganges:* likewise the natives of the north of Africa, of Greenland and the Esquimaux.
>
> (b). Brown (Homo Badius) of a yellowish-brown colour; has scanty hairs, flat features, and small eyes. This variety takes in the whole inhabitants of Asia *not included in the preceding division.*
>
> (c). Black (Homo Niger) of black complexion; has frizzly hair, a flat nose and thick lips. The whole inhabitants of Africa excepting those of its northern parts.
>
> (d). Cooper coloured (Homo Cuprens) . . .
>
> (e). Tawny (Homo Fuscus) . . .
>
> Vol. II; p. 393: Encyclopedia Britannica, 3rd Ed., 1797.
>
> ASIA: Asia is looked upon as that part of the world which, of all others, has been most peculiarly distinguished by heaven. There it was the first man was created; there the patriarchs lived, the law was given to Moses, and greatest and most celebrated monarchies were formed; from thence the first founders of cities and nations in other quarters of the world brought their colonies. Lastly in Asia Jesus Christ appeared; there it was that he wrought the salvation of mankind, that he died and rose again, and from thence it is that the light of the Gospel was diffused over all the world. Laws, arts, sciences and religion almost all had their origin in Asia.

After the first enactment of the words "white person" in 1790, they were re-enacted in 1870 when the words "and to aliens of African nativity and to persons of African descent" were added, yet again in 1875, when they were re-enacted to correct errors and omissions from the revised statutes of 1873. The meaning of the words which was current at the date of this last enactment is by the court's own holding the one that must be given to them in applying them to an individual applicant for naturalization. For the ascertainment of that meaning there is fortunately a readily available and unquestionable source. We turn to that institution in which for a century and more the language, usage and the opinion of the "common man" of the United States have been predominantly shaped—the common schools. In the textbooks of geography used in all American schools for three decades before and after the last enactment of the words of the test—both in the simply worded "primary geographies" and in the more comprehensive books used by older children—it was taught that there are five races of men: the white, or Caucasian race; the yellow, or Mongolian race; the red, or American Indian race; the brown, or Malay race; and the black, or African race. It was explained that the white, or Caucasian, race includes besides the peoples of Europe, the East Indians, or Hindoos (the word was spelled thus in all the earlier books), and the Arabs. . . . The children who were to become the "common men" of the 1870's stood in line before their teachers or sat upon the "recitation benches" of the elementary school rooms and recited these definitions until they became to them the common place response to any question concerning races of men. . . . Certainly no one can question that the meaning given to words in the daily teachings of those schools which were maintained for the forming of the thought habits of the children of the "common man" were the meanings those words definitely had for him and them! . . .

It should be noted further that the courts, both federal and state, up to the year 1917 and after, whenever certificates of citizenship were granted to Hindus, except in one reported opinion, had held *without exception that a Hindu is a white person* within the meaning of the statute. The popular mind accepted these decisions as a matter of course, according with common usage and the teaching of the common schools until a considerable influx of Hindu laborers upon the Pacific coast created an economic situation that led to agitation and the growth of prejudice against Hindus in the minds of certain classes whose interests were affected. This prejudice would in all likelihood never have become important if there had not already existed a prejudice against Chinese and Japanese laborers which was easily made to extend itself to a people identified with them as "Asiatics."

It is not possible to avoid the conclusion that the unfavorable attitude toward the naturalization of Hindus on the part both of the people at large (to the extent that such an attitude on their part exists—which we believe to be negligible outside of limited interested groups) and of the government is due to the anti-Asiatic agitation on the Pacific Coast and to the disposition to relate the matter of naturalization to the quite different one of immigration. Even Mr. Justice Sutherland makes this connection in the Thind decision (p. 215):

> It is not without significance in this connection that Congress, by the Act of February 5, 1917, c. 29, Sec. 3, 39 Stat. 874, has now excluded from admission into this country all natives of Asia within designated limits of latitude and longitude, including the whole of India. This not only constitutes conclusive evidence of the congressional attitude of opposition to Asiatic immigration generally, but is persuasive of a similar attitude toward Asiatic naturalization as well, since it is not likely that Congress would be willing to accept as citizens a class of persons whom it rejects as immigrants.

It is submitted that the inference here made is altogether illegitimate. It justifies by implication an interpretation of the will of Congress in 1875 in the light of an enactment made 42 years later to meet a set of conditions that no one could have foreseen in 1875, and that certainly no one did foresee. It suggests that the applications for citizenship of persons who had entered this country legally before the passage of the act of 1917 may be limited by that act, though that act does not deal with citizenship at all. This would manifestly be as inequitable as it would be illogical. It was unfortunate as applied to the case of Bhagat Singh Thind; it would be worse if applied to cases where the certificates actually issued several years before the law referred to was enacted.

The opinion in the Thind case suggests also the use of the altogether extra-legal test of assimilability in determining the intent of Congress.

This notwithstanding the distinguished justice had said in the Ozawa case (p. 197):

> Manifestly the test afforded by the mere color of the skin of each individual is impracticable, as that differs greatly among persons of the same race, even among Anglo-Saxons, ranging by imperceptible gradations from the fair blond to the swarthy brunette, the latter being darker than many of the lighter hued persons of the brown or yellow races. Hence to adopt the color test alone would result in a confused overlapping of races and a gradual merging of one into the other, without any practical line of separation.

The question, therefore, is one of race and not of color or complexion. And while there may be difference of opinion among ethnologists with regard to the position of certain small groups of Pacific islanders, for example, in the classification of races, there is practical unanimity among them with regard to the racial status of the Hindu. From Blumenbach, towards the end of the eighteenth century, to Prof. A. L. Krocher, head of the Department of Anthropology and Ethology at the University of California today, the consensus of scientific opinion is that Hindus are Caucasians and therefore of the white race, although their skins may be tanned or burnt by the torrid sun. . . .

"But," says the court (U. S. v. Thind, 261 U. S. 204, 209), "the term 'race' is one which, for the practical purposes of the statute, must be applied to a group of living persons now possessing in common the requisite characteristics."

It may be noted in opposition to this view that Congress in the amendment of what became Sec. 2169, R. S., making Africans eligible for citizenship, in 1870, speaks of "nativity" or "descent," thus giving to the term race its usual meaning, *in this very statute.* . . .

The Supreme Court in the Thind case, *supra,* at p. 215, adopts as the criterion of statutory race for naturalization purposes the test of assimilability, saying:

> It is a matter of familiar observation and knowledge that the physical group characteristics of the Hindus render them readily distinguishable from the various groups of persons in this country commonly recognized as white. The children of English, French, German, Italian, Scandinavian, and other European parentage, quickly merge into the mass of our population and lose the distinctive hallmarks of their European origin. On the other hand it cannot be doubted that the children born in this country of Hindu parents would retain indefinitely the clear evidence of their ancestry. It is very far from our thought to suggest the slightest question of racial superiority or inferiority. What we suggest is merely racial difference, and it is of such character and extent that the great body of our people instinctively recognize it and reject the thought of assimilation.

Any expert in biology and sociology could have saved the court from falling into the error clearly involved in the foregoing paragraph. To the extent that "the great body of our people" take the attitude attributed to them, they do so as the result of habit and tradition or out of experience of differences of culture and standards of living, not "instinctively." Whenever these differences disappear, or are so modified that they no longer have a powerful economic effect, the attitude rapidly alters. If by "assimilation" the court means "intermarriage," it must be admitted that an adverse sentiment in that regard may be found where the complexion happens to be very dark—though, even then, not any strong than it often is in considerable communities against intermarriage with special groups of Europeans or even with foreigners (or "furriners") in general. But this is clearly traceable to carrying over to other groups that prejudice against the Negro which is our heritage from the days of slavery, and which is perpetuated by the retention in the laws of some of our states of reprehensible enactments against inter-racial marriage.

Dr. E. H. Ross, professor of sociology in the University of Wisconsin, in his book, "Social Trends" (chap. I), defends the thesis that a considerable degree of homogeneity in its population is essential to the permanence of a nation. But his argument makes it clear that the homogeneity that is necessary is that of social structure, of cultural levels and standards of living, not of complexion or stature or structure of hair.

To hint at a lack of cultural assimilability in some Hindus would be unreasonable. Even in the eighteenth century it was recognized by Edmund Burke, who was among the best informed of his day about the population of India, that "This multitude of men does not consist of an abject and barbarous population. . . . [They are] a people for ages civilized and cultivated; cultivated by all the arts of polished life while we were yet in the woods." And nearly two hundred years of British association and tutelage in India has familiarized the Hindus more thoroughly with the prevailing ideals, standards and aspirations of the people of Western Europe. While the Hindus' racial and physiological assimilability with other whites is an established fact of anthropology and ethnology.

The opinion of the court, however, seems to be discussing not cultural, but biological assimilation. The descendants of Hindus will retain the physical characteristics of their ancestors. Quite likely—if they do not intermarry with persons of different characteristics! And the statement is true in exactly the same terms of the fair-haired Swede or the black-bearded Jew. There cannot be physical homogeneity in a nation made up of physically distinguishable groups, if intermarriage were prohibited. The opinion assumes that a high degree of physical homogeneity is desirable. The assumption is not necessarily correct—indeed, we believe it is not correct at all. But since the assumption is not pertinent, it is not necessary to argue the point. The court has pointed out that it is not the function of the judiciary to decide what sorts of persons should become citizens; it may merely ascertain what sorts legally may become citizens.

The Supreme Court said in Ebert v. Poston, 266 U. S. 548, 554, 45 Sup. Ct. 188, 190:

> The judicial function to be exercised in construing a statute is limited to ascertaining the intention of the legislature therein expressed. A *casus omissus* does not justify judicial legislation. Compare United States v. Wetzel, 246 U. S. 533, 543.

Says the court in its opinion in the case of Ozawa v. United States, *supra,* at page 198:

> We have no function in the matter other than to ascertain the will of Congress and declare it.

It may be respectfully submitted that it is quite impossible to discover in the naturalization laws of the United States any "will of Congress" toward a physical or racial homogeneity among citizens. Furthermore, the Constitution does not leave Congress free to exercise such a will. The much-quoted Sec. 2169, R. S., includes among those eligible for naturalization "Aliens of African nativity and persons of African descent."

Congress has also explicitly provided for the full citizenship of Indians who abandon their tribal life. The Constitution provides that all persons born in the United States and subject to the jurisdiction thereof are citizens of the United States. Under this provision descendants of Chinese and Japanese residents of the United States are recognized as citizens. Here plainly is no "will of Congress" for physical homogeneity.

It is true that by the terms of the Act of February 5, 1917, natives of India are no longer admitted to the United States as immigrant laborers; but that Act was passed because of considerations of cultural asimilability and possibility of economic absorption of Hindu labor. It has no bearing on the question of the eligibility to citizenship of Hindus who were in the United States before the passage of that Act or of those who belong to professional, artistic, scholarly or other occupations, who are expressly exempted from the exclusion provisions of the Immigration Act.

To sum up our discussion of the argument against the eligibility for naturalization of Hindus which is set forth in Mr. Justice Sutherland's opinion in the Thind case:

The court holds that the "popular" meaning of the term "white person" is intended by the naturalization law. The popular understanding has for years included Hindus in that class. . . .

The court rules that there is no question except: "Is a Hindu a white person within the meaning of the statute." All discussion of other questions is therefore irrelevant, and the decision is controverted by the very arguments advanced to support it.

The reference (Thind Case p. 209) to a meaning acquired during the last half century is also irrelevant, being subsequent to the enactment of 1875.

✺ E S S A Y S

The essays in this chapter highlight the causes and consequences of Asian immigration exclusion. In the first essay, historian and independent scholar Andrew Gyory argues that the first major exclusion of Asian immigrants, the Chinese Exclusion Act of 1882, was propelled by political aspirations and expedience. In the second essay, historian K. Scott Wong of Williams College, writing from the side of the excluded, analyzes the creative ways in which Chinese immigrants refused to be victimized. In the third essay, University of Chicago historian Mae M. Ngai, while exploring the later exclusion of Japanese and East Indians from immigration and citizenship, underscores the ultimate significance of racial ideology.

The Significance of Chinese Exclusion

ANDREW GYORY

The Chinese Exclusion Act of 1882 was the first law ever passed by the United States barring any group of people from American shores purely because of race or nationality. As many had foreseen, it provided a precedent for future restrictive legislation. "Hereafter," the *Chicago Times* noted, "we are to keep our hand on the door-knob, and admit only those whose presence we desire." For the next hundred

From *Closing the Gate: Race, Politics, and the Chinese Exclusion Act* by Andrew Gyory. Copyright © 1998 by the University of North Carolina. Used by permission of the publisher.

years Americans would indeed keep a "hand on the door-knob," barring the Chinese again in 1892, 1902, and 1904, and most Japanese and Koreans a few years afterward. The knob turned tighter in 1917 when the United States barred virtually all Asians and again in 1921 and 1924 when the United States all but closed the door to Europe and Japan. Not until World War II was the Chinese Exclusion Act repealed, but even then the United States restricted immigration to a quota of 105 Chinese per year. The door at last reopened in the 1960s, but shouts to close it again have grown shriller in recent years.

In tracing the origin of the Chinese Exclusion Act, both the California thesis and the national racist consensus thesis offer instructive points: the former illustrates how anti-Chinese sentiment developed in the West, and the latter suggests how Americans nationwide could readily accept anti-Chinese legislation. Both theses, however, essentially leave the politics out. And politics are at the core of the Chinese Exclusion Act. Anti-Chinese hostility, after all, had been rife in California for twenty-five years before the rest of the country took notice and began responding in the mid-1870s, and anti-Chinese imagery had long pervaded the nation during the nineteenth century without precipitating any adverse federal legislation. However racist the beliefs of politicians, workers, and other Americans in the post–Civil War years, Congress made no substantial effort to enact anti-Chinese laws in 1865 or 1870 or 1875. There was little demand for and little to gain from such legislation. But when the national railroad strike jolted the nation in 1877, just as Reconstruction was collapsing, a new era emerged that would make anti-Chinese politics possible nationwide. Suddenly the landscape had changed. Class conflict had forged this change and would keep generating and regenerating a changing political landscape for the duration of the Gilded Age. The fundamental question underlying the era's preeminent economic treatise—Henry George's *Progress and Poverty,* published in 1879—was, How in a nation of such wealth and abundance could there be so much poverty? It was this problem that politicians confronted throughout the Gilded Age and beyond, and in seeking answers, one of the first solutions they grasped was Chinese exclusion. This solution, politicians argued, would protect, uplift, and enrich the working person. As James Blaine said, "I feel and know that I am pleading the cause of the free American laborer and of his children and of his children's children." He was, he insisted, speaking "in defense and advocacy of the interests of the laboring classes." The Chinese Exclusion Act represented class politics on the cheap, a painless way for politicians to ensure working people's support without providing any genuine solution to their problems.

In the decade and a half following the Civil War, workers east of the Rocky Mountains carefully and repeatedly voiced their opposition to imported contract labor and their support for Chinese immigration. Only at the very end of this period, when exclusion became all but inevitable, did workers finally adopt the cause for their own. But at that point it really didn't matter, except that it enabled politicians to invoke the support of the working classes in whose name they convinced themselves, the nation, and ultimately workers that they were legislating. Their appeals to race and to class eventually struck a chord. As David Roediger, Alexander Saxton, and Gwendolyn Mink have argued, white working-class racism may indeed have been deep and pervasive in the middle and latter decades of the nineteenth century. The important question to ask, however, is not how racist workers were, but how did workers *act* on this racism? When issues of race arose at key historical moments, how did workers respond, and how did their entrenched racism influence their demands, their actions, and their political aims? The answer in this case is, surprisingly, not much. In the 1870s, a decade marked by depression, class conflict, and industrial upheaval, workers east of the Rockies—who composed the vast bulk of the working classes and the national labor movement—remained remarkably consistent in their tolerance toward Chinese immigration. From speeches made at rallies to resolutions passed at meetings, from letters sent to newspapers to slogans scrawled on banners, from offhand comments heard by reporters to prepared testimony delivered before Congress, from all the myriad working-class voices that can be rescued from the past, the great majority of workers who spoke out on the issue, contrary to the claims of countless historians, welcomed Chinese immigrants to America. After more than a dozen years of articulating their political demands for a ban on imported contract labor, legislation was at last passed—not the legislation most workers had wanted but the legislation politicians had fashioned. It was immigration—not importation, not contract labor—that politicians banned. Despite the avalanche of arguments by national politicians appealing to workers' self-interest, few workers in the East revealed much concern over Chinese immigration or Chinese exclusion. It was seldom an issue with which they chose to be associated. Immigration restriction rarely appeared on the working-class agenda in the 1860s and 1870s, and only when politicians placed it on the national agenda and trumpeted the issue in their name did workers finally accept it.

Politics, as Alexander Saxton has demonstrated, was the main channel for explicating and disseminating racial discourse. By spewing, amplifying, and propagating racist stereotypes of the Chinese and linking the well-being of workers to the exclusion of Chinese immigrants, politicians manipulated the two most volatile issues in American society—race and class—and combined them to produce the first race-based immigration act in American history. This manipulation is the essence of the Chinese Exclusion Act. Perhaps no better example of top-down politics exists than this 1882 statute. Both West Coast agitation and general racist tendencies nationwide were essential elements contributing to the climate conducive to Chinese exclusion, but the engine fueling and steering exclusion was politics. Politicians and national party leaders were the glue welding the active anti-Chinese racism of westerners within the nascent anti-Chinese racism of other Americans. In all senses of the term, Chinese exclusion was a *political* act.

Its impact, however, far transcended politics. By sanctioning racism, it perpetuated racism, and by sanctioning racist policy at the highest levels of government, it helped legitimize racist action at every level of society. The Chinese Exclusion Act was the foremost racist law passed after the Civil War. It both symbolized and facilitated the transition from Reconstruction to the Gilded Age, making discrimination more acceptable, more apparent, and more prevalent throughout the nation. All sections of the country, East and West, North and South, united in Congress to promote discrimination and legitimize segregation openly. Though westerners taunted a dwindling handful of eastern idealists for their "mawkish sentimentality" (as one California representative put it), the "equality gush" did not disappear entirely. It was simply redefined to suit the times. No one better captured this emerging ethos than Civil War veteran John Sherwin, an obscure two-term Republican congressman from

Aurora, Illinois, who sought to reconcile the ideals of an earlier age with the "stern realities" of the dawning era. "We do not deny the equality of man" Sherwin said, minutes before voting for the Chinese Exclusion Act. "We still assert that all men are born free and equal, but we claim the right to control our own workshops and choose our own associates." One could thus endorse equality in principle and discrimination in practice. Ideals were as malleable as words. But Sherwin did not go unchallenged. Cyrus Carpenter, an equally obscure Republican congressman from Iowa (as well as a Civil War veteran), predicted that a political backlash to the Chinese Exclusion Act would precipitate the law's repeal by 1890. "Common sense and not prejudice," he said, "will then prevail." Carpenter's vision was not borne out. After the Chinese Exclusion Act, prejudice prevailed and predominated, and Sherwin's words more perceptively codified the emerging philosophy of an increasingly segregated society. Equality could be proclaimed from the Capitol to the village square, but it would not be backed up by legislation or public policy. As the Jim Crow era of state-sponsored segregation dawned, more and more Americans, both nationally and locally, would "claim the right to control our own workshops and choose our own associates." From Sherwin's defense of Chinese exclusion in 1882 it was an effortless segue to *Plessy v. Ferguson* in 1896 and the institutionalization of racism in the twentieth century.

The Chinese Exclusion Act neither caused nor made inevitable later restrictions on immigration, but it certainly lent them legitimacy. It made future bans and quota systems easier to justify and easier to accept. By the early twentieth century, when many of the act's original sponsors had long since passed away, Chinese exclusion remained firmly embedded in the nation's laws. "Common sense" did not prevail, and renewals of the act passed with little opposition. The Exclusion Act legitimized racism, and racism legitimized further exclusion. As Senator William M. Stewart, the Nevada Republican who had boldly endorsed Chinese immigration and secured legal protections for all immigrants in 1870, remarked just days before the law's renewal in 1892; "There was a time when there was great diversity of opinion on the question of Chinese immigration to this country, but I think there is practically none now. The American people are now convinced that the Chinese can not be incorporated among our citizens, can not be amalgamated, can not be absorbed, but that they will remain a distinct element." Exclusion, this former defender of immigrant rights concluded, "seems to me a necessity." After permanent renewal in the early 1900s, exclusion no longer appeared an aberration of traditional American policy; it became American policy, it became American tradition, and thus had repercussions for generations to come. The law's legacy, in the form of future restrictions and anti-Asian racism, lingers to this day. Like the Fugitive Slave Act of 1850, the Chinese Exclusion Act of 1882 remains one of the most infamous and tragic statutes in American history. It must also remain one of the most ironic. No national sentiment arose to demand it, no broad effort emerged to prevent it. The Chinese Exclusion Act was a tool shaped and wielded by politicians who, in an era of burgeoning class conflict and razor-sharp electoral margins, championed an issue of paltry national importance in the false name of the working classes in the hopes of gaining a decisive handful of votes. In the name of morality, Gilded Age politicians used amoral tactics to enact an immoral law.

This point was not lost on contemporary observers. Kwong Ki Chiu, a Chinese scholar residing in Connecticut, identified the underlying motivation behind the

Chinese Exclusion Act. "I fear," he wrote on April 29, 1882, just days before 400 million of his fellow countrymen and countrywomen would for generations be excluded from the United States, "that some of the supporters of the anti-Chinese bills do not act from principle, but are seeking, under cover of this bill, to promote some ulterior and selfish end, such a their own reelection or their possible nomination for the Presidency."

In enacting the "anti-Chinese bill" in 1882, politicians not only closed the gate on an entire group of people but also set the standard for how Americans would both frame the immigration debate in the years that followed and come to accept greater and greater restrictions on foreigners seeking refuge and freedom in the United States. More than a century after its passage, the Chinese Exclusion Act still haunts the nation's treatment of immigrants and immigration.

Chinese Responses to Exclusion

K. SCOTT WONG

The anti-Chinese movement against which immigrants and American-born Chinese fought during the mid-nineteenth and mid-twentieth centuries existed simultaneously on several levels. In addition to the numerous mechanisms used to bar Chinese from mainstream American institutions and the physical intimidation and violence that they encountered regularly, the Chinese in America were confronted with an organized campaign to defame them in prose and in illustrations. Thus, the anti-Chinese movement was an early example of what is now often called a "culture war." Much of this "war" was a battle of words, waged in print as well as through other forms of public discourse. The exclusionists published an enormous number of pamphlets, essays, articles, novels, political cartoons, and other literary products advocating the exclusion of Chinese immigrants from the United States. This body of literature expressed the fears of what was known as the "Yellow Peril" in America.

In contrast, the Chinese had little recourse against their accusers. There is not much evidence to indicate that the Chinese physically retaliated against their attackers, although recent scholarship has revealed that the Chinese sought to challenge the discrimination that they faced by going on strike and by filing lawsuits in the American legal system. Another avenue of resistance open to the Chinese was print journalism. By adopting the same rhetorical tactics as their critics—writing in English and publishing in some of the same periodicals, such as the *North American Review* and the *Overland Monthly*—the Chinese elite in America attempted to gain some control over the images of the Chinese that were being presented to the American public. By offering alternative representations of themselves and by answering some of the charges levied against them, these writers hoped that attacks against the Chinese would lessen, that immigration legislation would be liberalized, and that the Chinese would eventually find acceptance in the American polity.

From the chapter "Cultural Defenders and Brokers: Chinese Responses to the Anti-Chinese Movement" by K. Scott Wong as it appears in *Claiming America: Constructing Chinese American Identities During the Exclusion Era*, ed. K. Scott Wong and Sucheng Chan. Reprinted by permission of Temple University Press. © 1998 by Temple University. All rights reserved.

These writings by Chinese spokespersons in America also revealed how they viewed themselves. Writing in self-defense, they used four distinct, yet overlapping strategies: They denied the anti-Chinese charges and paraded the virtues of Chinese history and culture; they sought equal treatment with other groups in America on the basis of class similarities; they defended the presence of the Chinese in America by comparing themselves favorably with others or be denigrating other immigrant and minority groups, often in Sinocentric terms; and they turned American democratic ideals back on their accusers, demanding that they live up to their own professed standards. The Chinese joined their critics in a "culture war of words" in an attempt to defend their presence in the United States. . . .

Of the Chinese foreign ministers assigned to the United States, Wu Tingfang (1842–1922) was the most active in writing and giving public lectures on behalf of the Chinese immigrant community in the United States. Rather than simply attack American exclusion policy as immoral or unjust, Wu tried to convince the American public that the policy was detrimental to U.S. interests. He first stressed the trade potential between the two countries. In the *North American Review,* a periodical that frequently printed anti-Chinese articles, Wu stated: "Let the products of American farms, mills, and workshops once catch the Chinese fancy, and America need look no further for a market. . . . I would suggest that American farmers and manufacturers might find it to their advantage to study the wants and habits of the Chinese and the conditions of trade in China."

Wu also encouraged using American capital to invest in China's future by providing aid for the construction of railroads and various public works. Wu argued that, seen in the light of reciprocal business relations between the two countries, such trade and investment not only would be a great benefit to both parties, but also would facilitate better relations.

However, full reciprocity could not exist if the United States maintained its exclusionary immigration policies toward China. This recognition framed Wu's second theme: equal treatment for the Chinese. He wanted American immigration policy to reflect parity between the two nations, and he demanded that Chinese immigrants be treated the same as others:

> Justice would seem to demand equal consideration for the Chinese on the part of the United States. China does not ask for special favors. All she wants is enjoyment of the same privileges accorded other nationalities. Instead, she is singled out for discrimination and made the subject of hostile legislation. Her door is wide open to the people of the United States, but their door is slammed in the face of her people. I am not so biased as to advocate any policy that might be detrimental to the best interests of the people of the United States. If they think it desirable to keep out the objectionable class of Chinese, by all means let them do so. Let them make their immigration laws as strict as possible, but let them be applicable to all foreigners.

Wu was careful not to challenge the right of the United States to determine the nature of its immigration laws, but he made a strong appeal to ideals of equal treatment. Thus, he placed the onus for the immigration crisis on the American government rather than on the supposed cultural flaws of the Chinese.

In his defense of the Chinese, however, Wu's class and racial biases became evident. His distance from the working classes and his belief in Chinese cultural superiority are obvious in many passages of his writings. While decrying the treatment of Chinese students and merchants in the United States, he drew a clear distinction between desirable and unwanted immigrants:

> It [the Chinese Exclusion Act] aimed to provide for the exclusion of Chinese laborers only, while freely admitting all others. As a matter of fact, the respectable merchant, who would be an irreproachable addition to the population of any country, has been frequently turned back, whereas the Chinese high-binders, the riff-raff and scum of the nation, fugitives from justice and adventurers of all types have too often effected an entrance without much difficulty. This is because the American officials at the entrance ports are ignorant of Chinese character and dialects and cannot always discriminate between the worthy and unworthy.

Not only did Wu sound like an anti-Chinese exclusionist at times, he also echoed sentiments held by nineteenth-century anti-immigrant nativists. In his published memoir, written in English, *America Through the Spectacles of an Oriental Diplomat,* he wrote:

> In a large country like America where a considerable portion of the land remains practically uncultivated or undeveloped, hardy, industrious, and patient workmen are a necessity. But the almost unchecked influx of immigrants who are not desirable citizens cannot but harm the country. In these days of international trade it is right that ingress and egress from one country to another should be unhampered, but persons who have committed crimes at home, or who are ignorant and illiterate, cannot become desirable citizens anywhere. They should be barred out of the United States of America.

Whether or not Wu included Chinese laborers in this group is uncertain, but clearly he embraced class attitudes similar to those of Americans who favored immigration restriction.

On the other hand, Wu often spoke of the Chinese in terms that placed them above other races. Speaking against exclusion, he stated, "So long as honest and steady workmen are excluded for no reason other than they are Asiatics, while white men are indiscriminately admitted, I fear the prosperity of the country cannot be considered permanent." More directly, he glorified the past achievements of Chinese civilization vis-à-vis Western achievements, claiming,

> It is too often forgotten that civilization, like religion, originally came from the East. Long before Europe and America were civilized, yet while they were still in a state of barbarism, there were nations in the East, including China, superior to them in manners, in education, and in government; possessed of a literature equal to any, and of arts and sciences totally unknown in the West. Self-preservation and self-interest make all men restless, and so Eastern peoples gradually moved to the West taking their knowledge with them; Western people who came into close contact with them learned their civilization. This fusion of East and West was the beginning of Western civilization.

Having "established" the origins of Western civilization, Wu took the moral high ground, using language rooted in Sinocentrism to condemn white supremacy:

> Those who support such a policy hold that they, the white people, are superior to the yellow people in intellect, in education, in taste, and in habits, and that the yellow people are unworthy to associate with them. Yet in China we have manners, we have arts, we have morals, and we have managed a fairly large society for thousands of years

without the bitter class hatreds, class divisions, and class struggles that have marred the fair progress of the West. We have not enslaved our lives to wealth. We like luxury but we like other things better. We love life more than chasing imitations of life.

Finally, Wu warned the exclusionists, "I only wish to give a hint to those white people who advocate an exclusive policy that in their next life they may be born in Asia or in Africa, and that the injury they are now inflicting on the yellow people they may themselves have to suffer in another life."

Educated primarily in Western institutions, Wu had adopted many Western attitudes, most notably his respect for the concepts of equal treatment under the law and reciprocity in international relations. In his defense of the Chinese and Chinese culture, however, his Sinocentrism surfaced. By claiming that the Chinese had developed a high civilization long before the West had done so and by castigating the exclusionists as morally deficient, Wu implied that Americans were inferior to the Chinese. Working constantly for the repeal of the exclusionary statutes, Wu was among the most articulate Chinese of his era in his efforts to defend the Chinese, but his writings also reveal the limits of his worldview. Unable to effect changes in U.S. immigration policy, Wu could only protest through his writings, often using Sinocentric rhetoric, unable to bridge fully the cultural gulf between the two nations. . . .

In addition to the appointed officials, the resident Chinese elite also published works in response to the exclusionists' rhetoric. Based primarily in San Francisco, but in cities such as New York as well, some of the individuals (often merchants) who served as spokespersons for the community had been educated in American schools or missionary institutions. This training not only provided them with the writing skills needed to challenge their accusers, but no doubt also informed their perception of their situation and shaped their response to it.

One of the earliest statements made by Chinese in San Francisco appeared in response to Governor John Bigler's letter of April 23, 1852, to the Senate and Assembly of the State of California calling for the exclusion of Chinese laborers. Bigler referred to the Chinese as Coolies," claiming that they were unfit to testify in American courts and, because of their culture and pecuniary interest in mining gold, did not want to become American citizens. In a letter dated April 29, 1852, and reprinted in the July issue of *Living Age,* two Chinese met Bigler's accusations and requests for immigration restriction head on. Hab Wa and Long Achick of Sam Wo Company and Ton Wo Company, respectively, claimed to have been educated in American schools and could therefore read the Governor's message and explain it to other Chinese in California. These authors first explained that the Chinese laborers in California were not "Coolies" in the pejorative sense of the word. Instead, they pointed out that the word "Cooly" *[sic]* was not a Chinese word, but one of foreign (Indian) origin. To the Chinese, the term had come to mean a common laborer, not one "bound to labor under contracts which they can be forcibly compelled to comply with." Keeping to this simple definition, the authors maintained, "The Irishmen who are engaged in digging down your hills, the men who unload ships, who clean streets, or even drive your drays, would, if they were in China be considered 'Coolies.'" Like the Chinese officials who came after them, these early writers sought to deflect criticism of the Chinese by pointed out that the Chinese were similar to the other working people in America. . . .

Most of the time, the local elite used the same approach as the appointed officials: They refuted the charges made against the Chinese and stressed the ideals of equality and fair treatment. Writing President Ulysses S. Grant in 1876, The Chinese Consolidated Benevolent Association (CCBA, also known as the Chinese Six Companies) declared that not all Chinese women in the United States were prostitutes and that white men were a part of this sordid business as well; that the Chinese diet, although different from that of many Americans, was hardly a cause for immigration restriction; that the Chinese Six Companies was not a secret tribunal; and that the Chinese in America were wage earners, not slaves. As the CCBA stated, "If these men are slaves, then all men laboring for wages are slaves." These authors also pointed out that the United States had a policy to "welcome immigration," that the Burlingame Treaty of 1868 provided for Chinese immigration to America, and that the Chinese had "neither attempted nor desired to interfere with the established order of things in this country, either of politics or religion." In other words, no cause existed for the Chinese to be singled out for exclusion.

These views on race and justice were apparently shared by some Chinese working people. One of the few writings left by a Chinese launderer from this period stated:

> Irish fill the almshouses and prisons and orphan asylums, Italians are among the most dangerous of men, Jews are unclean and ignorant. Yet they are all let in, while Chinese, who are sober, or duly law abiding, clean, educated and industrious, are shut out. There are few Chinamen in jails and none in the poor houses. There are no Chinese tramps or drunkards. Many Chinese here have become sincere Christians, in spite of the persecution which they have to endure from their heathen countrymen. More than half the Chinese in this country would become citizens if allowed to do so, and would be patriotic Americans. But how can they make this country their home as matters are now? They are not allowed to bring wives here from China, and if they marry American women there is a great outcry.
>
> All Congressmen acknowledge the injustice of the treatment of my people, yet they continue it. They have no backbone.
>
> Under the circumstances, how can I call this my home, and how can any one blame me if I take my money and go back to my village in China?

For the most part, however, the diplomats, intellectuals, and local elite who spoke out against exclusion and American attitudes toward the Chinese maintained a Sinocentric worldview, playing the role of cultural defenders. Coming from a country that had traditionally considered itself the center of the civilized world, these members of the Chinese elite protested American immigration policy because it offended their Chinese sensibilities. They demanded fair treatment for themselves and their lower-class compatriots on the basis of China's great civilization and past achievements. When seeking treatment equal to that of other immigrant groups, these individuals often resorted to denigrating the other groups to elevate the status of the Chinese. Even their appeals to American standards of justice and fairness were a tactic designed to make Americans live up to the rhetoric of democracy, but there is little indication that these Chinese spokespersons personally believed in democratic practices. One man, Yung Wing, however, stood in contrast to most of his peers. Acting as a cultural broker between Chinese and American worldviews, he rejected Sinocentrism, embraced American political and civic values, and made the United States his adopted home.

The Immigration Act of 1924

MAE M. NGAI

On February 4, 1929, Dr. Joseph A. Hill presented a plan for immigration quotas based on national origin to the United States Senate immigration committee. Hill was the chief statistician of the Census Bureau and chairman of the Quota Board, a committee under the departments of State, Commerce,and Labor. Congress had mandated the board to allocate the quotas under the Immigration Act of 1924. That law restricted immigration into the United States to 150,000 a year based on quotas, which were to be allotted to countries in the same proportion that the American people traced their origins to those countries, through immigration or the immigration of their forebears.

This was the third time in as many years that Hill had submitted a plan to Congress, and again members of Congress interrogated him as to the accuracy of the quotas. Hill's professional authority as one of the nation's leading demographers rested on a thirty-year tenure at the Census Bureau and was manifest in his patrician appearance. But determining the national origins quotas was arguably the most difficult challenge of his career. . . .

. . . [W]hile the national origins quota system was intended principally to restrict immigration from the nations of southern and eastern Europe and used the notion of national origins to justify discrimination against immigration from those nations, it did more than divide Europe. It also divided Europe from the non-European world. It defined the world formally by country and nationality but also by race, distinguishing between white persons from white countries and so-called colored races, whose members were imagined as having no countries of origin. This cross-cutting taxonomy was starkly presented in a table prepared by John Trevor, an advocate of immigration restriction and the chief lobbyist for a coalition of patriotic societies, on the national origins of the American people in 1924, which listed under the column "Country of Origin" fifty-three countries (from Australia to Yugoslavia) and five "colored races" (black, mulatto, Chinese, Japanese, and Indian). . . .

The system of quotas based on national origin was the first major pillar of the Immigration Act of 1924. The second was the exclusion of persons ineligible to citizenship. By one account, the provision barred half the world's population from entering the United States.

Ineligibility to citizenship and exclusion applied to the peoples of all the nations of the Far East. Nearly all Asians had already been excluded, either by the Chinese exclusion laws or by the "barred Asiatic zone" that Congress created in 1917. The latter comprised the area from Afghanistan to the Pacific, save for Japan, which the State Department wished not to offend, and the Philippines, a United States territory. In 1907 the Japanese government had agreed to prevent laborers from emigrating to the United States, but nativists complained that the diplomatic agreement was ineffective. The exclusion of persons ineligible to citizenship by the Immigration

From Mae M. Ngai, "The Architecture of Race in American Immigration Law: A Reexamination of the Immigration Act of 1924," *Journal of American History,* 86, no. 1 (June 1999); 80–81, 84–88. Copyright © 1999 Journal of American History. Used by permission of Organization of American Historians.

Immigration Quotas Based on National Origin (Annual Quota for Each Fiscal Year, Beginning July 1, 1929)

COUNTRY OR AREA	QUOTA	COUNTRY OR AREA	QUOTA
Afghanistan[a]	100	Muscat (Oman)[a]	100
Albania	100	Nauru (British mandate)	100
Andorra	100	Nepal[a]	100
Arabian peninsula	100	Netherlands	3,153
Armenia	100	New Guinea, Territory of (including	
Australia (including Tasmania, Papua,		appertaining islands) (Australian	
islands pertaining to Australia)	100	mandate)[a]	100
Austria	1,413	New Zealand	100
Belgium	1,304	Norway	2,377
Bhutan[a]	100	Palestine (with Trans-Jordan)	
Bulgaria	100	British mandate)	100
Cameroon (British mandate)	100	Persia	100
Cameroon (French mandate)	100	Poland	6,524
China[a]	100	Portugal	440
Czechoslovakia	2,874	Ruanda and Urundi	
Danzig, Free City of	100	(Belgian mandate)	100
Denmark	1,181	Rumania	295
Egypt	100	Russia, European and Asiatic	2,784
Estonia	116	Samoa, Western (mandate of	
Ethiopia (Abyssinia)	100	New Zealand)	100
Finland	569	San Marino	100
France	3,086	Siam[a]	100
Germany	25,957	South Africa, Union of	100
Great Britain and Northern Ireland	65,721	South West Africa (mandate of	
Greece	307	Union of South Africa)	100
Hungary	869	Spain	252
Iceland	100	Sweden	3,314
India[a]	100	Switzerland	1,707
Iraq (Mesopotamia)	100	Syria and the Lebanon	
Irish Free State	17,853	(French mandate)	123
Italy	5,802	Tanganyika (British mandate)	100
Japan[a]	100	Togoland (British mandate)	100
Latvia	236	Turkey	226
Liberia	100	Yap and other Pacific Islands under	
Liechtenstein	100	Japanese mandate[a]	100
Monoaco	100	Yugoslavia	845
Morocco (French & Spanish Zones			
and Tangier)	100		

SOURCE: *Proclamation by the President of the United States,* no. 1872, March 22, 1929, 46 Stat. 2984.
[a]Quotas for these countries available only for persons born within the respective countries who are eligible to citizenship in the United States and admissible under the immigration laws of the United States.

Act of 1924 achieved statutory Japanese exclusion and completed Asiatic exclusion. Moreover, it codified the principle of racial exclusion, incorporating it into general immigration law, albeit through the euphemistic reference to "persons ineligible to citizenship," which remained in effect until 1952.

Two major elements of twentieth-century American racial ideology evolved along with the racial requirement for citizenship: the legal definition of "white" and the rule of racial unassimilability. The origin of these concepts may be found in the Nationality Act of 1790, which granted the right to naturalized citizenship to "free white persons." After the Civil War and the passage of the Fourteenth Amendment, Congress amended the Nationality Act to extend the right to naturalize to "persons of African nativity or descent." The latter was a gratuitous gesture to the former slaves. No one seriously believed that "the [N]egroes of Africa [would] emigrate," a federal judge explained in 1880, "while the Indian and the Chinaman were in our midst, and at our doors and only too willing to assume the mantle of American sovereignty."

The Nationality Act of 1870 thus encoded racial prerequisites to citizenship according to the familiar classifications of black and white. European immigrants fit into that legal construct as white persons: between 1907 and 1924, nearly 1.5 million immigrants, nearly all from European countries, became American citizens. Although nativists commonly referred to southern and eastern Europeans as "undesirable races," their eligibility to citizenship as "white persons" was never challenged and the legality of naturalizing European immigrants was never an issue in public and political discourse. The Chinese Exclusion Act of 1882 declared Chinese ineligible to citizenship, but it remained unclear where Japanese, Asian Indians, Armenians, Syrians, Mexicans, and other peoples that immigrated into the United States in the late nineteenth and early twentieth century fit in the black-white construct of citizenship law. Although in 1906 the United States attorney general held Japanese and Asian Indians to be ineligible to citizenship, several hundred Japanese and Asian Indians obtained naturalized citizenship during the first two decades of the century. Between 1887 and 1923 the federal courts heard twenty-five cases challenging the racial prerequisite to citizenship, culminating in two landmark rulings by the United States Supreme Court, *Ozawa v. United States* (1922) and *United States v. Thind* (1923). In each case, the court's decision turned on whether the petitioner could be considered a "white person" within the meaning of the statute.

The judicial genealogy of the rules of racial eligibility to citizenship followed a racial logic different from that of the legislative discourse surrounding the quota laws. While the latter emphasized eugenics and the superiority of Nordics, scientific race theory proved inadequate to the classificatory challenge that eligibility to citizenship, and Asiatic exclusion generally, required of the law. As Ian Haney López has pointed out, the federal courts' rulings in naturalization cases increasingly rejected scientific explanations in favor of common understandings of race. No doubt this was because science was revealed to be an unreliable guide to racial exclusion. The few petitioners who successfully litigated their status as white persons did so with the aid of scientific race theories. In 1909 a federal court in Georgia ruled that George Najour, a Syrian, was eligible to citizenship. District Judge William Newman stated that "fair or dark complexion should not be allowed to control" determinations of race. He cited A. H. Keane's *The World's People* (1908), which divided the human race into four categories, noting that Keane "unhesitatingly place[d] the Syrians in the Caucasian or white division." Using similar logic, federal courts admitted Syrians, Armenians, and Asian Indians to citizenship as white persons in seven cases between 1909 and 1923.

In *Ozawa* the Supreme Court struggled with the problem of racial classification. The Court acknowledged that color as an indicator of race was insufficient, given the "overlapping of races and a gradual merging of one into the other, without any practical line of separation." Yet, the Court resisted the logical conclusion that no scientific grounds for race existed. It sidestepped the problem of classification by simply asserting that white and Caucasian were one and the same, concluding, with circular reasoning, that Japanese cannot be Caucasian because they are not white.

The Court resolved this problem in the *Thind* case, which it heard just a few months after *Ozawa*. Bhagat Singh Thind, a "high class Hindu," had argued his eligibility to citizenship as a white person based on his Aryan and Caucasian roots. Citing anthropological experts, Thind noted that the Aryans of India are a "tall, long-headed race with distinct European features, and their color on the average is not as dark as the Portuguese or Spanish." Because marrying outside of caste is strictly forbidden in India, Thind argued that he was a "pure Aryan."

The government rejected Thind's claim to whiteness as ridiculous. "In the popular conception," it stated, "he is an alien to the white race and part of the 'white man's burden'. . . . Whatever may be the white man's burden, the Hindu does not share it, rather he imposes it." The Court agreed, stating, "The word [Caucasian] by common usage has acquired a popular meaning, not clearly defined to be sure, but sufficiently so to enable us to say that its popular as distinguished from its scientific application is of appreciably narrower scope." In *Thind* the Court dismissed science altogether. The term "Caucasian," it said, "under scientific manipulation, has come to include far more than the unscientific mind suspects." Noting that Keane included Indians, Polynesians, and the Hamites of Africa in the Caucasian race, the Court commented dryly, "We venture to think that the average well-informed white American would learn with some degree of astonishment that the race to which he belongs is made up of such heterogeneous elements." The Court believed that the original framers of the law intended "to include only the type of man whom they knew as white . . . [those] from the British Isles and northwestern Europe . . . bone of their bone and flesh of their flesh." Furthermore, the meaning of white readily expanded to accommodate immigrants from "Eastern Southern, and Mid Europe, among them Slavs and the dark-eyed, swarthy people of Alpine and Mediterranean stock." Those immigrants were "received [as] unquestionably akin to those already here and readily amalgamated with them."

The Court's edict in *Thind*—"What we now hold is that the words 'free white persons' are words of common speech, to be interpreted with the understanding of the common man"—amounted to a concession to the socially constructed nature of race. Moreover, its acknowledgement of the assimilability of eastern and southern Europeans and its insistence on the unassimilability of Asians rendered a double meaning to assimilation. For Europeans, assimilation was a matter of socialization and citizenship its ultimate reward. Asians, no matter how committed to American ideals or practiced in American customs, remained racially unassimilable and unalterably foreign.

Although *Ozawa* and *Thind* applied to Japanese and South Asians, respectively, the Court made a leap in racial logic to apply the rule of ineligibility to citizenship to Koreans, Thais, Vietnamese, Indonesians, and other peoples of Asian countries who represented discrete ethnic groups and, in contemporary anthropological terms, different racial groups. This involved a measure of casuistry, which used retroactive and circular reasoning. In the last paragraph of *Thind* the Court applied the rule of ineligibility to citizenship to the natives of all Asian countries saying:

> It is not without significance in this connection that Congress, by the [Immigration] Act of 1917 . . . excluded from admission into this country all natives of Asia within designated limits of latitude and longitude, including the whole of India. This not only constitutes conclusive evidence of the congressional attitude of opposition to Asiatic immigration generally, but is persuasive of a similar attitude towards Asiatic naturalization as well,

since it is not likely that Congress would be willing to accept as citizens a class of persons whom it rejects as immigrants.

In 1923, on the heels of *Ozawa* and *Thind,* the Court issued four rulings upholding California and Washington state laws proscribing agricultural land ownership by aliens ineligible to citizenship. Those laws had been passed in the 1910s to drive Japanese and other Asians out of farming. In *Terrace v. Thompson,* the Court held that the alien land laws fell within the states' police powers to protect the public interest. Ironically, Japanese had taken up agriculture during the first decade of the century in the belief that farming would facilitate permanent settlement, civic responsibility, and assimilation. But if Japanese embraced the Jeffersonian ideal, the nativists who dominated Progressive politics on the Pacific Coast concluded that Japan was conspiring to take California away from white people. In a typical statement, United States senator James Phelan, formerly the mayor of San Francisco and for thirty years a leading California exclusionist, claimed in 1920 that Japanese land colonies in Merced County "would have destroyed that section for white settlement . . . and the desirable element."

In the alien land law cases, the Court did not address whether Japanese or other Asians were eligible to citizenship. That had already been decided—indeed, naturalized—by *Ozawa* and *Thind.* The Court contended that the alien land laws did not discriminate against Japanese because the laws applied to *all* aliens ineligible to citizenship, eliding the racial foundation of the concept. The Court held that it was logical and necessary to distinguish between citizens and aliens when considering land ownership, claiming, "Perfect uniformity of treatment of all persons is neither practical nor desirable. . . . [C]lassification of persons is constantly necessary [and] must therefore obtain in and determine legislation." The Court asserted, "One who is not a citizen and cannot become one lacks an interest in, and the power to effectually work for the welfare of the state, and so lacking, the state may rightfully deny him the right to own or lease land estate within its boundaries. If one incapable of citizenship may lease or own real estate, it is within the realm of possibility that every foot of land within the state may pass to the ownership of non-citizens." In this way the Court both refined and obscured the racial logic embedded in the concept of ineligibiltiy to citizenship, rendering invisible its premise of racial unassimilability.

Together, the naturalization and land cases solidified the concept "ineligible to citizenship," providing the basis for Asiatic exclusion in the Immigration Act of 1924. There is no direct evidence that the Supreme Court intended to influence the character of immigration legislation. But the timing of the decisions, coincident with the congressional debates over immigration restriction, is striking, especially since *Ozawa* and *Thind* had languished on the docket since World War I.

The Supreme Court rulings on Asians in 1922–1923 and the Immigration Act of 1924 thus completed the legal construction of "Asiatic" as a racial category. The "national origins" of Asians had become thoroughly racialized. This construct of race, based both on nationality and "common" or subjective understandings of race, differed from the language of eugenics that dominated the legislative discourse of immigration restriction, which was based on scientific race theory. Yet, the racialization of Asian nationalities was consistent with the overarching logic of the language in the Immigration Act of 1924, which, at the formal level, was based on categories of nationality and not of race. The act thus fit the modern tenor of classifying the world into nation-states and avoiding explicit racial language in the law. However, the underlying assumptions in the construction of those categories diverged in relationship to Europeans and Asiatics. The racial and national identities of the former became uncoupled while those of the latter became merged. The divergence pointed to a racial logic that determined which people could assimilate into the nation and which people could not. Thus, the shift in formal language from race to national origin did not mean that race ceased to operate, but rather that it became obfuscated.

FURTHER READING

Chan, Sucheng, ed. *Entry Denied: Exclusion and the Chinese Community in America, 1882–1943* (1991).

Coolidge, Mary Roberts. *Chinese Immigration* (1909).

Daniels, Roger. *The Politics of Prejudice: The Anti-Japanese Movement in California and the Struggle of Japanese Exclusion* (1962).

Gyory, Andrew. *Closing the Gate: Race, Politics, and the Chinese Exclusion Act* (1998).

Hess, Gary R. "The 'Hindu' in America: Immigration and Naturalization Policies and India, 1917–1946," *Pacific Historical Review* 38 (1969): 59–79.

Ichoika, Yuji. *The Issei: The World of the First Generation Japanese Immigrants, 1885–1924* (1988).

Iwata, Masakazu. *Planted in Good Soil: A History of the Issei in United States Agriculture,* 2 vols. (1992).

Jensen, Joan M. *Passage from India: Asian Indian Immigrants in North America* (1988).

Lee, Erika. "At America's Gates: Chinese Immigration During the Exclusion Era, 1882–1943," Ph.D dissertation, University of California at Berkeley (1998).

Mazumdar, Sucheta. "Racist Responses to Racism: The Aryan Myth and South Asians in the United States," *South Asia Bulletin* 9 (1989): 47–55.

McClain, Charles J. *In Search of Equality: The Chinese Struggle Against Discrimination in Nineteenth-Century America* (1994).

McKeown, Adam. *Chinese Migrant Networks and Cultural Change: Peru, Chicago, Hawaii, 1900–1936* (2001).

Modell, John. *The Economics and Politics of Racial Accommodation: The Japanese of Los Angeles, 1900–1942* (1977).

Moriyama, Alan Takeo. *Imingaisha: Japanese Emigration Companies and Hawaii, 1894–1908* (1985).

Ngai, Mae M. "The Architecture of Race in American Immigration Law: A Reexamination of the Immigration Act of 1924," *Journal of American History* 86 (June 1999): 67–92.

———. "Illegal Aliens and Alien Citizens: United States Immigration Policy and Racial Formation, 1924–1945," Ph.D dissertation, Columbia University (1998).

Peffer, George Anthony. *If They Don't Bring Their Women Here: Chinese Female Immigration Before Exclusion* (1999).

Sawada, Mitziko. "Culprits and Gentlemen: Meiji Japan's Restrictions of Emigrants to the United States, 1891–1909," *Pacific Historical Review* 60 (1991): 339–359.

Saxton, Alexander. *The Indispensable Enemy: Labor and the Anti-Chinese Movement in California* (1971).

Sayler, Lucy E. *Laws Harsh As Tigers: Chinese Immigrants and the Shaping of Modern Immigration Law* (1995).

Shah, Nayan. *Contagious Divides: Epidemics and Race in San Francisco's Chinatown* (2001).

Wakatsuki, Yasuo. "Japanese Emigration to the United States, 1866–1924: A Monograph," *Perspectives in American History* 12 (1979): 387–516.

Wong, K. Scott, and Sucheng Chan, eds. *Claiming America: Constructing Chinese American Identities During the Exclusion Era* (1998).

Yung, Judy. *Unbound Feet: A Social History of Chinese Women in San Francisco* (1995).

Imperialism and Anti-Imperialism in the Early Twentieth Century

The United States was late to the imperial game, taking its first colony in 1899, when it wrested control of the Philippines from the decaying Spanish empire. American imperialists, such as Assistant Secretary of the Navy and soon to be president Theodore Roosevelt, heralded the annexation of the Philippines as both a strategic victory for American authority in the Pacific and a moral imperative to bring American civilization to "backward" and "savage" peoples. But if Americans were a new colonial power, they were old hands at territorial conquest and the management of subordinated populations on the North American continent. Looking back to the "Indian Wars" earlier in the nineteenth century, Americans often portrayed Filipinos as simply another tribe of Indians to be subdued and, if possible, Americanized.

In colonizing the Philippines, however, American imperialists faced political opposition from prominent Americans that was rarely seen in the process of "Indian removal." The catalyst for much of this opposition was the Anti-Imperialist League, an organization of reportedly a half-million members, including the famous writer Mark Twain, Nation *editor E. L. Godkin, labor leader Samuel Gompers, and African American scholar and activist W. E. B. Du Bois. It was through the league's publications that many Americans learned about the atrocities American soldiers were committing in military campaigns to "pacify" the Filipino people, who supported the armed struggle for Philippine independence.*

The Anti-Imperialist League was an important signal that Americans were coming to accept the principle of national self-determination that President Woodrow Wilson would formalize as general philosophy in the peace settlement ending World War I. This anti-imperialist sentiment was also evident among smaller groups of East Indian and Korean immigrants and exiles in the United States. With some important exceptions, America for them offered a safe place from which to draw worldwide attention to the colonization of their respective nations, India and Korea.

☙ D O C U M E N T S

The first five documents address the American colonization of the Philippines. In Document 1, Senator Albert Beveridge argues that taking the Philippines was an economic necessity for U.S. trade with Asia and a moral imperative because the "barbarous" Filipinos were incapable of democratic self-government. Document 2 is a good part of the speech Theodore Roosevelt gave to the Republican National Convention in accepting the nomination as vice president. In this speech, Roosevelt justifies Philippine colonization as merely another form of westward expansion. Document 3 and 4 are photographs depicting, respectively, the surrender of Filipino soldiers to American troops and the continuation of fighting well after the U.S. victory in 1901. The persistent fight for Philippine independence is also made clear in Document 5, a written protest by Filipino nationalists against American imperialism that was reproduced and disseminated by the Anti-Imperialist League.

The next two documents provide anti-imperialist views of East Indians in the United States. Document 6 reveals the response by Indian nationalist Taraknath Das and his editors at the journal *Modern Review* to an American journalist's dismissal of nonviolence as an effective opposition to British rule in India. The criticism centers on the assumption of a fundamental and fixed difference between East and West. Document 7 is a brief life narrative based on an oral interview with Indian immigrant Mohan Singh. Singh was one of hundreds of young men in the first quarter of the twentieth century who escaped the repression of independence struggles in India by going to study in the United States. Many of these students would denounce British colonialism from the relatively safe harbor of American colleges and universities.

The final two documents focus on Korean Americans. Documents 8 is a transcript from the Korean Congress of 1919, which brought delegates from the United States, Korea, and other parts of the world to Philadelphia's Independence Hall to draw attention to Japan's wrongs in its colonization of Korea. The main speakers in this excerpt, Philip Jaisohn and Syngman Rhee, were two of the four best-known political leaders within the Korean immigrant community. Jaisohn (1866–1928), the first Korean to receive a medical degree in the United States, convened the Korean Congress and served at this time as an elder statesman to Korean immigrants. Rhee (1875–1965), who received a Ph.D. degree from Princeton University, believed strongly in cultivating American public opinion to support Korean independence and in 1948 served as the first president of the newly independent Korea. Document 9 provides an intimate look at the Korean independence movement by following the experience of one Korean immigrant who returns to Korea and plays an active role in a major anti-imperialist uprising.

1. Senator Albert Beveridge Champions Philippine Colonization, 1900

Mr. President, the times call for candor. The Philippines are ours forever, "territory belonging to the United States," as the Constitution calls them. And just beyond the Philippines are China's illimitable markets. We will not retreat from either. We will not repudiate our duty in the archipelago. We will not abandon our opportunity in the Orient. We will not renounce our part in the mission of our race, trustee under

From *Congressional Record,* Senate, January 9, 1900, 704–711; reprinted in *The Philippines Reader: A History of Colonialism, Neocolonialism, Dictatorship, and Resistance,* ed. Daniel B. Schirmer and Stephen Rosskamm Shalom (Boston: South End Press, 1987), 23–26.

God, of the civilization of the world. And we will move forward to our work, not howling out regrets like slaves whipped to their burdens, but with gratitude for a task worthy of our strength, and thanksgiving to Almighty God that He has marked us as His chosen people, henceforth to lead in the regeneration of the world.

This island empire is the last land left in all the oceans. If it should prove a mistake to abandon it, the blunder once made would be irretrievable. If it proves a mistake to hold it, the error can be corrected when we will. Every other progressive nation stands ready to relieve us.

But to hold it will be no mistake. Our largest trade henceforth must be with Asia. The Pacific is our ocean. More and more Europe will manufacture the most it needs, secure from its colonies the most it consumes. Where shall we turn for consumers of our surplus? Geography answers the question. China is our natural customer. She is nearer to us than to England, Germany, or Russia, the commercial powers of the present and the future. They have moved nearer to China by securing permanent bases on her borders. The Philippines give us a base at the door of all the East.

Lines of navigation from our ports to the Orient and Australia; from the Isthmian Canal to Asia; from all Oriental ports to Australia, converge at and separate from the Philippines. They are a self-supporting, dividend-paying fleet, permanently anchored at a spot selected by the strategy of Providence, commanding the Pacific. And the Pacific is the ocean of the commerce of the future. Most future wars will be conflicts for commerce. The power that rules the Pacific, therefore, is the power that rules the world. And, with the Philippines, that power is and will forever be the American Republic.

China's trade is the mightiest commercial fact in our future. Her foreign commerce was $285,738,300 in 1897, of which we, her neighbor, had less than 9 per cent, of which only a little more than half was merchandise sold to China by us. We ought to have 50 per cent, and we will. And China's foreign commerce is only beginning. Her resources, her possibilities, her wants, all are undeveloped. She has only 340 miles of railway. I have seen trains loaded with natives and all the activities of modern life already appearing along the line. But she needs, and in fifty years will have, 20,000 miles of railway.

Who can estimate her commerce then? That statesman commits a crime against American trade—against the American grower of cotton and wheat and tobacco, the American manufacturer of machinery and clothing—who fails to put America where she may command that trade. Germany's Chinese trade is increasing like magic. She has established ship lines and secured a tangible foothold on China's very soil. Russia's Chinese trade is growing beyond belief. She is spending the revenues of the Empire to finish her railroad into Pekin itself, and she is in physical possession of the imperial province of Manchuria. Japan's Chinese trade is multiplying in volume and value. She is bending her energy to her merchant marine, and is located along China's very coast; but Manila is nearer China than Yokohama is. The Philippines command the commercial situation of the entire East. . . . And yet American statesmen plan to surrender this commercial throne of the orient where Providence and our soldiers' lives have placed us. When history comes to write the story of that suggested treason to American supremacy and therefore to the spread of American civilization, let her in mercy write that those who so proposed were merely blind and nothing more.

But if they did not command China, India, the Orient, the whole Pacific for purposes of offense, defense, and trade, the Philippines are so valuable in themselves that we should hold them. I have cruised more than 2,000 miles through the archipelago, every moment a surprise at its loveliness and wealth. I have ridden hundreds of miles on the islands, every foot of the way a revelation of vegetable and mineral riches.

No land in America surpasses in fertility the plains and valleys of Luzon. Rice and coffee, sugar and coconuts, hemp and tobacco, and many products of the temperate as well as the tropic zone grow in various sections of the archipelago. . . . The wood of the Philippines can supply the furniture of the world for a century to come. At Cebu the best informed man in the island told me that 40 miles of Cebu's mountain chain are practically mountains of coal. . . .

I have a nugget of pure gold picked up in its present form on the banks of a Philippine creek. I have gold dust washed out by crude processes of careless natives from the sands of a Philippine stream. Both indicate great deposits at the source from which they come. . . .

And the wood, hemp, copra, and other products of the Philippines supply what we need and can not ourselves produce. And the markets they will themselves afford will be immense. Spain's export and import trade, with the islands undeveloped, was $11,534,731 annually. Ultimately our trade, when the islands shall be developed, will be $125,000,000 annually, for who believes that we can not do ten times as well as Spain? . . .

It will be hard for Americans who have not studied them to understand the people. They are a barbarous race, modified by three centuries of contact with a decadent race. The Filipino is the South Sea Malay, put through a process of three hundred years of superstition in religion, dishonesty in dealing, disorder in habits of industry, and cruelty, caprice, and corruption in government. It is barely possible that 1,000 men in all the archipelago are capable of self-government in the Anglo-Saxon sense.

My own belief is that there are not 100 men among them who comprehend what Anglo-Saxon self-government even means, and there are over 5,000,000 people to be governed. . . .

Mr. President, reluctantly and only from a sense of duty am I forced to say that American opposition to the war has been the chief factor prolonging it. Had Aguinaldo not understood that in America, even in the American Congress, even here in the Senate, he and his cause were supported; had he not known that it was proclaimed on the stump and in the press of a faction in the United States that every shot his misguided followers fired into the breasts of American soldiers was like the volleys fired by Washington's men against the soldiers of King George his insurrection would have dissolved before it entirely crystallized. . . .

But, Senators, it would be better to abandon this combined garden and Gibraltar of the Pacific, and count our blood and treasure already spent a profitable loss, than to apply an academic arrangement of self-government to these children. They are not capable of self-government. How could they be? They are not of a self-governing race. They are Orientals, Malays, instructed by Spaniards in the latter's worst estate.

. . . What alchemy will change the oriental quality of their blood and set the self-governing currents of the American pouring through their Malay veins? How shall they, in the twinkling of an eye, be exalted to the heights of self-governing peoples which required a thousand years for us to reach, Anglo-Saxons though we are? . . .

. . . The Declaration [of Independence] applies only to people capable of self-government. How dare any man prostitute this expression of the very elect of self-governing peoples to a race of Malay children of barbarism, schooled in Spanish methods and ideas? And you, who say the Declaration applies to all men, how dare you deny its application to the American Indian? And if you deny it to the Indian at home, how dare you grant it to the Malay abroad? . . .

. . . [T]he archipelago is a base for the commerce of the East. It is a base for military and naval operations against the only powers with whom conflict is possible; a fortress thrown up in the Pacific, defending our Western coast, commanding the waters of the Orient, and giving us a point from which we can instantly strike and seize the possessions of any possible foe. . . .

Mr. President, this question is deeper than any question of party politics; deeper than any question of the isolated policy of our country even; deeper even than any question of constitutional power. It is elemental. It is racial. God has not been preparing the English-speaking and Teutonic peoples for a thousand years for nothing but vain and idle self-contemplation and self-admiration. No! He has made us the master organizers of the world to establish system where chaos reigns. He has given us the spirit of progress to overwhelm the forces of reaction throughout the earth. He has made us adept in government that we may administer government among savage and senile peoples. Were it not for such a force as this the world would relapse into barbarism and night. And of all our race He has marked the American people as his chosen nation to finally lead in the regeneration of the world. This is the divine mission of America, and it holds for us all the profit, all the glory, all the happiness possible to man. We are trustees of the world's progress, guardians of its righteous peace. The judgment of the Master is upon us: "Ye have been faithful over a few things; I will make you rule over many things."

2. Theodore Roosevelt Justifies Philippine Colonization on the Basis of America's History of Westward Expansion, 1900

While paying heed to the necessity of keeping our house in order at home the American people cannot, if they wish to retain their self-respect, refrain from doing their duty as a great nation in the world. The history of the nation is in large part the history of the nation's expansion. When the First Continental Congress met in Liberty Hall and the thirteen original States declared themselves a nation, the westward limit of the country was marked by the Alleghany Mountains. Even during the Revolutionary War the work of expansion went on. Kentucky, Tennessee, and the great Northwest, then known as the Illinois country, were conquered from our white and Indian foes during the Revolutionary struggle, and were confirmed

From Roosevelt to Wolcott, September 15, 1900, in *The Works of Theodore Roosevelt,* vol. 14 (New York: Charles Scribner's Sons, 1926), 364–372.

to us by the treaty of peace in 1783. Yet the land thus confirmed was not then given to us. It was held by an alien foe until the army under General Anthony Wayne freed Ohio from the red man, while the treaties of Jay and Pinckney secured from the Spanish and British Natchez and Detroit.

In 1803, under President Jefferson, the greatest single stride in expansion that we ever took was taken by the purchase of the Louisiana Territory. This so-called Louisiana, which included what are now the States of Arkansas, Missouri, Louisiana, Iowa, Minnesota, Kansas, Nebraska, North and South Dakota, Idaho, Montana, and a large part of Colorado and Utah, was acquired by treaty and purchase under President Jefferson exactly and precisely as the Philippines have been acquired by treaty and purchase under President McKinley. The doctrine of "the consent of the governed," the doctrine previously enunciated by Jefferson in the Declaration of Independence, was not held by him, or by any other sane man, to apply to the Indian tribes in the Louisiana Territory which he thus acquired, and there was no vote taken even of the white inhabitants, not to speak of the negroes and Indians, as to whether they were willing that their Territory should be annexed. The great majority of the inhabitants, white and colored alike, were bitterly opposed to the transfer. An armed force of United States soldiers had to be hastily sent into the Territory to prevent insurrection, President Jefferson sending these troops to Louisiana for exactly the same reasons and with exactly the same purpose that President McKinley has sent troops to the Philippines. Jefferson distinctly stated that the Louisianians were "not fit or ready for self-government," and years elapsed before they were given self-government, Jefferson appointing the governor and other officials without any consultation with the inhabitants of the newly acquired Territory. The doctrine that the "Constitution follows the flag" was not then even considered either by Jefferson or by any other serious party leader, for it never entered their heads that a new Territory should be governed other than in the way in which the Territories of Ohio and Illinois had already been governed under Washington and the elder Adams; the theory known by this utterly false and misleading phrase was only struck out in political controversy at a much later date, for the sole purpose of justifying the extension of slavery into the Territories.

The parallel between what Jefferson did with Louisiana and what is now being done in the Philippines is exact. Jefferson, the author of the Declaration of Independence, and of the "consent of the governed" doctrine, saw no incongruity between this and the establishment of a government on commonsense grounds in the new Territory; and he railed at the sticklers for an impossible application of his principle, saying, in language which at the present day applies to the situation in the Philippines without the change of a word, "though it is acknowledged that our new fellow citizens are as yet as incapable of self-government as children, yet some cannot bring themselves to suspend its principles for a single moment." He intended that ultimately self-government should be introduced throughout the Territory, but only as the different parts became fit for it, and no sooner. This is just the policy that has been pursued. In no part of the Louisiana Purchase was complete self-government introduced for a number of years; in one part of it, the Indian Territory, it has not yet been introduced, although nearly a century has elapsed. Over enormous tracts of it, including the various Indian reservations, with a territory in the aggregate as large as that of the Philippines, the Constitution has never yet "followed the flag";

the army officers and the civilian agent still exercise authority, without asking "the consent of the governed." We must proceed in the Philippines with the same wise caution, taking each successive step as it becomes desirable, and accommodating the details of our policy to the peculiar needs of the situation. But as soon as the present revolt is put down and order established, it will undoubtedly be possible to give to the islands a larger measure of self-government than Jefferson originally gave Louisiana.

The next great step in expansion was the acquisition of Florida. This was partly acquired by conquest and partly by purchase, Andrew Jackson being the most prominent figure in the acquisition. It was taken under President Monroe, the after-time President John Quincy Adams being active in securing the purchase. As in the case of the Philippines, Florida was acquired by purchase from Spain, and in Florida the Seminoles, who had not been consulted in the sale, rebelled and waged war exactly as some of the Tagals have rebelled and waged war in the Philippines. The Seminole War lasted for many years, but Presidents Monroe, Adams, and Jackson declined for a moment to consider the question of abandoning Florida to the Seminoles, or to treat their non-consent to the government of the United States as a valid reason for turning over the Territory to them.

Our next question of territory was that of Texas, secured by treaty after it had been wrested from the Mexicans by the Texans themselves. Then came the acquisition of California, New Mexico, Arizona, Nevada, and parts of Colorado and Utah as the result of the Mexican War, supplemented five years later by the Gadsden Purchase.

The next acquisition was that of Alaska, secured from Russia by treaty and purchase. Alaska was full of natives, some of whom had advanced well beyond the stage of savagery and were Christians. They were not consulted about the purchase nor was their acquiescence required. The purchase was made by the men who had just put through a triumphant war to restore the Union and free the slave; but none of them deemed it necessary to push the doctrine of "the consent of the governed" to a conclusion so fantastic as to necessitate the turning over of Alaska to its original owners, the Indian and the Aleut. For thirty years the United States authorities, military and civil, exercised the supreme authority in a tract of land many times larger than the Philippines, in which it did not seem likely that there would ever be any considerable body of white inhabitants.

Nearly thirty years passed before the next instance of expansion occurred, which was over the island of Hawaii. An effort was made at the end of President Harrison's administration to secure the annexation of Hawaii. The effort was unsuccessful. In a debate in Congress on February 2, 1894, one of the leaders in opposing the annexation of the islands stated: "These islands are more than two thousand miles distant from our extreme Western boundary. We have a serious race problem now in our country and I am not in favor of adding to our domestic fabric a mongrel population (of this character). Our Constitution makes no provisions for a colonial establishment. Any territorial government we might establish would necessarily, because of the population, be an oligarchy, which would have to be supported by armed soldiers." Yet Hawaii has now been annexed and her delegates have sat in the national conventions of the two great parties. The fears then expressed in relation to an "oligarchy" and "armed soldiers" are not now seriously entertained by any human being; yet they are precisely the objections urged against the acquisition of the Philippines at this very moment. We are making no new departure. We are not taking a single step which in any way affects our institutions or our traditional policies. From the beginning we have given widely varying degrees of self-government to the different Territories, according to their needs.

The simple truth is that there is nothing even remotely resembling "imperialism" or "militarism" involved in the present development of that policy of expansion which has been part of the history of America from the day when she became a nation. The words mean absolutely nothing as applied to our present policy in the Philippines; for this policy is only imperialistic in the sense that Jefferson's policy in Louisiana was imperialistic; only military in the sense that Jackson's policy toward the Seminoles or Custer's toward the Sioux embodied militarism; and there is no more danger of its producing evil results at home now than there was of its interfering with freedom under Jefferson or Jackson, or in the days of the Indian wars on the plains. Our army is relatively not as large as it was in the days of Wayne; we have not one regular for every thousand inhabitants. There is no more danger of a draft than there is of the reintroduction of slavery.

When we expanded over New Mexico and California we secured free government to these Territories and prevented their falling under the "militarism" of a dictatorship like that of Santa Anna, or the "imperialism" of the real empire in the days of Maximilian. We put a stop to imperialism in Mexico as soon as the Civil War closed. We made a great anti-imperialistic stride when we drove the Spaniards from Porto Rico and the Philippines, and thereby made ready the ground in these islands for that gradually increasing measure of self-government for which their populations are severally fitted. Cuba is being helped along the path to independence as rapidly as her own citizens are content that she should go. Of course, the presence of troops in the Philippines during the Tagal insurrection has no more to do with militarism or imperialism than had their presence in the Dakatos, Minnesota, and Wyoming during the many years which elapsed before the final outbreaks of the Sioux were definitely put down. There is no more militarism or imperialism in garrisoning Luzon until order is restored than there was imperialism in sending soldiers to South Dakota in 1890 during the Ogillallah outbreak. The reasoning which justifies our having made war against Sitting Bull also justifies our having checked the outbreaks of Aguinaldo and his followers, directed, as they were, against Filipino and American alike.

The only certain way of rendering it necessary for our Republic to enter on a career of "militarism" would be to abandon the Philippines to their own tribes, and at the same time either to guarantee a stable government among these tribes or to guarantee them against outside interference. A far larger army would be required to carry out any such policy than will be required to secure order under the American flag; while the presence of this flag on the islands is really the only possible security against outside aggression.

The whole argument against President McKinley's policy in the Philippines becomes absurd when it is conceded that we should, to quote the language of the Kansas City platform, "give to the Filipinos first a stable form of government." If they are now entitled to independence, they are also entitled to decide for themselves whether their government shall be stable or unstable civilized or savage, or whether they shall have any government at all; while it is, of course, equally evident that under such conditions we have no right whatever to guarantee them against outside interference any more than we have to make such a guarantee in the case of the Boxers (who are merely the Chinese analogues of Aguinaldo's followers). If we have a right to establish a stable government in the islands it necessarily follows that it is not only our right but our duty to support that government until the natives gradually grow fit to sustain it themselves. How else will it be stable? The minute we leave it, it ceases to be stable.

Properly speaking, the question is now not whether we shall expand—for we have already expanded—but whether we shall contract. The Philippines are now part of American territory. To surrender them would be to surrender American territory. They must, of course, be governed primarily in the interests of their own citizens. Our first care must be for the people of the islands which have come under our guardianship as a result of the most righteous foreign war that has been waged within the memory of the present generation. They must be administered in the interests of their inhabitants, and that necessarily means that any question of personal or partisan politics in their administration must be entirely eliminated. We must continue to put at the heads of affairs in the different islands such men as General Wood, Governor Allen, and Judge Taft; and it is a most fortunate thing that we are able to illustrate what ought to be done in the way of sending officers thither by pointing out what actually has been done. The minor places in their administration, where it is impossible to fill them by natives, must be filled by the strictest application of the merit system. It is very important that in our own home administration the merely ministerial and administrative offices, where the duties are entirely non-political, shall be filled absolutely without reference to partisan affiliations, but this is many times more important in the newly acquired islands. The merit system is in its essence as democratic as our common-school system, for it simply means equal chances and fair play for all.

It must be remembered always that governing these islands in the interests of the inhabitants may not necessarily be to govern them as the inhabitants at the moment prefer. To grant self-government to Luzon under Aguinaldo would be like granting self-government to an Apache reservation under some local chief; and this is no more altered by the fact that the Filipinos fought the Spaniards, than it would be by the fact that the Apaches have long been trained and employed in the United States army and have rendered signal service therein; just as the Pawnees did under the administration of General Grant; just as the Stockbridge Indians did in the days of General Washington; and the friendly tribes of the Six Nations in the days of President Madison.

There are now in the United States communities of Indians which have so far advanced that it has been possible to embody them as a whole in our political system, all the members of the tribe becoming United States citizens. There are other communities where the bulk of the tribes are still too wild for it to be possible to take such a step. There are individuals among the Apaches, Pawnees, Iroquois, Sioux, and other tribes, who are now United States citizens, and who are entitled to stand, and do stand, on an absolute equality with all our citizens of pure white blood. Men of Indian blood are now serving in the army and navy and in Congress, and occupy high positions both in the business and the political world.

There is every reason why as rapidly as an Indian, or any body of Indians, becomes fit for self-government, he or it should be granted the fullest equality with the whites; but there would be no justification whatever in treating this fact as a reason for abandoning the wild tribes to work out their own destruction. Exactly the same reasoning applies in the case of the Philippines. To turn over the islands to Aguinaldo and his followers would not be to give self-government to the islanders; under no circumstances would the majority thus gain self-government. They would simply be put at the mercy of a syndicate of Chinese half-breeds, under whom corruption would flourish far more freely than ever it flourished under Tweed, while tyrannical oppression would obtain to a degree only possible under such an oligarchy.

3. Filipino Soldiers Pray Before Surrendering to Americans, 1900

Beyond the rhetoric of civilizing Filipinos, the reality of American colonization was bloody. Hundreds of thousands of Filipinos died in the undeclared American-Philippines War.

From National Archives at College Park, Md., Still Pictures Branch. Control Number NWDNS-395-PI-1 (50); found through NARA's web-based searchable collections database (NAIL).

4. American Troops Fight
in the Philippines, 1910

In 1901 American forces captured Filipino leader Emilio Aguinaldo and established a civilian government in the islands. But, as this photograph shows, outbreaks of fighting continued.

From National Archives at College Park, Md., Still Picture Branch. Control Number NWDNS-165-FS-16 (13634); found through NARA's web-based searchable collections database (NAIL).

5. Filipinos Demand Independence, 1908

Why should the Filipinos not be masters of their own destiny and arbiters of their own fate? Thus spake America, through the mouth of its leading statesmen, after having favorably decided the same question concerning the Cubans in the Gulf of Mexico. But this nation, free by tradition and by nature, this generous deliverer, found an answer in the discovery that we were incapable of self-government, and, since, according to oft-repeated and solemn statements, its object was to assist us in the realization of our national aspirations, it could only suggest that we might be granted our independence when we became capable of governing ourselves—the sovereign nation undertaking to prepare us suitably for such a condition.

Ten long years passed in this preparation, ten years of guardianship, ten years of painful experience, ten years of bitter deception, and as yet the problem remains unsolved. Very small indeed has been the progress made in this respect. Our advance is very slow; at least such is the opinion of Mr. Taft.

This old assertion of our incapacity is the stock argument of the smart imperialist politicians who clamor for American expansion. Among the most prominent of these is the President-elect of the United States. With what ingenuity does he evade the responsibilities of the situation!

In his report after enumerating the failures of the Filipinos in municipal government, which he calls the essence of self-government, Mr. Taft says:

> The result does not show that the Filipinos are capable of complete self-government, but it does not show, either, that they cannot reach a condition of capacity therefore and finally arrive at absolute self-government by means of the gradual extension of a partial self-government, extended as they gradually grow more and more capable of enjoying it.

Such is the manner in which Mr. Taft defines our political aptitude.

Incapable at present, yet endowed with qualities to attain final capacity by means of a slow preparation—so slow as to be simply disheartening.

Is this all the result realized by the Philippine nation in ten years of submission to a foreign guardianship? Sad destiny indeed for the Filipinos!

Furthermore, the sincerity of Taft may be doubted. In the imperialistic designs which betray themselves in the stronghold of genuine democracy the Philippine archipelago looms up as a most valuable prize, the open gate to China—the key of the Pacific—a strategical basis—a naval station—an inexhaustible source of coal and wood. Of course, therefore, ours must needs be a nation incapable for self-government for generations yet to come!

Let no one say that those who feel such sad presentiments and distrust are only the radicals—the theorists,—the demagogues among us; no, far from it; the most conservative Filipinos, the friends of the government, those who have been ardent partisans of the American sovereignty, do not hide their fear now lest the dominating

From *Taft's Term of Probation* (pamphlet), (Boston Anti-Imperialist League, November 30, 1908); reprinted in *The Philippines Reader: A History of Colonialism, Neocolonialism, Dictatorship, and Resistance,* ed. Daniel B. Schirmer and Stephen Rosskamm Shalom (Boston: South End Press, 1987), 50–51.

element today will before long be the owner of the entire country, and they do not hesitate to denounce the educational period of two generations which Taft has indicated.

The Philippine nation aspires more ardently with every passing day to be independent.

6. Indian Nationalists and American Journalist Disagree Over the Route to India's Independence, 1923

In reply to Mr. Saint Nihal Singh's splendid article in the *New York Evening Post,* Mr. Arthur Brisbane, one of the foremost American journalists, writes in the *Washington Herald:—*

"St. Nihal Singh, one of three hundred million Asiatics ruled in India by a few Englishmen thousands of miles away, has a grievance. When family members of the British empire meet, Canada, Australia and other colonies of European stock are represented by elected delegates. India's vast crowd is represented by men selected by English men.

"As usual, the trouble is within. It's the same if you lack force in yourself— some outside force will rule you. Among the 300,000,000 Asiatics of India dwell 100,000 Englishmen and they rule the 300,000,000 although they are outnumbered 3,000 to one. Could Mr. Singh imagine one Englishman keeping down 3,000 Irishmen? In these days you only get justice when you fight for it. Even then it is slow.

"In 5,000 years India has written millions of different books, and in all those books the word 'liberty' does not once appear. That's the trouble with India. Some day a man will come along, not a Gandhi trying to fight Manchester with a spinning wheel, but some person of mixed race with thick, hairy wrists, coarse hands, short, stubby fingers. He will not let England elect her delegates to the British empire's family reunion."

Mr. Brisbane bluntly gives expression to his sympathy for India's right to self-rule, but points out that India will not achieve self-government through the Gandhi method. The West does not care for Passive Resistance but wants to see an expression of manhood and womanhood through positive self-assertion. This attitude of the West is seen in appreciation of Kemal Pacha, fear of Lenin, and contempt for 300,000,000 of Indians ruled by less than 100,000 English soldiers.

TARAKNATH DAS.

Mr. Taraknath Das is no doubt aware, though Mr. Brisbane may not be, that in India there is a small number of men who believe in Ahimsā (non-killing, non-violence) as a spiritual principle which ought not to be violated even for the sake of political independence. They also believe that political freedom can be won by non-violent methods. We have not the least doubt that some at least of these men are among the

From Taraknath Das, "An American Attitude to Non-violent Non-cooperation in India," *Modern Review* 34 (1923): 751–752.

bravest on earth. In addition to the Ahimsāists on principle, there are adherents of Non-violence as a matter of right policy believed to constitute the majority, who do not advocate a war of independence because they believe that non-violent methods *may* suffice for the purpose of winning freedom and because fighting is impracticable and otherwise undesirable under present circumstances. Some at least of these men also are most fearless. The taunts of foreigners cannot deflect either class of Ahimsāists from their purpose and methods.

Mr. Brisbane is wrong in thinking that the Indian languages do not contain a synonym for "liberty," which itself is a word of Latin origin. But supposing there were no such Indian synonym; it would not prove the non-existence of love of liberty among Indians of ages past and present. The words "honour," "courtesy," "civility," "politeness," "gratitude," "patriotism," are not of Anglo-Saxon but of non-British origin. Does that prove that there were no honourable, courteous, civil, polite, grateful, or patriotic persons in English-speaking countries before the introduction of these words into the English language? If Mr. Brisbane and men like him would read even a school history of India before generalising they would find that Indians fought and died for their hearts and homes and liberty like other peoples. All the same, we confess with shame that our sacrifices for liberty are not what they ought to be.

7. Indian Immigrant Mohan Singh Recounts His Education in the United States, circa 1924

Mohan Singh was born in Amritsar, Punjab, India, April 1, 1901. In his family are his aged parents, one older brother, two younger brothers, and one married sister. His father, aged 64, gains his income from the ownership of three farm estates in different parts of the province. The largest farm consists of one thousand acres. These farms are leased and payment is received, either in a certain percent of the profits or perhaps one half of the crops raised. The father and sons will devote their time to travelling around seeing the condition of their estates, or in money-lending at home. The youngest son however is studying medicine at college. The family spends half of the time in town and the other half on a large farm six miles from the city. The products of this farm are used solely for the consumption of the family. The relatives are either in the military service, or in the same line of work as the Singhs, all of them being well-to-do, having gained their lands by inheritance. While in the country, now that the family has separated somewhat, leaving only the parents and one son at home, they have two servants whom they pay 12 or 15 rupees a month in addition to their board, room and clothing. The rupee, Singh said, is worth 33¢ in American money, but buys there, more than our dollar does here.

Singh had a private tutor till he was 12 years old, and then went to the middle school. There are very few government schools, so the people of means in the community contribute money and form a school for their children. Of course, only the wealthy children can attend. During high school the usual curriculum was studied:

From Miss Secord, "The Life History of Mohan." From the papers of William C. Smith (A-237, A-102, 84-A), Special Collections & University Archives, University of Oregon.

English, Persian, history, geometry, plane and solid, etc. In 1918 Mohan graduated from high school and entered Punjab University, which is financed by the people but under government control. Punjab is located about 200 miles from his home, so he lived in the dormitory, where all students not living in that town were compelled to live. No rooming with private families was permitted. During vacations, four or five times a year he returned home for visits. Punjab University, like the high school, is financed by the people, not through taxes but through special contributions by the wealthy people who wish an educational institution for their children. It is under government control, and receives small donations from the government. It is a school of liberal arts with a training school for grammar school teachers in connection with it. All the large provinces have their special schools for law, medicine and agriculture. Punjab has five buildings, a large central one and then smaller ones for chemistry, laboratories, etc. Students may also do their last two years of high school work at the college so that of the 1500 students only 1000 are actually doing college work. The teachers are natives with the exception of two Englishmen who teach English history and chemistry. The teachers gain their positions through graduation from the India college, or spending some time at Oxford and then returning. The curriculum includes chemistry, physics, Persian, English, philosophy, history, Sanskrit, mathematics, etc. Each subject must be continued for two years so that all its phases may be studied with thoroughness. Examinations are given every three months with finals at the end of the year and examinations covering the whole field at the end of two years. At the end of two years new subjects may be elected for the ensuing two years and a major may then be chosen.

The final examinations are not based on any text, but cover the field generally, necessitating wide reading in preparation. The high school examinations last a month and a failure in any subject means another year's work must be done and then examinations in all subjects repeated.

Life in the dormitories is rather rigidly outlined. As Freshmen, (called First Year Fools by the upper classmen) they live in rooms called cubicals, four in a cubical. The next year they are allowed separate rooms provided with bed, table, two chairs and book shelves, all extras being provided by the students from home. The school period is nine months. From April to June classes commence at 6 A.M. and continue until noon. During the winter months classes are hold from 9:45 to 4 P.M. "Everyone knows everyone else in school and there is very little snobbery," said Singh. "There are groups who go together but with no feeling of superiority to the rest." The First Year Fools are the foil of all jokes and pranks, but otherwise a fine sense of *comradeship* prevails. A few very wealthy students have their own special servants in addition to the ones provided in common by the college. Anyone can ring for a servant to go on errands, shine boots, etc.

There is a central building where all get together after classes to sing, play cards and talk. College sports form the principal diversion. They play hockey, cricket, tennis, football, volleyball, polo, and ride horse-back. Teams are formed with coaches to instruct much the same as in this country. The schools in India are not coeducational and the men's and women's colleges do not meet socially at all. Men do not dance there as all the dancing is done by professional girl dancers. Private homes entertain both boys and girls at parties, though none are allowed in public.

Singh went to college in the first place because his folks wanted him to become a lawyer, go to England to attend Oxford for two years and then come back and be a barrister. He would then be allowed to practice in the Supreme Court, a privilege not accorded ordinary lawyers. Titles count so much in India that if one does not have a noble name through inheritance it is absolutely necessary to acquire one by becoming a professional man, or one is doomed to obscurity regardless of wealth. Singh was more or less satisfied in college until an event occurred which changed his whole outlook. In 1919 the Rowlatt Act which was passed by England provided that no Nationalist could rise against the government and ask for dominion independence. The penalty for such an act was to be the forfeiture of life and property. The people held peaceful meetings of protest and sent petitions to Parliament. In 1919 a meeting of 53,000 people took place in an open air theatre. As it was a holiday the people all turned out. Fearing that the meeting would lead to a revolution, General Dyer and the governor of Punjab ordered the British troops to fire on the people. The meeting place was surrounded by a big wall and there was but one exit and the troops commanded that. They kept firing their machine guns into the crowd until their amunition gave out. As a result 935 men, women, and children were killed and this number included six students from Punjab College. Singh was present but saved himself by lying flat on the ground in a manner learned from military members of his family. When the firing ceased he jumped the wall and escaped.

After this there was a general feeling of hatred toward the English and Singh decided that he did not want to work for the British government and so refused to go to England to study. He saw that the Englishmen got all the good places even though better trained natives were available. Relatives of officials were given the first chance and no matter how long a native worked in a given position he was always liable to be removed so that a youngster just out of college might be given a position. Singh felt that if he could not work for the native government he would stay out of government work entirely.

Technical work did not appeal to Singh although relatives tried to interest him in engineering. He wanted a more liberal education, he said, and England being automatically eliminated from possible choices. America at once presented itself as a desirable place, for he was more familiar with the English language than with any other foreign language. He met an American professor who was teaching in a mission college who assured him that in America he could express himself quite freely without being put in prison as in India. He also met two Hindus who had studied in America while in political exile and after talking with them he decided to come to the United States. He felt that a greater variety of subjects would be available for study here and that eventually in India he would be able to use the liberal ideas gained even though at present they were too advanced to be safely advocated. In any event he thought the personal satisfaction gained would be worthwhile.

In July, 1920 Singh left home and went to California by way of China and Japan. He had a friend who was taking his Doctor's degree at the University of California in Berkeley and so joined him and registered as a Junior. He experienced no trouble in having his credentials accepted at the university. After one quarter there he decided that the classes, many of them having 800 and even 1000 students, were too large to give him the personal contacts with teachers and students that he wanted. His name started with "S," so he was always placed in a back row, which made it difficult for him to hear the lectures. He met a man who told him of Oregon Agricultural College so he went there and registered in the college of business administration and majored in money and banking. He enjoyed his stay at O.A.C. very much. The classes were small and he became intimate with the professors, and the Dean became one of his best friends. There were six other Hindus attending so they formed a club and lived together, read the newspapers together and discussed possible reforms they would try to inaugurate when they returned to India. In spite of the congenial group and friendliness of the professors, Singh was intensely homesick the first year, many times nearly giving up and going home but he would resolutely try to forget his home and go at his studying again. He had many difficulties. He could understand ordinary English but had not mastered English slang. One day a professor came to class and announced that "Tomorrow we will have a little banquet." Singh came to class the next day smiling and happy in anticipation of a good time and was most surprised to note that all the students around him were opening "blue books." He inquired why blue books were brought when the professor had said they would have a banquet instead of regular class, and was stunned to find that the professor had meant an examination. As a result he made a grade of 75. Later he went to the professor and asked him if he had said anything the day previous about giving a test. The professor said that he had announced it and Mohan reminded him that he had said they would have a party. The professor laughed heartily and promised to remember that foreigners did not understand slang, when he made up the grades.

Outside of talks with teachers and occasional remarks to the people sitting next to him in classes, he had no intercourse with the white people. He had expected the same politeness toward strangers here in America as he was used to in India and was greatly disappointed. In India any traveller is entertained in the village homes if there is no hotel, for the natives feel that hospitality should always be shown and never charge for the services they render. The Americans Singh knew in India were just as polite as his own people and he was surprised that the same qualities were not in evidence here. He remarked that people who had not travelled were very limited in their outlook and is convinced that their feelings are attributable to ignorance.

After graduating from the Oregon Agricultural school Singh desired to continue his studies in business administration and to take a Master's degree. O.A.C. did not offer graduate work in this field and while he was wondering where to go Dean Miller of the University of Washington came down there to dedicate a building and in his speech he told about the College of Business Administration at the University of Washington. Singh talked the matter over with his Dean and finally decided to come to Washington for his graduate work. While at the university in Seattle he has met quite a few Hindus, has taken part in the activities of the Cosmopolitan Club, composed of students of all nationalities who meet together with aim of becoming broad minded "citizens of the world," and of developing the international spirit among nations through a better understanding gained through comradeship and intellectual contributions of the type distinctive of each nation. This club has parties in private homes where Japanese, Chinese, Filipinos, Russians, Norwegians, Hindus, and Americans get together, play games, present stunts, put on musical programs in costume, show lantern slides of their countries, etc. At such gatherings no one thinks of anyone else's skin color. Each is liked or disliked for his personal qualities with no thought of nationality. Although Singh is but 23 years of age he has always worn a turban and a beard until last week when he removed both, making him less interesting looking, but probably more comfortable.

After obtaining his Master's degree in Money and Banking this June Singh plans to travel about the country for a year and perhaps work in a bank for a short time in order to study banking methods first hand. He will then return to India. He has no definite plans for work there but thinks he will either go into a bank or teach banking in some college. Later he wants to organize the farmers into a cooperative organization for purposes of production, marketing, etc. As it is, they lose all their money through the control of big companies. His family is influential among the farmers and the farm owners so he feels that he has a starting point. His plan is that this cooperative group should organize a bank as one feature of its activities.

Singh does not believe the British government will be in control of India for more than the next five years; that within that time India will at least have provincial autonomy, with real independence coming later. He feels it is the duty of the best men to go back to India and give to it the knowledge they have received elsewhere and he personally has never considered remaining in this country. His activities in banking in India he feels will be a good way to get into line for entrance into politics, his ultimate goal.

8. Korean Congress Declares Independence from Japanese Rule, 1919

An Appeal to America

We, the Koreans in Congress, assembled in Philadelphia, April 14–16, 1919, representing eighteen million people of our race who are now suffering untold miseries and barbarous treatment by the Japanese military authorities in Korea, hereby appeal to the great and generous American people.

For four thousand years our country enjoyed an absolute autonomy. We have our own history, our own language, our own literature and our own civilization. We have made treaties with the leading nations of the world; all of them recognized our independence, including Japan.

In 1904, at the beginning of the Russo-Japanese war, Japan made a treaty of alliance with Korea, guaranteeing territorial integrity and political independence of Korea, to co-operate in the war against Russia. Korea was opened to Japan for military purposes and Korea assisted Japan in many ways. After the war was over, Japan discarded the treaty of alliance as a "scrap of paper" and annexed Korea as a conquered territory. Ever since she has been ruling Korea with that autocratic militarism whose prototype has been well illustrated by Germany in Belgium and Northern France.

The Korean people patiently suffered under the iron heel of Japan for that last decade or more, but now they have reached the point where they are no longer able to endure it. On March 1st of this year some three million men, mostly of the educated class composed of Christians, Heaven Worshipers, Confucians, Buddhists, students of mission schools, under the leadership of the pastors of the native Christian churches, declared their independence from Japan and formed a provisional government on the border of Manchuria. Through the news dispatches and through private telegrams we are

From *First Korean Congress: Held in the Little Theatre, 17th and Delancey Streets (Philadelphia), 1919* (Sŏul Tŭkpyŏlsi: Pŏmhan Sŏjŭk Chusik Hoesa, 1986), 90–92, 31–36.

informed that 32,000 Korean revolutionists have been thrown into dungeons by the Japanese and over 100,000 men, women and children have been either killed or wounded so far. The Koreans have no weapons with which to fight, as the Japanese had taken away from them everything since the annexation, even pistols and fowling pieces. What resistance they are offering now against the Japanese soldiers and gendarmery is with pitchforks and sickles. In spite of this disadvantage and the horrible casualty among the Koreans, these people are keeping up their resistance and this demonstration is now nation-wide, including nearly all provinces. Japan has declared marital law in Korea and is butchering by thousands these unfortunate but patriotic people every day.

The Koreans in the United States and Hawaii have sent their representatives to Philadelphia, the Cradle of Liberty, to formulate a concerted plan with a view to stop this inhuman treatment of their brethren by the "Asiatic Kaiser," and to devise ways and means to help along the great cause of freedom and justice for our native land.

We appeal to you for support and sympathy because we know you love justice; you also fought for liberty and democracy, and you stand for Christianity and humanity. Our cause is a just one before the laws of God and man. Our aim is freedom from militaristic autocracy; our object is democracy for Asia; our hope is universal Christianity. Therefore we feel that our appeal merits your consideration.

You have already championed the cause of the oppressed and held out your helping hand to the weak of the earth's races. Your nation is the Hope of Mankind, so we come to you.

Beside this, we also feel that we have the right to ask your help for the reason that the treaty between the United States and Korea contains a stipulation in article 1, paragraph 2, which states as follows:

"If other powers deal unjustly or oppressively with either government, the other will exert their good offices, on being informed of the case, to bring about an amicable arrangement, thus showing their friendly feelings."

Does not this agreement make it incumbent upon America to intercede now in Korea's behalf?

There are many other good and sufficient reasons for America to exert her good offices to bring about an amicable arrangement, but we mention only one more, which is a new principle recently formulated at the peace conference in Paris. We cannot do better than to quote President Wilson's words, who is one of the founders of this new international obligation:

"The principle of the League of Nations is that it is the friendly right of every nation a member of the League to call attention to anything that she thinks will disturb the peace of the world, no matter where that thing is occurring. There is no subject that touches the peace of the world that is exempt from inquiry or discussion."

We, therefore, in the name of humanity, liberty and democracy and in the name of the American-Korean treaty and in the name of the peace of the world, ask the government of the United States to exert its good offices to save the lives of our freedom-loving breathren in Korea and to protect the American missionaries and their families who are in danger of losing their lives and property on account of their love for our people and their faith in Christ.

We further ask you, the great American public, to give us your moral and material help so that our breathren in Korea will know that your sympathy is with them and that you are truly the champions of liberty and international justice.

President Jaisohn: You have heard "The Appeal to America," as it has been read by Dr. Rhee. I would like to hear from you further on this appeal, as well as any delegate to the Convention who may wish to speak on the question.

Dr. Rhee: Mr. President, I don't believe that there is any need to make any changes at all in that resolution. I think the resolution should be adopted as read, and desire to make a motion to that effect.

President Jaisohn: Gentlemen, this is a Democracy. You do not want to take any important action unless you get the views of the people. We would like to get the views of this Congress, who represent their people. This is not old Korea; this is new Korea. We want to go by the will of the people, by the majority present. Speech is free, the press is free and that is one of the blessings we enjoy in this land.

Mr. Henry Chung: Mr. President, I agree with your views. I am sure that the government of the Republic of Korea will not use such a gag rule or any of those undesirable methods used in Japan. We have our friends in Korea who are defending our rights in a firm but passive manner. They cannot make any appeal to other powers, because the Japanese would not let such appeals go out of Korea. Therefore it is incumbent upon us who are in this free country to make this appeal known to the American people. I think our president made it clear to us this morning when he told us that thirty thousand of our fellow-countrymen fought on the Russian battlefront during the first period of the war in the cause of Democracy, and that our people contributed a large proportion of men and money to this cause. Therefore, I believe our appeal will receive favorable consideration from the American people.

A Delegate: Mr. President, I don't want my name known in the newspapers, and I can tell you afterward why I would not like my name to be recorded in the press.

President Jaisohn: If you wish to speak we must have your name. We cannot do that.

The Delegate: My reason for not giving my name is because I expect to return to Korea in a short time. However, my name is "Im."

President Jaisohn: The chair cannot recognize anybody who does not give his name. Now that you have given your name, I will state that I appreciate your position in the matter, but I tell you this, Mr. Im, if you lose your life for saying here what is right you lose your life worthily.

Delegate Im: The delegate delivered a short general address and concluded as follows:

I am heart and soul with you, my fellow-citizens. I asked that my name be not reported, but I did it because I thought it was not necessary and I merely wanted to say a few words in order to congratulate Dr. Rhee on the resolution presented by his committee as an "Appeal to America."

(There was further argument by Paihynk Kim in Korean, whom the president called to order because it was in a vein of needless criticism.)

Ilhan New: Mr. President, I understood as clearly as any gentleman here that there is not a delegate in this Congress, or that there is not a Korean in Korea, or in the world, who would not pass such a resolution. We all have our hearts in it and it is impossible for us to express in fitting terms what our feelings are, and I don't think it is necessary for us to consider this resolution any further.

President Jaisohn: We want to give everybody a chance to speak on the subject. That is the one business of this Congress, but we must confine ourselves to the subject that is before us, particularly in discussing the questions before this Congress and for the transaction of our business. If we go off on a tangent and go over the whole Encyclopedia of Government we won't get anywhere.

Mr. Syngman Rhee moved that this Congress adopt the resolution presented on "An appeal to America."

The motion was seconded by Mr. New and unanimously carried. . . .

At Independence Hall

President Philip Jaisohn led the delegates into the room in Independence Hall where the Declaration of Independence and the Constitution of the United States were signed. He then introduced the curator of Independence Hall, who in a brief address said:

> Ladies and gentlemen, in this room, with John Hancock sitting in the chair which you see here, with the table and the inkwell as it is here, with John Hancock presiding, the Declaration of Independence. was declared and signed, and the Liberty Bell which you saw as you entered the room proclaimed the event to all the world. The chair and the table are the same, and they are standing on the same spot just as they did when the Declaration of Independence was signed. In this same room also, with George Washington presiding, the Constitution of the United States was executed, declared and signed. It has been suggested that as you leave this room and pass by the Liberty Bell you touch it with you right hand.

President Jaisohn: I will now present to you Dr. Syngman Rhee, who will read the Korean Declaration of Independence.

Dr. Syngman Rhee then read the Korean Declaration of Independence by the Provisional Government of the Republic of Korea on March 1, 1919, which was adopted, followed by three cheers for the Republic of Korea and three cheers for the Republic of the United States.

The Declaration of Korean Independence

We, the representatives of 20,000,000 united people of Korea, hereby proclaim the independence of Korea and the liberty of the Korean people. This Proclamation stands in witness to the equality of all nations, and we pass it on to our posterity as their inalienable right.

With 4,000 years of history behind us, we take this step to insure to our children forever life, liberty and pursuit of happiness in accord with the awakening consciousness of this new era. This is the clear leading of God and the right of every nation. Our desire for liberty cannot be crushed or destroyed.

After an independent civilization of several thousand years we have experienced the agony for fourteen years of foreign oppression, which has denied to us freedom of thought and made it impossible for us to share in the intelligent advance of the age in which we live.

To assure us and our children freedom from future oppression, and to be able to give full scope to our national aspirations, as well as to secure blessing and happiness for all time, we regard as the first imperative the regaining of our national independence.

We entertain no spirit of vengeance towards Japan, but our urgent need today is to redeem and rebuild our ruined nation, and not to discuss who has caused Korea's downfall.

Our part is to influence the Japanese Government, which is now dominated by the old idea of brute force, so that it will change and act in accordance with the principles of justice and truth.

The result of the enforced annexation of Korea by Japan is that every possible discrimination in education, commerce and other spheres of life has been practiced against us most cruelly. Unless remedied, the continued wrong will but intensify the resentment of the 20,000,000 Korean people and make the Far East a constant menace to the peace of the world.

We are conscious that Korea's independence will mean not only well being and happiness for our race, but also happiness and integrity for the 400,000,000 people of China and make Japan the leader of the Orient instead of the conqueror she is at the present time.

A new era awakes before our eyes, for the old world of force has gone and out of the travail of the past a new world of righteousness and truth has been born.

We desire a full measure of satisfaction in liberty and the pursuit of happiness. In this hope we go forward.

We pledge the following:

1. This work of ours is in behalf of truth, justice and life and is undertaken at the request of our people to make known their desire for liberty. Let there by no violence.

2. Let those who follow us show every hour with gladness this same spirit.

3. Let all things be done with singleness of purpose, so that our behavior to the end may be honorable and upright.

The 4252d year of the Kingdom of Korea, 3d month, 1st day.

9. Korean Immigrant Margaret Pai Joins the Korean Independence Movement, 1919

Two years after she came to the new world Hee Kyung gave birth to her first child. She and her husband named her Chung Sook, meaning "straight and upright" and "clear and gentle like a brook." I was that daughter.

Although my father enjoyed learning his craft at the furniture shop, the wages he brought home still barely covered the necessities of life.

Home, church, and a society called the Youngnam Puin Hoe made up my mother's whole world. At her church she helped form the Methodist Ladies Aid Society, a powerful organization that provided a network of services reaching every Korean family in the community. Although the immigrants were all poor, so dedicated were the Society members that no family went without food or a roof over their heads (immigrant men often lost their jobs); a mother who became ill could depend on other mothers to help her; and a mother with a newborn baby did not have to rise from her bed until she was strong. All these services were rendered despite the fact that every woman was burdened with heavy responsibilities of her own.

From Margaret K. Pai, *The Dream of Two Yi-min*, pp. 7–9, 11, 17–21. © 1989 University of Hawaii Press. Used with permission.

The Youngnam Puin Hoe was a society that a good number of the immigrant women belonged to. The members were *yi-min,* from a province in Korea called Kyungsangdo. These lively, bright-eyed ladies laughed easily and talked incessantly when they got together. They met once a month on Sunday afternoons (they observed the Sabbath by attending church and by not working that day). They helped the poor and the sick as an extension of the Methodist Society's work but looked for other projects as well.

A project that captured their fancy and enthusiasm soon appeared. The desire for freedom of their country from Japanese rule was always in their hearts. They spoke often of possible ways Koreans could win liberty, and of hopes for Japan's ultimate destruction. One day they heard a rumor from Los Angeles that spread to Hawaii, Shanghai, Manchuria—wherever Koreans lived.

It was a plan for a massive demonstration in Korea that would bring freedom and relief from Japan's rule. The purpose of the demonstration was to show the imperialists of Japan that Koreans were a strong, unified people, not the weaklings the oppressors made them appear to be. The public expression would attract the world's attention and cause nations to come to the rescue of Koreans suffering from oppression and humiliation.

Month after month as new details of the plan were received by the Youngnam Puin Hoe, the members' interest grew. The women declared they would go to Korea and participate in the demonstration.

However, it wasn't long before their enthusiasm diminished and their group plans collapsed when they realized they lacked the funds to cover the boat fare. Furthermore, who would care for their husbands and babies while they were gone?

My mother begged her friends to find a way to Korea and persisted in fanning the fire of fighting for freedom. She told them of the disturbing letters from her parents, who reported that more and more oppressive measures were being imposed on Koreans by the Japanese military. She urged, "Let us go and do what we can to help. We cannot let these measures continue unchecked!"

But the ladies shook their heads. They admired my mother for her unflagging patriotism and determination to take part in the plan. They said, "He Kyung, we think you should go and represent all of us. We will pay for your trip."

In the summer of 1918 my parents agreed that I, then three-and-a-half years old, should accompany my mother to Korea while my father stayed behind. Because I had been ill for months with the whooping cough, I was thin and frail.

"I'm concerned about Chung Sook," Father said. "Hee Kyung, don't you think you should wait until she's stronger?"

"But we may not reach Korea in time for the demonstration." She was torn. Finally she added, "My brother is a physician back home. You know, we can't afford a doctor here. But as soon as we get there I will put our daughter under his care."

The Youngnam Puin Hoe publicly announced to the immigrant community that Hee Kyung Kwon was their emissary to the demonstration, although the date for it was yet unknown. The Koreans responded with generous donations from their hard-earned wages to the cause, and the funds gathered were entrusted to my mother to take with her. . . .

After the first week of our arrival, my mother left the house each morning and was gone for most of the day. She was becoming reacquainted with friends she used to know, she told us, and she hinted at meeting some important people. . . .

In September my mother decided to go to Seoul, the capital city. A week later she wrote to Grandmother that she was enrolling in Ewha College because that was where she found the people she needed to be with.

I did not know then that Ewha, a college for women, was seething with nationalism and that the majority of the students were revolutionaries. These young intellectual radicals detested the Japanese and were fomenting an overthrow of their rule. They secretly planned one day to join other political groups in the country in a massive show of patriotism.

"I don't know how long your mother will stay in Seoul," Grandmother said to me. "Shall we go and visit her?"

"Yes, yes," I answered. This was the first time I had been separated from my mother and I missed her.

One day in October when the weather was clear, with no anticipation of rain or snow, Grandmother and I, accompanied by one of the servant girls, Sook Cha, took the train to Seoul.

When we met my mother in her dormitory room, we found her in a blue military uniform. How strange she looked without her *chi-ma* and *cho-gori*. She removed the blue cap from her head and sat on the floor, crossing her legs as a man would. I wanted to be close to her and climbed on her lap.

"I'm so sorry you can't be with me every day, Chung Sook," she sighed, stroking my head.

"Please come home, Omoni," I begged.

Her chin grew hard. She looked tense. "Chung Sook, I can't. We're almost ready." She did not explain.

Grandmother seemed to understand. She did not say much. She did not try to persuade Mother to return home. She merely stared at her daughter with sad eyes. . . .

Several months passed. One day I was aware of a tense, cloying stillness hanging in the air. I was confused. I felt as if everyone were waiting for something dreadful to happen. Grandmother seemed preoccupied and did not care to entertain me. For long periods she merely sat on a flat pillow on the floor with needlework in her hands, which she barely looked at. Her usually serene face wore a frown—two little lines between her eyes.

"Why won't you talk to me, Grandma?" I asked several times. She'd turn to me and look as if she was about to say something, then stare off into space and forget to answer. I amused myself the best I could; because the weather was bad I could not go outside.

When the servant girl set up the low *sahng* and served our evening meal, Grandmother hardly touched her food. Nor did she prod me to eat as was her habit. Grandfather sat stolid at his own *sahng* and dined without his usual chatter. For some reason, he had not gone out that day.

I wondered what my grandparents were waiting for. They reminded me of frightened children who expected something terrible to happen to them because they had been naughty.

Suddenly we were jolted by a knock on the door.

"*Nu gu si o?*" Grandfather demanded. "Who are you?"

"Bong Chu it is, sir," came the reply. I recognized the voice of one of our servants.

Grandmother quickly rose and pushed open the papered sliding door. Gusts of icy wind blew into the room while Bong Chu removed his shoes. He walked in wearing his thick, padded white stockings. There was some snow still clinging to his coat and hair. His eyes were very wide, like those of a scared animal. Had he been naughty, I wondered?

He bowed respectfully. Then the words rushed out of his mouth: "Today, March 1, 1919, is a bad day for Korea! The Japanese have killed so many of our people!" Bong Chu began to sob.

"*Ai gu, ai gu!*" my grandparents moaned in shock.

"*A-ni-o!*" Grandmother cried. "No, no! Not my daughter, Hee Kyung!" She held her fists together tight as if in anguished prayer.

"*A-ni-o,*" Bong Chu said, comforting her. "I saw your daughter. She was marching near the front of the parade. Hundreds and hundreds—maybe thousands—of people lined the streets to watch. They shouted, '*Man sei! Man sei!*' Then the Japanese police came. They beat up the crowd—everybody in their path. They cut down our Korean flags the marchers carried. They used sabers, sticks, and rifles! It was terrible! People were falling all around. Blood on the street. Everybody trying to scatter and escape. And your daughter—I saw her. She was shoved into a police wagon with many others. I think she's in jail now."

"*Ai gu, ai gu. U chak ko?*" Both my grandparents looked helpless. "What shall we do?"

I was not able to follow Bong Chu's account. I asked, "What's happened to my mother? Is she coming home soon?"

Grandmother turned to me and beckoned. Tears were streaming down her cheeks. I moved over and sat next to her.

She spoke quietly, "Bong Chu, thank you for the news. You had a long journey to Seoul today. Were there many people on the trains?"

"Yes, so many! I had to push my way to get on one. Every train was packed." Bong Chu's flat young face was flushed. He was moving his body as if he were still on the train.

"Go now and have your supper." Grandmother motioned him to leave. Bong Chu bowed and went out the door.

The tense stillness of March 1 lingered through the next few days. Grandfather stayed at home. No one dared to go out to the street. The military commander's curfew rule forced people to remain in their homes.

But our servants were able to tread the back alleys and gather information, and they reported what they heard to my grandparents. They learned that the demonstrations for independence had taken place all over Korea, even in the small towns and outlying provinces. The largest parade, it was believed, was in Seoul. Thousands had joined in the marches, waved flags, cried for justice and an end to Japanese oppression. When the police started shooting and slaughtering the marchers, the Koreans wildly destroyed or damaged custom houses, police stations, and court buildings, especially those in the outskirts of the capital. The Japanese angrily retaliated by setting fire to many Korean churches and schoolhouses.

How quickly and brutally the Japanese suppressed the revolutionists! During the parade in Seoul a young woman's hand, proudly waving the Korean flag, was cut off by a Japanese sword. But before the flag touched the ground, she caught it with her other hand. More than 2,500 Koreans were thrown in prison in Seoul alone that day. Among the women activists incarcerated was my mother, Lee Hee Kyung.

⊕ E S S A Y S

In the first essay, Stefi San Buenaventura, who teaches Asian American studies at the University of California at Davis, shows how the colonization of the Philippines in words and deeds linked Filipinos with Native Americans and blacks in the American racial consciousness. The second essay, by New Mexico State University historian Joan M. Jensen, highlights the activism and surveillance of East Indian immigrant Taraknath Das. The peripatetic Das spread seeds of Indian nationalism among Indian immigrants and students in the early twentieth century. For this reason and his anti-imperialist publications, he was denied American citizenship and trailed by American, Canadian, and British intelligence agents. Such suspicion of Indian revolutionaries led a San Francisco federal jury in 1918 to convict twenty-nine Indian nationalists on charges of conspiring against America's World War I ally, Great Britain. Finally, the third essay, by Lili Kim, 2001 Ph.D. recipient and Visiting Assistant Professor of History at Hampshire College, addresses the Korean independence movement in Hawai'i and the United States, paying particular attention to the role played by ordinary people.

The Colors of Manifest Destiny in the Philippines

STEFI SAN BUENAVENTURA

When the United States took possession of the Philippine Islands in the aftermath of the Spanish American War, the Filipinos were in the middle of an unfinished revolution against more than three centuries of Spanish colonial rule. The Filipino struggle was essentially similar to the struggle of the Cuban people for whom the Americans had gone to war to liberate them from Spanish tyranny and establish their political independence. It seemed logical, therefore, for the Filipinos to assume that the Americans would assure the sovereign status of the Philippines once the war was over—but they were wrong.

Not having heard or known much of the Philippines before 1898, the Americans quickly realized that the Islands offered a wealth of accumulated benefits for U.S. expansionist interests that included: opening trade doors to China, establishing a strategic military outpost overseas, extracting Philippine natural resources, promoting American business interests and, of course, advancing the Anglo-Saxon cause. In the words of Republican Senator Albert Beveridge of Indiana, the most popular advocate of American imperialism during this time:

> The Philippines are ours forever. . . . And just beyond the Philippines are China's illimitable markets. We will not retreat from either. We will not repudiate our duty in the archipelago. We will not renounce our part in the mission of our race, trustee under God, of the civilization of the world.

Anti-imperialist Americans supported the Filipino revolutionary position and opposed the imposition of U.S. rule in the Philippines, as asserted in this paraphrase of Republican Senator George F. Hoar of Massachusetts, a most prominent voice of the anti-imperialist movement: "To annex foreign territory and govern it without

From Stefi San Buenaventura, "The Colors of Manifest Destiny: Filipinos and the American Other(s)," *Amerasia Journal* 24, no. 3 (winter 1998): 2–4, 6–10. Copyright © 1998 Regents of the University of California. Used with permission.

the consent of its population . . . is utterly contrary to the sacred principles of the Declaration of Independence and is unconstitutional. . . ." To the expansionists, however, the overall compelling drive to keep the Philippines as an American possession was deeply rooted in a national belief in the "God-given right" of the American Anglo-Saxon civilization to flourish and lead in the world, a canon which came with a racial corollary that viewed non-Anglo people as inferior and barbaric (which, in the case of the Philippines, applied not only to the natives but to their *Catholic* Spanish masters also). Thus, although the Philippine Islands "are so valuable in themselves that we should hold them," according to Beveridge,

> It will be hard for Americans . . . to understand the people. They are a barbarous race, modified by three centuries of contact with a decadent race. The Filipino is a South Sea Malay, put through a process of three hundred years of superstition in religion, dishonesty in dealing, disorder in habits of industry, and cruelty, caprice, and corruption in government. It is barely possible that 1,000 men in all the archipelago are capable of self-government in the Anglo-Saxon sense.

And, as far as the Declaration of Independence was concerned, it

> . . . applies only to people capable of self-government. How dare any man prostitute this expression of the very elect of self-governing peoples to a race of Malay children of barbarism, schooled in Spanish methods and ideas? And you, who say the Declaration applies to all men, how dare you deny its application to the American Indian? And if you deny it to the Indian at home, how dare you grant it to the Malay abroad? . . .

It was this critical question of what to do with a native population who were not considered "biologically fit" for the privilege of U.S. citizenship that defined the absolute power which the Americans had over the Filipino people. Not only were the natives dispossessed of their rights to self-sovereignty, now their colonial status was essentially a non-entity until the U.S. decided what it wanted to do. In Frederick Merk's words: "Inoffensively and inconspicuously a principle was thus adopted, new to the Constitution and revolutionary—the principle that peoples not candidates for equal statehood in the Union were annexed and their status as colonial subjects left to Congress. This was imperialism." . . .

White America and "Dissimilar" Peoples

The idea of annexing territory occupied by "dissimilar" peoples was not unfamiliar to the dominant Euro-Americans whose movement westward in building a continental republic began with the disposition and displacement of the Indian peoples who stood in the way of the white settlers, the land, and "progress." Its span included the conquest of Mexican lands in the U.S.-Mexican War of 1846–48, all the way to the U.S. military support of the 1893 overthrow of the Hawai'ian kingdom by American businessmen who wanted total control of the resources and governance of the islands and who finally succeeded, in 1898, in achieving their treacherous goal of making Hawai'i a territory of the United States.

The Filipinos resisted the American occupation of the Islands and the violation of their rights, in spite of obvious U.S. military superiority, in a brief but bloody war which ensued shortly after the transfer of the Spanish colonies in U.S. hands in the Treaty of Paris of December 10. It was not limited to a "Tagalog insurrection" in Luzon (a rationale given to undermine the seriousness of the revolution), but extended to the provinces of the Visayas and Mindanao regions among other Filipino ethno-lingusitic groups of the archipelago. Imbibed with a heightened sense of national consciousness and cognizant of the libertarian ideas of the Enlightenment and the democratic principles on which the American republic was created, Filipino revolutionary leaders who fought the Spaniards, particularly Apolinario Mabini, found it rather incomprehensible to accept American domination even under the guise of President William McKinley's policy of "Benevolent Assimilation." Refusing to sign an oath of loyalty to the United States, imprisoned, and banished to Guam, Mabini maintained his protest against the imposition of American hegemony on a people who wanted their own political self-determination. Mabini also believed that continuing the Filipino struggle for independence served as a reminder to the Americans "that they, once upon a time, found themselves in a position similar to that of the Filipinos when they were fighting Great Britain for their rights and eventual emancipation. Also, in the same manner that in their struggle against Great Britain, the Americans invoked the help of France, the Filipino[s] had hoped to see these very Americans help them defend their liberties instead of fighting them."

What Filipino nationalists failed to understand at this time was the permeating philosophy of Manifest Destiny which shaped white American perception of dissimilar natives. In the case of the Indian, Walter L. Williams provides a direct link between the Native American condition and the U.S. acquisition of the Philippines. He argues that the annexation of the Islands was not the first American experience with colonial rule because U.S. Indian policy during the nineteenth century showed "a clear pattern of colonialism toward Native Americans" and that "this policy served as a precedent for imperialist domination over the Philippine Islands and other islands occupied during the Spanish-American War."

> United States treatment of Indian groups after the passage of the frontier slowly evolved from the initial status of "nation," as represented by the treaty system. This form of international agreement implicitly recognized native sovereignty and nationhood. After white settlement had surrounded a native group, however, their status was seen by whites as something less than independent. In Cherokee Nation v. Georgia (1831) [Chief Justice John] Marshall admitted that the treaties did recognize the Cherokees as "a state" but he asserted that they were not a foreign state. . . . In what was to become the most quoted case relating to Indians in the nineteenth century, Marshall had established a de facto protectorate status for Indian "domestic dependent nations."

Williams also makes a distinction between "expansion" and "colonialism" by stating that the Indian tribes of "dissimilar" civilizations were not "merely pushed aside as expansion occurred" but "were enveloped under United States control without being given citizenship status. If we define colonialism in this way, to distinguish it from land ownership expansion, we might well conclude that Marshall's decision approached a conception of Indian 'wards' as colonial subjects as early as the 1830s."

Indian and Filipino "Wards"

Granting the Filipino natives "ward" status without citizenship rights was a very convenient solution to the problem of not having to assimilate a "barbarous" people living in a distant U.S. territory in the Pacific. More importantly, the Indian "colonial policy" offered a way out of a constitutional conundrum as imperialists argued that American western territories were, in fact, colonies and "that the Constitution gave Congress

supreme and total power over the territories . . . to rule as they pleased without granting citizenship or constitutional rights to the inhabitants" . . . or only "to some of the
inhabitants without granting rights to them all." Williams points out that Republican
Senator Henry Cabot Lodge of Massachusetts, a staunch imperialist, "made the comparison explicit between congressional power over Indians and over Filipinos" in a
statement documented in the *Congressional Record* of February 1, 1900:

> When our great Chief Justice John Marshall . . . declared in the Cherokee case that the
> United States could have under its control, exercised by treaty or the laws of Congress,
> a "domestic and dependent nation," I think he solved the question of our constitutional
> relations to the Philippines.

Unfortunately, the expedient application of this policy and the legal calculations
taken to manipulate the colonial status of the Filipinos came with all the beliefs
that racist American held against Indian peoples and indigenous populations. "Not
only did imperialists see Indians and island subjects as having a similar legal relations to the United States, but they saw behavioral similarities as well," writes
Williams. Like many journalists and observers who visited the Philippines immediately after its occupation to report about the people and island conditions, Phelps
Whitmarsh, for example, described the native Filipino as the "sleepy, forgetful,
servile Indian" in an article published in the *Outlook* in 1900. Theodore Roosevelt,
in particular, "made the most comparisons" and "habitually employed words like
'wild and ignorant,' 'savages,' 'Apaches,' and 'Sioux' to Filipinos."

The "Indian connection" to the Philippine situation was also evident in the military occupation of the Islands after Dewey accomplished his naval mission. For one
thing, the general who was sent to head the first expedition to the Philippines was
Wesley Merritt, a leading "Indian Fighter" of the 1870s, not to mention a long list
of others—generals, officers, and soldiers—who were veterans of the U.S. warfare
against the Indians and who were now face to face with a foreign indigenous people.
Williams adds:

> The impact of imperialist rhetoric on actual events in the Philippines, especially during
> the 1899–1902 insurrection, influenced the feeling among United States troops that this
> was merely another Indian war. In the first place, most of the regiments in the islands
> were from the western states, where memories of Indian wars were strongest. . . . Those
> troops who did not already accept the analogy were taught upon arrival "that the Filipinos
> were savages no better than our Indians."

Imperialism and Negro "Citizenry"

Just as the Indian peoples were the expedient object of continental destruction and
colonial control, a major "other" American population at home played a crucially
parallel role in the formation of American imperialism and annexation. Rubin
Francis Weston argues that in post–Civil War development, political accommodation between North and South and white racial instincts prevented the "nationaliza-
tion of civil liberties" as the nation proceeded forward after slavery was abolished.
"It was in this atmosphere of national unity that imperialism was born," a unity that
"had been achieved at the expense of the Negro people," adds Weston. Consequently, the state laws that challenged the Fourteenth Amendment and the growth
of Jim Crow laws leading to the *Plessy* v. *Ferguson* decision of 1896, finally led to
the institutionalization of segregation and second-class citizenry to which the

American Negro was relegated and which constituted a convenient precedent in the treatment of dissimilar peoples as the U.S. proceeded to claim their native lands:

> It is important to note the degree to which the new nationalism extended to encompass the thinking and actions of Americans and the manner in which minority rights were concomitantly compromised by the United States, in the atmosphere of the new nationalism, as it annexed dissimilar peoples.

Although there was great apprehension at the turn of the century about annexing territories of (and with) nonwhite populations because of all the implications for their possible but unwanted entry into American society, the U.S. had constructed a "protective" policy based on the precedent of the Indian colonial issue discussed earlier whereby the natives of these annexed territories were designated *in*eligible for citizenship. Consequently, their treatment as second-class citizens—a Negro precedent, in Weston's position—became the subsequent "logical" phase in this racial construct of American imperialism and overseas venture.

> The actions of the federal government during the imperial period and the relegation of the Negro to a status of second-class citizenship indicated that the Southern point of view would prevail. The racism which caused the relegation of the Negro to a status of inferiority was to be applied to the overseas possessions of the United States.

Domestically, however, the unequal treatment of Negro Americans had extended to other nonwhite immigrants, especially the "colored" peoples from Asia who first came to the United States in mid-nineteenth century. In the case of the Filipinos, their journey to America as "nationals" at the beginning of the 1900s came as a direct result of the American crossing of the Pacific to claim possession of the Philippine Islands.

As the U.S.'s "furthest frontiers," the remote but extremely rich Philippine archipelago titillated the economic appetite and imperial designs of the emerging global power of the twentieth century. However, although this acquisitive venture was completely and totally an Anglo-American imperial blueprint *vis a vis* dissimilar, native populations, it inevitably invoked the national racial thinking on the two American others, the Indians and the Negroes. The Native Americans served as the prototype for American colonial policies and administrative strategy in the governing of the Filipino *indios* in the archipelago. The African Americans represented the justification and model for extending "second-class citizenry" and Jim Crow segregationist behavior in the Philippines.

Exporting Independence to Colonial India

JOAN M. JENSEN

The first colony in which the British engaged in political surveillance was India. That surveillance followed Indians who immigrated to the West Coast and began to organize. From 1908 through the 1930s, the British, either directly through their own agents, through Canadian agents, or through United States officials, kept a close eye on the Indian community. . . .

From Joan M. Jensen, *Passage from India: Asian Indian Immigrants in North America*, 163–166, 170–174. © 1988 Yale University Press. Used by permission.

. . . In January 1909, the [Canadian] Laurier government employed W. C. Hopkinson to conduct political surveillance within the Indian community. Hopkinson built his career around the desire of the British to know what Indians were doing to oppose their rule in India. . . .

. . . Hopkinson established an elaborate surveillance system within the immigrant community. Offering his translating services to the United States immigration authorities in Vancouver and Montreal in return for free entry into the United States for himself and for his Indian informants, he was soon watching Indian activities on both sides of the border. He also provided U.S. immigration authorities with information on suspects in Canada in return for information on Indians entering the United States. Copies of his reports went to the Canadian government as well as to the British colonial office in London.

Hopkinson investigated and reported on many Indians between 1909 and 1914, but perhaps the two best known were Taraknath Das and Har Dayal, both of whom attempted to organize Sikh dissent against British rule in India. While other government officials frequently stressed Sikh opposition to British rule in India, Hopkinson believed that nationalist students were the real cause of unrest among the normally loyal Sikhs and was hence absorbed with the activities of the young intellectuals Das and Dayal.

Hopkinson may have been watching Das long before his official job as a Canadian agent began in 1909. It is possible that Hopkinson may have been sent to Canada by British India officials to watch just such student radicals as Das. Born near Calcutta, Das was one of the young Indians allowed by the British to receive a university education in order to qualify for the Indian civil service. Caught up in the politics of the antipartition movement in Bengal, Das never graduated. He left college in 1905 to become what he later called "an itinerant preacher, explaining the economic, educational, and political conditions to the masses of the people." When the Indian government put out a warrant for his arrest, Das fled to Japan. There, he joined other dissident students who hoped to continue their political activities while obtaining industrial training that would be useful in reviving ancient industries in India or developing new ones in their place. A number of Indian students had congregated at the University of Tokyo, and Das joined them, preaching the cause of Indian freedom. The British ambassador, noting students' criticism of British rule in India and their new freedom with the Japanese students, asked that they be deported. Faced with an inhospitable host, Indian students in Tokyo began to look about for a new place to study. "If you want to see the civilized use of machinery, go to America," one Indian student advised a friend. Japanese students told Das that he could also seek political asylum in the United States.

Das was twenty-two when he arrived in Seattle on 16 July 1906, alone and broke. After working for a while as an unskilled laborer, he drifted down to California, where he worked in the celery fields along with other Indians. Then he worked in a hospital and read books in his spare time, until a professor of medicine helped him get work at the chemistry laboratory at the University of California at Berkeley. Das enrolled as a student and tried to file a declaration of intention to become an American citizen; after being turned down, he took a competitive examination for the position of translator with the United States immigration service. His rating won him a job in Vancouver in July 1907. . . .

. . . In early 1908, as the Canadian government was moving to exclude Indian workers, Das published the first issue of *Free Hindusthan,* in which he urged Indians both in Canada and in India to resist exclusion. If Canada excluded them, he warned, so would the United States. He also warned that Canadian exclusion would affect British rule in India: "The foundation of the British Empire is undermined on the very day when the legislative body unjustly supports measures, owing to which the natives of Hindusthan cannot go freely to other parts of the British Empire."

Vancouver immigration officials had no difficulty in tracing the newspaper to Das. McInnes, then in Vancouver to investigate the riot, reported to Laurier that Das was using the threat of revolt in India as a bluff to make the Canadian government hesitate in establishing an exclusion policy. The Canadian government promptly protested to Washington about Das's attacks on "British prestige." The American immigration official in Vancouver called Das into his office soon after to inform him that he must either cease editing the *Free Hindusthan* or resign. Das refused to do either. On 18 April 1908, the United States government dismissed him. Das continued to organize. . . .

Hopkinson . . . discovered that Das was encouraging students to organize. Das joined the students at the University of Washington at Seattle in January 1910, where, with the help of a history professor, he organized the Association for the Promotion of Education for the People of India. He also organized a Hindustan club for Indians. From Seattle, Das went on to organize students at the University of California at Berkeley. The routine for Indian students traveling to Berkeley was already well established by the time Das arrived in 1910. The *Modern Review* of Calcutta gave explicit advice for students who wished to study in the United States. They must arrive with a good knowledge of English, a hundred dollars in pocket, and the government certificate of identity. Students had already organized to help others make the trip. One Berkeley student wrote an article for the *Modern Review* outlining how to study on the Pacific Coast. He advised a year of high school in the United States, which could be obtained without fee at Berkeley High School, only an eight-minute walk from the university. Prospective students could get a letter of recommendation from the American consul general to the immigration inspector at Seattle and identification papers from the organization sponsoring the student. When the immigration inspector asked whether the student believed in polygamy, he should answer no. At Seattle, a friendly American would meet the newcomer and take him to New India House. From Seattle, the student was to write to Berkeley, and another student would arrange to meet him. It was best to leave India at the end of February, arrive in Berkeley at the end of April, and then work during the summer or take a summer course. At Berkeley, students could live on twelve dollars a month. A student could get by on $250 a year; for $350 he could live in luxury. He could make twenty-five or thirty cents an hour working, or he could sell shawls or other Indian products.

Das found more than thirty Indian students enrolled at Berkeley in 1910. Students chose Berkeley primarily because tuition was only fifteen dollars per semester. Classes were large at Berkeley, some over five hundred, and often students were assigned seats alphabetically. There were thus few personal contacts between professor and students—a difficult adjustment for students who had experienced small classes in India, close rapport with their Indian professors, and emphasis on wide reading rather than on textbook cramming for exams. Those who asked for special attention from American professors with heavy teaching loads sometimes received an unsympathetic response from faculty members annoyed with students who did not willingly conform to convention. Nor were most Berkeley professors at that time sympathetic to Indian students' criticisms of the university or of British imperialism. "They are generally revolutionaries, or if not such when they come, are soon taken in hand by their fellows and converted to revolutionary ideas," complained one Pacific Coast professor.

Students at Berkeley had already encountered West Coast discrimination before Das arrived. In the Northeast, a turban could be a passport to high society. When travelling in the Southeast, Indians had to wear their turbans lest they be taken for black Americans and encounter even more discrimination. Because of the opposition to Indian laborers in West Coast cities, however, most students learned not to wear turbans. Hotels and boarding houses, including the YMCA, usually turned students away regardless of their head covering because of their color. One student remembered spending a cold winter night in a Southern Pacific depot in northern California after being turned away from a dozen hotels. When students found rooms, they were often refused use of the kitchen to prepare their own food. Most public restaurants, including those at the University of California, which were run by students, refused to serve Indians. Typical fare for the Indian college student was graham bread, fruit, milk, eggs, and nuts. In an era when college clubs determined all social activities on campus, Indians were refused membership in the clubs. A few Berkeley Indians formed a fraternity, but they were refused admission to the interfraternity council.

Such discrimination made students feel, sometimes for the first time, that political organizing might be necessary. Many had been sponsored by societies that looked forward to a nationalism that would eliminate caste in India, and students writing for the *Modern Review* had warned Indians to leave their caste prejudices behind if they wanted to come to America to study. Although many of the students had not worked in India, they often accepted the tradition of working their way through college at Berkeley. One student worked cleaning house in return for room and board. Another became a linen keeper in a San Francisco hospital. Many students joined Sikh laborers doing summer farm work in the fields. In answer to the question of caste, one Berkeley student wrote, "We do not pay any more respect to a Brahman than we do to Pariah, Hindu or Muhamadan, Christian, Brahman or Khsatriya, Namasudra or Chandall, all are equally welcome in this Temple of Lord Jagannath. In fact, we never know or care to know to what caste anyone belongs." To find the earmarks of caste in a country that provided an example of political democracy seemed wrong, then, and being treated as outcasts deepened the students' nationalism. Discrimination led to a growing consciousness of their common political oppression. They now felt like Indians and were ready to act collectively as Indians.

Students had already found their way to the Vedanta temple in San Francisco, an elaborate three-story edifice that combined Gothic, Hindu, Shiva, and Muslin designs in an aggregation of towers, minarets, and colonnades topped by a precariously perched American eagle. Because it housed the Vedanta Society, the building also became a home for new students. Euro-American women who attended services at the temple often helped students to find jobs and lodging, and Unitarian ministers often invited them to speak to congregations about India. At these church lectures, Indian students from Berkeley felt free to speak out against British rule. At one YWCA meeting, where missionaries denounced the Hindu religion and praised British rule, sixteen Indian students stationed themselves in the front row and arose one after another to defend their culture until the speaker abruptly closed the meeting. Life for these student exiles in California, wrote a Swiss student at Stanford who later married one of the men, was "rather pathetic, an uncertain hovering between two worlds, permeated by a sense of irremediable hopelessness and futility."

Nationalism was a powerful antidote to the feeling of helplessness. When Das arrived in the Bay Area, he told students about restrictions on immigration, collected funds to fight cases in court, and urged students to remain vocal in their opposition to British rule. When the Friends of Hindustan was formed in September 1910 to help poor students, Das urged that the group become political. By March 1911, the students community was split between loyalists who wished to support the British in India and nationalists such as Das who continued to speak out against British rule. The Friends of Hindustan dissolved that month. Some students joined California radicals, but most nationalist students concentrated on getting more students to join them. The nationalists formed the Hindustan Association of the United States. Das returned to the University of Washington, where he obtained his master's degree in 1911. He then applied for citizenship again.

Hopkinson's informants told him about Das's citizenship attempt late in June. He immediately advised the Canadian minister of the interior, W. W. Cory, asking him to interrupt the proceedings by giving information to the American government that Das was an anarchist agitating against British rule in India. Das, he claimed, wanted to return to India at the time George V was to be crowned emperor of India, claim the protection of the American flag, and raise international complications. Cory informed Bryce of these predictions, and Bryce in turn informed the state department informally that this was why Das was seeking naturalization. In a letter to secretary of state Philander Knox, Bryce warned that Das was suspected of being an anarchist and a revolutionist. The state department replied to Bryce that it had no evidence that Das was trying to obtain citizenship papers or that he was an anarchist. Das was allowed to file his application for citizenship. He then applied to the University of California at Berkeley to work on a doctorate in political science and moved to Berkeley.

Informants within the Indian student community, now regularly reporting to Hopkinson, noted Das's departure for Berkeley. Late in September 1911, Hopkinson arrived in San Francisco, where he went to Angel Island to find out what officials knew about Das and other nationalist Indian students. These officials said they were surprised that the British government had not been aware of the situation created in California by the Indian students. Hopkinson then saw the secretary of the AEL, who provided him with clippings of lectures made by Das. Back in Seattle, Hopkinson obtained the promise of immigration inspectors to testify against Das if he proceeded with his application for citizenship. There, Hopkinson also discovered that on 16 October, Indians had called a mass meeting to commemorate the anniversary of the partition of Bengal. The Indian national flag was hoisted, and the meeting ended with the singing of "Bande Mataram." Hopkinson dutifully reported all this information and warned that Indian students had been influencing white women to help them in the name of humanity. When he made a report in early October 1911, he also suggested that the British consulate in San Francisco should take more note of the Berkeley students. An agent should be assigned specifically to watch Das, who was gaining prominence by assisting immigrants to secure their "alleged rights" when they received no protection from consular officers. The situation in the Bay Area was a good opportunity for agitators, Hopkinson concluded. There was no doubt in his mind that Berkeley was now the main center of agitation.

In Washington, Bryce was still attempting to prevent Das from becoming a citizen, but the state department insisted that there was not sufficient evidence to deny Das citizenship. Bryce then wrote to Connaught asking for information on Das that could be used officially in court to oppose naturalization on the grounds of "anarchist tendencies." In December 1911, Das left Berkeley and moved to Bandon, Oregon. There he purchased sixty acres of land and opened the Bandon Clay Products Company. Then, on 10 January 1912, he appeared in the circuit court of Coos County at Coquille, Oregon, and filed a petition of intention to become a citizen. Connaught sent a secret telegram to Bryce, saying that all the evidence was in the hands of Hopkinson, who was to use it at his discretion, in cooperation with Hunter in Seattle, in opposing Das's naturalization. Hopkinson was still not sure whether the bureau of naturalization would reject Das's application, but the Seattle office forwarded the information to Washington, D.C., and the department of commerce and labor notified the justice department that its files suggested that Das would not make a desirable citizen. The department asked the United States attorney at Portland to oppose Das's naturalization. There is no evidence that Das engaged in any political activity for the next two-and-a-half years.

Korean Independence Movement in Hawai'i and the Continental United States

LILI KIM

For pioneer Korean immigrants in Hawai'i and the continental United States the most devastating experience of their immigrant lives was Japan's colonization of their beloved homeland in 1910. More than any harsh working conditions they faced, the news of Japan's annexation of Korea delivered a crushing blow. As one man recalled, learning the news of the Japanese colonization robbed him and other fellow Korean immigrants of the last source of inspiration and hope for enduring the harsh realities of their lives:

> Dear Friends . . . We left our home country to make money in America, the land of prosperity. Didn't we promise that we would go back after we made our fortune? To fulfill that promise, we swallowed our pride and sweated our blood in the sugarcane fields. We almost died of dehydration in the grape plantation. We constructed new railroads, and we worked in coal mines. . . . But wasn't it our promise of going back that inspired us to endure all this? But not too long after we left, how the news of the fall of

"Korean Independence Movement in Hawai'i and the Continental United States" is an original contribution by Lili Kim, Visiting Assistant Professor of History at Hampshire College, written 2001.

our country tore our hearts apart! Just thinking about it now gives me warm tears in my eyes. How we cried in our plantation fields and mining stations. And how we could not help running around like we had lost our minds!

Without a home country to go back to, Korean immigrants felt "orphaned," even though many originally had planned to stay and try their luck in America. They felt that being stateless and having no legitimate government to protest on their behalf left them vulnerable to abuses by their employers and other nationals. Aside from these practical concerns surrounding their own lives, Koreans in Hawai'i and the continental United States genuinely mourned the devastating impact Japanese colonialism would have on Korea's culture and history.

As a result, Koreans at home and abroad mobilized to fight Japanese colonial powers after World War I. Joining forces with the wider movement of Koreans abroad—including those in China, Cuba, Russia, and Mexico—Korean immigrants in Hawai'i and the continental United States launched an extensive independence movement away from the watchful eyes of the colonizers. Their active and zealous participation in the Korean independence movement in turn heightened their Korean nationalism and strengthened their identity as Koreans in the United States.

The first major wave of Korean immigrants began in 1903 with the recruitment of workers for Hawai'ian sugar plantations. The American plantation owners found a key ally in Horace Allen, the United States minister to Korea, whose close ties to the Korean emperor made him an effective recruiter of Korean laborers. Hoping to better their economic condition and looking for a place more hospitable to their newly adopted Christian beliefs, over 7,000 Koreans migrated to Hawai'i between 1903 and 1905. In contrast to their inflated expectations of the opportunities awaiting them in Hawai'i, what they found when they arrived was over ten-hour days of back-breaking labor in the sugar plantation fields that paid a mere 67 cents a day. Gradually, many Koreans migrated to cities like Honolulu to open their own tailor shops and shoe-repair shops, as well as to the West Coast, where they sought construction and mining jobs with slightly better pay.

Japanese Colonialism in Korea and U.S. Culpability

Japan had been eyeing Korea since 1876, when this island nation forced Korea to sign the Treaty of Kanghwa, which commercially opened Korea to Japan. Following its victory over China in the Sino-Japanese War of 1895, Japan asked Korea to sign a provisional agreement that required Koreans to accept Japanese reform. On the face of it, the reform called for the modernization of Korean educational, judiciary, and fiscal systems as well as its government, but in actuality it translated into disassociating Korea from Chinese social, cultural, and political influences. While Japan's attempt to replace China as the dominant power in Korea failed because of international pressure on Japan to surrender the Liaotung Peninsula and withdraw from Korea, Japan again forced Korea to sign a treaty that gave Japan the right to use Korea for military purpose in the Russo-Japanese War of 1904 despite Korea's declaration of neutrality. The treaty ending that war in September 1905 promised the independence of Korea but required that Korea incorporate Japanese recommendations on international administration.

American leadership, or lack thereof, helped Japan to penetrate Korea even further. When Japanese victory in the Russo-Japanese War became evident, Horace Allen, still the United States minister to Korea, urged President Theodore Roosevelt to intervene so the Japanese would not take complete control over Korea. Roosevelt, however, purposely ignored the request, believing that the Japanese occupation of Korea would prevent further expansion of Russian power elsewhere. Moreover, in the secret Taft-Katsura Agreement of July 1905, Roosevelt had already acknowledged Japan's dominance over Korea in exchange for Japan's acquiescent recognition of U.S. hegemony in the Philippines. With such negotiations with Japan, the United States knowingly violated the Korean-American Treaty of 1882, which stipulated that "[t]here shall be perpetual peace and friendship between the President of the United States and the King of Choson (Korea) and the citizens and subjects of their respective governments. If other powers deal unjustly or oppressively with either government, the other will exert good offices, on being informed of the case, to bring about an amicable arrangement, thus showing their friendly feelings." Despite this promise of mutual aid, the United States simply looked the other way while Japanese imperial power over Korea expanded, and even anticipated Japan's full dominance over Korea.

In September 1905, a defeated Russia acknowledged Japan's interest in Korea and promised not to interfere with its plans to conquer Korea. With Russia out of the way, Japan quickly moved to establish protectorate over Korea. The Protectorate Treaty of 1905 gave Japan complete power to administer Korea's internal and external affairs. The Korean emperor, Kojong, protested the Protectorate Treaty and appealed for international help. Japan then cleverly forced Kojong to step down and pass the throne to his imbecile son Sunjong in 1907. Finally on August 29, 1901, Emperor Sunjong was forced to relinquish Korea to Japan. Japan thus realized its long-dreamed goal of annexing Korea and went on to exercise cruel and harsh colonial rule in Korea.

The Korean Presence in Hawai'i and the Continental United States

After Japan established a protectorate over Korea in 1905, numerous organization with an explicitly political purpose sprang up within the overseas Korean community. Although many of these organizations were short-lived and did not exercise much influence, the sheer number of them indicates how prolific Koreans were in organizing, as well as how fragmented the community was, especially given the relatively small number of Koreans living in Hawai'i and the continental United States at the time. New political organizations in Hawai'i included the Kongniphoe, or Mutual Aid Society, founded in April 1905; the Changanhoe, or Self-Strengthening Society, founded in October 1905; and the Noso Tongmaenghoe, or Young and Old Alliance, founded in February 1907. Koreans in the continental United States also began forming various political organizations, including branches of the ones already established in Hawai'i and others, such as the Kongjehoe, or Mutual Salvation Society, founded in New York in 1907; the Tongmaeng Sinhunghoe, or Newly Rising Alliance, founded in Seattle in 1907; and the Taedong Pokukhoe, or All-Together Protecting the Nation Society, founded in San Francisco in 1907. In total, no fewer than twenty-four Korean political organizations existed by 1907, all with the same purpose of fostering Korean nationalism and retaliating against the growing power of Japanese colonialism in Korea.

The problem of fragmentation was not lost on Korean community members. In December 1907, thirty delegates from the twenty-four organizations held a unification meeting and agreed to form one single umbrella organization called the Hanin Hapsonghoe, or United Korean Society, which later became a branch of the Korean National Association. Its headquarters was located in Honolulu and had forty-seven chapters and over 1,000 members. This was the first of many attempts of unification to come.

One major political event that further unified Korean Americans was the 1908 assassination by two Koreans of a pro-Japanese U.S. advisor to Korea, Durham White Stevens. Stevens, while visiting San Francisco, had publicly declared that Koreans were not capable of self-governing and that they benefited from the protection of the Japanese government under the protectorate. Outraged by what they considered a humiliating and condescending statement, Koreans in San Francisco unsuccessfully attempted to intimidate Stevens into retracting his comment. On March 23, 1908, two Korean men, In-hwan Chang and Myong-won Chon, shot Stevens, who died two days later in the hospital. When the two men were arraigned for the murder of Stevens, Koreans from all organizations in Hawai'i and the continental United States—as well as from Mexico, China, and Japan—contributed a total of $7,390 in defense funds. Chon was released before the trial, since it was Chang who had actually fired the shot that fatally wounded Stevens, and there was no evidence to prove that the assassination attempt was a conspiracy. Chang was convicted of second-degree murder and sentenced to twenty-five years. He served only ten years and was later released for good behavior. With such a publicized case, Koreans in the United States made their nationalism known and their sentiments toward Japan clear to American officials and the American public.

The formation of the Korean National Association (KNA) marked another major effort to unite Koreans in the United States. The Korean National Association was founded in San Francisco in 1909, later electing Chang-ho Ahn as its first president in 1910. Discouraged by the corruption in Korean government, Ahn espoused what he called "educational nationalism" to cultivate able Korean leaders, which he firmly believed was the key to developing a stronger Korea. Ahn founded the Hungsadan, or Young Korean Academy, in San Francisco in 1910 to train Korean American leaders to serve in the Korean National Association. The Korean National Association went on to have an influential branch in Hawai'i, as well as 116 chapters in Mexico, Siberia, Cuba, and Manchuria.

Korean Independence Activities After Annexation

After Japan officially colonized Korea in 1910, the Korean independence movement in the United States picked up steam dramatically. Hawai'i, where the majority of pioneer Korean immigrants still resided, became the hotbed of the Korean independence movement. After the Hawai'i branch of the Korean National Association was established in 1910, Young-man Pak, a well-respected proponent of military training for Korean independence, joined the organization, leadership in 1912 as the editor of its newspaper, the *Korean National Herald*. Serious about creating a powerful Korean independence movement in Hawai'i, Pak invited Syngman Rhee to join him shortly after his arrival. Rhee had just completed his doctoral studies at Woodrow Wilson's Princeton University. Because of his education and connections to prominent U.S. officials, Rhee was regarded with deep respect and had a large loyal following in Hawai'i.

Pak and Rhee soon became archrivals. They clashed over strategies to restore Korean independence and competed for power and respect in the community. While Pak believed that military training was the key to fighting back against Japan, Rhee firmly supported education and diplomacy as the most pragmatic ways to regain Korean independence. When Pak successfully founded the Kundan, or military academy, in 1914, Rhee quickly maneuvered to curtail Pak's popularity by spreading rumors that Pak was a traitor. Not to be outdone, Pak and his supporters accused Rhee of mishandling the Korean National Association's finances.

The March First Movement in 1919, the most notable (and bloodiest) resistance effort in Korea, helped to unify factions in Hawai'i. On March 1, 1919, thirty-three patriots in Korean signed the Declaration of Korean Independence, and more than a million people participated in a peaceful march, shouting *"Teahan Toknip Manse"* ("Long Live Korean Independence"). Caught by complete surprise, Japanese officials met the Korean demonstration with brutality. Between March and December 1919, when such protests recurred repeatedly, over 7,500 Koreans were killed and 15,000 injured, while some 45,000 people were arrested. In the meantime, an independent Korean provisional government was set up secretly in Shanghai, and later moved to Chungking, China, where it continued to exist in exile.

Inspired by the heroic acts of so many ordinary Korean men and women who fearlessly put their lives on the line during the March First Movement, Koreans in Hawai'i and the continental United States revitalized their anti-Japanese spirit and rededicated themselves to the common goal of Korean independence. Philip Jaisohn, one of the few Koreans who came to the United States as a political refugee before the mass migration of 1903, and the first Korean to earn a medical degree in the United States, organized a three-day liberty conference in Philadelphia. The conference site was a strategic attempt to link the Korean struggle with the birth of American independence. On April 14, 1919, about 150 Koreans from Hawai'i and the continental United States met to reaffirm their support for Korean independence and the new Korean provisional government in China. The conference ended on April 16 with a delegate parade to Philadelphia's Independence Hall, where Rhee read the Declaration of Korean Independence signed in Korea.

Ordinary People as Ardent Nationalists

While the elite male leaders jostled for power and visible positions in the community, ordinary Korean immigrants quietly toiled in the background to fund and support the independence movement. It was their hard-earned money and their grassroots participation on which the Korean independence movement was built. Making weekly or monthly contributions to independence funds in their respective independence organizations and churches, pioneer Korean immigrants put their faith (sometimes much too blindly) in their leaders to make something of their contributions and energy toward achieving Korean independence. Given their meager salaries, coming up with extra money for contributions was not easy. Yet they did not hold back on fulfilling what they considered as their duty. Recognizing the importance of and need for money to fund the independence activities, Koreans conscientiously gave what they could.

Sometimes the thorny issues of finances—how much one needed to survive and how much one could realistically contribute—were a source of intense arguments between husbands and wives. Women, who usually had a more realistic sense of how much money was needed to run the household, often resisted their husbands' contributions, which were generous beyond their means. Inez Park-Soon Kong recalled a particularly heated argument her parents had over donations to the independence cause. In 1933 Rhee insisted on attending the League of Nations meeting in Geneva to make a case for Korean independence. Thus, his followers were asked to make a bigger contribution than usual to fund the trip. As one can imagine, this kind of economic burden put a strain on Koreans' already strapped finances. Kong remembered:

> Syngman Rhee went to Geneva to plead the case for Korean independence. Money needed to be raised and I had just returned from Korea at age sixteen. My father decided to give Syngman Rhee a thousand dollars. My mother blew her top. "We can't afford that kind of money!" she said. She was so much more practical than my father. She thought Rhee was crazy. I could hear my parents having that argument. My father said, "*We* have to support him."

Husbands often won such arguments, and wives had to adjust their home finances to make ends meet.

Not only making contributions, but attending organization meetings also required a certain level of financial stability and class standing. Those who had multiple jobs or had to work long hours could not afford the time to attend meetings. For example, Pun Cho Yu, a picture bride whose husband could not work because of his heart condition, spoke of the financial hardship that prevented her from active participation in the independence movement: "I worked day and night. I was too busy working to participate. Other women would curse me for not coming when they saw me. I was too busy working. I had not time." Yu's inability to attend meetings said more about her class status than about the level of her patriotism for Korea.

Pioneer Korean immigrant women stepped out of their traditional gender roles as wives and mothers to help the independence cause. While by no means immune from factional divisions within the community, Korean women substantially contributed to the goal of Korean independence. Maria Hwang, leader of the Korean Women's Relief Society of Hawai'i, was someone whom the community people typically called a "warrior" woman for immigrating to Hawai'i by herself *with her children* after leaving her husband, who had a concubine. Although Korean husbands commonly kept concubines in the early 1900s, Hwang did not accept it as a part of her marriage. She allegedly told her husband before leaving him: "I can no longer live under these circumstances with you. I am taking our children to America and will shame you in the future. These children shall become educated and I shall become a wonderful person. You can remain as you are."

Under Hwang's leadership, the Korean Women's Relief Society, founded in 1919, contributed in no small way to the Korean independence movement. The members collected money through membership fees of $1 and annual dues of $3. They sponsored various fundraisers by selling homemade Korean cuisine. They also raised money but going door-to-door to sell copies of the Declaration of Korean Independence of 1919. They sent money to families whose members were killed or injured in the March First Movement, and to victims of famine and flood in Korea. They also contributed to the Korean Provisional Government in China, the Korean Commission in Washington, D.C. (set up by Rhee for his publicity efforts), and the Korean Independence Army in China and Manchuria.

The Korean Women's Patriotic Society of California, also founded in 1919 after the March First Movement, had a similar purpose and function. Members organized fundraisers in conjunction with their campaign to boycott Japanese products by selling homemade soy sauce and bean paste. Their strict personal code required that members give up meat on Tuesdays and Fridays, and soy sauce on Wednesdays, to contribute to the Thrift Fund. The money collected was used to fund various independence projects in coordination with the Korean National Association. Although women of both the Korean Women's Relief Society and the Korean Women's Patriotic Society took on more feminine projects like sale of Korean food to raise funds, the extent to which they were able to contribute financially to the independence movement through their organizations was a tribute to Korean women's ability to redefine the boundaries of traditional gender roles.

Despite the bitter factions that curtailed the effectiveness of the Korean independence movement, Korean immigrants never gave up on their hope of someday seeing Korea liberated. Doing their part for the Korean independence movement, pioneer Korean immigrants, in the meantime, slowly established themselves as upstanding residents—or more accurately, a model "Orientals." As a 1930 U.S. military intelligence report on Koreans in Hawai'i declared, "Koreans on the whole" were "law abiding" and "a desirable section of the Oriental population." Occupying the ironic lot of trying to prove themselves as desirable "Orientals" in the country that readily supported Japanese colonialism in Korea, pioneer Korean immigrants embraced their identity as proud Koreans in mourning the loss of their motherland. Not surprisingly, Koreans in Hawai'i and the continental United States welcomed the shocking news from Pearl Harbor on December 7, 1941, and the declaration of war on Japan by the United States.

✎ F U R T H E R   R E A D I N G

Brody, David. "Building Empire: Architecture and American Imperialism in the Philippines," *Journal of Asian American Studies* 4 (2001): 123–145.

Bulosan, Carlos. *America Is in the Heart: A Personal History* (1943).

Charr, Easurk Emsen. *The Golden Mountain* (1961).

Choy, Bong-Youn. *Koreans in America* (1979).

Compomanes, Oscar V. "New Formations of Asian American Studies and the Question of U.S. Imperialism," *Positions: East Asia Cultures Critique* 5 (1997): 523–550.

Hess, Gary R. "The 'Hindu' in America: Immigration and Naturalization Policies and India, 1917–1946," *Pacific Historical Review* 38 (1969): 59–79.

Jacobson, Matthew Frye. *Barbarian Virtues: The United States Encounters Foreign Peoples at Home and Abroad, 1876–1917* (2000).

Jensen, Joan M. *Passage from India: Asian Indian Immigrants in North America* (1988).

Kim, Min-Jung. "Moments of Danger in the (Dis)Continuous Relation of Korean Nationalism and Korean American Nationalism," *Positions: East Asia Cultures Critique* 5 (1997): 357–389.

Lee, Mary Paik. *Quiet Odyssey: A Pioneer Korean Woman in America* (1900).

Leonard, Karen Isaksen. *Making Ethnic Choices: California's Punjabi Mexican Americans* (1992).

———. *The South Asian Americans* (1997).

Letters in Exile: An Introductory Reader on the History of Filipinos in America (1976).

Lyu, Kingsley K. "Korean Nationalists Activities in Hawai'i and the Continental United States, 1900–1945, Part I: 1900–1919," *Amerasia Journal* 4, no. 1 (1997): 23–90.

———. "Korean Nationalist Activities in Hawai'i and the Continental United States, 1900–1945, Part II: 1919–1945," *Amerasia Journal* 4 no. 2 (1977): 53–100.

Melendy, H. Bret. *Asians in America: Filipinos, Koreans, and East Indians* (1977).

Merk, Frederick. *Manifest Destiny and Mission in American History: A Reinterpretation* (1963).

Miller, Stuart Creighton. *"Benevolent Assimilation": American Conquest of the Philippines, 1899–1903* (1982).

Pai, Margaret K. *The Dreams of Two Yi-min* (1989).

Posadas, Barbara M. *The Filipino Americans* (1999).

Rafael, Vicente L. *White Love and Other Events in Filipino History* (2000).

Savage, Timothy L. "The American Response to the Korean Independence Movement, 1910–1945," *Korean Studies* 20 (1996): 189–231.

Stephanson, Anders. *Manifest Destiny: American Expansionism and the Empire of Right* (1995).

Welch, Richard E., Jr. *Response to Imperialism: The United States and the Philippine American War, 1899–1902* (1979).

Williams, Walter L. "United States Indian Policy and the Debate over Philippine Annexation: Implications for the Origins of American Imperialism," *Journal of American History* 66 (1980): 810–831.

CHAPTER
6

Orientalism and Popular Culture, 1904–1930s

The movements to exclude Asian immigration and the colonization of the Philippines coincided with the prominence of eugenics, a field of scientific racism predicated on the assumption that among humans there exists an innate racial hierarchy in which whites, especially "Anglo-Saxons," are on top. The political significance of eugenics as a justification for immigration exclusion and colonial conquest, as well as for white working-class social mobility, is well documented in Chapter 3–5. What remains to be considered, however, is how such racist theories about Asians took on mass appeal. It is too simplistic to assume that all whites were predisposed to see Asians as dangerously different from themselves. A better alternative is to ask how the vast majority of Americans came to accept this perspective as a fact of nature. In the first third of the twentieth century, institutions of popular culture did much of the work of propagating racial understandings of Asians to American consumers.

There was no better example of this than the world's fair, which by the St. Louis exhibition in 1904 attracted millions of visitors to its massive and ostensibly authentic displays of "backward" racial groups. But it is important to remember that world's fairs were made possible by the rapid rise in urbanization, wage labor, and its attendant leisure time. In this context, even traditional cultural mediums, such as newspapers and literary publications, took on much more significance and capital as they catered to the rapidly expanding populations in American cities. And the editors of such publications realized then, as they do now, that manipulating racial fears can sell products. Another dimension of popular culture to consider is the dawn of the motion picture industry. The movies, of course, would become the ultimate showcase of the consumer society, selling everything from automobiles to dishwashing detergent. But films also "sold" less tangible products like beauty, lifestyles, and racial sensibilities. In this sense, Hollywood popularized American Orientalism from the early days of silent film.

DOCUMENTS

The documents in this chapter reveal how Asians were portrayed in ways that were entwined with the domination of Asian immigrants in the United States. Yet equally important here is the fact that Asian Americans too were culture makers, whose writings embodied the dilemmas and possibilities of their experiences. Document 1 reveals writer Jack London's take on the "Yellow Peril" after serving as a war correspondent during the Russo-Japanese War. The most dangerous outcome of Japan's victory over Russia, London warned *San Francisco Examiner* readers, was that the Japanese, whom he referred to as a "Brown" race, were now in a position to strengthen their hand vis-à-vis the West by allying with the much more numerous and thus more feared "Yellow" Chinese. Document 2 is a photograph of the "living exhibition" of Filipinos at the St. Louis World's Fair in 1904. To many in attendance, the natives' scantily clad costumes confirmed their "savagery." Document 3 is an excerpt from an oral history interview conducted in 1924 with a Filipino immigrant who discusses the interconnection between anti-Filipino images and his negative experiences in the United States. Document 4 is an excerpt from Wallace Irwin's *Seed of the Sun,* a novel seeking to warn Americans about the evils of Japanese immigration.

The final four documents concentrate on various depictions of the Chinese. Document 5 is a portrayal of Chinese merchant wives by the first American novelist of Chinese descent, the Eurasian Sui Sin Far. Document 6 is a Chinese American student's list of American beliefs about the Chinese. Document 7 is a movie studio proposal regarding the promotion—what in Hollywood was known as exploitation—of *The Painted Veil,* a 1934 film set in China. Finally, in Document 8, anthropologist Harold R. Isaacs analyzes the influence of famous author Pearl S. Buck in shaping the image of the Chinese in the American imagination.

1. Writer Jack London Decries the New Yellow Peril, 1904

Here we have the Chinese, four hundred million of him, occupying a vast land of immense natural resources—resources of a twentieth century age, of a machine age; resources of coal and iron, which are the backbone of commercial civilization. He is an indefatigable worker. He is not dead to new ideas, new methods, new systems. Under a capable management he can be made to do anything. Truly would he of himself constitute the much-heralded Yellow Peril were it not for his present management. This management, his government, is set, crystallized. It is what binds him down to building as his fathers built. The governing class, entrenched by the precedent and power of centuries and by the stamp it has put upon his mind, will never free him. It would be the suicide of the governing class, and the governing class knows it.

Comes now the Japanese. On the streets of Antung, of Feng-Wang-Chang, or of any other Manchurian city, the following is a familiar scene: One is hurrying home through the dark of the unlighted streets when he comes upon a paper lantern resting on the ground. On one side squats a Chinese civilian on his hands, on the other side squats a Japanese soldier. One dips his forefinger in the dust and writes strange, monstrous characters. The other nods understanding, sweeps the dust slate level with his hand, and with his forefinger inscribes similar characters. They are talking. They cannot speak to each other, but they can write. Long ago one borrowed

From Jack London, "The Yellow Peril" (1904), in London, *Revolution and Other Essays* (New York: Macmillan, 1910), 277–289; reproduced in S. T. Joshi, ed., *Documents of American Prejudice* (New York: Basic Books, 1999), 439–444.

the other's written language, and long before that, untold generations ago, they diverged from a common root, the ancient Mongol stock.

There have been changes, differentiations brought about by diverse conditions and infusions of other blood; but down at the bottom of their being, twisted into the fibres of them, is a heritage in common—a sameness in kind which time has not obliterated. The infusion of other blood, Malay, perhaps, has made the Japanese a race of mastery and power, a fighting race through all its history, a race which has always despised commerce and exalted fighting.

To-day, equipped with the finest machines and systems of destruction the Caucasian mind has devised, handling machines and systems with remarkable and deadly accuracy, this rejuvenescent Japanese race has embarked on a course of conquest, the goal of which no man knows. The head men of Japan are dreaming ambitiously, and the people are dreaming blindly, a Napoleonic dream. And to this dream the Japanese clings and will cling with bull-dog tenacity. The soldier shouting "Nippon, Banzai!" on the walls of Wiju, the widow at home in her paper house committing suicide so that her only son, her sole support, may go to the front, are both expressing the unanimity of the dream.

The late disturbance in the Far East marked the clashing of the dreams, for the Slav, too, is dreaming greatly. Granting that the Japanese can hurl back the Slav and that the two great branches of the Anglo-Saxon race do not despoil him of his spoils, the Japanese dream takes on substantiality. Japan's population is no larger because her people have continually pressed against the means of subsistence. But given poor, empty Korea for a breeding colony and Manchuria for a granary, and at once the Japanese begins to increase by leaps and bounds.

Even so, he would not of himself constitute a Brown Peril. He has not the time in which to grow and realize the dream. He is only forty-five millions, and so fast does the economic exploitation of the planet hurry on the planet's partition amongst the Western peoples that, before he could attain the stature requisite to menace, he would see the Western giants in possession of the very stuff of his dream.

The menace to the Western world lies, not in the little brown man, but in the four hundred millions of yellow men should the little brown man undertake their management. The Chinese is not dead to new ideas; he is an efficient worker; makes a good soldier, and is wealthy in the essential materials of a machine age. Under a capable management he will go far. The Japanese is prepared and fit to undertake this management. Not only has he proved himself an apt imitator of Western material progress, a sturdy worker, and a capable organizer, but he is far more fit to manage the Chinese than are we. The baffling enigma of the Chinese character is no baffling enigma to him. He understands as we could never school ourselves nor hope to understand. Their mental processes are largely the same. He thinks with the same thought-symbols as does the Chinese, and he thinks in the same peculiar grooves. He goes on where we are balked by the obstacles of incomprehension. He takes the turning which we cannot perceive, twists around the obstacle, and, presto! is out of sight in the ramifications of the Chinese mind where we cannot follow.

The Chinese has been called the type of permanence, and well he has merited it, dozing as he has through the ages. And as truly was the Japanese the type of permanence up to a generation ago, when he suddenly awoke and startled the world with a rejuvenescence the like of which the world had never seen before. The ideas of the West were the leaven which quickened the Japanese; and the ideas of the West, transmitted by the Japanese mind into ideas Japanese, may well make the leaven powerful enough to quicken the Chinese.

We have had Africa for the Africander, and at no distant day we shall hear "Asia for the Asiatic!" Four hundred million indefatigable workers (deft, intelligent, and unafraid to die), aroused and rejuvenescent, managed and guided by forty-five million additional human beings who are splendid fighting animals, scientific and modern, constitute that menace to the Western world which has been well named the "Yellow Peril." The possibility of race adventure has not passed away. We are in the midst of our own. The Slav is just girding himself up to begin. Why may not the yellow and the brown start out on an adventure as tremendous as our own and more strikingly unique?

The ultimate success of such an adventure the Western mind refuses to consider. It is not the nature of life to believe itself weak. There is such a thing as a race egotism as well as creature egotism, and a very good thing it is. In the first place, the Western world will not permit the rise of the yellow peril. It is firmly convinced that it will not permit the yellow and the brown to wax strong and menace its peace and comfort. It advances this idea with persistency, and delivers itself of long arguments showing how and why this menace will not be permitted to arise. To-day, far more voices are engaged in denying the yellow peril than in prophesying it. The Western world is warned, if not armed, against the possibility of it.

In the second place, there is a weakness inherent in the brown man which will bring his adventure to naught. From the West he has borrowed all our material achievement and passed our ethical achievement by. Our engines of production and destruction he has made his. What was once solely ours he now duplicates, rivalling our merchants in the commerce of the East, thrashing the Russian on sea and land. A marvellous imitator truly, but imitating us only in things material. Things spiritual cannot be imitated; they must be felt and lived, woven into the very fabric of life, and here the Japanese fails.

It required no revolution of his nature to learn to calculate the range and fire a field-gun or to march the goose-step. It was a mere matter of training. Our material achievement is the product of our intellect. It is knowledge, and knowledge, like coin, is interchangeable. It is not wrapped up in the heredity of the new-born child, but is something to be acquired afterward. Not so with our soul stuff, which is the product of an evolution which goes back to the raw beginnings of the race. Our soul stuff is not a coin to be pocketed by the first chance comer. The Japanese cannot pocket it any more than he can thrill to short Saxon words or we can thrill to Chinese hieroglyphics. The leopard cannot change its spots, nor can the Japanese, nor can we. We are thumbed by the ages into what we are, and by no conscious inward effort can we in a day rethumb ourselves. Nor can the Japanese in a day, or a generation, rethumb himself in our image.

Back of our own great race adventure, back of our robberies by sea and land, our lusts and violences and all of the evil things we have done, there is a certain integrity, a sternness of conscience, a melancholy responsibility of life, a sympathy and comradeship and warm human feel, which is ours, indubitably ours, and which we cannot teach to the Oriental as we would teach logarithms or the trajectory of projectiles. That we have groped for the way of right conduct and agonized over the soul betokens our spiritual endowment. Though we have strayed often and far from righteousness, the voices of the seers have always been raised, and we have harked back to the bidding of conscience. The colossal fact of our history is that we have made the religion of Jesus Christ our religion. No matter how dark in error and deed, ours has been a history of spiritual struggle and endeavor. We are preëminently a religious race, which is another way of saying that we are a right-seeking race.

"What do you think of the Japanese?" was asked an American woman after she had lived some time in Japan. "It seems to me that they have no soul," was her answer.

This must not be taken to mean that the Japanese is without soul. But it serves to illustrate the enormous difference between their souls and this woman's soul. There was no feel, no speech no recognition. This Western soul did not dream that the Eastern soul existed, it was so different, so totally different. . . .

The religion of Japan is practically a worship of the State itself. Patriotism is the expression of this worship. The Japanese mind does not split hairs as to whether the Emperor is Heaven incarnate or the State incarnate. So far as the Japanese are concerned, the Emperor lives, is himself deity. The Emperor is the object to live for and to die for. The Japanese is not an individualist. He has developed national consciousness instead of moral consciousness. He is not interested in his own moral welfare except in so far as it is the welfare of the State. The honor of the individual, per se, does not exist. Only exists the honor of the State, which is his honor. He does not look upon himself as a free agent, working out his own personal salvation. Spiritual agonizing is unknown to him. He has a "sense of calm trust in fate, a quiet submission to the inevitable, a stoic composure in sight of danger or calamity, a disdain of life and friendliness with death." He relates himself to the State as, amongst bees, the worker is related to the hive; himself nothing, the State everything; his reasons for existence the exaltation and glorification of the State.

The most admired quality to-day of the Japanese is his patriotism. The Western world is in rhapsodies over it, unwittingly measuring the Japanese patriotism by its own conceptions of patriotism. "For God, my country, and the Czar!" cries the Russian patriot; but in the Japanese mind there is no differentiation between the three. The Emperor is the Emperor, and God and country as well. The patriotism of the Japanese is blind and unswerving loyalty to what is practically an absolutism. The Emperor can do no wrong, nor can the five ambitious great men who have his ear and control the destiny of Japan.

No great race adventure can go far nor endure long which has no deeper foundation than material success, no higher prompting than conquest for conquest's sake and mere race glorification. To go far and to endure, it must have behind it an ethical impulse, a sincerely conceived righteousness. But it must be taken into consideration that the above postulate is itself a product of Western race-egotism, urged by our belief in our own righteousness and fostered by a faith in ourselves which may be as erroneous as are most fond race fancies. So be it. The world is whirling faster to-day than ever before. It has gained impetus. Affairs rush to conclusion. The Far East is the point of contact of the adventuring Western people as well as of the Asiatic. We shall not have to wait for our children's time nor our children's children. We shall ourselves see and largely determine the adventure of the Yellow and the Brown.

2. Dance of the Igorrotes, Louisiana Purchase Exposition, St. Louis, 1904

Igorrote village at the Louisiana Purchase Exposition, St. Louis, 1904. This was one of the exposition's most popular living exhibitions of the "races" of mankind.

3. Filipino Immigrant Condemns Representation of Group, circa 1924

I was born in a town called Candon, in the province of Ilocos Sur, Philippine Islands, in 1900. When the United States occupied the Philippines, the first thing she did was to establish public English schools in all parts of the archipelago. So, when I was at an age of schooling I attended the public school. In my high school years I attended the provincial high school, located at the capital of my province. In my senior high school year I graduated in the Seminary High School, a school of the Evangelical churches at Manila. Then I finished my two years' college work in the Union Schools of the same Evangelical church.

In all of my schooling in the Philippines I attended different [schools] and I have mingled with different peoples. In my sophomore and junior years in high school, I took charge of a small congregation. That work gave me a chance to feel the joy of service to my people; awakened me to the greatest needs of my people

From J. W. Buel, ed., *Louisiana and the Fair,* vol. 5 (World Progress Publishing Co.: St. Louis, 1904), p. 1721. Missouri Historical Society.

From *Orientals and Their Cultural Adjustment: Interviews, Life Histories and Social Adjustment Experiences of Chinese and Japanese of Varying Backgrounds and Length of Residence in the United States* (Nashville: Social Science Institute, Fisk University, 1946), 127–129, 136–137.

and a possibility of a worthy life's investment and lastly, it gave me the great desire for further education. Because of this ambition to serve my own people, the missionaries took me to the Evangelical schools at Manila for further education. I then felt that to be in the ministry of the Gospel one must be fully prepared to meet all phases of human life. The desire for further training and more education caused me to come to this great country, the United States.

I first heard of America from the first American missionaries that came to my home town. Then in my early school in the grammar grades I studied Geography and the people of America. In my high school course I studied the history, government, and the institutions of America. The missionaries have been telling us of the riches, beauty, and grandeur of the country. Then in our text-books in schools we saw pictures of the big buildings, beautiful streets and parks, big factories, great men, etc. In short, we have known the best of America. We have heard much of America as a land of the brave and the free, land of opportunity, and we pictured her as a land of "Paradise." The results of the American administration in the Philippines showed us the greatness of America, and we typified all the American people in the United States as like those missionaries and teachers who are working with the spirit of love among my people.

As I am in this country now, I am absorbing the best of the American life so that when I will go back to my people I will show and teach all of these good qualities and in that way my people will always adore and respect the American people because of the living good example that they show to the other peoples.

It is indeed a great disappointment to me and it breaks my heart to think that many of the good Americans who have been in my country have misrepresented my people to their own people. I have seen exhibitions in the museums and in the windows of the banks and big stores of the primitive utensils, furniture, implements, etc., of the backward and ignorant Filipinos. Some books are full of pictures of the naked Igorots and their primitive ways of living—people who only number about one-twentieth of the whole population. Even the missionaries themselves, in their lectures and in their articles published in the papers, talk of the dark side of the Filipino life. Through all of these, the American people in this country formed their opinion that the Filipino are nothing but backward, uncivilized, wild and naked people. If so, the noble works of Spanish civilization that have influenced my people for three and a half centuries and the progress done by the American administrations have been discredited. Have not these European and Western civilizations done anything good to my people? May any foreigner who comes to my country please note the best of my people and thus tell so to anybody wherever they may be. This is one cause of race prejudice—of misunderstanding of other people.

America is being looked upon by all the countries of the world as their leader. America has a wide door of opportunity for leadership training, not only among her own people but to the other peoples as well. Hundreds and thousands of my fellow country-men come to this country with me and only one purpose and that is to be prepared for leadership in her schools, colleges and universities. Only the young men and women then come to this country. I, also, came to California for the same reason. Hawaii, Australia, Mexico, or other countries could not give me such opportunities as I am now enjoying here. California is the first place that I stopped at because of the wonderful climates, such that I don't feel so much different than that of my country. . . .

The Americans have their own ways of thinking and of doing things. Some one said that there is an instinctive racial and national pride and each nationality considers herself superior along certain lines. Too much self-esteem and national pride might cause trouble with other peoples because there is then the sense of superiority without recognizing the good qualities in other races. Such prejudice spirit in a certain nationality might cause it not to be able to know the psychology, philosophy of life and the environment of the ones considered inferior. I find out that *misunderstanding* causes prejudice. The average American reads the daily papers about the bad side of an oriental individual, then he draws a conclusion that all of the Orientals are like that. For example, I met the other day an American woman whose uncle has been among the mountain tribes in the Philippines. This uncle sent her pictures of the headhunters. She asked me if the Filipinos are all headhunters. It is indeed dangerous if we all have our opinions about a certain nation by induction.

I am planning to go back to my country as soon as I will be prepared for a greater service in the schools of America. I will send my children to this country for their education. Surely, we have all of the schooling we want in the Philippines, but there is a greater advantage of being in the schools of this great educational land.

I am now slowly but surely realizing my ambition in this country. I am now getting along in my university work and I hope I could be in the school year after year until I finish my course.

I fail to realize the high expectation of seeing the people and their conditions in life as I have heard before I came over. The cities, towns, people, and everything were pictures to us in the Philippines as the best place with all comforts and enjoyment of life. We look upon America as a heaven on earth. Anyway, I am enjoying my life here, although I found it different from what I expected, because I am looking for the best people to associate with.

4. Anti-Japanese Monologue in Wallace Irwin's *Seed of the Sun*, 1926

"Killed any Japs this week, Artie?" he sang out, addressing a plump young man who seated himself beside Zudie with a second helping of everything on the bill.

"Don't mention 'em!" he growled, reddening with rage. "I'm through—get me?—through! I'm playing Hindus now, and getting a day's work out of 'em, too."

"Artie had a gang of Japs walk out on him last week," explained Dunc as soon as he found time to occupy the vacant chair at Anna's side. "He got so sore that I thought he was going to declare war right away."

"Is there any danger?" asked Anna, scared at the thought.

"Of war?"

Dunc and his belligerent friend Artie grinned at the thought.

From Wallace Irwin, *Seed of the Sun* (New York: Arno Press, 1978), 144–145.

"My dear lady," said Artie, after a mouthful of chile con carne, "the war is on right now. I don't mean machine guns and battleships and tin Kelleys. The hard-thinking, intellectual old gentlemen running the Japanese Government don't want any more of that sort of rough stuff. They'll never run amuck the way the Kaiser did and bleed themselves to death with a fool military program. All this newspaper talk is merely a smoke barrage to keep our minds off what Japan is really putting over."

"Artie was an officer in our Siberian job," interjected Dunc.

"Well, what are they putting over?" asked Anna, seeing here another aspect of the deep-rooted California race prejudice.

"Peaceful war. The conquest of the world by agriculture, commerce, immigration, secret treaties, counterfeit labels, soft words, hard bargains and the Japanese genius for teamwork. To accommodate their little expedition into Siberia I saw them build barracks that looked big enough to put up half the imperial army. What for? To send in more troops and fight it out? Not on your life! Pretty soon the Japanese troops will fade away and those comfortable barracks will be full of farmers, tradesmen and mechanics. Shan-tung all over again. They're the greatest real-estate men in the world. They took Shan-tung for the good of humanity, and they're keeping it for the good of Japan. I don't blame them. If I were a Jap I'd do the same. There's standing room only in Japan, and the race is suffocating."

5. Writer Sui Seen [Sin] Far Reveals Private Lives of Chinese Merchant Wives, 1897

With her quaint manners and old-fashioned mode of life, she carries our minds back to times almost as ancient as the earth we live on. She is a bit of olden Oriental coloring amidst our modern Western lights and shades; and though her years be few, she is yet a relic of antiquity. Even the dress she wears is cut in a fashion designed centuries ago, and is the same today as when the first nonfabulous Empress of China begged her husband to buy her a new dress—of a tunic, a pair of trousers and a divided skirt, all of finest silk and embroidered in many colors. A Chinese woman in a remote age invented the divided skirt, so it is not a "New Woman" invention.

The Chinese woman in America differs from all others who come to live their lives here, in that she seeks not our companionship, makes no attempt to know us, adopts not our ways and heeds not our customs. She lives among us, but is as isolated as if she and the few Chinese relations who may happen to live near were the only human beings in the world.

So if you wish to become acquainted with her, if you wish to glean some knowledge of a type of which very little is known, you must seek her out. She will be pleased with your advances and welcome you with demure politeness, but you might wait for all eternity and she would not come to you.

Having broken the ice, you find that her former reserve was due to her training, and that she is not nearly so shy as report makes her. You also find, despite the

From Sui Seen Far, "The Chinese Woman in America," *Land of Sunshine* 6, no. 2 (January 1897): 59–64; reprinted in *Unbound Voices: A Documentary History of Chinese Women in San Francisco*, ed., Judy Yung, (Berkeley: University of California Press, 1999), 158–163.

popular idea that the Chinese are a phlegmatic people, that she is brimful of feelings and impressions and has sensibilities as acute as a child's. That she is content to live narrowly, restricted to the society of one man and perhaps a couple of females, does not prove lack of imagination; but merely that she is ignorant of any other life.

She was born in China, probably in Canton or near that city. When a little girl, she played Shuttlecock, Guessing Pennies and Blind Man's Buff with childish playfellows, boys and girls; and grandfather and uncles kept her awake, when her mother put her to bed, by telling her stories of hobgoblins and ghosts. Amongst her memories of home are little pagodas before which she and her brothers and sisters were taught to burn incense, and an image of a goddess called "Mother," to whom she used to kneel till her little knees ached.

Until about twelve years old, she enjoyed almost as much healthful liberty as an American child; but in China it is not deemed proper for girls beyond that age to have boy playmates.

Then she learned to sew and embroider, to do light cooking and sing simple ballads. She was taught that whilst with them, her first duty was obedience to her father and mother; and after marriage, to her husband and his parents. She never had a sweetheart, but with girl friends would pass the hours in describing the beauties and virtues of future husbands.

In spite of these restraints, her years slipped away happily until time came for her to become an American bride—for the Chinese woman who comes to America generally comes as a bride, having been sent for by some Chinamen who has been some years in the States or in Canada and has prospered in business.

She has never seen her future husband, she has never perhaps ventured outside her native village; yet upon being apprised that for good and valuable consideration—for the expectant bridegroom, like Isaac of old when courting Rebecca, sends presents of silver and presents of gold to the parents or guardians of his chosen—she must leave home and friends and native land, she cheerfully sets about preparing for her journey. She may shed a few tears upon her mother's breast and surreptitiously hug her little sisters; but on the whole, she is pleased.

Her companions and friends usually regard her with envy. None but a well-to-do Chinaman could afford to send for a bride across the sea. The chief reason, however, is that the girl who goes to America does not become subject to her husband's mother, as when a girl marries in China. In that strange land she is obliged to live with her husband's parents and obey them as a daughter; and unless she is of yielding disposition, or the mother-in-law of extraordinary good nature, the result is often unhappiness. If there is a disagreement, it is the duty of the husband and son to take his mother's part, and the wife is made to acknowledge herself in the wrong. The Chinese woman who comes to America is favored also in that she can dress in richer costumes. In China her ordinary attire would consist of cotton, or a combination of silk and cotton, plainly made. The richly embroidered dresses which the Chinese women who come to America are allowed to bring with them are in China worn only by women of rank and position.

The bride comes from a respectable middle-class Chinese family. Aristocratic or wealthy people would not give a daughter to a man living in exile; and Wah Ling, being a big enough man to keep a wife in America, feels himself too big to take a girl from the laboring classes. He wishes his friends to think that he marries well; if he were to choose a girl of mean condition he might be ridiculed. The Chinaman knows little of natural selection; though in his youth he has a sweetheart, when he wants a wife he sends for a stranger.

In China it is deemed altogether wrong for girls "in society" to have men acquaintances; but very poor girls choose their associates as they please without causing remark. Now and then a poverty stricken or outcast maid wins the heart of a Chinaman brave enough to marry her in spite of what his world may say; but such cases are rare. Very few Chinamen are introduced to their wives until after marriage.

The Chinese woman in America lives generally in the upstairs apartments of her husband's dwelling. He looks well after her comfort and provides all her little mind can wish. Her apartments are furnished in American style; but many Chinese ornaments decorate the tables and walls, and on the sides of the room are hung long bamboo panels covered with paper or silk on which are painted Chinese good-luck characters. In a curtained alcove of an inner room can be discerned an incense vase, an ancestral tablet, a kneeling stool, a pair of candlesticks—my lady-from-China's private chapel. She will show you all her pretty ornaments, her jewelry and fine clothing, but never invite you near her private chapel. There she burns incense to her favorite goddess and prays that a son may be born to her, that her husband may be kind, and that she may live to die in China—the country which heaven loves.

She seldom goes out, and does not receive visitors until she has been a wife for at least two years. Even then, if she has no child, she is supposed to hide herself. After a child has been born to her, her wall of reserve is lowered a little, and it is proper for cousins and friends of her husband to drop in occasionally and have a chat with "the family."

Now and then the women visit one another; and when they are met together, there is such a clattering of tongues one would almost think they were American women. They laugh at the most commonplace remark and scream at the smallest trifle; they examine one another's dresses and hair, talk about their husbands, their babies, their food; squabble over little matters and make up again; they dine on bowls of rice, minced chicken, bamboo shoots and a dessert of candied fruits.

The merrymaking over, they bid good-by by clasping their own hands, shaking them up and down and interlacing their fingers—instead of shaking hands with one another.

If it is necessary to pass a room occupied by men, they do so very demurely, holding open fans before that side of the face—not because they are so shy, but because it is the custom of their country.

Although she does not read nor go out to see the sights, the Chinese woman does not allow time to hang heavy on her hands in America. There are many little thoughts in her mind, and she gives expression to them in beautiful fancy-work, representations of insects, flowers and birds most dexterously wrought from silk and beads. This is not useless, from her point of view, for it can be used as presents to distant relations, for the ornamentation of caps for her husband and little son, and also on her own apparel.

She loves flowers, natural or artificial: and if not supplied with the former, makes herself great quantities of the latter and wears them on hair and breast.

She bestows considerable pains on the plaiting of her hair; and after it is done up flat at the back of her head, she adorns it with flowers and large fantastic pins.

Her tresses are shining, black and abundant, and if dressed becomingly would be attractive; but the manner in which she plasters them back from her forehead would spoil the prettiest face.

While there are some truly pleasant to behold, with their little soft faces, oval eyes, small round mouths and raven hair, the ordinary Chinese woman does not strike an observer as lovely. She is, however, always odd and interesting.

Needless to say she is vain. Vanity is almost as much part of a woman's nature as of a man's; but the Chinese woman's vanity is not that of an American woman. The ordinary American dresses for the eyes of her friends and enemies—particularly the latter—and derives small pleasure from her prettiest things unless they are seen by others. A Chinese woman paints and powders, dresses and bejewels herself for her own pleasure; puts rings on her fingers and bracelets on her arms—and carefully hides herself from the gaze of strangers. If she has Golden Lily feet (Chinese small feet) she is proudly conscious of it; but should she become aware that a stranger is trying to obtain a glimpse of them, they quickly disappear under her skirt.

She is deeply interested in all matters of dress; and, if an American woman calls on her, will politely examine the visitor's clothing, with many an expression of admiration. She will even acknowledge the American dress prettier than her own, but you could not persuade her to adopt it. She is interested in all you may tell her about America and Americans; she has a certain admiration for the ways of the foreigner; but nothing can change her reverence for the manners and customs of her own country.

"Why do you do that in such a way?" she is asked, and her answer is, "Oh, because that is Chinese way."

"Do it like this," she is told. She shakes her head smilingly: "No, that not Chinese way."

As a mother, she resembles any other young mother—a trifle more childish, perhaps, than young American matrons, but just as devoted. When the baby seems well, she is all smiles and Chinese baby-talk; when he is ill, or she fancies so, she weeps copiously and cannot be comforted. She dressed him in Chinese dress, shaves his head and strings amulets on his neck, wrists and ankles.

She is very superstitious with regard to her child, and should you happen to know the date and hour of his birth, she begs with tears that you will not tell, for should some enemy know, he or she may cast a horoscope which would make the child's life unfortunate.

Do not imagine for an instant that she is dull of comprehension and unable to distinguish friendly visitors from those who merely call to amuse themselves at her expense. I have seen a little Chinese woman deliberately turn her back on persons so ignorant as to whisper about her and exchange knowing smiles in her presence. She is very loyal, however, to those she believes to be her real friends, and is always seeking to please them by some little token of affection.

More constant than sentimental is the Chinese woman. She has a true affection for her husband; no other man shares any of her personal thoughts. She loves him because she has been given to him to be his wife. No question of "woman's rights" perplexes her. She takes no responsibility upon herself and wishes none. She has perfect confidence in her man.

She lives in the hope of returning some day to China. She feels none of the bitterness of exile—she was glad to come to this country—but she would not be a daughter of the Flowery Land were she content to die among strangers.

Not all the Chinese women in America are brides. Some were born here; others are merely secondary wives, the first consorts of their husbands being left in China; and there are a few elderly women who were married long before leaving home. The majority, however, are brides; or as the Chinese call young married females, "New Women."

6. Sociology Graduate Student Rose Hum Lee Lists American Beliefs About the Chinese, 1927

The favorite delicacies of the Chinese are rats and snakes.

The Chinese say yes for no and vice versa. . . .

They eat soup with chopsticks.

Chop suey and chow mein are their national dishes and that besides these dishes they eat nothing but rice.

Chinese men wear skirts and women pants.

A Chinaman never gets drunk.

A Chinese is properly a Chinaman and that the word "Chinee" is singular for "Chinese."

The Chinese are a nation of laundrymen yet have a highly developed civilization. . . .

All Chinese are cunning and crafty.

All Chinese are honest and absolutely trustworthy.

The Chinese never lose their tempers.

The United States is the friend and protector of China.

All Chinese look alike.

The Chinese have no nerves and can sleep anywhere. . . .

They have no souls because they are not Christians.

They never say what they mean and abhor straight lines.

The Chinese invented pretty nearly everything that was ever invented.

The Chinese all hate water and never bathe.

They are a mysterious and inscrutable race and that they do everything backwards.

From Rose Hum Lee, "Social Attitudes Toward Chinese in the United States, Expressed in Periodical Literature from 1919 to 1944," in *Scratches on Our Minds: American Images of China and India* by Harold Isaacs, pp. 117–118. Copyright © 1958, 1980 by Harold Isaacs. Reprinted by permission.

7. MGM Studios Strategizes Advertisement
for *The Painted Veil,* 1934

Cooperative Tieups (Advertising and Displays)

Due to the Chinese background of "The Painted Veil," there is an excellent opportunity to tie up with stores featuring Chinese merchandise. And there is a preponderance of Chinese-influence merchandise on the market. A cooperative page devoted to the following items should be discussed with the advertising manager of your newspaper. We are not unmindful of the difficulties encountered in "putting over" the average cooperative page but we sincerely believe that a "Chinese Page" has possibilities, particularly so should you find it convenient to exhibit the Chinese merchandise somewhere in your theatre . . . perhaps a Chinese Bazaar display which might even be used as an advance plug for "The Painted Veil." Consider these articles:

Chinese Mandarin Coats . . . Pajamas . . . Dressing Gowns

Chinese Rugs

Chinese Jade Jewelry

Chinese Silks and Laces

Chinese Lacquer Tables

Chinese Tapestries and Lanterns

Chinese Buddha and incense novelties

Chinese Sandals

Chinese "high collar" fashions (as worn by GARBO)

China-ware

Chinese Bamboo novelties

Chinese Marriage Proposal Contest

The flowery English and the customary parable parlance of the educated Chinese was perhaps best exemplified in "The Son Daughter." In "The Painted Veil" this manner of speech is employed intermittently. This might be the basis for a Chinese "Marriage Proposal" contest, whereby the "proposals" are presented in "Chinese-English," limiting same to 25 words. A sample "proposal" could be submitted so that contestants might better understand the requirements.

"The Painted Veil" from Howard Dietz, *Advertising Approach, Box Office Analysis: Exploitation, Synopsis,* pp. 21–24, 27–28. Copyright © Warner Bros. Used with permission.

Tea and Wafer Tieup

Arrangements may be made with a tea merchant for a theatre display of attractive matted tea casks with the original Orient shipping stamps, this, in conjunction with the serving of tea and tea wafers on your mezzanine floor. For such a display and opportunity to exhibit their wares, the tea and wafer dealers should take a cooperative newspaper ad announcing this feature.

Tea Cup Readings

The tea tieup also suggests a Chinese-costumed tea cup reader . . . one who foretells the future by "reading" the tea leaves. This may be used as a mezzanine or foyer stunt in advance of your opening.

Jinrikisha Ballyhoo

Where a street ballyhoo is desired we would suggest the characteristic jinrikisha. Where not available one may be built . . . a wicker chair, mounted on light weight wheels, with a bamboo shaft for the coolie-costumed attendant. In the 'riksha may be an attractive "Chinese" girl in costume, carrying a Chinese parasol, the top of which may read, "GARBO in 'The Painted Veil' . . . Loew's State."

Chinese Fireworks Demonstration

For your opening night, a Chinese fireworks demonstration would make an excellent marquee attraction, granting you have the permission of local authorities. Do not use anything explosive . . . anything that will create a loud report. Your demonstration may be handled by Chinese-costumed girls . . . using sparklers, red fire, etc.

Chinese Paper Novelty

There is a peculiar type of red paper used by the Chinese. It is colored on one side and white on the other. As a novelty feature have a Chinaman write the name "G A R B O" in Chinese characters. This may be made into a cut and imprinted in black on the red paper, as per:

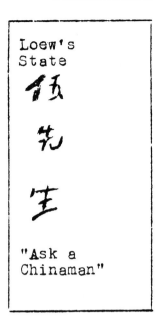

Travel Agencies

Steamship companies featuring sailings to the Orient should be contacted for co-operation. Several "shots" which were actually made in China appear in "The Painted Veil." Railroad agencies, affiliated with Oriental steamship lines, may also be approached.

Keye Luke Art

Keye Luke, a young Chinese who portrays the role of a physician in "The Painted Veil," is an artist of note. His pen and ink sketches have appeared repeatedly in the Los Angeles dailies. He has drawn a beautiful "head" of GARBO, which was accorded a 4-col. layout in the L.A. Times. In metropolitan cities where unusual high-class art is used, your dramatic editor will welcome the Keye Luke sketches. A photo of Luke at his easel, together with the GARBO sketch, are both available. The GARBO sketch may also be used for "Coloring Contest" purposes. Incidentally, Loew's State Theatre, Los Angeles, recently featured a mezzanine exhibit of Luke art which attracted unusual attention.

Chinese Promotion

Due to the fact that "The Painted Veil" was made with the cooperation of the Chinese government and because of the presence in its cast of the artist Keye Luke, and the

Chinese Garbo, Soo Yong, be sure to contact your Chinese newspapers, should you be located in a metropolitan city.

Buddhas

As an advance theatre display, feature incense-burning Buddhas throughout your house, with a "head" of GARBO and poster copy, reading, "An Event . . . GARBO in 'The Painted Veil' starts Sunday."

Chinese Lobby Display

"The Painted Veil" and its Chinese angles present possibilities for a colorful lobby display. You may give thought to Chinese lanterns, pagoda-topped box offices, bamboo, Chinese idols, dragon characters and coolie hat designs. Also, a Chinese gong may be sounded at intervals.

8. Harold R. Isaacs Addresses the Historical Significance of Pearl Buck's Portrayal of the Chinese, 1958

Of all the Sinophiles who have tried to depict and interpret the Chinese for Americans, none has done so with more effect than Pearl Buck. No single book about China has had a greater impact than her famous novel, *The Good Earth.* It can almost be said that for a whole generation of Americans she "created" the Chinese, in the same sense that Dickens "created" for so many of us the people who lived in the slums of Victorian England. The extent of her influence is illustrated in our own panel by the fact that 69 individuals spontaneously mentioned Pearl Buck as a major source of their own impressions of the Chinese and these were almost uniformly impressions of a wonderfully attractive people.

Pearl Buck happened "quite accidentally" to be born in the United States while her missionary mother was home recuperating from an illness. She was carried back to China when she was three months old and lived there most of her next forty years. Of her childhood in a missionary compound she has written these illuminating lines:

> I had a few dolls, but my "children" were the small folk of the servants quarters and the neighbors and we had wonderful hours of play. . . . I remember going to bed at night replete with satisfaction because the day had been so packed with pleasurable play. . . .

She early abandoned the missionary claims and creed, seeking her satisfaction in both private and public life in a more encompassing emotional attachment. In her relations with Chinese, in particular and in general, and indeed, with the whole world and all the people in it, Pearl Buck has tried to be warmly, competently, and for the most part undemandingly, maternal. There is more than this, to be sure, in the

From Harold R. Isaacs, *Scratches on Our Minds: American Images of China and India*, 155–158. Copyright © 1958, 1980 by Harold Isaacs. Reprinted by permission.

books she has written, but it is the thread that links her to the whole pattern of American-Chinese relationships.

Her single most successful book, *The Good Earth,* a novel about a Chinese peasant and his wife and their struggle against adversity, against the cruelties of men and the angers of nature, appeared in 1931. It had an instant and immense popular success. According to its publishers, the John Day Company, its many editions and reprintings ran up to an eventual total of more than 2,000,000 copies. In 1937, it appeared as a remarkably powerful and successful film that was seen over the ensuing years, according to its makers, by some 23,000,000 Americans and by an estimated 42,000,000 other people all over the world.

Book and film together, *The Good Earth* almost singlehandedly replaced the fantasy images of China and the Chinese held by most Americans with a somewhat more realistic picture of what China was like and a new, more intimate, and more appealing picture of the Chinese themselves. Indeed, *The Good Earth* accomplished the great feat of providing faces for the faceless mass.

One of our panelists—a journalist who later in his life spent several years in China—described the Buck influence this way:

> My first exposure to Asia came through Pearl Buck. China was a place on the map to me, with 400 million people who wore inverted dishpans for hats, rode rickshas and ate rice with chopsticks. This much I got in high school. Then I read *The Good Earth.* Pearl Buck made people out of the Chinese for me. . . .

This seemed to have been an experience shared by many. In the hours that it took to read or to watch, it transformed the blurred subhumans into particular human beings for whom a great and moving sympathy was evoked by a momentary sharing in the universal experiences of mating, parenthood, suffering, devotion, weakness, aspiration. The Chinese girl in the story, O-lan, bride, mother, and grandmother, and the man, Wang, dogged, strong, weak, and sometimes sinning, are certainly the first such individuals in all literature about China with whom literally millions of Americans were able to identify warmly.

This achievement was something new in American writing about China. Pearl Buck did not, for one thing, write about Chinese in relation to foreigners, but about Chinese in relation to one another. Nor, like Lin Yutang in *My Country and My People,* which enjoyed its own much smaller vogue in this same period, did she concentrate on the charm of Chinese ways and wisdom. Pearl Buck chose instead to write about the lowliest of all Chinese, the peasant, and to deal with the harshness of his struggle for existence. Some Chinese critics complained of this, often out of envy and discomfort, suggesting that the book was no adequate picture of Chinese life because neither they nor their prototypes appeared in its pages. But what Pearl Buck was really after was to humanize the Chinese peasant and to cast him in the universally understood role of the man rooted in the soil, and this she succeeded in doing for most of her large audience. For some of her missionary readers, indeed, the book was a bit too earthy, but this had no adverse effect on its popularity.

The times were ready with a welcome for *The Good Earth.* It appeared coincidentally with Japan's attacks on China. In a way that never could have been accomplished by event or propaganda, it humanized the people who became Japan's principal victims. The film based on the book appeared when Japan's piecemeal attacks had broadened into a full-scale war and American sympathy for the Chinese had become a powerful national emotion. Although it did not deal with the war itself, it gave the quality of individual recognition to the figure of the heroic Chinese peasant or peasant-soldier who offered battle to the Japanese against such great odds in the years just before Pearl Harbor. This film, indeed, set the molds for a long series of imitative sequels that followed during the war years, dramatizing the war itself and China's stand. One of these was a filming of one of Miss Buck's own later books, *Dragon Seed.* In all of them, however, Dorothy Jones observes, "the character of the Chinese peasant in general follows that dramatized in *The Good Earth*—he is hardworking, strong, persevering, and able to withstand the most severe adversities, kind toward children, respectful toward elders, all in all an admirable [and] warmly lovable character."

The impressions left on the minds of our panelists, re-evoked after the passage of nearly twenty years, suggest that they retained from Pearl Buck not the memory of any individual Chinese, but a broad notion of what Chinese in general were like. By creating the first Chinese individuals capable of impressing themselves on American minds, Pearl Buck in effect created a new stereotype. Nobody remembered the evil and wickedness and cruelty also portrayed in her book; what they had retained was an image of the Noble Chinese Peasant, solid, wonderful, virtuous, admirable.

It is no accident that the reader of Pearl Buck's novels about China acquires an impression of the Chinese in general which is sharper and more memorable than any individual character she has created. For Pearl Buck herself, when asked directly, willingly generalizes, and it is interesting to note that, so often charged herself with sentimentality, the Chinese virtue she values above all else is unsentimentality:

> When I think of the Chinese, I think of a kind of person I like. He is not poetic, but extremely realistic, practical rather than artistic. The Chinese artist is never an artist for art's sake. Art is always a means or a philosophy with the Chinese. China could not produce a Matisse or a Gauguin, certainly not a Picasso. There are no Chinese cubists. The Chinese is a loyal father and friend. But this has its limits. He is not fantastically loyal. This loyalty will come to an end if occasion demands it. He is common-sensible about everything. . . . The Chinese can be terribly cruel. He never loves an animal. He will never die of love. He is not egocentric. He is remote from the maudlin in everything. He is a man of principle, but not to the point of folly, for his goal is larger than any one principle or any one situation. I see these as features of the basic character of the Chinese, the basis of all the characters I have created, the variety occurring as I discover deviations and combinations of so many different kinds. There is some mixture of some or all of these qualities in every Chinese I have ever known. Americans seem to me to differ more in individual personalities than Chinese do. I feel a greater uniformity among them. Their corners are much more smoothed off than ours have been. I don't know if under a Communist-controlled society the Chinese is becoming a different kind of man. I find it difficult to think so. I continue to think of the Chinese who sees everything against the background of eternity. . . .

The chances are that even now, for those who read and are influenced by the books of Pearl Buck, it is the image of the Chinese peasant that she created that rises to the forefront of their minds whenever they think of the Chinese people marshaled under the demanding leadership of the Communist zealots.

⟡ *E S S A Y S*

In the first essay, historian Robert Rydell, professor at Montana State University, describes the Filipino exhibit at the St. Louis World's Fair, arguing that its breakdown into different anthropological "types," including Visayans, Moros, Negritos, and Igorots, embodied the American colonial policy of giving privileges to those Filipino groups whom they thought to be the most civilized and civilizable. The second essay moves the analysis of Orientalism from World's Fairs to the Hollywood screen. Here historian Karen Janis Leong, Assistant Professor at Arizona State University, examines the complex racial identity of silent film star Anna May Wong. The argument reveals Orientalism to be a useful fiction that can both benefit and limit Asian Americans.

The Filipino Village at the 1904 World's Fair

ROBERT RYDELL

The Louisiana Purchase Exposition featured the most extensive Anthropology Department of any world's fair. The directors expressed their intent to establish "a comprehensive anthropological exhibition, constituting a Congress of Races, and exhibiting particularly the barbarous and semi-barbarous peoples of the world, as nearly as possible in their ordinary and native environments." These plans received enthusiastic endorsement from leading anthropologists around the country, including Frederic Ward Putnam, former head of the Department of Anthropology at the World's Columbian Exposition, who tendered the directors his "hearty approval" for their plans. To head the department, the directors turned to W J McGee, who had become one of the nation's preeminent anthropologists during his tenure at the Bureau of American Ethnology before charges of financial irregularity forced him to resign. His reputation was blemished, but by no means demolished. He regarded the exposition as an opportunity not only to maintain his stature in the anthropology profession, but to fashion the national identity out of his own well-developed theory of racial progress.

McGee had organized the substance of his theory about progress into two 1899 addresses: "The Trend of Human Progress," delivered at the Washington Academy of Sciences, and "National Growth and National Character," one in a series of lectures on national expansion sponsored by the National Geographic Society. In "The Trend of Human Progress," McGee developed a broad overview of human history, observing the existence of a "trend of vital development from low toward the high, from dullness toward brightness, from idleness groveling toward intellectual uprightness." The driving forces behind this upward movement, he explained, were "cephalization"—the gradual increase in the cranial capacity of different races—and "cheirization"—the regular increase of manual dexterity along racial lines. The proof, he believed, was self-evident: "It is a matter of common observation that the white man can *do* more and better than the yellow, the yellow man more and better than the red or black." As a consequence of cheirization and cephalization, the "advance of culture" proceeded along lines of racial achievement:

> Classed in terms of blood, the peoples of the world may be grouped in several races; classed in terms of what they do rather than what they merely are, they are conveniently grouped in the four culture grades of savagery, barbarism, civilization, and enlightenment.

This division of humanity into racially based cultural grades did not signify a static universe for McGee. Far from it. He saw the turn of the century as a time when "perfected man is over-spreading the world." By "perfected man" he simply meant "the two higher culture-grades—especially the Caucasian race, and (during recent decades) the budded enlightenment of Britain and full-blown enlightenment of America." Caucasians, he argued, were ushering in a new era in world history when "human culture is becoming unified, not only through diffusion but through the extinction of the lower grades as their representatives rise into higher grades." The net effect of this process was "that the races of the continents are gradually uniting in lighter blend, and the burden of humanity is already in large measure the White Man's burden—for, viewing the human world as it is, white and strong are synonymous terms. . . .

When McGee arrived in Saint Louis in August 1903, he made it clear that he would fashion the exhibits in his charge into an exemplum of his theory of racial progress, "The aim of the Department of Anthropology at the World's Fair," McGee stated, "will be to represent human progress from the dark prime to the highest enlightenment, from savagery to civic organization, from egoism to altruism." "The method," he added, "will be to use living peoples in their accustomed avocations as our great object lesson," with particular emphasis on "Indian school work, America's best effort to elevate the lower races." . . .

By opening day, . . . McGee had converted the western portion of the exposition grounds into a field research station for the study of nonwhite "types." Groups of pygmies from Africa, "Patagonian giants" from Argentina, Ainu aborigines from Japan, and Kwakiutl Indians from Vancouver Island, as well as groups of Native Americans gathered around prominent Indian chiefs including Geronimo, Chief Joseph, and Quanah Parker, were formed into living ethnological exhibits. They were supplemented by an adjoining United States government exhibit of nearly one thousand Filipinos and by separate ethnological concessions along the Pike. McGee assembled the nonwhites directly under his charge into a "logical arrangement" of living "types" stretched out between the Indian School Building and the Philippines display. . . .

The Philippine Reservation, according to William P. Wilson, chairman of the United States government's Philippine Exposition Board, constituted "an exposition within an exposition; the greatest exhibition of the most marvelous Exposition in the history of the world." With nearly twelve hundred Filipinos living in villages on the forty-seven-acre site set aside for the display, the exhibit climaxed the efforts of earlier exposition promoters to establish, under federal government auspices, a large-scale exhibit of the people and resources of the Philippine Islands. But the size of the exhibit at Saint Louis far exceeded the wildest dreams of the directors of previous fairs. It was also unique in having the full support of the federal government at the outset.

The directors' hopes for government participation in the planned Philippine showing received an early endorsement from William Howard Taft while he was civil governor of the islands. According to the *World's Fair Bulletin,* Taft believed that the proposed exhibit would have a "moral effect" on the people of the islands and that "Filipino participation would be a very great influence in completing pacification and in bringing Filipinos to improve their condition." President Theodore Roosevelt and Secretary of War Elihu Root supported Taft's position and encouraged his efforts to organize "as comprehensive an exhibit as possible of the products and resources, manufactures, art, ethnology, education, government of the Philippines Islands, and the habits and customs of the Filipino people."

Responsibility for the success of the undertaking centered on William Powell Wilson, Taft's appointee to direct the Philippine Exposition Board. At the time of his selection, Wilson had a national and international reputation as the founder and head of the Philadelphia Commercial Museum—an institution that wedded science to the interests of American business expansion overseas. . . .

One of Wilson's first steps as head of the Philippine Exposition Board was to recommend that his associate at the Commercial Museum, Gustavo Niederlein, be appointed director of exhibits for the board. Like Wilson, Niederlein was a naturalist and scientist devoted to the advance of Western imperialism. . . .

In late 1902 Niederlein and Wilson put their scientific and business talents to work in the Philippines. With the cooperation of several prominent Filipinos and numerous United States colonial officials—including Clarence R. Edwards, chief of the Bureau of Insular Affairs, Albert E. Jenks, former ethnologist at the Bureau of American Ethnology and head of the War Department's Ethnological Survey of the Philippine Islands, Daniel Folkmar, anthropologist and lieutenant-governor in charge of the Philippine civil service, and Pedro A. Paterno, president of the Philippine senate—they proceeded to arrange material for the colonial exhibit at the Louisiana Purchase Exposition. Simultaneously, in accordance with the congressional act authorizing establishment of the Exposition Board, Wilson and Niederlein collected materials for a permanent commercial museum in Manila and for a preliminary exposition that would show Filipinos the exhibits that would be sent to Saint Louis. The museum, intended primarily to provide American business interests with commercial data about the economic possibilities of the islands, opened in February 1903 but closed in May when it became apparent that the exhibits would be needed to complete the display for Saint Louis. The preliminary exposition never materialized for the same reason. Yet the motives behind the Manila exposition and museum informed the plans for the exhibit at Saint Louis and revealed the overall goal of the government to institutionalize American colonial rule, to bring to the Philippines "the impelling power of modern civilization," as Niederlein termed it, and to show the Filipinos how America would aid the development of the islands through "the consumption of the raw material of this archipelago in [America's] well developed and increasing industries."

To emphasize to Filipinos the long road they would have to travel before achieving the capacity for self-rule, the short-lived museum included a division of ethnology illustrating "tribal and racial exhibits in every detail" and "showing the state of culture and growth of civilization" on the islands. This ethnological feature not only reappeared in the exhibit at Saint Louis, but dominated the Philippine

Reservation to such an extent that McGee, as early as November 1903, informed the *New York Times* that the display from the islands would be "to all intents and purposes ethnological in character." When the experienced midway organizer Edmund A. Felder, joined the board as an executive officer in March 1904, it became clear that the Exposition Board would draw upon the decade-long tradition of midway ethnological concessions as well as upon received scientific wisdom en route to establishing what amounted to a federally sanctioned ethnological village on the site of the reservation.

Under the primary direction of government-appointed scientists, the reservation affirmed the value of the islands to America's commercial growth and created a scientifically validated impression of Filipinos as racially inferior and incapable of national self-determination in the near future. No exhibit at any exposition better fulfilled the imperial aspirations of its sponsors. As David R. Francis observed at the official dedication of the million-dollar exhibit in mid-June, the display from the Philippines alone justified the expense and labor that went into the entire fair. From start to finish he believed it was the "overshadowing feature" of the exposition. Francis noted, moreover, that ninety-nine out of a hundred fairgoers visited the reservation.

The pervading imperial message of the reservation was inescapable and apparent from the moment visitors set foot on the forested acreage set aside for the display. The moss-covered Bridge of Spain, the main entrance to the reservation, conveyed visitors into an immense War Department exhibit in the Walled City—a replica of the fortification around Manila—where fairgoers could relive the recent military triumphs by the United States.

Beyond the Walled City, the Philippine Exposition Board engineered the circular ground plan of the reservation into a series of three cultural spheres depicting the civilizing influence of the Spanish past, the current ethnological state of the islands, and the beneficent results that Filipinos and Americans alike could expect from the United States takeover. At the center of the reservation the board established a "typical" Manila plaza, surrounded by four large Spanish-style buildings. These structures, consisting of an upper-class residence, a government building, an educational building, and a reproduction of the commercial museum in Manila, reminded visitors of the Spanish legacy on the islands and at the same time laid out the attributes of civilization—social and political order, education, and commerce—that the federal government considered essential to the future well-being of the islands.

Radiating from the central plaza were a series of ethnological villages, often placed adjacent to exhibit buildings depicting the wealth of natural resources on the islands. The villages portrayed a variety of Filipino "types," including Visayans, "the high and more intelligent class of natives," Moros, "fierce followers of Mohammed," Bagobo "savages," "monkey-like" Negritos, and "picturesque" Igorots. In the third cultural sphere, at the farthest outreach of the reservation and concentrated behind the Igorot and Negrito villages, the board located encampments of Philippine Scouts and Constabulary—collaborationist police forces enlisted by the American military to aid in suppressing the ongoing insurrection in the islands against the United States. The function of these units at the fair extended beyond policing the reservation. As one official guide to the reservation explained, the Constabulary and Scouts were juxtaposed to the Igorots and Negritos to bring out the "extremes of the social order in the islands." Numbering nearly seven hundred, or over half the total number of Filipinos on the reservation, these paramilitary forces were intended to illustrate the "result of American rule" and to suggest the possibility for cultural advance under America's colonial administration of the islands.

This possibility was also the subject of an ethnological museum situated on the reservation. Directed by Albert Jenks, this institution, "with cloisters like a convent," contained exhibits devoted to "an interpretation of the habits and life of the Philippine tribes." Jenks concentrated on the Igorots, Moros, Bagobos, and Negritos and declared that they were "true savages." Jenks, however, stressed that they "represent only about one-seventh of the entire population of the Archipelago, and their culture is almost entirely of their own development."

Their relative numerical insignificance in the islands and at the fair notwithstanding—there were 38 Bagobos, 41 Negritos, 114 Igorots, and 100 Moros—the exhibits of the "wild tribes" became the most popular displays on the reservation. From the start of the fair, the Igorot and Negrito villages, especially the former, caught the fancy of fairgoers and of the nation to a degree unsurpassed by any exhibit at any fair since the summer of 1893 when Fatima had danced the hootchy-kootchy on the Midway at the World's Columbian Exposition. The perceived simplicity of Igorot life doubtless accounted for part of their appeal and made some fairgoers long for a less complicated way of living than that represented by the monuments to industrialization contained in the White City palaces. But the immediate impetus to see the Igorot exhibit stemmed less from preindustrial longings than from a powerful mixture of white supremacist sexual stereotypes and voyeurism.

Nothing propelled the Igorots and Negritos into prominence more rapidly than the controversy that erupted in June, shortly after the opening of the exhibit, over what one visitor termed "their dusky birthday robes." With a presidential campaign under way and with anti-imperialists in the Democratic party on the verge of including a plank in the party's platform stating that the Filipinos were "inherently unfit to be members of the American body politic," the Roosevelt administration became concerned that local press reports emphasizing the absence of clothing on these Filipinos would undermine the government's efforts at the fair to show the possibilities for progress on the islands. On 23 June Taft wired Edwards to avoid "any possible impression that the Philippine Government is seeking to make prominent the savageness and barbarism of the wild tribes either for show purposes or to depreciate the popular estimate of the general civilization of the islands." In a follow-up telegram, Taft suggested "that short trunks would be enough for the men, but that for the Negrito women there ought to be shirts or chemises of some sort." Taft also ordered: "Answer what you have done immediately. The President wished to know." Edwards lost no time in cabling his response, telling Taft that the Negritos "wee until recently dressed up like plantation nigger[s], whom they diminutively represent, recently . . . [the] men have discarded these clothes and put on their native loin cloth." Furthermore, Edwards informed the secretary of war, signs had been put up showing the low number of "wild tribes" relative to the overall population of the Philippines. The administration, however, remained unsatisfied. The following day Taft's private secretary wired Edwards: "President still thinks that where the Igorot has a mere G string that it might be well to add a short trunk to cover the buttocks and front." Taft, moreover, instructed Edwards to obtain a written statement from the Board of Lady Managers, an adjunct to the general directorship of the exposition, assuring the administration that the appearance of the Igorots and Negritos was unobjectionable. In the meantime Edwards ordered Niederlein to have Truman K. Hunt, former lieutenant-governor of the Lapanto-Bontoc province and manager of the Igorot village, put breechclouts on the Igorots and "allow no child to go naked."

The government's efforts at overnight civilization provoked much mirth, brought an outcry from anthropologists, and generated a great deal of publicity for the exposition. The Saint Louis *Post-Dispatch* carried a cartoon showing Taft carrying a pair of pants, in hot pursuit of an Igorot clad only in a G-string. The editor of the same newspaper dispatched a letter to the "Department of Exploitation" at the reservation, declaring: "To put pants on [the Igorots and Negritos] would change a very interesting ethnological exhibit which shocks no one into a suggestive sideshow." An irate Frederick Starr seconded these thoughts in a memo to Wilson: "The scientific value of the display is unquestionably great. Such value would be completely lost by dressing these people in a way unlike that to which they are accustomed." Starr also added that clothing might actually kill the Igorot and Negrito villagers, given the heat of the Saint Louis summer. By mid-July the Board of Lady Managers concurred in the need for maintaining the apparent genuineness of the exhibits, and the Roosevelt administration abandoned its plans to compel the Igorots and Negritos to wear bright-colored silk trousers.

Authenticating these villagers as "savages," however, left the administration with the original problem. If fairgoers perceived the villagers as utterly backward and incapable of progress, the displays would actually buttress the racist arguments used by anti-imperialists to oppose annexation of the islands. But the Philippine Exposition Board had already circumvented this dilemma by driving an ethnological wedge between the Igorots and Negritos. The Negritos, according to various official descriptions of their village, were "extremely low in intellect," and "it is believed that they will eventually become extinct." To reinforce this idea, one of the Negritos was named Missing Link. The Igorots, on the other hand, were judged capable of progressing. "Scientists," according to an official souvenir guide, "have declared that with the proper training they are susceptible of a high stage of development, and, unlike the American Indian, will accept rather than defy the advance of American civilization." Igorot women, one American official hastened to point out, "are the most expert ore-sorters" in the world. The possibility for uplift was highlighted when Roosevelt visited the reservation and a missionary schoolteacher led her class of Igorots in a chorus of "My Country 'Tis of Thee." The *Globe-Democrat* recorded the president's satisfaction. "It is wonderful," Roosevelt declared. "Such advancement and in so short a time!" In conceding that the Igorots might be capable of cultural advance, however, the government did not suggest that they were capable of achieving equality with Caucasians. Rather, the schools in operation on the reservation suggested that the place of the Igorots and other members of the "wild tribes" in the American empire would closely resemble the place mapped out for Native Americans and blacks in the United States.

With the exception of the Negritos, who were placed on the road to extinction by government ethnologists, the Philippine Exposition Board crowded other "grades" of Filipinos into the wagon of progress—to borrow McGee's metaphor—without permitting them to ride horseback. As several members of the Scouts and Constabulary discovered, any attempt to cross the forward limits of the racial hierarchy

imposed on the riders down the road to utopia would meet with serious consequences. Members of the Scouts and Constabulary who accepted the invitation of
young white women schoolteachers from Saint Louis to accompany them on tours
of the fairgrounds and of the city were taunted as "niggers." When taunts failed to
halt the promenades, several United States Marines, with the active cooperation of
the exposition's police force, known as the Jefferson Guards and composed
largely of southern whites, took matters into their own hands. As couples walked
around the grounds, a contingent of Marines and guards—the latter had been
issued slingshots "heavily loaded with lead" in lieu of revolvers—threatened to
arrest the white women and kicked their Filipino escorts to the ground. When the
Scouts returned to their camp, an even larger group of Marines arrived on the
scene determined to show the Filipinos that the lynch law was not limited to
southern blacks. They charged the Filipinos, shooting revolvers into the air and
shouting, "Come on boys! Let's clean the Gu-Gus off the earth!" Edwards deplored
the racial clashed, "in view of the fact that there are none of the negro blood in the
Scouts or Constabulary." But the outburst of violence against the "highest grade"
of Filipinos represented on the reservation underscored the success of the exhibit
in confirming the impression that Filipinos were savages at worst and "little
brown men" at best.

On the occasion of Philippine Day at the fair, held to commemorate the surrender of Manila, "a great step in the diffusion of freedom over the globe," a local paper
summarized the overall meaning of the reservation: "For the sake of the Filipinos and
for the credit of our own country we retained control of the Philippines, with the determination to educate their people into the nearest approach to actual independence
which they can have with safety to themselves." As the reservation made clear, that
"nearest approach to actual independence" entailed instructing Filipinos in the
ethnological limitations operating to hamper their progress—limitations that in turn
mandated that Filipinos be willing workers and consumers in the burgeoning overseas market being established by American commercial interests. "The Filipinos
themselves learned from their St. Louis experience that they were not ready for self-
government," the *Portland Oregonian* reported on the eve of the Lewis and Clark
Centennial Exposition, which also would include an exhibit of Filipinos. Americans,
the newspapers added, "who talked with [the Filipinos] and studied the tribesmen
disabused themselves of any impression that the natives could take care of themselves" The newspaper conceded that "[t]here are intelligent Filipinos. But the
majority are comparatively helpless. They are children. . . . Burdened with a problem
of government, they would be hopelessly lost." Two homes missionaries who visited
the exhibit similarly commended the government officials in charge for "a grand
affair—wisely planned, well adjusted to enable Americans to see the several tribes
in their various stages of development and to note the capabilities and possibilities
of the race." The reservation, they continued, "has strengthened our confidence in
the wisdom of our government's general policy respecting the Philippines and their
people, and in the hopeful outlook for the Filipinos under American jurisdiction."
The missionaries, moreover, promised to do everything in their power to advertise
the exhibit as they traveled around the country on the National Home Mission lecture
circuit. It remained for the *New York Post* to sum up: "There probably was never such
a colonial exhibit gathered in the world."

The Racialized Image of Anna May Wong

KAREN JANIS LEONG

Anna peers into the mirror, then looks intently at the magazine on her dressing room table. "For the thoroughbred American GIRL—a skin as white as milk! You can have it!" the advertisement promises, featuring a full-length figure of the "Typical" American young woman on the margin. Her gaze drawn back to her own reflection, Anna frowns at her "brown" arm and, directing her attention again to the mirror, attempts to "massage out her Oriental lines." Finally she reaches for a bottle of lotion, "Malhofsky's Milk-White Magic." She again gazes in the mirror, imitating the "Typical American girl" pictures on the lotion's label.

Anna is not destined to transform herself. In this screenplay scenario of Paramount's *Forty Winks* (1925), Annabelle Wu—referred to in the scenario as "Anna"—schemes to aid the cad she loves in his plot to blackmail the heroine into marriage. She does this out of her desire to be white. She hopes that the treacherous Le Sage in turn will desire her because of her "whiteness." But this is not to be. After Le Sage realizes she has failed him, he is furious. "You yellow fool! Do you know what this means to me? It means prison—for life!" Anna hysterically indicates that they should flee together. His response, as written in the scenario, is to literally fling her from himself and out of the picture. "You! I hope I may never see your stupid, slant-eyed face again—you damned Chink!" Thus Anna May Wong exited one of her earlier films.

The role of Annabelle Wu appears to have been written with Anna May Wong in mind. One of a handful of Asian actresses in Hollywood, the similarity of Wong's name with Wu's was more than coincidental. [Journalist] Zelda Crosby's 1919 synopsis of "Lord Chumley," the initial title of the Paramount feature, mentioned no Asian character, no Annabelle Wu. By the time "Lord Chumley" was filmed as *Forty Winks* six years later, however, Annabelle Wu had become the pivotal character, her desire to be white as central a tension in the story as the romance between the heroine and hero. The scenario of Bertram Millhauser's screenplay makes stunningly clear the producer's perception of a "typical" Asian woman. In the scene where Annabelle Wu first appears, a note explains her character:

> We intend to characterize Anna as a girl who would give her last drop of blood to be considered a "white" girl. She loves to think of herself as looking thoroughly American. To point this, we must make certain that all her dress (negligees, etc.) and her head-dress, in fact everything intimate and personal about her be done in American fashion. Her instinctive reactions are *always* Oriental.

These "oriental" reactions, according to the screenplay, included wanting to be "white" and acting in a conniving and duplicitous matter. No matter how much she strives, Anna will always remain innately "oriental."

The effects of racial prejudice were painfully obvious in the film roles of Anna May Wong, and are likewise evident in a survey of her career. In her "private" life

---

as well as her film roles, Wong would publicly and persistently be cast as a woman struggling between two cultures, between tradition and modernity. Wong's career undoubtedly was shaped by her racial heritage and appearance, and her celebrity relied on her relatively unique status as an actress of Chinese descent. Magazine interviews with Wong focused on her cultural conflicts, which she freely discussed. These representations capitalized on what set Wong visibly apart from other Hollywood hopefuls. Wong profited in some ways from this strategy; she clearly suffered in other ways. Certain aspects of her story resonate with the stories of numerous other Chinese Americans, except that hers was uniquely much more public. In order to be recognized in American society, Wong had to perpetuate or at least participate in mainstream stereotypes of the Chinese. For herself and the Chinese Americans community, socioeconomic mobility and public visibility powerfully limited the possibilities of representation.

Over the course of her career, Wong's roles would undergo slight but significant changes that reflected America's, and Wong's own, changing relationship with China. Popular perceptions of Chinese and Chinese Americans in United States society shaped her opportunities and roles. Although Wong's early roles from 1919 as an extra to the late 1920s as a character actor were relatively minor, her presence onscreen significantly aided the audience in accepting the fictive "authenticity" of the imagined, often foreign, locale. Yet Wong herself was not foreign, but American.

Anna May's parents, Sam Sing Wong and his wife Lee Gon Toy Wong, both claimed to be native-born Californians of Chinese descent. They owned and operated a laundry on Figueroa Street in Los Angeles, in which they also resided with their seven children—Lulu, Anna May, James, Mary, Frank, Roger, and another daughter, who presumably died at a young age. Anna May, the second eldest, was born in 1905. Beginning in 1919, while still a high schooler, she began working as an extra in several silent films. She was a featured player in the Technicolor-produced *Toll of the Sea* in 1922, but thereafter continued to play minor or supporting roles in a variety of American films.

Unable to get a contract in Hollywood, Wong set sail for Europe in 1927 after a German production company chose her to star in two films. After these films, Wong received feature roles in three British productions. Wong enjoyed great popularity in Europe during this time, and also starred in a Viennese operetta and a London stage play. In 1930, Wong returned to the United States and signed a three-picture contract with Paramount Studios. Before beginning any film projects, Wong reprised her London role in the Broadway version of the same play, *A Circle of Chalk*. This was cut short with news that her mother had been killed in an auto accident, and Wong returned immediately to Los Angeles to be with her family. Paramount cast her in two mediocre thriller pictures; these did little to enhance her career. Due to the lack of opportunities, Wong again set off for Europe where she appeared on the European theatre circuit. Abroad, Wong starred in *Tiger Bay, Chu Chin Chow,* and *Java Head.* After those films Paramount signed her to appear in *Limehouse Nights.*

In 1934, Wong again returned to America. That same year her father decided to return to retire in China, taking the four youngest children with him. Soon after Wong unsuccessfully auditioned in 1935 for a role in MGM's *The Good Earth,* she announced plans "to return to China" to visit her family. At the end of 1936, ten months later, Wong returned once more to the United States, where she again was signed to a multi-picture contract with Paramount Pictures.

During the late 1930s Wong's changing roles began to reflect Americans' changing views of China. Paramount Studios now cooperated with the Chinese consul in producing films set in China. A series of three films featuring Wong as an independent, proactive Chinese American woman resulted. By 1939, however, Wong's film career again declined. Simultaneously, her activism on behalf of China increased. Beginning in 1938, and continuing through the end of the war she devoted her efforts to publicizing and fundraising for China's war of resistance.

From 1941 to the end of the war, Anna May Wong starred in two films about China, attempted some stage plays, and made several United Service Organization (USO) appearances. She seemed to retire semi-officially from films by 1943. In the later 1940s and early 1950s, Wong appeared in a few films and hosted a short-lived mystery theater series on television. She was on the verge of yet another career transition when she was signed to a role in Rodger's and Hammerstein's musical *Flower Drum Song* in 1961. Before the production about Chinese American assimilation and generational conflict in San Francisco commenced, however, Wong at the age of fifty-six died in her sleep at the home of her youngest brother.

"A part, yet not a part . . . ": Anna May Wong's "Own" Cultural Conflict

Anna May Wong was more successful in crossing national borders than she was in breaking through those barriers to her career posed by race and gender. Her publicized "personal" life, so necessary to maintaining a star personality, only confirmed and entrenched expectations on the part of producers (and possibly even audiences) of the characters Wong could convincingly portray. A selective personal history complemented the marketing of Anna May Wong as an actress occupying a unique niche.

The focus on Wong's romantic life extended her "existence already laid out in films." Wong's 1931 starring vehicle, *Daughter of the Dragon,* focused on the tragedy of illicit romance. The daughter of the evil Fu Manchu (portrayed by Swedish actor Warner Oland), Wong's character falls in love with a young Englishman. Her feelings are reciprocated, and he professes his love for her in the film. The article quoted her character's response in the film. "But does that change the color of my skin? . . . Does that make my straight black hair turn to yellow curls and my black eyes to blue?" The interviewer, Audrey Rivers, added, "[Wong] might have been talking of her own tragedy." Rivers noted the irony of Wong's "inability" to be kissed on film because of her race, "even though she has become so Westernized that she is now almost a stranger to her own race. She thinks in terms of penthouses and speeding cars, not in terms of bamboo huts and ox-carts. She reveals in the freedom of the Western woman—in clothes, in habits, in speech." In another interview that same year, Wong recalled visiting with "some Chinese friends . . . and their wives did nothing but gossip about their babies, their neighbors and their housework. "Nothing like that for me," declared Anna May, "I could not live such narrow life." Wong's youthful reflection of married home life was cast as rejection of Chinese culture.

Movie magazines reflected the nature of Hollywood's fascination with Anna May Wong. By the 1920s, magazines marketed at movie fans constituted a particularly important mechanism for perpetuating personalities. Interviews and articles "revealed" personal details of the star's ostensibly "private" life, individualizing his or her identity. Publicists provided stories intended to fulfill the audience member's perceived desire to focus on and identify with the "star," focusing on what made the individual unique and what kept her ordinary. The actor's "individual" thoughts and feelings only entered the public sphere as they were channeled through the star system and subjected to its requirements. So while these magazines articles constitute the majority of what is known about Wong, their content also was shaped by the needs of the industry itself.

As a relatively successful movie actress and the only Chinese American woman to be thus, Wong's hybrid identity formed the basis of her unique star personality. Anna May Wong both affirmed and challenged preconceived notions of Asian difference in her public stagings. Significantly, the few feature articles about Wong exploited these divergent narratives. Wong's conflict of cultures and her attempt to reconcile her American and Chinese backgrounds were central to her picture personality as developed in movie magazines. This polarization manifested itself most conspicuously in discussions [of] Wong's romantic life. Although numerous interviewers observed that Wong maintained an aura of mystery and distance, Wong appeared to speak freely about marriage, dating, and the conflict she felt between cultures.

Feature stories about Wong supported white privilege—non-whiteness resulted in suffering—and reinforced racial separation. The conspicuous absence of publicized romance, a topic that immediately connoted a private life, constituted the core of Wong's public image. Melodramatic articles portrayed her as continually divided and terribly lonely. According to [Fan magazine writer Audrey] Rivers, Wong explained to her that "no American man will marry me. . . . I have become too American to marry one of my own race. What is there for me?" [Journalist Helen] Carlisle similarly reported Wong's conjectures about her marital status, heightening her own privileged status as confidante and Wong's "oriental" status. "In a burst of confidence, exceedingly rare among her people, she said to me one day: 'I don't suppose I'll ever marry. Whom could I marry? Not a man of your race, for he would lose caste among his people and I among mine.'"

The public discourse of Anna May Wong's private life thus was constructed about the gendered differences between the cultures of the West and the opposing, nebulous East. Wong's "emancipated" status as an Americanized woman prevented her from a relationship with a Chinese man. Her marginalized status as a Chinese woman, however, legally prevented her from marrying a European American. This "strange problem," which "seemingly has no solution," fastened itself to Wong's image. "Yet, Hollywood wonders, what true romance—and romance should go hand in hand with youth—can come to this girl who is a part, yet not a part? . . . She was "a little Oriental girl" enclosed by the Occident, a society in which she longed to fully participate but could not.

Discussions of Wong's cultural conflict set up a divergence of identity for Wong and the generic fanzine reader. On the one hand, the reader might partly identify with Wong's story to wanting to fit in, be popular, and to live her own independent life. On the other hand, presumably few readers could identify with the object of Wong's conflict—her Chinese ancestry. Movie magazines consciously appealed to middle class and white adolescent women, attempting to influence opinions and attitudes, and to market advertisers' beauty products. Romance and marriage persistently presented themselves in most movie magazine features. Anna May Wong's publicized private life reflected some Americans' fascination with oriental exoticism, and the stereotypical "all American" girl's desires of (heterosexual) love, romance, and marriage.

In "The Tragic Real Love Story of Anna May Wong," subtitled "Oriental Beauty Compelled to Choose Between Heritage of Race and Her Performance for an American Husband," the question of why Wong *had* to choose between race and nationality never presented itself. Conflict between Asian and American cultures was assumed to be inevitable. Race was perceived to be the essential and defining factor of one's identity. As one caption read, "Anna May Wong finds it difficult to keep *her real Chinese self* separate from her westernized personality."

At stake in this narrative is the possibility of cultural interaction beyond racial appearances and cultural differences. According to these interviews, assimilation is not possible. . . . Wong represented a test case in which the person who enters into another social, cultural, and racial milieu is subsequently rejected by both cultures, resulting in pathological internal conflict and alienation. One article escalated from a specific story of why Wong does not marry to a general discussion of why individuals should not attempt to mix with different groups, a cautionary tale against attempting to transcend one's own "tribal" affiliation. The dramatization of difference paralleled the narratives against modernity and urban attractions magnified through the exaggerated differences of race that Wong enacted onscreen.

Yet what little Wong revealed regarding her own thoughts on marriage suggests an alternative perspective. Anna May Wong enjoyed the mobility that her career and subsequent wealth supported. Although unmarried, Wong did not lack for companionship or social activities, moving across the intellectuals and sophisticates of Europe and cosmopolitan New York with grace and apparent ease. Her lower-case background and racial heritage notwithstanding, Wong gained access to these social circles because of her appearance and her status.

Wong may have chosen to play up to her racial difference to quiet speculation on why she did not appear interested in marriage. At one point, she and her good friend, actor Philip Ahn, were rumored to be engaged. Representing these two Asian American actors as romantically attached reflected an important aspect of Hollywood publicity. Heterosexual romance served as a functional and fictional construction to meet the expectations and needs of a segment of the moviegoing public. A star's romance in private life therefore was a necessary aspect of his or her public personality. Attributing her never having been photographed on a date with a man to anti-miscegenation law enhanced her heterosexual identity whether based in actual practice or not.

Ironically, Wong could openly refer to racial barriers to explain her lack of a public(ized) romantic life. The narrative of "Success," of "Celebrity," thus was interrupted conspicuously by intrusion of social reality—racial division. Wong's prominent discussions of race suggest that the existence of racial barriers to an interracial romance in fact may have been more publicly accepted than a public romance with a non-Asian man. Conrad Doerr, who rented an apartment from Wong in the late 1940s, recalled, "Her one big love was a Caucasian . . . it was imperative that their romance remain clandestine. He was married."

Working within the parameters of public expectations, Wong could explain her single status along racial or gender lines and disclose nothing more. Stating her reluctance to discuss her own views on marriage, Wong admitted that she wasn't sure "it would work with her, for she wants, above all things, to travel widely. . . . As a bachelor girl she has one consolation, 'I do so enjoy my independence!' " Tellingly, even the article writer could not fully believe she enjoyed her independence, calling it her "one consolation."

There are many gaps in the publicized life of Anna May Wong. Examining two specific events that did not enter into the discourse of her public image is instructive as to what constituted a public personality and what remains private. Wong's attempts to purchase a new home in 1946 were documented by a telegram addressed to gossip columnist and occasional actor Hedda Hopper. Desiring to relocate, Wong had sold her home to Hedda Hopper. Upon looking at homes for sale, Wong soon found that she could not purchase other homes because racial restrictions had been written within the housing contracts. In desperation, she tried to contact Hopper by telephone. Failing to reach Hopper at home or the office, Wong resorted to a telegram.

> Sorry could not reach you by phone at office or home yesterday. Wanted to see you and beg of you to relinquish my property. Perhaps when I explain situation you will understand it is not for any gain or profit but after covering the real estate field thoroughly I discovered there are racial restrictions on everything we looked at. This can be verified by the real estate offices. Therefore please see my unusual situation and make the generous gesture due to seriousness of my position. . . .

Hopper apparently was sympathetic. One week later, Hopper conceded Wong's house by not closing escrow, and Wong was able to regain the deed to her house. Even though relatively affluent and well known, Anna May Wong's movements were circumscribed by prejudice.

Wong never publicly discussed her personal losses. When Wong's mother was killed by a driver in front of the house or when Wong's sister Mary committed suicide in the garage, neither became part of her public image for understandable reasons. But she did not discuss her mother's death with any interviewer. Clearly, the details of these events would not add luster to Wong's star persona, and might even diminish her stature. "Reality" in star discourse as [film scholar Richard] de Cordova has shown, is a construction in concert with the fabricated image of the star herself. Although Wong's Chinese heritage was romanticized, any potentially "negative" aspects that did not enhance her image as a tragic yet romantic figure were omitted. Thus, while Wong might mention travelling abroad to China to visit her family or the anti-miscegenation laws that prevented her from ever marrying a man of another race, little else of her experiences as a Chinese American person was subject for discussion.

Early in her career, Wong attracted media attention because she looked "alien," yet fully participated in the conspicuous consumption of American popular culture. Wong presented herself as more American than Chinese in her dress, slang and attitudes. [Film journalist] Margery Collier commented on this in 1930, concluding that Wong featured "the face and figure of a Chinese girl and the mind of an American flapper." Wong was a combination of stereotypes of both Chinese and American women. Although Collier asserted that "Hybridism is inherent" in Wong's "screen interpretation," Wong realized greater marketability in emphasizing her "Chinese" identity. Wong' stage routine in Europe further exploited her perceived hybridity and exotic Orientalism, as well as her marginal status in Hollywood. The novelty of "appearing foreign" yet sounding "continental," alongside her "American flapper" image, contributed to Europeans' fascination with Wong. An article announcing her 1931 return to Hollywood described how "Wong was the toast of the continent, according to stories brought back by film player who visited Europe. She made appearances in England, Germany, and France and speaks fluently the languages of these nations."

By the early 1930s, Wong tired of being typecast. She herself desired better roles. She had only made two pictures, *Daughters of the Dragon* (1932) and *Shanghai Express* (1932) since her return to the United States in 1932. Before departing for England yet again, in 1933, Wong agreed to be interviewed by the *New York Herald Tribune*'s Marguerite Tazelaar. She explained that "after going through so many experiences of roles that don't appeal to me, I have come to the point of finding it all pretty futile to repeat poor things. I feel that by now I have earned the right to have a little choice in the parts I play." Wong would not be considered for non-Asian roles, yet also could lose Chinese roles to non-Chinese actresses. The *Los Angeles Times* reported in September 1932 that Wong was the leading consideration to star in *The Son-Daughter,* adapted from a stage play. However, Helen Hayes was cast for that role.

Diplomacy also contributed to a lack of suitable roles that Wong could play as a Chinese American. Although 1932 seemed to promise more Chinese roles, the Chinese government's threat to ban Paramount and other studios from exhibiting films in China further dampened Wong's prospects for roles. [As Wong stated:]

> The Chinese government has appointed a Chinese Consul in Hollywood to censor the most objectionable scenes in all Chinese pictures. This puts some limitations upon stories for Chinese players. I suggested to the consul that I make a picture for China, but that is still pending.

Wong explained that the Chinese government's protests over Hollywood depictions of Chinese had resulted in "some limitations upon stories for Chinese players." Chinese nationalism surged in the 1930s in response to Japan's occupation of Manchuria in 1931 and the League of Nation's refusal to respond with sanctions. One manifestation of this was a sharpened governmental critique of Hollywood's negative portrayals of Chinese. In addition, the tendency of films featuring Asian characters or locales to rely on sordid or violent plots also contributed to a decline in roles. Church groups, such as the Catholic Legion, began to boycott Hollywood films because of the perceived immoral intent.

Wong herself hoped that changing depictions of Asians might result from the diverse pressures converging on Hollywood. "[I]n between the films they object to and the wishy-washy films they will certainly get, if the producers get panicky and go to extremes of innocent entertainment, is the kind of picture I've been wanting to do for years." Wong, currently reading Durin Byrne's *Messer Marco Polo,* expressed her interest in making a film based on Marco Polo's experiences in Asia.

> It would help me correct the impression moviegoers have of me as sinister Oriental figure—why, the children were afraid to come near me in London! —it would present a beautiful, entertaining and adventurous picture, and it would make for greater understanding between America and China.

Wong also approached some studios with a proposed film series inspired by the Charlie Chan series, featuring herself as a detective. Studios did not respond positively until three years later, with the success of the Charlie Chan series.

Wong clearly understood that the cultural uniqueness that she represented on screen reflected the very uniqueness that inspired prejudice and discrimination. Despite Wong's frustration with the stereotypical roles she portrayed, she also recognized that her options were greatly limited. In 1937, she explained to an admirer, "As to the medium I am playing in, I have no choice in the matter. One has to take that which is available." As one whose economic livelihood correlated with her ability to project a commodifiable, easily identified image—Wong often was limited to those roles that were available to her as a non-white actress. The need to maintain her celebrity status, in order to enhance her ability to be cast in film roles, required her to accommodate the expectations of audiences and studio executives.

Within the limited range of possible roles available to her, Wong chose to participate in her own exoticization as an Oriental performer. After completing *Limehouse Blues* in Hollywood, no further roles materialized for Wong. She departed again for Europe in 1934, where she already established her reputation, in an attempt to revive her career. Before she left, Wong apparently sought the advice of her Hollywood friend Rob Wagner on how to cultivate her celebrity abroad. Wagner suggested that Wong could actively increase her value in the culture of film and celebrity by being "different." According to Wagner, "Among other things, I urged her to 'can' her Hollywood feathers and be Chinese. I suggested that she even burn incense in her hotel room, to add to her exotic charm."

Wong appears to have followed Wagner's advice and, by all accounts, enjoyed great success in Europe. [Journalist] Vivien North described for the British readers of *Picturegoer Weekly* the mysterious quality surrounding the actress:

> sitting there against the Oriental background of her room, with its bowls of big flowers, its mirrors and soft lighting, her hands—with their lacquered finger nails matching the Chinese red of her jumper—folded, her ankles crossed and every feature composed— almost physically feeling her complete stillness.

[Fan magazine writer] John K. Newnham made similar observations of Wong in a 1930 *Film Weekly* feature, comparing Wong to a "Chinese Puzzle." Newnham asserted that Wong's "American mentality" worked in concert to promote her "Chinese features." This unique combination of American initiative enabled her to "play Hollywood's game well."

> She retains a deliberate atmosphere of subtle mystery. There is always a faint aroma of perfume about her. But in her conversation and outlook on life, she is smartly Western.
> No genuine Chinese woman could boast the attribute she possesses: women haven't been emancipated long enough in China. So you can see why Anna May Wong is so

unique and why she can always step back to starring roles. She has a corner which is uniquely her own.

Newnham's analysis suggests that Wong succeeded because she could use her multiple identifications to her advantage. Presenting herself in more overtly orientalist fashion, Wong's primary selling point continued to be her racialized identity.

FURTHER READING

Cheng, John. "Amazing, Astounding, Wonder: Popular Science, Culture, and the Emergence of Science Fiction in the United States, 1926–1939, Ph.D. dissertation, U.C. Berkeley (1997).

Dower, John W. *War Without Mercy: Race and Power in the Pacific War* (1986).

Isaacs, Harold R. *Scratches on Our Minds: American Images of China and India* (1958).

Jones, Dorothy B. *The Portrayal of China and India on the American Screen, 1896–1955* (1995).

Lee, Robert G. *Orientals: Asian Americans in Popular Culture* (1999).

Leong, Karen Janis. "The China Mystique: Mayling Soong Chiang, Pearl S. Buck and Anna May Wong in the American Imagination," Ph.D. dissertation, U.C. Berkeley, (1999).

Ling, Amy. *Between Worlds: Women Writers of Chinese Ancestry* (1990).

Marchetti, Gina. *Romance and the 'Yellow Peril': Race, Sex, and Discursive Strategies in Hollywood Fiction* (1993).

Moy, James S. *Marginal Sights: Staging the Chinese in America* (1993).

Palumbo-Liu, David. *Asian/American: Historical Crossings of a Racial Frontier* (1999).

Rydell, Robert. *All the World's a Fair: Visions of Empire at American International Expositions, 1876–1916* (1984).

Said, Edward W. *Orientalism* (1978).

Takaki, Ronald T. *Iron Cages: Race and Culture in 19th-Century America* (1979).

Tchen, John Kuo Wei. *New York Before Chinatown: Orientalism and the Shaping of American Culture, 1776–1882* (1999).

White-Parks, Annette. *Sui Sin Far/Edith Maude Eaton: A Literary Biography* (1995).

Wong, Eugene Franklin. *On Visual Media Racism: Asians in the American Motion Pictures* (1978).

Wong, K. Scott. "Liang Qichao and the Chinese of America: A Re-evaluation of His Selected Memoir of Travels in the New World," *Journal of American Ethnic History* 11 (1992): 3–24.

———. "Transformation of Culture: Three Chinese Views of America," *American Quarterly* 48 (1996): 201–232.

Yu, Henry. *Thinking Orientals: Migration, Contact, and Exoticism in Modern America* (2001).

CHAPTER
7

Interethnic Tensions
and Alliances in the
1920s and 1930s

The 1920s were a period of transition in the story of Asian Americans. It was this decade that the long-standing movement to exclude Asian immigration culminated with the passage of the restrictionist Immigration Act of 1924. It was also at this time that the Supreme Court settled the lingering legal question of whether Asian immigrants could become American citizens by deciding that Japanese and East Indians (and by logical extension all other Asian groups) were not "white" and therefore were barred from the naturalization process. But if the 1920s marked the end of some critical themes in Asian American history, it also witnessed two developments that would recast relations among Asian American groups and across the color line. The first of these was the maturation of Asian settlement, including increasing marriage rates, growth of indigenous institutions, rising numbers of American-born generations, and the crucial movement from agricultural labor to agricultural proprietorship. The blossoming of ethic communities was especially true for Japanese Americans but was shared in a more limited sense by Chinese, Korean, and East Indian Americans. The second new development in the 1920s was the influx of Filipino immigrants, who began arriving in large numbers just as the Immigration Act was being passed. This was no coincidence, since exclusion did not apply to American colonial subjects and the demand for immigrant labor remained strong in the American West.

Filipino immigrants confronted the same racist and nativist sentiment and attacks the bedeviled earlier Asian groups. Another similarity emerged as Filipinos lost the safeguard of colonial status, becoming "aliens" ineligible for immigration and citizenship after the process of Philippine independence began in 1934. Yet the timing of their arrival just before and during the Great Depression prevented most Filipinos from climbing out of farm labor, and, as a result, they would have the deepest ties to the labor movement of all Asian immigrants. Another factor that distinguished the Filipinos' was their racial sensibility, which after centuries of intimate contact with Spanish and, more recently, American colonizers better prepared them

*than other Asian immigrant groups for relations with white Americans. This may
explain, in part, why anti-Filipino race riots and the movement for Filipino exclusion were fueled to a much greater degree than before by fears about Filipino sexual
relations with white women.*

◐ D O C U M E N T S

The first three documents address questions of interethnic and interracial marriage.
In Document 1 an American-born Chinese American women explains her marriage to
a Japanese immigrant as the result of "turning against my own people" because of their
strict "Oriental" traditions. Document 2 is the testimonial of a "cosmopolitan" white
women regarding her marriage to a Chinese immigrant and, after he died, her marriage
to a Japanese immigrant. In her story, class, rather than culture, was the deciding
factor in marrying both husbands. Document 3 is a brief life narrative of Inder Singh,
who explains the pragmatic reasons why he married a Mexican woman and not someone of another race.

The next three documents capture different perspectives on the question of Filipino
immigrant sexuality. Document 4 is an excerpt from an oral history in which a Filipino
immigrant turns the charge of Filipino lasciviousness on its head by condemning the
shockingly liberal sexual practices of American women. Document 5 is a contemporary
description of an anti-Filipino race riot in Watsonville, California, written by University
of Southern California sociologist Emory Bogardus. According to Bogardus, the riot was
sparked by an incident in which Filipinos danced with nine white dance hall women.
Document 6 is an excerpt from a *Time* magazine report on the sexual fears behind the
American government's campaign to return Filipino immigrants to the Philippines.

The final three documents shed light on the intersection between race, labor, and
economics. Document 7 is a narrative of an interview with E. E. Chandler, a landholder
in southern California's Imperial Valley, and an observer of race relations in this agricultural community. Document 8 is a brief passage from author Carlos Bulosan's
fictionalized memoir *America Is in the Heart* in which he describes the dangers of
labor organizing in 1930s California. Finally, Document 9 is an account by Communist
labor leader Karl Yoneda of his organizing Japanese immigrants into multiracial labor
unions in the 1930s.

1. A Chinese American Woman Identifies with Japanese American Marriage Practices, circa 1924

I was born in Los Angeles but was raised in strictly Oriental fashion. My mother died
while I was quite young and my grandmother raised me. My father was dominated
by the Chinese idea that the man was the head of the family and that the children
were to be entirely submerged in the family—we were not considered as having
any individuality of our own. When I was in school I was told that my position was a
subordinate one even in cases where I had more information than father on account

From Fisk University, Social Science Institute, *Orientals and Their Cultural Adjustment: Interviews, Life
Histories and Social Adjustment Experiences of Chinese and Japanese of Varying Backgrounds and Length
of Residence in the United States* (Nashville: Social Science Institute, Fisk University, 1946), 24–26.

of my school work, but he would never admit anything like that. I was kept closely at home and restrained until I began to revolt against this situation. I saw the freedom of the American children and saw that some other Chinese girls had more freedom than I had.

In school I had no particular hardships but at times I was hurt by expressions to the effect that the Chinese were inferior. While I went to school I did not really have any close American friends but associated with some Chinese girls. I had to learn the Chinese language because father told me time and again that I could never be an American because my skin was yellow and only white people could be Americans.

While I was in school I also made friends with some Japanese and became interested in them. I began to see that the Japanese were less rigid in holding to their Oriental customs and were really more assimilable. I began to turn against my own people and became more interested in the Japanese. I married a Japanese and since then I have come in contact with many Americans and I have been much happier. My husband worked for several years at an English club in Vancouver, B.C., where he learned the English ways, and so he has been quite free in mingling with white people.

When I was married the Chinese group cut me off and it hurt me, but I have been taken into the Japanese group so heartily that I am perfectly satisfied. I used to attend the Chinese Methodist Church, but after my marriage there was a decided coolness shown toward me. I now attend the Japanese Reformed Church, where I receive the heartiest welcome, and even though I understand but very little Japanese I enjoy the service because I feel the spirit of it. I am frequently asked to sing at church; I am glad to help in any way I can.

When I was married my own father refused to recognize my husband as his son-in-law. My husband told me not to worry because when my father needed him he would be Johnny-on-the-spot, and then all would be well. The time did come, and now father thinks there is no one quite like my husband.

The young people among the Chinese have a harder time than among the Japanese. The parents retain their Oriental ideas longer and try to impose them upon the children and to prevent their Americanization. The Chinese do not co-operate with the young people as the Japanese do. This makes it quite difficult for some persons in the group.

Dr. Margaret Chung, a relative of mine, who graduated from the University of Southern California medical college, could get no practice in Los Angeles because she was unmarried. She is now practicing in San Francisco where the Chinese are more liberal. In Los Angeles an unmarried women cannot converse with a group of married women. Before I was married, if I approached a group of married women they would close up like clams, but immediately after I was wedded I could approach them. Chinese women do not teach their daughters anything about the marriage relations, but the Japanese do.

My half-brother . . . has made several appearances in the Juvenile Court. He has been going around with a group of American boys and has been the "goat." They have taken several autos for joy rides, after which they have returned them. The home condition, without doubt, has much to do with Edward's delinquencies. The home is too oriental and repressive and does not attract him so that he spends too much time on the street.

I have noticed a great deal of change in my father's home since I was a child. The younger children now do not obey him as I had to do. One day I said to my half-brothers that they had a chance to attend school and should make the most of their opportunities so they would be able to take care of father in his old age. One of them spoke up and said, "I'll have all I can do to take care of myself." In China such an expression would be considered disgraceful, because the children take care of their aged parents."

2. A White American Woman Compares Marriage to Chinese and Japanese Husbands, circa 1924

Since my marriage to an Oriental nearly a quarter of a century ago, among the various adjectives, complimentary and otherwise, that have been employed to describe me, none has seemed more apt than that used by a Berkeleyan the other day when he spoke of me as "Cosmopolitan." In fact, I am a product of San Francisco, the great cosmopolitan city of the West, and among my most treasured possessions is a silver medal awarded to me for scholarship upon my graduation from the North Cosmopolitan Grammar School. I always loved that name and regret that the school has since been rechristened the Hancock.

Many nationalities were represented in that district at North Beach, and my classmates were largely the children of foreigners. Although myself of pure English stock, race prejudice was foreign to my nature. The struggles of those children to learn English awakened my sympathies, and it was through helping a Spanish girl to get her lessons that I discovered my talent for teaching. I was popular with these young Americans of the first generation and was frequently the only person at a party or social gathering who was not an Italian, a Spaniard, a Dane, or a German, as the case might be. Nevertheless, I was perfectly at home in any one of these groups.

The Japanese population in San Francisco at that time was practically nil, and my only point of contact with the Chinese during my grammar and high school days was through the laundry man, the day worker and the vegetable huckster. Nevertheless, at the age of five I had expressed great indignation at the persecution of the Chinese consequent upon the Dennis Kearny agitation, and later, when about ten years old, at which time we were residing in the Mission district. I had been delighted to find that there was a Sunday school for Chinese men in Bethany Congregational Church. I remember having asked my Sunday school teacher whether she thought that Dr. Pond would let me teach some of those Chinese when I grew older.

Having been graduated from high school at the age of 17 I entered Stanford University, where I majored in history, with sociology and education as my minors. In the economics class I met a most brilliant foreigner in the person of Rev. Walter Ngon Fong, pastor of the Methodist Mission of San Jose and president of the Western Debating Society of Stanford University. He was an upper classman, but we

From Fisk University, Social Science Institute, *Orientals and Their Cultural Adjustment: Interviews, Life Histories and Social Adjustment Experiences of Chinese and Japanese of Varying Backgrounds and Length of Residence in the United States* (Nashville: Social Science Institute, Fisk University, 1946), 42–50. 72–73.

were attracted to each other from the first. However, the thought that we should even become man and wife did not occur to either of us. He was very well known at Stanford and I had a number of student friends. I walked the mile through the arboretum to and from Palo Alto sometimes with one and sometimes with another, really being partial to none. Gradually, however, I began to realize that there was something deeper and broader about him. He seemed to have the education of two men. Although his well-stored mind was exceptionally keen, he was humble and retiring in disposition, and I became enamored with his visions of service.

Mr. Fong was the only Chinese student in Stanford at that time, and, as he was a general favorite with the women as well as the men students, my companying with him aroused no comment. It was not until a few days before his graduation in May, 1896, that he asked me to share his future. I was unprepared for the question and took an indefinite time to think about it, much to his discomfort.

It was then that the race question and popular prejudice against the Chinese loomed up before me, hideously black and threatening. All the sunshine seem to go out of the sky, a blight seemed to settle upon the flowers, and the birds to cease their singing. For three terrible months the struggle raged within my locked breast, for there was none but the Almighty in whom I could confide. My parents, while not narrow-minded themselves, had not felt quite comfortable about my going with Mr. Fong, for fear that there might be unfavorable comment. My mother had given a sigh of relief when he had bid us good-by and packed his trunk and departed from Palo Alto.

I knew that public opinion would condemn the marriage and prophesy divorce and other horrors. I analyzed every possible objection, treating it impersonally and scientifically. Finally, I was convinced beyond a doubt that there was no reasonable ground for one member of the human family to regard himself as superior to another no matter what the race or the color of the skin of that individual might be. The Scripture verse: "Man looketh upon the outward appearance, but God looketh upon the heart," sang itself into my heart.

During all this time I had not seen Mr. Fong, although we had corresponded, and I had continued to go out with the other young people as usual. The proposal had been sudden and unexpected, but by the close of the summer I was very certain that I loved this young Chinese graduate to the exclusion of all others and that it would be cowardly for me to break his heart and blight his future, because I feared to face popular opinion. We became engaged on Admission Day, September 9.

Chapter II

As I desired to complete my school year, the wedding was set for the following June. Meanwhile Mr. Fong established himself in the practice of law in San Francisco and incidentally became the head of the Chinese Revolutionary Party in America, the object of which was to drive the Manchus out of China. While longing to tell my mother, though not daring to, as I wanted to shoulder the entire responsibility for the step myself, I provided myself with a serviceable trousseau, and, leaving a letter of explanation behind, entrained early one June morning for Denver, Colorado.

By way of explanation as to why we went to Denver to get married instead of having the ceremony performed in San Francisco, I would say that there are laws in all the Pacific Coast States forbidding the issuing of licenses for marriages between whites and Orientals, but that none of the other states have any such restrictions.

The ceremony was performed on June 19, 1897, by Dr. Camden Coburn of Chautauqua fame. The "Rocky Mountain News" published a very good item regarding us, and incidentally wired the news to all part of the United States. Early next morning we received a telegram of congratulation from San Francisco. My uncle in Chicago, my aunt in Detroit and numerous other relatives in the Eastern States read the news with astonishment, as they had no idea that I had been thinking of marriage. Without exception, however, they welcomed the man of my choice as a relative, and some sent pretty wedding gifts. In Denver, a wedding reception was prepared for us by some Americans who had known my husband in San Jose. People treated us finely wherever we went, and upon our return to California the San Francisco Chinese gave us a grand reception and a whole tableful of useful gifts.

We established our home in Berkeley, my husband continuing his law practice in San Francisco, and specializing at the University of California in international law, in which he later took a higher degree, while I kept house and continued my undergraduate work. The following year he accepted the pastorship of the Chinese Methodist Episcopal Mission in Oakland and I engaged to help him teach in the evening school. We still continued to take some work at the university and thus two busy, happy years sped by.

Mr. Fong had been looking forward to a professorship in the Chinese National University at Peking, and in fact the agreement had been entered into when the Boxer uprising took place and the University was closed for some time. He therefore accepted an appointment at the University of California to teach the Chinese language, which appointment was announced at the same time as that of his friend, Yoshi S. Kuno, as instructor in Japanese. We then abandoned all hope of going to China, and built a home on Francisco Street, two sons being born to us later.

The first one was a most precocious child, talking and carrying a tune at six months, and at nine forming short sentences and replying to questions. Strangers from all parts of Berkeley came to our home saying that they had heard of that marvelous baby and asking if they might hear him talk. He was a very sociable baby, loving company, and delighted all who came. He is still an entertaining talker and his love for his fellow-men has never forsaken him, for he will share his last dollar with the man that is down. Unlike his father he has no desire for a higher education. His craving is to be among people; to be doing something out in the world. For the past four years he has been connected with the Stewart Fruit Company at San Dimas, Los Angeles county. He was one of the eight who distinguished themselves in that district in 1919 in fighting the forest fires that threatened the orange groves.

The younger son, while not so precocious as a child as was his brother, is of a more quiet, retiring disposition and is a deeper thinker. He is now 15 years of age and will enter the University of California this fall.

Chapter III

NOTE:—After spending some years in their home on Francisco street, Mr. Fong received a call from the Revolutionary Party in China to go to Hongkong to establish a Revolutionary College. There Mrs. Fong met with a very cosmopolitan atmosphere.

She met people from India, Annam, Siam, the Straits Settlements, Japan, the Philipines and other parts of Asia, as well as from every nation in Europe.

Early in May of the third year of their residence in Hongkong, however, Mr. Fong was stricken with Bubonic plague, and shortly died. That summer Mrs. Fong returned to San Francisco.

Chapter IV

In the group of San Francisco, Palo Alto and Berkeley people who met at the pier stood Professor Yoshi S. Kuno, one of my dead husband's closest friends, for despite the fact that one was Chinese and the other was Japanese, these two scholarly Orientals had loved each other as brothers. Upon hearing of the death of President Fong, Professor Kuno had been prostrated with grief, and there had come over him an intense desire to do something for his dead friend's family.

Finally, after about a year I became the wife of Professor Kuno, a strong bond between us being affection for the one that was gone and a desire to make a home for the children. It seemed like living again to go back to my home on Francisco street, and with a husband and children to help me to dig weeds in my own back yard.

Chapter V

Differences in husbands may be attributed to differences in social inheritance, environment, disposition, education and ideals; and secondarily to their reactions upon the behavior of their wives. Perhaps no two individuals of the same nationality assume precisely the same attitude toward their mates. Therefore it would scarcely be reasonable to expect men who have been brought up under widely varying conditions to regard their wives in exactly the same way.

The task of comparing Oriental with American husbands, who themselves are so unlike, would be a heroic one, for as everybody knows American husbands of French, Italian, English and German descent differ widely. Speaking broadly, however, it would be easier to find the counterparts of Oriental husbands in Europe than in America. Furthermore, the gulf between the Japanese and the Chinese husband is much greater than that between the American and European. This disparity may be traced directly to the national inheritance of these two neighboring peoples of the yellow race. The position of woman in the two countries has been different throughout the ages. For instance, feudalism was abolished in China about two and one-half centuries B.C. while that institution lingered in Japan until 1872 A.D.

There are instances in Japanese history where an emperor has sometimes given a concubine of great beauty to a loyal supporter for faithful service or to a general as a guerdon for some deed of valor. Even today, despite the great advance toward freedom that has been made by woman in Japan, the Japanese husband looks upon his wife as "belonging to him" and considers it his prerogative, in addition to enjoying perfect freedom in the management of his own affairs, to dictate with regard to every detail of the home. He selects his wife's associates and arranges her schedule for her, and although, perhaps, he does not say so in so many words, he still considers himself her lord and master and takes it as a matter of course that she should find her highest job and satisfaction in complying with his desires.

I have in mind a cultured Christian Japanese wife, a woman of noble family, wedded to a gentle, unassuming graduate of a Japanese university, who provided for her well, was faithful and affectionate, and stood high in business circles. This lady rose in good time every Sunday morning to prepare breakfast and get her little American-born daughter ready for Sunday school. She would have liked to accompany her or go to the morning church service, but, as her husband enjoyed staying in bed until about 10:30 Sunday mornings, it was her duty to remain at home in order that she might get a special breakfast for him when he chose to get up. She frequently had to prepare dinner for his men friends and be on hand to wait upon them in the evening. Thus her Sabbath, which had been so precious to her before marriage, generally meant a day in the kitchen. She bore it uncomplainingly and with a patience and stocism foreign to the average American wife.

Both of my husbands came to California when comparatively young. Having mingled constantly with cultured Americans, they early absorbed the best ideals of American life and became accustomed to regard woman from an Occidental standpoint. Nevertheless, though not in extreme degree, it has been easy for me to detect the racial characteristics in their respective attitudes toward me. . . .

Chapter XVIII

Upon hearing that it had been said that I had disgraced my family by marrying a Chinese, Dr. David Starr Jordan announced it as his opinion that any family in the State of California might be proud to have Walter Fong as a member. The comment of the various members of the Stanford faculty was equally favorable. I once saw a written statement regarding our marriage made by Professor Mary Barnes, under whom we had both studied history, in which she said that I had been signally honored.

In Berkeley, while the faculty and students at the University of California were free from prejudice, ours being a pioneer marriage of this kind, there was considerable undesirable publicity in the town. Women in their clubs and various chit-chat societies raked me over unmercifully. Occasionally some of their findings reached my ears, but I was too busy with things worthwhile to pause to inquire the names of the authors of these bursts of eloquence.

There have been many American girls married to Orientals since I blazed the trail in 1897. Some of these have held up their heads, been proud of their husbands, and have won respect, while others have tried to conceal, from all but their immediate associates, the fact that the head of the house was an Oriental. They have never appeared in public with their husbands nor mentioned them to acquaintances except in a very general way.

I know of one such case here in Berkeley where both the Chinese husband and his beautiful young American wife were students at the University of California. In registering, she spelled the family name a little differently from what he did. Although they went to school at the same hour she never walked with him neither did she recognize him on the campus. She made many friends among the women students, but she never dared invite any of them to her home, and she lived in mortal fear that some day they would find out that her husband was a Chinese and banish her forever from their society. She didn't do very well in college and the joy gradually faded from her expressive blue eyes. I frequently talked to her about the falseness of her position, but she said that having started in that way she couldn't do otherwise.

For my own part, I feel that through my marriages I have been brought into contact with a type of people morally and intellectually superior to the average. Of one thing I am certain, and that is that at the present time I am receiving more than my share of invitations to social gatherings and to the homes of people of culture who are interested in my husband because of his broad scholarly attainments. Therefore, I consider that through my marriages to Orientals I have been helped up socially rather than dragged down.

3. Indian Immigrant Inder Singh Discusses His Marriage with a Mexican Woman, 1924

Fifteen years ago when I was at the age of 24 I left my home in India and came to America. In India I was a Sikh missionary, but the Government did not like me and interferred with my activities. When I received a letter from a friend of mine in America I sailed for San Francisco where I intended to carry on my missionary work, but finding no opportunity for such activity I turned to manual labor for a livelihood. For several years I worked on ranches near Los Angeles and now for the past 5 years I have been farming in the Imperial Valley. Two years ago I married a Mexican woman and through her I am able to secure land for farming. Your land law can't get rid of me now; I am going to stay. Several Hindus have married Mexican women. The Hindu group accepts the Mexican women that come in through intermarriage, but should a Hindu marry a Negro woman he would have his head cut off. There is no advantage in marrying an American woman because she loses her citizenship on marriage to an alien. My wife's family live in Calexico. She went there to visit them today and at times I go with her. My wife is inclined to be like the American women to a certain degree. The American woman is entirely too free; she is the boss and if a woman tells a man to kill some one he will do it. My wife would like to boss me, but I am not disturbed by that and we get along very well. Should she at any time want to leave me I would tell her, "The road is wide; go ahead." There is entirely too much divorce here because the women are so free. At first I was really shocked by the freedom of the women. I have now grown accustomed to the practice of men and women going along the streets together. If I were to return to India I believe I would carry out this practice over there, I should like to return to India to secure a position in the immigration office so that I might treat some Americans as they have treated me. I have applied for American citizenship but this has been denied me. Were I in the immigration service in India, when an American would apply for entry I would prefer him to his Consul, and that would be of no avail. He would then have to apply to Washington and even to London but it would avail him nothing. Of course, this treatment accorded me is only in perfect accord with many other things in America. Justice is quite uneven, for the man with

"Interview with Inder Singh." From the papers of William C. Smith (A-237, A-102, 84-A), Special Collections & University Archives, University of Oregon.

money can kill another and get off. I am interested in India and am keeping in touch with conditions there. India will be free in 1925. I hope to see the caste lines break down. Here in America, we all eat together, so why should they not in India. Of course, not all the Hindus in America are alike. The Hindu who wears the *pugree* on his head still holds to his old religion, but I who have taken to wearing a hat and shaving my beard, have lost my religion. So far as my relations with Americans are concerned they have been quite good. I have several American neighbors now with whom I an on good terms. I also have some very good Japanese neighbors. There are some Swedes in the community, but damn them, they are bad; I don't know of any good Swedes. The Mexicans are usually no good. A Mexican will come and borrow five dollars which he will never repay. My father-in-law and brother-in-law, however, are pretty good; they are better than most Mexicans. But no matter what my neighbors may be I should really like to quit farming and go into a store; farming is entirely too hard.

4. A Filipino Immigrant Is Shocked by Sexual Freedom in the United States, circa 1924

I have been shocked with some of the things that I saw here for the first time. Most of all was the girls in their bathing suits. I first saw an American lady in her bathing suit in the boat where I rode. Then I went to the beach for the first time. I have seen girls and boys (young people) in their bathing suits, catching each other, and playing without any delicacy on the part of the girls. Some of the girls were almost naked. This freedom and enjoyment of the young people has not yet been comprehended by our young people at home. The girls are so delicate that they are very careful not to expose their legs especially before young men.

Again, in the movie, I have seen young people (lovers and sweethearts) who sit together and have the arms of the young men around the necks of the young women. Their actions shocked me very much. Those actions might be done in their private rooms. Even in the street and in the street cars, the intimacy between lovers is too much for the public.

The freedom of young women is beyond my comprehension. Some ladies are let by their parents to go anywhere. They do as they please. They are free to go with their boy friends, even late at night. They go out riding even at nights. I have been staying in a house where there was a lady. A boy friend comes to visit even late at night, and when the friend comes the parents leave her in the living room with him and the girl and the boy stay alone together. Such freedom has never yet been given to the girls at home. They are carefully watched for who know what will happen, for they, the young people, are in their impulsive and sensitive nature!

I was talking with a lady friend about the freedom of young girls in this country and about their love affairs, and she said that a girl might go out riding in the machine with a boy whom she meets the first time in the street. She said that most of the

From Fisk University, Social Science Institute, *Orientals and Their Cultural Adjustment: Interviews, Life Histories and Social Adjustment Experiences of Chinese and Japanese of Varying Backgrounds and Length of Residence in the United States* (Nashville: Social Science Institute, Fisk University, 1946), 132–134.

American girls, when the boys take them out to a show or riding, give those boys a good time, that is, by kissing and all sorts of happy good time, because if not the boys would not take them out again for the next time. When the girls get together, they talked of what they did to the boys and how they gave them a good time. These statements were a great surprise to me. Surely the moral life is degrading. She also said that these young people make love for the time being. They are engaged for the time being without any thought of getting married afterwards. The young people at home never do this. When they make love and are engaged, they are sure that they will marry. In the newspapers we read about the effects of this free love making. Marriage is very cheap because divorce is easily taken. Love stories, suggestions for young people about love affairs, are read in the press. One time I read, "A young beautiful lady who is supporting a father wants a husband." Love is even advertised! Almost all of the movies are full of love stories. I believe that all of these read in the newspapers and seen in the movies have a great moral effect upon the lives of the young people.

I observe that the independence of women in this country is too much. The center of life here is the individual, while at home the family is the center. I don't see any conflict of these young people with their parents in this country. I believe in the freedom of the young people to think for themselves, to act for themselves. But oftentimes the young people do not do just the right thing because of inexperience in life or because of their acting upon their impulse at the moment. The individual freedom must not go so far as to disregard the opinions, advice, and suggestions of older people.

5. Sociologist Emory Bogardus Analyzes an Anti-Filipino Riot, 1930

Before an analysis is attempted of the riots, an account will be given of antecedent factors. . .

(1) A few cases of Filipinos had been brought into court of the justices of peace of Pajaro township, and into the country court at Salinas (of Filipinos living in the Watsonville district). The offenses were usually "reckless driving" of automobiles.

(2) On January 10, 1930, there appeared newspaper accounts of a set of Resolutions passed in Pajaro (adjoining Watsonville) by the Northern Monterey Chamber of Commerce and written it is stated by the justice of peace of Pajaro township. The article in the *Pajaronian*, appeared under a double column, first page headline which read: "Resolution Flaying Filipinos Drawn by Judge D. W. Rohrback." The article began as follows:

From Emory S. Bogardus, *Anti-Filipino Race Riots: A Report Made to the Ingram Institute of Social Science of San Diego* (San Diego: Ingram Institute of Social Science, 1930); reprinted by permission of author's daughter, Mrs. Ruth Bogardus Allen, in *Letters in Exile: An Introductory Reader on the History of Philipinos in America* (Los Angeles: UCLA Asian American Studies Center, 1976), 51–62. This last reprint was reprinted in *The Philippines Reader: A History of Colonialism, Neocolonialism, Dictatorship, and Resistance,* ed. Daniel B. Schirmer and Stephen Rosskamm Shalom (Boston: South End Press, 1987), 59–62.

Coming out square-toed and flat-footed in an expression on the Filipino question, the Northern Monterey Chamber of Commerce adopted a resolution Wednesday night (January 8) designating the Filipino population of this district with being undesirable and of possessing unhealthy habits and destructive of the wage scale of other nationalities in agricultural and industrial pursuits.

The article continued:

When interviewed this morning Judge Rohrback said the move of the Monterey Chamber of Commerce was but the beginning of an investigation of a situation that will eventually lead to the exclusion of the Filipinos or the deterioration of the white race in the state of California.

The charges made against the Filipinos in this Resolution were as follows: (1) Economic. They accept, it is alleged, lower wages than the American standards allow. The new immigrants coming in each month increase the labor supply and hold wages down. They live on fish and rice, and a dozen may occupy one or two rooms only. The cost of living is very low, hence, Americans cannot compete with them. (2) Health. Some Filipinos bring in meningitis, and other dangerous diseases. Some live unhealthily. Sometimes fifteen or more sleep in one or two rooms. (3) Intermarriage. A few have married white girls. Others will. "If the present state of affairs continues there will be 40,000 half-breed in California before ten years have passed,"— is the dire prediction.

The Resolutions included the following statement about sending the Filipinos home.

We do not advocate violence but we do feel that the United States should give the Filipinos their liberty and send those unwelcome inhabitants from our shores that the white people who have inherited this country for themselves and their offspring might live.

It is evident that the Northern Monterey Chamber of Commerce did not speak for other Chambers of Commerce for the Resolutions contained the following challenge:

Other Chambers of Commerce have probably passed resolutions endorsing the use of Filipino labor as being indispensable. If that is true, better that the fields of the Salinas Valley should grow into weed patches and our wonderful forests be blackened.

These and similar statements speak for themselves regarding the impassioned tone of the Resolutions.

Upon the publication of the Resolutions sensitive Filipino leaders promptly replied. A four-page pamphlet entitled "The Torch" appeared within a few days from Salinas. It contained a detailed reply to the Resolutions, by a member of the editorial staff of the *Three Stars,* Stockton, California. It questions vigorously the truth of a number of statements in the Resolutions and replies sharply to the insinuations of others. . . .

A few days later, January 19, a mass meeting of 300 Filipinos was held in a hall at Palm Beach, a few miles west of Watsonville, according to a half page paid advertisement in the Watsonville evening newspaper. As indicated by the statements in this article the reactions of the Filipinos to the Pajaro Resolutions had now reached the state of formal group action.

On January 11, 1930, a new angle to the race situation in and around Watsonville developed. A small Filipino club leased a dance hall from two Americans at Palm

Beach (four or five miles west of Watsonville), imported nine white dance hall girls, and set up a taxi dance hall for the Filipino members. Definite rules of propriety were apparently maintained. The American owners of the property stated that the Filipinos conducted their dances in more orderly fashion than did many American groups who had leased the dance hall property. But the idea of Filipinos dancing with white girls (no matter who the latter were) incensed white young men of Watsonville, and they determined to break up the procedure. As one white person said to the writer:

> Taxi dance halls where white girls dance with Orientals may be all right in San Francisco or Los Angeles but not in our community. We are a small city and have had nothing of the kind before. We won't stand for anything of this kind.

On Sunday, the 19th, the anti-Filipino demonstrations began and lasted until the early hours of Thursday morning, the 23rd. Early Sunday afternoon it is said "that several machine loads of American youths went out to the resort (the dance hall at Palm Beach), but were barred by deputies hired to guard the place." Later that evening several fights occurred on the streets of Watsonville between Americans and Filipinos. On Monday evening, the 20th, the disturbances continued. "Possibly 200 Americans formed Filipino hunting parties, running in groups from 25 to over 100 persons." On Tuesday evening, the 21st, "a mob (of white men and boys) attempted to storm the Palm Beach premises. Word had been passed among boys of the town that a mass meeting of the Filipinos was to be held at Palm Beach. The boys were aware that several white girls were living on the premises and working in the dance hall there. This fact infuriated them and at eleven o'clock last night full thirty machines, filled with flaming youth," went to Palm Beach, but were met by the owners of the beach resort who held them at bay with guns until "shortly after midnight" when the sheriff, deputies, and constables arrived and "made short work of the mob." Before the arrival of the officers there was some shooting but no one was seriously hurt.

On Wednesday evening, the 22nd, the rioting reached its climax. Violence developed into destroying property, beating Filipinos, and finally one Filipino was killed.

> Forty-six terror-stricken Filipinos beaten and bruised, cowered in the City Council room . . . after being rescued from a mob of 500 infuriated men and boys who, being robbed of their prey, shattered windows and wrecked the interior of the brown men's dwellings.

Further light on the rioting is given:

> To the accompaniment of pistol shots, clubbings and general disorder . . . it is believed that 700 trouble-seekers, armed with clubs and some firearms, attacked Filipino dwellings, destroyed property, and jeopardized lives. The most serious rioting occurred on the San Juan road in Pajaro about 10 o'clock . . . when a mob estimated at 250 men entered several Filipino dwellings and clubbed the occupants.

Then came the fatal shot, and the ending of the rioting. A headline and an opening sentence tell the story tersely: "Wild Rioters Murder Filipino in Fourth Night of Mob Terror," and "Mob Violence in Watsonville Is Ended." A published account reads:

> Near midnight a carload of rowdies drove to the ranch (Murphy) and began firing into it. The unfortunate men (or boys) trapped like rats were forced into a closet where they huddled and prayed.

One of the Filipino boys, Fermin Tober, did not follow the others. The next morning, "it was discovered that a heavy bullet, tearing through the walls and a door of the bunkhouse had pierced Tobers' heart." . . .

Somewhat belatedly the leading citizens of Watsonville came to the rescue of the reputation of the city, and of the Filipinos. The headline in the *Evening Pajaronian* summed up part of the reactions: "Volunteer Deputies Bring Welcome Peace to Turbulent Town." The American Legion, the Rotary, the Kiwanis, and other organizations took action in support of law and order, and of protection of the Filipinos.

The *Evening Pajaronian* of the 24th reports that seven (white) boys were brought into the court of the justice of the peace of Pajaro township for preliminary hearing on the charge of rioting. At the hearing a total of eight boys were bound over to the Superior Court of Monterey County. The justice is quoted as stating that he hoped "with all his heart that the judge of the superior court would be lenient in handling their cases as he did not consider them criminals." On February 17, six of the eight youths pleaded guilty at Salinas for attacking Filipinos. On February 25th, the eight were sentenced to serve two years in the county jail. Probation was granted four. The other four were sent to the county jail for thirty days; then put on probation for two years, during which time they must keep away from pool halls, abstain from intoxicating liquors; they must never molest Filipinos and on the other hand they are to lead sober, industrious lives. At the inquest over the body of Fermin Tober it was decided that the person who had fired the fatal shot was unknown.

6. *Time* Magazine Reveals Sexual Basis for Filipino Repatriation, 1936

This week a special train chartered by the Department of Labor will start from Manhattan, proceed to Cleveland, Chicago, St. Louis, on across the plains and the Rocky Mountains to San Francisco picking up passengers as it goes. Four weeks later these same passengers will all debark from the *President Coolidge* at Manila, having enjoyed a trip halfway around the world entirely at the expense of the U.S. Government. Anyone in the U.S. may join the party provided he is a Filipino born in the Philippines.

Last week few people east of the Continental Divide knew or cared that such a trip was about to take place, but on the Pacific Coast it was an object of interest. Reason for the free ride was that last summer Congress passed and President Roosevelt signed a bill for the Treasury to pay the transportation back to his native land of any Filipino who would accept. A backer of this law was Pacific Coast Labor, which saw in the creation of the Philippine Commonwealth a good excuse for inviting Filipino workers to go home rather than stay in the U.S. selling their services for 10¢ an hour in competition with white men.

The Pacific Coast was interested in this subsidized exodus not only from the standpoint of labor but also from the standpoint of race and sex. In many places Filipinos are "problem children" for Pacific Coast authorities. To the intense dismay

From "Lovers' Departure," *Time*, April 13, 1936, p. 17. Copyright 1936 Time Inc. Reprinted by permission.

of race-conscious Californians these little brown men not only have a preference for white girls, particularly blondes, but have even established to many a white girl's satisfaction their superior male attractions.

Last January into San Francisco Municipal Court went a white girl with the charge that a Filipino boy had held her while a rival white girl battered her nose, blacked both her eyes. Said Judge Sylvain Lazarus from the bench: "This is a deplorable situation. . . . It is a dreadful thing when these Filipinos, scarcely more than savages, come to San Francisco, work for practically nothing, and obtain the society of these girls. Because they work for nothing, decent white boys cannot get jobs."

Promptly Filipinos held a mass meeting in San Francisco, passed a resolution denouncing this description of them as savages, sent a copy to Quintin Paredes, Philippine Resident Commissioner in Washington. Before the Philippine Commonwealth was set up Commissioner Paredes, short, swart, swank, suave and banjo-eyed; was Speaker of the Insular House of Representatives and one of the Islands' leading politicians. When Manuel Quezon became the first Philippine President, he made it plain that he would brook no rivals in political power. The once-powerful Speakership was reduced to an office of no importance, and able Señor Paredes reluctantly accepted the job of Commissioner in Washington.

Statesman Paredes answered his San Franciscan countrymen with restraint: He believed the judge had not meant to call all Filipinos savages—"but there are savages everywhere." Finally he urged his compatriots to "avoid occasions for rebuke" and sent a copy of his reply to Judge Lazarus accompanied by a note saying, "I cannot believe that you had in any way intended to refer to my people as a whole."

Last fortnight Señor Paredes received a reply from Judge Lazarus: "I intend to be as straightforward with you as you have been considerate with me. Basing my conclusions on years of observation, I regret to say that there is probably no group in this city, proportionate to its members, that supplies us with more criminal business than the local Filipino colony. It is no compliment to the predominant race that most crimes committed by Filipinos have as background intimate relations with white girls. Jealousy between rivals for the affections of the same girl leads to assaults, knifings, and shootings; a desire to provide gifts for the objects of their affections offers temptations for thievery. I am making allowance for the fact that there is a scarcity—I imagine almost a total absence—of Filipino girls in this country and that the kind of white girls who associate with these Filipino lads is not calculated to provide the best influences for them. However, the girls are satisfied and generally very happy in their relations with these boys. Their sweethearts are working—all of them—as waiters, elevator operators, janitors, bell boys, etc. and are able to supply them, according to their notions, with abundant attentions and diversion. . . .

"Some of these boys, with perfect candor, have told me bluntly and boastfully that they practice the art of love with more perfection than white boys, and occasionally one of the girls has supplied me with information to the same effect. In fact some of the disclosures in this regard are perfectly startling in their nature."

"Well," said Señor Paredes urbanely, "the Judge admits that Filipinos are great lovers."

7. White Landowner Dr. E. E. Chandler Describes an East Indian Agricultural Community, 1924

I have been interested in the Imperial Valley since 1909, and have had opportunity to become quite well acquainted with a number of Hindus. I have a ranch east of Brawley which I rented to white tenants several years and lost money by so doing. Three years ago I leased it to Hindus, and since then the land has yielded good returns. The first year I received $9,000 and last year $10,000 as my share. The white tenants raised barley, but the Hindus have been raising cotton.

The land owners in the Valley are very favorable to the Hindus, while the U.S. trainees or pensioners are opposed to them—but at the same time the latter are not making a success of their agricultural operations. The main factor is that the white man is not willing to do the hard work needed in the Imperial Valley. The Hindu will get up at one o'clock in the morning and haul his cotton a distance of thirteen miles to the gin with his four-horse team and be there ahead of the American who lives nearer town. The latter does not like this.

In reality, I do not believe the Imperial Valley is a white man's country and I am willing to hand it over to the Hindus and Japanese. The Negro is not nearly so industrious: when he has accumulated a small bank account he moves to town.

For the first two years the Hindus worked my land under the crop-rent system, but now that has been declared illegal. The four Hindus are now working for me and I am planning to pay them about the same amount as they received from their share of the crop before. We have only a verbal agreement, but they are working as industriously as ever. When they came to my place they were in rather difficult circumstances but I helped them out to a certain extent and they have made good. I have tried to deal squarely with them. On several occasions I could have taken advantage of them but I did not, and so I believe that they have confidence in me now. I have found the Hindus to be honest in their dealings, and in fact several other persons have given like reports to me. A merchant in Brawley told me that he never lost anything on the Hindus, but considerable on the Mexicans. J. A. Harris, who owns the gins in the Valley, secures money from Los Angeles which he loans to the cotton producers at 10 per cent interest, taking as security a mortgage on the crops. In this way he exercises a considerable amount of control over them. He has said that the Hindu is more satisfactory to deal with than the white man, because he does not go into bankruptcy as does the white man.

Prior to 1920 the Hindus could get money from the banks more readily than the whites—they work harder and spend less. The Hindus have also been able to secure better land than the whites, all of which has aroused opposition on the part of many whites. The whites in the Valley seem to like the Japanese better than the Hindu. The Hindu is quite serious and stoical, while the Japanese is more jovial and can take things as a joke in a better way.

The Hindus and Japanese do not work well together because both are business men and want to run their own establishment; neither group wants to work for others,

"Interview with Dr. E. E. Chandler." From the papers of William C. Smith (A-237, A-102, 84-A), Special Collections & University Archives, University of Oregon.

and in fact before the anti-alien land law went into effect neither was available for day labor.

The Japanese in the Imperial Valley raise berries and cantaloupes in the main and are located near the towns, while the Hindus raise cotton and are located for the most part on the east side of the valley.

The Hindus get along well with the Mexicans, who are available for day labor. The Mexicans go from place to place in automobiles and live in camps while picking cotton. They do not work well as they are quite wasteful but the Hindus are very watchful and are able to handle the Mexicans remarkably well.

The Hindus are quite shrewd business men. Before making a business proposition it has usually been quite thoroughly threshed out in a group, after which a designated spokesman presents the matter.

In Brawley the Hindus go to the part of town where the white loafers stay only to attend to any necessary business. If they stay in town they remain in the Mexican section. Hindus may not eat in white restaurants in Brawley, and so they go to the Japanese eating places. They would prefer to deal with the whites, but recognize that there is prejudice against them. They are doing their best to avoid trouble and so do not try to break over any of the taboos which have been raised against them. There are many whites from the southern states who have come there with their prejudice against the Negro and this has been turned against all the groups with any color.

A report has been circulated that two Hindus figured in an automobile accident when one was killed and the other badly injured. The injured man was taken to Brawley where the white doctor refused to attend him. The Hindus then tried to get the ambulance to take him to El Centro for which they were willing to pay a good price, but they had to take him there in a Ford car.

Many whites take advantage of the Hindus when they can. The Hindus on my ranch have told me that even though I have paid for the water they have to pay "tips" to the ditch tenders in order to get the necessary water. I understand that this practice is quite widespread in the valley. Then the whites say that the Hindus do this in order to secure special favors.

During the period that the Hindus were receiving a big price for their cotton they raised their heads and put on some show, for which the whites criticized them. But they lost heavily in 1920 and that deflated any pride they may have had.

A part of this prejudice against the Hindu is no doubt due to the fact that he is a keen competitor, but I think there is also another factor which enters in here. I believe that we are prejudiced against him because he is so much like us. We fondle a dog, but not a monkey because he resembles us so closely. The Hindu resembles us except that he is black—and we are shocked to see a black white man.

At first the Hindus had a lot of law-suits and much litigation among themselves. Several Hindus are now in the penitentiary on account of crimes of violence among themselves. This gave them much unfavorable publicity and they then began to take matters into their own hands to improve the situation by organizing an association for handling their own cases, in the settlement of which they would at times call in an arbitrator. They are now quite well organized and cling together in matters of interest to their group.

During my last Christmas vacation I visited the ranch when some 200 Hindus met there to talk over the conditions created by the land law. For some time they had their headquarters in Brawley, but of late they have been holding their meetings in the country. In this group Pritam Singh was the leader. He was at one time the head of the municipal jail in Shanghai, China, and speaks English fluently. At one time I helped him secure a lease on a tract of land, for which he still shows his appreciation by writing letters to me.

Another quite prominent man is named Bhagwan Singh, who is a sort of silk-shirt aristocrat. He now signs his name S. Bhagwan instead of Bhagwan Singh and it seems that this change will admit him into any hotel.

Tija Singh is still another outstanding member of the Hindu group. He has been arrested on suspicion of smuggling in Hindus from Mexico. The case cost him $7,000 when it was dismissed. The attorneys and immigration inspectors have been hounding and bleeding him. He has been here since he was a mere boy.

The Hindus are interested in their own affairs here, in addition to which they take a lively interest in affairs in India. They have made contributions toward the support of nationalist schools in India. The majority of these Hindus are Sikhs, of which sect Amritsar is the holy city. They say that the temples and schools have passed from the control of the Sikhs into the hands of the British, and they, the American group, are now trying to regain this control.

I know one Hindu who married a red-headed Irish woman from Los Angeles. Several Hindus have married Mexican women. A Mexican woman considers that she has stepped up when she marries a Hindu, because he is industrious and thrifty as compared with the Mexican men.

A number of the Hindus hold to their old religion, but some have broken away from it. So long as the Hindu wears the turban he keeps to his religion, is a good fellow, and is in good standing with his group; but when he adopts a hat he seems to drop down.

8. Writer Carlos Bulosan Conveys the Dangers of Filipino Labor Organizing (1930s), 1943

Upon my return to the Santa Maria Valley, I found that the Filipino Workers' Association, an independent union, was disintegrating. I rushed to join José in Lompoc, where he had gone with Gazamen to see if there was a possibility of establishing a workers' newspaper. The three of us decided to form a branch there and to make it the center of Filipino union activities in Central California.

Salinas was still the general headquarters of the Association, but it was fast losing its authority and prestige. There was a mad scramble for power in the Association among the national officers, and their bitter rivalries wrecked our chance toward the establishment of a more cogent labor organization. Actually, however, it was the birth of progressive leadership in the Filipino labor movement.

The membership of the Filipino Workers' Association was tremendous, considering the myriad difficulties it met in the campaign to spread throughout the agricultural areas of California. The vigilant Filipino workers—their whole-hearted

From Carlos Bulosan, *America Is in the Heart* (Seattle: University of Washington Press, 1973), 194–197.

support of the trade union movement, their hatred of low wages and other labor discriminations—were the direct causes that instigated the persecutions against them, sporadic at first and then concerted, but destructive to the nation's welfare.

In Salinas, for instance, the general headquarters were burned after a successful strike of lettuce workers, and the president of the association was thrown in jail. Upon his release, he moved to Guadalupe, in the south, and the campaigned for the purchase of a new building. Always alert, the Filipino agricultural workers throughout the valley rallied behind the proposal, and after a few months a new national office was established. Again, striking for better wages, the Filipino lettuce cutters and packers succeeded, but lost the building and their right to build another in Guadalupe.

Finally, José and I made the office in Lompoc the temporary general headquarters. It was unconstitutional, of course, but the moment called for drastic action. Our move was without precedent, but we hoped to accomplish something, and we did.

It was during our membership campaign that I came in contact with fascism in California. The sugar beet season was in full swing in Oxnard, but the Mexican and Filipino workers were split. The companies would not recognize their separate demands, and although there were cultural and economic ties between them, they had not recognized one important point: that the beet companies conspired against their unity.

I contacted a Filipino farm-labor contractor and a prominent Mexican, and José, who joined us later, planned a meeting in the town park. I felt a little elated; harmony was in the offing. But in the evening, when we were starting the program, deputy sheriffs came to the park and told us that our right to hold a meeting had been revoked. I did not know what to do. I was still a novice. An elderly Mexican told us that we could hold a meeting outside the city limit.

There was a large empty barn somewhere in the south end of Oxnard. A truck came and carried some of the men, but most of them walked with us on the highway. They were very serious. I glanced at José who was talking to three Filipinos ahead of me, and felt something powerful growing inside me. It was a new heroism: a feeling of growing with a huge life. I walked silently with the men, listening to their angry voices and to the magic of their marching feet.

I was frightened. But I felt brave, too. The Mexicans wanted a more inclusive union, but that would take time. We were debating the issue when I heard several cars drive into the yard. I signaled to the men to put out the lights and to take cover. They fanned out and broke through the four walls, escaping into the wide beet fields.

I rushed upon the improvised stage and grabbed José, whose wooden leg had become entangled in some ropes and wires.

"This is it!"

"Yeah!"

"Follow me!"

"Right!"

I jumped off the stage, José following me. Then there was the sudden patter of many feet outside, and shooting. I found a pile of dry horse manure in a corner of the barn. I told José to lie down; then I covered him with it, exposing only his nose. I lay beside him and covered myself with it, too. When I tried to talk, the manure went into my mouth and choked me. I lay still, waiting for the noise outside to subside.

A man with a flashlight came inside and stabbed the darkness with the steely light, cutting swiftly from corner to corner. He came near the pile of manure, spat on it, and searched the ceiling. A piece of manure tickled my throat, and I held my breath, bringing tears to my eyes. The man went outside, joined his companions, and drove off to town.

I pushed the dung away and jumped to my feet.

"Did you see his face?"

"No!"

"I saw it. He is a white man, all right."

"Let's run. There is still time."

I crept to the wall and crouched in the darkness. I wanted to be sure that every man had gone. The way was clear. José followed me outside. Then we were running across a beet field, our feet slapping against the broad leaves that got in our way. The moon came up and shone brightly in the night. As I ran, I looked up to see it sailing across the sky.

Then my fear was gone. I stopped running and sat down among the tall beets. José sat beside me. There were no words to describe the feeling in our minds and hearts. There was only our closeness and the dark years ahead. There was only the dark future.

9. Labor Leader Karl Yoneda Recalls Japanese Interethnic Organizing (1930s), 1978

I decided to join and volunteered to be an organizer for the Agricultural Workers Organizing Committee of Southern California (AWOCSC) established by the Los Angeles Japanese Labor Association in the spring of 1927; also on May 1st became a member of the Communist Party using the name Karl Hama, in both organizations. All organizers were either Issei (Japan born) or Kibei (U.S. born but raised in Japan). We signed up over a thousand workers among Mexican, Filipino and Japanese strawberry, tomato and bean pickers and conducted strikes for 25 to 35 cents pay and union recognition. . . .

We found during organizing drives that Japanese were last to sign-up, in contrast to quick responses from Mexican and Filipino laborers. Our successes filled us with enthusiasm, though we realized that more Japanese were behind picket lines—in other words scabbing where strikes occurred. AWOCSC efforts continued till 1929, when the militant Agricultural Workers Industrial Union of the Trade Union Unity League (AWIU-TUUL) emerged in California taking in all farm workers regardless of race, color, creed or nationality. Its membership switched to the new union, later Japanese Sections were established to meet the need for Japanese language material.

Imperial Valley, one of California's most fertile areas, had over 10,000 farm workers—7,000 Mexicans, 1,000 Japanese, several hundred Filipinos and 1,000 others—employed there in 1930. In January the AWIU sent ten organizers, including

From Karl Yoneda, "A Partial History of California Japanese Farm Workers," in Foner, *Racism, Dissent, and Asian Americans from 1850 to the Present: A Documentary History.* Copyright © 1993 Greenwood Press. Reproduced with permission of Greenwood Publishing Group, Inc., Westport, CT.

Tetsuji Horiuchi, Issei, and Danny Roxas, Filipino, in the valley to start the union. They raised five demands:

25 cents per hour pay; Doing away with all labor contractors;

Elimination of piecework; Improvement of labor camps;

Recognition of camp (union) committees,

at the same time appealing to workers to walk off if growers rejected them, which many did but once again most of these were from small farms.

However, 400 members of the all white AFL shed workers took advantage of the strike situation and shut down a packing house after their demands of $1.00 per hour for lettuce packers and 75 cents for trimmers were turned down. . . .

Seventeen million unemployed were looking for jobs and food during the massive U.S. economic crisis which began in 1929. The Socialist Party had collapsed ideologically many years before, the IWW was no longer an active force, AFL leaders were collaborating with employers by betraying those who dared to strike and [were] not interested in the unemployed. The Communist Party was the only organization which helped to establish National Unemployed Council branches encompassing unemployed workers from all industries. . . .

In '31 and '32, due to prevailing unbearable working conditions such as low pay, long hours, indiscriminate firing and poor housing on California farms where only Japanese were hired, more than 20 strikes, led by the AWIU Japanese Section, were conducted in Chico, Lodi, Walnut Grove, Fresno, Visalia, Bakersfield down to Stanton and San Gabriel Valley among strawberry, raspberry, pea, peach, asparagus, grape and lettuce pickers. Significantly, these strikes were always supported by their fellow union members who helped "man" the picket lines, strike kitchens, etc. . . .

AWIU Japanese Sections in Sacramento, Stockton and Los Angeles acted as coordinators of union activities between all farm workers. During 1933, more than 15 AWIU strikes were recorded. In a round figure there were 35,000 Mexican, Filipino, Japanese, Negro, white, small number of Korean and East Indian participants. Over 100 strike leaders were arrested; among them were a Korean and five Kibei organizers. At the Martin Ranch in Visalia, where 250 Japanese grape pickers went on strike for higher pay. I, along with the Korean and seven others, were picked up by a dozen or so deputies and told by the sheriff "Get out of town or go to jail."

☙ E S S A Y S

In examining the Asian American past, historians have concentrated on race relations between Asians and whites. But increasingly they are paying attention to tensions and alliances contained within seemingly distinct racial groups. The following essays attest to the significance of class as an identity that has both united and divided different ethnic groups. In the first essay, historian Eiichiro Azuma, assistant professor at the University of Pennsylvania, contends that Japanese immigrant nationalism among small farmers in the California delta advanced their economic interests at the expense of Filipino farm workers. Addressing the same depression era in California, Rhacel Salazar Parrenas, assistant professor of women's studies and Asian American studies at the University of Wisconsin at Madison, examines the romantic relations between these same Filipino farm workers and white working-class women.

Labor Conflict Between Japanese and Filipinos in the California Delta

EIICHIRO AZUMA

On the evening of February 8, 1930, Japanese in Stockton, California, were stunned when FIlipinos boycotted their businesses, resulting in a virtual shutdown. According to the local Japanese press, this clash between the two ethnic groups resulted from "a personal affair"—the secret marriage of an American-born Japanese(Nisei) woman and a Filipino laboring man. The woman's father had strongly opposed the marriage, telling her that, "racial and cultural differences" between Japanese and Filipinos doomed the relationship. She soon left her Filipino husband, an action that he, his friends, and his relatives blamed on the entire Japanese community, because Japanese allegedly believed "the Filipinos [we]re inferior." Infuriated, Filipinos called their "sympathy boycott."

As the boycott dragged on for a second week and merchants' losses escalated, frustrated Japanese immigrant (Issei) residents came to see the conflict as a "war" between two "races," a perception reinforced by news reports. A Stockton correspondent of the *Nichibei Shimbun* (Japanese American News) reported that Filipino store owners, doctors, and newspaper executives actively supported the boycott. The Filipino community, he wrote, "seems to have learned the weakness of the Japanese." Most Japanese businesses in the delta relied heavily on the Filipino trade. The Japanese business community feared that Filipinos might develop an ethnic entrepreneurship of their own and thus achieve economic independence, patronizing their fellow merchants instead of Japanese establishments. To avoid such a development, Japanese community newspapers urged all Japanese in Stockton to withstand this boycott at any cost.

Issei businessmen moved quickly to diversify their customer base. To reduce their reliance on Filipinos, merchants decided to bring Mexican laborers into the San Joaquin delta. In mid-March, a special committee, formed within the Japanese Association, dispatched representatives to gain support from Japanese farmers, urging them to hire Mexican laborers. The merchants stressed the advantages for local farmers. Mexican workers would stabilize Japanese agriculture because they were regarded as more "docile" and "better" than Filipinos, who had already struck against farmers elsewhere in California. Although the plan was abandoned when the boycott ended in April, what Issei called "Japanese consciousness" (*minzoku ishiki*) continued to run high in the delta. The emotional response of Issei to the Filipino boycott merely presaged an ever-growing nationalism spurred by local interethnic conflict. . . .

A localized form of Issei nationalism and ethnic identity developed in the San Joaquin delta from a series of clashes between Japanese and Filipinos from 1930 to 1941. The decade of the 1930s commenced with the Filipino boycott. As the first interethnic conflict, the incident marked a watershed in Japanese-Filipino relations.

From Eiichiro Azuma, "Racial Struggle, Immigrant Nationalism, and Ethnic Identity: Japanese and Filipinos in the California Delta," *Pacific Historical Review* 67, no. 2 (May 1998): 163–164, 168–176. © 1998 by Pacific Coast Branch, American Historical Association. Used with permission.

Japanese immigrants began to perceive their relationship with Filipinos in racial more than in economic terms, although the two were always intertwined. Underlying the rise of racial discourse was the rapid transformation of the local agricultural labor market in the last half of the 1920s, when Filipinos became an integral part of the Japanese-immigrant economy. The Japanese dependence on Filipinos derived mainly from state and federal discriminatory legislation that drastically affected the Issei socioeconomic position. In the San Joaquin delta, the pattern of interethnic relations was characterized by the process of replacement and succession caused by legal exclusion. Surrounded by the San Joaquin and Sacramento rivers, the region was an agricultural center in which a handful of white landlords used different groups of Asian tenant farmers and laborers in succession—first Chinese until the turn of the century, then Japanese, and finally Filipinos following the mid-1920s. Starting with the Chinese Exclusion Act of 1882, anti-immigration legislation always played a pivotal role in this transition.

The California Alien Land Law of 1920 and the Immigration Act of 1924 brought to the delta an influx of Filipinos, who quickly dominated the local labor market and gradually threatened Japanese tenancy. First, the Alien Land Law, which prohibited Japanese tenancy and landholding, compelled many Issei to give up farming and deprived laborers of employment. According to a report compiled by the Japanese Consulate, there had been 995 Japanese farmers in the delta in 1920, but 575 of them left the region within three years. Issei laborers, too, had to go elsewhere, reducing their number from 750 to 400 between 1920 and 1925. The remaining farmers worked primarily as foremen who received fixed salaries from white landlords, thereby evading the Alien Land Law. Second, the Immigration Act abruptly terminated Japanese immigration. Filipino immigrants, who as colonized American nationals were exempt from the law, filled the labor vacuum. Although no population statistics are available for the delta proper, Census figures indicate that that number of Filipinos in California increased during the 1920s from 2,674 to 30,470. Japanese farmers came to depend on the "cheap but valuable [Filipino] labor" that they perceived would carry them through the depression, while Japanese commercial establishments catered to Filipinos for their own survival.

In the eyes of Issei, who were fully aware of the ramifications of such a change in the delta, the 1930 boycott signified Filipinos' attempt to accelerate the process of replacement and succession. Of course, as the *Nichibei Shimbun* correspondent reported, some Issei leaders recognized both that Filipinos waged the boycott specifically against Japanese merchants, not against *all* Japanese, and that the Filipino business sector sought to profit from the situation. Nevertheless, a majority of Issei interpreted the boycott as a collective racial challenge by the Filipino population. In the Japanese community, mass meetings and the vernacular press further propagated such an interpretation and helped to ignite ethnic nationalism. With the veiled threat of social ostracism and persecution, the delta's Issei leaders demanded that all the community members maintain Filipinos under Japanese control. Here, the racial rhetoric overshadowed the class dimension of the conflict.

The 1930 incident also awakened the Japanese community to what was called the "racial menace" of Filipinos, which continued to haunt them until Pearl Harbor. To the dismay of Issei, it appeared that the root of the incident—a marriage between a Nisei woman and a Filipino man—foreshadowed more "interracial" unions. Many

Nisei came to adulthood in the 1930s, and their parents believed that male Filipino laborers posed a serious threat to the chastity of Nisei women. According to Japanese newspapers, Filipino men were trying to "seduce" Nisei women, for few Filipina women lived in the delta. Besides, many Issei parents dreaded the alleged "sexual laxness" and "uncontrollability" of young Nisei women, which they usually attributed to negative "American" influences. Fearing the recurrence of Japanese-Filipino marriages, a local reporter of the *Shin Sekai* (New World) alarmed the community shortly after the boycott with this figurative language:

> This incident [marriage], I often hear, points to the fact that many more problems like this have already "struck root" and are about to "put forth buds." It is our responsibility—parents, social leaders, and community at large—to make sure to raise our children properly [so as to avoid interracial marriage].

Filipino laborers, albeit indispensable for local Japanese agriculture, now represented a "racial peril" to Nisei young people.

Japanese immigrants worried about intermarriage because it signified Filipino "contamination" of their "pure" bloodline. This racial doctrine derived from the racism of Imperial Japan, which sought to dominate "backward races" in Asia. During the years of militarist aggression in Asia, a number of government officials and intellectuals expressed a faith in the "purity of blood," and they frequently admonished imperial subjects against miscegenation with the dominated, on the grounds that it would "destroy the 'national spirit' of the Yamato race" and spoil their racial superiority. These ideas crossed the Pacific through imported Japanese publications, lectures by writers and scholars from Japan, and frequent visits by Issei to their native villages in Japan.

It is, however, important to note that other perspectives on racial purity also existed in Imperial Japan. As recent Japanese-language scholarship on race and nation points out, intermarriage between Japanese and colonized Koreans and Taiwanese was *encouraged* rather than discouraged after the early 1920s in Japanese assimilation policy. To rationalize a colonial social structure that required the inclusion of newly dominated populations into the Japanese nation, bureaucrats and other ideologues who favored assimilationism propagated the notion of the Japanese race as a hybrid, consisting of Korean, Chinese, Ainu, Okinawan, Micronesian, and core imperial elements. While Issei were grappling with emerging racial problems, in Japan itself the discourse on racial hybridity was actually as influential as the racial purity argument. Why, then, did the latter predominate in California?

Issei leaders both adopted and adapted the racial purity position because it best fit the sociohistorical context in which immigrants found themselves after the mid-1920s. In the United States, where they had been subjected to a series of discriminatory laws as "aliens ineligible to citizenship," the Issei envisaged a better future not in their own lifetimes but for their children. They believed that American citizenship would allow Nisei to restore what they saw as the golden age of the Japanese community prior to 1920. Such a view was grounded solely in their *belief* in the purported superiority of the Japanese race. Without state military power to create the situation of Japanese supremacy over Filipinos and other "lesser" groups, the protection of racial purity was defined as *the* precondition for a Nisei victory in racial competition and for future prosperity. Therefore, immigrant publications repeated this argument throughout the 1930s. For example, a *Nichibei Shimbun* editorial warned of the enormous implications of racial transgressions for the future of Japanese Americans:

> The Japanese race, possessing superior racial traits unparalleled in the world, is destined for ceaseless development and prosperity. On the other hand, those people [Filipinos], whose homeland contents itself with being a third-class nation, . . . would see nothing but poverty and misery in their lives. If their lazy blood becomes part of the Japanese race through interracial marriage, it would eventually offset the racial superiority of the Japanese. . . . Racial purity is a precondition for the welfare of the second generation.

What is clear in this line of reasoning is the sharp contrast between the Japanese race/state, on the one hand, and the colonized Filipinos and their dominated homeland, on the other—a contrast reflected in Issei views of Filipinos in the delta. Japanese immigrants conflated state and ethnic dimensions of nationalism through the concept of "overseas racial development." Embracing both the state and overseas communities as interwined components of "the Japanese race . . . destined for ceaseless development and prosperity," the concept enabled Issei to imagine race relations in the delta as a manifestation of the hierarchical power relations of nation states. As Japan enjoyed supremacy over all other Asian nations, so Japanese in the delta should keep Filipinos and other "third-class" races in a subordinate position. Or course, whites were excluded from this picture, for they represented the real power in the delta.

White American racism further strengthened Issei repugnance for intermarriage. Based on the bourgeois liberalism and fictive racial hierarchy of eighteenth-century Europe, American racial ideology defined miscegenation as causing the degeneration of race, nation, and class. In order to prevent such a crisis, managing the sexuality of children was considered crucial not only for personal well-being but for society itself. In California, as in other states, interracial unions were legally banned, and "mixed-blood" children were excluded from the ruling circle of the white race. This white ideology gave Issei a scientific justification for their own views. Like white Americans, Japanese immigrants stressed the value of childrearing and the need to protect the chastity of their daughters from "inferior" races, but they also linked these conditions to the survival and development of the Japanese race in the United States. Nisei were not allowed to encounter other groups as their free individual selves but only as racialized selves whose utmost responsibility was to their "brethren in America" (*zaibei doho*).

Therefore, following the 1930 boycott, the issue of race occupied the central position in Japanese attitudes toward Filipinos. The contrast between the economic value of Filipino labor and the "racial peril" Filipinos represented became widely discussed topics, and Issei contemplated how to exploit the former and yet circumvent the latter. They characterized their relationship with Filipinos as a "race war," a decisive struggle for Japanese survival in the United States. Essays written by Issei readers for a 1933 *Nichibei Shimbun* contest on the topic of "the expansion of Filipino influences and our preparation" reveal these concerns. The winning essays were selected by Issei leaders according to content rather than style, and the assertions in them represented the orthodoxy in the immigrant community. Indeed, their main theses were strikingly similar: first, the Nisei mission to win a total victory in their competition with Filipinos, and second, the Issei duty to lay the economic foundation for that final battle.

One prize winner, a Stockton immigrant, spoke specifically of the delta situation. He wrote emphatically about the dangerous trend of Filipino settlement on area farms (as opposed to migratory labor) and Filipino encroachment into small businesses. In his opinion, such changes hindered the development of the Japanese community, and it was necessary for "all our Japanese brethren to mobilize" against them. To protect Japanese farming and commerce, he insisted that Japanese laborers be used for long-term farm work and that Issei farmers and merchants expand their capital base. Until Nisei could finally "expel" them from the delta. Filipinos must always be harmless workers and customers, never contenders or equals. These viewpoints expressed a consensus in the delta. They appeared in other writings time and time again; indeed, the community actually started one program in response to them.

Known as the Kibei movement (*kibei undo*), the program attempted to return to the delta American-born men who had gone to Japan with their parents or had been sent alone for education (Kibei). Issei leaders in the delta anticipated two major benefits from this program. First, it would help to reduce relationships between Nisei women and Filipino men. Because of the number of boys sent to Japan for education, there was an imbalance between the numbers of Nisei men and women. In 1935, there were almost 15 percent more second-generation females (1,230) than males (1,070) in the delta. Kibei males, Issei expected, would be perfect mates for the "surplus" females who were most likely to consort with Filipino laborers.

Second, the Kibei movement would add youthful Japanese to the local ethnic labor force, thereby enabling it to compete more successfully with Filipino labor. Issei generally viewed Kibei far more favorably than American-educated Nisei, for they thought the returnees had internalized the "Japanese spirit" (*nippon seishin*), reminding the first generation of the vigor and ambition of their own youthful years. Whereas Issei sometimes found Nisei too "Americanized" and lax in their thought and behavior, they saw Kibei as embodying the physical and mental strength of the invincible Japanese empire. The presence of Kibei laborers later proved crucial during another series of interethnic conflicts.

The Issei quest to gain the upper hand over Filipinos, which gave shape to the delta's Japanese identity, can be characterized by what Michael Omi and Howard Winant call "a racial war of maneuver" under white hegemony. Drawing upon Antonio Gramsci, Omi and Winant contend that a war of maneuver involves "a situation in which subordinate groups seek to preserve and extend a definite territory . . . and to develop an internal society as an alternative to the repressive social system they confront." In the 1930s, Japanese immigrants, too, attempted to protect their own "internal territory" that they had established within the delta's racial order. To do so, they had to fight Filipinos, who increasingly threatened the Japanese "territory" in their own war of maneuver. The resultant conflict was a clash between two simultaneous wars of maneuver mounted by the Asian immigrant groups for their respective survival.

Alliances Between White Working-Class Women and Filipino Immigrant Men

RHACEL SALAZAR PARRENAS

During the 1920s and 30s, taxi dance halls flourished as sites of commercial amusement in Filipino labor migrant communities. From the rural areas of Fresno and Wastonville to the urban cities of Chicago, Seattle, and Los Angeles, Filipino labor migrants—numbering approximately 40,000 in the mainland patronized taxi dance halls to enjoy the company of mostly white working class female hostesses. In taxi dance halls, "hostesses (were) obliged to dance with any man who request(ed) it, and for as long a time as he (chose) to pay for their company." Costing the Filipino male patrons "ten cents a dance," the taxi-dance hall served as the primary institution which allowed Filipino men to interact socially with women. Taxi dance halls boomed in a time of racial segregation and stringent anti-miscegenation in the United States while eugenicists advocated for the segregation and complete separation of "lesser" races from mainstream society. Believed to be "unassimilable" and "brown monkeys," Filipinos had been excluded from owning property and patronizing "white-owned" businesses and establishments, and, in some cases, even churches. Anti-miscegenation laws were also enacted as the number of Filipinos in the United States increased to a more visible portion of the population. Not surprisingly, taxi-dance halls were objects of public scrutiny and scorn. As Mr. Birmingham, a member of the Fruit Grower's Supply Company management and employer of many Filipino farm workers, stated quite frankly:

> It is natural that most Americans hate to see a Filipino associate with a white woman whether she be good, bad, or indifferent.

Upper-class white women leaders of the community formed special city commissions designated to better control the interaction and possible "promiscuity" in the dance halls while white working class men raised their fists and initiated anti-Filipino race riots to protect white women's "purity" and "morality" from Filipino men. Considering the staunch racist dogma against Filipinos that permeated the dominant society during the peak period of taxi dance halls, the close physical proximity of white female and brown male bodies in itself represents an interracial phenomenon. It is the phenomenal "close interaction," a simultaneously racialized and gendered case, that I interrogate in this article. . . .

"Little Brown Monkeys": The Racial Subordination of Filipino Male Migrants in the 1920s and 30s

. . . Limited to menial and unskilled jobs, many Filipino male migrants found themselves working for no more than "a dollar a day" as farm workers in the rural areas, cannery workers in Alaska and low-wage service workers (e.g., bellboys, janitors,

From Rhacel Salazar Parrenas, "'White Trash' Meets the 'Little Brown Monkeys': The Taxi Dance Hall as a Site of Interracial and Gender Alliances Between White Working Class Women and Filipino Immigrant Men in the 1920s and 1930s," *Amerasia Journal* 24, no. 2 (summer 1998): 115–116, 119–130. Copyright © 1998 Regents of the University of California. Used with permission.

and domestic workers) in urban areas. At best, their jobs could be described as demeaning and backbreaking. Magnos Cabreros of San Francisco recalled the harrowing ordeal of his day-to-day experience in the 1920s labor camps in California:

> 1927 . . . ten hours at the time . . . it's hardly daylight when we moved to the fields and come back after sundown . . . it was hard. . . . [A]t night, I'd feel all kinds of pain in my body . . . my back, my arm. . . . Imagine, less than 15 years old . . . after I got to my bed, I'd be crying. . . . .

Filipino laborers like Magnos Cabreros could not seek higher level jobs even if endowed with college degrees from the United States. Occupational segregation relegated them to jobs disdained by more racially privileged members of society. The recruitment of Filipinos to the United States was primarily billed to fill the need for "single able-bodied men" to perform rough physically excruciating labor in the plantations of Hawaii and agricultural fields on the Pacific Coast. From the demands and expectations of employers, Filipino men were subjected and disciplined through the maximization of their bodies as machines, what Foucault describes as "anatomo-politics of the human body" and defines as the body's "disciplining, the optimization of its capabilities, the extortion of its forces, the parallel increase of its usefulness and its docility, its integration into systems of efficient and economic controls." For employers, Filipino men came to be machine-like bodies, disciplined to maximize their capabilities and expected to produce and harvest crops—

> "asparagus . . . tomatoes . . . spinach . . . strawberries . . . beets" from "four o'clock in the morning . . . with flashlights on their heads like miners" until the sun sets, when they are left docile from exhaustion.

While Filipino men faced the physical control and discipline of "anatomo-politics" in the workplace, another form of physical subjection of their bodies came through the denial of female members in a community made-up of mostly heterosexual and virile ("able-bodied") men. Filipina women constituted less than 10 percent of the Filipino American population in 1930. The absence of Filipina women in the community is of no surprise considering that single women were less likely to migrate on their own during that time and that the wages of Filipino men could ill afford to meet the standard of living for raising families in the United States. Moreover, the passage of the Tydings-McDuffie Act in 1934, which curtailed Filipino migration to fifty persons per year and declared Filipinos "aliens" ineligible for citizenship, all together prevented women and families migrating to the United States from the Philippines. As a result, Filipino Americans remained restricted to primarily bachelor communities.

For Filipino men, the racial subordination of forced bachelorhood meant their physical repression and asexuality. Forced bachelorhood for Filipinos made them an unreproductive population or in Foucauldian terms, an unproductive species body. The absence of women and, later on, the imposition of anti-miscegenation laws can be seen as "regulatory controls" over Filipino men in "a biopolitics of the population." As the body is "imbued with the mechanics of life and serving as the basis of the biological processes: propagation, births and mortality, the level of health, life expectancy and longetivity," Filipino social reproduction had been carefully controlled and prevented. . . .

Interestingly, taxi dance hall activities functioned as main forms of resistance against the dual subjection of bodily control, specifically the racialized construction of their bodies as machine-like cheap laborers and the racialized imposition of asex-uality, on Filipino men. Not surprisingly, Filipino men felt released by dancing as "many obviously enjoy dancing for its own sake." The physical activity of dancing in taxi dance halls physically opposed the more uniform, repetitive motions involved in their daily "stoop" labor. In contrast, movements in the dance hall are described as non-uniform and chaotically diverse:

> Some couples gallop together over the floor, weaving their way in and around the slow dancers; others seek to attain aesthetic heights by a curious angular strut and a double shuffle or a stamp and a glide. Still others dance the "Charleston," and are granted un-challenged pre-emption of the center of the floor. Some couples are content with a slow, simple one-step move about the hall.

The space of the taxi dance hall enabled Filipino men to take control of their cor-poral, physical bodies and counter the mechanically conditioned bodily actions of repetitive motions that they performed as low wage laborers.

In addition, the taxi dance hall provided a means by which Filipino men could counter the racialized imposition of asexuality as their activities in the dance hall enabled them to show their sexual prowess and virility. Dancing styles in taxi dance halls also included sexualized movements:

> At times certain dancers seem to cease all semblance of motion over the floor, and while locked tightly together give themselves up to movements in nature and obviously more practiced than spontaneous. These couples tend to . . . mill about in a compressed pack of wriggling perspiring bodies.

The close access to women that the taxi dance halls provided Filipino men also prompted self-images of being irresistible studs. In interviews, Filipino men in the 1920s and 30s often described themselves to be great romancers who could have a "girlfriend in every hall."

While the racial oppression of Filipino men as asexual seemed to unavoidably necessitate the counter stance of establishing their sexual prowess and virility, this form of resistance against racism unfortunately relied on the physical control of female bodies. As Filipino men used taxi dance halls to strategically counter the method of asepsis in their racial subordination, they unfortunately did so at the ex-pense of perpetuating patriarchy and establishing themselves as rightful beneficiaries of gender inequality. In the taxi dance hall, women were the usual objects of pleasure of the "male gaze." In the dance halls, women would often be physically objectified by roving male eyes as "ogling, in fact, seems . . . to be the chief occupation of the male." The "male gaze" and the objectification of the usually white female bodies illustrate an intersecting locus of race and gender as female subordination meant resisting race oppression for these Filipino men.

"White Trash": White Working Class Women in the Early Filipino American Community

In his ethnographic study of taxi dance halls in Chicago, Paul Cressey found that most taxi dancers were "immigrant girls seeking economic and social adjustment in the new world" and of Southern European descent—Italian and Polish. Predom-inantly working class, the women of the taxi dance halls usually danced at night to subsidize the small wages they earned in factories during the day. As members of impoverished immigrant families, white working class women in the taxi dance halls had often been expected to work since their early teens to help support widowed mothers "in desperate financial straits" or to just be self-supporting to ease the financial responsibilities of their parents. In the 1920s and 30s, poor, single, white women also provided a cheap labor pool, a sharp contrast to the idealized role of homemaker and relegation of middle and upper class women to the private sphere. Without a doubt, poor working class immigrant women, including whites, provided a strong base for cheap labor in the pre–World War II period.

Jobs held by the white women of the taxi dance halls were usually expected to be "temporary," i.e., to be abandoned after marriage. Most worked as low-paid factory workers or as "female service workers," for example as waitresses and retail clerks. The restricted mobility in such occupations usually rendered them unchallenging dead-end jobs. For example, Wanda, a former cigar factory workers turned to the dance hall to break free from the monotony of a job where "all day long she wrapped cigars." For women like Wanda, the dance hall offered, similar to that of the Filipino patrons, a release from the monotonous and repetitive labor imposed on their individual bodies. With the lesser degree of physical control on their bodies also came the incentive of higher salaries. Alma Heilser gave her story as an example:

> I was working as a waitress in a Loop restaurant for about a month. I never worked in a dance hall like this and didn't know about them. One day the "boss" of this hall was eating in the restaurant and told me I could make twice as much money in his "dancing school." I went there one night to try it and then quit my job at the restaurant. I always liked to dance anyway, so it was really fun.

While employment as a taxi dancer garnered relative economic stability, this was gained in lieu of the commodification of the female body to male pleasure and the "respectability" of the women in their respective working class communities. . . .

Yet, the bodies of these particular white women had a different value than their richer counterparts. What is clear is that these women are not those white women whom Jacquelyn Dowd Hall refers to as "the forbidden fruit, the untouchable property, the ultimate symbol of white male power." Being of the working class and often of immigrant communities, white women who associated with Filipino American men were not protected from men of color but actually economically pushed to a shared marginal site with them. As "white trash" these women's bodies had a lesser value than other white female bodies and could have been seen as more expendable than others because as women they "mean less or mean differently than those against white women from the middle and upper classes." . . .

"White Trash" Meets the "Little Brown Monkeys": The Politics of Interracial Unions in the Midst of Anti-Miscegenation

While gender and class oppression led some white working class women to the marginal site of the taxi dance hall, it was race oppression that directed Filipino men in the 1920s and 30s to the halls. Nevertheless, the different trajectories landing these two groups in the taxi-dance hall brought forward the possibilities for intimate relationships, cohabitation, marriages, and love to blossom for the heterosexual patrons and employees of the dance halls.

Promoted by their close interaction in the "closed" spaces of the taxi dance hall, sexual alliances between Filipino men and white women were thought to be of a "larger proportion . . . than any other racial minority" in Los Angeles. In his study of anti-race riots in Watsonville, California, Emory Bogardus found the threat of intermarriage to be the most immediate concern of proponents for the exclusion of Filipinos. In the 1930s, James Wood observed that "the sex problem," i.e., the absence of women, in the Filipino American community, was greatly alleviated by the presence of white women:

> But although the Filipino and the white are not allowed to intermarry in this and in four other Pacific states, nevertheless, some of these couples wishing to be joined in wedlock have solved their problem by going to a state which does not prohibit this union. . . . Other ways (other than the legal) in which sexual relationships are carried on are through illicit cohabitation and through other relationships of a promiscuous character. The statements that "some of these white girls are crazy for these Filipinos," and also that "the Filipino is attracted strongly by the white girl," are recurrent in almost every conversation that touches on the sex problem. *As a matter of fact, it is common knowledge (possessed by individuals in contact with and observing the situation) that a sexual relationship between the Filipino "boy" and "a certain type of white girl" materializes very easily.*

The actual number of intermarriage between Filipinos and white women in difficulty to establish. Benicio Catapusan, a doctoral student in sociology at the University of Southern California in the 1930s, found evidence of 1,778 intermarriages with Filipinos from official records and publications of various Filipino organizations. Moreover, the 1930 Census reveals that the number of married Filipino men (7,409) far exceeded the number of Filipina women (1,640) in the U.S. mainland. The unaccounted 6,151 married Filipino men suggests the strong possibility of intermarriage in the community. While these men may have been married to women they left in the Philippines, they may have also been attached to non-Filipino women in the United States.

Considering the staunch eugenicist views during the time, it is really quite a surprise that a number of Filipino men had the opportunity to have sexual relations with white women. Testifying in the Congressional hearings for the exclusion of Filipino immigration to the United States, V.S. McClatchy of the exclusionist group Native Sons of the Golden West exclaimed in reference to the taxi dance halls of Northern California: "These places have been a provocative cause of the intense feelings against the Filipinos on the part of Caucasians in many communities." The possibility for these unions to flourish makes better sense if we consider why those in a position to prevent such interactions allowed the activities of the taxi dance hall to even take place. City officials, state legislators, and congressional members may have listened to the complaints of white working class men sooner if middle or upper class white women had been involved with Filipinos. Shaped by their status as working class or immigrant women, the women involved with Filipino men had not been considered worthy of protection immediately enough to prevent the possibilities for the formation of intimate relations. In actuality, the white working class women of the dance halls had not been seen as women whose "morality" needed protection from the racially "impure" Filipino.

Gathered from interviews conducted by James Wood in California in the 1930s, many middle class community members, who had contact with Filipinos and observed their interaction with white women, came to the conclusion that Filipino men were actually in need of more protection from the white working class woman. A Salvation Army coordinator in Los Angeles, for example, mentioned his distress for the Filipino who had been foolish enough to fall in love with a white woman:

> When I was working among Filipinos, there was one very good looking educated boy who was planning to marry a white girl who was, I thought, very *inferior to him*. I tried to break them up by discouraging him. He didn't appreciate it, I'm sure and it did no good.

In other instances, Filipino men were construed to be victims of troublesome white girls:

> . . . he has to do the dirtiest work in the world. . . . These "white" girls are always bothering the Filipino. I have one working here (a Filipino boy) and these girls are always phoning for him. One day some of them came in here and I had to run them out.

Reiterating the view of some that the "Filipino is far superior to this white trash," Mr. Orlanes, an importer based in Los Angeles, saw the taxi dance hall girls as bad influences on Filipinos:

> The taxi dances are schools of crime. These boys spend all their money there and are then induced to steal by these taxi dance hall girls. . . .

White working class women were not just "white trash" but also "sexual vixens." As dangerous immoral women, they were considered dirtier and socially lower than Filipino men.

Because white working class women were neither pure nor moral, sexual alliances with Filipino men could neither disrupt the racial order nor threaten the masculinity of white men. Categorically identified as less worthy than other women, white working class women involved with Filipino men were seen as expendable and degenerate. The racial hierarchy of protecting white women as the prized possessions of society remained intact because these women, not worthy of protection, simply joined Filipino men at the bottom of the existing social order.

Still, the vehemence of some reactions could not be subdued as "the pressure from the white community was always there for both the Filipino and his white bride. Couples were often victims of public ostracism and scrutiny. While both had been seen as belonging in the lowest position in the racial order of society, the gender and race dynamics among these couples weave along a complex web of power relations. For white working class women, involvement with Filipino men meant the loss of community and alienation from their families. The court case of *Stella F. Robinson v. L. E. Lampton, County Clerk of LA* is one such example of a mother who so vehemently opposed the marriage of her daughter to a Filipino that she took her case to court, petitioning "the court for a writ of prohibition, which would have restrained the county clerk from issuing the marriage license." Successful cases like Mrs. Robinson's usually led to the alienation of young white women from their families; many, we can speculate, may have run away from home and married Filipinos regardless of their parents' approval.

The alienation of these women from their communities can also be seen through the "scarlet letter" imposed on them as used goods of Filipino men. A taxi dancer explained that "most of the white fellows won't dance with (her) if they learn (she goes) out all the time with Flips." With women symbolizing a man's status in the racial order, a white woman associated with a Filipino man could therefore not be good enough for any white man; a white woman must be "the forbidden fruit, the untouchable property" to be worthy of the white man's legitimate affections. In the same way, white women who were branded as used goods of Filipinos faced rejection in the Filipino community:

> If a girl dances with too many Flips they think she's common, so they won't keep on coming to her for dances. . . . I've got to dance with some good-looking white fellows once in a while so the Filipinos will keep on dancing with me.

Additionally, marrying Filipinos cost white women the higher price of citizenship and accordingly certain legal protection and benefits. By declaring Filipinos "aliens" ineligible for citizenship, the Tydings McDuffie Act of 1934 extended to include Filipinos in the Cable Act of 1922 which established "that any woman citizen who marries an alien ineligible to citizenship shall cease to be a citizen of the United States." Marriages with Filipinos relatively stripped white women of legal rights and protection. While one court case gives proof of a woman Lola Butler successfully divorcing her husband in order to testify against him in court, we have the case of *Ilona Murillo v. Tony Murillo, Jr.* which denied Ilona her petition to divorce her Filipino husband. Although stripping white working class women of their legal rights, these unions also brought benefits to the lives of white women. With the advantage of race privilege over their husbands and partners and the hunger for women in a largely bachelor community of "single, able bodied" Filipino men, white women, we can speculate, could have negotiated to be treated with more respect by their husbands. Women leaving their husbands was an ominous threat for Filipino men.

Marriages and intimate relations between Filipinos and working class white women in the period of the taxi dance halls served as strategies against dominant power relations in society for both groups. Although these unions definitely compromised their racial privileges, white female partners of Filipino men may have gained a more equal gender relation in their marriages and sexual alliances. On the other hand, Filipino men were able to compromise their gender privilege to alleviate their experiences of racism in the U.S. because relations with white women directly questioned and resisted imposed racist policies promoting the asexuality of Filipino men. The mutual compromise involved in these two groups establishes their political alliance to a certain degree. They enabled each other to alleviate, but certainly not get rid of, their qualitatively distinct experiences of race and gender oppressions. Within these relationships that occurred in a specific historical moment, the juxtaposition of race and gender subordination and privilege forced the negotiation that had led to the political alliance of these two groups in society.

F U R T H E R   R E A D I N G

Almaguer, Tomás. *Racial Fault Lines: The Historical Origins of White Supremacy in California* (1994).

Azuma. Eiichiro. "Racial Struggle, Immigrant Nationalism, and Ethnic Identity: Japanese and Filipinos in the California Delta," *Pacific Historical Review* 67 (1998): 163–199.

Bulosan, Carlos. *America Is in the Heart: A Personal History* (1943).

Charr, Easurk Emsen. *The Golden Mountain* (1961).

Hellwig, David Johns. "The Afro-American and the Immigrant, 1880–1930: A Study of Black Social Thought," Ph.D. dissertation, Syracuse University (1973).

Ichioka, Yuji. "Japanese Immigrant Nationalism: The Issei and the Sino-Japanese War, 1937–1941," *California History* 69 (1990): 260–275.

Leonard, Karen Isaksen. *Making Ethnic Choices: California's Punjabi Mexican Americans* (1992).

Parrenas, Rhacel Salazar. "'White Trash' Meets the 'Little Brown Monkeys': The Taxi Dance Hall as a Site of Interracial and Gender Alliances Between White Working Class Women and Filipino Immigrant Men in the 1920s and 1930s," *Amerasia Journal* 24 (1998): 115–134.

Pascoe, Peggy. *Relations of Rescue: The Search for Female Moral Authority in the American West, 1874–1939* (1990).

Posadas, Barbara M. *The Filipino Americans* (1999).

Spickard, Paul R. *Mixed Blood: Intermarriage and Ethnic Identity in Twentieth Century America* (1989).

Taylor, Quintard. "Blacks and Asians in a White City: Japanese Americans and African Americans in Seattle, 1890–1940," *Western Historical Quarterly* 22 (1991): 401–429.

Yung, Judy. *Unbound Feet: A Social History of Chinese Women in San Francisco* (1995).

CHAPTER
8

Americanization and the Second Generation, 1920–1942

The process of becoming American, or Americanization, has been a perennial concern in American politics. One of the first responsibilities of Congress was to establish citizenship qualifications for the new nation. The result was the Naturalization Act of 1790, a measure that explicitly reserved the naturalization process to "free whites." The consequences of this statute, as Chapter 3 reveals, formed the bedrock of anti-Asian discrimination throughout the nineteenth and early twentieth centuries. But seen from a different angle, another significance of the Naturalization Act lay in its failure to be the final word on who could become an American citizen. The issue of Americanization had always been too politically charged for Americans to simply accept the letter of the 1790 statute. As a result, each generation since then has added a new layer of meanings and debates to the living legacy of the Naturalization Act.

Three general orientations have proved to be the most durable in the interpretation of American citizenship. First is the image of the melting pot, which at its most literal connotes a mixing of all the world's peoples and cultures to create an entirely new one—the American. Related, and often confused, with the melting pot is the idea of "assimilation," which has meant the expectation that newcomers conform to the dominant Anglo group. Both the melting pot and Anglo conformity have been contrasted with a third perspective that is best recognizable to the twenty-first-century American. This is the notion of pluralism, a vision of society as a mosaic of irreducible ethnic, racial, and cultural differences.

An important interest among Asian American historians has been how Asian Americans have engaged the issue of Americanization. How could Asians in the United States prove to the white majority that they could become American? This question, which generations of Asian immigrants had struggled (and largely failed) to answer, continued to perplex Asian Americans from the 1920s to the start of World War II. But, at the same time, this period witnessed a profound demographic change that would come to have major political significance; this was the coming of age of the immigrants' children, the second generation of Asians in the United States.

Born on American soil, members of the second generation were American citizens and as such were legally protected from the public policies discriminating against their "alien" parents. Another crucial difference from their parents was that the second generation usually had no serious cultural or linguistic handicaps that might promote misunderstanding between themselves and whites. The foundation of similarities between the second generation and whites was often the public schools, where the children of immigrants were taught to think like Americans and where they came to be familiar with interacting with whites and other racial minorities. This is not to say that the second generation faced no racial prejudice. They clearly did, and many abhorred their common predicament with the immigrant generation. But it was no coincidence that the second generation would play a deciding role in the dismantling of anti-Asian racism after World War II. The roots of this postwar revolution in race relations reach back to the pre-war second generation experience.

How did the American-born generation engage the process of becoming American before World War II? What was it like for them to grow up Asian American? What impact did they have on society and vice versa?

☻ D O C U M E N T S

The documents in this chapter focus on the retention or abandonment of Old World traditions in the context of specific international, political, economic, and personal motivations. Documents 1 and 2 offer contrasting perspectives by two second-generation women on their parents' immigrant culture. The first, by Chinese American Flora Belle Jan, sees old-fashioned immigrant traditions as stultifying her creative individuality, while the second, by Connie Tirona, provides a warm remembrance of her small tight-knit Filipino American community. Dora Yum Kin, in Document 3, provides a brief account of the early childhood socialization of a second-generation Korean American girl who experiences a "pan-Asian" solidarity with Chinese and Japanese Americans.

The remaining six documents focus on second-generation Japanese Americans, the largest cohort of American-born Asians before World War II. In Document 4, an editorial in a Japanese American newspaper, Taishi Matsumoto bemoans the racial exclusion of the second generation, or Nisei, from most jobs outside the ethnic enclave. Documents 5 and 6 show different Nisei responses to the Sino-Japanese War (1937–1945). Document 5 is a brief exchange regarding the editorial policy of the English section of a leading Japanese American newspaper. One side wants to continue to be sympathetic toward Japan's involvement in the war, whereas the other side, represented by Tokutaro Slocum, insists that the Nisei must sever all ties to their parents' homeland and identify only with the United States. Document 6, a newspaper editorial from 1940, presents the appearance and talents of a Nisei beauty queen as a cultural bridge between the increasingly belligerent nations Japan and the United States. An alternative view of the Nisei is put forth in Document 7 by an American intelligence officer who in the early 1940s had studied whether the Nisei, and their immigrant parents, would be loyal to the United States in the event of a U.S.–Japan war. Finally, Documents 8 and 9 provide visual testimony to the cultural adaptation of Japanese Americans on the eve of their imprisonment in internment camps during World War II.

1. Flora Belle Jan Longs for Unconventionality and Freedom, 1924

Miss Jan is a graduate of the Fresno High School and has taken two years in the Fresno State College. She is a leader among the native born Chinese, very much interested in writing, dramatics and social life.

She entertained me [investigator Merle Davis] in her father's upstairs restaurant for about an hour. My first approach was through Miss Purcell, but was unsuccessful and I finally saw her by presenting my card directly.

She said, "Would you like to hear something about my life? I will tell you if you are interested. I was born here in Fresno Chinatown and attended the city schools and graduated from the High School and have had two years in the State College. When I was a little girl, I grew to dislike the conventionality and rules of Chinese life. The superstitions and customs seemed ridiculous to me. My parents have wanted me to grow up a good Chinese girl, but I am an American and I can't accept all the old Chinese ways and ideas. A few years ago when my Mother took me to worship at the shrine of my ancestor and offer a plate of food, I decided it was time to stop this foolish custom. So I got up and slammed down the rice in front of the idol and said, 'So long Old Top, I don't believe in you anyway.' My mother didn't like it a little bit.

"As I grew older I came to see that American life is also full of conventionality and foolish customs and it has become a fad of mine to study these things and to write about them. I long for unconventionality and freedom from all these customs and ideals that make people do such ridiculous and insincere things.

"I have written a good deal in local papers about Chinese life. Much of this had displeased the Chinese people of Fresno. My article on 'The Sheiks of Chinatown' (a description of the young sports of China Alley) was a takeoff on certain well known native-born Chinese. It made a terrible fuss in Chinatown. I have had three blackmailing letters sent me for writing so openly about Chinese life. One of the Chinese students from North China became very angry at my article on the Sheiks and wrote me a very long, fat letter attacking me and picking to pieces everything that I had said. He thought that I was trying to disgrace China, which I distinctly was not, but only trying to have a little fun with my Chinese friends. All Chinatown got very excited and two of the boys, one from North China and the other from South China, fought a kind of a duel over it. North boy said that I had disgraced China. South boy said No, that we should be too proud to let a little dust like this hurt us. A delegation of Chinese students met me at college and I challenged them to show what I had said that disgraced anybody or anything. They put on their spectacles and after ten minutes could not find anything. I said, 'Ta ta, Kiddos, when you find any disgrace you just put me wise. I can't wait all day.'

"It is very funny to watch the snobbishness of the girls at the state college. I listen to the Sorority girls talk over possible candidates to membership in their sorority.

From "Interview with Flora Belle Jan . . . ," June 5, 1924, Box 28, Folder 225, Survey of Race Relations Collection, Hoover Institution on War, Revolution, and Peace, Stanford University, Stanford Calif. reprinted in Judy Yung, *Unbound Voices: A Documentary History of Chinese Women in San Francisco* (Berkeley: University of California Press 1999), 311–314.

It runs something like this, 'Girls, what do you suppose, Jane Smith whom we've been rushing is impossible. We've just found out that her father once drove a delivery wagon. They live in such a nice house and she wears such pretty clothes, who would have dreamed it. My, she's such a nice girl, it is really too bad.' I happen to know that some of these very girls have families where the men are working at shop work and day labor and where the mothers do their own work. They judge people entirely by the clothes they wear and the amount of money they spend, and they get awfully stung in this way sometimes. Of course being a Chinese girl, I'm not eligible to membership in a sorority, but some of the girls are awfully good to me.

"I have written a sketch of American girls, called 'Old Mother Grundy and her brood of unbaptized nuns,' which takes off some of the characteristics of the modern flapper in American society.

"At the Community House last week our Chinese Club gave a play called, 'Miss Flapper Vampire,' that I wrote. I was the leading character and about five young men played in it with me. There was a large audience of Americans. Afterward we danced and the American girls danced with the Chinese boys and I danced with American young men."

2. Connie Tirona Recalls Growing Up Filipino American (1930s and 1940s), 1995

Childhood Memories of the Manongs

When my parents landed on Angel Island in San Francisco Bay, their friends were in the Delano area working in the grape fields. My parents did not know where Delano was. A Japanese grower from Stanford decided to hire them (Part of Stanford at one time was all a nursery owned by this Japanese farmer.) So my parents had a place to stay.

But their friends from Delano contacted them again and asked them to join them there, where they could earn more money. So my parents decided to move to Delano to be near their *kababayans* (countrymen) from Hawaii. My father said there was a lot of Bombays (East Indians) but not as many Mexicans in Delano. However, the Bombays were moving on to El Centro. My parents stayed in that area for quite some time, until I was born, and then my father decided to move the family back to northern California.

I was born in 1929 in Selma, which is right next to Fresno. I remember many Filipinos as I was growing up. They still had their cockfights. The cockpit arena was really the gathering place for all the Filipinos. Even if some didn't like to bet on the cockfights, everybody was there. I remember the women having little stalls, with their little tables filled with individual special delicacies they had cooked. And of course, the men who were single at the time were so happy to have Filipino food because they lived in these barracks, while the families lived in cottage and could prepare their own food. These cottages were really dilapidated shacks, but they were always kept neat and immaculate.

From Connie Tirona, "Sometimes, I Am Not Sure What It Means to Be an American," in *Filipino American Lives,* ed. Yen Le Espiritu, pp. 66–71. Reprinted by permission of Temple University Press. © 1995 by Temple University. All rights reserved.

Even when they were following the seasonal crops, all of them—there were three families in my parents' group—would pitch in to buy a car so they could travel from camp to camp. And we would all go in that car, and I can remember sometimes there was not enough work for everyone, and the ones who got the work would buy the groceries. And everyone would pitch in to get a small place where we all lived together. It was somewhat crowded, but we always kept it clean. Everybody would cook and help.

I can remember one time, they were down to their last fifty cents. They were going to another place where there was an opening for pruning grapes. So, the other two families would stay behind in the place that they had rented, while the rest would go seek jobs. Well, they only had fifty cents. Two chickens crossed the road. Let me tell you, those chickens did not stay alive for very long. They plucked them and cleaned them that night. They gathered vegetables from their garden; they always had a garden wherever they went. They threw everything in a pot. Those two chickens fed three families that night. Soon they were able to get jobs again. Not one of us ever went hungry.

When I was about four or five years old, my parents moved up to Oakland. With his experience working in the shipyard in Hawaii, my father eventually got a job at a shipyard. So he was able to leave the agricultural job environment. He was a rigger and retired from the Mare Island shipyard after twenty years. And guess what? He went back to work as a foreman in the fields again. I think he was one of the first who wanted to organize a union against the growers. He was always fighting for the rights of workers.

In the 1930s, most of the *manongs* were still on the farms. The *manongs* were those men who came here from Hawaii without any families. They were bachelors. And they were the best dancers, the best dressers. There was just something very suave about them. . . .

There were about thirty *manongs* in the labor camps in the Sacramento—San Joaquin area that we would visit. Sometimes the *manongs* would come and visit us. They were so homesick for family. They always looked up to my father because he had a "government job" in the shipyard. We went to see them almost every week or every other week. My mother would bake all her delicacies all week long for such visits, and the *manongs* enjoyed eating them.

It was so beautiful there when we visited them. They built what looked like a Japanese bathhouse. They installed a huge metal tub with hot coals underneath to warm the water. Of course, you had to bathe outside first. That was the biggest treat! And the *manongs* would fix up their rooms immaculately. They scrubbed their place because "the families were coming!" They picked fresh corn and cooked good, wholesome food. Their big thing was fishing in the delta's rivers. We would go up there and fish, and they would be roasting pigs.

After eating they would play guitars and mandolins, and we, as little children of the families, would sing and dance. The *manongs* liked to hear the little kids sing. They had a small makeshift stage for us, and we would go up there with our curly hair and cute little dresses. And they would throw coins at us. It was the biggest thing for them. You could just see tears of joy on their faces. They would come up and hug us. And I was thinking, "Gosh! Just a little joy that we brought to them." But they were so happy.

I especially remember when we sang the Visayan songs. You could see the tears on the faces of those grown men. Usually, Filipino men are not like that. I don't think Asian men really show their feelings. I remember my younger sister had a beautiful soprano voice, and she would sing this one Visayan song that said something about how hard life was in a strange land. It was like a love song. As they listened to her song, tears would form and slowly flow from their eyes. They would drink their wine and cry softly. They would say to my parents, "Thank you for teaching your daughter to sing that song."

Soon it was time for us to go to bed. As I was drifting off to sleep, I could hear them laughing as they started to sing nostalgic songs from the Philippines. Lying on a small cot, it just lulled me to sleep. The next morning, we would go fishing again and do the same thing. Breakfast was prepared and served. We would leave for home on Sunday evening. After such weekends, the *manongs* prepared for another grueling week of hard work.

The *manongs* bought me my first bike. They wanted to have snapshots taken so they could send them back to their families in the Philippines. When they received mail from the Philippines, they would ask me to read it to them. Some of them did not read well. Their families probably had someone write the letters in English for them. One of the letters said, "Thank you for the picture of your adopted daughter with the bicycle you got her. Thank you for the money that you sent." And I would end up writing back to them. The *manongs* would keep the mail they received until it became so frayed and torn because of so many readings. You could tell that they read it at night when loneliness overcame them.

I wish for those days again. If I could relive one day in the past, I would love to see them again.

Growing Up in the 1930s and 1940s

At this time, Filipinos were experiencing much prejudice and discrimination. We could not buy homes in certain areas. My parents bought a home in Vallejo on the other side of town by the waterfront, where all of the people of color lived. We would take walks on Saturday nights to pass the time away. We could not afford anything else. We just wanted to see people. We could see all the Filipinos all dressed up with no place to go, except the dance halls. My mother would say, "No, no! We don't go this way," as if I didn't know what was down there.

Where we lived there was one certain block that you could go up to and feel comfortable. You could go to this one theater, and that was all right because that was where all the people of color would go. But if you went beyond to the next block, people would stare at you. They would look at you when you went into a department store. My father would say to us, "Well, we don't have to go there. Things are so expensive up there anyway."

Being foolhardy, I told my sister, "Well, I am going up there." She told me that I should not. When I asked her why, she told me what had happened to her. She had gone into a department store because it fascinated her. The manager told her she did not belong in there and to get out. She told the manager she was just looking around and was not doing anything wrong.

I guess that when you are a child and curious, you would do anything. Since I could not go into that department store, I remembered that there was a Sees candy store in the same block. So I went there to buy a piece of candy. The lady in the store asked if I had any money. When I showed her my money and pointed to the piece of chocolate candy I wanted, I remember her taking double pieces of paper so she wouldn't touch my hands. Being the child that I was, I purposely dropped the money on the floor. She had to come around the counter to pick it up. I was about eight at the time.

Then I decided I would be more adventurous, so I went down to another block and into another department store. Again, I was kicked out. Then I went into a Chinese-owned store, and they welcomed me with open arms. They asked me what I was doing at that end of town. I told them I was just curious and wanted to find out what it was like, since we were told that we could not go there.

Of course, I got a spanking afterward because I disobeyed my parents. My father sat me down and asked, "Well, what did you learn?" I replied, "Everything you said was true, Papa." He said, "I just wanted you to know that you can do these things. You can go anywhere; it's just that you may not be treated as good as other people. So you have to learn how to respond and react in that situation." I told him about dropping the money on the floor in the candy store, and he laughed.

I went to a Catholic school. The reason we were able to attend this school was because the sisters said that we only had to pay so much. Our home was five miles away from the school I attended. But that was all right, since I had many friends that I picked up on my way to school. I can remember walking to elementary school and being taunted at times.

My sister and I were the only ones of color in the school. But that never bothered me because I thought I could play just as well as anyone could, and I was equally as bright as the other students, if not brighter. I used to bring rice and fish to school for lunch because I love to eat both. It was a great meal for me. The little girls would not sit by me, and I wondered why, because their lunch was not as good as mine. The nuns would come over and say, "They don't understand."

In high school, some of my friends were Greeks and Italians. They were white people but never thought about color. The only problem that I had was when they had a school dance. They did not allow people of color to attend. My friend, who was the captain of the basketball team, invited me. I told him I could not go, and he said he would not go either. All my friends said they would not go also, but I told them it was the rule and rules are not made to be broken.

3. Dora Yum Kim Recalls Growing Up Korean American in Chinatown (1920s, 1930s, and 1940s), 1999

I started going to school at Lincoln Grammar School in Oakland. Then we moved back to San Francisco when I was in second grade, where I started going to the Jean Parker School. When I started going to school, my mother told us that she had tried to take English lessons. She had gone to the ESL classes they had at a Chinese church located a block down from where we lived. But she said it just wouldn't go into her head, and so, . . . I knew I was on my own. I ended up translating for my mother. . . . I don't remember how old I was, but I think by the time I was in second or third grade I was writing notes for my mother excusing me from school when I and, later, my brothers were sick.

When I was in grammar school my mother had two Korean friends who spoke good English. And this one woman was just beautiful. This family owned a cleaning shop, and she sewed, so she dressed up her four daughters just beautifully. And her English . . . I think I used to envy the girls because their mothers would come to the PTA meetings and talk with the teachers. My mother couldn't do that. She was so busy at the business that she probably couldn't have come anyway. But even if she did come, she couldn't communicate with anybody. In fact, most of the parents from Chinatown couldn't speak English and were fully engaged in minding their businesses. And I remember envying these girls because their mothers spoke English. When I was older, I learned that they spoke such good English because they were raised in Christian orphanages in Korea. But I didn't know that as a child. All I felt was the envy. . . .

What did going to school teach you about where you fit in America?

Going to school was a real eye-opener. When I was young, before I went to school, I never thought about what I was or anything like that. But when I started going to school in Oakland, I realized I was different from most of the other kids at school—I was Oriental. But they never taught us about Orientals in America. I suppose by the time I was in second grade I already knew not to expect that. But what they did teach us about was China and Japan. I came to realize that there was no mention of Korea in geography or history. I couldn't find out anything about my background. So as a Korean I was invisible outside the small Chinatown Korean community. At that time the Koreans in the area were so actively involved in events in Korea, yet there was no mention of it in school.

I was really curious about my heritage, so I started cutting out anything I read in newspapers or magazines that had anything to do with Korea. These articles are where I learned how to talk about Korea and being Korean I recall one picture of two Korean girls standing, instead of sitting, on a seesaw. I showed it to my mother, and she said, "I used to be really good at this. I could jump really high."

The caption read, "Public Education for Girls in Korea."

I look at it now and think, "What a joke." For centuries Korean women have been virtual slaves. This would be a good article for the feminists, you know, in terms of the irony. Education of any kind used to be an extraordinary innovation for the ordinary Korean girl.

I'm confused. Why did you rely on newspaper and magazine articles? I thought you said that your parents taught you about Korean heritage.

My parents did teach us about Korea. I think they did a pretty good job of it. When I was growing up, I wanted to visit Korea because I felt proud to be Korean. But I wasn't quite sure what being Korean meant because we were different from our parents. Our parents' ideas of being Korean had to do with their experiences growing up and living in Korea. But we American-born Koreans didn't have that experience; all we had was secondhand information about it. Since I am Korean and not Chinese or Japanese, I found myself having to explain what I was at a young age. When I was in grammar school, it was hard for me to explain where Korea was and what the people were like. The articles and clippings I saved in my scrapbook helped me explain these things in English to my classmates.

There are other differences between my parents' perspectives and mine. They were anti-Japanese because of the situation at home, but for the children it was different. It's different to be American. You know that your parents hate the Japanese, and that it's a sore point with them, but if your own experience doesn't support the hatred, it's all hearsay. Your parents tell you that in Japan the Japanese hate the Koreans and they still fingerprint them even though they have Japanese names and all that. But within the community of people we knew, we had a Japanese doctor, Dr. Clifford Uyeda, who went to Japan to try to fight against that. It didn't do any good, but as Americans we have different feelings than we're supposed to have. You can't tell what people believe based on appearance.

I also had close Japanese girlfriends. But as far as having Japanese friends, I was restricted. I couldn't bring a Japanese friend home. And I understood, and I just didn't bring them home. But I associated with lots of Japanese people.

I know you can read and write Korean. When did you learn that?

By the time I was in second grade, I could read and write Korean even though I couldn't understand everything I read. I don't actually remember learning to read and write, but I think my parents must have initially taught me. You know, from 1924 to 1965, when immigration laws were relaxed, no Koreans could come over except missionaries or students. The missionaries or students who did come over didn't have any money. So when they came to the restaurant, my parents felt so sorry for them and fed them. Anyway, I guess my dad must've made a deal with them. "Hey I'll feed you free if you'll teach my children Korean." So that's where I got some additional training in Korean. A few of them did come by to say hello after they got their Ph.D.'s.

I also remember going to Korean school with other Korean children. There were only about half a dozen kids of school age at any given time since there were no more than half a dozen total families here. I used to think that it was pretty terrible that the children would always cut classes. You would think that since we knew each other and their families they wouldn't just cut classes like that. . . . We had what they call *kuku hakyo* [Korean language school] at the church. The class was actually an organized tutorial. We tried to have that during summer vacations and other breaks. I don't remember studying very hard, but I remember all my Korean. In fact, even now I run into people who used to teach there. Not so long ago I ran into this man, and when we were introduced to each other, this guy says, "I taught her Korean." I remember reciting *kakya kokyo koekyoe ku kyu keu ki* [literally, the manner in which children recite the vowels with the first consonant (k/g) of the Korean alphabet] and all the other basics. I'm glad it stuck with me because I can read the Korean paper now and get the gist of it. . . .

What did you do after school and weekends other than work?

Growing up in Chinatown, most of my girlfriends were Chinese, and they had to go to Chinese school after school. All the Chinese kids went to the Hip Wo school after school. So there wasn't really time to play with them. I have wondered if it's because they had to go to Chinese school every day that many of the Chinese who were born here still had accents. I actually think it's because the Chinese kids went to Chinese school that many of them really didn't have much time to study for American school.

In terms of the Korean girls, there were very few, and I was the youngest of the girls around my age. Often they wouldn't bother with me because I was younger than they were. So I didn't play with them much either. There were just a few girls who were younger, but they were much too young for me to play with.

So when I was growing up, I lived in the library. None of my girlfriends really used the library because they didn't have the time. But I would sometimes go twice a day. I'd read one book, bring it back, bring another book home. I was drawn to books. I enjoyed reading about other people's lives because I would get so absorbed when I read that I lived the parts. I still do. I remember being Jo in Louisa May Alcott's *Little Women.* Maybe it was because there was nothing else to do in Chinatown in those days. The library was right down on Powell Street, where it still is. I used to like Nancy Drew books, the whole set, then the Five Peppers. I remember reading all of those. That's what I did after school when I didn't go down to my parents' restaurant. . . .

So who did you socialize with in junior high?

I still continued to hang around with the girls from Chinatown when I was a teenager. And on Saturday night the Chinese girls would all play mahjong. It was part of their culture, and they really enjoyed it. But I couldn't see playing mahjong, so I would study in the corner while they played. I think part of the reason I studied instead of playing with the girls is that I had this thing about finishing school before I turned eighteen. Normally you start kindergarten when you're five, but I didn't start until I was six. I don't know how come. So I really wanted to graduate when I was seventeen, like everyone else. It was kind of crazy but that's what motivated me to get out of school really quickly. . . .

During high school . . . [m]y social life was . . . affected by discrimination. When I was at Girls' High School, there were dances. The girls used to be invited to dances at all boys' high schools. So my Chinese girlfriend and I decided to attend one of these dances just to see what it would be like. We talked about the fact that nobody was going to ask us to dance, but we decided to go just to see. Sure enough, every white girl was asked to dance, but this girl and I were never asked.

I didn't feel inferior or anything like that. I knew that not being asked to dance was part of discrimination and that it was a learned thing. And I knew that all those white boys were not going to have anything to do with Asians. I mean, my girlfriend and I were disgusted. I'm really glad I went with my girlfriend because imagine how I would have felt if I had gone there alone as the only Asian girl, being ostracized like that. It also could have been worse if we didn't know that we would be hurt. But we knew. We just went to see what it would be like anyway. And it hurt anyway. Back then I didn't think too long on being hurt. I thought it was just a part of life. We knew that we were Asians, and we couldn't do the things Caucasians did. We accepted that fact. And we were sheltered from the worst of the discrimination in Chinatown. But now I often think about these kinds of incidents that we had growing up when I read about the different effects of discrimination. When you grow up with it, it stays with you.

I didn't go to any more Girls' School functions. Instead, we went to the Chinese dances every Saturday night. I used to go around with a Chinese girl. All the high schools like Galileo High School, George Washington High School, Lowell High School, Commerce High School, Balboa High School, Polytechnic [a couple of those are no longer in existence] had a Chinese club with all Chinese members. And each week one club would give a dance with a live band. They, Chinatown, had a good band that played at the dances, and everybody [all the Asian teenagers] would look forward to that. It was mostly Chinese, and all the Koreans went, what few there were. Then toward the end of high school all the Japanese started to come because they didn't have anything like that. I would dance with any of the boys who would ask me—Chinese, Korean, Japanese.

4. Taishi Matsumoto Bemoans Limited Employment Opportunities for Nisei, 1937

I am a fruit stand worker. It is not a very attractive nor distinguished occupation, and most certainly unappreciated in print. I would much rather it were doctor or lawyer . . . but my aspirations [were] frustrated long ago by circumstances, social and financial. . . . I am only what I am, a professional carrot washer.

My work can be very pleasant at times. That is, if [I] make no complaints of long hours and little pay, thereby impressing my subdued qualities upon my employer who so approves of this virtue among his employees. He often goes out of his way to humor me, for he realizes that I am of a rebellious nature. He approaches me beaming, and plants a hearty slap on my shoulder . . . attempting to create a comradely atmosphere. He attributes this familiarity to his and my parent's prefecture, Hiroshima, of which he may take advantage of once too often. After all, what is Hiroshima ken [prefecture] to me? It is a mere name without meaning only that my parents had drifted from thence seeking a livelihood here in America. What so important connection is there here that my employer should make so much of it? I can almost say without due contempt that the man [i]s exploiting my labor in the name of an alien country. What sort of spineless fool am I to be accepting this daily hypocrisy? . . .

Disillusioned men, well on in their years, work with me side by side. They make no complaints; they make no progress; they accept the days as they unfold, following [in] [their] wake as though it were their undisputable lots. Yet what can they expect and what can be expected of them with their underdog complexes? Will I, and the rest of the nisei youths contract their attitude and inherit their lot?

I grit my teeth at the drudgery, the unending hours of the hopelessness of fruit stand work, and its meagre compensation. This cannot go on forever, much less can I go on.

From Taishi Matsumoto, "The Protest of a Professional Carrot Washer," *Kahsu Mainichi [newspaper]* (Los Angeles), August 4, 1937, English language section, editorial page. Used with permission.

It seems that I started out in life on the wrong foot. I feel [like] a square peg in a round hole. . . . An optimist would undoubtedly make the best of it, but even the most optimistic, after several years of market work[,] will begin to notice the hole.

I understand my position and realize that I am stagnating; that I am making no progress, and most keenly do I realize that . . . I am getting older.

The little optimism that is left in me refuses to accept my ever increasing conviction that market work may have to be my career after all. It goads me on with the hope that when I have a few shekels saved that I can call my own, and only God knows when that will be, I will invest it in an enterprise which will be, through habit and familiarity rather than choice, most likely another market.

But until then, and it will be a long time till then, [are] there no inspired Messia[h]s, no strong organizations to whom I can appeal not only for myself, but for others like me, so that life will be less miserable, that we may bear fewer blisters on our hands and less corns on our toes?

5. Tokutaro Slocum Debates Nisei Stand on Sino-Japanese War, 1938

Minutes of The *Rafu Shimpo* English Section editorial board meeting, July, 1938, at Rosslyn Hotel: "In the discussion about the Nisei stand on the Sino-Japanese war, members felt that it was only natural that the Nisei should have pro-Japanese sympathies. It was the general feeling that "even you [Tokutaro] Slocum, if you were honest with yourself, would recognize the fact you are ultimately Japanese; you are not 100% American; you are barred from inter-marrying racially; you are barred from exclusive country clubs; you are discriminated against in many ways; this is a de facto situation. Because we know this, as proud of our American citizenship as we are, we know it it something different from that of a white American citizen. Officially we are Americans, but inevitably we are treated as Japanese." To this Slocum, leaping to his feet and bringing his fist down upon the table, shouted: 'I don't like that statement that officially we are American and actually we are Japanese. We are all Americans and Japanese only to the extent we want to be. I do recognize that we are discriminated against but I do not let this resentment stand in my way. Our policy must look to the future. This Sino-Japanese war will not last forever, whereas the Nisei and Sansei will probably outlive it, so we cannot and must not jeopardize our future by participating too actively in a militant pro-Japanese campaign. I am going to have a resolution passed to tax the export of any fund raised for any foreign countries to be used for unpeaceful purposes; I'm going to do this through the American Legion and the V.F.W. Remember we are dealing with Anglo-Saxons, and they deliver the blow first.'"

From Minutes of the *Rafu Shimpo* [newspaper], English language section editorial board meeting, July 1938, at Rosslyn Hotel, Los Angeles, California, as quoted in Togo Tanaka, "History of the JACL [Japanese American Citizens League]," unpublished manuscript, circa 1945, chap. 4, p. 33, folder T 6.25, Japanese American Evacuation and Resettlement Records (67/14c), Bancroft Library, Berkeley, Calif.

6. Japanese American Newspaper *Kashu Mainichi* Heralds Biculturalism of Beauty Queen, 1940

She's lovely and charming, wears a quiet smile. Her age is twenty-two and she likes to collect dolls.

Have you guessed who she is? That's a thumbnail sketch of Queen Shizue Kobayashi, who reigned over one exciting week of fun and festivity in Little Tokyo. Her term of office, however, doesn't end with the last performance of the busy Nisei Week program. She will be known, henceforth, as the nisei Queen of 1940 and will rule undisputedly in Nihonmachi until another maiden is chosen again next year.

"It's so exciting and wonderful, says Miss Kobayashi when asked how she felt being a queen. "Words can't describe how I felt, meeting so many people—and they've all been wonderful—going to so many occasions."

In her quiet dignified charm, Miss Kobayashi represents the best of nisei womanhood. When you meet her, you are impressed with her courteous manner and her unassuming personality. When you ask her what she likes to do, she smiles and says she likes movies, ballets and [to] play a little tennis.

Shizue is a native Los Angeles girl, having attended Maryknoll grammar school and Lincoln High School. She is also a graduate of a local sewing school, the result of which you will see in the dress she is wearing, which she designed and made herself.

And what does she do in the evenings? Well, the queen is very busy evenings. Three nights out of the week, she will tell you, she goes to sewing school; two nights every week, she goes to master the intricate Japanese musical instrument called Koto; and one night she studies Japanese. All of which keeps her quite busy, thank you.

Her winning modesty doesn't permit her to talk very much about herself. She would rather listen to you. But that shouldn't fool you because she is a very accomplished young lady. She reads Japanese with facility and visited Japan about five years ago. Shizue knows her Japanese manners as well as American etiquette.

They say nisei are a bridge between Japanese and Occidental culture. Well, that just about sums up the situation in the person of this petite miss.

"I'm just an old fashioned girl," she admits quite frankly. But, that only applies when it comes to jitterbug—she hasn't learned to jitterbug yet, and doesn't intend to either. However, she does want to learn to play golf and will take it up when she gets around to it, she says.

For a whole week, she's lived in a fairyland of entertainments and personal appearances. She has been acclaimed by thousands and has become the toast of the town. Shizue went all through it without becoming affected by it—that's how she is, takes it in her quiet way.

Oh, yes. What about all these offers by merchants who promise so many things in case she decides to walk up the altar during the next year? She smiles and says

---

From "Her Majesty, The Queen," *Kashu Mainichi* [newspaper] (Los Angeles), August 11 1940, English language section, editorial page. Used with permission.

she has no intentions of marching to the tune of Lohengrin, at least during the next few years. But, who knows?

"My employer, Dr. Sakiyama, has been very considerate," says the Queen. "He's given me a week's vacation during the festival, and he's going to give me another week to 'recuperate.'" At present she is working as a secretary for the doctor.

And so after a brief interview, we take leave of her majesty the Queen of the Nisei Festival, wishing her the best of luck for the coming years.

She's a very lucky girl, you might say. Well, she is, but you mustn't forget that her training for queen started in early years, and she thoroughly deserves the honor. You'll also agree with me on that point.

7. American Intelligence Officer Promotes Nisei Americanization, 1942

I

Within the past eight or ten years the entire "Japanese question" in the United States has reversed itself. The alien menace is no longer paramount, and is becoming less important every day as the original alien immigrants grow older and die, and as more and more of their American-born children reach maturity.

Three words are commonly used in identifying the Japanese in the United States:

Issei (pronounced ee-say) meaning "first generation." The word refers to those who were born in Japan—hence, alien Japanese in the United States.

Nisei (pronounced nee-say) meaning "second generation." The word identifies the children, born in the United States, of *Issei.*

Kibei (pronounced kee-bay) meaning "returned to America." The word refers to those *Nisei* who spent all or a large portion of their lives in Japan and who have now returned to the United States.

The primary present and future problem is that of dealing with the American-born United States citizens of Japanese ancestry. I consider that at least seventy-five per cent of them are loyal to the United States.

As a basic policy tending toward the permanent solution of this problem, the American citizens of Japanese ancestry should be officially encouraged in their efforts toward loyalty and acceptance as bona fide citizens; they should be accorded a place in the national effort through such agencies as the Red Cross, U.S.O., civilian defense, and such activities as ship- and aircraft-building or other defense production activities, even though subject to greater investigative checks as to background and loyalty than Caucasian Americans.

My opinion has been formed largely through personal contact with the *Nisei* themselves and their chief organization, the Japanese American Citizens League. It has also been formed through interviews with many people in government circles, law enforcement officers, and business men who have dealt with them over a period

Excerpt from "The Japanese in America: The Problem and the Solution," *Harpers Magazine* 185 (October 1942), 490–496. Copyright 1946 by *Harper's Magazine.* All rights reserved. Reproduced from the October issue by special permission.

of many years. Many of the *Nisei* voluntarily contributed valuable anti-subversive information to this [the author's] and other governmental agencies. The Japanese Consular staff, the Central Japanese Association, and others known to have been sympathetic to the Japanese cause did not themselves trust the *Nisei*. A great many of the *Nisei* had taken legal steps through the Japanese Consulate and the Government of Japan to divest themselves officially of Japanese citizenship (dual citizenship) even though by so doing they became legally dead in the eyes of the Japanese law and were no longer eligible to inherit any property which they or their families might have held in Japan.

The United States recognizes these American-born Orientals as citizens, extends the franchise to them, drafts them for military service (it is estimated that approximately 5,000 *Nisei* in the State of California have entered the United States Army as a result of the Selective Service Act), forces them to pay taxes, perform jury duty, and so on, and has extended to them the complete protection afforded by the Constitution and the Bill of Rights. At the same time it has viewed them with considerable suspicion and distrust, and so far as is known to the writer, has made no particular effort to develop their loyalty to the United States, except by permitting them to attend public schools. They have been segregated as to where they may live by zoning laws, discriminated against in employment and wages, and rebuffed in nearly all their efforts to prove their loyalty to the United States. There has been a great deal of indiscriminate anti-Japanese agitation—the work of lecturers, radio commentators, newspaper editors, and others. There were just enough half-truths in these articles and statements to render them exceedingly dangerous and to arouse a tremendous amount of violent anti-Japanese feeling among Caucasians of all classes who were not thoroughly informed. Many of those agitating against the *Nisei* and *Issei* have done so from ulterior motives. An example is the anti-Japanese agitation of Yugoslav fishermen in California who frankly want to eliminate competition in the fishing industry.

The only practical permanent solution of this problem is to indoctrinate and absorb these people and accept them as an integral part of the United States population, even though they remain a racial minority, and officially to extend to them the rights and privileges of citizenship, as well as to demand of them its duties and obligations. The *Nisei* could be accorded a place in the national war effort without risk or danger. Such a step would go farther than anything else toward cementing their loyalty to the United States.

II

Of the *Japanese-born alien* residents [the *Issei*], the large majority are at least passively loyal to the United States.

There are among the Japanese, both aliens and United States citizens, certain individuals, either deliberately placed by the Japanese government or actuated by a fanatical loyalty to that country, who would act as saboteurs or enemy agents. This number is estimated to be less than three per cent of the total, or about 3,500 in the entire United States.

The most potentially dangerous element of all are the *Kibei*—those American citizens of Japanese ancestry who have spent the formative years of their lives, between ten and twenty, in Japan and have returned to the United States to claim their legal American citizenship within the past few years. These people are essentially and inherently Japanese and may have been deliberately sent back to the United States by the Japanese government to act as agents. In spite of their legal citizenship and the protection afforded them by the Bill of Rights they should be looked upon as enemy aliens.

[It must be remembered that the *Kibei* are a part of the much larger group of *Nisei,* all of them native-born citizens of the United States. Quite apart from the *Kibei,* some of the other *Nisei* have occasionally gone back to Japan to visit or to work. Most of these have made the journey to Japan after they have reached the age of seventeen. The reception given to these Japanese-Americans in Japan is very different from the welcome extended to the *Kibei.*]

They [these other *Nisei* who went back to Japan after they had grown up] found themselves viewed with more distrust in Japan than was the case in the United States; in Japan they were looked on with more suspicion than if they had been white persons. They were laughed at for their foreign ways; they were called American spies. In other ways they didn't conform and found themselves unable to conform. They couldn't live on the Japanese standard of living or the Japanese diet; they couldn't accustom themselves to Japanese ways of life. The majority of them returned after a short time, thoroughly disillusioned with Japan and more than ever loyal to the United States. It is my firm belief that the finest way to make a pro-American out of any *Nisei* is to send him back to Japan for one or two years after he is seventeen. Often a visit of a few months, in the past, has been sufficient to do the job.

The parents of a maid who worked for me had taken her back to Japan to a small farming village when she was sixteen. She was utterly miserable. She did not speak the Japanese language very well—which is the case with most *Nisei.* She was laughed at and talked about and ridiculed by the entire village for her American way of thinking and American mannerisms. She was so miserable that she finally prevailed upon her parents to allow her to return to the United States alone. She was under the nominal charge of an aunt who lived in Los Angeles. Since the girl, who was a high school graduate in the United States, had a talent for home economics, she entered domestic service, where she was most happy and contented until the evacuation. At that time she was forced back into the family of her aunt, where she is none too contented, and at the moment [May, 1942] she is interned in the Santa Anita Assembly Center.

It is the *Kibei* who are a dangerous group. It seems logical to assume that any child of Japanese parents who was returned to Japan at an early age, grew up there, studied in Japanese schools, possibly did military service in the Japanese army or navy, and then as an adult returned to the United States, is at heart a loyal citizen of Japan and may very probably have been deliberately planted here by the Japanese government. . . .

III

The Americanization of the *Nisei* is far advanced. The attitude of the *Issei* parents has had a great influence on the *Nisei* children. The last *Issei* to enter the United States did so in 1924—eighteen years ago. American influences have affected these *Issei,* consciously or unconsciously, directly or indirectly, since that time. It must be remembered that one of the chief factors affecting the Americanization of the parents has been the children themselves—in the reports they bring back from their school life, their play, and their association with white American children.

These factors have worked to a greater or lesser degree on the individual *Issei* parents. The real conflict between the two ideologies, American and Japanese, is in the *Issei,* for they have their background of life in Japan and must struggle to reconcile these two very different phases of their lives.

It must therefore be conceded that the Americanization of the *Nisei* children has proceeded with at least the tacit consent, if not the active co-operation, of many of the Japanese-born parents. The degree to which the parents oppose it [Americanization] is a measure of the strength of the loyalty to Japan of the parents. That there have been factors in America tending to strengthen that loyalty is conceded—the Japanese Associations, the Japanese consular system, and most of all, the fact that the parents cannot become citizens of this country though they have the status of legal residents. That some of the *Nisei* children are more Americanized than others is not so much a measure of the success of an Americanization program as it is a measure of the strength of the opposition to such a program, usually on the part of the parents. Unless there is a conscious, active, continuous opposition, the child will absorb Americanization as naturally as he breathes.

It is a Japanese characteristic to have a very great reverence and thirst for knowledge and education. The teacher is a person of importance to the Japanese mind; the words and teachings of the teacher are greatly respected. The school influence carries over into the home and to the hours outside the school through such mediums as schoolbooks, school magazines, sports contests, hygiene, diet, dress, and so on.

The Japanese is a great conformist. The *Nisei* children have always been in the minority in schools and community life and have naturally and very consciously striven to conform to the American standards of the majority. This is far more than a surface conformity. The expression "That thing is or is not done" applies to the *Nisei* in far greater degree than would be the case with the average American.

This idea of conformity can be illustrated by a story told by Fred Tayama of Los Angeles. "My parents came over here many years ago," he said. "They desired quite earnestly to adapt themselves to the ways and customs and life in this country. They were poor and had to work very hard. They were anxious that we attend American schools, that we children who were born here and were citizens should have every opportunity to make our own place in this country. Nevertheless, we suffered somewhat in that our parents could not fully bridge the gap, largely because of language, and were not able to take effective part in American activities like the Parent-Teacher Association and so on. We *Nisei* feel that we have bridged that gap. My little girl is ten years old. She plays the violin in the school orchestra and works in the school library. We are members of the Parent-Teacher Association and freely and frequently consult with our daughter's teacher. As far as we are able to tell, she mingles with her Caucasian schoolmates on terms of absolute equality. She can understand a very little bit of Japanese which she has picked up from her grandmother, but cannot and will not speak the language at all. We value her association with her teacher and playmates above everything else, and those are the things which we are being asked to give up by this evacuation program."

I believe that this is a typical sentiment with these people.

The position of women is far, far higher in America than it is in Japan. The *Issei* mother in nearly all cases desires this higher position not only for herself but for her daughters. Even in opposition to the father, she will encourage her daughter to adopt the American standard and encourage her sons to accord women the position they occupy in American life. Co-education [goes much farther] in this country than in Japan; boys and girls learn to know and understand each other to a degree that is completely impossible in Japan. The girls themselves demand and receive from the boys the deferential treatment accorded to American women in general. The Japanese marriage system [has broken down] on this account. In Japan marriages are arranged by family contracts, usually by means of a marriage broker. The parties very seldom, if ever, know each other before the marriage. In America this has been among the first Japanese customs to be broken down. The forms still persist, to some degree, largely as a sentimental concession to the parents, but in nearly all cases the boys and girls are well acquainted and in love on their own, and they themselves, as a rule, arrange the formalities of "go-between" and contact between families.

Difference will be noted in dress. The *Issei* women have universally adopted Western costume. It is true that on certain ceremonial occasions they do resort to the Japanese kimono. This, however, is a sort of fancy-dress costume. I have never seen in the United States a Japanese girl use the Japanese style of hairdress or the Japanese style of make-up even on the most ceremonious occasions.

The Christian religion as practiced in the United States is a powerful influence toward Americanization. In order to persist, the Buddhist religion is conforming to the American way of life and now includes Young Men's and Young Women's Buddhist Associations, modeled on the Y.M.C.A. and Y.W.C.A. That many of the priests are alien importations who have deliberately used their influence in favor of Japan, and who may have been planted here by the Japanese government for that very purpose, is freely admitted and must always be borne in mind. Most of the pro-Japanese *Issei* are members of the Buddhist faith. Nevertheless, the tenets of the faith are perfectly acceptable and cannot be classed as anti-American.

In the Japanese community of Terminal Island, the Baptist Church was the center of community life. The Sunday School was the social center of all *Nisei* activities. It conducted cooking and sewing classes, had church suppers, baseball games, and picnics in the American way. The pastor of the church was himself a *Nisei,* educated in the United States. The contrast between the activities at the Baptist Church and those surrounding the Buddhist Temple, less than a block away, was startling. The Christian church always had at least five times as many people participating in its activities as did the Temple.

In general, the caste system does not exist among the Japanese in America, [chiefly] because all of the *Issei* who came to America came from the same social group. Hence the caste lines were not imported. There did and do exist social distinctions, but they are essentially the same as those in any American community and are based on business success, the degree of education, and so on. The breakdown of caste [may be seen in the case of] Walter Taukamoto, a very brilliant young *Nisei* attorney from Sacramento, who has been voted the outstanding *Nisei* in the United States and who is admired as a speaker and as a lawyer. He came from the "Eta" class, the untouchables who are almost pariahs in Japan.

There is among the *Nisei* a desire to rise above their environment and to separate themselves from a purely Japanese community. There were, for example, two young men from Terminal Island, both college graduates and both young men of considerable ability. One of them asked me point-blank what I thought his chances were of getting employment as a machinist in the shipbuilding plants in Los Angeles harbor. He stated that he had a degree in engineering, that he was a good machinist with considerable knowledge and experience with Diesel engines, and that in the past few years he had made his living as an engineer of a fishing boat. He could see no future in his present employment; as long as he remained on Terminal Island in the fishing industry he was classed as "just another damn Jap." He thought he saw in the demand for skilled laborers in the shipyards an opportunity to separate himself from this Japanese environment, to do a patriotic service for his country, and to establish himself in a recognized trade. I told him I thought his chances were slim, not because of his race but because he belonged to a minority group of whose loyalty and integrity the people at large were not sure. He replied, "Well, thanks for the answer. It's at least an honest one and nobody can stop me from trying." But he did *not* get the job.

Loyalty is a rather predominant characteristic of these people. Loyalties are rather slow in being given, but once conferred are conferred without reservation. The Japanese themselves do not consider the *Nisei* loyal to Japan. This has been reflected in many of the official acts of the Japanese Consul at Los Angeles. The Japanese Consulate was considerably alarmed at my apparent and open friendship with the *Nisei*.

It may be asked why the views expressed [in this memorandum] are not more common. This is attributable to the extreme youth of the *Nisei,* and, as a class, to their economic dependence on the *Issei* to date. This dependence forced many *Nisei* to do many things which otherwise they would not have done. The holding of jobs was sometimes made contingent upon regular contributions by *Nisei* toward the purchase of Japanese war bonds; upon joining some Japanese society and the like. Also, Americans of power and influence whose opinions and decisions carry weight are the same people who—rightly at the time—brought about the Exclusion Act, and who see in all Oriental faces, *Issei* and *Nisei* alike, the very alien and incomprehensible type of peasant who was entering the country twenty-five or thirty years ago. The white contemporaries of the *Nisei,* the young people who were their schoolmates, are not yet in positions of influence in politics or business. Ten to fifteen years from now, when both groups have matured, these conditions would no longer obtain; they would meet on grounds of mutual acquaintance and understanding.

Had not this war come along at this time, in another ten or fifteen years there would have been no Japanese problem, for the *Issei* would have passed on, and the *Nisei* taken their place naturally in American community and national life.

8. San Francisco Japantown, 1942

Business district of San Francisco's Japantown before the World War II internment.

From National Archives at College Park, Md., Still Pictures Branch. Control Number NWDNS-210-G-A67; found through NARA's web-based searchable collections database (NAIL).

9. Middle-Class Japanese American Family Before Evacuation, 1942

This is a photograph of the Shibuya family of Mountain View, California, taken just before they were interned in a concentration camp during World War II. Before the war the father was a successful grower and distributor of chrysanthemums and four of the six American-born children had already attended leading universities of California.

◉ *E S S A Y S*

The first essay, by historian Judy Yung, American Studies professor at the University of California at Santa Cruz, illustrates how Chinese American women in San Francisco steered a path between their family traditions and the American culture they were exposed to outside the home. The second essay, by University of Southern California historian Lon Kurashige, focuses on the changing identity of the Nisei who created a community festival that sought to assuage anti-Japanese prejudice by presenting the Nisei as a bicultural bridge between the United States and Japan.

From National Archives at College Park, Md., Still Pictures Branch. Control Number NWDNS-210-G-A60; found through NARA's web-based searchable collections database (NAIL).

Second-Generation Chinese American Women

JUDY YUNG

The marriage pattern of Chinese American women differed from that of European American women. In 1920, only 14 percent of foreign-born women in America over age fifteen were single, but 37 percent of the second generation remained unmarried. According to Doris Weatherford, the general pattern in the United States had been that immigrant women often married young; third-generation women had the second highest marriage rate after the first generation; and those who were most likely to be unmarried were second-generation women (those born in America of foreign parents). She attributed the second generation's reluctance to marry to the harsh married lives of their mothers or the need for daughters to delay marriage in order to help out their families, as in the case of Irish women. This was not the same for second-generation Chinese women in the insulated community of San Francisco Chinatown in the 1920s, who still considered marriage and motherhood as their destiny. Just when and how they married, however, depended upon their class background, degree of acculturation, and the historical circumstances at the time.

Prior to the 1911 Revolution, it was not unusual for poor, working class parents to marry off their daughters early in order to better provide for the rest of the family. The marriage was arranged through a matchmaker, and according to Chinese custom, the bride had no say in the choice of her partner. She was not even allowed to see him until the wedding day, when, dressed in red silk and beaded headdress, she was carried from a carriage into her husband's home. Because of the skewed Chinese sex ratio in America, the husband was usually older, China-born, and conservative. Life for most of these young brides proved to be as harsh and socially restrictive as it had been for their immigrant mothers. The case of Rose Jeong serves as an example of such a traditional marriage. Her sister Bessie Jeong described how it all happened:

> In a way, she had two men to choose from, but as she had never seen either of them, only their photographs, she took her parents' advice. One was young, about twenty, and her parents put it this way: "This man is young, he has his way to make, and he has a large family of brothers and sisters. You would be a sort of slave to all of them. This other man is fifty years old, but he can give you everything, he has no family. Better to be an old man's darling than a young man's slave," or words to that effect. They told her, too, that a young man would not be constant, he would be running around with other women, it was far safer to take an older man, who would settle down. Of course she was married in the Chinese way, that is, the man handed over to her parents a sum of money. Naturally that would be far larger with an older and richer man, but the parents did not speak of that.

Having already endured a hard life as the eldest daughter responsible for housework and the care of her younger siblings, sixteen-year-old Rose dutifully agreed with her parents' choice, even though the man was thirty-four years her senior. After the wedding she followed him to the lumber camp of Weed, California, where he worked as a cook. He was a "hard taskmaster," according to Bessie, who also went to

From Judy Yung, *Unbound Feet: A Social History of Chinese Women in San Francisco*, pp. 164–177. Copyright © 1995 Judy Yung. Used by permission of University of California Press.

live with them in their poorly insulated log cabin. "He had a horrible disposition, suspicious and jealous, and my sister's life was one long tragedy with him." Rose worked alongside her husband in his many business ventures. He first ran a boardinghouse, then a laundry, and at another time, five different dining places in town. When his businesses later failed, he sold all of Rose's wedding jewelry. In 1918, Rose died during the flue epidemic at the young age of twenty-six.

Learning from her sister's example, Bessie was determined not to suffer the same fate. When her father, who had returned to China with the rest of the family after the 1906 earthquake, came back to fetch Bessie and, as she believed, marry her off in China, she refused to go with him. "I knew that my father was determined to take me back that time. He was going to realize money out of it or he was fulfilling his duty as a father. But I still would be on the auction block. Prized Jersey—the name 'Bessie' always made me think of some nice fat cow!" At the suggestion of her sister Rose, Bessie ran away to Donaldina Cameron and the Presbyterian Mission Home. "I had been away from my father for so long that I was not much afraid of him. . . . I was resolved not to marry, to have an education instead." With a bit of legal maneuvering, Cameron was made her legal guardian, and Bessie was able to stay at the Mission Home and pursue an education, becoming a physician. She later married a man of her choice, Dr. Ying Wing Chan, the Chinese consul in San Francisco, and was in private practice in the San Francisco Bay Area for nearly forty years.

After the 1911 Revolution, the second generation—particular those of middle-class background—began to take a different course from that of their mothers with regard to courtship and married life. Inspired by the example of the "new woman" in China, many resisted arranged marriages and chose to follow Western courtship and marriage customs. Initially, their attempts were cause for social ostracism. "Remember when young men and women were never seen together on the streets of Chinatown?" wrote Chingwah Lee in 1936. "Even as late as 1910, when the bold experiment of 'spooning' along Dupont Street (generally immediately after school, and always in droves) [happened], business would be momentarily at a standstill, and there would be a lot of [rubber]necking—on the part of the giggling spectators." . . .

King Yoak Won Wu, whose family was strongly influenced by Chinese nationalism and Christianity, claimed to be among the first Chinese women to have a Western wedding, in 1913. She met her husband, Rev. Daniel Wu, in church, where she worked as a volunteer rolling bandages for Dr. Sun Yat-sen's army. "He came by often when we were rolling bandages, telling us how patriotic we were. I guess he was impressed with our dedication. At other times, I would attend his lectures in church." After three years of meeting in church and at the park across from the church, they decided to get married at Grace Cathedral outside Chinatown. "My family had switched to the 'new way of thinking' for a long time. . . . We did not need a matchmaker or any of the other Chinese rituals. There was no loud crying or colorful layers of clothes. We just decided to have a Christian wedding and I even made my own wedding dress and veil." According to a newspaper account of the wedding, the ceremony was conducted in Chinese and English, and the large gathering consisted of both Chinese and European American friends. . . .

Most large weddings in the 1920s took place in either a church, a hotel, or a public hall. Caroline Chew wrote in 1926, "The bride and groom and all the attendants appear in conventional Western garb and the famous Wagnerian and Mendelsohnian strains are played in true Western fashion." After the ceremony, coffee and cake were served, and the bride was driven to her new home in a limousine decorated with red paper and silk. The day after the wedding, the parents usually hosted an elaborate wedding feast in Chinatown, consisting of fifteen to twenty courses. Most important, the bride did not live with her husband's family after her marriage but established her own home, "where she reigns supreme from the very outset."

Although more second-generation women were allowed to choose a groom after 1911 than before, they found their decisions encumbered by discriminatory laws that discouraged their marriage to foreign-born Chinese and prevented marriage to white Americans. The Cable Act of 1922 reversed the Expatriation Act of 1907, which had required women to assume their husband's nationality upon marriage. The 1922 act provided that a female citizen would no longer lose her citizenship by marrying an alien and, conversely, that an alien woman would no longer gain U.S. citizenship by marrying a citizen. However, section 3 of the Cable Act stipulated that "any woman citizen who married an alien ineligible to citizenship shall cease to be a citizen of the United States." Although section 4 allowed that "a woman who, before the passage of this Act, has lost her United States citizenship by reason of her marriage to an alien eligible for citizenship, may be naturalized," section 5 stated that "no woman whose husband is not eligible to citizenship shall be naturalized during the continuance of the marital status." The Cable Act, in effect, stripped any American-born Chinese woman of her citizenship status should she choose to marry a foreign-born Chinese with no hope of naturalization, since she herself, by virtue of her race, thereby became an "alien ineligible to citizenship." Moreover, once a woman lost her citizenship, she could no longer confer derivative citizenship to any of her children who might be born outside the United States. She also lost her rights to own property, vote, and travel abroad freely. . . .

Aside from the Cable Act, anti-miscegenation attitudes and laws that prevented interracial marriage between Chinese and whites discriminated against Chinese women as well. Compounding the problem was ostracism in the Chinese community with respect to intermarriages. Tye Leung, who had run away to the Presbyterian Mission Home to avoid an arranged marriage, found herself the target of such shunning. While employed as an assistant to the matrons at Angel Island, she met and fell in love with an immigration inspector, Charles Schulze. They had to travel to Vancouver, Washington, to become legally married. "His mother and my folks disapprove very much, but when two people are in love, they don't think of the future or what [might] happen," she wrote later in an autobiographical essay. After their marriage both had to resign from their civil service jobs because of social ostracism. Charles went on to work for many years for the Southern Pacific Company as a mechanic, and Tye found a job as a telephone operator at the Chinatown Exchange. Although they were "the talk of Chinatown," according to one of her contemporaries, the Schulzes chose to live close to Chinatown, and Tye remained active in the Chinese Presbyterian church. Their children, Fred and Louise, recalled that they were one of the few interracial families in Chinatown, and although they as children were sometimes called *fan gwai jai* (literally, foreign devil child), they were accepted in the community, most likely because their mother spent many hours volunteering in the community. Her son Fred said, "She was very kind and always willing to help other people go see the doctor, interpret, go to immigration, and things like that.

Very often she would take the streetcar and go out to Children's Hospital to interpret on a volunteer basis."

Discriminatory laws such as the Cable Act and the Anti-Miscegenation Act went hand-in-hand with other anti-Chinese measures and practices that sought to stop Chinese immigration and the integration of Chinese into mainstream America. Such laws were often both racist and sexist in character and created hardships for Chinese American women already hampered by cultural conflict at home. They were painful reminders of the vulnerable existence of the second generation, who, in spite of their rights as U.S. citizens, could easily become disenfranchised on the basis of race alone.

Other American laws, however, such as divorce laws, gave Chinese American women leverage and latitude in changing their marital circumstances. Although few cases of divorce among Chinese Americans were reported in the local newspapers, Caroline Chew wrote in 1926 that "divorce among Chinese in America has become comparatively common, and although it is still looked upon with a little distaste, if it is quite justifiable, no one has anything disparaging to say." She added that, unlike in China, wives in America had just as much right as husbands to sue for divorce. According to local newspapers, one major source of information on divorce patterns in the Chinese American community, important causes of divorce among second-generation women included wife abuse and polygamy. In 1923, for example, Emma Soohoo sued her American-born husband, Henry, for divorce on grounds that he "cruelly beat her and then deserted her," and she requested sole custody of their twenty-month-old baby. As another example, in 1928 Amy Quan Tong, the owner of a manicuring parlor in Chinatown, filed for divorce from her American-born husband, Quan Tong, because, as she told the judge, he had put her to work at low wages in his Hong Kong candy store and taken a second wife.

Like second-generation European American women, Chinese American women who married men of their own choice often embarked on a life quite different from that of their immigrant mothers. To start, they were not as confined to the domestic sphere, as Caroline Chew points out:

> She is perfectly free to come and go as she pleases and has free access to the streets. She goes out and does her own marketing; goes calling on her friends when she so desires; dines at restaurants occasionally; and even ventures to go beyond the precincts of "Chinatown" quite frequently—all of which have hitherto never been done by a Chinese woman. Fifteen or twenty years ago such conduct would have been considered most outrageous and would have caused a woman to be all but ostracized.

There was also more equality, mutual affection, and companionship in second-generation marriages. Not only did couples go out together, but they were not afraid to express their affection in public. Because both worked and contributed to the family income, they tended to discuss matters and make joint decisions regarding the family's welfare. Second-generation husbands were also less resistant to helping with the housework and sharing their outside concerns with their wives. . . .

Jade Snow Wong shared a . . . close and equal relationship with her husband, Woody Ong, about whom she wrote in *No Chinese Stranger,* the sequel to *Fifth Chinese Daughter.* Old family friends, the two become reacquainted after they had both established their businesses in Chinatown and were thrown together by a family emergency. As Jade Snow put it, "Each grew in awareness of the other, and devotion flowered." Their married life was wedded to their work life, as they lived and worked together on the same premises.

> In this first year of marriage, they often walked the three blocks to Chinatown for a restaurant lunch, after which they would purchase groceries for that night's late Chinese dinner at home. The division of their studio work was natural. Financial records and bank deposits, mechanical problems, chemical formulas, checking kiln action, packing, pickup, and deliveries naturally fell into Woody's hands while Jade Snow stayed close to home, working on designs, supervising staff schedules, and keeping house. True to tradition, once Woody had locked the studio door and come upstairs, he was home as a Chinese husband, expecting their house to be immaculate and to be waited upon and indulged. They could consult with each other on just about every subject without disagreement. Kindness, devotion, protection with strength new to her, and extravagant gifts were privileges that gladdened Jade Snow's heart, while her husband's physical comfort and mental relaxation were her responsibility.

Although their marriage revealed a traditional gender division of labor, neither partner dominated the other. As their family grew to four children and they added an active travel business to their ceramics work, Woody proved a supportive partner, helping with the children and household chores, encouraging Jade Snow's career in ceramics and writing, nursing her back to health when she became ill, and sharing responsibilities with her on the many tours to Asia that they cosponsored.

Similarly, Type Leung's marriage to Charles Schulze, despite being handicapped by the taboo against interracial marriage, was successful because it was both egalitarian and interdependent. According to their son, Fred, "We had good family relations. I never heard arguments, fights, or anything." Both parents were kind and mild tempered, and both worked to provide for the family. Tye did most of the cooking and housework, but in the evenings, when she was working at the telephone exchange, Charles would take care of the children and of Tye's mother, who lived with them. Fred fondly recalled: "Before we went to bed each night, my father would always bring us a cup of cocoa. Then after he gave us our cocoa, he would take the dishes out to the kitchen, wash them, and put them away."

Both parents loved music and led an active social life. Tye played the piano and Chinese butterfly harp and attended the Chinese Presbyterian church regularly; Charles played the French horn with a military band and was active at Grace Cathedral. Tye would often go to the Chinese opera, weddings, and birthday parties in Chinatown accompanied by her children, while Charles played with various musical bands in the city and attended regular meetings of the Odd Fellows Lodge. Although they led different social lives, they were a close family. They always ate and played together at home on Sundays, Fred recalled. Not only was the marriage a happy one, but the children benefited from the cultural strengths of both parents and the warm family life they provided.

Further factors that distinguished between traditional and modern marriages among Chinese Americans included the size of the family and the quality of home life. Unlike their mothers, second-generation women knew about and had access to birth control, which became more available to American women in the 1920s. "My friends were very good to me and told me what to do," said Gladys Ng Gin. "When it was time to have my first baby, a good friend of mine said, 'Gladys, you have to go to the hospital,' and she introduced a woman doctor to me." Most of her contemporaries—both European and Chinese American—limited their families to two or three children and had them in the hospital. However, some "modern" husbands proved uncooperative. Flora Belle Jan's health was ruined after five abortions because her husband refused to practice birth control. She confided to Ludmelia:

> I have been thinking that I have given the six best years of my life to a man who is not worth it. . . . When I first met him, I was idealistic and enthusiastic and ambitious. I had a body that was sound and healthy. Now I am completely disillusioned, entirely lacking any enthusiasm, and utterly devoid of ambition. . . . I had my first abortion in September, 1928, at a time when I was pathetically struggling with some editorial work for which I was never paid. The next abortion came the following spring. Then in September, 1929, I was fortunate enough to get a job at the Methodist Book Concern, the salary from which helped [my husband] to go back to school. In January, 1930, I had my third abortion. My memory is a bit hazy but I think the fourth came in December of 1931. I struggled with contraceptives, begged [my husband] to use condoms for added precaution but he stubbornly refused. Then I had a fifth abortion in January, 1932. For these abortions, I have pawned my mother's jewelry, modeled in art schools, slaved at office routine, stood the boresome company of a Chinese newspaper editor whom I taught English, neglected [my son] to go out to work, gone without the decencies of life and the clothes I long for with all the fever of youth. Why have I had to undergo this torture? Because of a man who prides himself on his intelligence [but] is hopelessly lacking in understanding.

Despite her husband's shortcomings, Flora remained married to him and bore him three children, two of whom were born in China. The last pregnancy almost cost her her life. That was when she finally insisted on having a tubal ligation.

Although they faced discrimination in the labor market and in their search for decent housing, second-generation Chinese were still able to take advantage of their education and achieve a degree of upward mobility. The combined income of this generation of middle-class Chinese American couples afforded them modern apartments outside of Chinatown, albeit on the fringes. Chew Fong Low, frustrated by housing discrimination in San Francisco, spent a quarter of a million dollars constructing the Low Apartments on the outskirts of Chinatown in order to give her family and "her people an opportunity to live in true American style in a building constructed by American workmen from American plans." The apartment building was made of steel frame and concrete and contained twenty-five apartments, all featuring modern kitchens, tiled bathrooms, separate shower cabinets, French doors and windows, built-in mirrors, hot water heaters, and outlets for radio and private telephone lines. Other Chinese American couples, like the Schulzes, were able to rent accommodations, complete with running water and a private bathroom, above Powell Street in the 1920s. They were also among the first in Chinatown to have modern appliances such as a radio, toaster, iron, and refrigerator.

Although they preferred to live in modern apartments, young Chinese American couples generally tried to combine Chinese and Western customs in their home life. The Schulzes, for example, had Western food for breakfast and lunch but Chinese food for dinner. They celebrated Thanksgiving and Christmas but also Chinese New Year and the Moon Festival. They spoke both Chinese and English at home with the children. They went to church, but every year at Ching Ming, Tye took the children to the Chinese cemetery to pay proper respect to her parents. Nor did Tye physically punish her children, as was the practice among Chinese parents then. Fred and Louise Schulze could not remember ever being spanked. "She was always very gentle. She never raised her voice," said Fred.

Although Jade Snow Wong had spent her college years away from home and Chinatown, after her marriage she chose to live close to Chinatown so that her children might learn from their grandparents and come to appreciate their bicultural heritage. The children attended Chinese school and were introduced to Chinese foods, holidays, and the arts, but they were also raised on Christmas parties, Easter egg hunts, trips to museums and libraries, and vacations in Hawaii and Canada. Ultimately, Jade Snow instilled the same traditional values of honor, courage, honesty; personal conviction, and service to fellow humans in all her children that she had been taught by her parents. Representative of her generation, she had come full circle in her search for a new ethnic and gender identity conditioned by the discrimination she had experienced as a dutiful daughter at home and a young woman growing up in a prejudiced society. As she wrote in *No Chinese Stranger,* a work that compares socialist life in China with democratic life in America:

> Each Chinese-American like me has the opportunity to assess his talents, define his individual stature, and choose his personal balance of old and new, Chinese and Western ways, hopefully including the best of both. Father Wong's prize, more meaningful than gold, has also been the legacy he gave his children and grandchildren: he, and others like him, first gave us our cultural identity and then, by remaining in this country, permitted us the American freedom to attain individual self-images which ought to be constructive for the state but not subordinate to it. My own children may be potential revolutionaries who will throw their javelins earnestly and strongly; and I hope their targets will be the alleviation of mankind's miseries. When they drink water, as the old Chinese saying goes, I hope that they will think of its source, so that when they reach out to drop *their* aerial roots, their growth will bear the fruit of the banyan tree—wisdom.

She concluded her second autobiography on an optimistic note:

> My future is in this land where Daddy and his progeny have sunk their roots around the rocks of prejudice, rather than closer to the shelter of the mother trunk. As I encourage my children's roots, I take heart from that "Foolish Old Man" in Ming Choy's lesson. With strong belief in our purpose, it may not be folly for the determined, with the hearts of children, to attack the high mountain of prejudice in our own way. When we die, our children and grandchildren will keep on working until, some day, the mountain will diminish. Then there will be no Chinese stranger.

By the time of the Great Depression, second-generation women under the influence of Chinese nationalism, Christianity, and acculturation had indeed taken the first steps toward challenging traditional gender roles and racial discrimination in the larger society. Compared to their mothers, they were better educated, more economically mobile, socially active, politically aware, and equal partners in marriage. Although they still had a difficult time assimilating into mainstream society, they had learned to accommodate racism and establish a new bicultural identity and lifestyle for themselves. As the Great Depression loomed before them, they would draw strength from the wellspring of their bicultural heritage to weather the storm ahead.

The Problem of Nisei Biculturalism

LON KURASHIGE

Buy Cultural

A surge of advertising was the first sign that the Nisei Week festival was about to begin. Little Tokyo merchants flooded the vernacular press with sales announcements
and redesigned display windows to appeal specifically to the second generation. In
1934 one retailer proclaimed that preparations were done "All for the Satisfaction
of the Nisei!" Such appeals masked a fear among Little Tokyo merchants that the
second generation had developed consumption tastes that lured them outside the enclave particularly to department stores whose economies of scale allowed them to
undercut small businesses. Some shop owners criticized Nisei who, they said, were
embarrassed to wear clothing made in Japan. Others simply bemoaned the loss of
an estimated half a million dollars a year that could be spent by Nisei shoppers. How
would the merchants stop the hemorrhaging of money from the ethnic enclave?

That was the question that pushed the Issei leadership to place unproven second-
generation businessmen in charge of Nisei Week. Never before had Little Tokyo
been turned on its head, with the Nisei—albeit temporarily—in command. Sei Fujii,
an Issei leader and newspaper publisher, challenged the JACLers [Japanese American Citizen League] "to show their old folks how much of an asset they are instead
of being [a] burden as they used to be." The youngsters, for their part, welcomed the
chance to run what they called the "greatest civic project undertaken by a second
generation group." Nisei Week was a rite of passage that continued the JACL's initiation into community leadership. With solid Issei backing, the organization was
founded in 1930 and mirrored the extensive and tightly organized network of
Japanese immigrant associations throughout the West Coast. By 1936 thirty-eight
chapters, governed by a national headquarters in San Francisco, supported the older
generation's economic endeavors and efforts to fight anti-Japanese discrimination.
"The early devices of the rising Nisei organization," one member observed, "were
in many instances mild imitations of the Issei."

While the JACLers patterned themselves after the immigrant leadership, they
differed significantly from the bulk of their own generation. They were over-
whelmingly male despite equal numbers of Nisei women in Los Angeles and were
about a decade older than the majority of their peers in the second generation.
Moreover, they were almost twice as likely to have attended college and to be in
management positions than most of the Nisei men their age. Thus the organization
was made up of the second generation elite—lawyers, dentists, medical doctors,
and entrepreneurs who relied upon the ethnic enclave for their businesses and practices and therefore had vested interests in enhancing and protecting Little Tokyo.
The exceptional status of the JACLers was doubly true for the organization's leaders.

From Lon Kurashige, "The Problem of Biculturalism: Japanese American Identity and Festival Before
World War II," *Journal of American History* 86, no. 4 (March 2000), 1636–1640, 1650–1654. Copyright
© 2000 Journal of American History. Used by permission.

Consider the success story of Keiichi "Kay" Sugahara, the first president of the Los Angeles chapter. Born in 1909, Sugahara was thirteen when he and his younger siblings were orphaned. To help provide for his brother and sister, he worked at a fruit stand from junior high through his years at the University of California, Los Angeles (UCLA). In 1932, as a senior, the young Sugahara teamed with white partners to launch the first customs brokerage firm in Little Tokyo. As someone who could bridge American and Japanese cultures, he capitalized on the needs of business importing good from Japan. The success of this venture, he claimed, made him a millionaire before the age of thirty.

Under Sugahara's command, the theme of the first Nisei Week festival was "Buy in Lil' Tokyo." Sugahara's brother, Roku, promised his generation that Little Tokyo stores would have the lowest prices and the highest-quality Japanese and American merchandise. Just in case competitive prices and products were not enough, the JACLers linked enclave purchases with Nisei Week participation. Admission to festival events required receipts from Little Tokyo stores, and by the late 1930s, purchasing merchandise enabled shoppers to cast votes for their favorite beauty contestants.

But even the most successful of such gimmicks ended with Nisei Week. In order to secure year-round patronage, the organizers of Nisei Week strove to give the second generation a stake in the future of the immigrant enclave. The logic was straightforward: If the Nisei benefited materially from Little Tokyo, they would have more reason to shop there. The most compelling incentive Issei merchants could offer the younger generation was employment. While free to patronize white owned businesses, Nisei usually could not work for them. Most white employers refused to hire Japanese Americans, and major labor unions denied them membership. One field open to the Nisei was higher education, but only a select few followed this route since even college graduates faced racial barriers that forced them back to the restricted world of the ethnic enclave. On the eve of World War II, most Nisei were working in the ethnic enclave's primary sectors: agricultural production, retail enterprise, and domestic service. While Issei leaders looked to them to calm anti-Japanese antipathy in white America, the Nisei relied upon the older generation for employment opportunities.

Yet most Little Tokyo retailers refused to hire Nisei for sales positions because of their inability to meet the needs of Japanese-speaking clients. To spur Nisei employment, Nisei Week organizers persuaded enclave merchants that Nisei salespersons would boost their business by attracting second-generation shoppers. In 1934 the festival's employment bureau placed thirty-five workers in just three days, and although their jobs, like the sales and the beauty pageant, typically ended with Nisei Week, the employment agency attained a permanent place in Little Tokyo.

The strongest appeals for Nisei patronage relied upon a sense of fictive kinship. According to Roku Sugahara, Little Tokyo offered a pleasanter shopping experience than the stores outside its protective borders. There was, he suggested, "a better understanding, a feeling of freedom and congeniality, and friendliness" because the "seller knows the background and characteristics of the buyer much better." The winner of the Nisei Week essay contest in 1938 also viewed Little Tokyo as an ethnic sanctuary. Answering the question "Why I should buy in Little Tokyo," he listed the enclave's unique benefits for Nisei customers:

Japanese can serve Japanese people with good taste. They know what type of clothing or merchandise would be best suited, whereas an American family naturally would not. And, too, they are inclined to be more personal and understanding, as there are no barriers of speech or race. This results in friendly, sociable business tactics, and not cold ruthless negotiations.

Festival leaders used ethnicity as both carrot and stick to attract Nisei shoppers. While they played up the "natural" affinities among Japanese Americans, they also stressed the obligations that such ties entailed. "If the Nisei expect to see Lil' Tokio exist and rise out of its present depression," the *Rafu Shimpo* newspaper commanded, "they must cooperate and help build Lil' Tokio by putting some funds into the business" and "buy all necessities at Japanese stores and only buy those things which are not carried in Lil' Tokio at American stores." The result of "this extensive trading," explaining the 1938 essay contest winner, "will be a closer union of our race—drawn together by the cohesive force of economic and social dependency." Roku Sugahara's do-or-die scenario best characterized the invocation of group obligation: "It all depends on the nisei, whether they will aid in strengthening our economic foundation or will stand idly by while it crumbles into oblivion."

Despite these appeals, Nisei Week leaders were aware of the pitfalls of attempts to attract second-generation customers. The *Kashu Mainichi* newspaper cautioned against any business strategy that promoted ethnic insularity as not only unfeasible, but "un-American." During the depression, the paper insisted, hoarding money within Little Tokyo was "un-American," since the nation's recovery required pumping money into the broader economy. Carl Kondo, the runner-up in the Nisei Week essay contest in 1935, criticized the futility of the "buy in Lil' Tokio" campaign. He warned that Japanese merchants should not rely on Nisei consumption because their mom-and-pop establishments could not compete with the department stores in nearby downtown Los Angeles. Even if prices were slashed in Little Tokyo, Kondo argued, the Nisei were too influenced by American culture to be interested in Japanese merchandise or to be swayed by invocations of racial responsibilities.

Kondo maintained that Japanese business should cultivate external, rather than internal, markets. He believed that the nation's increasing interest in Japan as a rising world power and United States trading partner created a favorable climate for purveying Japanese artifacts, services, and cultural displays to the exotic tastes of white America. The *Kashu Mainichi* also championed the benefits of the tourist market. It pointed with envy to Chinatown and the Mexican-inspired Olvera Street as two of Los Angeles's successful ethnic attractions and lamented that "one cannot immediately feel the foreign atmosphere or distinction upon entering Lil' Tokyo."

Nisei Week proved the optimal occasion to dress up Little Tokyo for white consumption. Here the Oriental-styled street displays, decorations, music, dance, and fashions assumed dual meanings: symbols of ethnic pride for Japanese Americans but also exotic enticements for outsiders. The kimono, in particular, attracted so much interest that Nisei Week leaders in 1936 added a second fashion show, where those Japanese garments were modeled exclusively for White Americans. The festival booklet billed the event as "an exhibition of Japanese pajamas and lounging clothes" with refreshments served by "petite Japanese maidens in picturesque kimonos." The JACLers invited hundreds of "leading women in Los Angeles society" and selected kimono styles that would "appeal particularly to American women."

Enclave merchants also proposed that Nisei women wear kimonos while serving as tour guides who provided a "night of adventure to Americans in Little Tokyo." The hostesses were to greet tourists as they entered the enclave, answer questions about Japanese culture, including flower arrangements and the tea ceremony, and assist them in purchasing merchandise. Nisei Week leaders in 1940 redesigned the festival booklet to increase the enclave's tourist appeal. A glossy full-page advertisement especially greeted white Americans. "WELCOME TO LITTLE TOKYO" appeared in orientalized script inserted within a photograph of the community's main thoroughfare. The night scene featured a group of well-groomed, entertainment-seeking white Americans chaperoned by four smiling, kimono-clad women. Fluorescent Little Tokyo storefronts, particularly the Fuji-kan Theater's elaborate neon marquee, in front of which the group stood, radiated an energy and enthusiasm that seemed to overwhelm the tourists. The smiling Japanese women reflected the enclave's warmth and hospitality, while the flood of bright lights and signs symbolized its entrepreneurial vigor—a shopper's paradise. . . .

American Front

The economic motives that began Nisei Week and the concerns about Little Tokyo's Americanization were inexplicably tied to the demonstration of the second generation's civic virtue and political allegiance. "Through the medium of this festival," John Maeno declared in 1936, "the JACL hopes to present, acquaint, and connect you directly with the young Japanese American citizen, his life and environment." Maeno, the organization's second president, was one of the few Nisei lawyers in Little Tokyo. A graduate of the University of Southern California, he used his college ties to make inroads into Los Angeles political circles. He explained that as a "new American," the Nisei was a "true and loyal citizen of the United States" who sought to take "part in civic development and community progress."

The JACLers used the Nisei's citizenship to gain advantages in the political arena. They, like the leaders of African Americans and many urban immigrant groups, attempted to gain electoral power by combining Japanese American votes into one large ethnic bloc. This way, as increasing numbers of Nisei's came of age, they could expand their impact on local elections. A flock of white officer seekers took the Nisei vote seriously and showed up at the festival's inauguration in 1934, their large number even raising concerns in Little Tokyo that the festivities would turn into a "political rally." Nisei Week was also an occasion to pay respects to the highest elected official in Los Angeles. In the opening ceremony in 1936 a colorful procession moved through the streets of Little Tokyo on its way to Los Angeles's city hall two blocks away. The ethnic community's "leading citizens" accompanied the Nisei Week queen and "her pretty and charming attendants" as they were carried along in Japanese rickshaws. The ceremony concluded with these "kimono clad, dark-eyed beauties" presenting the mayor of Los Angeles" with an official invitation to attend this gala event in Lil' Tokyo."

Such a visible display of goodwill toward the Los Angeles community illustrated the type of citizenship the JACLers espoused. Being American, to them, meant not just possessing legal entitlements, but performing a wide range of civic duties. The winner of the JACL's oratorical contest in 1938 placed the responsibility of resolving "our race problem" squarely on the Nisei's shoulders. He encouraged the Nisei to engage in "active citizenship" by voting and involving themselves in public affairs. Civic involvement, he asserted, would prove that the Nisei are a "racial group worthy of being accepted on an equal plane" because "it will show to the white citizenry that we are not a culturally or mentally inferior race . . . , that we are beneficial to America's social and economic welfare, and that we desire to cooperate with the white race in solving our community and national problems." The ultimate significance of active citizenship, the orator explained, was that eventually it would compel "the white race, themselves, to take down the racial barriers that have been erected against us."

But the JACLers did not equate proving loyalty to the United States with severing ties to Japan. Despite America's opposition to Japanese imperialism, they sided with their parents, who, like most expatriates, reveled in the military victories of their homeland. The formal declaration of the second Sino Japanese war in 1937 heightened ties to the motherland, as both generations sent money, supplies, and well-wishes to Japanese soldiers. Issei leaders called upon the JACLers to counteract the American public's overwhelming support for the Chinese (President Franklin D. Roosevelt, in fact, disobeyed his own policy of neutrality in foreign wars by sending American arms to Chinese troops). The older generation, with assistance from the Japanese consulate, briefed the young leaders on the necessity and righteousness of Japan's foreign policies and helped to establish a Nisei "speakers bureau" to inform Americans about Japan's side of the story. Togo Tanaka, writing in the 1940s, confirmed that the English section of his newspaper, *Rafu Shimpo,* based its editorials and coverage of the Sino-Japanese war on information provided by Issei who blamed Japan's negative image on Chinese propaganda. The staff of the paper's Japanese section prepared pamphlets for their Nisei colleagues about Japan's plight in the West—the subtitle of one read, "How about Giving Japan a Break?" Thus Tanaka concluded that the JACLers, despite their strong commitment to American political institutions, were mindful "not to disparage the cultural values of Japan, nor to antagonize Issei feelings in the latter's sympathies for Japan. JACL leaders even rationalized their Americanism as being rooted in Japanese culture."

But opposition in the United States only grew when Japanese troops captured Beijing and pressed on to victory. In 1939 FDR abrogated the treaty that had safeguarded United States–Japan trade and, a year later, in response to Japan's Tripartite Alliance with Germany and Italy and its apparent movement into Southeast Asia, threatened to cut off the shipment of about 80 percent of the island nation's war supplies. The growing opposition to Japan buoyed antagonism to Japanese Americans. By 1938 Lail Thomas Kane was in the habit of sharing his opinions with *Rafu Shimpo* editor Togo Tanaka, who duly noted them as an alarming indication of popular sentiment. "By this time," Tanaka later noted, "Kane's attitude toward the Nisei as 'Jap-stooges' appears to have crystallized." This was evident in Kane's telling Tanaka, "I'm rapidly being convinced that the JACL which represents the Nisei leadership is nothing more than an instrument of the Issei. You really take your orders from Japan." Thus Kane, still backed by the American Legion, continued to lobby for legislation against Japanese American fishermen. He told Tanaka that if the JACLers, who he referred to as "jackals," were really loyal "you would support this fishing bill which is a national defense, patriotic proposal"—"you should know that the security of the United States is menaced by the presence of fishing boats manned by naval reserve officers of the Imperial Japanese Navy." These fears reached a national audience through Kane's publications, including an article in the *Saturday Evening Post,* and spread beyond the issue of Japanese American fishermen. The immediate problem for Little Tokyo was that increasing anti-Japanese sentiment gave rise to boycotts against Japanese businesses that placed the depression-weary enclave in even further jeopardy.

"A direct coorelation exists," asserted Togo Tanaka in an analysis of JACL history he wrote in the 1940s, "between the growing intensity of America-Japan friction and the increasing frequency of Nisei and even Issei loyalty pledges." The Issei old guard responded to anti-Japanese affronts as they had done before: they had the Nisei reassure Americans that their support for Japan was in no way at odds with their commitment to living and raising their children in the United States. But mounting United States–Japan hostility forced Nisei Week's leaders to retreat from the idea of biculturalism. The *Rafu Shimpo's* English-language staff, for example, veered away from Japanese nationalism. Togo Tanaka claimed that the decision was based on both the fallout from the rescinding of the trade agreement and the results of a survey that revealed the impressive Nisei commitment to the United States. The English section split from the paper's Japanese staff to launch an editorial policy encouraging the Nisei to drop biculturalism in favor of a "single American political loyalty." The Nisei were urged to support the JACL's Americanism, buy United States defense bonds, and forgo dual citizenship with Japan.

Nisei Week now became a forum to ensure that Japanese Americans would not be confused with their relatives overseas. The *Kashu Mainichi* in 1940 assured the people of southern California of the Nisei's eagerness to participate "in the building of this great country, to assume responsibility for its defense against all enemies and to safeguard its great institutions." A year later the Nisei Week crowd was steered away from dressing in Japanese garb. "From the American point of view," the leading vernacular newspaper asked, "how can one be expected to be impressed by any profession of loyalty via a 'native Japanese kimono'? The two don't jibe." The call for patriotic expression was especially evident in the festival's parade. Old Glory replaced the "rising sun" flags so prevalent at earlier celebrations, while beauty contestants, draped in white evening gowns, floated through the streets of Little Tokyo perched beneath a replica of the Capitol dome. A sedan resplendent with red, white, and blue streamers carried a flowered marquee that left the Nisei's identity unambiguous. Displayed beneath the facsimile of a spread-winged dove were the words "USA, Our Home."

It was difficult to gauge the extent to which the patriotic activities paid off. No amount of flag-waving or swearing of loyalty oaths could convince Kane and other die-hard racists that the Nisei were trustworthy. But the JACL's patriotism made such a favorable impression on Kenneth Ringle, the naval intelligence officer responsible for assessing the loyalty of the ethnic community, that he concluded "the entire Japanese Problem' had been magnified out of its true proportion, largely because of the physical characteristics of the people." Japanese Americans also received support from the *Los Angeles Times,* which encouraged its readers to attend Nisei Week because its sponsors "had no part in and no responsibility for causing war clouds to gather in the Orient." Fletcher Bowton, the mayor of Los Angeles in

1941, echoed this sentiment. In the speech that opened what became the last Nisei Week before World War II, the mayor not only implored Japanese Americans to show their patriotism but reassured them, "we know you are loyal."

Yet after the bombing of Pearl Harbor and the United States' declaration of war on Japan, Bowron did not hesitate to call for the mass evacuation of 110,000 Japanese Americans from the West Coast. The mayor, along with most public officials in California and other western states, confessed his utter distrust of Japanese Americans and did not think twice about denying them their constitutional rights. In early February 1942, he warned a radio audience about the Japanese American threat: "Right here in our own city are those who may spring into action at an appointed time in accordance with a prearranged plan wherein each of our little brown brothers will know his part in the event of any possible attempted invasion or air raid." Two weeks later, despite intelligence reports that deemed the overwhelming majority of Japanese Americans loyal to the United States, President Franklin Roosevelt signed Executive Order 9066, sanctioning their removal to concentration camps. Not long after that, over 33,000 Japanese Americans were forcibly removed from southern California, and with their departure ended a chapter in Nisei Week history.

During World War II the JACLers took control of the ethnic community precisely because they had failed to fulfill Nisei Week's twin goals of ameliorating anti-Japanese racism and securing the future of the ethnic enclave. While neither biculturalism nor the switch to Americanism could prevent the internment, the latter identity proved more pragmatic amid the extreme anti-Japanese sentiment that gripped the nation during World War II. The JACLers, pushed by government officials, adopted a new language of identity predicated on the eradication, not celebration, of ethnic difference. To prove their loyalty to the nation, they, as an organization and individually, cooperated with American intelligence agencies by informing on "suspicious" elements within the ethnic community. Their surveillance activities, which the ethnic press highlighted often, generated deep animosities against JACL (particularly its most boisterously anti-Japanese leaders) that led to the intimidation, beating, and attempted murder of JACLers within the internment camps. While military authorities saw the ethnic group as a monolithic (enemy) race, Japanese Americans experienced World War II more divided than ever.

FURTHER READING

Chin, Soo-Young. *Doing What Had to Be Done: The Life Narrative of Dora Yum Kim* (1999).

Espiritu, Yen Le. *Filipino American Lives* (1995).

Hayashi, Brian Masaru. *"For the Sake of Our Japanese Brethren": Assimilation, Nationalism, and Protestantism Among the Japanese of Los Angeles, 1895–1942* (1995).

Ichioka, Yuji. "Japanese Immigrant Nationalism: The Issei and the Sino-Japanese War, 1937–1941," *California History* 69 (1990): 260–275.

———. "The Meaning of Loyalty: The Case of Kazumaro Buddy Uno," *Amerasia Journal* 23 (1997): 45–71.

———. "A Study in Dualism: James Yoshinori Sakamoto and the Japanese American Courier, 1928–1942," *Amerasia Journal* 13 (1986): 49–81.

Kurashige, Lon. *Japanese American Celebration and Conflict: A History of Ethnic Identity and Festival in Los Angeles, 1934–1990* (2000).

———. "The Problem of Biculturalism: Japanese American Identity and Festival Before World War II," *Journal of American History* 86 (2000): 1632–1654.

Matsumoto, Valerie. "Desperately Seeking 'Dierdre': Gender Roles, Multicultural Relations, and Nisei Women Writers in the 1930s," *Frontiers* 12 (1991): 19–32.

———. *Farming the Home Place: A Japanese American Community in California, 1919–1982* (1993).

———. "Redefining Expectations: Nisei Women in the 1930s," *California History* 73 (1994): 44–53.

Miyamoto, S. Frank. *Social Solidarity Among the Japanese in Seattle* (1981; originally published in 1939).

Modell, John. *The Economics and Politics of Racial Accommodation: The Japanese of Los Angeles, 1900–1942* (1977).

Posadas, Barbara M. *The Filipino Americans* (1999).

Siu, Paul C. P. *The Chinese Laundryman: A Study in Social Isolation* (1987; originally published as Ph.D. dissertation, University of Chicago, 1953).

Sone, Monica. *Nisei Daughter* (1953).

Spickard, Paul R. *Japanese Americans: The Formation and Transformations of an Ethnic Group* (1996).

Stephan, John J. "Hijacked by Utopia: American Nikkei in Manchuria," *Amerasia Journal* 23 (1997): 1–42.

Takahashi, Jere. *Nisei/Sansei: Shifting Japanese American Identities and Politics* (1997).

Tamura, Eileen H. *Americanization, Acculturation, and Ethnic Identity: The Nisei Generation in Hawaii* (1994).

Wong, Jade Snow. *Fifth Chinese Daughter* (1950).

Yoo, David K. *Growing Up Nisei: Race, Generation, and Culture Among Japanese Americans of California, 1924–49* (2000).

Yu, Henry. *Thinking Orientals: Migration, Contact & Exoticism in Modern America* (2001).

Yu, Renqiu. *To Save China, to Save Ourselves: The Chinese Hand Laundry Alliance of New York (1992)*.

Yung, Judy. *Unbound Feet: A Social History of Chinese Women in San Francisco* (1995).

Yung, Judy. *Unbound Feet: A Documentary History of Chinese Women in San Francisco* (1999).

CHAPTER
9

War, Race, and the
Meaning of Citizenship,
1941–1988

World War II had a profound impact on Asian American views of colonialism, nationalism, patriotism, democracy, and citizenship. Korean Americans and Chinese Americans who had earlier campaigned against Japanese colonialism rejoiced when America declared war against Japan after the attack on Pearl Harbor in December 1941. To counter Japanese propaganda about American racism and recognize China's contributions as an ally, Congress repealed Chinese exclusion in 1943, provided China with an annual immigration quota of 105, and granted Chinese immigrants naturalization rights. No longer denounced as a "Yellow Peril," Chinese Americans embraced new educational and occupational opportunities throughout the wartime era.

Americans also praised Filipino Americans as "little brown brothers" in the fight against Japan. A 1941 executive order by President Franklin D. Roosevelt conscripted the Philippine Commonwealth Army into the U.S. forces. Filipino Americans continued to serve as stewards in the U.S. Navy and enlisted in segregated Filipino regiments created in 1942. Displaying great heroism at Corregidor and Bataan, these servicemen helped liberate the Philippines from Japanese control. The U.S. government promised Filipino soldiers naturalization rights and full veterans' benefits but allowed only a small number to become citizens before 1946. In 1990, the United States finally passed legislation to fulfill its wartime pledge, and thousands of Filipino veterans became U.S. citizens.

Japanese Americans living on the West Coast found that the U.S. government could disregard their citizenship rights during the war. Identified with the Japanese enemy, 70,000 American-born citizens and 40,000 immigrants of Japanese ancestry were uprooted from their homes and incarcerated in internment camps in 1942. Japanese Americans responded to life behind barbed wire in different ways. Some fought for the right to join the armed forces to demonstrate their patriotism and improve the treatment of Japanese Americans. Others protested against internment by refusing to sign a loyalty questionnaire, failing to comply with draft procedures,

*and, in some cases, even renouncing their citizenship. Dividing families and the
ethnic community, internment left deep wounds that began to heal when the community came together in the 1980s to win an apology and monetary redress from
the government.*

☙ D O C U M E N T S

The following documents provide different views of loyalty, patriotism, and citizenship during World War II. The first two documents illustrate a change in Chinese
American and Filipino American perspectives on economic opportunities and political
rights during the war. In Document 1, Rose Hum Lee, a sociology graduate student at
the University of Chicago, describes how Chinese Americans found well-paying jobs
in the defense industry and the private sector, enlisted in the military, and called for
the repeal of discriminatory legislation. In Document 2, drawn from a 1943 magazine
article, Filipino regiment member Manuel Buaken celebrates American ideals, notes
America's failure to live up to those ideals, and recounts his feelings as one of 1,200
Filipino soldiers who became U.S. citizens in a wartime ceremony at Camp Beale in
northern California.

The next five documents provide different views of racism that led to the incarceration of Japanese Americans during the war. In Document 3, the commander in charge
of West Coast security urges the War Department in 1942 to remove all Japanese
Americans because he assumes that racial ancestry determines loyalty. Document 4
presents selections from the 1942 congressional testimony of Mike Masaoka, the
national secretary of the ultrapatriotic Japanese American Citizens League (JACL),
pledging cooperation with any government removal orders. Journalist James Omura's
condemnation of Masaoka's stance is excerpted from the same congressional hearings
in Document 5. In Document 6, the "Fair Play Committee," led by Kiyoshi Okamoto
and other internees at the Heart Mountain internment camp, denounces the mass
incarceration and the creation of a segregated combat unit. Urging Japanese Americans to defend the constitution and democracy "here at home," the Fair Play Committee calls on internees to resist the draft to protest the violation of their citizenship
rights. Associate Supreme Court Justice Frank Murphy's searing dissent to the 1944
Supreme Court opinion upholding the constitutionality of mass removal is excerpted
in Document 7.

More than three decades passed before the government provided substantive
redress for internment. Many former internees found it too painful to remember or
discuss their wartime experiences until the Commission on Wartime Relocation and
Internment of Civilians held twenty days of hearings throughout the country in 1981.
In 1982, the commission's report, excerpted in Document 8, proclaimed that internment
had been unjustified and had caused tremendous suffering. The commission's recommendation of an official apology and payments of $20,000 to each surviving internee
was implemented by the passage of the Civil Liberties Act of 1988. Document 9 provides excerpts from the 1984 decision by District Court Judge Marilyn Hall Patel
vacating the wartime conviction of Fred Korematsu for violating mass removal orders,
on the grounds that the Justice Department had deliberately concealed Federal Bureau
of Investigation, intelligence, and Federal Communications Commission evidence from
the Supreme Court.

1. Sociology Graduate Student Rose Hum Lee Describes How World War II Changed the Lives of Chinese Americans, 1942

One hundred and thirty million Americans were very little aware on December 7 [1941] of the eighty thousand Chinese in the United States. But by noon of December 8, the country's declaration of war on Japan and similar action by the Republic of China had made the two nations allies. Since then the outlook of the Chinese living in this country has been considerably changed by Pearl Harbor.

One half of our Chinese population lives on the West Coast. San Francisco and the Bay Region have approximately 30,000, Los Angeles 4,500, Seattle 3,500, Portland 2,000. Most of the others are located in large cities in the East and Midwest; New York, Chicago, Cincinnati, Detroit, and Cleveland have sizable Chinatowns. In out-of-the-way towns are lonely laundrymen silently washing and ironing. Wherever the Chinese are, it has been possible to count the variations in ways they can earn their living on the fingers of the hand—chop suey and chow mein restaurants, Chinese art and gift shops, native grocery stores that sell foodstuffs imported from China to the local Chinese community.

In San Francisco's Chinatown, merely from force of habit, signs saying, "This is a Chinese Shop" are still displayed. But they no longer are needed; the section today is completely Chinese. The fifty Japanese shops fringing upon or in Chinatown have had to liquidate and Chinese have rented the stores. One of the most attractive shops is being run by a second generation Chinese-American young woman.

Throughout the Chinatowns in the United States there is a labor shortage. For the first time since Chinese labor exclusion began, absorption of the Chinese into American industry has been significant. Whether in New York, Los Angeles, San Francisco, Chicago, or in Butte, Mont., the service in Chinese restaurants is slow. Four restaurants in New York's Chinatown have closed their doors in the past few months. The proprietor of Li Po, an up-to-date cocktail-chop-suey place located in "Chinatown on Broadway" in Los Angeles, said sadly: "I was just ready for another venture. But I can't now. No men to run it."

They have gone in the army and navy, into shipbuilding and aircraft plants. Even the girls are getting jobs. A personal column of the *Chinese Press* notes: "The newest on the defense payrolls are Jane Sai, stenographer; Rose Hom, timekeeper; Jimmy Hom, welder; J. Eric Hom, carpenter." And another item says; "In Fresno, Chinese boys and girls are training at the NYA resident project for employment with Consolidated Aircraft."

The same issue carried the announcement that the associate editor, William Hoy, is donning a uniform. This brilliant young inductee is one of the best informed persons on the history of the Chinese in California.

From *Unbound Voices: A Documentary History of Chinese Women in San Francisco*, pp. 419, 444.

In War Industries

In Portland, Ore., the Chinese Consul, Silwing P. C. Au, and his wife have done much to promote interracial understanding. For three years they have worked to get Chinese assistants and cooks into the hospitals at Vancouver Barracks. The Chinese make good workers: they are taciturn, orderly, and perform their duties well. Meetings with the union leaders have smoothed out some labor difficulties and paved the way for absorption of many Chinese-Americans into war industries. Recently the restaurant unions invited the Chinese restaurant employees to join their ranks. Although very few Chinese have joined so far, the invitation is significant. Mrs. Au is active in the League of Women Voters, the American Association of University Women (she was recently invited to be the program chairman for the coming season), in the National Federation of Women's Clubs, as well as in the Chinese American Women's League, and in all organizations aiding in relief for China.

Only a handful of stores dot the so-called Chinatown in Minneapolis. In June, when the city turned out to welcome fifteen war heroes from the East Coast, tiny Chinese-Americans wearing their gay costumes waved welcome to the visiting celebrities. The flag of the Republic of China elicited thundering applause. The proprietor of the city's only Oriental gift shop liquidated his business last winter at the height of a busy Christmas season and entered a war industry. His wife, likewise a Chinese-American, works in the same plant. An American-born University-of-Minnesota-trained master in architecture found work in a war industry—the first technical job he has held since his graduation fifteen years ago. Previously he had to be satisfied with managing his father's restaurant, but now, his American-born, business-trained wife is doing that.

In the Pittsburgh and Philadelphia communities, shortage of help has been acute for so long that not even labor imported from other cities can ease the situation. In New York, students who used to earn money as "extra waiters" during the weekends have found employment in industries working on lease-lend material for China. The China Institute in America has placed many trained young men in American industry as technicians, chemists, and engineers.

An officer of the China Institute, Dr. B. A. Liu, has been making a tour of the large universities to get in touch with Chinese students, many of them stranded in this country as a result of the war. The Department of State announced in April that such students would be given opportunities to gain practical experience or be assisted financially to complete their technical training. The response of American industry has been heartening. Industrial, transportation, and scientific organizations have absorbed many scientific and technical students. Other students hope for employment in educational institutions, libraries, foundations, hospitals, publishing houses; and as translators. . . .

In the Armed Services

Portland's Chinese community sent a contingent of thirty-three trained pilots to Generalissimo Chiang Kai-shek before December 7. With America in the war as an ally, those now in training will be pilots in the United States Air Force. The Generalissimo has urged Chinese men here to enlist in the armed forces of the United States as a demonstration of China's complete cooperation with the United Nations.

The removal of restrictions in the United States Navy and Naval Reserve has started a drive for 500 Chinese as apprentice seamen. Heretofore, Chinese were restricted to enlistment as messmen and stewards. The recent requirements for enlistment are American citizenship; ability to pass the navy's physical examination; age seventeen to thirty-one for the navy and seventeen to fifty for the naval reserve.

New York's Chinatown cheered itself hoarse when the first draft numbers drawn were for Chinese-Americans. Some below-age boys tried to pass on their "Chinese age," which is often a year or two older than the American count. Since their birth certificates told a different tale, they had to be patient and wait.

There were only eleven Chinese-Americans of draft age in Butte, Mont., and all enlisted or are serving Uncle Sam in some other way. One in the army was promoted to be sergeant, and has gone overseas. A family with three sons has one in the medical corps, another in the army air corps, the third in the navy. In another family with three sons one, an engineer, is in the East in a lease-lend organization, and the other two, both engineering students, are reserves in the air corps until they graduate.

K. S. Jue, president of the Shiu [Sue] Hing Benevolent Society, speaking of home front activities, said: "San Francisco has gone over the top in its recent Red Cross drive. We raised $18,000 for the campaign. In the Defense Bond Drive, we bought over $30,000." This is in addition to all the war relief the Chinese here have been sending to China and in response to the demands of relatives across the Pacific.

Civil Rights for Our Chinese Allies

This year, at the recent convention of the California League of Women Voters in San Francisco, the following resolution was passed:

> Recognizing the racial discrimination shown in several Asiatic Exclusion Acts passed by our government over a period of sixty years, the California League of Women Voters accepts its responsibility for education as to the history and effects of the Exclusion Acts leading toward effective opposition to racial discrimination in immigration laws, and asks that the National League send material to all State Leagues.

It is significant that this step towards righting an old wrong should come from California, where the Chinese exclusion movement first saw birth as a state issue, gradually to become national policy. While the exclusion sections of the Immigration Act of 1924 were aimed primarily at rapidly increasing immigration of Japanese picture-brides in the early years of the twentieth century, they worked even more hardship among the Chinese immigrants. The solution to the problem of Oriental immigration promises to be not exclusion by law, but intelligent restriction and selection of those who desire admittance into the country. It seems to the Chinese that those of us not born here should be eligible to become citizens through a process of naturalization as do those who come from other lands; and that the right to own property as citizens should be acknowledged. Surely racial discrimination should not be directed against those who are America's Allies in the Far East and are helping here in every way to win the war.

It has long been recognized that "cheap labor" was not eliminated by the series of exclusion laws. Immediately after the passing of those laws, "cheap labor" was supplied by incoming Mexicans and Filipinos.

Every thinking Chinese in this country and in China hopes that the American people will advance the social, political, and economic status of the Chinese in the United States. To be fighting for freedom and democracy in the Far East, at the cost of seven million lives in five years of hard, long, bitter warfare, and to be denied equal opportunity in the greatest of democracies, seems the height of irony. With the absorption of the Chinese in industry and the proof that they are good workers, loyal citizens, and faithful to the United Nations' cause, racial barriers and prejudices should break down now and for all time.

In California, today, there are fourth generation Americans—Chinese-Americans who speak no Chinese. They live on close terms with their American neighbors, enjoy the same recreation and health facilities offered to their fellow citizens. For them the present crisis is another stepping stone toward complete assimilation. No longer do Americans think of the Chinese as mysterious Orientals from a little known land. Most of these Chinese living among them are fellow citizens. The rest of them, as well as their cousins in the old country, are Allies. The crisis of December 7 has emancipated the Chinese in the United States. It is up to the American people to effect the emancipation by law.

2. Filipino Regiment Member Manuel Buaken Fights for Freedom, 1943

The eyes of the world were upon us that day of our world premiere as citizens of the United States. We were spotlighted before the cameras and microphones of the nation. The place of our debut was the parade ground of Camp Beale, on the wet red clay of northern California. The time, February 20, 1943.

We are soldiers, members of the First Filipino Infantry, United States Army. We are Mount Mayor's men, as you can see by our insignia symbolizing our oath of vengeance against the invaders of our homeland—a brilliant yellow disk upon which is the volcano Mount Mayon in black, erupting black smoke, with three bright stars shining through, to represent the three principal islands of the Philippines.

While we, the twelve hundred candidates for citizenship, stood proud and silent in a V formation, Colonel Cowley began the ceremony, saying in part, "Officers who returned from Bataan have said there are no finer soldiers in the world than the Filipinos who fought and starved and died there shoulder to shoulder with our troops. I can well believe it as I look at the men before me. On those faces is quiet determination and a consciousness of training and discipline with a definite end in view. I congratulate them on their soldierly appearance and on their approaching citizenship."

The post's public relations officer, Captain Sprague, described the scene to the radio audience ". . . fine looking, well disciplined Filipino soldiers. Their faces are immobile but their eyes are gleaming with anticipation. In exactly eight minutes they will become officially what they have long been in their hearts—Americans. They

---

From Manuel Buaken, "Our Fighting Love of Freedom," *Asia and the Americas* vol. 43, no. 6 (June 1943): 357, 359.

are waiting at this moment for the only reward they have asked—citizenship—real live nephews of the Uncle Sam they revere."

Next to come to the microphone was Colonel Offley, who simply said, "They are fine soldiers and I am proud to be their commander."

The concluding speech was made by Judge Welsh: "Citizenship came to us who were born here as a heritage—it will come to you as a privilege. We have every faith you will become and remain loyal, devoted citizens of the United States, and we wish you God speed and success."

Then the oath was solemnly administered by Judge Welsh, and as solemnly pledged by us.

Came the singing of "On to Bataan," our stirring regimental song, then "The Star Spangled Banner" and our salute to the flag. And we were citizens of the United States.

We have not taken this step lightly, but with serious consideration, and much debate among ourselves. We did not renounce our citizenship in the Philippines. We have accepted a wider citizenship, a greater responsibility. As Pfc. Jose Trinidad said, in one of our discussions in our barracks, "I cannot give up my citizenship in the Philippines, it is my heart. But America is also in my mind. I wish to have both loyalties." One phase of this wider responsibility was voiced by Corporal Manuel Luz, of Company I, when he said, "This is a step toward our dream of a world citizenship, of a United States of the Orient. And we are preparing now the pattern of this citizenship, by this leadership that America has set for us, and has taught us."

That is the consensus of our convictions—that America has set the pattern this day, with this grant of citizenship to us, as we have granted it to Americans in the Philippines long ago—on a dual basis—*giving you full participation in our country's political and economic life without asking you to renounce your share in America.*

So you ask me, what is the Philippine interpretation of the meaning of citizenship?

With us, it is a growth, a summary of all our traditions, our folk-lore—it has taken elements of meaning from all our diverse racial strains, it has been molded by all our history. . . .

Our citizenship concept has been tolerant—we have assimilated Chinese, modern Malayans, Spanish and other Europeans such as the Portuguese. And in some ways our citizenship standards are higher than yours. We have begun our national life with the protection of all our natural resources from exploitation and ruthless destruction. We shall have no denuded forests as you have, no exhausted lands or heavy concentration of wealth in the hands of the ruthless few. Our citizenship is foresighted.

More than that, we have taken your best ideals and made them our own. These twelve hundred Filipino soldiers, now citizens of America, are here because they were fired by American ideals and determined to learn the best democratic principles and practices, to make them a part of our country's heritage. We are here because we have studied your books, have made your patriotic leaders our heroes—Washington, Lincoln, Woodrow Wilson and, not least, Franklin Delano Roosevelt.

What Captain Sprague said is true: we have long been Americans in our hearts. We are thankful now for the privilege of becoming legally entitled to participate in your democracy. To us it is the fruition of Filipino-American friendship. It is the flower of the bloodless freedom, an achievement almost unparalleled in history.

But alas, how many Americans are truly sincere in granting us this privilege? We know that you have long denied it to us and that military expediency is a large factor in the gift you have made to us.

But you must know us by our unwavering loyalty to you. We came to the United States to learn the best, and we found that our place here was in the blind spot of America. We believed in your ideals, we expected you to practise them. But we were barred from the best in your society, we were barred from economic advancement, held to the most menial of your unwanted tasks, kept from labor unions, denied access to skilled jobs or professions, prevented from learning those things that would be of value to our country when we returned home, condemned here for our dark skins, the light of our high ideals ignored and shunned. Yet we have not become bitter. No Filipino in the United States harbors hatred against the Americans in spite of all the stupidities with regard to race prejudice. We have always been loyal to your ideals to the extent of tolerating the un-American dealings of some Americans. We have held to the hope in our hearts that some day you would know us for what we are—*and now that day has come.* It came by way of Bataan—but it is here—this citizenship ceremony proves it.

It was to perfect our citizenship that we came to America. And the work done by Filipinos on California ranches, in Alaskan fisheries and canneries, in the movie industry, on railroads, in mills, factories and in homes all over America has been a contribution to the economic welfare of the United States, but primarily apprenticeship for us in service and useful arts. Here, as well as in your American schools and colleges, we have absorbed the lessons of America. Now we advance another step. We are soldiers now, soldiers of freedom, who go to take back a free citizenship to our country. When this war ends, when reconstruction comes to our homeland, the Filipino citizen of the United States will go back home, not to renounce his oath to the American people but eager to fulfill his duty to the Philippines. The Philippines will need men who have been trained in your modern ways to rebuild the shattered Orient, to be the leaders of the new order. All that we learn now will one day be put to use for our country.

We are taking on a broad responsibility, a triple responsibility, really. We are responsible for our loyalty to the United States. Our duty to the Philippines means that we must take the leadership there. And we must also lead in the rebuilding of the new Orient. The Malayan lands, freed, must have leadership they trust and understand. We Filipinos must have trade and cooperation with our neighbors: we cannot live isolated from the rest of the Orient. The United States has already set up trade barriers against us. Furthermore, America has taught us well; now it is our duty to pass the teachings on to these other lands that will be freed from the Japanese invader, and freed also from European "colonizers," by the same army of the United Nations.

All this was bound up in the oath that we took at Camp Beale, as we stood in our Victory formation, as we saluted the American flag, proud American soldiers!

We are the Advance Echelon of the Army of the United States of the Orient.

Photograph of members of the First Filipino Infantry becoming citizens of the United States, 1943.

3. Lieutenant General John L. DeWitt Recommends the Removal of Japanese Americans from the West Coast, 1942

The area lying to the west of the Cascade and Sierra Nevada Mountains in Washington, Oregon and California, is highly critical not only because the lines of communication and supply to the Pacific theater pass through it, but also because of the vital industrial production therein, particularly aircraft. In the war in which we are now engaged racial affinities are not severed by migration. The Japanese race is an enemy race and while many second and third generation Japanese born on United States soil, possessed of United States citizenship, have become "Americanized," the racial strains are undiluted. To conclude otherwise is to expect that children born of white parents on Japanese soil sever all racial affinity and become loyal Japanese subjects,

From Manuel Buaken, "Our Fighting Love of Freedom," *Asia and the Americas* 43, no. 6 (June 1943): 358. Hansel Mieth / TIMEPIX.

From United States Department of War, *Final Report: Japanese Evacuation from the West Coast, 1942* (Washington, D.C.: U.S. Government Printing Office, 1943), 34–37.

ready to fight and, if necessary, to die for Japan in a war against the nation of their parents. That Japan is allied with Germany and Italy in this struggle is no ground for assuming that any Japanese, barred from assimilation by convention as he is, though born and raised in the United States, will not turn against this nation when the final test of loyalty comes. It, therefore, follows that along the vital Pacific Coast over 112,000 potential enemies, of Japanese extraction, are at large today. There are indications that these are organized and ready for concerted action at a favorable opportunity. The very fact that no sabotage has taken place to date is a disturbing and confirming indication that such action will be taken.

c. Disposition of the Japanese

(1) *Washington.* As the term is used herein, the word "Japanese" includes alien Japanese and American citizens of Japanese ancestry. In the State of Washington the Japanese population, aggregating over 14,500, is disposed largely in the area lying west of the Cascade Mountains and south of an east-west line passing through Bellingham, Washington, about 70 miles north of Seattle and some 15 miles south of the Canadian border. The largest concentration of Japanese is in the area, the axis of which is along the line Seattle, Tacoma, Olympia, Willapa Bay and the mouth of the Columbia River, with the heaviest concentration in the agricultural valleys between Seattle and Tacoma, viz., the Green River and the Puyallup Valleys. The Boeing Aircraft factory is in the Green River Valley. The lines of communication and supply including power and water which feed this vital industrial installation, radiate from this plant for many miles through areas heavily populated by Japanese. Large numbers of Japanese also operate vegetable markets along the Seattle and Tacoma water fronts, in Bremerton, near the Bremerton Navy Yard, and inhabit islands in Puget Sound opposite vital naval ship building installations. Still others are engaged in fishing along the southwest Washington Pacific Coast and along the Columbia River. Many of these Japanese are within easy reach of the forests of Washington State, the stock piles of seasoning lumber and the many sawmills of southwest Washington. During the dry season these forests, mills and stock piles are easily fired.

(2) *Oregon.* There are approximately 4,000 Japanese in the State of Oregon, of which the substantial majority reside in the area in the vicinity of Portland along the south bank of the Columbia River, following the general line Bonneville, Oregon City, Astoria, Tillamook. Many of these are in the northern reaches of the Willamette Valley and are engaged in agricultural and fishing pursuits. Others operate vegetable markets in the Portland metropolitan area and still others reside along the northern Oregon sea coast. Their disposition is in intimate relationship with the northwest Oregon sawmills and lumber industry, near and around the vital electric power development at Bonneville and the pulp and paper installations at Camas (on the Washington State side of the Columbia River) and Oregon City, directly south of Portland.

(3) *California.* The Japanese population in California aggregates approximately 93,500 people. Its disposition is so widespread and so well known that little would be gained by setting it forth in detail here. They live in great numbers along the coastal strip, in and around San Francisco and the Bay Area, the Salinas Valley, Los Angeles and San Diego. Their truck farms are contiguous to the vital aircraft industry concentration in and around Los Angeles. They live in large numbers in and about San Francisco, now a vast staging area for the war in the Pacific, a point

at which the nation's lines of communication and supply converge. Inland they are disposed in the Sacramento, San Joaquin and Imperial Valleys. The are engaged in the production of approximately 38% of the vegetable produce in California. Many of them are engaged in the distribution of such produce in and along the water fronts at San Francisco and Los Angeles. Of the 93,500 in California, about 25,000 reside inland in the mentioned valleys where they are largely engaged in vegetable production cited above, and 54,600 reside along the coastal strip, that is to say, a strip of coast line varying from eight miles in the north to twenty miles in width in and around the San Francisco bay area, including San Francisco, in Los Angeles and its environs, and in San Diego. Approximately 13,900 are dispersed through-out the remaining portion of the state. In Los Angeles City the disposition of vital aircraft industrial plants covers the entire city. Large numbers of Japanese live and operate markets and truck farms adjacent to or near these installations. . . .

I now recommend the following:

(1) That the Secretary of War procure from the President direction and authority to designate military areas in the combat zone of the Western Theater of Operations, (if necessary to include the entire combat zone), from which, in his discretion, he may exclude all Japanese, all alien enemies, and all other persons suspected for any reason by the administering military authorities of being actual or potential sabo-teurs, espionage agents, or fifth columnists. Such executive order should empower the Secretary of War to requisition the services of any and all other agencies of the Federal Government, with express direction to such agencies to respond to such requisition, and further empowering the Secretary of War to use any and all federal facilities and equipment, including Civilian Conservation Corps Camps, and to ac-cept the use of State facilities for the purpose of providing shelter and equipment for evacuees. Such executive order to provide further for the administration of military areas for the purposes of this plan by appropriate military authorities acting with the requisitioned assistance of the other federal agencies and the cooperation of State and local agencies. The executive order should further provide that by reason of military necessity the right of all persons, whether citizens or aliens, to reside, enter, cross or be within any military areas shall be subject to revocation and shall exist on a pass and permit basis at the discretion of the Secretary of War and implemented by the necessary legislation imposing penalties for violation.

4. Japanese American Mike Masaoka Vows to Cooperate with Government Removal Plans, 1942

We have been invited by you to make clear our stand regarding the proposed evac-uation of all Japanese from the West coast. When the President's recent Executive order was issued, we welcomed it as definitely centralizing and coordinating defense efforts relative to the evacuation problem. Later interpretations of the order, how-ever, seem to indicate that it is aimed primarily at the Japanese, American citizens

---

From Testimony of Mike Masaoka, House Select Committee Investigating Defense Migration, 77th Cong. 2nd Sess. (1942), 1137, reprinted in *Asian Americans: Opposing Viewpoints,* ed. William Dudley (San Diego: Greenhaven Press, 1997), 151–154.

as well as alien nationals. As your committee continues its investigations in this and subsequent hearings, we hope and trust that you will recommend to the proper authorities that no undue discrimination be shown to American citizens of Japanese descent.

Our frank and reasoned opinion on the matter of evacuation revolves around certain considerations of which we feel both your committee and the general public should be apprised. With any policy of evacuation definitely arising from reasons of military necessity and national safety, we are in complete agreement. As American citizens, we cannot and should not take any other stand. But, also, as American citizens believing in the integrity of our citizenship, we feel that any evacuation enforced on grounds violating that integrity should be opposed.

If, in the judgment of military and Federal authorities, evacuation of Japanese residents from the West coast is a primary step toward assuring the safety of this Nation, we will have no hesitation in complying with the necessities implicit in that judgment. But, if, on the other hand, such evacuation is primarily a measure whose surface urgency cloaks the desires of political or other pressure groups who want us to leave merely from motives of self-interest, we feel that we have every right to protest and to demand equitable judgment on our merits as American citizens. . . .

I now make an earnest plea that you seriously consider and recognize our American citizenship status which we have been taught to cherish as our most priceless heritage.

At this hearing, we Americans of Japanese descent have been accused of being disloyal to these United States. As an American citizen, I resent these accusations and deny their validity.

We American-born Japanese are fighting militarist Japan today with our total energies. Four thousand of us are with the armed forces of the United States, the remainder on the home front in the battle of production. We ask a chance to prove to the rest of the American people what we ourselves already know: That we are loyal to the country of our birth and that we will fight to the death to defend it against any and all aggressors.

We think, feel, act like Americans. We, too, remember Pearl Harbor and know that our right to live as free men in a free Nation is in peril as long as the brutal forces of enslavement walk the earth. We know that the Axis aggressors must be crushed and we are anxious to participate fully in that struggle.

The history of our group speaks for itself. It stands favorable comparison with that of any other group of second generation Americans. There is reliable authority to show that the proportion of delinquency and crime within our ranks is negligible. Throughout the long years of the depression, we have been able to stay off the relief rolls better, by far, than any other group. These are but two of the many examples which might be cited as proof of our civic responsibility and pride.

In this emergency, as in the past, we are not asking for special privileges or concessions. We ask only for the opportunity and the right of sharing the common lot of all Americans, whether it be in peace or in war.

This is the American way for which our boys are fighting.

5. Journalist James M. Omura Condemns the Mass Exclusion of Japanese Americans, 1942

I requested to be heard here due largely to the fact that I am strongly opposed to mass evacuation of American-born Japanese. . . . I suppose you understand that I am in some measure opposed to what some of the other representatives of the Japanese community have said here before this committee. . . . I specifically refer to the J.A.C.L. It is a matter of public record among the Japanese community that I have been consistently opposed to the Japanese-American Citizen League. I have not been opposed to that organization primarily in regards to its principles, but I have felt that the leaders were leading the American-born Japanese along the wrong channels, and I have not minced words in saying so publicly. . . .

It is doubtlessly rather difficult for Caucasian Americans to properly comprehend and believe in what we say. Our citizenship has even been attacked as an evil cloak under which we expect immunity for the nefarious purpose of conspiring to destroy the American way of life. To us—who have been born, raised, and educated in American institutions and in our system of public schools, knowing and owing no other allegiance than to the United States—such a thought is manifestly unfair and ambiguous.

I would like to ask the committee: Has the Gestapo come to America? Have we not risen in righteous anger at Hitler's mistreatments of the Jews? Then, is it not incongruous that citizen Americans of Japanese descent should be similarly mistreated and persecuted? I speak from a humanitarian standpoint and from a realistic and not a theoretical point of view. This view, I believe does not endanger the national security of this country nor jeopardize our war efforts. . . .

Are we to be condemned merely on the basis or our racial origin? Is citizenship such a light and transient thing that that which is our inalienable right in normal times can be torn from us in times of war? We in America are intensely proud of our individual rights and willing, I am sure, to defend those rights with our very lives. I venture to say that the great majority of Nisei Americans, too, will do the same against any aggressor nation—though that nation be Japan. Citizenship to us is no small heritage; it is very precious and jealous right. You have only to look back on our records in social welfare and community contributions to understand that.

May I ask the committee members if any or all of you are acquainted with the Nisei? I believe that much of this distrust of citizen Japanese is based on ignorance. It would seem more compatible in the sense of fair play and justice that we should not be prejudged and that racialism should not be the yardstick by which our loyalty is measured. Our words, in current times, have no meaning, and so I ask you to examine our records, for there I believe that to a large measure, if not necessarily so, lies the true determination of our oft-questioned loyalty.

From Testimony of James M. Omura, House Select Committee Investigating Defense Migration, 77th Cong., 2nd Sess. (1942), 11229; reprinted in *Asian Americans: Opposing Viewpoints,* ed. William Dudley (San Diego: Greenhaven Press, 1997), 156–159.

6. The Fair Play Committee Calls on Nisei, Second-Generation Japanese Americans, to Resist the Draft Within the Heart Mountain Internment Camp, 1944

We, the Nisei have been complacent and too inarticulate to the unconstitutional acts that we were subjected to. If ever there was a time or cause for decisive action. IT IS NOW!

We, the members of the FPC [Fair Play Committee] are not afraid to go war—we are not afraid to risk our lives for our country. We would gladly sacrifice our lives to protect and uphold the principles and ideals of our country as set forth in the Constitution and the Bill of Rights, for on its inviolability depends the freedom, liberty, justice, and protection of all people including Japanese-Americans and all other minority groups. But have we been given such freedom, such liberty, such justice, such protection? NO!! Without any hearings, without due process of law as guaranteed by the Constitution and Bill of Rights, without any charges filed against us, without any evidence of wrongdoing on our part, one hundred and ten thousand innocent people were kicked out of their homes, literally uprooted from where they have lived for the greater part of their life, and herded like dangerous criminals into concentration camps with barbed wire fences and military police guarding it, AND THEN, WITHOUT RECTIFICATION OF THE INJUSTICES COMMITTED AGAINST US NOR WITHOUT RESTORATION OF OUR RIGHTS AS GUARANTEED BY THE CONSTITUTION, WE ARE ORDERED TO JOIN THE ARMY THRU <u>DISCRIMINATORY PROCEDURES</u> INTO A <u>SEGREGATED COMBAT UNIT</u>! Is that the American way? <u>NO!</u> The FPC believes that unless such actions are opposed <u>NOW,</u> and steps taken to remedy such injustices and discriminations <u>IMMEDIATELY</u>, the future of all minorities and the future of this democratic nation is in danger.

Thus, the members of the FPC unanimously decided at their last open meeting that until we are restored all our rights, all discriminatory features of the Selective Service abolished, and measures are taken to remedy the past injustices thru Judicial pronouncement or Congressional act, we feel that the present program of drafting us from this concentration camp is unjust, unconstitutional, and against all principles of civilized usage. Therefore, WE MEMBERS OF THE FAIR PLAY COMMITTEE <u>HEREBY REFUSE TO GO TO THE PHYSICAL EXAMINATION OR TO THE INDUCTION IF OR WHEN WE ARE CALLED IN ORDER TO CONTEST THE ISSUE.</u>

We are not being disloyal. We are not evading the draft. We are all loyal Americans fighting for JUSTICE AND DEMOCRACY RIGHT HERE AT HOME. So, restore our rights as such, rectify the injustices of evacuation, of the concentration, of the detention, and of the pauperization as such. In short, treat us in accordance with the principles of the Constitution.

From Frank Abe, "One for All—All for One," 1944; reprinted at www.resisters.com/documents/FPC_Bulletin_3.htm. Reprinted by permission of the author.

If what we are voicing is wrong, if what we ask is disloyal, if what we think is unpatriotic, then Abraham Lincoln, one of our greatest American President (sic) was also guilty as such, for he said, "If by the mere force of numbers a majority should deprive a minority on any Constitutional right, it might in a moral point of view justify a revolution."

Among the one thousand odd members of the Fair Play Committee, there are Nisei men over the draft age and Nisei girls who are not directly affected by the present Selective Service program, but who believe in the ideals and principles of our country, therefore are helping the FPC in our fight against injustice and discriminations.

We hope that all persons whose ideals and interests are with us will do all they can to help us. <u>We may have to engage in court actions but as such actions require large sums of money, we do need financial support and when the time comes we hope that you will back us up to the limit.</u>

ATTENTION MEMBERS! FAIR PLAY COMMITTEE MEETING SUNDAY, MARCH 5, 2:00 PM. BLOCK 6-30 MESS. PARENTS, BROTHERS, SISTERS, AND FRIENDS INVITED.

7. Justice Frank Murphy Criticizes the Supreme Court's "Legalization of Racism," 1944

Mr. Justice MURPHY, dissenting

This exclusion of "all persons of Japanese ancestry, both alien and non-alien," from the Pacific Coast area on a plea of military necessity in the absence of martial law ought not to be approved. Such exclusion goes over "the very brink of constitutional power" and falls into the ugly abyss of racism.

In dealing with matters relating to the prosecution and progress of a war, we must accord great respect and consideration to the judgments of the military authorities who are on the scene and who have full knowledge of the military facts. The scope of their discretion must, as a matter of necessity and common sense, be wide. And their judgments ought not to be overruled lightly by those whose training and duties ill-equip them to deal intelligently with matters so vital to the physical security of the nation.

At the same time, however, it is essential that there be definite limits to military discretion, especially where martial law has not been declared. Individuals must not be left impoverished of their constitutional rights on a plea of military necessity that has neither substance nor support. Thus, like other claims conflicting with the asserted constitutional rights of the individual, the military claim must subject itself to the judicial process of having its reasonableness determined and its conflicts with other interests reconciled. . . .

From *Korematsu v. United States,* 323 U.S. 233, 235, 239–242; reprinted in *Racism, Dissent, and Asian Americans from 1850 to the Present A Documentary History,* ed. Philip S. Foner (Westport, Conn.: Greenwood Press, 1993), 254–257.

The judicial test of whether the Government, on a plea of military necessity, can validly deprive an individual of any of his constitutional rights is whether the deprivation is reasonably related to a public danger that is so "immediate, imminent and impending" as not to admit of delay and not to permit the intervention of ordinary constitutional processes to alleviate the danger. . . . Civilian Exclusion Order No. 34, banishing from a prescribed area of the Pacific Coast "all persons of Japanese ancestry, both alien and non-alien," clearly does not meet that test. Being an obvious racial discrimination, the order deprives all those within its scope of the equal protection of the laws as guaranteed by the Fifth Amendment. It further deprives these individuals of their constitutional rights to live and work where they will, to establish a home where they choose and to move about freely. In excommunicating them without benefit of hearings, this order also deprives them of all their constitutional rights to procedural due process. Yet no reasonable relation to an "immediate, imminent, and impending" public danger is evident to support this racial restriction which is one of the most sweeping and complete deprivations of constitutional rights in the history of this nation in the absence of martial law.

It must be conceded that the military and naval situation in the spring of 1942 was such as to generate a very real fear of invasion of the Pacific Coast, accompanied by fears of sabotage and espionage in that area. The military command was therefore justified in adopting all reasonable means necessary to combat these dangers. In adjudging the military action taken in light of the then apparent dangers, we must not erect too high or too meticulous standards; it is necessary only that the action have some reasonable relation to the removal of the dangers of invasion, sabotage and espionage. But the exclusion, either temporarily of permanently, of all persons with Japanese blood in the veins has no such reasonable relation. And that relation is lacking because the exclusion order necessarily must rely for its reasonableness upon the assumption that *all* persons of Japanese ancestry may have a dangerous tendency to commit sabotage and espionage and to aid our Japanese enemy in other ways. It is difficult to believe that reason, logic or experience could be marshalled in support of such an assumption.

. . . The main reasons relied upon by those responsible for the forced evacuation, therefore, do not prove a reasonable relation between the group characteristics of Japanese Americans and the dangers of invasion, sabotage and espionage. The reasons appear, instead, to be largely an accumulation of much of the misinformation, half-truths and insinuations that for years have been directed against Japanese Americans by people with racial and economic prejudices—the same people who have been among the foremost advocates of the evacuation. A military judgment based upon such racial and sociological considerations is not entitled to the great weight ordinarily given the judgments based upon strictly military considerations. Especially is this so when every charge relative to race, religion, culture, geographical location, and legal and economic status has been substantially discredited by independent studies made by experts in these matters.

The military necessity which is essential to the validity of the evacuation order thus resolves itself into a few intimations that certain individuals actively aided the enemy, from which it is inferred that the entire group of Japanese Americans could not be trusted to be or remain loyal to the United States. No one denies, of course, that there were some disloyal persons of Japanese descent on the Pacific Coast who did all in their power to aid their ancestral land. Similar disloyal activities have been engaged in by many persons of German, Italian and even more pioneer stock in our country. But to infer that examples of individual disloyalty prove group disloyalty and justify discriminatory action against the entire group is to deny that under our system of law individual guilt is the sole basis for deprivation of rights. Moreover, this inference, which is at the very heart of the evacuation orders, has been used in support of the abhorrent and despicable treatment of minority groups by the dictatorial tyrannies which this nation is now pledged to destroy. To give constitutional sanction to that inference in this case, however well-intentioned may have been the military command on the Pacific Coast, is to adopt one of the cruelest of the rationales used by our enemies to destroy the dignity of the individual and to encourage and open the door to discriminatory actions against other minority groups in the passions of tomorrow.

No adequate reason is given for the failure to treat these Japanese Americans on an individual basis by holding investigations and hearings to separate the loyal from the disloyal, as was done in the case of persons of German and Italian ancestry. . . . It is asserted merely that the loyalties of this group "were unknown and time was of the essence." Yet nearly four months elapsed after Pearl Harbor before the first exclusion order was issued; nearly eight months went by until the last order was issued; and the last of these "subversive" persons was not actually removed until almost eleven months had elapsed. Leisure and deliberation seem to have been more of the essence than speed. And the fact that conditions were not such as to warrant a declaration of martial law adds strength to the belief that the factors of time and military necessity were not as urgent as they have been represented to be.

Moreover, there was no adequate proof that the Federal Bureau of Investigation and the military and naval intelligence services did not have the espionage and sabotage situation well in hand during this long period. Nor is there any denial of the fact that not one person of Japanese ancestry was accused or convicted of espionage or sabotage after Pearl Harbor while they were still free, a fact which is some evidence of the loyalty of the vast majority of these individuals and of the effectiveness of the established methods of combatting these evils. It seems incredible that under these circumstances it would have been impossible to hold loyalty hearings for the mere 112,000 persons involved—or at least for the 70,000 American citizens—especially when a large part of this number represented children and elderly men and women. Any inconvenience that may have accompanied an attempt to conform to procedural due process cannot be said to justify violations of constitutional rights of individuals.

I dissent, therefore, from this legalization or racism. Racial discrimination in any form and in any degree has no justifiable part whatever in our democratic way of life. It is unattractive in any setting but it is utterly revolting among a free people who have embraced the principles set forth in the Constitution of the United States. All residents of this nation are kin in some way by blood or culture to a foreign land. Yet they are primarily and necessarily a part of the new and distinct civilization of the United States. They must accordingly be treated at all times as the heirs of the American experiment and as entitled to all the rights and freedoms guaranteed by the Constitution.

8. A Government Commission Proclaims Internment a "Grave Injustice," 1982

The exclusion, removal and detention inflicted tremendous human cost. There was the obvious cost of homes and businesses sold or abandoned under circumstances of great distress, as well as injury to careers and professional advancement. But, most important, there was the loss of liberty and the personal stigma of suspected disloyalty for thousands of people who knew themselves to be devoted to their country's cause and to its ideals but whose repeated protestations of loyalty were discounted—only to be demonstrated beyond any doubt by the record of Nisei soldiers, who returned from the battlefields of Europe as the most decorated and distinguished combat unit of World War II, and by the thousands of other Nisei who served against the enemy in the Pacific, mostly in military intelligence. The wounds of the exclusion and detention have healed in some respects, but the scars of that experience remain, painfully real in the minds of those who lived through the suffering and deprivation of the camps. . . .

The Effect of the Exclusion and Detention

The history of the relocation camps and the assembly centers that preceded them is one of suffering and deprivation visited on people against whom no charges were, or could have been, brought. The Commission hearing record is full of poignant, searing testimony that recounts the economic and personal losses and injury caused by the exclusion and the deprivations of detention. No summary can do this testimony justice. . . .

The promulgation of Executive Order 9066 was not justified by military necessity, and the decisions which followed from it—detention, ending detention and ending exclusion—were not driven by analysis of military conditions. The broad historical causes which shaped these decisions were race prejudice, war hysteria and a failure of political leadership. Widespread ignorance of Japanese Americans contributed to a policy conceived in haste and executed in an atmosphere of fear and anger at Japan. A grave injustice was done to American citizens and resident aliens of Japanese ancestry who, without individual review or any probative evidence against them, were excluded, removed and detained by the United States during World War II.

From Commission on Wartime Relocation and Internment of Civilians, *Personal Justice Denied: Report of the Commission on Wartime Relocation and Internment of Civilians.* Washington, D.C.: U.S. Government Printing Office, December 1982), 3, 10–11, 18.

9. A District Court Acknowledges Government Misconduct Before the Supreme Court During World War II, 1984

[19] The substance of the statements contained in the documents and the fact the statements were made demonstrate that the government knowingly withheld information from the courts when they were considering the critical question of military necessity in this case. A series of correspondence regarding what information should be included in the government's brief before the Supreme Court culminated in two different versions of a footnote that was to be used to specify the factual data upon which the government relied for its military necessity justification. The first version read as follows:

> The Final Report of General DeWitt (which is dated June 5, 1943, but which was not made public until January 1944) is relied on in this brief for statistics and other details concerning the actual evacuation and the events that took place subsequent thereto. *The recital of the circumstances justifying the evacuation as a matter of military necessity, however, is in several respects,* particularly with reference to the use of illegal radio transmitters and to shore-to-ship signalling by persons of Japanese ancestry, *in conflict with information in the possession of the Department of Justice. In view of the contrariety of the reports on this matter we do not ask the Court to take judicial notice of the recital of those facts contained in the Report.*

> Petitioner's Exhibit AA, Memorandum of John L. Burling to Assistant Attorney General Herbert Wechsler, September 11, 1944 (emphasis added).

The footnote that appeared in the final version of the brief merely read as follows:

> The Final Report of General DeWitt (which is dated June 5, 1943, but which was not made public until January 1944), hereinafter cited as Final report, is relied on this brief for statistics and other details concerning the actual evacuation and the events that took place subsequent thereto *We have specifically recited in this brief the facts relating to the justification for the evacuation, of which we ask the Court to take judicial notice, and we rely upon the Final Report only to the extent that it relates to such facts.*

> Brief for the United States, *Korematsu v. United States,* October Term, 1944, No. 22, at 11.

The final version made no mention of the contradictory reports. The record is replete with protestations of various Justice Department officials that the government had the obligation to advise the courts of the contrary facts and opinions. Petitioner's Exhibit A-FF. In fact, several Department of Justice officials pointed out to their superiors and others the "willful historical inaccuracies and intentional falsehoods" contained in the DeWitt Report. . . .

. . . Omitted from the reports presented to the courts was information possessed by the Federal Communications Commission, the Department of Navy, and

From *Korematsu v. United States,* United States District Court, Northern District of California, 1984 584 F. Supp. 1406; reprinted in *American Justice: Japanese American Evacuation and Redress Cases,* ed. Nobuya Tsuchida (Minneapolis: University of Minnesota, Asian/Pacific American Learning Resource Center, 1988), 129–131.

the Justice Department which directly contradicted General DeWitt's statements. Thus, the court had before it a selective record.

Whether a fuller, more accurate record would have prompted a different decision cannot be determined. Nor need it be determined. Where relevant evidence has been withheld, it is ample justification for the government's concurrence that the conviction should be set aside. It is sufficient to satisfy the court's independent inquiry and justify the relief sought by petitioner.

✦ E S S A Y S

The following two essays examine the multiple perspectives of Filipino Americans and Japanese Americans during World War II. The first essay, by Theo Gonzalves, American Studies professor at the University of Hawai'i at Manoa, analyzes why some Filipino and Filipino American veterans believed they were fighting for freedom and the liberation of the Philippines while others viewed the war as an intracolonial conflict between the United States and Japan. Drawing on interviews with veterans in 1992, Gonzalves explores different interpretations of citizenship and obligation to the Philippines and America. The second essay, by historian Alice Yang Murray of the University of California at Santa Cruz, reviews the causes and consequences of Japanese American internment. Murray discusses the role of anti-Asian racism and hysteria following Pearl Harbor in the decision to intern Japanese Americans and describes conditions within the camps. The essay also recounts how conflicting views of cooperation, loyalty, patriotism, and protest tore apart the ethnic community during the war.

Filipino Veterans of World War II on Citizenship and Political Obligation

THEO GONZALVES

Leonardo de Guzman pushes up his glasses and wipes away tears from his eyes; a tiny American flag sits in the front pocket of his coat. The United States government originally promised citizenship for Filipino World War II era veterans like de Guzman, who served with armed forces in the Philippines. Such promises were to remain unfulfilled for almost fifty years. On December 16, 1991 de Guzman and 194 other veterans, the first batch of the estimated fifty thousand eligible, were sworn in as United States citizens. These men, who answered a call for the defense of their country, the Philippines, continued to fight additionally for nearly fifty years more—to become "Americans.". . .

This is a survey of two cohorts of veterans. From the Philippines, members of Philippine units are represented by men whose stories are similar to de Guzman's. From the United States, members of the First and Second Filipino Infantry Regiments are highlighted for their crucial and distinctive role in the United States' military history. Constituted specifically as a unit to be commissioned for duty in the Philippines, this under-heralded cohort clamored for a chance to liberate their

From Theo Gonzalves, "'We Hold a Neatly Folded Hope': Filipino Veterans of World War II on Citizenship and Political Obligation," *Amerasia Journal* 21, no. 3 (winter 1995/1996): 155–156, 158–164, 169–171. Copyright © 1995 Regents of the University of California. Used with permission.

"homeland." They would perform this service—and with distinction—in American uniform. My aim is to take up both cohorts simultaneously without erasing their respective historical locations in an effort to link the notion of belonging across colonial and neo-colonial formations. . . .

"We had to fight. We had to do something. That was our home."

Nearly a half-century after the imperial campaign in the Philippines, the United States reacted, now as a foe of Japanese imperialism. At the outbreak of war, the call to arms rang loudly among Filipinos residing in the U.S. From factories, farms, offices, university campuses, canneries—nearly one-third of the Filipino male population clamored for the opportunity to defend their homeland. "Remember Bataan!" was the rallying cry for the state-side Filipino, as he once again (echoing the Katipunero) summoned the trace of nationalism to counter imperialism. However, their peculiar legal status as "nationals" proved to be a delicate political issue for a whole generation of men, demonstrating the indeterminacy of what was afforded them under American "protection."

And while a handful of material has been written concerning the legal and political status, very little attention has been paid to Filipinos' orientations—personal, local, national *and theoretical*—concerning questions of political obligation and expectation. Thousands of Filipinos were unable to enlist because they were not citizens. Raising their protestations to the Philippine Commissioner and the administration in Washington, stateside Filipinos pressed for inclusion. They held local meetings, addressed inquiries to Washington, and eventually won the support of the U.S. President to allow for their service. Debates grew out of long-held racist attitudes against the Filipino. Many "Americans" argued that Filipinos should stay on farms instead of defending national interest. Less than a generation preceeding their service, Filipinos were seen as threats—both economically and socially—to American society. Despite vigorous anti-Filipino campaigns, especially nativist initiatives popular throughout the West coast, Filipinos fought exclusion.

On April 8, 1942, the First Filipino Infantry was activated in San Luis Obispo, California. As word of mouth spread, the infantry grew dramatically, achieving overstrength capacity, resulting in the creation of two regiments. At that moment, an ambiguity of national obligation surfaced among the new inductees. Who were they defending? The primary mission of the Filipino Regiments was to enter the Philippine theater with highly trained units of Filipinos. If they hoped to fight for the liberation of the Philippines, did they find contradiction wearing American uniforms? i.e., was a nationalism for the Philippines being asserted, or was the opportunity to serve the U.S. Armed Forces a logical progression of the civic orientation received from the Philippines?

On the other side of the Pacific, Filipino military units had already been under United States military control since the quelling of the Philippine "Insurrection" at the turn of the century. Originally organized against the U.S. military, the Philippine Scouts were reorganized under American auspices, with many rewarded for their loyalty and devotion to the "Americanos." The passage of the 1934 Tydings-McDuffie Act granted the Philippines its "independence" by 1946. The interim commonwealth government, inaugurated on November 15, 1935, raised indigenous military forces, receiving direction from the U.S. Army. Assuming control as military advisor to the

Philippines, General Douglas MacArthur established the Philippine Army in 1936. Ten years later, the War Department created the United States Armed Forces in the Far East (USAFFE), promoting MacArthur to Lieutenant General and commander of the Forces. As a vestige of resistance to colonial incursion in the form of localized militia, the peasant guerilla movement remained scattered throughout the Archipelago. Treated in memory either as marauders or as heroes, guerillas organized local resistance, sabotaged Japanese troop movements, and prevented confiscation of the rice harvests. For Filipino veterans who fought in the Philippines, national obligation surfaces as a question most poignantly *after* the war. President Roosevelt offered citizenship to those whose service benefited Allied forces and for those called into service at the request of Washington, such as the Philippine Army, guerillas, Scouts, and so forth. However, at the close of World War II, the American government provided for a narrow six-month window of opportunity for soldiers to apply for American citizenship in the Philippines. Frustrated by debates over a Philippine government's fear of mass migration from the country at the end of hostilities or the monetary drain on the American economy that was expected from a crush of applications for veterans' benefits, many veterans continued to press the courts and federal agencies to honor a long-forgotten commitment. The Second World War ineluctably provided the forum for the transformation of civic agency, a defining moment to articulate the multiple obligations of Filipinos—in the Philippines and in the United States. . . .

Before the War. The veterans approached the conflict with different occupational skills and levels of education. Those in the Philippines were more likely to have been attending or finishing school at the outbreak of war. Some were professionals who had just begun their careers. In the U.S., many had a variety of jobs, usually service-related, indicative of the low level of access to professional and non-professional jobs. With an economy thriving on racially segmented labor groups, Filipino Americans were often found "following the crop." Ernesto Balaga worked all over the country—in the canneries of Alaska, on the railroads of Montana, in an iron-plate molding factory in Chicago, on vegetable farms in Toledo, Ohio. But it was in Florida, while working on the fields, where he was drafted. From either side of the Pacific, these men approached agency in one of the most urgent forms, in defense of their "homeland." Filipinos witnessed the simultaneous attack on Pearl Harbor and the Philippines. The call to defense was clear.

Perceived Objectives of the War. This line of inquiry seeks a sense of how the veterans understood their purpose as soldiers in an international conflict. Eugenio Galarza's motives reflect a nationalistic urgency, citing the necessity "to defend your country against aggressors . . . and to defend our countrymen from tyranny." The location of his obligation is the Philippines. The Japanese attack made clear his mandate. Abstracting from Galarza's understanding, Hilario K. Linosa intellectualizes the conflict:

> It was a fight for supremacy between two ideologies, democracy on the one hand, and communism on the other. However . . . it was a veritable war of attrition wherein the belligerents were the losers and civilization the victim.

A law student prior to the war, Linosa served with the USAFFE. Balaga's perspective reflects familiarly propagated themes resulting from the U.S. involvement as well as his location as a soldier with the First Filipino Infantry Regiment:

Freedom is the most important thing here in America. Freedom, your freedom, my freedom, that's the best. . . . [It] is the most sacred thing we must keep.

Missing from Balaga's comments is an emphasis on the mission of national liberation as a central motivation for Filipinos. Instead, agency is driven by an abstracted notion of a "sacred" (American) freedom. Manuel Quiñones, however, injects this statement concerning the war's objectives: "I had no idea [what they were]. The war was not ours." Simmering under the nationalistic fervor in the Philippines is a nascent colonial—in this case, neocolonial—critique. From Quiñones's vantage, the war fought on Philippine soil had more to do with an intra-colonial conflict than with one between agents of democracy and communism. Yet attention during the war focused on the choice which many Filipinos felt compelled to address: between and "American democracy" and its pan-Asian, Japanese challenger.

Transitions of War. For many, the interruption of war proved to be irrevocably unsettling. Necitas Iglesias was a second year high school student when the Japanese began [the] Occupation. "The war destroyed my education. . . . After I got out of the Army in 1949, I wanted to get settled." The careers of many veterans, professional as well as academic, were often similarly affected. Indeed, the lessons afforded by the war provided a new perspective, replacing academic and professional training with the civic duty of the patriot. Veterans noticed attitudinal changes also occurring with respect to the Filipino presence in America's regular forces. Anticipating such changes, Fernando Taggaoa wrote:

> Oh Emancipating War! Gone will be the thousands of Filipinos, particularly in California, relieved of the brunt of prejudice and injustice. No more shall the illiterate workers be oppressed, exploited and made to live in shacks and hovels, for they will have gone to fight and die for their freedom. . . . By their hands will arise a New Philippines consecrated in the blood of Americans and Filipinos alike.

Describing the Filipino as "inconsequential" to the larger American polity, Taggaoa saw war as an opportunity to deliver the lot of Filipino Americans from political and social ambiguity. While Augusto Florencio believes that "war made the U.S. the most powerful nation," Balaga asserts that the contemporary success of Filipino Americans is due in large part to the war. Media attention reinvented the image of the Filipino in American memory: from the violent, lazy, (white) womanizing, foreigner seeking instant gratification through gambling, cars, clothes and taxi dances ("Little Brown Monkey"), to the hard-working, Christian ally from the Pacific ("Little Brown Brother").

Valuing American Citizenship. The veterans of the Philippine Army generally view the acquisition of citizenship positively. These men, some waiting nearly fifty years, persisted through numerous hearings before immigration boards and the legal system. The passage of the Naturalization Act of 1990 opened the door for many veterans to gain citizenship. For many, U.S. citizenship has meant "a chance for a new life," a "dream come true," or an opportunity to improve the lives of family members. Absent the legal designation, Quiñones imagines an attenuated relationship to a community which enlisted his service years ago. He has been unable to convince immigration and defense officials of his service without the proper written documentation: "I haven't crossed the bridge yet. By this time, I feel still as a 100% Filipino citizen. I still long for home."

The Duality of Obligation. Separating allegiances can be a difficult task. During wartime, this often becomes a necessity. Generations following the McCarthy era America muddled through a Cold War effectively dividing international interests for almost half a century. In the Philippines, resistance to Japanese occupation was coordinated by American officers. And in the United States, Filipino Americans reconstituted notions of "homeland." In response to the question, "Were you fighting for the Philippines, the U.S., or both? Guerrero speaks for nearly all of the participants' attitudes concerning a dually-constructed obligation: ". . . my mission was to serve *both* the United States and the Philippines in time of war." [Emphasis added.] Many responses also indicate how this Filipino and American "friendship" has been extended beyond its original construction at the turn of the century. This indication should be seen in light of the "special relationship" of American involvement with Philippine history at the beginning of the century. Negotiating an ambiguous symbiosis of their countries' histories of dependence and dominance, veterans have pointed out many shared experiences between the two: from Christianity to democracy to free market capitalism. However, the contest for Philippine independence left some veterans having to acknowledge the neocolonial subordinate relationship remaining in place, pointing out the consequences of being an American "ally." Quiñones, a member of the USAFFE, discusses this:

> Before the USAFFE surrendered to the Japanese, I believed I was fighting for the Philippines. When the Philippines was liberated by the American forces and the Filipino soldiers were ordered to report for military control at Palo, Leyte, I began to think that I was fighting for the U.S.

Iglesias, a member of the guerilla movement, echoes the sentiment:

> I thought I was fighting for my country. Only at that time our country was under the U.S. when I joined the Philippine Scouts. Ultimately, I had to serve the U.S., with loyalty, sincerity, and with my last blood. Luckily, life was spared on me.

Role Requirements for Citizenship and the Actualization of Citizenship Orientation. Thus far, veterans' comments speak to ambiguous national attachments, with varying degrees of personal obligation. Their commitments reveal the embedded "political unconscious" of the veteran's generation—how conflicting moments of resistance, neocolonial expansion and tutelage produced a wide variety of responses, from a personal and political wholesale identification with America to an urgent neocolonial critique of yet another military power. At the same time, many veterans recognize the stated promise of democracy, certainly a by-product of a transferred education system reflecting the cultural bias of its importer. Marcelo Abanda lists major components of American government: that it is democratic, that it has a triumvirated separation of powers across branches, that it attends to the welfare of the people, that it encourages scientific inventions, and that it promotes scientific explorations. However idealized Abanda's view on American government may be, the following responses concerning his understanding of Americans suggests a strong effect of exogenous tutelage. Americans, Abanda believes, are: "hardworking, scientifically minded, particular of time and health habits and practices, and *belong to the white race*" [emphasis added].

Indeed, the preparation of civic agency provided by American instructors in the Philippines underscores the possibility, if not the inevitability, of a *dualistic* obligation to the two countries. The American flag, a G.I.'s cigarettes, the military jeep—icons of a shared defense. The wartime struggle synonymously situated their identification as well. With the U.S. as his "adopted" country, Nestor Cereño felt lucky "to be under two flags."

> Opening the school [in the Philippines], we only sang the 'Star Spangled Banner' " and saw the American flag. There was no Filipino flag when I went to school. I think the Philippine flag was introduced—they called it the Commonwealth in 1916—when the American and the Philippine flag[s] [were] flying together; before that it was just only the American flag. . . .

Pedro M. Padua: This Side of the Diaspora

The discovery of 1st Filipino Infantry Regiment member Pedro M. Padau's essay, "Why Filipino-American Citizens?" adds to the discussion of a construction of citizenship. This piece highlights and precedes a growing tension with an American community, namely that of an intra-ethnic distinction between Filipinos and Filipino Americans. In his essay, Padua takes up a number of issues: the importance of cultural centers as sites of community development, greater exchange of information between the Philippines and the U.S., and a critique of self-appointed, self-serving community "leaders." Most important, Padua sketches an early genealogy of a Filipino American consciousness—politically invested on the U.S. terrain, and distinctive from a Philippine orientation.

Padau reflects on the Congressional discussion of legislation enabling Filipinos to attain full citizenship. In answering the question posed by the title of his essay, Padua identifies three groups of Filipinos, each expressing divergent opinions of and motivations to acquire American citizenship. *The super-nationalist* "despises the Filipinos, who become American citizens." Padua quotes an official from the Philippine Consulate General's Office. He finds it "unfortunate" that a government official would employ "coercion" in encroaching upon an "individual's moral judgments and decisions." Padua teases out a suspicion of the Philippine government official: that Filipino Americans are not loyal to the Philippines. An economic consideration has also been offered to explain the source of such a critique; namely, that the acquisition of American citizenship would result in the draining of the skilled labor from the Philippines. Thousands of able-bodied men and women, it was feared, would seek brighter prospects in America. Padua characterizes the *nationalist* as one who suffers from a severely colonized mentality. Insecurity concerning an American future working in tandem with "low self-worth," produces for the nationalist a tenuous connection to an American ethos. Padua sees in the nationalist simultaneously a dependence upon the Philippines for a source of cultural identity which is "fixed" and "authentic," while holding the United States as the standard for a "civilized people."

The *Filipino* (I take Padua to mean "Filipino American" in terms of the political sensibility and orientation discussed earlier) resonates, upon cursory inspection, with characteristics of more familiar articulations. For Padua, the Filipino is "rational, unbiased, and impartial." He emphasizes the importance of freedom of choice as an indication of the Filipino American citizen's newly acquired social currency. He is celebrating nothing less than what he sees as the emergence of a wholly new subjectivity. The above characteristics distinguish the Filipino American from his two previous examples. Both the super-nationalist and nationalist, he claims, speak to a subjectivity hopelessly attached to a Philippine national orientation. This is not to say that Padua's emphasis of rationality and individual freedom is a wholesale adoption of American classical liberalism. He writes,

> . . . the fact that they are citizens of this great country does not necessarily mean that their sentiments, aspirations and thoughts are entirely changed and Americanized. Like many other divergent ethnic groups here, they also have the freedom to call themselves Filipinos.

For Padua, freedom is not merely what pertains to the individual, but also to the collective. Submitted in his comments is an acknowledgement of the notion that the United States is as much a product of groups as much as it is the labor of the individual. Padua links this celebration of individuated (plural, not individual) democratic pragmatism with the "rich traditions and backgrounds" of Filipino Americans, arguing for the expression of ethnic identification remaining consonant with the attainment of citizenship. While celebrating the possibility of sustaining substantive communities of Filipinos in the United States as active participants in America's urban post-war future, Padua's parochialism ultimately forecloses an analysis of community-formation as a function of imperial relations between the U.S. and the Philippines. Susceptible to a chauvinistic privileging of the "Filipino American," Padua sacrifices too much in his analysis to the logic of "Americanization."

Afterword

Choices made during war are of great interest to students of American cultural history. The sophisticated political obligations as envisioned by . . . these veterans . . . suggests a number of points: that "citizenship" is not simply a matter of belonging to a single country (contrary to the classical contractarian doxa recited in Rousseau, Locke, and so forth); that struggles in the Philippines are synonymous with, though not necessarily identical to, Filipino Americans' struggles for the contestation of political identities and precious resources; and consequently, that these veterans share insurgent histories of service and sacrifice.

The Internment of Japanese Americans

ALICE YANG MURRAY

On the morning of December 7, 1941, Japanese Americans learned the shocking news that Japan had attacked Pearl Harbor in Hawaii. Like most Americans, they were stunned by the surprise assault that destroyed America's Pacific fleet. As Americans of Japanese ancestry, however, these immigrants and their children, American citizens by virtue of their birth in the United States, also feared retaliation.

Even before the smoke had cleared from the ruins at Pearl Harbor, Federal Bureau of Investigation agents began rounding up suspected "enemy aliens" throughout Hawaii and the West Coast. Most of those arrested were male immigrants put under surveillance a year before the attack because they were leaders of the ethnic community—Japanese Association officials, Buddhist priests, Japanese language teachers, and newspaper editors. In the weeks following the declaration of war, the FBI arrested more than two thousand of these Japanese immigrants and ten thousand immigrants from Germany and Italy suspected of belonging to pro-Nazi or fascist organizations.

The FBI interrogated these immigrants and sent those considered "dangerous" to internment camps administered by the Department of Justice. . . . The largest of these camps, the one in Crystal City, Texas, also interned many of the 2,264 Japanese Latin Americans deported from their countries so that the United States might exchange them for Americans held by Japan in 1942 and 1943.

The Justice Department camps held about 10 percent of all Japanese immigrants from the West Coast. Many of these immigrants questioned the fairness of the hearings. . . . All hopes of returning home, however, were dashed when they learned in March 1942 that all Japanese Americans on the West Coast would be interned in separate camps run by the War Relocation Authority (WRA).

Ultimately, 120,000 Japanese Americans, two-thirds of whom were citizens, were interned in one of ten WRA camps. Why did the U.S. government decide to remove and confine people from the West Coast solely on the basis of their Japanese ancestry? Most scholars now agree that this decision was not simply the product of wartime hysteria but reflected a long history of anti-Japanese hostility fueled by economic competition and racial stereotypes. . . .

The attack on Pearl Harbor and the rapid succession of victories by Japanese forces in the Pacific rekindled the embers of anti-Japanese sentiment. . . . As Americans struggled to make sense of these losses, news accounts of the attack on Pearl Harbor fanned the flames of hatred against Japanese Americans. Secretary of the Navy Frank Knox told the press of an effective "fifth column" in Hawaii, even though his official report contained no such charges. The report remained classified, and the government did nothing to allay the fears spawned by Knox's remarks as headlines blared "Secretary of Navy Blames Fifth Column for the Raid" and "Fifth Column Treachery Told." Further misleading the public and contributing to the "official" validation of sabotage suspicions were declarations by a committee of inquiry on Pearl Harbor, led by Supreme Court Justice Owen J. Roberts, that Japanese spies had helped the enemy during the "sneak" attack. Newspapers began reporting wild rumors about the bombing of Pearl Harbor as "facts." The *Los Angeles Times,* for example, announced that Japanese fliers shot down over Pearl Harbor were wearing class rings of the University of Hawaii and Honolulu High School. The paper even claimed that a Japanese resident painted himself green and "camouflaged himself so he could hide in the foliage and aid attacking Japs."

As reports of Pearl Harbor "treachery" proliferated, West Coast politicians stoked the fires of anti-Japanese prejudice and began clamoring for the removal of Japanese immigrants and citizens. . . The advocates of internment found a receptive audience in the commander of the Western Defense Command, Lieutenant General John L. DeWitt. In charge of protecting West Coast security, DeWitt was more impressed by the dire warnings of California politicians and Allen Gullion, provost marshall general for the army, than by reports from Naval Intelligence, the FBI and the Army General Staff dismissing any threat of sabotage, espionage, or invasion.

On February 14, 1942, DeWitt sent a memo to Secretary of War Henry Stimson recommending the removal of all immigrants and citizens of Japanese ancestry from the West Coast. DeWitt's memo declared, "The Japanese race is an enemy race," and "racial affinities are not severed by migration." Even second- and third-generation Japanese Americans who were citizens and "Americanized" could not be trusted, according the DeWitt, because "the racial strains are undiluted." Taking for granted that all "Japs" were disloyal, DeWitt concluded that the "very fact that no sabotage has taken place to date" was a "disturbing and confirming indication that such action will be taken."

Why did Washington accept DeWitt's recommendation? Members of the government who knew there was no need to remove Japanese Americans mounted a tepid response to the advocates of internment. FBI director J. Edgar Hoover wrote a memo to Attorney General Francis Biddle noting that the public hysteria was groundless. Biddle argued against mass exclusion at a luncheon conference with President Roosevelt. But neither one publicized their objections or criticized plans for mass removal on constitutional grounds. Once it became clear that the War Department and the president supported DeWitt's request, Biddle even proceeded to help implement the plans for mass removal.

President Roosevelt accepted Secretary of War Stimson's advice to endorse DeWitt's plans and ignored the advice of his own intelligence specialist. . . .

Instead, Roosevelt signed Executive Order 9066 on February 19, 1942, authorizing the War Department to designate military areas from which "any and all persons may be excluded." Although this order never specifically named Japanese Americans, it soon became clear that they would be the only group targeted for mass removal. DeWitt also wanted to exclude German and Italian "enemy aliens" from the West Coast, but his civilian superiors at the War Department overruled him. . . .

Individuals of Japanese ancestry in Hawaii were spared from mass exclusion despite the fact that the islands were more vulnerable to an invasion than the West Coast. The 158,000 people of Japanese ancestry in Hawaii were, however, viewed with suspicion and suffered special restrictions under martial law. "Enemy aliens" in Hawaii were required to carry a registration card at all times and endured travel and work limitations. Almost fifteen hundred "suspects" of Japanese ancestry were arrested and interned in camps run by the U.S. Army or the Department of Justice because of their activities within the ethnic community. Yet General DeWitt's counterpart in Hawaii, General Delos Emmons, recognized that Japanese labor was critical to both the civilian and the military economies of the islands. Japanese Americans made up less than 2 percent of the population of the West Coast and could be removed without much difficulty. But removing more than 35 percent of the population of Hawaii not only would be a logistical nightmare but also would cripple many industries needed for the war effort. . . .

DeWitt, by contrast, quickly implemented plans for mass exclusion on the West Coast. At first, he simply ordered Japanese Americans to leave Military Area 1, which consisted of southern Arizona and the western portions of Washington, Oregon, and California. Yet "voluntary evacuation" was short-lived because public officials in the mountain states condemned the prospect of their states becoming "dumping grounds" for California "Japs." If they were too dangerous to roam freely in California, why weren't they too dangerous to let loose in Idaho and Wyoming? With the exception of Governor Ralph Carr of Colorado, the governors of these western states unanimously opposed voluntary migration and urged that Japanese Americans be placed in "concentration camps."

Consequently, at the end of March, "voluntary evacuation" was replaced with what the government called a "planned and systematic evacuation." The government used such euphemisms to mask the fact that immigrants and citizens would be incarcerated behind barbed wire. Even the three thousand Japanese Americans who had moved from Military Area 1 to Military Area 2 in the eastern half of California, based on government assurances that this area would remain a "free zone," were forced into internment camps.

The Internment Camps

The government developed a two-step internment program. Japanese Americans were first transported to one of sixteen "assembly centers" near their homes and then sent to one of ten "relocation centers" in California, Arizona, Utah, Idaho, Wyoming, Colorado, or Arkansas. Most Japanese Americans had less than a week's notice before being uprooted from their homes and community. Instructed to bring only what they could carry, most had little choice but to sell businesses, homes, and prized possessions for a fraction of their value. Internment also disrupted educational and career plans. But for many Japanese Americans, the stigma of suspected disloyalty and the loss of liberty inflicted the deepest wounds. As one internee later recalled, "The most valuable thing I lost was my freedom."

A few Japanese Americans defied DeWitt's orders. Lawyer Minoru Yasui, still outraged by the internment of his father, Masuo Yasui, decided to walk the streets of Portland, Oregon, at night deliberately disobeying the curfew order. After failing to get a policeman to arrest him, he turned himself in at a police station so the he could contest DeWitt's authority in court. Yasui was soon joined by Gordon Hirabayashi, a twenty-four-year-old University of Washington student, who went to an FBI office to report his refusal to comply with removal orders. The third Japanese American to wage a legal challenge did not initially plan to be a protester. Fred Korematsu had simply wanted to remain in Oakland and San Francisco to be with his Italian American fiancée. But after he was discovered and arrested for violating the Army's exclusion order, Korematsu also decided to battle the government in court. Yasui, Hirabayashi, and Korematsu forced the Supreme Court to consider the constitutionality of the government's curfew and exclusion policies. When the Court affirmed the legality of the "mass evacuation," it established a legal precedent for the wartime removal of a single ethnic group that has never been officially overturned. Only in the case of Mitsuye Endo did the justices acknowledge a limitation to the government's powers to detain Japanese Americans. On December 18, 1944, the Supreme Court ruled in the Endo case that camp administrators had "no authority to subject citizens who were concededly loyal to its leave restrictions" and made it possible for at least some Japanese Americans to return to the West Coast.

Although a few individuals went to court to fight the removal and detention orders, most Japanese Americans complied with DeWitt's instructions. Few had any idea of their destinations when they were labeled, like luggage, with numbered identification tags at designated departure points in April and early May 1942. Most of the "assembly centers" were located at racetracks and fairgrounds, and many families stayed in hastily converted horse stalls that reeked of manure. Then, at the end of May, they were sent to camps run by the WRA, where barbed wire, watchtowers, and military police reminded them that they were prisoners who could not leave without the administrators' approval. Even those who received permission to leave the camps could not return to the West Coast until the exclusion order was lifted in December 1944.

Most internment camps were located on desert or swamp-like terrain. In some camps, winter temperatures dropped to 35 degrees below zero, and summer temperatures soared as high as 115 degrees. The hot and humid summers in the Arkansas camps bred swarms of chiggers and mosquitoes. The assistant project director of Minidoka, a camp in Idaho, described the camp as "hot, dusty, [and] desolate" and remarked on the "flat land, nothing growing but sagebrush, not a tree in sight." A WRA official noted a common problem in many camps: "a dust storm nearly every day for the first two months. . . . Fine, choking dust . . . swirled over the center. Traffic was sometimes forced to a standstill because there was no visibility."

Facilities differed from camp to camp, but all were spartan. Internees were assigned to a block consisting of fourteen barracks subdivided into four or six rooms. The average room for a family of six measured twenty by twenty-five feet. Privacy within the barracks proved elusive because room dividers often stopped short of the roof. Many internees, especially older women, were mortified by the lack of partitions in the communal bathrooms. Families constantly battled the dust that seeped through the barracks planks. The WRA supplied only canvas cots, a potbellied stove, and a lightbulb hanging from the ceiling. Resourceful internees later constructed makeshift furniture from scrap lumber and cultivated their own gardens to supplement the unfamiliar and unappetizing food served in the mess halls. Standing in line became an integral part of camp life. The WRA's assistant regional director once reported counting three hundred people waiting outside a mess hall.

At first, no internee could leave the center except for an emergency, and then only if chaperoned by someone not of Japanese ancestry. Regardless of education or training, Japanese American workers were subordinate to WRA personnel and received vastly lower wages of $12, $16, or $19 a month. For example, a WRA librarian might earn $167 a month, whereas her Japanese American staff members were paid only $16 for doing similar work. Moreover, wages and clothing allowances were often delayed, and the WRA failed to fulfill its promise to ship household goods to arriving internees. There were even rumors that WRA staff members at several camps stole food and other supplies.

WRA policies also exacerbated pre-existing tensions between Issei (first generation) and Nisei (second-generation) community leaders. The government named Nisei leaders in the Japanese American Citizens League (JACL) as representatives of the entire ethnic community. Even though this middle-class, second-generation organization had fewer than eight thousand members before the war, government officials were pleased by JACL ultrapatriotic statements praising "American Democracy," vowing cooperation, and expressing gratitude for benevolent internment

policies. Camp administrators accepted JACL advice to limit community government positions to citizens, to ban Japanese-language schools, and to prohibit the use
of the Japanese language at public meetings. Whereas JACL leaders believed that
cooperation, assimilation, and regaining the right to serve in the military were necessary to combat racism, many disgruntled internees, especially the disempowered
Issei, derided JACL leaders as "inu" or dogs who collaborated with the government
against the interests of the community.

As hostility toward the WRA grew, some internees vented their anger against
JACL leaders suspected of being informers. The arrests of individuals accused of
beating up suspected "inu" generated protests against the administration at the
Poston and Manzanar Camps at the end of 1942. When the project director at Poston
refused to release two men arrested for an attack, internees waged a general strike
that shut down most camp services. Deciding to negotiate with the strikers, camp
administrators agreed to release one suspect and to try the other within the camp
rather than in an Arizona court. In return, strike leaders agreed to try to stop assaults
against suspected "inu" and to promote harmony with the administration.

Similar protests at Manzanar, however, ended in bloodshed. The project director
summoned the military police to put down a mass demonstration calling for the
release of an arrested internee. When the crowd refused to disperse, military police
sprayed tear gas, which was ineffective due to the wind. A member of the crowd
started a car and aimed it at the police. While witnesses disagree about whether the
police began firing before or after the car was started, all agree that they opened fire
directly on the crowd, killing two people and wounding at least nine others. Even after the administration removed JACL leaders from the camp and moved suspected
agitators to isolation camps, tensions remained high.

Turmoil enveloped all of the camps in February 1943, when the WRA instituted a loyalty review program with little or no notice and without a clear explanation as to how the information gathered would be used. All internees over the age
of seventeen were told to fill out a "leave clearance" application, which included
ambiguously worded questions that confused many internees. Ironically, the WRA
mistakenly assumed that the internees would be grateful for this expedited "leave
clearance" program, which would allow them to move to the Midwest or East and
volunteer for military service. JACL leaders had fought for the opportunity to serve
in the armed forces and praised the War Department's decision to allow Japanese
Americans to volunteer for a segregated combat unit on January 28, 1943. But
many other internees resented being asked to shed blood for a country that had
imprisoned them.

Unaware of the depth of internee fear and anger, WRA officials were shocked
by the controversy generated by two of the questions on the leave application. Question 27 required internees to say whether they were "willing to serve in the armed
forces of the United States on combat duty, wherever ordered." Question 28 asked,
"Will you swear unqualified allegiance to the United States of America and faithfully defend the United States from any or all attack by foreign or domestic forces,
and forswear any form of allegiance or obedience to the Japanese emperor, or any
other foreign government, power or organization?" Taking for granted that both
questions would be answered positively, the WRA didn't contemplate how foolish it
was to ask elderly Issei to serve in combat. Some Nisei suspected that question 28
was designed to trap them into admitting an "allegiance" to the emperor they never

had. The injustice of asking immigrants ineligible for American citizenship to become stateless by forswearing "any form of allegiance or obedience to the Japanese emperor" was recognized only belatedly. But even after WRA officials rephrased these questions, some internees still refused to complete the "leave clearance" forms to avoid being force to resettle. After losing their businesses and property and being told that they could not return to the West Coast, some embittered internees were skeptical that they could start over in predominately white communities in the Midwest and East.

Although about some 68,000 internees answered the two loyalty questions with an unqualified yes, approximately 5,300 answered "no no" and about 4,600 either refused to answer or qualified their responses. One WRA staff member noted how difficult it was to distinguish.

> the No of protest against discrimination, the No of protest against a father interned apart from his family, the No of bitter antagonism to subordinations in the relocation center, the No of a gang sticking together, the No of thoughtless defiance, the No of family duty, the No of hopeless confusion, the No of fear of military service, and the No of felt loyalty to Japan.

Far from measuring "loyalty" to the United States or Japan, the questionnaire, another staff member noted, "sorted people chiefly into the disillusioned and the defiant as against the compliant and the hopeful."

Some of "the compliant and the hopeful" followed WRA procedures to leave camp for military service, jobs, or college programs. But of the almost 20,000 men in the camps who were eligible for military service, only 1,200 actually volunteered from behind barbed wire. Later, at the beginning of 1944, the Selective Service began drafting Japanese Americans. More than 300 men refused to comply with the draft while they and their families were still incarcerated. Many of these draft resisters served prison terms of two to four years, but they were pardoned by President Harry Truman in 1947. Other Japanese Americans agreed to offer "proof in blood" of their loyalty to the United States. Ultimately, approximately 23,000 Nisei, more than half from Hawaii, served in the 100th Infantry Battalion, the 442nd Regimental Combat Team, and the Military Intelligence Service during World War II. Fighting seven major campaigns in Italy and France, the 442nd suffered almost 9,500 casualties (300 percent of its original complement) and became the most decorated unit in American military history for its size and length of service. . . .

Other Japanese Americans left the camps through the WRA's "seasonal leave" program, developed in the summer of 1942 to address a shortage of farmworkers. In 1942 and 1943, more than eight thousand internees obtained work release furloughs. The WRA encouraged internees who passed the "loyalty test" to resettle in the interior states after February 1943. By December 1943, the National Japanese American Student Relocation Council was able to place more than two thousand Nisei in colleges in the Midwest and East. Then, on December 17, 1944, officials announced the termination of mass exclusion one day before the Supreme Court declared in the Endo case that the United States could no longer detain loyal citizens against their will. Once allowed to go back home, more than two-thirds of the internee population chose to return to the West Coast.

A significant number of "the disillusioned and the defiant, " however, remained in camps even after the war ended in August 1945. The Tule Lake camp in northern California, which had been transformed into a "segregation center" for "disloyals," did not close until March 1946. Approximately one-third of the eighteen thousand residents at Tule Lake were people the WRA deemed "disloyal"; another third were members of their families; and the final third were "Old Tuleans," who, when the camp was designated as a segregation center in 1943, chose to remain with the "disloyals" rather than be forced to move a second time. The combination of this diverse internee population and a repressive administration created an explosive atmosphere at the segregation center. On November 4, 1943, the Army was called in to quell a demonstration, took over the camp, and declared martial law, which remained in effect until January 15, 1944. In the last half of 1944, the WRA allowed "resegregationists," who demanded a separation of those wanting to leave the United States for Japan and those at Tule Lake for other reasons, to dominate the camp. Using rumors, beatings, and in one case murder, the resegregationists intimidated inmates considered "fence-sitters" or "loyal" to the United States. By the time the WRA brought the camp back under control, seven of every ten adult Nisei had renounced their citizenship.

The Department of Justice received more than 6,000 applications for renunciation of citizenship and approved 5,589 of them. This number represented 12.5 percent of the 70,000 citizens interned during the war. But even before many of these applications were processed, most of the "renunciants" tried to withdraw their requests. In fact, 5,409 citizens attempted to rescind their applications but the government ignored these attempts and proceeded with plans to deport these people to Japan. In August and September 1945, the renunciants who wanted to fight for their citizenship rights organized the Tule Lake Defense Committee and hired attorney Wayne M. Collins to represent them. Collins resisted pressure from the national American Civil Liberties Union to withdraw from the case and spent more than a decade fighting on behalf of the renunciants. In his suit, Collins argued that the Nisei had been coerced into renouncing their citizenship. He said that the government's forced removal and incarceration of Japanese Americans had subjected internees to "inhuman" treatment and extreme duress. To compound this injustice, the government had known about but had done nothing to restrain a small group of Japanese Americans at Tule Lake who terrorized many of the Nisei until they renounced their citizenship. Finally after fourteen years, citizenship rights were restored to 4,978 Nisei.

Perhaps the most tragic example of "defiance" against the authorities was opposition to the closing of the camps. Instead of celebrating the prospect of freedom, many demoralized internees demanded that the government continue to provide for them or at least increase the amount of assistance given to resettlers. Many were afraid to leave the camps after hearing reports of how Japanese Americans outside the camp were subjected to arson, vandalism, and even gunfire. Many Issei men in their sixties didn't relish the prospect of starting over and felt that they were "entitled to receive compensation from the Government for the losses which they experienced at the time of evacuation." Rejecting these calls for substantive redress, the WRA gave recalcitrant internees $25 and put them on trains back to their hometowns.

☙ F U R T H E R   R E A D I N G

Buaken, Manuel. *I Have Lived with the American People* (1948).

Bulosan, Carlos. *America Is in the Heart* (1946).

Chang, Gordon. *Morning Glory, Evening Shadow:Yamato Ichihashi and His Internment Writings, 1942–1945* (1997).

Collins, Donald E. *Native American Aliens: Disloyalty and the Renunciation of Citizenship by Japanese Americans During World War II* (1985).

Cordova, Fred. *Filipinos: Forgotten Asian Americans* (1983).

Daniels, Roger. *Concentration Camps, U.S.A.: Japanese Americans and World War II* (1972).

Daniels, Roger, Sandra C. Taylor, and Harry H. L. Kitano, eds. *Japanese Americans: From Relocation to Redress* (1986).

Drinnon, Richard. *Keeper of Concentration Camps: Dillon S. Myer and American Racism* (1987).

Duus, Masayo Umezawa. *Unlikely Liberators: the Men of the 100th and the 442nd* (1987).

Espiritu, Yen Le. *Filipino American Lives* (1995).

Hansen, Arthur A., and David A. Hacker. "The Manzanar Riot: An Ethnic Perspective," *Amerasia Journal* 2 (1974): 112–157.

Hansen, Arthur A., and Betty E. Mitson, eds. *Voices Long Silent: An Oral Inquiry into the Japanese-American Evacuation* (1974).

Hatamiya, Leslie T. *Righting a Wrong: Japanese Americans and the Passage of the Civil Liberties Act of 1988* (1993).

Hayashi, Brian. *"For the Sake of Our Brethren": Assimilation, Nationalism, and Protestantism Among the Japanese of Los Angeles, 1895–1942* (1995).

Hirabayashi, Lane Ryo, ed. *Inside an American Concentration Camp: Japanese American Resistance at Poston* (1995).

Hohri, William Minoru. *Resistance: Challenging America's Wartime Internment of Japanese-Americans* (2001).

Ichioka, Yuji, ed. *Views from Within: The Japanese American Evacuation and Resettlement Study* (1989).

Irons, Peter. *Justice at War: The Story of the Japanese American Internment Cases* (1983).

Kurashige, Lon. *Japanese American Celebration and Conflict: Ethnic Orthodoxy, Options, and Festival in Los Angeles* (2002).

Maki, Mitchell T., Harry H. L. Kitano, and S. Megan, Berthold. *Achieving the Impossible Dream: How Japanese Americans Obtained Redress* (1999).

Matsumoto, Valerie. *Farming the Homeplace: A Japanese American Community in California, 1919–1982* (1993).

Nakano, Mei. *Japanese American Women: Three Generations, 1890–1990* (1990).

Okihiro, Gary Y. *Storied Lives: Japanese American Students and World War II* (1999).

San Juan, E. *From Exile to Diaspora: Veterans of the Filipino Experience in the United States* (1998).

Spickard, Paul R. *Japanese Americans: The Formation and Transformations of an Ethnic Group* (1996).

———. "The Nisei Assume Power: The Japanese Citizens League, 1941–1942," *Pacific Historical Review* 52, no. 2 (1983): 147–174.

Takahashi, Jere. *Nisei/Sansei: Shifting Japanese American Identities and Politics* (1997).

Takezawa, Yasuko. *Breaking the Silence: The Redress Movement in Seattle* (1995).

Tateishi, John. *And Justice for All: An Oral History of the Japanese American Detention Camps* (1984).

Weglyn, Michi. *Years of Infamy: The Untold Story of America's Concentration Camps* (1976).

Wu, Judy Tzu-Chun. "Mom Chung of the Fair-Haired Bastards: A Thematic Biography of Dr. Margaret Chung, 1889–1959," Ph.D. dissertation, Stanford University (1998).

Yoo, David. *Growing Up Nisei: Race, Generation, and Culture Among Japanese Americans of California, 1924–49* (2000).

Yu, Renqiu. *To Save China, To Save Ourselves: The Chinese Hand Laundry Alliance of New York* (1992).

Yung, Judy. *Unbound Feet: A Social History of Chinese Women in San Francisco* (1995).

CHAPTER 10

Asian Americans and the Cold War, 1945–1965

World War II ended when Japan surrendered in 1945, but international affairs con-
tinued to have a major impact on the lives of Asian Americans. American diplomatic
relations with Japan and China in the 1950s provided a stark contrast with those
of the World War II era. Once a hated foe and an occupied country, Japan became
a vital friend of America in the "cold war" between capitalism and communism. The
United States established strategic bases in Japan to "contain" Communist aggression
in Asia, and U.S. military personnel brought back Japanese "war brides" to Amer-
ica. China, on the other hand, went from being a World War II ally to a Communist
adversary after Mao's victory in 1949. Tension escalated during the Korean War in
1950, when Chinese Communists joined North Koreans in combat against South
Korean and American forces. The popular media resurrected exclusion-era images of
"yellow hordes" bent on world conquest. The American government, however, distin-
guished between mainland Communist China and the Chinese nationalist forces, or
the Kuomintang, in Taiwan. Designating Asians as admissible refugees for the first
time, Congress passed the Refugee Relief Act of 1953 and provided 2,000 visas for
Chinese refugees approved by the government of Taiwan.

The intense ideological war between communism and capitalism during the late
1940s and 1950s also affected American immigration and naturalization policies.
Mindful of Communist indictments of American discrimination against minorities,
U.S. politicians began to call for the removal of racial barriers to immigration and
naturalization. The 1952 McCarran-Walter Act provided a mixed response to these
reform efforts. The act reaffirmed and extended the national origins quotas that
limited Asian immigrants to just 2 percent of the total number allowed entry each
year. Some Japanese Americans, however, praised the act for ending Japanese ex-
clusion, granting Japan a token annual immigration quota of 185, and allowing
Japanese immigrants to become citizens. As a result of changes in national and state
laws in the late 1940s and early 1950s, Asian immigrants were no longer relegated
to the status of "aliens ineligible for citizenship" or subjected to "alien land laws"
that denied them the right to own property. Yet although the McCarran-Walter Act
encouraged these reforms, it also promoted several repressive measures in the name of
protecting national security. A prime example of cold-war legislation, the act instituted

loyalty tests to prevent "subversives" from entering America. It also expanded the ideological and moral criteria for preventing admission to the United States and facilitating the deportation of "undesirable" immigrants.

Leftist Asian Americans were especially vulnerable in the 1950s, a decade in which Senator Joseph McCarthy led a witch hunt for Communist agents and the list of dangerous "subversives" came to include civil rights activists, trade unionists, and critics of the American government. Leftists mistrusted government motives in establishing a Chinese "confession program" in 1957. Ostensibly, the program was designed to help illegal immigrants from China who arrived during the exclusion era regularize their status. After admitting to having entered the country by fraud or misrepresentation, they would not face deportation as long as a spouse, parent, or child was a citizen or permanent resident. Some Chinese Americans, however, worried that officials would use these "confessions" to deport other "paper sons," especially those involved in leftist politics. In this period of heightened anxiety, some Chinese Americans even feared they might be interned during a conflict with Communist China after the 1950 Internal Security Act granted the attorney general the authority to "detain" suspected threats to "national security" during an "internal security emergency."

☙ D O C U M E N T S

The first three documents illustrate how the occupation of Japan and the expansion of military bases throughout Asia affected American perceptions of race and gender. In James Michener's 1953 novel *Sayonara,* Major Ace Gruver jilts his American sweetheart for being too independent and is drawn toward a passive Japanese woman who is eager to fulfill his every desire, even though her father and brother had been killed by Americans. An excerpt from this popular novel, included as Document 1, describes Gruver's fascination with actress/dancer Hana-ogi and his views of a supposedly exotic Japanese culture. Document 2, a 1957 poster for the movie adaptation of the novel, shows Hollywood marketing the romantic metaphor of a strong, virile, and masculine America rescuing a submissive and feminine Japan. This image of transcendent love is undermined by Document 3, the government testimony of a social worker that recounts the actual problems many "war brides" experienced in their home countries and America throughout the 1950s and 1960s.

The next two documents examine the impact of cold-war legislation on immigration and naturalization policies. In 1946 U.S. legislation granted Filipino and Indian immigrants the right to become citizens and reflected the government's commitment to cultivating anticommunist allies in Asia and South Asia. Document 4 consists of excerpts from President Harry Truman's speech explaining his veto of the McCarran-Walter bill, excerpted in Document 5. Truman criticized the measure, which was passed over his veto, for failing to eliminate the national-origins quota system that limited immigration from non-Western countries. Truman's speech and the actual legislation also show that Asian immigrants, unlike other immigrants, were counted not by the place of their birth or last residence but by their racial ancestry. Thus, an individual of half Indian ancestry who was born in Britain was included in India's immigration quota.

The last four documents illustrate the intense conflict within Asian American communities generated by the cold war. In Hawai'i, business leaders and conservative politicians used fears of communism to attack a growing labor movement and charged that a 1946 strike by sugar workers and a 1949 strike by the International Longshoremen's and Warehousemen's Union (ILWU) were instigated and controlled by Communists. Former Communist Ichiro Izuka's pamphlet *The Truth About Communism in Hawaii,* excerpted in Document 6, helped fuel these charges. Izuka, a former vice president of the

ILWU on Kauai, declared that he left the union because the Communist Party controlled the union, was loyal only to the Soviet Union, and was leading the workers astray. The House Un-American Activities Committee held hearings in Honolulu in 1950 and then indicted seven people for violating the Smith Act by advocating the overthrow of the U.S. government in 1951. In Document 7, Koji Ariyoshi, one of the seven arrested because he was the editor of the radical labor newspaper the *Honolulu Record,* denounced the indictment as an assault on union activism. Although the seven were convicted, the verdict was overturned in 1958 after the Supreme Court ruled that advocating revolution or government change was protected by the First Amendment. Battles between supporters of the Chinese Communist Party and supporters of the Kuomintang in San Francisco's Chinatown are revealed in Documents 8 and 9. In Document 8, Franklin Woo remembers how leftist Min Ching members were beaten up by Kuomintang supporters and investigated by the FBI throughout the 1950s. In Document 9, Pei Chi Liu describes why he helped found the Chinatown Anti-Communist League.

1. Novelist James Michener Portrays Romance Between Japanese Women and White Soldiers in *Sayonara,* 1953

It came unexpectedly. On a warm day in May I waited for Hana-ogi at the Bitchi-bashi but she did not appear and disconsolately I wandered down to the railroad station to purchase a ticket back to Itami, but as I approached the cage I saw Hana-ogi standing off to one side, holding a ticket in her hand and impulsively, even though we were in the heart of Takarazuka, she came to me and we went to the ticket cage together and we bought two tickets for a small town at the end of the line, and on this lovely day we walked for the first time through the ancient Japanese countryside.

Hana-ogi, unable to speak a phrase of English, and I quite as dumb in Japanese, walked along the rice fields and across the little ridges that ran like miniature footpaths beside the irrigation ditches. We nodded to old women working the fields, laughed at children, and watched the white birds flying. Hana-ogi wore her green and white kimono and her cream zori and she was a bird herself, the May wind catching at her loose garments and the branches of trees tousling her delicate hair.

Wherever we went the land was crowded. Where in Texas there would be one farmer here there were forty. Where the footpath in New Hampshire might be crowded with three people, here it was overwhelmed with fifty. There were no vacant fields, no woodlots, no mossy banks beside the wandering streams. On every foot of land there were people and no matter how far we walked into the countryside there were always more people. More than any day I ever lived in my life I treasure this day because I discovered not only Hana-ogi's enormous love but I also discovered her land, the tragic, doomed land of Japan, and from it I learned the fundamental secret of her country: too many people.

In Korea we used to joke about enlisted men who bought Japanese girls of sixteen or seventeen—a man could buy a young girl anywhere in Japan—and we thought it a horrible reflection on Japan, but today I saw that it would always be possible to find some Japanese farmer who would be eager to sell his daughter to a kind man, for if she stayed at home and had to fight for her share of the skimpy rice in the family bowl she could never do as well as if she went off with a man who could buy rice for her. All the problems we used to laugh about as being so strange—so unlike America—I saw explained this afternoon. The Japanese were no different from us. Their farmers loved their daughters exactly as Iowa farmers love theirs. But there was not enough land. There was never enough food.

I thank God for that May evening walking among the rice fields while the crickets droned at us, for if I had not seen this one particular old man tending his field I am sure that when I finally learned the terrifying truth about Hana-ogi I could not longer have loved her; but having seen this old man and his particles of soil I loved her the more.

He stood where a trail turned off from the main road, leaving in the joint a thin sliver of useless land that in America would have been allowed to grow up in burdock. In Japan this tragic triangle was a man's field, the sustenance of one man's large family. On this May night he was bent over the field, digging it to a depth of fourteen inches. The dug soil he placed reverently to one side until his tiny field was excavated. Then, as we watched, he took each handful of soil and gently pulverized it, allowing it to return to its bed. Pebbles he tossed aside and sticks and foreign things, and in the two days that followed this man would finger each item of his soil. Not for him a plow or a harrow, but the gnarled fingers and the bending back.

It is difficult for me to report these things, for I cannot explain how Hana-ogi explained them to me. By pointing, by gestures, by little pantomimes with the old man she explained that he was like her father except that her father's field—before the American bombs killed him—was slightly bigger. But her father had nine children.

It was breathlessly apparent to us as the sun sank below the distant hills that in terribly crowded Japan Hana-ogi and I were seeking a place in which to make love. There was now no thought of Japanese or American. We were timeless human beings without nation or speech or different color. I now understood the answer to the second question that had perplexed me in Korea: "How can an American who fought the Japs actually go to bed with a Jap girl?" The answer was so simple. Nearly a half million of our men had found the simple answer. You find a girl as lovely as Hana-ogi—and she is not Japanese and you are not American.

As we walked into the twilight we drew closer together. She took my hand and also took my heart and as dusk fell over us we searched more urgently from side to side. We were no more looking at the white birds or the old men bending over their fields. We were looking for a refuge—any kind of refuge—for we were desperately in love.

I remember that once I thought I saw a grove of trees, but they were houses, for random trees were not allowed to grow in Japan. Again Hana-ogi pointed to a barn, but it was occupied. In Japan there was not even spare land for love.

But at last we came to a structure that was familiar to me, two inclined massive poles with two more set across them at the top like an enormous capital A, flat at the point. It was the timeless symbol of a Shinto shrine and here there were trees, but as always there were people too. We watched them come through the towering A, stand silently before the shrine, clap their hands three times, bow and depart, the torn white paper and the rice ropes of the religion fluttering quietly in the wind above them.

Hana-ogi took my hand and led me past the shrine until we came to a grassy bank partially protected by four trees. Villagers passed ten feet from us and dogs barked nearby. Across the mound we could see the dim lights of houses, for there was no empty countryside as I had known it in America. There was no place where there were not people. But at last we had to ignore them and it seemed to me as I sank beside Hana-ogi in the May twilight that we were being watched by the million eyes of Japan.

I remember vividly two things that happened. I had no conception of a kimono and thought it a kind of wrap-around dress but when we embraced and it was clear that Hana-ogi intended that we love completely, I tried to undo this gossamer dress, but it led to another and then another and to still more and although we could not speak we fell to laughing at my astonishment. Then suddenly we laughed no more, for I was faced with the second vast occurrence of the day, for when in the fading light I at last saw Hana-ogi's exquisite body I realized with shock—even though I was prepared to accept it—that I was with a girl of Asia. I was with a girl whose complete body was golden and not white and there was a terrible moment of fear and I think Hana-ogi shared this fear, for she caught my white arm and held it across her golden breasts and studied it and looked away and then as quickly caught me to her whole heart and accepted the white man from America.

We returned at last to Takarazuka and as we approached that lovely place we went into separate cars and I waited long till Hana-ogi had disappeared across the Bitchi-bashi before I appeared on the streets, heading for the Marine Barracks. Mike Bailey was in the shower and when he heard me go by he yelled and brought me back to military life with a fearful bang.

He said, "Mrs. Webster saw me in Kobe today and asked me a lot of questions."

"About you and Fumi-chan?" I asked, nonchalantly.

"Don't play coy, son. About you and Eileen."

"What'd'j tell her?"

"It isn't so much what I told her as what she asked." He waited for me to press the point, but I called downstairs for some cold beer and he said, "She asked me if you were going with a Japanese girl."

I sort of gulped on my beer and Mike said promptly, "Of course I said no. You aren't, are you?"

I took another drink of beer and pondered a long time what I ought to say. Then the pressing desire to talk with someone overcame me and I said, "I've been walking with Hana-ogi. We must have walked for five miles and I'm so deep in love . . ."

Mike was a fine character to talk with at a time like this. He laughed and said, "I feel like a traitor, Ace, getting you into this. Hell, I'm the one who's supposed to be in love."

I said, "It hit me like a propeller zinging around when you aren't looking. Jesus, Mike, I tell you the truth, I'm desperate."

Mike laughed again and said, "No need for a guy to be desperate in Japan. If you can't cuddle up to Hana-ogi because she's an actress, there's always the Tiger of Takarazuka. Better men than you . . ."

I started to say boldly, "But we . . ." My voice trailed off and I ended lamely, "The stars came right down and knocked me out."

Mike looked at me quizzically, then said without joking, "Look, Ace, I know better than most men around here how sweet a Japanese girl can be. But don't get involved. For the love of God, Ace, don't get involved."

"I am involved."

"Mrs. Webster said the M.P.'s have instructions to pick up officers seen holding hands with indigenous personnel. That's a lovely phrase, isn't it?"

"I just don't give a damn, Mike. To hell with the M.P.'s (sic) and to hell with Mrs. Webster."

"I agree with you, Ace. But while I was talking with the general's main tank division her daughter came up and I got a good look. For Christ sake, Ace, that girl's a ravin' beauty. Why do you have to mess around with a Japanese actress if this Eileen is on tap?"

I put the beer down and stared at the floor. That was the question I had not wanted Mike to ask. I saw Eileen as I had known her at Vassar, bright, eager, a wonderful sport. I saw her that winter in Texas when her father was a colonel at San Antonio and I was at Randolph Field. Why hadn't I married her then? Why had she turned down the other young officers and insisted upon waiting for me? I felt like the announcer who asks the burning questions at the end of each radio program about breaking hearts, but I knew that you could turn my radio on the next day and still not get the answers.

I looked up at Mike and said, "I don't know."

He asked me directly, "Are you afraid of American women?"

I said, "I hadn't thought of it."

He said, "I've been over here a long time, what with one thing and another. I've watched lots of our men go for these Japanese girls . . . Hell, I wont' be superior about it. I do myself. Frankly and all kidding aside, Ace, I'd a damned sight rather marry Fumiko-san than Eileen. But I just wondered why you felt that way?"

"I don't feel that way. At least if I do I don't know about it. But why do you?"

"With me it's very clear. One thing explains it all. You ever had your back scrubbed by a Japanese girl? Not a bath attendant mind you. That's simple. But a girl who really loved you?"

"What's back scrubbing got to do with it?"

"Ace, either you understand or you don't."

"What are you driving at?"

"I'm trying to say there are hundreds of ways for men and women to get along together. Some of the ways work in Turkey, some work in China. In America we've constructed our own ways. What I'm saying is that of them all I prefer the Japanese way." He laughed and saw that I didn't entirely understand, so he banged his beer down and shouted, "All right! One easy question! Can you imagine Eileen Webster scrubbing your back?"

It was a crazy question, a truly hellish shot in the dark, but I could immediately visualize fat little Katsumi Kelly the other night, taking her sore and defeated husband into the bath and knocking the back of his neck and getting him his kimono and quietly reassuring him that her love was more important than whatever Lt. Col. Calhoun Craford had done to him, and I saw runty, sawed-off Joe Kelly coming back to life as a complete man and I had great fear—like Mike Bailey—that Eileen Webster would not be able or willing to do that for her man. Oh, she would be glad to storm in and fight it out with Lt. Col. Craford, or she would take a job and help me earn enough so that I could tell Lt. Col. Craford to go to hell, or she could do a million other capable things; but I did not think she could take a wounded man and make him whole, for my mother in thirty years of married life had never once, so far as I knew, done for my father the simple healing act that Katsumi Kelly had done for her man the other night.

2. A Hollywood Poster Sells Interracial Love and the Exoticism of Japan in the Film *Sayonara*, 1957

Hollywood celebrates interracial romance and the exoticism of Japan in this 1957 poster for the film *Sayonara.*

From Gina Marchetti, *Romance and the "Yellow Peril": Race, Sex, and Discursive Strategies in Holly-wood Fiction* (Berkeley: University of California Press, 1993), 127. PHOTOFEST/JAGARTS.

3. Social Worker Bok-Lim C. Kim Describes the Social Isolation and Alienation of War Brides (1947), 1979

Today there are an estimated 20,000 Asian women who have immigrated to the United States as wives of U.S. servicemen. These women are scattered all over the Nation and are largely invisible, both from our majority society and from Asian and Pacific American communities, because of their social isolation.

The immigration of Asian wives of American soldiers began in 1947 when the United States Congress granted immigration rights to Japanese wives of U.S. service-men stationed in Japan. This initial wave of Japanese wives was followed by Korean wives, and later by Vietnamese and Thai women. Intermarriage and immigration of Philipino wives of both U.S. Navy and civilian personnel have always been sizable because of prolonged U.S. presence in the Philippines.

Attitudes towards these unions range from caution to outright hostility among the relatives and home communities of Asian women and their American husbands. The attitude of the U.S. military establishment towards these marriages can be characterized as "negative." These attitudes and behaviors of the respective parties do not usually improve over a period of time and such negative reactions often con-tribute to or exacerbate marital problems such as spouse abuse, desertion, separation, and divorce. . . .

Communication within these marriages is greatly handicapped by the Asian wives' lack of proficiency in English and their unfamiliarity with lifestyles and val-ues in American society. The situation is further aggravated by their husbands' ignorance of and failure to learn about the language and culture of their wives.

The psychosocial isolation and alienation of the Asian wives are the result of social isolation and a language barrier which is often exacerbated by insensitivity or inaction on the part of their husbands and those around them who have failed to sup-port and guide Asian wives in dealing with their new environment. The Asian wife has left her family, friends, culture, everything with which she is familiar, when she immigrated to the United States. She was part of a family and community system in which she had status and roles which provided her with self-esteem. In new and unfamiliar surroundings, handicapped by her limited English and without anyone to guide her, she is helpless. She needs a supportive and caring person to teach, guide, and assist her in acculturation. Unfortunately, among the women and families who have been referred to me for services, the husbands have failed in this task. Often the husband is not even aware that such assistance and support are needed. He ex-pects a speedy and miraculous transformation of his wife into a competent wife and homemaker in her newly adopted land. He becomes impatient and frustrated with her helplessness and dependency, and with what appears to him to be her slowness in learning. He often becomes verbally and physically abusive toward his wife.

The couple's failure to anticipate these adjustment tasks and the temporary "role strains" generated by a wife's dependency are often key factors in marital dis-ruption, spouse abuse, and desertion.

From Bok-Lim C. Kim, "Military Wives/Emerging Roles of Asian Immigrant Women," in United States Commission on Civil Rights, *Civil Rights Issues of Asian and Pacific Americans: Myths and Realities,* May 8–9, 1979 (Washington, D.C.: U.S. Government Printing Office, 1980), 149–151.

Psychosocial isolation and alienation, which are the consequences of the failures mentioned above, also act as further hindrances to a host of other psychosocial adjustments for the couple or their children. I need not repeat the deleterious effect of alienation on the psychological well-being and on the social functioning of individuals and society. The only difference, in the case of Asian wives, is that their isolation and suffering are hidden and unknown to the majority society. Thus, remediation is not possible. The Asian wives must become full, participating members of our society as wives, mothers, and useful citizens.

As the common saying goes: Eastern and Western cultures and value systems are often diametrically opposed. Nowhere is such a difference more apparent than in the area of the management of conflicts and disputes in personal, social, and commercial transactions in the two societies. Contracts and agreements are sealed in legal written documents in the West, while similar agreements are consummated verbally in the East. Harmony and compromise (based upon the moral and ethical code in teachings of Confucius) are the ideals to which many Asian societies still aspire; resorting to court for settlement of conflicts is still frowned upon and despised in Asian culture. This explains the different mindset of Asian wives who must now deal with a different and highly complex legal system which regulates and often governs daily life in America, affecting even the most intimate marital and parent-child relationships.

Ignorance and lack of familiarity with the American legal system severely handicap the Asian wife and place her at a great disadvantage in this country. Asian wives whose husbands are still with the Armed Forces are unfamiliar with the rules and regulations that affect their lives, and, as a rule, do not know the benefits and privileges accorded to them as dependents of military personnel. The consequences of such ignorance include divorce without the woman's knowledge; loss of rights as a legal spouse; loss of child custody and financial support; in some cases, commitment to a mental hospital without knowledge or consent; threat of or actual deportation; loss of permanent residency; and loss of the opportunity to become a naturalized American citizen. I could even enumerate more of these dire and often tragic consequences of not knowing or not having a bilingual advocate who can protect these rights.

4. President Harry S Truman Vetoes an Immigration and Naturalization Bill, 1952

I want our residents of Japanese ancestry, and all our friends throughout the Far East, to understand this point clearly. I cannot take the step I would like to take, and strike down the bars that prejudice has erected against them, without, at the same time, establishing new discriminations against the peoples of Asia and approving harsh and repressive measures directed at all who seek a new life within our boundaries. I am sure that with a little more time and a little more discussion in this country the public conscience and the good sense of the American people will

From President Harry S Truman's Veto of McCarran-Walter Act (June 25, 1952), *Public Papers of the Presidents* (June 25, 1952): 441–447; reprinted in *U.S. Immigration and Naturalization Laws and Issues: A Documentary History* ed. Michael Lemay and Elliot Robert Barkan (Westport, Conn.: Greenwood Press, 1999), 226, 228–231.

assert themselves, and we shall be in a position to enact an immigration and natu-ralization policy that will be fair to all. . . . The bill would continue, practically without change, the national origins quota system, which was enacted into law in 1924, and put into effect in 1929. This quota system—always based upon assump-tions at variance with our American ideals—is long since out of date and more than ever unrealistic in the face of present world conditions. . . .

The only consequential change in the 1924 quota system which the bill would make is to extend a small quota to each of the countries of Asia. But most of the beneficial effects of this gesture are offset by other provisions in the bill. The coun-tries of Asia are told in one breath that they shall have quotas for their nationals, and in the next, that the nationals of the other countries, if their ancestry is as much as 50 percent Asian, shall be charged to these quotas.

It is only with respect to persons of oriental ancestry that this invidious dis-crimination applies. All other persons are charged to the country of their birth. But persons with Asian ancestry are charged to the countries of Asia, wherever they may have been born, or however long their ancestors have made their homes out-side the land of their origin. These provisions are without justification.

I now wish to turn to other provisions of the bill, those dealing with the quali-fications of aliens and immigrants for admission, with the administration of the laws, and with problems of naturalization and nationality. In these provisions, too, I find objections that preclude my signing this bill.

The bill would make it even more difficult to enter our country. Our resident aliens would be more easily separated from homes and families under grounds of deportation, both new and old, which would specifically be made retroactive. Admission to our citizenship would be made more difficult; expulsion from our citizenship would be made easier. Certain rights of native born, first generation Americans would be limited. All our citizens returning from abroad would be sub-jected to serious risks of unreasonable invasions of privacy. Seldom has a bill ex-hibited the distrust evidenced here for citizens and aliens alike—at a time when we need unity at home, and the confidence of our friends abroad. . . .

I am asked to approve the reenactment of highly objectionable provisions now contained in the Internal Security Act of 1950—a measure passed over my veto shortly after the invasion of South Korea. Some of these provisions would empower the Attorney General to deport any alien who has engaged in or has had a purpose to engage in activities "prejudicial to the public interest." No standards or definitions are provided to guide discretion in the exercise of power so sweep-ing. To punish undefined "activities" departs from traditional American in-sistence on established standards of guilt. To punish an undefined "purpose" is thought control.

These provisions are worse than the infamous Alien Act of 1798, passed in a time of national fear and distrust of foreigners, which gave the President power to deport any alien deemed "dangerous to the peace and safety of the United States." Alien residents were thoroughly frightened and citizens much disturbed by that threat to liberty.

Such powers are inconsistent with our democratic ideals. Conferring powers like that upon the Attorney General is unfair to him as well as to our alien residents. Once fully informed of such vast discretionary powers vested in the Attorney General,

Americans now would and should be just as alarmed as Americans were in 1798 over less drastic powers vested in the President. . . .

Native-born American citizens who are dual nationals would be subjected to loss of citizenship on grounds not applicable to other native-born American citizens. This distinction is a slap at millions of Americans whose fathers were of alien birth. . . . Children would be subjected to additional risk of loss of citizenship. Naturalized citizens would be subjected to the risk of denaturalization by any procedure that can be found to be permitted under any State law or practice pertaining to minor civil law suits. Judicial review of administrative denials of citizenship would be severely limited and impeded in many cases, and completely eliminated in others. I believe these provisions raise serious constitutional questions. Constitutionality aside, I see no justification in national policy for their adoption. . . .

In these and many other respects, the bill raises basic questions as to our fundamental immigration and naturalization policy, and the laws and practices for putting that policy into effect.

Many of the aspects of the bill which have been most widely criticized in the public debate are reaffirmations or elaborations of existing statues or administrative procedures. Time and again, examination discloses that the revisions of existing law that would be made by the bill are intended to solidify some restrictive practice of our immigration authorities, or to overrule or modify some ameliorative decision of the Supreme Court or other Federal courts. By and large, the changes that would be made by the bill do not depart from the basically restrictive spirit of our existing laws—but intensify and reinforce it.

These conclusions point to an underlying condition which deserves the most careful study. Should we not undertake a reassessment of our immigration policies and practices in the light of the conditions we face in the second half of the twentieth century? The great popular interest which this bill has created, and the criticism which it has stirred up, demand an affirmative answer. I hope the Congress will agree to a careful reexamination of this entire matter.

To assist in this complex task, I suggest the creation of a representative commission of outstanding Americans to examine the basic assumptions of our immigration policy, the quota system and all that goes with it, the effect of our present immigration and nationality laws, their administration, and the ways in which they can be brought in line with our national ideals and our foreign policy.

Such commission should, I believe, be established by the Congress. Its membership should be bi-partisan and divided equally among persons from private life and persons from public life. I suggest that four members be appointed by the President, four by the President of the Senate, and four by the Speaker of the House of Representatives. The commission should be given sufficient funds to employ a staff and it should have adequate powers to hold hearings, take testimony, and obtain information. It should make a report to the President and to the Congress within a year from the time of its creation.

Pending the completion of studies by such a commission, and the consideration of its recommendations by the Congress, there are certain steps which I believe it is most important for the Congress to take this year.

First, I urge the Congress to enact legislation removing racial barriers against Asians from our laws. Failure to take this step profits us nothing and can only have serious consequences for our relations with the peoples of the Far East. A major contribution to this end would be the prompt enactment by the Senate of H.R. 403. That bill, already passed by the House of Representatives, would remove the racial bars to the naturalization of aliens.

Secondly, I strongly urge the Congress to enact the temporary, emergency immigration legislation which I recommended three months ago. In my message of March 24, 1952, I advised the Congress that one of the gravest problems arising from the present world crisis is created by the overpopulation in parts of Western Europe. That condition is aggravated by the flight and expulsion of people from behind the iron curtain. In view of these serious problems, I asked the Congress to authorize the admission of 300,000 additional immigrants to the United States over a three year period. These immigrants would include Greek nationals, Dutch nationals, Italians from Italy and Trieste, Germans and persons of German ethnic origin, and religious and political refugees from communism in Eastern Europe. This temporary program is urgently needed. It is very important that the Congress act upon it this year. I urge the Congress to give prompt and favorable consideration to the bills introduced by Senator Hendrickson and Representative Celler (H.R. 3109 and H.R. 73765), which will implement the recommendations contained in my message of March 24.

I very much hope that the Congress will take early action on these recommendations. Legislation to carry them out will correct some of the unjust provisions of our laws, will strengthen us at home and abroad, and will serve to relieve a great deal of the suffering and tension existing in the world today.

Harry S Truman.

5. Congress Expands Immigration and Naturalization Rights for Asian Immigrants, 1952

Chapter 1—Selection System/Numerical Limitations

Sec. 201. (a) The annual quota of any quota area shall be one-sixth of 1 per centum of the number of inhabitants in the continental United States in 1920, which number, except for the purpose of computing quotas for the quota areas within the Asia-Pacific triangle, shall be the same number heretofore determined under the provisions of section 11 of the Immigration Act of 1924, attributable by national origin to such quota area: *Provided,* That the quota existing for Chinese persons prior to the date of enactment of this Act shall be continued, and, except for as otherwise provided in section 202(e), the minimum quota for any quota area shall be one hundred. . . .

[Sec. 202. (b)] (4) such immigrant born outside the Asia-Pacific triangle who is attributable by as much as one-half of his ancestry to a people or peoples indigenous to not more than one separate quota area, situate wholly within the Asia-Pacific triangle, shall be chargeable to the quota of that quota area. . . .

From Act of June 27, 1952: The Immigration and Nationality Act, 66 Stat. 163; reprinted in *U.S. Immigration and Naturalization Laws and Issues: A Documentary History* ed. Michael Lemay and Elliot Robert Barkan, (Westport, Conn.: Greenwood Press, 1999), 220–223.

Sec. 203. (a) Immigrant visas to quota immigrants shall be allotted in each fiscal year as follows:

(1) The first 50 per centum of the quota of each quota area for such year, plus any portion of such quota not required for the issuance of immigrant visas to the classes specified in paragraphs (2) and (3), shall be made available for the issuance of immigrant visas (A) to qualified quota immigrants whose services are determined by the Attorney General to be needed urgently in the United States because of the high education, technical training, specialized experience, or exceptional ability of such immigrants and to be substantially beneficial prospectively to the national economy, cultural interests, or welfare of the United States, and (B) to qualified quota immigrants who are the spouse or children of any immigrant described in clause (A) if accompanying him.

(2) The next 30 per centum of the quota for each quota area for such year . . . shall be made available for the issuance of immigrant visas to qualified immigrants who are the parents of citizens of the United States, such citizens being at least twenty-one years of age or who are unmarried. . . .

(3) The remaining 20 per centum of the quota . . . shall be made available . . . to qualified immigrants who are the spouses or unmarried sons or daughters of aliens lawfully admitted for permanent residence. . . .

(e) Every immigrant shall be presumed to be a quota immigrant until he establishes to the satisfaction of the consular officer, at the time of application for a visa, and to the immigrant officers, at the time of application for admission, that he is a nonquota immigrant. Every quota immigrant shall be presumed to be a nonpreference quota immigrant until he establishes to the satisfaction of the consular officer . . . that he is entitled to a preference status under paragraph (1), (2), or (3) of subsection (a) or to a preference under paragraph (4) or such subsection. . . .

Chapter 2—Nationality through Naturalization

Sec. 311. The right of a person to become a naturalized citizen of the United States shall not be denied or abridged because of race or sex or because such a person is married. Notwithstanding section 405(b), this section shall apply to any person whose petition for naturalization shall hereafter be filed, or shall have been pending on the effective date of this Act.

Sec. 312. No person except as otherwise provided in this title shall hereafter be naturalized as a citizen of the United States upon his own petition who cannot demonstrate—

(1) an understanding of the English language, including the ability to read, write, and speak words in ordinary usage in the English language. . . .

(2) a knowledge and understanding of the fundamentals of the history, and of the principles and form of government, of the United States.

Sec. 313. (a) Notwithstanding the provisions of section 405(b), no person shall be naturalized as a citizen of the United States—[the act lists subsection (1) through (6) which prohibit the naturalization of anarchists, communists, totalitarians, and those who believe or publish such, etc.]. . . .

Sec. 316. (a) No person, except as otherwise provide for in this title, shall be naturalized unless such petitioner, (1) immediately preceding the date of filing his petition for naturalization has resided continuously, after being lawfully admitted for permanent residence, within the United States for at least five years and during the five years . . . has been physically present therein for periods totaling at least half of that time, and who has resided within the State in which petition is filed for at least six months, (2) has resided continuously within the Untied States from the date of the petition up to the time of admission to citizenship, and (3) during all the periods referred to in this subsection has been and still is a person of good moral character, attached to the principles of the Constitution of the United States, and well disposed to the good order and happiness of the United States.

6. Former Communist Party Member Ichiro Izuka Denounces Communists in Hawai'i, 1947

Wherever I go in these Islands, I find people who are disturbed by all the rumors and the radio propaganda about Communists in Hawaii. Some think every labor leader who fights for better wages and working conditions is a Communist. Others who calls themselves liberals scoff at the idea that Communists have influence in Hawaii Nei. The Communists themselves are loud in their assertions that talk of Communism is merely anti-labor, red-baiting.

You good people need to know the truth about the Communist situation in Hawaii. You need to know where and how they operate. Hawaii must wake up. **Especially union members must wake up.** If you are a union member it is exceedingly important that you know what the Communist Party is, and whether Communists are in your union today, getting control over its membership and property.

I am an ex-Communist. I know what the Party in Hawaii is doing. I know it from the inside. Only last November I left it after nine years association with the Communists named in the pages which follow. I was treasurer of the Communist cell to which I once belonged, and was also an active worker on Kauai while I lived there, having joined the Party in 1938 while I was an employee of Kauai Terminal, Ltd. at Port Allen.

I believed in the sincerity of the Party's efforts to help the workers of Hawaii. I knew how much they needed help, and I mistakenly thought the Party was the only place to aid them. My faith was strong for a long time, but this story will tell you how it was undermined. I see the Party now as it really is, a conspiratorial party, working against the welfare of the people of my native Islands.

Because of all that I did to strengthen the Party in the days of my blindness, I desire now to tell you the truth of my experience whatever the consequences may be to myself. You must know what is among you before it is too late. This is my warning.

During these months when I have been openly opposing the Party there have been threats against me, and my character has been attacked. When this story is printed the threats and lies will increase on every side. There may be libel suits. Hate is a weapon the Party knows how to use and does use to the fullest extent.

From Ichiro Izuka, *The Truth About Communism in Hawaii,* preface, pp. 30-31, © HFAF, 1947.

But here is the truth about Communism as I know it in Hawaii. . . .

I quit the Communist Party because it is not **honest** with the workers. With Adolph Hitler, the Party believes that the lie is a very useful means for gaining its ends. The bigger the lie, the better it works. The Communists propagandize the workers with any story, true or false, which aids their cause. Just as the Kremlin tells the Russian people it was the Soviets alone who defeated the Japanese, so the Communists have now told their victims in the pineapple unions, not that they lost a strike, but that they won a lockout. What an insult to the intelligence of our Hawaiian workers!

The Party has never undertaken a broad American style of program of worker education. The Party does not want an intelligent, well-informed rank and file in the unions. The Party will do the thinking for the masses. All the Party wants are handpicked Charlie McCarthys who know how to carry out orders. Prospective victims are sent to San Francisco for training and indoctrination. Then they come back to the paid positions in the unions.

Moreover, the Communist Party is not interested in the workers in Hawaii as human beings or as individuals. Nor is it interested in this community as a place in which to grow up and live. It is merely interested in Hawaii as a favorable battle ground on which to wage the class struggle and win converts to Communism. Its loyalty is not to Hawaii or to America, but to the Soviet Union. For this reason it will sacrifice American men and women, even its own existence as a "local party," if Soviet policy and needs so dictate.

Communist Party leaders, always deceitful and contemptuous of truth, will denounce anyone opposing their program or methods as a "fascist" or "enemy of labor." Character assassination and vilification are their standard weapons and they are ever alert to use them to shift the spot light from themselves.

But the truth comes out despite their frantic efforts to cover up and fabricate. The American people including the rank and file of labor are beginning to see the light.

I served the Hawaiian labor movement proudly and faithfully and believe in the American labor movement and social progress. Our American trade unions must be preserved. They are a vital part of our democracy but the termites who would undermine and destroy them must be exposed if democracy is to survive.

The rank and file Hawaiian workers, now innocent pawns of the Communist Party, must free themselves of the Communist leadership whose first loyalty is not to the American labor movement but to the political doctrines and policies of the Soviet Union.

I am hoping that they will not wait too long.

The Communist Party in Hawaii is a secret, underground organization. It works in the dark—fears the light of day. It takes advantage of the simple faith of our people and of their lack of knowledge and experience. We do not need that kind of influence in our growing Hawaiian democracy. Indeed, it is a serious threat to our American ideals, for it makes a mockery of democratic action and subverts it to its undercover objectives.

For these reasons I am doing my bit in exposing the Communist Party of the United States of America as it operates in the Territory of Hawaii.

7. *Honolulu Record* Editor and Labor Leader Koji Ariyoshi Describes the Arrest of Seven Suspected Communists in Hawai'i (1951), 2000

The early morning arrest of seven members of this community, including the editor of the *Record,* raises the curtain in Hawaii on the intensified campaign to stifle independent thinking and free speech, a suppression which is becoming more urgent in the whipped-up war program, highly profitable to the big employers but not popular with the great masses of the people.

The attack upon the constitutional rights of the seven individuals who are charged under the notorious Smith Act of advocating certain ideas, but not of committing any overt act of crime, comes at the crucial moment of the sugar negotiations between Hawaii's Big Five and the ILWU [International Longshoremen's and Warehousemen's Union]. On Lanai, 750 workers are on strike, and have been now for more than half a year, and Hawaiian Pineapple Company is letting a $25,000,000 crop rot to break the union.

One of the seven is the ILWU regional director. The others have been alleged by fingermen, stool pigeons and disgruntled former labor leaders to have influenced the policies of the union, a union in whose democracy its participating members take great pride.

As the longshoremen from Maui have already said, this is a move to discredit the ILWU which, nationally and locally, has not kow-towed to the war mobilization program that results in higher taxes and less pork chops, while destruction and death take place far from our shores to keep the pumps primed for the highly profitable war industry that benefits only big employers.

The arrest of the seven is said to fall into the "national pattern" by Justice Department propagandists. It is significant that the top publicity man of the Justice Department was brought here to drum up the allegation of "conspiracy" and the teaching of the overthrow of the government by force and violence.

Such preparation of the propaganda barrage was necessary to strike fear into the people, even after all these years of red-baiting the labor movement, particularly the ILWU, in order to isolate the leadership of the union from the membership, and the union itself from the rest of the island community.

A large segment of the people who have had close association with the seven must realize from their own experiences that the allegation of teaching the overthrow of the government by force and violence is fantastic. Subscribers to the *Record* have read views of the editor as expressed in the editorial column week after week for more than three years. . . .

What is this "national pattern"? Those who ride the bandwagon of the witch-hunters say it is the arrest and incarceration of Communists, alleged Communists and non-conformists.

From *Kona to Yenan: The Political Memoirs of Koji Ariyoshi* by Koji Ariyoshi, pp. 1–5, © 2000 University of Hawaii Press. Used with permission.

Photograph of six suspected Communists and their lawyer. The six were arrested in 1951, convicted in 1953, and had their convictions overturned in 1958. *Right to left:* Dwight Freeman, John Reinecke, Koji Ariyoshi, Jack Kimoto, lawyer Richard Gladstein, and Charles and Eileen Fujimoto.

Let us look at the picture from the other side and ask a few questions: "Why the arrests?" "What crime or crimes harmful to the populace have these people committed?" "What purpose and whom do the arrests serve?"

Actually, the "national pattern" today is the attack against trade unions, the buying off of some top leaders, attempting to crush militant unions that do not conform, loyalty purges, a war scare to condition the people for continued mobilization, unprecedented profits for big industrialists and financiers whose key men run the government. We have big steals in war contracts, corruption and graft in government even involving the President's immediate staff—now the chairman of the National Democratic Party is implicated.

All these go on as the industrialists, who postponed a recession setting in two years ago by the war program, grab profits in the most ruthless manner. They dodge taxes, get plants built free with taxpayers' money, and constantly fight to raise taxes of the low-income earners, 10,500,000 families of whom live, according to a recent government report, on less than $2,000 a year.

From Richard Borreca, "Fear of Communist Infiltrators Engulfed Postwar Hawai'i, *Honolulu Star-Bulletin,* October 18, 1999. Provided by The *Honolulu Advertiser.*

More and more people are beginning to realize that the war program is a phony, despite the increasing attempts to instill fear and timidity to voice their disapproval. . . .

Now, what has the *Record* done to bring similar attacks upon its editor? It is not a Big Five controlled newspaper. Last week, for instance, it reported that Davies & Company is laying off its 25-year men, all of Japanese ancestry. No other newspaper has reported this major news in the community where job security is disdainfully ignored by big employers. The *Record* has criticized plantation conditions and has brought about improvements in housing on certain plantations. And the *Record* is the only newspaper that supports unions and the workers in the Territory.

The jailing of its editor will not suspend its publication. There will be others to carry on, and there being no monopoly of ideas, there are many more coming up who will see the injustices in these islands and raise their voices against them in order to improve conditions. . . .

The hope lies in the people, here and on the Mainland. We have deep faith in them to struggle for progress. It is the duty of those who understand the situation, including those who have been silenced, to awaken the conscience of the whole populace.

8. Franklin Woo Remembers Attacks on Chinese Immigrant Leftists Who Supported Communist China (1950s), 1973

[B]y 1947 I gradually realized more and more the corruption and ineptness of the Nationalist government. I felt that it was crumbling, certainly China needed a change. At the time, the Communists were the only ones who could promise that kind of change, that kind of honest government. And China needed an honest government.

I think by 1949 it was clear to most people in Chinatown that Chiang [Kai-shek] was going to lose the civil war, and I would say that many of us wanted a new government for China by then. You know, there had always been criticism of Chiang in some of the Chinatown papers, papers which I began reading myself by that time, and there was a lot of enthusiasm, actually a lot of knowledge, about Mao's writings among the leftist groups of students and workers at that time. Well, in October 1949, when the People's Republic had just been established, I heard that the Chinese Workers' Mutual Aid Association was going to hold a celebration of the victory as part of its twelfth anniversary program. . . .

That night, October 9, the celebration drew a full house. I would say about five hundred people showed up at the CACA [Chinese-American Citizens Alliance] hall and we filled the whole place, even the balcony. It was a pretty exciting moment, actually. There were a lot of new faces, including workers from the Longshoremen's Union. But during the second speech we heard a shout from the door, then all of a sudden two lines of men ran through the aisles to the speakers' platform, tore down the red flag, knocked over the vases of flowers, and began throwing some kind of

Excerpt from *Longtime Californ'* by Victor G. Nee and Brett de Bary Nee. Copyright © 1973 by Victor G. Nee and Brett de Bary Nee. Used by permission of Pantheon Books, a division of Random House, Inc. pp. 213–217.

blue dye around the audience. There was some scuffling and I remember one Caucasian guy who tried to protect a poster got beat up pretty badly, he got a broken rib. The men didn't stay long, though, maybe about five minutes, and there were just twenty of them. I guess it was because it came so suddenly, and when everyone was caught up in the excitement of beginning the celebration, that it kind of caught us off guard and we panicked. After about fifteen minutes we pulled ourselves together, somebody began singing the "March of the Volunteers," the Chinese national anthem, and we all joined in. But by that time a lot of people had left because the thing shook them up. The rest of us stayed and continued the program. Jerry Ja finished his speech. Then William Kerner spoke about the founding of a new, democratic China. It wasn't until I heard the Yellow River Cantata that I felt a spirit of celebration again. Then we all went home. . . .

. . . You see, the Kuomintang had had the upper hand in Chinatown since the Second World War. We were only students in the *Min Ching* and besides, we only had about forty active members. The Chinese Workers' Mutual Aid Association, even though they must have had about five hundred members, were nowhere near being strong enough to take on the Six Companies, the family associations, the merchants, and the Bing Kung Tong. They were just much stronger than the left. Then in a few years, with the McCarthy terror, the Chinese army in Korea, and this immigration business, they had all the cards. You know, a lot of the people in *Min Ching* came in on false papers. Obviously, they played that to the hilt. So in a few years, the left was just smashed.

The McCarthy terror didn't affect Chinatown as much as it could have, I guess, but still I was very careful about circumventing things when I talked. You had to make sure you didn't sound anti-American. Actually, I think the Korean war had a greater impact on Chinatown than McCarthyism. The whole atmosphere here then was fear. If you weren't careful, you could be thrown into a concentration camp. That was when the FBI stepped up its activities in Chinatown. The only left-wing paper, the *Chinese Weekly,* folded then under the new pressure. The Chinese Workers' Mutual Aid Association also began to fall apart about that time, although it didn't disband completely until 1956. A lot of the men there were hounded by the immigration service and a couple were deported. The *Min Ching* kept up its weekly discussion periods down in our basement on Stockton Street. We continued our Mandarin classes, dance group, choir, plays, even though we were all getting more and more apprehensive. We knew the FBI was keeping a close eye on us, and we even suspected there was an informer among us. I guess that's one thing all of us feel bad about now, that we had to be suspicious of each other. The FBI people began coming to our homes, going to talk to our relatives, friends, where we worked. I guess when they got the Immigration Office working on us, though, we knew the *Min Ching* was coming to an end. I remember the immigration people would stop *Min Ching* members on the street and demand to see their papers, just to harass us. Once they discovered somebody had false papers, they would begin proceedings for deportation. I guess I've never been able to explain that well to people who haven't experienced it, how painful this immigration harassment can be to Chinese. Say, if a *Min Ching* member is discovered to have false papers, his whole family will be affected because probably they didn't have the proper papers either. So they'll go from you, to the uncle who brought you in, his wife, and it

Immigration and Naturalization Service officials investigate Seattle's Chinatown, 1963.

goes on and on. Well, too many of us had illegal entries somewhere along the line. It wasn't a quick thing or a big decision. People just slowly stopped coming down to the basement. A couple of people every few months. Then we'd lose touch with people who had dropped out, although some of us have still kept up our friendships, I

From *Annual Report of the Immigration and Naturalization Service, 1963* (Washington, D.C.: U.S. Government Printing Office, 1963).

guess my closest friends are the three or four members I still see. But by 1958 the lease on the basement had run out, the Anti-Communist League had pressured the owner not to renew, and there weren't enough of us left anyway to make it worth keeping. In the end, just a few people were actually deported. But I know former *Min Ching* members who even today have no permanent residence status because of their *Min Ching* affiliation. They just live here as stateless people.

9. Pei Chi Liu Recalls Why He Campaigned Against Communism as a Leader of the San Francisco Chinatown Branch of the Kuomintang Party (1950s), 1973

All through the Second World War the people in Chinatown were supporting the government in China, they were sincerely supporting it. The Six Companies organized fundraising, and the Chinese people here sent more than twenty million dollars to China. Medicine, too. Then when the Communists took over, the people in Chinatown hated this, but they didn't know what to do. After the takeover, they just received a letter from the government, but they didn't know about Communists. What were Communists to them? They felt there was no hope. Then the Communist propaganda came, on radio broadcasts, in the newspapers, and it began to affect people here, too. Our newspaper was still against the Communists, but after a while our business went down. People bought the *Chinese World,* got all the news from the Communists, and they were affected by the propaganda. Our *Young China Daily's* business went down. After two years, the Communists decided no Chinese people could come to Hong Kong, and they purged all the people. People here received letters that their relatives had been killed by the Communists. Then they all knew what communism meant. I knew that. I told the people at first but they didn't believe me.

There really wasn't much of an organized group that supported the Communists during the civil war. Mainly it was just individuals. I remember, by October 1949, the Communists had taken over more than ninety percent of China. Their troops were making inroads to Canton City. The Chinese Communist supporters here, not many, just about one or two hundred people, were very happy. On October 9, they rented the CACA [Chinese American Citizens Alliance] Hall to hold a celebration of Communist victory in China. But some of our people went inside and beat them, you know, knocked them down. . . .

Of course, as a member of the Kuomintang committee I was very much concerned about the situation in 1949. But for a while there was nothing much I could do. I just tried to report the news correctly, even when our circulation went down. It wasn't until the Korean War that I had a chance. Before the Korean War I hadn't said much, but after the Chinese Communists crossed the Yalu River, I could see the Communists were coming up. Even the American people began to be afraid. There was a lot of trouble in Chinatown with people looking for communists among us. Some people stopped coming to Chinese restaurants. The Six Companies was searching for a way to show that the Chinese are not all communists. I saw a good chance to organize. Do you know Mr. Doon Wong? He was a member of the Six Companies, a big member. I suggested to him that we should set up an anti-communist league in Chinatown to prove to the American people that we are against communism. He talked to all the other members, and after that it was easy to organize. Each organization in Chinatown sent two representatives to the first meeting. Then Los Angeles and many Chinatowns in the United States set up their own organizations.

The primary aim of the league was to let the American people know that the Chinese are not communists. The other thing was to rally all overseas Chinese people against the Communists and to support the Republic of China.

Mr. Doon Wong helped me. He's in the Kuomintang, and he's been my partner all these thirty years. Since 1940, he has been manager of this newspaper. I was editor-in-chief. He's a very important man in Chinatown, you know. When there are big problems, big things, people always ask Mr. Wong to help. He's the leader of the Chinese people here. The Chinese people believe in him. His name is very well-known.

You see, one thing is he has a big family, a big district. He's from Toishan. In the Kuomintang he represents Toishan, too. This gives him a lot of influence with the government of China. They believe in him, and they gave him a very high official position in the government—National Political Advisor to Chiang Kai-shek. So he's a member of the National Assembly of Taiwan, representing the Chinese people here. And then, he's a member of so many other groups! He's an elder in the Bing Kung Tong. And three days ago, when there was a convention in Los Angeles, he was elected president of the Wong Family Association. He didn't want to do it, you know. But there were too many candidates, and he was the only one who could beat all of them. They made him president to settle the dispute.

He's something more powerful than even the president of the Six Companies. The president changes every two months, you know, so it's not so important. The permanent influence is on the Board of Directors. They decide everything the president carries out. Mr. Wong is on that. And he represents the Ning Yung District Association, which happens to be the largest district association in the United States. So he has the main power there. He's quite popular and everyone usually agrees with him.

ESSAYS

The first essay, by Paul R. Spickard, professor of history at the University of California at Santa Barbara, analyzes why America's military, economic, and cultural power in Asia cultivated the growth of interracial marriages and recounts the discrimination "war brides" endured in both Asia and the United States. In the second essay, Arleen de Vera, assistant professor of history at the State University of New York at Binghamton, describes the persecution of Filipino immigrant union leaders accused of being Communists during the McCarthy era. De Vera shows how these attacks eroded labor solidarity on the West Coast and created conflict within the Filipino American community during the 1950s. The final essay is by Xiaojian Zhao, associate professor of Asian American Studies at the University of California at Santa Barbara. Zhao examines divisions within the Chinese American community that lasted well into the 1960s as government informants and a "confession program" exposed a history of illegal immigration during the exclusion era. Planning to deport "paper" sons and daughters, the government subpoenaed family association records, scrutinized medical blood tests, interrogated family members, and created turmoil within families and the Chinese American community.

Marriages Between American Men and Japanese Women After World War II

PAUL R. SPICKARD

When the war ended in 1945, American soldiers took over Japan as a conquered province. By the time they gave it back in 1952, tens of thousands of American men had become involved with Japanese women. Some enjoyed casual dates, some transient affairs, some temporary living arrangements, some enduring marriages. Harassed at first by Americans and Japanese alike, many couples split rather than endure the pressure. Others stuck it out and lived together in Japan or in America. Thousands of children came from these marriages and fleeting unions. Some never knew their fathers, growing up under their mothers' care alone. Others did not know their mothers either. They were orphans, cast upon the uncertain benevolence of relatives, children's homes, or private families. . . .

. . . The fabric of Japanese society had been rent, as much by wartime shortages as by the bombs that levelled Japanese cities. Economic life was at a standstill. Food was scarce. Hundreds of thousands were homeless. People were dead, wounded, or demoralized, and the living harbored deep resentments toward their conquerors. . . .

In such a climate of barely suppressed mutual fear and hatred, it is remarkable that some intimate, personal relationships came into being. Japanese men and women worked with their conquerors in rebuilding their country. Some became friends. Others formed recreational relationships. Very soon after the troops landed, early in the fall of 1945, bars, nightclubs, and houses of prostitution appeared around American bases. There, encounters between GIs and Japanese women often became intimate long before they became personal. Just how intimate was clear on June 28, 1946, when Japanese radio announced the first recorded birth of a baby of mixed parentage. Some Japanese women took up with American men as an extension of their wartime professions; more entered prostitution or shady entertainment out of a desperate need for food and shelter. Japan's utter devastation, with people starving in the streets, drove previously respectable women to barter their bodies for food and shelter for themselves or their families. . . . Out of these shadowy encounters on the outskirts of American military posts came an image that has endured; the Japanese woman as sexually enthusiastic courtesan. . . .

Alongside these informal connections there also grew in 1946 and 1947 more enduring relationships between GIs and Japanese women. Some of these ultimately

From *Mixed Blood: Intermarriage and Ethnic Identity in Twentieth-Century America*, Paul R. Spickard, © 1989. Reprinted by permission of The University of Wisconsin Press.

became marriages. More were long-term living arrangements, where the woman would live near a military base and keep house for her GI partner as long as he was in Japan. Some of the women who were involved in such unions sought or were willing to accept the companionship of American men for much the same reasons as those who went into prostitution. They needed to eat, and American soldiers could help them do that. Some were able to extract a measure of financial security not only for themselves but for their families as well. . . .

Other Japanese women chose American men in part because there were so few Japanese men available. Hundreds of thousands of young Japanese men died in the war, and many more did not return from China or the Pacific until many months after the end of hostilities. For some Japanese in their middle and late twenties, marriage to an American was preferable to no marriage at all. Some evidence of this situation may be found in the fact that on average, the Japanese women who married American men were older than their sisters who married Japanese. . . .

. . . Ijichi Junsei wrote at the time that " the emancipation of women [was] much encouraged by the Occupation regime." He described the groping of Japanese women for a "new interpretation and philosophy of love and marriage . . . to achieve free love and free marriage with their newly-gained freedom," and concluded that "the impact of American culture upon Japanese women is undermining the foundations of their manners and morals." Ijichi complained that some Japanese women wanted to know a wider range of experiences than was appropriate to their traditional situation, wanted higher status than had previously been their lot, and wanted to be treated like Western ladies by their men. . . .

. . . Ritsuko Parks reported that similar qualities attracted her to her husband: his care for her as a person and his ability to take her away from Japan. She told a reporter for *Ebony* magazine, "I like being married to an American man. In most things my husband puts me first. In Japan the husband is the boss. It is true that many Japanese girls married Americans just to get away from Japan and come to this country, but most of us love our husbands."

The women who chose American men, then, tended to be urban dwellers from a variety of backgrounds, who were united in their interest in pursuing life beyond the restrictions that bound their more traditional sisters. . . . Most of the men seem to have come from blue-collar homes. A surprising number, perhaps as many as half, came from farms and small towns. These concentrations in the lower middle class and in rural environments were not fully representative of the American population at large. In other demographic aspects—age and education, for example—the men who took Japanese mates do not seem to have differed greatly from their fellows. . . .

. . . One GI told an *Ebony* reporter what attracted him to his wife: "Man, try to find a girl on Seventh Avenue that is as kind and sweet as these little mooses. They appreciate the least thing you do for them. . . .

GIs met Japanese women, then, in circumstances guaranteed to yield romance. Young men far from home, possessing the power and status of conquerors, encountered women who badly needed a square meal. Add to this the fact that many of the women were highly Westernized and sought the nurturant husband more typical in America, while many of the men were looking for women to wait on them, and the prospects for dating and mating were good. The prospects for successful marriage, however, were not so good. Many of the men were looking for the docile Asian women that American stereotypes had led them to expect, while many of the women were looking for men who would allow them to leave that role. It was a situation ripe for conflict. . . .

Insofar as they addressed the interracial romance issue at all, the military (and the U.S. government, generally) bent their energies toward keeping GIs from marrying the Japanese women they loved. When they failed in this, the government tried to keep the Japanese spouses out of the United States. In December 1945 Congress passed Public Law 271, which came to be known as the War Brides Act. It was designed to enable American GIs to bring back the spouses and children they had acquired overseas by waiving the usual immigration quotas, visa requirements, and restrictions on "physical and mental defectives" in their cases. But Congress assumed that American soldiers, sailors, and airmen would be marrying Caucasians. The law was based on studies of GI needs in Europe and excluded spouses of "racially ineligible races"—i.e., Japanese. This distinction was based on the 1924 act that forbade Asian immigration. That act was amended during the war to allow Chinese immigration, because it was not seemly for the United States to continue to deny entry to its Asian allies. But the Japanese were another matter. They must stay out, including the wives and children of U.S. servicemen in Japan. The effect was that Germans and Italians were free to marry American servicemen and come to the United States, but Japanese were not.

By 1947, however, many American GIs had married Japanese women and were clamoring for permission to bring them home. In response, Congress passed an amendment to the War Brides Act that allowed Japanese spouses to enter during 1947 and 1948. That act expired before more than a tiny number of husbands could fight through bureaucratic opposition and bring their families home. After another series of protests by intermarried GIs, Congress approved another period, from August 1950 to February 1952, during which soldiers might take their families to America. But during those months most American troops were tied down in Korea and unable to take their brides home. Moreover, if a soldier died in Korea, his wife had to stay in Japan. If he was wounded, he was likely to be sent straight home from Korea, leaving his wife stranded. Finally, in late 1952, Congress passed the McCarran-Walter Act, which removed overt racial restrictions on immigration and put narrow, racially motivated national quotas in their place. That meant no increase in immigration by most of the world's darker peoples, for their countries were given tiny allotments. The Japanese war brides fared better, however, for they were designated nonquota immigrants and were now legally free to come.

Legal restrictions were only one impediment to intermarriage. The military's unparalleled ability to create bureaucratic obstacles was another. To get permission to marry a Japanese women, a soldier had to fill out an endless parade of documents. . . .

If a couple could get permission from the husband's commanding officer, their application still had to be approved by higher military authorities. The government would check the groom's background to make sure he was single, a U.S. citizen, and able to support a wife. They would ask Japanese officials to run a security check on his fiancee. All the paperwork usually took about six weeks, but it could easily take twice that. By the time the papers came through, many soldiers had been transferred away from their sweethearts, sent to the front, or shipped home. . . . If the husband was killed or shipped home, his wife and children were left without benefits and unable to enter the United States. More than a few husbands were sent home before they were able formalize their marriages. Many of these men had to make two or three trips back to Japan before they could arrange for their families to come to America. Some gave up and abandoned their families in Japan.

The total effect of the U.S. policy and practice with regard to marriages to Japanese nationals during the Occupation and the years that followed was to prevent intermarriages wherever possible and encourage GIs to opt for informal, unstable relationships—even prostitution—instead of marriage.

The Japanese government and people were no more kindly disposed toward intermarriages. The new Japanese government, installed and directed by the Americans, cooperated with its overlords in this area, as in others. Japanese officials published U.S.-ordered regulations for intermarriages and did much of the legwork in background checks on the prospective brides. Some Japanese families disowned daughters who consorted with American men. Others seemed more concerned for their daughter's welfare than outraged. They were afraid—rightly, in many cases—that the American suitors were not serious in their attentions, but were merely out for some fun at their daughters' expense. One soldier had to take drastic steps to convince his girlfriend's father of his sincere intentions: he invited the old man's friends along on their dates. The father set a strict, early curfew and lifted it only gradually over more than a year's time until finally he came to trust the boy. For many families the thought of an intermarriage brought visions of shame and defilement. . . .

Other Japanese opposed intermarriages and did their best to make mixed couples unhappy. They stared at the couples on the street with undisguised hatred, insulted them, spat on them, and shut them out of social groups. Some Japanese felt that the women had betrayed their country and challenged the rule of Japanese men by consorting with the conquerors. . . .

Despite opposition from both Americans and Japanese, international couples did marry. This was when the hardships set for in many. Few military bases provided housing for dependents of enlisted men, and nearly all those units went to women from the States. But Japanese houses remained off limits to GIs for some months after Congress passed the first bill allowing Japanese-American marriages. Husbands and wives often had to live apart. Many times a baby would come before a couple could start living together, or before they were formally married. Those who lived together off base often had trouble getting medical care. Wives of servicemen were supposed to be able to shop at PXs, but sometimes they were denied admission.

Whatever logistical problems couples faced, they also had to deal with the fact that they came from very different cultures. Almost no GI spoke any Japanese, and few Japanese women spoke English well. One soldier said, "At first I needed an interpreter to talk to her." Lacking an interpreter, many couples could communicate only by gestures. This led to all manner of misunderstandings. Eventually, many women learned enough English to handle daily affairs, but few ever were able to share their innermost feelings with their husbands. Almost none of the husbands ever learned more than pidgin Japanese. Cut off from other Japanese, many of the women felt a loneliness they had never known. . . .

In general, Japanese Americans quickly withdrew their welcome from Japanese wives of American men, whether the husbands were Nisei or non-Japanese Americans. Especially those women married to White and Black men were stigmatized as immoral women. They were denied access to many Japanese American community institutions. Only a tiny percentage, for example, ever felt comfortable enough to attend Japanese American churches. The intermarried women's problems were ignored by most Japanese Americans. Only with the rise of pan-Asian activism in the 1970s did a significant number of Japanese Americans begin to address the special problems faced by the Japanese brides of American men.

In sum, American-Japanese marriages in the immediate postwar years suffered intense opposition from the military and from private citizens in America and Japan. When a couple did succeed in marrying, they faced an arduous adjustment period. They were pressed by economic insecurity, loneliness, an inability to communicate deeply held feelings, cultural differences, family demands, hostility from some Americans, and a lack of support systems. Did these so-called war bride marriages weather the storm? Were the individuals involved able to make the necessary adjustments? . . .

. . . Anselm Strauss surveyed American-Japanese marriages for the University of Chicago in the early 1950s and concluded that such unions stood a good chance of success, precisely because of the "severe selective process for those who did marry." Concerted opposition from Americans, Japanese, and the military, said Strauss, had kept all couples apart except those whose members were most dedicated to each other. The couples he studied looked long and hard before marrying. As individuals, they were less likely than others to feel the pressures exerted by family, religious institutions, and the general public, for most had long since cut outside ties. They adjusted well to each other's circles of friends and career aspirations. In short, Strauss found American-Japanese marriages that showed every sign of succeeding. . . . Without question, there were couples who experienced tremendous difficulties. The cultural chasm between East and West was hard to bridge, and not a few marriages fell to destruction in the middle. Yet many unmixed marriages failed, too. Severe though the problems of individuals and couples were, there is little evidence to show that the rate of failure was higher for war bride couples than for others.

The United States Government Tries to Deport Filipino Labor Leaders

ARLEEN DE VERA

Between 1949 and 1953, the United States Immigration Service investigated Local 7 and accused its Filipino members of communist party membership or other subversive activities. The union's success in raising cannery workers' wages tenfold and in organizing California agricultural workers and its militant brand of left politics made Local 7 suspect during the McCarthy years. . . . So concentrated was the Service's ensuing campaign of red-baiting and arrests against Local 7 that one national civil rights organization described it as "without parallel anywhere else in the country." . . .

From Arleen de Vera, "Without Parallel: The Local 7 Deportation Cases," *Amerasia Journal* 20, no. 2 (1994): 1–2, 5–16. Copyright © 1994 Regents of the University of California. Used with permission.

. . . [T]he spring of 1949 began ominously. Hundreds of Local 7 members in Seattle and Portland, mostly Filipino nationals, began to receive letters from the Immigration and Naturalization Service "requesting" their appearance at immigration offices for questioning. A report in the *Philippines Mail* accused the Service of having ulterior motives:

> In Seattle alone more than one hundred rank and file members were called by the Immigration office either by letter, telephone or personal calls [on workers' homes] by immigration inspectors in an effort to coerce the men to swear or sign affidavits that certain officials are "communists." The same situation is taking place in Portland where scores of rank and filers were questioned by immigration inspectors.
>
> In Seattle . . . immigration authorities have subpoenaed George Minato, a member of the Local's executive board, to "testify and to bring all records and documents" to prove that "Chris Mensalvas [Local 7 Publicity Director and candidate for union President] and Ernie Mangaoang [business agent for Local 7]" are members of the Communist Party.

Those initial signs foreshadowed what was to come. On August 2, shortly after business agent Ernesto Mangaoang came into the Local 7 offices, two immigration service agents arrested and charged him with membership in the communist party, a "crime" punishable by deportation. Mangaoang, a union member since 1937, had served as business agent for two years, and had served briefly as an assistant regional director for the International.

Union officials and international representatives were convinced that his arrest had been timed to disrupt the union's organizing drive in Southeastern Alaska. International Representative Ken Howard wrote to the FTA [Food, Tobacco, Agricultural, and Allied Workers of America] International offices back in Philadelphia:

> The date of the first issuance of the warrant [July 6] coincides with our drive in Bristol Bay. July 1st Bob [Kinney] left for the Bay to prepare for strike action; Ernie demanded a meeting with the industry on the 5th. The warrant was issued on the 6th, and the meeting took place on the 8th. But meantime, or by the 11th at the latest, the industry knew that we had called off the action.
>
> Intensive negotiations with the industry over the [southeastern Alaska] situation took place on the 29th of July, [when] it became clear to them that we meant business in [southeastern] Alaska; the warrant was served on the 2nd of August.

Local 7 rallied to Mangaoang's defense. The day after his arrest, one hundred and fifty Filipinos picketed and chanted outside the immigration offices at Airport Way. A special union bulletin railed against his jailing as a wholesale violation of civil rights:

> This is a flagrant attack against the labor movement and our union—Local 7, FTA-CIO [Food, Tobacco, Agricultural, and Allied Workers of America Congress of Industrial Organizations] . . . The arrest of Brother Mangaoang is a definite threat against the civil rights of non-citizens and citizens!

In view of the need for its ace negotiator during contract discussions with the industry, the union posted the $5,000 bail out of the treasury's general fund. Mangaoang was out by the night of August 3.

By the end of August, the INS [Immigration and Naturalization Service] had arrested three more officers on charges of Communist Party membership. Jailed were publicity director Chris Mensalvas, and executive board member Ponce Torres, both in Seattle; and election committee member Casimiro Bueno Absolor in Portland. Bail for the three was set high: for Mensalvas, $5,000; Absolor, $500; Torres, $1,000.

The International insisted, however, that the reasons for the arrests and intimidation were Local 7's record of fighting militancy and trade union reforms—not communism:

> Before the salmon workers were organized in Local 7, FTA, wages averaged around $25 a month. Today, the average is $250 a month. Before the union, hiring was done under a vicious contract system that robbed and victimized the workers. Today, hiring is done by rotation through the union.

The Local 7 defense committee was even more blunt. The committee charged the Alaska Salmon Industry, Inc. with a part in the deportation drive:

> Where the industry has failed to demoralize the membership and break the union with the Taft-Hartley club, it has now turned to the U.S. Immigration Service for service and assistance. The bosses know that a great majority of the members of Local 7 are non-citizens. This is the hidden card up the sleeve of the employers. The crimes of the arrested workers are simple—they fought for years to organize the workers. . . .

Fellow Local 7 member Carlos Bulosan added his voice in criticism. By then, a fifth member, Joe Prudencio, a militant rank and filer and World War II veteran, had been arrested in Seattle, also on charges of Communist Party membership:

> The deportation proceedings against the five members of Local 7, FTA, should be halted by all those who want to live in freedom and see an America where the individual is not in constant fear of his life and security. It should be stopped before our constitutional rights are destroyed by an ever expanding machinery of our government, now bent on spying [into] the deepest recesses of our private lives. . . .

. . . The INS hearings on the deportation case of President Chris Mensalvas illustrate the ease with which one could be accused of communist sympathies and held for deportation. Government witnesses were from Local 7's rival unions, namely the American Federation of Labor Seafarers union and the Congress of Industrial Organization's Local 77 Packinghouse Workers. In presenting its case against Mensalvas, one government witness, Pete Bautista, swore that he himself was a member of the Communist Party, that he knew that Mensalvas was a communist, and that he had seen Mensalvas present at closed communist meetings. Yet upon cross-examination by Mensalvas's attorney, Bautista admitted he had never seen a Communist Party membership book or card, had never seen Mensalvas pay dues to the Party, and had never heard him say anything to indicate membership. Bautista also indicated his testimony was in part motivated by self-interest, as his own petition to the Department of Justice for naturalization was still pending. The testimony of a second government witness proved so faulty that Immigration Service attorney Robert DeMoulin had it struck from the record, stating, "I am unable to rely on anything he has said at this hearing," and recommended that the witness be investigated for perjury. Despite the unreliability of the testimony, deportation proceedings against Mensalvas continued.

Meanwhile, the union defense committee stepped up its lobbying campaign on behalf of its embattled members. At an ILWU [International Longshoremen's and

Warehousemen's Union] convention representing some eighty thousand workers, members unanimously adopted a resolution calling for a Congressional investigation of the Immigration Service's "union-busting" campaign against Local 7:

> The Immigration Service patently operates upon the theory that no foreign-born person has the right to engage in trade union activities or take any step in concert with fellow workers in order to achieve security and better conditions. To the service such activity is a crime, and since there is no law to support its theory the service resorts to framed, perjured testimony. . . .

The second phase of the union's strategy was to file legal challenges to the deportation orders. As legal expenses mounted, defense committee members wrote letters of appeal for loans and pledges, and collected donations for a defense fund (five hundred dollars alone was collected from one longshoreman's local). Members also turned their attentions to *Mangaoang* v. *Boyd,* which was shaping up as a test case for the McCarran Act. Mangaoang's attorneys hoped to use the ambiguity of U.S. colonial law to the Local 7 deportees' advantage, as at the time of their "subversive activities," Filipinos were not aliens but American nationals. If the United States District Court accepted such an interpretation, union lawyers hoped the court would rule the Immigration Service's deportation campaign invalid. . . .

Internally, the deportation cases became a major issue in the 1953 union elections. Former union president Trinidad Rojo campaigned against Mensalvas on a platform or reforming, not repealing, the McCarran-Walter Act, and advocated non-involvement in progressive causes:

> If some of our officers do not stop irritating Uncle Sam with regards to subversive cases, if we identify the Union officially [with] any and all deportation cases relating to a handful of members, and if the international tension worsens, Local [7] runs the risk of being listed as a subversive organization.
>
> That risk is fraught with disaster. . . . In the event of war between Russia and America, our members may be interned in concentration camps. Let us be valiant fighters but for the cause of the greater number, for a real union cause, not for the private ideas of a few, not for the outside affiliations of whatever nature. . . . Let us work for the revision of the Law and not defy it. . . .

. . . On July 25, immigration agents intercepted five cannery workers returning from Bristol Bay, interrogated and then jailed them for two days. A Local 7 bulletin warning members what to expect listed the questions put to the five while in screening:

"Have you ever been arrested before?

"Have you ever been a pimp?

"Have you ever lived with a woman, not your wife?

"Have you ever been drunk?

"Have you ever murdered [anyone]?

"Why [didn't] you get a new Alien Registration Card?

"Have you ever been in a hospital?

"Have you ever been convicted of a traffic violation?

"Are you now, or have you ever been, a member of the Communist Party?"

The bulletin urged the men to ask for an interpreter, and to answer "no" to most of the questions. A "yes" to any one question, the union warned, could mean grounds for deportation under the McCarran-Walter Act. The bulletin cautioned, "Remember that the Immigration does not know . . . [the] jail records of [everyone]. It is none of their business in the first place. . . .

The screenings and arrests continued until the end of the season in November. All together, the Immigration Service screened some two thousand Filipinos returning to Seattle. In those few months, more than a hundred were jailed, and eventually, over a dozen singled out for exclusion.

While the grounds for exclusion varied, it is clear that their basis had little to do with expionage or treason. One man's offense against national security was that he had stolen a chicken during the Depression some twenty years ago. . . .

Supreme Court Decisions, 1953–1955: *Mangaoang* v. *Boyd*, *Gonzales* v. *Barber, Alcantra* v. *Boyd*

The first legal victory came later that fall. On November 9, 1953, the Supreme Court upheld the lower court's ruling for Mangaoang. The high court reasoned that for the McCarran Act to apply, Mangaoang had to be simultaneously an alien and a member of the Party. Since the years of his alleged membership occurred before the Philippines' independence from the United States in 1946, Mangaoang, and by extension, the others similarly accused, were not deportable.

With the Mangaoang decision, resolution of the remaining McCarran and McCarran-Walter cases came quickly. The next summer, on June 7, 1954, the United States Supreme Court ruled in Gonzales's favor in *Gonzales* v. *Barber*. Filipinos, the court decreed, who had committed crimes of "moral turpitude" before 1946 were not deportable under the Internal Security Act of 1950. The final case, *Alcantra* v. *Boyd*, reached the Supreme Court the next spring. On May 10, 1955, the court struck down the McCarran-Walter exclusion provisions as unconstitutional. In so doing, the court argued that the exclusion would unfairly burden Alaska's economy, and might adversely affect its fishing and canning industry:

> Many thousands of workers residing in the continental United States are annually employed in that industry; and one may well assume that substantial numbers of them are aliens who would be put in peril of exclusion and deportation upon their return home.

With the Alcantra decision, the legal battles were over. The Immigration and Naturalization Service dropped the remaining deportation and exclusion cases, and ended its screening program. Local 7 members could now travel freely back and forth from their homes to their work without fear of harassment. The union had won.

Conclusion

The Immigration Service's deportation campaign had an impact greater than the union's legal victories alone would indicate. Its use of intimidating letters, phone calls, and visits to pressure members into naming union leaders as communists; arrests; immigration hearings in which officials could act with impunity; and the screening program took their toll. The union's base of support eroded under such pressures, and splits formed within the union's ranks over the future direction of the local, and specifically, whether to challenge the deportation orders and to continue

with its "political" cause of repealing the Walter-McCarran Act. The legal costs in-
curred as a result of the deportation campaign also led to severe financial losses.
Bail and attorney's fees for the deportees caused such a drain on resources that
union officials postponed, then abandoned, a plan to recruit California agricultural
workers and expand Local 7's base. Ironically, after its legal victories, union leaders
returned to the basics of survival: recruiting members and paying off debts. . . .

To understand the larger significance of labor organizing, the individual story
of what happened to Local 7 and its leaders must be multiplied by the hundreds.
Accusations and arrests for alleged Communist Party membership or subversion
became an all too common feature during the McCarthy years. But in the end, what
was put down was not a conspiracy of traitors, but the freedom to dissent, to disagree,
and to organize.

The Immigration and Naturalization Service's Campaign Against Chinese Americans During the Cold War

XIAOJIAN ZHAO

In the early 1950s the Immigration and Naturalization Service (INS) had pushed
some Chinese Americans to confess. Through meetings held in Chinatowns in large
cities, investigators had told their subjects that should they be aliens, not citizens as
reflected in the records, they might be eligible for an adjustment of status according
to the Immigration and Naturalization Act of 1952 if they cooperated. Successful
criminal proceedings against some Chinese were often made possible after investigators secured confessions from other members of the Chinese American community,
and in exchange for information, the INS sometimes adjusted the status of confessors
who subsequently appeared as government witnesses.

Seeking cooperation from Chinese Americans and at the same time making
itself look good, the INS began to advertise the so-called Confession Program in
mid-1956. No official policy or guidelines were issued at the time; instead, the program was announced through "informal and unwritten publicity" to civic leaders
and Chinese Americans. Under this program, Chinese who in the past had fraudu-
lently established U.S. citizenship were encouraged to come forward, and they were
told that the Immigration and Nationality Act of 1952 would allow some of them to
adjust their status. Every effort was made to convince Chinese Americans that they
were the ones who could gain from the program.

As part of its internal policy, the INS tried to make the Confession Program as
ambiguous as possible. The government said in public that it had "no desire to en-
trap" Chinese Americans, although immigration authorities never promised favorable action to any prospective confessors. The Chinese were told only that they
should seriously consider the relief available and secure adjustment of status prior
to further proceedings, which gave the impression that confessors would have more
to gain than to lose. In a memo to the regional chief of investigations, the service's

From Zhao, Xiaojian, *Remaking Chinese America: Immigration, Family, and Community, 1940–1965.*
Copyright © 2002 Rutgers University Press. Reprinted by permission of Rutgers University Press.

assistant commissioner of the Investigations Division pointed out that a "wider application" of the program would be "beneficial to the Service." The commissioner was particularly satisfied, noting with "approval" that his staff had not made "promises of immunity from prosecution or commitments that discretionary relief will be granted," and he reiterated "every medium is used to advise Chinese in the United States regarding the possibilities of adjustment under the law."

Because there was no written policy, the INS was able to decide arbitrarily whom it would allow to stay and whom it would deport. Ralph E. Stanley, an INS investigator in San Francisco, wrote in late 1956, "It must be admitted that there have been cases wherein this Service has ultimately found it necessary to institute deportation proceedings against Chinese, even though they had appeared as government witnesses in criminal proceedings involving other Chinese."

The INS used grand jury investigation as a threat to press Chinese to participate in the program. The agents approached individuals based on leads from informants, anonymous sources, and letters and coaching materials seized by government agencies. Should they persist in the fraudulent pattern, the Chinese were told that they might ultimately involve themselves and their family members in criminal charges.

Chinese American veterans from the U.S. armed forces, who were eligible for relief under the law, were seen by the INS as easy prey. One lead from the consulate in Hong Kong, for example, indicated that Lew Bok Yin, who had established himself as a native-born U.S. citizen by means of a habeas corpus proceeding in 1902, had been born in China. The INS records revealed that seventeen persons had gained entry as Lew's sons and grandsons and their wives. In addition, the family had claimed another seventeen members in China and Hong Kong as being eligible for nonquota status. Immigration authorities suspected that some members of the family were not Lew's descendants. To prove their cases, investigators approached several family members who had served in World War II or the Korean War. The veterans were told that they were eligible for relief according to the law and would not be in danger of deportation if they told the truth. The entire family eventually went to the INS office and made full confessions.

The group confession of the Lew family could hardly be seen as voluntary, for the family members could no longer conceal their identities. Chinese Americans well understood the disturbing and terrifying experiences that the veteran members of the Lew family had gone through. They not only had to reverse their own early sworn testimonies, but also had to provide information that would put relatives and friends in jeopardy. Two members of the Lew family were faced with deportation proceedings as the result. The process to receive relief was also convoluted. The veterans were naturalized first, but their wives had to wait until the husbands' status was adjusted before they could attempt to adjust their legal status under 8 CFR 235 of the act. Other family members had to seek relief under section 244. Most damaging to the family was that once the members admitted their fraud, they gave up the hope of bringing in family members who were still in China. All the slots that they had created on paper would be closed.

The INS gave considerable publicity to the war veterans of the Lew family when they were naturalized in 1956 under the provisions of section 329 of the 1952 Immigration and Naturalization Act. Each time a group of Chinese veterans was naturalized, the INS would furnish a press release to the Chinese American community.

The government tried to advertise what it called the humanitarian aspect of the program, that is, to free those otherwise law-abiding persons from the constant pressure of living with a lie, while its obvious purpose was to "terminate permanently the machinery which facilitated a steady influx of illegal aliens." The Chinese community press printed these news releases, but no attempt was made to elaborate upon the Confession Program, and neither the CCBA [Chinese Consolidated Benevolent Association] nor the press called upon Chinese Americans to participate in it.

Chinese Americans soon came to realize that they could not trust the INS despite its honeyed words and oblique promises. The Immigration and Naturalization Act of 1952 subjected aliens who entered the United States by fraud to deportation, and even though an amendment passed on September 11, 1957, provided that such a person might be granted permanent U.S. residency if he or she admitted the commission of such a perjury, this required the consent of the attorney general. Although the Chinese were pushed to admit perjury and fraud, the INS would not promise its forgiveness for such criminal offenses, which were prerequisite for the Chinese to receive the discretionary relief.

As it turned out, some confessors brought disaster upon their own families. In late 1955, acting on an FBI request, the INS investigated Lee Ying, the co-owner of the World Theater in San Francisco. The FBI had received information that the theater was an outlet for Artkino, a company that imported movies from Russia and China, and that it had sponsored benefits for newspapers and organizations that were listed as Communist or pro-Communist. Lee Ying had entered the United States as a paper son of Hui Suey (Fong Suey). Under pressure, Hui Suey admitted that Lee Ying was really his son-in-law. The confession implicated other family members who had made false claims, including Hui Suey's wife, his two sons, and his daughter. Although Hui Suey had cooperated fully with the investigators, he could not protect his family. A week after his father-in-law testified, Lee Ying was arrested and his home searched. The arrest warrant charged that he did not possess a valid immigration visa. On January 30, 1957, the grand jury in San Francisco filed four criminal indictments against him for document fraud and giving false testimony. Lee Ying admitted his guilt and left the United States.

The case of Lee Ying reflected another internal INS policy, which held that no relief would be granted to a person who had been investigated by another government agency. While this policy was especially effective in punishing leftist Chinese Americans, it did not guarantee that other members of the community would not be targeted.

The fear of prosecution haunted Chinese Americans who had never violated any laws other than those related to immigration. On September 24, 1956, Poon Bok Shing of San Francisco wrote a confession for INS officials admitting that he and Poon Gon On had gained entry as sons of natives, although they were in fact sons of citizens of China. The circumstances under which Poon Bok Shing confessed are unclear, but the humiliation, the realization that he had committed perjury and some fraud, and the guilt over betraying a friend were so overwhelming that Poon Bok Shing took his own life that same day. Agents later requested full relief for Poon Gon On.

To escape any contact with INS investigators, many Chinese changed their addresses and telephone numbers, and some closed down their businesses. Shirley Wong, born in San Francisco in 1949, recalled years of living in fear while her parents and relatives tried to hide from immigration authorities. Investigators eventually found her father in 1962 and pressed him and his wife to confess. According to Shirley's mother-in-law, Mary Yee, everyone was scared at the time. Mary's husband Eddie was a paper son, and although he was a World War II veteran and therefore eligible for relief, he knew that telling the truth might result in the deportation of his relatives. Eddie confessed when his paper family was exposed in 1962.

Even for those who were confident of getting relief, confessing would make their lives more complicated. In a letter to the *Chinese American Weekly* in 1960, a woman expressed fear upon learning that immigration authorities had obtained her name and her whereabouts from her paper father. "I am so scared," she said. "Should I go confess?" The woman had been in the United States for more than twenty years, but because her husband, the son of a merchant, was not a citizen when they married and was therefore not qualified to buy property, all family assets had been purchased under her name. Even if relief were granted, it would take at least three years for her to be naturalized. What would happen to her family property then? What could the government do if she did not cooperate with the INS?

Editor Wu Jingfu encouraged the woman to go forward. He said that since she had lived in the United States for twenty years and her husband and children were all citizens, deportation would be unlikely. Given that she had come as a minor, she might also be able to demonstrate that she had not understood what she had done. Once a family was under investigation, cooperating with the government seemed to be the only solution. Many slots would be closed, but it was hoped that the individuals already in the United States would be able to stay; people simply had to make the best of the grave situation. If there was an unwritten internal principle among the Chinese Americans faced with the Confession Program, it was to go forward only when they could no longer hide.

The Confession Program, which encouraged Chinese Americans to testify against one another, had a mixed impact on many families. The program led to mistrust among family members, tearing some families apart. Jat Fang Lew, who entered as a paper grandson of Lew Chuck Suey, confessed in 1962, pointing INS investigators to his paper father and brothers. To this day, members of the Lew family consider Jat Fang Lew's confession unwise and unnecessary, and he declined to be interviewed. But to some extent, the investigation also brought family members together. Few individuals acted alone. Once there was any indication that the INS was after a certain person, the person would inform everyone in his family. The entire family would then consult a lawyer and go to confess together. In 1962 Maurice Chuck, a former Min Qing member who had written for the *China Daily News,* was indicted for making a false statement to obtain a certificate of citizenship in 1954. The INS brought Hwong Jack Hong, Chuck's father, to court against him. They shared a hotel room during the trial. For the first time, father and son gained some understanding of each other. After Chuck was sent to jail, it was Hwong Jack Hong who helped Chuck's wife to get through the difficult time.

As the INS used court charges to intimidate Chinese Americans and tried to force them to leave the country, it confronted persistent resistance. In 1961, following a lead from a relative's confession, the INS filed criminal charges against Dear Kai Gay, a former member of Min Qing who had entered the United States in 1933 as a paper son. Dear Kai Gay was convicted on three charges, including knowingly making a false representation of a matter within the jurisdiction of a U.S. agency.

After his jail sentence was set, the INS reduced it to six months on the condition that he would leave the United States. Using what were described as "voluntary" departure cases, the service tried to demonstrate that it was sending Chinese people back to China to be with their families.

By then, however, many of those who were on the deportation list had already established families in the United States. Leaving the country meant that a married man like Dear Kai Gay would have to part from his wife and children and gave up the right to return. In an effort to block or delay forced deportations, lawyers for the Chinese deportees pooled information, evidence, and witnesses to claim that their clients would be physically threatened and persecuted if they were deported to China. Even though the INS believed that only those who had been affiliated with the Nationalist government or who had opposed the Communist regime would face such dangers, it failed to establish a case in court to prove it was safe for most Chinese to go back to China. The INS then tried to deport some Chinese to Taiwan, but since many of those targeted were sympathizers of the PRC, it was difficult to prove they would not face persecution by the Nationalist government. Dear Kai Gay appealed. A year later, the judge for the Ninth Circuit Court of Appeals declared the sentence "cruel and unusual." Such a punishment, the judge ruled, was unconstitutional, and the district court was ordered to resentence him according to the law.

When Gilbert Woo, the editor of the *Chinese Pacific Weekly,* called for an end to the community's preoccupation with China politics and asked Chinese Americans to get involved in political reform in the United States in the late 1940s, not many people listened. His friends thought that he was being intimidated; supporters of the Nationalist government accused him of being pro-Communist. In 1951, after the Kang Jai Association was raided by the police, one reader wrote to the *China Daily News,* urging a "united action of all the Chinese." At that time, however, the Guomindang controlled CCBA was still eager to exterminate all leftist groups. In the midst of the government's investigation into immigration fraud, the CCBA finally called for united action. The Guomindang's mouthpiece, the *Chinese Journal,* told Chinese Americans that they "should not act like 'a plate of loose sand,' [*yipan sansha*]," for everyone's life would be affected if the government were able to use the investigation to further restrict Chinese immigration.

The investigation of immigration fraud in the 1950s also compelled the Chinese American community to find new ways to deal with discriminatory government policies: their old strategy of circumventing immigration laws was no longer working. During the exclusion era, many Chinese Americans believed that making China strong would be the key to improving their status in the United States. Now it was clear that neither the PRC [People's Republic of China] nor the government of Taiwan could protect them.

In March 1957 the CCBA in New York called a national conference. One hundred and twenty-four Chinese American representatives from thirty-four cities throughout the United States gathered in Washington, D.C. A few participants proposed that the thrust of the conference should be anti-Communist and pro-Taiwan, but it soon became clear that such an agenda would go nowhere. Chinese American journalists put pressure on the conference organizers. Gilbert Woo wrote:

If some people enjoy a conference on [China] politics, let them go. I strongly advise all citizens of the United States not to be involved. . . . For decades, involvement in China's political struggle has caused endless conflict in the Chinese American community and brought about zero benefit. . . . If the primary purpose of this conference is a political power struggle rather than an attempt to benefit the entire community, our delegation should withdraw and hold a conference of its own. If they are too myopic to see the harm, why should we follow them down this path?

Seeing that they had few followers, the organizers shifted the focus of the conference and passed resolutions to lobby Congress for immigration reform. This meant not that the CCBA had finally decided to relinquish its involvement in the political struggle between the PRC and Taiwan, but that the majority of Chinese Americans had decided that they did not want to be manipulated by a few community leaders, and that they wanted to exercise their political power to secure the protections provided by the U.S. Constitution.

Once again, legislative reform on immigration brought Chinese Americans together, and the Chinese American Citizens Alliance [CACA] again played an active role working together with CCBA and other community organizations. Throughout the late 1950s and early 1960s, the Chinese American community had its lobbyists stationed in Washington, D.C., working together with other Asian American groups. A great effort was made to amend the McCarran-Walter Act of 1952, which retained the national origins quota system of 1924. Both the CCBA and the CACA especially urged their members to vote and write to their representatives in Congress to draw attention to the interests of the Chinese American community.

Although relatively few deportation proceedings went through, the INS viewed the Confession Program as one of its greatest accomplishments. Paper families were rooted out one after another, and the number of slots closed was featured in the service's annual report between 1957 and 1965. It was indeed an impressive record for the INS: 13,895 Chinese participated in the program, leading to the exposure of 22,083 persons and the closing of 11,294 slots.

The success of legislative reform in the late 1950s and early 1960s would require a reevaluation of the Confession Program. The 1965 Immigration Act, signed into law by President Lyndon B. Johnson in front of the Statue of Liberty on October 3, repealed the Asian-Pacific triangle provisions of the 1924 Immigration Act. Instead of requiring quotas based on racial ancestry, as it was provided by the 1943 repeal act, the new law used place of birth to determine an immigrant's origin, and a new system was established to grant each country the same immigration quota. The act also provided special protection for the family unit, allowing American citizens' immediate relatives, including their children, spouses, and parents, to come outside the quota limit, and gave quota preference to their other relatives. The new law changed the face of Chinese immigration entirely. Many Chinese Americans, paradoxically, now found that their participation in the Confession Program enabled them to claim immediate family members and relatives in China using their true identities.

On February 2, 1966, the INS decided that it would no longer solicit confessions. The service could not, however, reject Chinese Americans who wanted to confess voluntarily in order to take full advantage of the new immigration act. Under the new domestic and international political climate of the late 1960s, the government finally decided that "no special treatment is to be given to aliens of that nationality [the Chinese] not accorded to all others."

⟡ F U R T H E R   R E A D I N G

Ariyoshi, Koji. *From Kona to Yenan: The Political Memoirs of Koji Ariyoshi* (2000).
Chan, Sucheng. *Asian Americans: An Interpretive History* (1991).
Cordova, Fred. *Filipinos: Forgotten Asian Americans* (1983).
Daniels, Roger. *Asian America: Chinese and Japanese in the United States Since 1850* (1988).
Fong, Timothy. *The First Suburban Chinatown: The Remaking of Monterey Park, California* (1993).
Heine, Steven. "Sayonara Can Mean 'Hello': Ambiguity and the Orientalist Butterfly Syndrome in Postwar American Films," *Post Script: Essays in Film and the Humanities* 16, no. 3 (1997): 17–35.
Hing, Bill Ong. *Making and Remaking Asian American Through Immigration Policy, 1850–1990* (1993).
Holmes, Michael T. *The Specter of Communism in Hawaii* (1994).
Kang, K. Connie. *Home Was the Land of the Morning Calm* (1995).
Kent, Noel J. *Hawaii: Islands Under the Influence* (1983).
Kim, Bok-Lim C. Asian Wives of US Servicemen: Women in Shadows," *Amerasia Journal,* 4, no. 1 (1977): 91–115.
Kim, Haeyun Juliana. "Voices from the Shadows: The Lives of Korean War Brides," *Amerasia Journal* 17, no. 1 (1991): 15–30.
Kwong, Peter. *The New Chinatown and Chinatown, New York: Labor and Politics 1930–1950* (1987).
Lai, Him Mark. "The Chinese Marxist Left in America to the 1960s," in Chinese Historical Association of America, *Chinese America: History and Perspectives* (1992), 3–82.
Lee, Robert G. " The Hidden World of Asian Immigrant Radicalism," in *The Immigrant Left in the United States* ed. Paul Buhle and Dan Georgakas (1996), 256–288.
Leonard, Kevin Allen. "'Is That What We Fought For?' Japanese Americans and Racism in California, The Impact of World War II," *Western Historical Quarterly* 21, no. 4 (1990): 463–482.
Lyman, Stanford. "Red Guards on Grant Avenue," in *The Asian in North America* (1977), 177–199.
Marchetti, Gina. *Romance and the "Yellow Peril": Race, Sex, and Discursive Strategies in Hollywood Fiction* (1993).
National Committee Concerned with Asian Wives of U.S. Servicemen. *Women in Shadows: A Handbook for Service Providers Working with Asian Wives of U.S. Military Personnel* (1981).
Nee, Victor G., and Brett de Bary Nee. *Longtime Californ': A Documentary Study of an American Chinatown* (1972).
Patterson, Wayne. *The Ilse: First-Generation Korean Immigrants in Hawaii 1903–1973* (2000).
Riggs, Fred Warren. *Pressures on Congress: A Study of the Repeal of Chinese Exclusion* (1950).
Sung, Betty Lee. *Chinese American Intermarriage* (1990).
Thornton, Michael C. " The Quiet Immigration: Foreign Spouses of U.S. Citizens, 1945–1985, in *Racially Mixed People in America,* ed. Maria P. P. Root (1992), 64–76.
Tung, William L. *The Chinese in America, 1820–1973* (1974).
Vallangca, Caridad Concepcion. *The Second Wave: Pinay & Pinoy, (1945–1960)* (1987).
Williams, Teresa K. "Marriage Between Japanese Women and U.S. Servicemen Since World War II," *Amerasia Journal* 17, no. 1 (1991) 135–154.

Post-1965 Immigration

and

Asian America

The Immigration and Nationality Act of 1965 dramatically reshaped Asian American communities by allowing streams of new immigrants to enter the United States from countries throughout Asia. Also known as the Hart-Cellar Reform Act, this legislation was part of a wider package of civil rights laws in the mid-1960s banning racial discrimination in voting, education, and other areas of public life. The landmark legislation abolished the 1924 national origins system that heavily favored northern Europeans and severely restricted Asian, as well as southern and eastern European immigrants. The act provided a set quota of 170,000 immigrants from the Eastern Hemisphere, with no more than 20,000 from a single country, and 120,000 from the Western Hemisphere, without any country limitations. The law also established a preference system for family members of citizens and resident aliens and individuals with educational or job skills needed in the United States.

Perhaps most significant for Asian Americans, however, was the fact that spouses, unmarried minor children, and parents of U.S. citizens could enter as nonquota immigrants without any numerical limits. Policymakers never antici- pated that large numbers of Asians and Latin Americans would use these family reunification provisions to swell the ranks of new immigrants. In the mid-1960s, citizens of Asian ancestry constituted only 0.5 percent of the U.S. population. But naturalization classes quickly filled with Asian immigrants who took the oath of citizenship and then sent for their relatives abroad. These nonquota immigrants profoundly changed immigration patterns in ways never envisioned by the archi- tects of the 1965 law. In 1960, 75 percent of all immigrants came from Europe, 9 percent from Latin America, and 5 percent from Asia. By 1999, 51 percent of all immigrants living in the United States came from Latin America and 27 percent from Asia, while only 16 percent came from Europe.

Immigration fueled the tremendous growth of the Asian American popula- tion, which leaped from 490,000 in 1940, to 3.5 million in 1980, to 10.8 million

*in 1999. Infusing new life into existing ethnic enclaves, these immigrants also
established new settlements and changed the ethnic composition of the Asian
American population. Before the 1960s, most Asian immigrants were likely to be
of Chinese, Japanese, or Filipino ancestry, although there were small communities
of Korean and Indian immigrants. The arrival of large numbers of immigrants
from the Philippines, Korea, China, and India after 1965, along with the influx
of Southeast Asian refugees after 1975, made obvious the remarkable ethnic diversity of "Asian America."*

☙ D O C U M E N T S

Taken together, the following documents reveal how post-1965 Asian immigration has
been shaped by changes in U.S. immigration legislation and by political, social, and
economic relations established after World War II between the sending countries and
the United States. Document 1 excerpts the Immigration and Nationality Act of 1965,
which replaced the national origins quota system with a seven-category system of pref-
erences. The graph and table in Document 2 show how this new immigration policy
led to a tremendous increase in Asian immigration after 1965. Perla Rabor Rigor provides a personal account of the migration experience in Document 3. Arriving in 1957
as an exchange visitor from the Philippines, Rigor describes promotional difficulties
and problems with housing discrimination that many immigrants experienced in the
1950s and 1960s.

The second set of documents illustrates the influence of new immigrants on
American educational and religious institutions, Asian American communities,
and Asian homelands. Document 4 provides excerpts from the 1974 Supreme Court
decision requiring the San Francisco school district to provide English language
instruction to 1,800 students of Chinese ancestry within the public school system. In
Document 5, journalist Bill Wong describes diverse Asian American views of California's Proposition 227, also known as the Unz initiative, to eliminate most bilingual
education programs in public schools and place limited-English-proficient students
in English immersion classes. After the 1998 passage of Proposition 227, bilingual
programs were available to students only if their parents applied for waivers to the
law at their schools, and in 2002, just 12 percent of the state's 1.5 million students
were in bilingual programs.

Document 6 notes how Christian, Buddhist, and Hindu immigrants from Asia
have marked the religious landscape in America. The 1994 journal article describes
the role of new immigrants in financing and constructing the approximately 1,500
temples, shrines, monasteries, and retreat houses throughout the United States. Document 7 contains excerpts from a 1998 *Social Justice* article by Elaine Kim. Kim, a
professor of ethnic studies, exhorts Asian Americans to critically examine the impact
of U. S. policies on Asian migration experiences, to condemn racial rhetoric that
positions Asian Americans between blacks and whites, and to recognize the need
for cross-racial alliances. Finally, in Document 8, Sarita Sarvate describes the economic underdevelopment of India caused by the migration of scientists, engineers,
technicians, and other professionals and calls on American corporations to establish
a "brain trust" to compensate for this "brain drain." This document further demonstrates how many immigrants maintain cultural, economic, and political ties with
their native countries.

1. The Immigration and Nationality Act of 1965 Repeals Discriminatory Policies Toward Asian Immigrants, 1965

Be it enacted by the Senate and House of Representatives of the United States of America in Congress assembled, That section 201 of the Immigration and Nationality Act . . . be amended to read as follows:

Sec. 201. (a) Exclusive of special immigrants defined in section 101 (a) (27), and of the immediate relatives of United States citizens specified in subsection (b) of this section, the number of aliens who may be issued immigrant visas or who may otherwise acquire the status of an alien lawfully admitted to the United States for permanent residence, or who may, pursuant to section 203 (a) (7) enter conditionally, (i) shall not in any of the first three quarters of any fiscal year exceed a total of 45,000 and (ii) shall not in any fiscal year exceed a total of 170,000.

(b) The "immediate relatives" referred to in subsection (a) of this section will mean the children, spouses, and parents of a citizen of the United States: *Provided,* That in the case of parents, such citizen must be at least twenty-one years of age. . . .

Sec. 2. Section 202 of the Immigration and Nationality Act . . . is amended to read as follows:

(a) No person shall receive any preference or priority or be discriminated against in the issuance of an immigrant visa because of his race, sex, nationality, place of birth, or place of residence, except as specifically provided in section 101 (a) (27), section 201 (b), and section 203: *Provided,* That the total number of immigrant visas and the number of conditional entries made available to natives of any single foreign state . . . shall not exceed 20,000 in any fiscal year. . . .

"(b) . . . For the purposes of this Act the foreign state to which an immigrant is chargeable shall be determined by birth within such foreign state. . . .

Sec. 3. Sec. 203 of the Immigration and Nationality Act . . . is amended as follows:

Sec. 203 (a) Aliens who are subject to the numerical limitations . . . shall be allotted visas or their conditional entry authorized, as the case may be, as follows:

(1) Visas shall be first made available, in a number not to exceed 20 per centum of the number specified in section 201 (a) (ii), to qualified immigrants who are the unmarried sons or daughters of citizens of the United States.

From Immigration and Nationality Act of October 3, 1965, 79 Stat. 911; reprinted in *U.S. Immigration and Naturalization Laws and Issues: A Documentary History,* ed. Michael Lemay and Elliot Robert Barkan (Westport, Conn.: Greenwood Press, 1999), 257–259.

(2) Visas shall next be made available, in a number not to exceed 20 per centum of the number specified in section 201 (a) (ii), plus visas not required to be classes specified in paragraph (1), to qualified immigrants who are spouses, unmarried sons or unmarried daughters of an alien admitted for permanent residence.

(3) Visas shall next be made available, in a number not to exceed 10 per centum . . . to qualified immigrants who are members of the professions, or who because of their exceptional ability in the sciences or arts will substantially benefit prospectively the national economy, cultural interests, or welfare of the United States.

(4) Visas shall next be made available, in a number not to exceed 10 per centum . . . to qualified immigrants who are the married sons or married daughters of citizens of the United States.

(5) Visas shall next be made available, in a number not to exceed 24 per centum . . . to qualified immigrants who are the brothers or sisters of citizens of the United States.

(6) Visas shall next be made available, in a number not to exceed 10 per centum of the number specified . . . to qualified immigrants who are capable of performing specified skilled or unskilled labor, not of a temporary or seasonal nature, for which a shortage of employable and willing persons exists in the United States.

(7) Conditional entries shall next be made available by the Attorney General, pursuant to such regulations as he may prescribe and in a number not to exceed 6 per centum . . . to aliens who satisfy an Immigration and Naturalization Service officer at an examination in any non-Communist or non-Communist-dominated country, (A) that (i) because of persecution or fear of persecution on account of race, religion, or political opinion they have fled (I) from any Communist or Communist-dominated country or area, or (II) from any country within the general area of the Middle East, and (ii) are unable or unwilling to return to such country or area on account of race, religion, or political opinion, and (iii) are not nationals of the countries or areas in which their application for conditional entry is made; or (B) that they are persons uprooted by catastrophic natural calamity as defined by the President who are unable to return to their usual place of abode.

2. Statistics on Immigration Trends

Immigration Trends by Race and Decade, 1820–1980 (in millions)

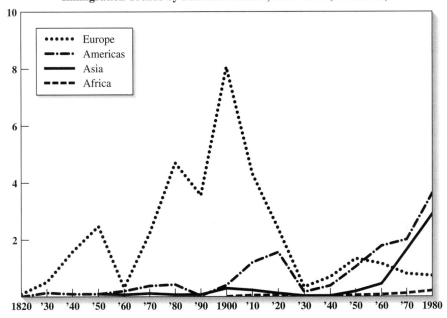

Source: Data for 1981 to 1990 are from U.S. Immigration and Naturalization Service (INS), *Statistical Yearbook of the Immigration and Naturalization Service, 1991* (Washington, DC: U.S. Government Printing Office, 1992), table 3, p. 32. Data for 1820 to 1980 were adapted from Leon F. Bouvier and Robert W. Gardner, "Immigration to the U.S.: The Unfinished Story," *Population Bulletin* 41, no. 4 (November 1986); table 1, p. 8. Primary source: INS, *Statistical Yearbook* (Washington, DC: U.S. Government Printing Office, 1986), table IMM 1.2.

Immigration by Country of Origin, 1850–1990

DECADE	CHINESE	JAPANESE	ASIAN INDIAN	KOREAN	FILIPINO	VIETNAMESE
1850–1860	41,397	-	43	-	-	-
1861–1870	64,301	186	69	-	-	-
1871–1880	123,201	149	163	-	-	-
1881–1890	61,711	2,270	269	-	-	-
1891–1900	14,799	25,942	68	-	-	-
1901–1910	20,605	129,797	4,713	7,697	-	-
1911–1920	21,278	83,837	2,082	1,049	869	-
1921–1930	29,907	33,462	1,886	598	54,747	-
1931–1940	4,928	1,948	496	60	6,159	-
1941–1950	16,709	1,555	1,761	-	4,691	-
1951–1960	9,657[a]	46,250	1,973	6,231	19,307	-
1961–1970	34,764	3,998	27,189	34,526	98,376	3,788
1971–1980	12,326	49,775	164,134	271,956	360,216	179,681
1981–1990	366,622[b]	43,248	261,841	338,824	495,271	401,419

Sources: For 1851–1980, U.S. Commission on Civil Rights, *The Economic Status of Americans of Asian Descent: An Exploratory Investigation* (Washington, DC: U.S. Commission on Civil Rights Clearinghouse Publication 95, October 1988), table 2.2, p. 21. For 1981–1990, selected from U.S. Immigration and Naturalization Service (INS), *Statistical Yearbook of the Immigration and Naturalization Service, 1991* (Washington, DC: U.S. Government Printing Office, 1992), table 3, p. 32. Primary source: For 1851–1980, INS, *Statistical Yearbook of the Immigration and Naturalization Service,* various years. Data on Filipino migration to mainland United States for the decades 1911–1940 were derived from the INS *Report of the Commissioner General of Immigration.* A dash (-) represents less than 0.5 percent. *Notes:* (a) Beginning in 1957, Chinese total includes immigration from Taiwan. (b) Beginning in 1982, Taiwan was no longer included in the Chinese total. Immigration from Taiwan to the United States from 1982 to 1990 was 118,105. These immigrants are not included in the total for Chinese which appears in the table.

3. Perla Rabor Rigor Compares Life as a Nurse in the Philippines and America, 1987

I didn't want to stay in one place. It was always my desire for adventure and the place I really wanted to visit was the U.S. There is so much opportunity with all the modern facilities and technology. What we saw back home was always the good part about America. The movies always showed the best.

I am a registered nurse. I graduated in Southern Island Hospital in the Philippines. After graduation, I worked in Manila in various hospitals. I was a staff nurse at St. Lazarus Hospital. It was always my dream to take postgraduate courses in the U.S., thinking that I would return to the Philippines and share my knowledge. But this did not happen.

I came here as an exchange visitor—a professional exchange. At that time, I was accepted at the Margaret Haig Hospital in New Jersey to take postgraduate study in obstetrics and gynecology. In the Philippines, my background was surgery. At the time I was trying to come to the States all the programs that I wanted were

From Susan B. Gall and Timothy L. Gall, *Statistical Record of Asian Americans,* p. 411. Copyright © 1993 The Gale Group. Reprinted by permission of The Gale Group.

Excerpt from Caridad Concepcion Vallangca, *The Second Wave: Pinay and Pinoy (1945–1960),* pp. 162–165. Copyright © 1987 Strictly Books. Used with permission.

closed; only OB was available. Besides, I would then be close to Jersey City where my brother was. I stayed at the Margaret Haig Hospital for six months. I also took postgraduate courses and finished advanced supervision and management. After that I went to Polytechnic Clinic in New York to take postgraduate study in operating room nursing. Then, after that, I applied in Chicago at Cook County Hospital. This is a big hospital. I worked in OB/GYN, in the operating room.

After a year, I got married—I met my husband here. His father is Filipino and his mother is Russian. When I came to Chicago, he had just come out of the U.S. Navy. We lived with his father, who already has a place. Later, we bought our own place on the West Side. Since my husband looks like an Italian, we happened to be in an Italian neighborhood. We loved it. People in that area did not even know where I came from. They did not even know where the Philippines is. Then we moved. We looked for an apartment, and that was the hardest part. It was rough. We did not buy because we wanted to be sure we really liked the place. We wanted to be close to the hospital. When they see you, they just slam the door in your face. Finally, my husband found a place—when we bought the place, no problem at all. . . .

When I came to Cook County Hospital, Filipino nurses were highly regarded as hard working, but to get into a better position, to me there was still a bit of prejudice. Regardless of your qualifications, the opportunity for us Filipinos has been suppressed and that is what I felt—it happened to me. I could see that I was well qualified to be the head nurse. I was not given that opportunity. Another incident was when I was in West Suburban Hospital in Oak Park. The reason I went from one hospital to another was to learn different types of techniques. At Suburban Hospital, I was never given a chance. I know how qualified I am, I am an aggressive person, I can verbalize. I was in the delivery room, in the operating room, in the emergency room, more like a pinch hitter, but not given a chance. Somebody resigned and I should have been the next person in line, but they picked a person who was a new graduate—it was a slap in the face—there was complete discrimination. So, I quit that place. I moved to Swedish Covenant Hospital. This is a missionary hospital. When I applied, there was no hesitancy at all to hire me—they accepted Filipinos as one of the best.

It looks to me like nursing in the Philippines has become like a diploma mill. It could happen in the States, too. The training that we had during my time was really rigid, clinically as well as theoretically. The language barrier was not too bad—but in the third wave, it seems to me that, with most of the nurses that come here, there is a difficulty in understanding them when they speak English. There is something there—it could be that the educational system in the Philippines no longer stresses English, but only the use of the national language. They can understand, but not express themselves. Some of them are afraid, so meek, afraid to accept responsibility. They are smart, but they are just not aggressive, it makes me mad. Filipinos are smarter than other Asian groups, we are well educated, but they keep on using their language. The new arrivals do not speak English—and they just *have* to speak English. Not that we want to lose our own heritage. . . .

I am very satisfied—it was a rough time for me when I started here, because being from a foreign land you have to push yourself to get your ability recognized. During my time, no matter how good you were in your work, you had to be the best. So, I went to school and I finally finished in 1975, got my degrees in psychology and in education from St. Francis College in Joliet, Illinois. I got my diploma all on my own. To me, even dealing with people, success is not measured by the position the person has reached in life, but by the obstacles she or he has overcome.

The Second Wave has passed the test—we are now recognized.

4. The Supreme Court Endorses Bilingual Education, 1974

The failure of the San Francisco school system to provide English language instruction to approximately 1,800 students of Chinese ancestry who do not speak English, or to provide them with other adequate instructional procedures, denies them a meaningful opportunity to participate in the public educational program and thus violates 601 of the Civil Rights Act of 1964, which bans discrimination based "on the ground of race, color, or national origin," in "any program or activity receiving Federal financial assistance," and the implementing regulations of the Department of Health, Education, and Welfare. Pp. 565–569. . . .

The Court of Appeals reasoned that "[e]very student brings to the starting line of his educational career different advantages and disadvantages caused in part by social, economic, and cultural background, created and continued completely apart from any contribution by the school system," 483 F.2d, at 797. Yet in our view the case may not be so easily decided. This is a public school system of California and 71 of the California Education Code state that "English shall be the basic language of instruction in all schools." That section permits a school district to determine "when and under what circumstances instruction may be given bilingually." That section also states as "the policy of the state" to insure "the mastery of English by all pupils in the schools." And bilingual instruction is authorized "to the extent that it does not interfere with the systematic, sequential, and regular instruction of all pupils in the English language." [414 U.S. 563, 566] . . .

Under these state-imposed standards there is no equality of treatment merely by providing students with the same facilities, textbooks, teachers, and curriculum; for students who do not understand English are effectively foreclosed from any meaningful education.

Basic English skills are at the very core of what these public schools teach. Imposition of a requirement that, before a child can effectively participate in the educational program, he must already have acquired those basic skills is to make a mockery of public education. We know that those who do not understand English are certain to find their classroom experiences wholly incomprehensible and in no way meaningful. . . .

It seems obvious that the Chinese-speaking minority receive fewer benefits than the English-speaking majority from respondents' school system which denies them a meaningful opportunity to participate in the educational program—all earmarks of the discrimination banned by the regulations. . . .

From *Lau v. Nichols*, 414 U.S. 563 (1974); reprinted at http://caselaw.lp.findlaw.com/scripts/getcase. pl?court=us&vol=414&invol=563.

We accordingly reverse the judgments of the Court of Appeals and remand the case for the fashioning of appropriate relief.

5. Asian Americans Debate the Pros and Cons of Bilingual Education, 1998

About 1.4 million California public school students are classified as limited-English proficient, or LEP. About 80 percent are Spanish-speaking Latinos. According to the California Department of Education, students whose primary language is an Asian one (Vietnamese, Hmong, Cantonese, Filipino, Mandarin, Khmer, etc.) make up 15 percent of the LEPs, or about 210,000 students. Some Asian American bilingual-ed experts put the number closer to 250,000, or approximately 40 percent of all Asian American students in the state's public schools.

It is perhaps ironic that the contemporary bilingual education movement was triggered in part by a U.S. Supreme Court case brought by San Francisco Chinese American families. In the landmark 1973 Lau vs. Nichols case, the high court said public schools had to offer students who weren't proficient in English equal educational opportunities, which educators have broadly interpreted to mean bilingual programs.

These days, it's not clear whether Asian Americans support or oppose bilingual education, or even how much they care. Some polls have shown majorities as high as 70 percent in favor, but bilingual advocates question whether the sampling is large enough to be statistically significant. Among public officials, proponents include Garden Grove Councilman Ho Chung, and Westminster Councilman Tony Lam, as well as state Treasurer Matt Fong, who is seeking the Republican nomination for the U.S. Senate.

"The education issue cannot be distorted by ethnic sensibilities or political opportunism," said Chung, a Korean American. "Children are our future. We have to educate them. We have to have one common language for everybody to be able to communicate."

However, Judy Chu, a Democratic candidate for the state Assembly from the Monterey Park–San Gabriel area east of Los Angeles, says the Unz initiative would hurt kids.

"The massive dismantling of bilingual programs under Unz would do a great disservice to limited-English-proficient students in our area," said Chu, adding she isn't concerned that her stance could hurt her at the polls. "This is a very diverse area. Lots of people come from other countries."

Jean Quan, a member of the Oakland School Board, worries about losing Asian-language-speaking classroom aides who translate between teachers on one end and students and their parents on the other. If they are cut from school budgets, there will be no one to translate for the parents, she said.

From Bill Wong, "The Lessons of Bilingual Education," *AsianWeek,* May 20, 1998. Copyright © 1998 AsianWeek. Used with permission.

Leland Yee, a San Francisco supervisor and former San Francisco School Board member, said he opposes 227, but criticizes the political and educational establishment for doing a "terrible job" on behalf of limited-English-speaking children.

"The Unz Initiative says we can't have non-English primary language instruction. I can't accept that. But I can't accept business as usual "because policymakers have not exercised sufficient political will to hire enough qualified bilingual teachers and provide enough primary-language textbooks. Yee said.

"If I were the parent of a limited-English-proficient student, I would think twice about putting my kid into a bilingual class," he added.

If Proposition 227 becomes law, limited-English-proficient students would be placed in English immersion classes, possibly with kids of other ages, for up to one year. After that, students are to be placed in classrooms where English is the only language of instruction. Exceptions could be made if enough parents show up in person to request that their children be enrolled in bilingual classes.

Advocates of bilingual education say that core subjects would not be taught during the immersion period and that one year is not enough time for most students to learn the language well enough to grasp core subjects taught in English. Some educators fear that some students will drop out.

"We know from the research that [non-English-speaking students] can't learn English well enough in one year to be put into an academic setting to understand subject matter content taught in English," said Gay Wong, an associate professor at California State University at Los Angeles who specializes in literacy and biliteracy. Wong said it takes three to four years to learn "social" English, and five to seven years to learn the more abstract "academic" English.

Experts say many factors determine a student's speed in acquiring English: academic background in the student's native culture, socioeconomic status of the family, age of arrival. Stanford education professor Kenji Hakuta, speaking at a forum last month in San Francisco, said it is a myth that young children magically learn English quickly.

"If we take into account socioeconomic status, transitional bilingual programs are more effective than English-only programs," when it comes to reading and math, he said. About half of Asian LEP students are poor; among all limited-English-proficient youngsters, 80 percent are under the poverty line, he said.

A child's native language also affects how long it takes to learn English, he said. Cambodian immigrant students, for instance, have more difficulties, in part because of economic status, in part because of a lack of certified Cambodian-language bilingual instructors. Hmong immigrant children can have a harder time learning English because many come from a non-literate culture. . . .

Have bilingual programs worked for Asian Americans? Experts say there haven't been enough studies done. On May 1, San Francisco school officials issued a study showing that bilingual students who completed the district's program did as well, if not better, in reading and math scores, grade-point average and attendance as students not in the program. Unz criticized the study for looking only at students who had completed the program and not at those who hadn't.

Absent broad, conclusive studies, Tammy Leung's experience, like that of many others, sheds insight. Leung immigrated to the United States from Hong Kong in 1978, when she was 15. She could read and write English, but couldn't speak it or understand it. She took bilingual classes at Oakland High, including core subjects taught in Cantonese and English.

"It worked for me," she said in barely accented English. "It gave me confidence when I did well in classes. It gave me a feeling I could do well in the United States."

Eventually, she got her bachelor's degree in nursing at San Jose State University and is now a registered nurse.

When asked how she thinks she would have done had she been placed in an English-only immersion program, she said, "I would have dropped out of school."

6. Asian Immigrants Transplant Religious Institutions, 1994

When Vietnamese refugees in battered wooden boats battled ocean currents in the 1970s on a long, tortuous journey to what they hoped would be a life of freedom in America, they carried hardly any worldly possessions. However, many of the refugees, devout Buddhists, did carry religious icons, often secured to their bodies.

Chrys Thorsen, an official of the Buddhist Sangha Council in Los Angeles, explains: "They were afraid there would be no Buddhist temples here for them. The one thing they were not going to leave behind was their religion."

They did not know it, but there already were Buddhist houses of worship in the United States, but mainly by Chinese and Japanese Buddhists, and open to all believers. But the influx of new immigrants from Southeast and South Asia since the 1970s has led to the construction of many more temples. Experts put the number of Asian temples, shrines, monasteries and retreat houses in the U.S. today at 1,500. Some sit on sprawling estates spread across hundreds of acres while others are merely areas set aside in private homes.

An estimated US$200 million has gone into the purchase of the land and construction of these temples. Part of the money has come from overseas Buddhist temples, while a substantial amount has been raised from the immigrants. And at least US$100 million is currently being raised for new temples and the expansion of the existing ones.

The Immigration Act of 1965, which ended national origin quotas, was followed by an influx of thousands of immigrants from the Indian Subcontinent and Southeast Asia. According to Ron Takaki, professor of ethnic history at the University of California at Berkeley, the arrival of the immigrants led to a boom in Buddhist, Hindu and Sikh temples. "It took them about a decade to settle down, and once they had made their homes and saw their children doing well in schools and colleges, they began building temples," he said. There are at least 3 million Buddhists and 1 million Hindus in the U.S.

Some of the temples were built from scratch; some were converted from dilapidated churches, and in one case, a former mental institution on a 237-acre property in Talmage, California was transformed into a temple complex called City of a Thousand Buddhas.

Arthur J. Pais and Etta Sanders, "Transplanting God: Asian Immigrants Are Building Buddhist and Hindu Temples Across the U.S.," *Far Eastern Economic Review* (June 23, 1994): 34–35. © Dow Jones & Co. Inc. Reprinted by permission.

The new immigrants even brought about a revival of Buddhism across America. Second-and third-generation Asian Americans had, for various reasons, lost interest in the religion of their parents and grandparents. Even those who continued to practise their religion made accommodations "to appear less foreign," according to the Reverend Himaka, a director of the Buddhist Churches of America. Japanese Buddhists, for example, began using the word "church" instead of "temple." But now, a move is being made to revive the use of the word "temple."

As the Buddhists went about their temple-building, so did Hindus and Sikhs. The monthly magazine *Hinduism Today* until recently listed temples and ashrams across America under the heading "Find God and Gods in your City." It gave the locations of more than 75 Hindu temples and ashrams across America but, even as the list was updated each month, unknown to the magazine a coconut or two was broken amidst the chanting of mantras at a ground-breaking ceremony for another temple.

In Memphis, Elvis Presley's home town, last year the *nadaswavam* (Indian reed music) was heard when a temple costing US$3 million was consecrated. Some Hindu temples, cast in the mould of famous Indian structures, sit on sites exceeding 100 acres. According to conservative estimates, Hindu immigrants have donated US$125 million in the last decade for temples. (Apart from these temples, about two dozen other facilities such as the Hare Krishna temples and ashrams costing over US$100 million and built mostly with donations of American devotees have come up.) In addition, more than a dozen *gurudwaras* have emerged to serve the Sikh community.

"Immigrants have always brought their religions and reshaped them in America," says Raymond Brady Williams, author of *Religions of Immigrants From India and Pakistan.* "When they build the temples, it shows that they are no more sojourners. They have found their roots in this country."

But immigrants have also encountered opposition from the local people. For example, a few years ago, barely a week after Bochanaswami Swaminarvan Sanstha, an affluent religious sect from India, announced plans for a US$100 million temple complex in Independence, a small New Jersey town, opposition began brewing. Video cassettes of a tape, *Gods of New Age,* produced by a fundamentalist Christian group, began circulating among the 3,000 residents.

The tape described yoga as mind control. Mahatma Gandhi was depicted as a sex pervert, and devotion to a guru was associated with Nazism. There were references to Shree Rajneesh, the controversial free-sex Indian guru who had established a commune in rural Oregon, and to the Hare Krishna commune in New Vrindaban, West Virginia, which was embroiled in sex and murder scandals. The town's zoning laws were suddenly changed to restrict new buildings to single-family dwellings.

"Zoning is often used as a thinly veiled way of exerting prejudice." Thorsen says. Adds Malti Prasad of The Hindu Temple in Livermore, California: "On the surface, they bring the argument of congestion. But in their hearts they fear we will establish a cult like the one in Jones Town" where hundreds died in a mass suicide. It took over six years for the Hsi Lai Temple project in Hacienda Heights to get permission from zoning authorities. The US$30 million temple, consecrated four years ago and perched atop a hill overlooking an affluent Los Angeles suburb, was partly financed by the Taiwanese mother temple.

Some temple-builders have become smarter. "On one hand we try to buy the houses and the property around the proposed temple," says a leader of The Hindu Temple in New York "And on the other hand, we sit down across the table and discuss the tenets of our religion and convince the opposition that we are not a suicidal cult."

Even after opposition is overcome and a temple is built, it is frequently confronted with other problems, principally vandalism. The Bharatiya Temple in Troy, Michigan, was vandalised five years ago soon after it was consecrated. The attack took place on the anniversary of Kristallnacht in 1938, when Nazi gangs in Hitler's Germany burned synagogues and destroyed Jewish businesses. A Nazi swastika was painted on the temple's outer walls. The walls of the Hindu Temple in New York, the first such facility in the U.S., were daubed with such slogans as: "Hindus Go Back Home."

Some critics question how long the temples can sustain themselves. "Many of them have taken loans from banks owned by the Indian Government," says one. "And right now, they cannot pay the interest, for they are dependent on donations from devotees and fees." There has been a steady attrition in donations at Sikh temples following political problems between Sikhs and Hindus, and the latter have stopped visiting them.

Others question the relevance of the temples to life in America. The late Surendra Saxena, who was president of the Association of Indians in America, asked "what appeal these temples will have to the second and third generation of Hindus?" He said: "Ask the rich doctors and businessmen who cough up money for temples to fund a community hall or contribute to a social cause or a scholarship, and many will refuse." Many say that while the temples dwell on rituals, they have mostly eschewed social responsibilities. "There are hundreds of Indian women who are battered, and who are afraid to go into shelters," says A. Bhattaryajee of Sakhi, an organisation for South Asian women. "Temples could help to get them temporary abodes. But they won't."

But some temples are slowly getting to recognise their social responsibilities. The Sri Venkateswara Temple in Pittsburgh, for example, has funded many medical camps in India and has donated thousands of dollars to such causes as the Ethiopian famine relief.

Supporters of the temple movement say that temples will continue to survive as long as new immigrants keep coming. "And precisely because we fear the second and third generations will lose their faith, we must have temples and educational centres," says Manshueh of Hsi Lai Temple. Ram Chandran, till recently an executive director of The Hindu Temple in New York, says: "We have achieved the first task the construction. Now comes the challenge, how to keep the faith alive, especially among the young." To this end, the New York temple and others have organised children's camps and seminars. "The older generation is used to the chanting of mantras in Sanskirt or an Indian language," says Uma Mysorekar, a doctor who has donated US$3 million to the New York temple. "We are trying to get priests who can perform the rituals in English and converse with our children."

L. N. Raghava Bhattar, a priest at the New York temple who arrived from India about a decade ago, predicts that American-born Indians will join the priesthood as the community is growing—and temples are gearing to get young men and women involved in their activities.

7. Korean American Professor Elaine Kim Discusses Problems in Building Coalitions Between Asian Immigrants and Other Communities of Color, 1998

It is often said that by the year 2015, people of color will constitute a majority of Californians. Those fearful of this future have been vociferously supporting a variety of measures and policies aimed at dismantling affirmative action programs and restricting services for racial minorities and immigrants of color, based on the idea that paying any attention to race is racist and perpetuates racism. Asian Americans are frequently positioned as the racial minority that proves that we have attained a color-blind society, since they have higher educational attainment and incomes than Latinos and African Americans, who have presumably not succeeded as well because programs like affirmative action and bilingual education have made them lazy.

In many ways, Asian Americans are positioned on the in-between—on the cusp, at the interstice, in the buffer zone—of Asia and America, between black and white, between old-timer and newcomer, between mainstreamed and marginalized. Yet the in-between is a precarious and dangerous position to occupy if we are not fully cognizant of where we are and what our position means in the larger picture. Armed with that cognizance, we have the potential to participate creatively and courageously in the shaping of the social, political, and cultural environment.

Current Asian American history is not marked by the blatantly discriminatory laws of the past, which prevented them from immigrating, becoming naturalized citizens, marrying, owning land, and testifying against white Americans in court. However, phobic attitudes and discriminatory policies persist. As Richard Fung has observed, old racist stereotypes of Asian inscrutability, unfair competition, cultural unassimilability, and sexual perversity are displaced onto every new group of Asian immigrants and in every new crisis: the most recently arrived refugees of U.S. wars in Southeast Asia find themselves being called "Chinks" and "Japs" as they step into a historical situation they had no part in making. In recent years, resentment and hatred have become ever more visible against Asians and Latinos, who are still thought by many to be inferior, alien, and all alike. As in the past, Asian Americans today are still seen as metonyms for Asia and are forcibly distanced from U.S. national culture, which defines its citizenry—or who can be American—as well as which histories and experience are to be remembered and which ones forgotten.

I am old enough to have experienced various kinds of pre–Civil Rights Movement racial bigotry. Growing up in Maryland in the 1950s, I was continually taunted and subjected to racial gestures and epithets. Sometimes people tried to spit on me. Classmates' mothers sometimes scolded them for befriending me. People told my parents, my brother, or me to go back to our country. People continually joked about how "all Orientals look alike." Asians were assumed to be foreign, since "Asian" and "American" were popularly thought to be mutually exclusive. Even my

---

From Elaine Kim, "'At Least You're Not Black': Asian Americans in U.S. Race Relations." Reprinted by permission from *Social Justice* 25, no. 3 (fall 1998): 3.

graduate seminar professor at Columbia University complimented me on my ability to speak English at the end of a four-month semester.

A pair of comments that white people often made remains stubbornly in my memory: "At least you are not black," or "You should be grateful that you are not black." These comments, I think, convey the particular kind of racism Asian Americans should recognize and challenge. While being encouraged to feel superior to African Americans, Asian Americans are being positioned in a racial hierarchy meant to perpetuate white privilege at the expense of both Asian and African Americans.

What seems to infuriate some people the most is the thought of an ungrateful Asian American siding with other people of color, presumably against whites. They want to hold onto their notion of Asian Americans as docile honorary white people whose very existence proves that other people of color are lazy and stupid and that racism does not exist in U.S. society. If you love African Americans so much, why don't you go back to Asia? According to this logic, Asian American affinities with African Americans and acknowledgement of the history of enslavement, segregation, and discrimination equal negation of "America," which can only be coded as "white." . . .

Asian Americans share with African Americans and other Americans of color a long, complex, and little-discussed relationship. This reminds me a little of the relationships between Korean provinces and villages, linked by roads built by the Japanese colonizers not to each other but to the sea, from which Korean natural resources were taken and into which Japanese manufactured goods are pumped. The political, economic, and cultural histories of Mexico and the Philippines have much to share, but the discussion, instead of being direct, is siphoned through the U.S. and Spain. Likewise, there are many parallels between Asian Indian and Korean American histories rendered invisible by British, Japanese, and American narratives. Unlike the assimilationist attempt to study Japanese-Anglo interracial marriages in recent decades, a long history of Chinese–Native American, Filipino–Native American, Filipino-Mexican, Sikh-Mexican, Chinese–African American, and indeed Japanese-Filipino and Chinese-Korean interracial marriage was simply swept aside and ignored, so that we know about it mostly from our own experiences or from stories the old-timers tell us. . . .

To forge our links in the face of these forces, we need to unearth the buried history of coalition work and activism in the past. For instance, Afro-Asian friendship had hidden roots in our society. No one talks much about how people of the African American community stood, practically alone and certainly at no direct gain to themselves, against the abrogation of Japanese Americans' civil rights during World War II. Or how three-quarters of a century ago the mostly black Brotherhood of Sleeping Car Porters issued a public statement of solidarity with Filipino workers who, they said, "have been used against the unionization of Pullman porters just as Negroes have been used against the unionization of white workers."

Asian Americans have a proud if subterranean legacy of fighting economic and social injustice. Since the 19th century, Chinese Americans fought every piece of discriminatory legislation, sometimes all the way to the Supreme Court. Indeed, Chinese and African American court cases against segregation inspired and propelled each other forward over the decades. The spectacular pan-ethnic labor organizing activities between Japanese and Filipinos in Hawaii at the turn of the century and the cross-racial labor organizing between Japanese and Mexicans in California in the first decades of this century and then between Filipinos and Mexicans from the 1960s have provided a legacy for Asian American labor organizing taking place in various parts of the country today. Examples are the multiracial San Francisco hotel maids' strike in the early 1980s and the pan–Asian American Jessica McClintock boycott of the 1990s that included many Korean American participants and was strongly supported by Latina garment workers. The movement beyond narrow nationalism was clearly seen several years ago in Los Angeles, when Korean Immigrant Workers Advocates (KIWA) organizers fought against the South Korea–based corporation that acquired the Radisson Plaza Hotel and planned to replace unionized Latino workers with cheaper, nonunionized immigrant workers.

Besides divesting ourselves of the old dominant versus marginal binary thinking, we must also try to resist the temptation to see ourselves and our relationships with each other through rose-colored glasses. We must reach far beyond simple-minded celebrations of identity and resist the seductive claims of victimhood. We must scrutinize our warts. We need to be critical and self-critical. If building concrete coalitions with other communities of color is at the top of the agenda for Asian Americans right now, we need to look closely at how this crucially important work is made difficult by a number of factors.

First, U.S. immigration policies historically favored middle-class Asian immigrants: merchants and foreign students, not laborers before 1965, and urban professionals until the 1980s. Proportionally, the middle class is better represented among Asian Americans, including South Asians and Filipinos, than is the case with other groups of color, which reinforces the primacy of middle-class concerns that always predominate anyway because poor and working-class people have less access to power. Moreover, U.S. immigration policies favor those who oppose socialism and communism, and many immigrants and refugees from Korea and other parts of Asia have been staunchly anticommunist and, thus, both lacking in sympathy for the poor and ripe for alignment with conservative Republicans who traditionally opposed many of the programs supported by other people of color in the U.S.

A second and related point is that many recent Asian immigrants are from countries colonized by the U.S. and other Western nations. Although anti-U.S. sentiment is growing all over Asia, the "colonial mentality" is a frequent outcome of colonization, and many immigrants are held back from questioning injustices by ingrained old notions about the predominance and superiority of everything "American," which for many of them is coded as "white." Today, burgeoning Korean nationalism and anti-U.S. sentiments notwithstanding, Western cultural influences can be seen everywhere in South Korea. A good friend tells me how the newspapers and TV talk shows there recently carried programs on "postmodernism." When she went to a small village video store to find a video to rent, the owner advised her to rent Terminator II because it was very "postmodern." . . .

Another thing that has dramatically separated Asian Americans from other people of color has been in terms of attitudes toward what we call "America." We know that for many Native Americans, America means stolen land. For many Chicanos, it means occupied territory conquered and taken from Mexico 150 years ago. For many African Americans, it means the country built with slave labor brought here by force. For a large number of Asian Americans, especially of the

recent immigration generation that escaped from war, political upheaval, colonization, and barriers to social and economic mobility in the homeland, America has
meant "promised land" or "dream country."

Having immigrated or come as refugees from colonized countries, often escaping from socialist and communist governments, many Asian Americans still feel
like guests in the house or a daughter-in-law in her mother-in-law's house. Like a
guest or a new bride living with her mother-in-law, she needs to be grateful, obedient,
and uncomplaining. She needs to be mindful of the rules and of her host's generosity,
without which where would she be? . . .

. . . . Even though many of today's Asian immigrants can't claim the U.S. Civil
Rights Movements as their legacy, organizing efforts among them could stress heritages in the Asian homelands that are also rooted in struggles for justice and equality, such as the long and bloody movement against martial law in the Philippines and
Taiwan and the democracy movements in China, India, and Burma. Every Japanese
American can be proud of the huge peace movement in Japan, where the atomic
bomb was dropped. In addition, for the past three decades, the most spectacular
labor movement in the world has been taking place in South Korea, the country
that boasted the world's longest work week, and where murder and assault of labor
leaders have been legendary. . . .

If we don't watch out, Asian Americans may find ourselves one day schooled,
credentialed, and trapped in the old "buffer zone" or "middleman" position, attempting an ultimately impossible mediation between those mostly white people who
have the power to make the rules and those mostly black and brown people who are
oppressed by them. Whether as professors, newscasters, attorneys, or middle managers, we could be positioned to serve as apologists for and explicators, upholders,
and functionaries of the status quo.

8. Indian Immigrant Sarita Sarvate Criticizes the "Brain Drain" from the Third World, 2000

Recently, a bill was introduced in Congress called the "Brain Act" to allow foreign
students with higher degrees in science and engineering to work in the U.S. To us
immigrants, the bill seems to legitimize the policy that the U.S. industry has surreptitiously implemented for nearly four decades—the stealing of brain from the
third world.

During the sixties and the seventies, the politicians in my native India used to
brandish the slogan "Stop Brain Drain," to describe the departure of the cream of India for the lucrative shores of England and America. That was the post-independence
era, when everything foreign smacked of colonialism. So we talked of cottage industries and economic imperialism. We threw Coca Cola out and invented Thumbs Up.
But it was also the era of Sputnik and Neil Armstrong, of nuclear power and the
green revolution. On Independence Day, our Prime Minister Jawaharlal Nehru stood
on the ramparts of the Red Fort and spoke of the benefits of science and technology.

From Sarita Sarvate, "The Last Word: 'Brain Act' or 'Brain Drain?'" *India Currents* 13, no. 11 (February 28, 2000). Used by permission of India Currents, www.indiacurrents.com.

And our institutes of technology, built with European and American aid, offered students free room and board, even stipends. The Indian taxpayer footed the bill, in the hope that one day the graduates would reconstruct the nation.

I was one such student. Poring over textbooks in the General Theory of Relativity late at night in the library of the Indian Institute of Technology (IIT), I would dream, not of India, but of America, the land of opportunity. Many students like me indeed left during the sixties and the seventies, never to return.

So our government set up special programs to tempt foreign graduates back. There were parallels, our leaders believed, to the independence movement, which had been founded by people like Nehru and Gandhi, who, after imbibing Western political ideology at institutions like Eton and Oxford, returned home to serve the motherland. But few foreign graduates came home to "redeem their pledge," as Nehru had put it.

What our leaders failed to foresee was the fact that the emphasis on symbol manipulation in the education at IIT left little room for social ideology and much scope for capitalistic greed.

Over the next two decades, California's Silicon Valley was founded off the backs of our graduates, educated at our taxpayer's expense. Later, the personal computer revolution, and the internet, mushroomed the demand for skilled labor to such gigantic proportions that even if every American child were to study science from now on, we would be unable to keep pace with it.

Contrary to American public perception, therefore, the Brain Act, or the officialization of "brain drain," benefits not foreign workers but American industry, which would be crippled without it.

Back at home in the meantime, the education system of an entire nation has shifted gears to feed the demands of the American computer industry. IIT graduates cannot suffice a single corporation like Microsoft, let alone an entire cyber-revolution. So every street corner in India sports billboards now for computer academics offering diplomas in software engineering. At the Book Show in my hometown of Nagpur recently, hordes of young people pored over books on engineering and computer science.

Children are raised with a singularity of purpose; to help them forsake their ancestral land at the earliest opportunity. An entire nation stands poised to leave, for the brighter shores of America. Rhetoric about Brain Drain doesn't hold much water when every politician has a son or a daughter aspiring to go abroad.

And why bother rebuilding the nation when the only goal is to abandon it? At the Book Show, the latest American social treaties were conspicuous by their absence. The elite of yesteryears has been replaced by a new kind of elite, riding on the wave of the internet revolution, making fortunes within a span of years.

This new elite has abandoned all talk of economic imperialism in favor of market economics. Today, Thumbs Up is a subsidiary of Coca Cola. Indians now put garlands around Bill Gates' neck and offer him the kind of reception once offered only to British royalty.

The reasons are not hard to understand. Mid-sized cities like Bangalore are now the Silicon Valleys of India. Workers there generate demand for the goods they produce, creating a feedback loop.

But the nation is slowly disintegrating. India's population recently hit the one billion mark; its infrastructure in water, transportation, and healthcare is fast crumbling. The largest number of AIDs cases now reside within its boundaries. Its air is dangerously polluted.

India has gone from an agrarian society to the cyber revolution, bypassing intermediate stages such as the new deal, the welfare state, and the creation of social services. Perhaps it is time to enact a voluntary Brain Act; one that will encourage corporations like Microsoft and Intel, who have drained India for decades of its technical brains, to finance the creation of a new "brain trust," which will study, not symbol manipulation, but the creation of a social infrastructure for a population of a billion.

☙ E S S A Y S

The first essay, by University of Minnesota historian Catherine Ceniza Choy, analyzes the "transnational" identity of Filipino nurses who have migrated to the United States. Choy also traces the links between more recent migration practices and American colonial policies established at the turn of the century. The second essay, by Edward Park, a sociologist at the University of California at Riverside, examines the impact of the 1992 Los Angeles "civil unrest" (riots) on Korean Americans. Park compares campaigns by Democrats and Republicans to recruit Korean immigrants by offering different interpretations of the causes of the destruction of Koreatown and the systematic targeting of Korean stores in South Central Los Angeles.

A Transnational History of Filipino Nurse Migration

CATHERINE CENIZA CHOY

The contemporary international migration of Filipino nurses is inextricably linked to the history of American imperialism and the early-twentieth-century U.S. colonization of the Philippines. As a part of the establishment of an Americanized training hospital system in the Philippines during the colonial period, new standards were instituted to improve the professional skills and standing of the nursing labor force. These changes included an Americanized nursing-school curriculum, English language fluency, and professionalization of the nursing work culture. . . .

The socioeconomic and cultural significance of experience abroad for Filipino nurses changed dramatically in the mid-twentieth century. During this period, several exchange programs served as vehicles for the transformation of nursing into an internationally recognized profession. While new international work programs in Germany and Holland recruited Filipino nurses to work outside of the Philippines, the U.S. Exchange Visitors (EVP) facilitated the first wave of mass migration of Filipino nurses abroad by providing several thousand Filipino nurses with the opportunity to work and study in the United States. Between 1956 and 1969, more than eleven thousand Filipino nurses participated in the EVP. Under the EVP, the experience of going abroad was transformed from an opportunity reserved for the few into one available to any Filipino registered nurse.

From Catherine Ceniza Choy, "Exported to Care: A Transnational History of Filipino Nurse Migration to the United States," in *Immigration Research for a New Century: Multidisciplinary Perspectives,* eds. Nancy Foner et al., © 2000 Russel Sage Foundation, New York, New York.

In 1948, the Exchange Visitor program was established by the American government, through the U.S. Information and Educational Act. The general objectives of the program were "to promote a better understanding of the United States in other countries and to increase mutual understanding between the people of the United States and the people of other countries." However, the motivations for establishing the program were rooted in Cold War politics. According to Senate reports, "hostile propaganda campaigns directed against democracy, human welfare, freedom, truth, and the United States, spearheaded by the Government of the Soviet Union and the Communist Parties throughout the world," called for "dynamic measures to disseminate truth." One of the "dynamic measures" the Senate proposed was an educational exchange service involving the interchange of persons, knowledge, and skills.

Exchange Visitor Program participants from abroad engaged in both work and study in their sponsoring American institutions, for which they received a monthly stipend. Several thousand U.S. agencies and institutions, including the American Nurses Association and individual hospitals, served as sponsors. The American government issued EVP visas for a maximum stay of two years. Upon completion of the program, both the American and the sending-country governments expected the EVP participants to return to their countries of origin. In all, between 1956 and 1969, nurses made up more than 50 percent (11,136) of the total number (20,420) of exchange visitors from the Philippines.

Filipino nurses may initially have perceived the Exchange Visitor Program as "a dream come true," but exploitation in U.S. hospitals complicated romanticized Philippine narratives about work and study in America. Many sponsoring American hospitals actively recruited exchange nurses to alleviate growing nursing shortages in the post–World War II period. Some American hospital administrators took advantage of the exchange status of Filipino nurses by assigning them the work of registered nurses and compensating them with a minimal stipend. Other American hospital administrators abused the educational and professional component of the EVP by assigning Filipino exchange nurses the work of nurse's aides.

By the mid-1960s, the use of exchange nurses as employees appeared to be more the rule than the exception. A Philippine Department of Labor study committee characterized the EVP as "a handy recruitment device" and "a loophole for the circumvention of United States immigration laws." In 1966, the Philippine congressman Epifanio Castillejos, visiting the United States to survey the situation of Filipino exchange nurses, severely criticized the program: "Almost every Filipino nurse I met had problems which ran the gamut from discrimination in stipend, as well as in the nature and amount of work they are made to do, to the lack of in-service or specialized training in the hospitals they work in." However, reports of discrimination and exploitation did not discourage further Filipino nurse migration to the United States through the EVP. Between 1967 and 1970, more than three thousand Filipino nurses participated in the program. . . .

Filipino nurses working in the Philippines also earned low wages and little professional respect. At some government agencies, nurses were paid lower wages than janitors, drivers, and messengers. In the mid-1960s, Filipino nurses earned between two hundred and three hundred pesos monthly for a six-day workweek, including holidays and overtime if required. In the United States, in the mid-1960s, general-duty nurses earned twice as much, from four hundred to five hundred dollars a month.

Filipino nurses were also attracted to the prestige attached to studying and working in the United States, a prestige originally created by the American colonial scholarship programs in the early twentieth century and revived in the mid-twentieth century. The Filipino Nurses Association contributed to the re-creation of this idealization through news stories in their official publication, the *Philippine Journal of Nursing (PJN)*. Simply participating in the EVP was newsworthy. In 1960, the journal published the names and alma maters of the more than one hundred Filipino exchange nurses leaving for the United States every two to three months. The *PJN* also reported on the professional recognition that Filipino nurses had gained in the United States. When Chicago's American Hospital honored Juanita Jimenez as "Best Nurse of the Year," the *PJN* featured Jimenez as "a silver lining in our profession."

The ability of Filipino exchange nurses to improve their socioeconomic status through their earnings in American dollars, the acquisition of material goods unobtainable in the Philippines, and new forms of leisure also contributed to the prestige of work and study in the United States. Independent of wage differentials, which were considerable, the devaluation of the Philippine peso further increased the earning power of Filipino nurses working in America. The devaluation of the Philippine peso began in 1946 with the Tydings Rehabilitation Act, and by 1971, one American dollar was equivalent to six and a quarter pesos. As exchange nurse Ofelia Boado observed, "the pay [in the United States] was good compared to what I was getting in the Philippines. . . . It became so clear to me that many nurses come here not for advancement but for pay, for really good pay."

Some Filipino exchange nurses manipulated the exchange visitor program to serve their own agendas, for example, by working sixteen-hour shifts to earn more money. With their stipends in American dollars, American credit cards, and layaway plans, the exchange nurses purchased stereos, kitchen appliances, and cosmetics unobtainable for all except the affluent elite in the Philippines. They enjoyed forms of leisure completely unavailable in the Philippines: Broadway shows, performances at Lincoln Center, travel within the United States and to Europe. They lived in their own apartments and stayed out late at night. According to Ofelia Boado, "You're very independent. You have your own apartment. In the Philippines, you live in the dorm where everything closes at 9:00 P.M. Or even if you stay at home, you don't go home late in the night or anything like that."

Given these opportunities abroad, Filipino exchange nurses created a folklore of an America filled with social and economic promise. In their letters to Filipino nursing friends back in the Philippines, boasting of high salaries and "good living" in the United States, Filipino exchange nurses encouraged other Filipino nurses to follow their example.

Going abroad became a trend among Filipino nurses. One study reveals that between 1952 and 1965 an average of slightly more than 50 percent of the 377 graduates from the University of the Philippines College of Nursing went abroad. Filipino exchange nurses, directly or by example, encouraged not only thousands of other Filipino nurses to go to the United States but also other young Filipinas to enter nursing school. In 1962 there were more student applicants for nursing studies than Philippine colleges and schools of nursing were able to accommodate; and going abroad after the study of nursing figured prominently in the plans of most of them. . . .

By the early 1960s, many Filipino nurses hoped to remain indefinitely in the United States, as well. In 1960, Alvarez reported that many Filipino exchange nurses in Chicago complained about the length of their visits, claiming that a two-year period was insufficient time to "avail [themselves of] the benefits of the program." They asked if it were possible to extend their visit to a period of three to five years. When extensions of the exchange visits did not materialize, some Filipino exchange nurses returned to the Philippines after their two-year stay. Others, however, attempted to bypass the two-year exchange limit and their mandatory return to the Philippines altogether and to change their "exchange" visa status while they were still in the United States.

According to the U.S. Mutual Educational and Cultural Exchange Act of 1961, exchange visitors were unable to apply for permanent residence until they had returned to their countries of origin and lived there for a period of at least two years after their departure from the United States. Yet Filipino exchange nurses employed multiple strategies to avoid returning to their homeland. Some married American citizens. Others immigrated to Canada. Filipino exchange nurses also exited the United States through Canada, Mexico, or St. Thomas and reentered on student visas. Some utilized a combination of requests by American universities, the Philippine Consul General, and American hospital employers to petition the Exchange Visitor Waiver Board of the Department of Health, Education, and Welfare for a waiver of the foreign residence requirement. When even these strategies failed and the Immigration and Naturalization Service (INS) set their dates for departure, some Filipino exchange nurses brought their cases to the U.S. Court of Appeals in an attempt to overturn INS rulings.

The widespread desire of Filipino exchange nurses to remain in the United States became a cause for alarm for Philippine government officials and nursing leaders. They interpreted nurses' duties as an integral part of Philippine nation-building. Songs, such as "The Filipino Nurses' Hymn," promoted this relationship between nursing and Philippine nationalism: "We pledge . . . to build a better nation that is healthy and great." The hymn conjures images of Filipino nurses "traveling on" to all regions of the Philippines: "In towns and upland terraces/In plains, in hills and mountains."

Philippine government officials and nursing leaders took pride in the professional achievements of Filipino nurses abroad and empathized with their desire to go to the United States and to remain there, given the potential social and economic opportunities. They also continued to endorse participation in the EVP and to believe that Filipino nurses' training abroad was necessary for the national development of the Philippines.

However, government health officials and nursing leaders also harshly criticized the new lifestyles of Filipino exchange nurses abroad, employing a rhetoric of spirituality and morality in their efforts to persuade Filipino nurses to return to or to remain in the Philippines. They characterized the economic ambitions of some Filipino exchange nurses to accumulate American dollars and to purchase American goods as a dangerous obsession. Critics charged that some Filipino exchange nurses had become financially as well as morally bankrupt—that they miscalculated their expenditures and, using credit and layaway plans, overspent their earnings. Others associated the nurses' new lifestyles in America with licentiousness. They claimed that the women smoked, drank, and talked behind each other's backs. The harshest criticism was leveled against Filipino exchange nurses who used marriage to American citizens to remain in the United States. The editor of the *Philippine Journal of Nursing* likened those nurses who "marr[ied] any American they could entice, if only to stay in the country of their husbands," to prostitutes: "This is 'selling" themselves."

The national problem that Filipino exchange nurses had become only worsened when it became clear that the vast majority of returning Filipino exchange nurses planned to go back eventually to the United States. If they contributed at all to Philippines nation-building, it was not for very long. They compared their salaries, nursing facilities, equipment, and research opportunities in the United States with those of the Philippines and found the latter sorely lacking.

By the early 1960s, the international migration of nurses, particularly Filipino nurses, seemed unstoppable. Hospitals in Holland, Germany, the Netherlands, Brunei, Laos, Turkey, and Iran recruited Filipino nurses to alleviate their nursing shortages. Although Filipino nurses had to adjust to the different languages and foods as well as some new nursing procedures, nursing practices in Europe, such as the emphasis on bedside nursing, were generally similar to those in the Philippines. When officers of the Filipino Nurses Association visited hospitals in the Netherlands that had recruited Filipino nurses, they concluded that Filipino nurses in those hospitals were safe and well taken care of, and these reports—which also publicized favorable work conditions and bonuses—inspired further migration abroad.

Producing Nurses, Exporting Women

In 1965, the U.S. Congress passed the Immigration and Nationality Act, which expedited a process that was already under way among Filipino nurses. The new law created a more equitable system of immigration involving worldwide ceilings and per country quotas. One major impact of the new legislation was the increased migration of highly educated and skilled persons into the United States through occupational preference categories. These categories dramatically affected Filipino professional immigration. Between 1966 and 1970, 17,134 Filipino professionals emigrated to the United States, constituting almost one-third of all Filipino immigrants.

In the 1960s and 1970s, engineers, scientists, and physicians as well as nurses made up the bulk of professional immigrants from the Philippines. However, the demands for foreign-trained nurses to fill critical U.S. nursing shortages (exacerbated by the creation of Medicare and Medicaid programs in the mid-1960s), in combination with Filipino nurses' professional skills and historically shaped desires to work abroad, made the Philippines a dominant force in the international migration of nurses. By 1967, the Philippines became the world's top sending country of nurses to the United States, ending decades of numerical domination by European and North American countries. In 1967, Filipino nurses received the highest number of U.S. nursing licenses among foreign-trained nurses—1,521 licenses out of a total of 5,361.

New American legislation also facilitated the adjustment of exchange visitor's status to that of permanent resident. A new law, passed in 1970, enabled exchange visitors to waive their two-year foreign residency requirement. Between 1966 and 1978, 7,495 Filipino exchange visitors adjusted their status to become U.S. permanent residents. The growing exodus of Filipino nurses abroad through new avenues of immigration created new problems for nursing in the Philippines. . . .

As the number of nursing schools increased, so too did the demand for nursing school faculty. At the same time, the socioeconomic rewards of working abroad depleted the supply of Filipino nursing instructors. Although the Philippine Board of Examiners for Nurses required a ratio of one faculty member to ten to twelve students during clinical supervision, according to one nursing dean, Rosario S. Diamante, the ratio was "not possible due to the rapid turnover of faculty. This was mainly due to an exodus abroad either as immigrant or as participant of the Exchange Visitors Program or under a working visa." . . .

As new avenues of entry to the United States exacerbated the trend of migration abroad, as the aggressive international recruitment of Filipino nurses continued unabated, and as nurses' wages in the Philippines lagged behind those of nurses abroad, Filipino nursing leaders, in collaboration with the Philippine government, employed new strategies to retain Filipino nurse graduates, if only temporarily. In the early 1970s, mandatory health service requirements for new nurse graduates replaced emotional appeals to nurses' selflessness and humanitarianism. However, these service requirements were only temporary. Decrees by Philippine president Ferdinand Marcos mandating several months of health service in rural areas were token gestures to alleviate the maldistribution of Filipino health personnel in the country. At the same time, Marcos also committed the Philippines to an export-oriented economy, which included the export of people and skills as well as goods. Government officials thus promoted the export of laborers, including Filipino nurses, when the shortage of Filipino nurses serving the general population was most acute.

By the early 1970s the Marcos government was promoting "employment contracts" of Filipino laborers and a "dollar repatriation program" as a way both to alleviate unemployment and to revitalize a failing Philippine economy. Marcos' address to the Philippine Nurses Association at their 1973 convention in Manila revealed the government's new commitment to exporting womanpower: "And so, in short, what is the policy of nursing? . . . It is our policy to promote the migration of nurses. . . . We encourage this migration, I repeat, we will now encourage the training of all nurses because, as I repeat, this is a market that we should take advantage of. Instead of stopping the nurses from going abroad, why don't we produce more nurses? If they want one thousand nurses we produce a thousand more?" Like the revenue earned from agricultural exports, the earnings of Filipino nurses working abroad, deposited in Philippine banks, would help to build the Philippine national economy. Marcos encouraged Filipino nurses abroad to "earn for the country" as well as for themselves.

Given the shift to an export-oriented economy, Filipino nurses abroad were no longer seen as having abandoned their role in Philippine nation-building; rather, they were now considered integral to the process. Once criticized in the 1960s by the Philippines secretary of health for "turning their backs on their own people when the almighty dollar beckons," Filipino nurses abroad now became the new national heroes. Their work as nurses abroad continued to be associated with prestige. However, this time the prestige derived from indefinite working sojourns abroad, during which they would return a portion of their "precious dollars" to their country of origin. In his 1973 address to visiting Filipino nurses from abroad, a new Philippine health secretary, Clemente S. Gatmaitan, proclaimed, "We in the Health Department are happy that you have elected to stay and work abroad. . . . While in other countries, you give prestige to the Philippines because you are all virtually ambassador of good will. . . . Another benefit that accrues from your work is the precious dollar you earn and send back to your folks at home. In this manner, you help indirectly in the improvement of our economic condition."

These changes in the attitude of Philippine government officials toward the mass migration of Filipino workers abroad led to the implementation of an official overseas labor policy. In 1974, the government created the Overseas Employment Development Board and the National Seamen Board. These agencies publicized the availability of Filipino labor in overseas labor markets, evaluated overseas employment contracts, and recruited Filipino laborers for work abroad.

Conclusion

At the close of the century, the Philippines continued to export its people as contract workers overseas through government agencies such as the Philippine Overseas Employment Administration. Filipinas have played a significant role in this phenomenon. In 1991, they constituted a larger proportion of the Philippine's overseas workforce (41 percent) than its domestic workforce (36 percent). Significant numbers of overseas Filipino workers in domestic services (housecleaning), entertainment, and the sex industry, in addition to the overseas working force, form a worldwide diaspora of Filipinas working in Japan, Canada, the Middle East, and several European countries, as well as the United States. This diaspora is a late-twentieth-century phenomenon, but a transnational history, of Filipino nurse migration to the United States reveals that the migration of Filipino nurses has its roots in practices established earlier in the century. Although contemporary U.S. and Philippine government policies have facilitated migration in the tens of thousands since 1965, American educational policies during the U.S. colonial period in the Philippines and the U.S. Exchange Visitor Program of the 1950s and 1960s laid the social, economic, and political foundations for the Philippine export of nurses in the late twentieth century.

The Los Angeles Civil Unrest Transforms Korean American Politics

EDWARD J. W. PARK

Civil Unrest and the Transformation of Korean American Politics

The Civil Unrest has had a transformative effect on Korean Americans. Along with unprecedented devastating economic and human loss, the Civil Unrest and the ensuing politics of rebuilding brought the first major political crisis to the Korean American community. As a political crisis, the Civil Unrest has generated two different, but ultimately interrelated, changes in the Korean American community leadership. The first change occurred at the level of political legitimacy of community leadership, brought on by the discourse surrounding the Civil Unrest and, more

From Edward J. W. Park, "Competing Visions: Political Formation of Korean Americans in Los Angeles, 1992–1997," *Amerasia Journal* 24, no. 1 (1998). Copyright © 1998 Regents of the University of California. Used with permission.

concretely, the politics of rebuilding. The second change has been the increasing division among the emerging political leadership, and for the first time within the Korean American community, a prominent injection of openly partisan politics. These changes have transformed Korean American politics and have set the stage for future political development.

The political discourse surrounding Korean Americans and their strained relationship with African Americans was a major contributing factor to the events of April 29, 1992. At the center of this discourse was the utilization of the Soon Ja Du Incident of 1991 [involving a Korean storeowner who shot African American teenager Latasha Harlins] as the central metaphor for a decade of Black-Korean tensions in the inner-city. Many observers—from journalists and academics to elected politicians and persons on the street—cited the Soon Ja Du Incident as a major factor that not only led to the Civil Unrest, but, in some cases, justified the inordinate economic loss suffered by Korean Americans. Particularly within the mass media, the Soon Ja Du Incident was invoked in a casual and reckless way, with some outlets replaying the video footage of the actual shooting as they showed the live footage of burning Korean American stores. Indeed, KPFK, the Los Angeles radio affiliate of the Public Broadcasting System and one of the few progressive media outlets in the city, celebrated the looting of Korean American stores as a "pay back."

From the Korean American perspective, the invoking of the Soon Ja Du Incident and the Black-Korean tension to explain both the cause of Sa-I-Gu [4-29-92] and the ethnic pattern of looting was seen as a case of scapegoating Korean Americans. Many Korean Americans felt "re-victimized" by this discourse. A Korean American student at UCLA recalls being told by a number of non–Korean American students, "Korean Americans got what they deserved," linking the Soon Ja Du Incident with the Civil Unrest. K. W. Lee, a long-time journalist and observer of the Korean American community, argued that "this scapegoating was the real victimization that Korean Americans were made to suffer. We were told in a backhanded way that we were to blame for the riots and that we should rightly bear the burden."

As frustration and anger within the community grew, the existing political establishment within the community—represented most powerfully by the Korean Federation whose political legitimacy came with its close identification with the South Korean government—could not defend the community. Bound by language barriers and lack of institutional ties, the Korean Federation vented its frustration within the confines of the Korean American media, with little impact on the mainstream discourse. Members of the Korean Federation also charged local African American politicians for turning their backs on the Korean American community even though they had received financial support for their political campaigns from various Korean American organizations, including the Korean Federation. However, their bitter charges only underscored the failure on their part to influence the mainstream political system. A Korean American volunteer at a senior citizen center stated:

> I lost all respect I had for the Korean Federation. They have always claimed that they were the leaders of the community, even calling the President the "Mayor of Koreatown." But during the riot, our mayor could not even come on the television and tell the rest of America that Korean Americans should not be blamed for the riots and that our suffering is as real as anyone else's.

While Korean American were frustrated and angered by what they perceived to be an effort to blame them for the Civil Unrest, the politics of rebuilding further demonstrated the ineffectiveness of the existing Korean American community political power structure. In the aftermath of the Civil Unrest, Korean Americans had little or no representation in the official rebuilding efforts. In the creation of "Rebuild Los Angeles" (RLA), the sole official response to the Civil Unrest from the city hall, Korean Americans were notably absent from the leadership. Even after RLA's leadership was diversified with the creation of four co-chairs, the "Asian co-chair went to Linda Wong, a Chinese American. In addition, as both of the Presidential candidates—George Bush and Bill Clinton—made their tours of Los Angeles in the midst of election year politicking, Korean Americans were notably absent in the entourage as locally elected officials took the spotlight and articulated the rebuilding agenda. The Korean community, confronted with unprecedented crisis, keenly felt their marginality in the politics of rebuilding. A first-generation Executive Director of a community food distribution center recalled:

> When these rebuilding efforts were going on, it really showed the shortcomings of the established Korean American leadership right after the riots. We didn't have anyone who had the ability to work effectively with people outside the Korean American community. I'm a good example. During Sa-I-Gu, I was an assistant minister at one of the largest Korean American churches in Korea-town, and I once served as an officer in Korean Federation. But, even though I lived in the U.S. for 15 years, I can't speak enough English, let alone speak English with lawyers and government bureaucrats. So, people like us stood by and hoped for new leaders to come in.

Literally, overnight on the May 6, 1992 broadcast of ABC's "Nightline," the Korean American community found a new leader in Angela Oh. A second-generation Korean American criminal defense lawyer who had been active in liberal circles in Los Angeles politics but an unknown within the Korean American community, Oh finally articulated a Korean American perspective on the Civil Unrest. With enormous poise, she protested the media's coverage of Korean Americans as dehumanized gun-toting vigilantes and faulted the media for failing to discuss the decades of neglect of the inner-cities that created the conditions for the Civil Unrest. While her appearance on "Nightline" did little to reshape the discourse on the Civil Unrest, her entry into the debate nonetheless marked an important turning point in Korean American politics: for the first time in the community's short history, a spokesperson emerged whose political ties lay outside of the entrenched community power structure. And, by winning the support of Korean Americans who saw in her an articulate spokesperson who could advocate the mainstream media on behalf of the community, Oh created a space for others to fill the political vacuum. Oh was quickly joined by other Korean Americans such as Marcia Choo and Ryan Song who spoke for the first time as representatives of the community. . . .

With a benefit of six-year hindsight, it is clear that the shift in the Korean American political leadership has occurred along two dimensions. Most visibly, the shift represents a generational change whereby many of the immigrant-generation leaders stepped aside as second-generation and the so-called 1.5-generation (those who immigrated to the U.S. as young children) emerged as key political leaders. The political ascendancy of Angela Oh, Bong Hwan Kim, Roy Hong, Cindy Choi, . . .

and Michelle Park-Steel (Republican activist and a key figure in the Korean American Coalition's Youth Leadership Conference) represents this generational shift within the Korean American political leadership. A concurrent, less visible transition saw the decline of those whose political base was rooted in "homeland" politics and the rise of others (first-generation included) who had political ties with mainstream political institutions. These included Congressman Jay Kim (R-Diamond Bar) and Tong Soo Chung (a Democrat activist and a Clinton appointee to the Department of Commerce), first-generation Korean Americans who leveraged their careers to unprecedented levels of Korean Americans. As an unequivocal sign of concession to the changing political realities within the Korean American community, the Korean Federation changed their main organizational mission from "representing the collective interest of Koreans living in the U.S." to "supporting the effort of Korean Americans for political representation."

Community Divided

While Korean Americans in Los Angeles agree on the necessity to participate in mainstream politics, they have been divided over how to best channel their political resources and energies. At the center of this division lies the explicit partisan politics that have emerged within the community. This partisanship division reflects both the change in the community's leadership and developments facing the community since the Civil Unrest. New leaders had clear party loyalties. Liberals such as Angela Oh and Bong Hwan Kim were clearly identified with the Democratic Party, while conservatives such as Jay Kim and Michelle Park-Steel brought with them institutional ties to the Republican Party. In this way, a central component of the shift in the community's political leadership was the introduction of explicit partisan politics within the Korean American community.

As Korean Americans embark on their road to political empowerment, Korean American liberals have argued that the community ought to align themselves with the traditional Civil Rights Coalition within the Democratic Party. In particular, they argue that Korean Americans are victims of racial oppression in America who have been excluded from the mainstream economy and from equal protection under the law. At the same time, they also argue that whatever rights and equality Korean Americans currently enjoy have originated largely from the Civil Rights struggles of the African Americans and Latinos, including the passage of Hart-Celler's Act (1965) which finally removed racial barriers to immigration. From this vantage point of racial oppression and historical linkages with other racial minority groups, Korean American liberals argued that the Civil Unrest of 1992 was a culmination of racial injustice in America where decades of inner-city neglect and racial oppression resulted in the explosion that victimized all communities of color. Liberals believed that the best hope for Korean Americans in their effort to find lasting political empowerment is to join other communities of color and white liberals who are committed [to] issues of racial equality and justice. In practical terms, this vision of Korean American political incorporation urged the community to join the Democratic Party and its established structure of racial minority incorporation. . . .

This vision of political incorporation emerged within the Korean American community immediately after the Civil Unrest. Angela Oh became one of the first openly liberal political leaders within the community by linking the Civil Unrest with the Republican neglect of the inner-cities and racial inequality on the part of mainstream political institutions, including the criminal justice system. In the massive "Peace Rally" organized by Korean Americans and attended by 30,000 participants on May 11, 1992, placards such as "Justice for Rodney King," "Justice for All People of Color," and "More Jobs for the Inner-City" implicated institutional racism and economic inequality as primary causes of the Civil Unrest. Moreover, these messages reflected a sense of common victimization and destiny that Korean Americans felt with the African American and Latino communities. . . .

While liberals urged Korean Americans to join other communities of color through the Civil Rights Coalition within the Democratic Party, conservative Korean American activists have urged the Korean American community to align itself with the conservative politics of the Republican Party. Whereas liberals cite racial injustice and inner-city neglect as the cause of Civil Unrest, Korean American conservatives have argued that the root of the Civil Unrest can be found in the failure of the liberal welfare state and the Civil Rights Coalition. Moreover, they argued that the Korean American community, with its large segment of small entrepreneurs and accelerating residential sub-urbanization, could best pursue their political interests through the Republican Party that has championed fiscal conservatism and law and order. While appealing to material interests of Korean Americans, they also pointed out the recent changes within the Republican Party itself. More specifically, they cited the rise of racial minorities such as Colin Powell, Ward Connerly (an African American member of the University of Carolina Regents and a key architect of

Korean Americans march for peace after the Los Angeles Riots, 1992.

Photograph courtesy of Alice Yang Murray.

undermining the state's affirmative action programs), Jay Kim, and Wendy Gramm (a Korean American appointee to the Department of Commerce under Bush and the wife of Senator and Presidential Candidate Phil Gramm) within the Party as evidence that the Party was now inclusive of racial minorities and "legal" immigrants. While Korean American liberals pointed to the Civil Rights Coalition and the Democratic Party for removing past discriminatory policies, Korean American conservatives pointed to the symmetry of the Republican political agenda and the material interests of the Korean American community and the new politics of inclusion within the Republican Party. . . .

Conclusion

The Civil Unrest of 1992 marked a fundamental shift in Korean American political formation, resulting in the efforts to find empowerment through a commitment to mainstream political process. New leaders must participate and work in multiracial and multiethnic settings. Korean Americans, however, remain profoundly divided along partisan lines. At the center of this division lies conflicting "racial visions" of where Korean Americans fit into America's racial landscape as well as conflicting assessments over the Civil Rights Coalition. Liberals have argued that Korean Americans are an oppressed racial minority group and their rights and interest can be best protected by joining the Civil Rights Coalition and the Democratic Party. In contrast conservatives have insisted that Korean Americans have fundamental economic and political differences with key members of the Civil Rights Coalition and that Korean Americans can better meet their interests through the Republican Party and its commitment toward fiscal conservatism, law and order, and the dismantling of the welfare state. . . . Clearly, it is too early to tell which one of these partisan efforts will succeed in leaving lasting impact on Korean American political formation. As the Korean American community has become transformed in its search for political empowerment, the inclusion of Korean Americans and other new immigrant groups have posed new challenges for the mainstream political system and its more established participants. As the Democratic Party attempts to revise the traditional Civil Rights Coalition to include Korean Americans, the Republican Party seeks to reinvent itself as an inclusive Party in the face of America's changing demography. As the massive entry of African Americans into the mainstream political system transformed the American political system during the post–World War II era, the entry of Korean Americans into the American political system will lead to yet other transformations.

☛ *F U R T H E R   R E A D I N G*

Abelman, Nancy, and John Lie. *Blue Dreams: Korean Americans and the Los Angeles Riots* (1995).
Chang, Edward T., and Russell Leong, eds. *Los Angeles: Struggles Toward Multiethnic Community* (1994).
Cheng, Lucie, and Philip Q. Yang. "Global Interaction, Global Inequality, and Professional Migration to the United States," *International Migration Review* 32, no. 3 (1998): 626–653.

Dasgupta, Shamita Das, ed. *A Patchwork Shawl: Chronicles of South Asian Women in America* (1998).

Fawcett, James T., and Benjamin V. Carino, eds. *Pacific Bridges: The New Immigration from Asia and the Pacific Islands* (1987).

Fenton, John. *Transplanting Religious Traditions: Asian Indians in America* (1988).

Finn, Michael. *Foreign-National Scientists and Engineers in the U.S. Labor Force, 1972–1982* (1985).

Hamamoto, Darrell Y., and Rudolfo D. Torres, ed. *New American Destinies: A Reader in Contemporary Asian and Latino Immigration* (1997).

Hing, Bill Ong, and Ronald Lee, ed. *Reframing the Immigration Debate* (1996).

Hurh, Won Moo, and Kwang Chung Kim. *Korean Immigrants in America* (1980).

Khare, Brij B. *Asian Indian Immigrants: Motifs and Ethnicity and Gender* (1997).

Kim, Illsoo. *New Urban Immigrants: The Korean Community in New York* (1981).

Kim, Elaine H., and Eui-Young Yu, eds. *East to America: Korean American Life Stories* (1996).

Kwong, Peter. *The New Chinatown and Chinatown, New York: Labor and Politics 1930–1950* (1987).

Leadership Education for Asian Pacifics: Asian Pacific American Public Policy. *The State of Asian Pacific America: Policy Issues to the Year 2020* (1993).

Leonard, Karen. *Making Ethnic Choices: California's Punjabi-Mexican Americans, 1910–1980* (1991).

———. *The South Asian Americans* (1997).

Light, Ivan, and Edna Bonacich. *Immigrant Entrepreneurs: Koreans in Los Angeles, 1975–1982* (1988).

Lui, John M., and Paul M. Ong, and Carolyn Rosenstein. "Dual Chain Migration: Post-1965 Filipino Immigration to the United States," *International Migration Review* 25, no. 3 (1991): 487–513.

Min, Pyong Gap. *Caught in the Middle: Korean Merchants in America's Multiethnic Cities* (1996).

Ong, Paul, ed. *The State of Asian Pacific America: Economic Diversity, Issues and Policies* (1994).

Ong, Paul, Edna Bonacich, and Lucie Cheng, eds. *The New Asian Immigration in Los Angeles and Global Restructuring* (1994).

Ong, Paul, Lucie Cheng, and Leslie Evans. "Migration of Highly Educated Asians and Global Dynamics," *Asian and Pacific Migration Journal* 1 (1992): 543–567.

Park, Kyeyoung. *The Korean American Dream: Immigrants and Small Business in New York City* (1997).

Pedraza, Silvia, and Roben G. Rumbaut, eds. *Origins and Destines: Immigration, Race and Ethnicity in America* (1996).

Reimers, David M. *Still the Golden Door: The Third World Comes to America* (1985).

Williams, Raymond Brady. *Religions of Immigrants from India and Pakistan* (1989).

Yoo, David K., ed. *New Spiritual Homes: Religion and Asian Americans* (1999).

Yoon, In-Jim. *On My Own: Korean Businesses and Race Relations in America* (1997).

Zhou, Min. *Chinatown: The Socioeconomic Potential of an Urban Enclave* (1992).

CHAPTER

12

Refugees and Their Struggles in Asia and America, 1975–2000

Unlike most immigrants, refugees who began arriving from China in the 1950s and from Southeast Asia in the mid-1970s were forced to leave their native countries with little notice or advance planning. Many suffered extreme physical, emotional, and psychological trauma before and during their escape that continued to haunt them in the United States. Refugees from Vietnam, Cambodia, and Laos fled countries devastated by decades of war and could testify about the terror of bombing campaigns, the destruction of homes, and the death of family members. Accounts by Southeast Asian and Chinese refugees reflect the diverse political, educational, and cultural backgrounds that shaped their experiences of war, escape, resettlement camps, and life in the United States. For example, most of the 130,000 refugees who fled Vietnam as part of a "first wave" in 1975 shared characteristics that distinguished them from later waves of refugees. Many of these first-wave refugees were South Vietnamese military personnel and their relatives, who were more likely to be well educated, to have lived in urban areas, and to have had contacts with Americans. Approximately 40 percent of these refugees were Catholic, and two-thirds spoke English. Many were airlifted out of the country and escaped before the fall of Saigon to the Communists in 1975.

Refugees who fled after the Communists assumed power throughout Vietnam, Cambodia, and Laos in 1975 endured the loss of businesses that were nationalized by the government, physical and psychological abuse within Communist "reeducation" camps, and forced migrations to the countryside. Cambodians under the Khmer Rouge also suffered from mass executions, starvation, and disease, which killed somewhere between half a million to 3 million people in a country that had a population of 7 million in early 1975. Hmong hill tribespeople in Laos were targeted for reprisals by the Communist regime for participating in a secret army of 40,000 organized by the U.S. Central Intelligence Agency (CIA) in the 1960s.

A "second wave" of refugees began arriving in 1978 and included "boat people" from Vietnam and land refugees from Cambodia and Laos who had fled to Thailand.

This second wave was both ethnically and economically more diverse than the first wave. Approximately 70 percent of the Vietnamese boat people were ethnic Chinese, and the Laotian refugees included lowland Lao and highland Hmong. Many second-wave refugees came from rural areas, were Buddhists or animists, and spoke little English. Not surprisingly, many of these refugees had greater difficulty finding jobs and adjusting to life in America. Congress passed the 1980 Refugee Act to limit the massive influx of refugees and provide funding for resettlement programs. Setting an annual quota of 50,000 refugees, the act reimbursed state spending on refugees for a period of up to thirty-six months. In 1982, the time limit was reduced to eighteen months. After eighteen months, however, refugees became eligible for general welfare benefits.

☙ D O C U M E N T S

The first five documents reflect the diverse backgrounds and experiences of Southeast Asian refugees. In Document 1, Lang Ngan describes being airlifted out of Vietnam in July 1975 as part of the first wave of refugees. Ngan notes that she and her English-speaking siblings have had a much easier time than her parents in adapting to America. In Document 2, a poor peasant who chose the fictitious name Bun Thab recounts how his wit and determination helped him escape from the brutal Khmer Rouge in 1977. A ninth-grader when Saigon fell in 1975, Le Tan Si left his family and his country as a boat person four years later. Excerpts from his college essay depicting several harrowing encounters with pirates during his escape are included in Document 3. Documents 4 and 5 shed light on Hmong cultural conflicts in refugee camps and America. Journalist Anne Fadiman describes in Document 4 how American doctors did not understand that Hmong religious beliefs in traditional healers and shamans and their fear of hospitals, blood sampling, and anesthesia might affect their response to American medical care within a Thai refugee camp in 1982. In 1994, Xang Mao Xiong gave his daughter an oral history of his life in Laos and America. In the excerpts from this oral history included in Document 5, Xiong recounts his problems in learning English after he arrived in 1978, in finding a job as an electronics assembler, and in raising his children in a culture with different views of discipline and respect.

The last three documents illustrate how refugees have often spoken out and attempted to influence politics in their former homelands. Vietnamese refugees in America have held many anticommunist rallies and demonstrations. Chinese refugees have appeared before the U.S. government to condemn the 1989 massacre of demonstrators in Tiananmen Square, attacks on Christians, and the sale of items produced by forced prison labor in China. Individuals charged with being illegal Chinese immigrants have sought political asylum by claiming to be victims of religious persecution and the government's planned-birth policies that limit the number of children within a family. Document 6 describes how a group of Chinese women launched an unsuccessful fifty-day hunger strike to protest government rejection of their claims that they deserved asylum because they faced forced abortions and sterilization in China. Some of these women were survivors of the *Golden Venture,* a notorious ship that tried to smuggle nearly three hundred illegal Chinese immigrants into the United States but ran aground off the shore of Queens, New York, in 1993.

Harry Wu is probably the most famous refugee to campaign against the Chinese government. After spending nineteen years in the Laogai, China's forced-labor system, Wu dedicated himself to investigating and publicizing torture, abuse, and human rights violations in China. Documents 7 and 8 provide contrasting views of Wu's campaign to prevent the expansion of trade relations between China and the United States. In Document 7, George P. Koo, a business consultant and chair of the Asian American Manufacturers Association, accuses the media of promoting Wu's sensationalist charges and failing to investigate his misrepresentations of Chinese policies. Wu's testimony before Congress in 2000, excerpted in Document 8, disputes those who claim that providing China with "most favored nation" status will improve conditions in China and calls for the United States to withhold economic investment until China improves its human rights record.

1. Lang Ngan, A First-Wave Refugee, Compares Life in Vietnam and the United States (1975), 1991

On April 25th, near the end of the war, my supervisor called me in, and told me that by six o'clock that evening, we had to meet, to get to the airport by nine the next morning. I had worked for the U.S. Embassy in Saigon for seven years. If we had stayed, we would have been persecuted by the new government.

There was no time to talk to friends or relatives because the evacuation was supposed to be secret, and we were not allowed to tell our relatives. We couldn't even take our money out of the bank. We weren't prepared to come to this country. It was a last minute thing. We had to make our decision overnight. We didn't have any time to think about it.

I was allowed to take my family, because I was single. My father, my mother, myself and six brothers and sisters—the nine of us. We were so frightened because we didn't have any friends or relatives in this country to help us. We couldn't sell our property. We literally left with the clothes on our backs. I was twenty-nine when I came to the U.S., one brother was twenty-three, and one was nineteen. The youngest only eight. The rest were in their teens.

I didn't have the Golden Mountain dream [a Chinese term for America, where making lots of money fast is believed possible]. I knew life wouldn't be easy, especially since we didn't receive a high education in Vietnam. I told my brothers and sisters on the plane coming here that I didn't know whether I could support all of them. If not, then I would have to give them up for adoption. They said they understood but asked that before I left, I give them my address so that when they grew up, they could look for me.

We were transported by military cargo plane. At the time, the evacuation was so sudden the U.S. government didn't have a chance to prepare for our arrival. So we were taken to a military camp in the Philippines for a few days. From there, some of the refugees were sent to Guam. We were sent to Wake Island, and screened for admittance. We left Vietnam April twenty-fifth. We arrived at the camp in Arkansas on May fourth.

At the beginning, there wasn't enough food. There was a shortage because the U.S. government wasn't prepared for us. But really it wasn't bad. It was actually

From Lang Ngan, "The Success Story" from *Asian American Experiences in the United States: Oral Histories of First to Fourth Generation Americans from China, the Philippines, Japan, India, the Pacific Islands, Vietnam, and Cambodia.* © 1991 Joann Faung Jean Lee by permission of McFarland & Company, Inc., Box 611, Jefferson, NC 28640. www.mcfarlandpub.com.

much better than the first asylum camps in Malaysia and Thailand. We felt we were the luckiest. A month later, the government contracted a company to provide food for us, so after that, there was plenty of food. The living situation wasn't bad. The housing was used by soldiers in training, and the facilities were good like staying in dorms. There were bunk beds. The volunteer agencies—refugee resettlement agencies—started sending people to process us. Some of the agencies, such as the one I work for now, are partially funded by the State Department. Currently they provide five hundred twenty-five dollars for the initial resettlement cost. Part of the funding is also provided by public donations, or foundations. These resettlement agencies and the immigration office sent people in to screen us, to see if the refugees have relatives or friends in the country they could go to, and to process them. Because I could speak English, I started helping many of those who couldn't, translating for them. I met the representative from the International Rescue Committee, and started to work as a volunteer for IRC. I ended up in New York because the IRC offered me a job. Southeast Asian refugees were calling the office, and no one could understand what they were saying. I was so happy that I could get a job right away. I asked my boss if he thought that I alone could support a whole family of nine. And he said, "Probably not. Why don't I hire your sister, too?" She was only nineteen at the time, and we've worked for the IRC ever since.

My sister and I left the camp first, and we started work as soon as we got to New York. We started looking for apartments, but at the time, my salary was only one hundred fifty dollars a week, and my sister made one hundred twenty-five dollars. Someone took us to look for an apartment in Flushing, Queens. A two bedroom was two hundred fifty dollars, and a one bedroom was one hundred ninety dollars, and even with a family of nine, we took the one bedroom, because we tried to save as much as possible. Fortunately, the building superintendent was a refugee—from Cuba—and he helped us. He said he wouldn't tell the landlord that there were nine people living there as long as we didn't make any noise, and kept the children quiet. So he helped us get the apartment. He lied to the landlord for us by saying there were only two girls in the apartment—my sister and myself. The superintendent was very helpful. He tried to get some used furniture for us, and used clothes and dishes. He collected them from other tenants and his friends. That is how we started.

Half a month later, we had the rest of our family join us. Even though there was only my sister and I working to support nine, life wasn't bad. We were quite happy. But the only frustration was our parents. They had a lot of difficulty adjusting. They felt isolated, because there were no Cantonese-speaking people in the building, and in the daytime, when all the children were in school, there was nothing for them to do but sit. In the beginning, I wanted to go back to Vietnam, because life was easier there. Here, we had no friends or relatives, and the lifestyle was so different. Even the mailbox was different. Every evening, we opened it and it was full of papers and envelopes. I was afraid to throw away anything in case it was important, so I would read every word—thinking they were letters—not realizing that this was advertising, junk.

As for my siblings, they knew that if I couldn't support them I would give them away. So they were very happy when I didn't have to do that. They felt lucky. So they worked hard. They didn't think about many of the things children think about today—expensive toys, expensive clothes, fixing their hair. We wore whatever people gave us. Today I tell my refugee clients, I wore the same used clothes people gave me until two years ago. I finally threw them out because there were so worn.

The first books we bought were dictionaries. We got three or four of them. We used them a lot. We didn't have any friends or relatives here, but at least we were together as a family. The children studied very hard to catch up in school. We had only one table, and they all had to study together around the same place, and all of them still feel this closeness to this day. We helped each other. I helped the children at that time, but not now. Now they correct my accent.

We had no furniture—just a few chairs and a used sofa that the supervisor gave us, and broken TV. And the rest were mattresses. We had no beds, only mattresses. In the evening, we had to carry all the mattresses to the living room for the males to sleep. All the females slept in the bedroom. And we lived in this condition for two and a half years, until we were able to get a two-bedroom apartment. We waited till we felt financially secure to do this. We had saved some money over the two and a half years, and because I was getting married, I felt that with my husband's income, we could afford to move. My husband and I got a one bedroom apartment and my family moved to a two bedroom place in the same building. We were very happy. We felt that we were one family unit. We were really together, and sharing. There was no privacy, but we all remembered the times we had gone through together, and we were able to work things out with each other without problems.

All my younger sisters and brothers have done very well in school. And the teachers and school counselors have shown them what is the best way for them to go. Actually, we didn't give them that much counselling. They all got it from school. Even though they don't act the same way I did when I was going to school in Vietnam, they still have certain values—such as respect, and obeying teachers, and therefore the teachers like them, and tried to help them. My sister got a full scholarship to MIT from Bell Labs. I have one brother who got an electrical engineering degree from Columbia, and the other finished at City College. One other brother is going to medical school at New York Med.

I think the problems we had when we first came to this country helped our success. We're not like other people who were born here, and had everything. We went through all those difficulties, so when we have a chance, we grab it. We now own a two family house. My husband and I live in one side, my parents in the other.

2. Cambodian Refugee Bun Thab Remembers the Atrocities of the Khmer Rouge, 1993

I learned that to survive the regime, I had to be a good worker. I didn't talk to people, I didn't defy the soldiers, I just acted dumb, and after we finished building the dam, I was made a junior group leader. . . .

. . . I also had to write down people's life stories each month, and if what they said this month was different from what they had said the previous month, I had to report them to the leader. That was enough to get them killed.

From "Bun Thab: A Khmer Rouge Escapee," in Usha Welaratna, *Beyond the Killing Fields: Voices of Nine Cambodian Survivors in America,* pp. 117–135. Copyright © 1993 by the Board of Trustees of the Leland Stanford Junior University. Used with permission.

I had been with the old monk for about a year when a new group of Communist soldiers came to our village. They were a lot meaner than the old leaders, and killed many of the old leaders because they had asked for more freedom. They also killed a lot of "New People" that the soldiers had brought to our village in 1976. One of them was my cousin, who had lived in the city and couldn't do hard labor because he got tired very quickly. A chlop followed him around for a few days, and one morning the chlop said, "You have been called to attend a special meeting. Come with me." That was all. My cousin just disappeared, and we knew he was killed because two or three days later the soldiers brought his clothes back and gave them to his own wife to mend. When she realized what had happened, she became so upset and depressed, but she had to pretend that nothing was wrong; if she had cried or asked any questions, she would have been killed too.

None of us knew when we would be killed. . . . One evening, we had just sat down to eat when two soldiers came and chose three people to go to a meeting in the soldiers' house. First they called a man who had been a monk but had been forced to unfrock and marry. Next they called my friend, and then they called me. We knew that the night before they had killed two people in my group.

Running for Life

The two soldiers escorted us back to the soldiers' house, where four or five others had cooked us a very good dinner. They invited us to eat as much as we wanted, but we didn't know why they gave us such good food. After we ate, they gave me an ax, and gave my friend a long knife. Then the leader announced, "Tonight we have three enemies here." We knew that they meant us. Two soldiers grabbed my friends, pulled their arms behind their backs and started to tie them up tightly. I was terrified because I knew what was coming. I needed to urinate. A soldier took me outside. It was dark and raining a little, but suddenly the rain came pelting down, I ran into the darkness. . . .

When I was sure that all of them had gone, I started running again, and in the distance, I saw two other people running away also. Their arms were tied behind their backs; when I got closer I recognized my friends. I called out to them, and they stopped. Using the ax the Khmer Rouge gave me, I cut the ropes that bound them, and we decided to escape from Cambodia together. . . .

We tried to avoid meeting any Pol Pots by escaping through the jungle, and we always kept very close to one another so we would not get separated. We kept going day and night, and after we ran out of food, we lived on fruits and leaves from the forest trees. . . . Everywhere we looked we saw only trees, and they all looked the same. We had no choice but to keep going, taking turns to climb trees every now and then to see if we could see the mountains of Thailand.

One afternoon, the old monk had just reached the top of a tree to look for the mountains when I heard a faint sound of dry leaves crackling. "Khmer Rouge, lie down!" I whispered fiercely to my friend. We dropped down and waited, hardly daring to breathe. A shot rang out. Our friend fell from the tree, screaming with pain. While we watched, the Communist walked up and he chopped our friend to pieces with his ax. We fled, and he shot at us too, but I don't know where the bullets went. We kept on running and we came to a river. We jumped in, and hid under water. I know the Communist kept running after us because once, as I looked up from under the water, he jumped right over my head. I still have nightmares of that Khmer Rouge jumping over my head, and I wake up, shivering with fear.

After some time we came out of the water. Our friend had been killed, we had no more food, and we had lost the ax and the knife we carried. . . . But we had to go on. We decided, "If we die, we will die together," and started walking again, holding hands.

We walked for two days with nothing to eat. Our feet were cut from the bamboo splinters that covered the ground, and they were swollen and smelly, and really painful. But we kept on going, and suddenly, we saw a huge turtle. At last, we had found real food! We couldn't believe our luck for we even had a lighter to make a fire.

But neither my friend nor I could bring ourselves to kill the turtle. Instead, we prayed and promised the turtle, "If you bring us good luck and take us to Thailand, we will not kill you. We will let you go." We started walking again, carrying the turtle.

The following day we heard a new sound. It was the whirring of an engine, and we thought it came from Communist planes that were searching for us. We threw ourselves into the bushes, and looked at the sky. The sound continued, but we couldn't see any planes. Very slowly, my friend and I crawled in the direction of the sound.

After a while we began to hear peoples' voices. We stopped and listened hard, thinking we had come to another Pol Pot camp, but we couldn't understand what the people were saying. After a while we realized that we couldn't understand them because they were speaking Thai! We had reached Thailand! We thanked the turtle and set him free.

I crawled up to an old man who was digging by himself and spoke to him very softly. But when he saw me, he got such a fright that he jumped and screamed, and people came running from everywhere. When the old man realized we had escaped from the Khmer Rouge, he took us to his house, and his family gave us rice. We hadn't eaten for three days, and we ate until our stomachs bulged. But although our stomachs were full, our hearts were heavy; we couldn't forget our friend who got killed.

3. Le Tan Si Writes a College Essay About His Terrifying Escape by Boat from Vietnam (1979), 1989

Around 9:00 P.M. on June 4, 1979, our boat departed in good weather with fifty-eight people on board. Our boat operated safely for the next two days. However, although I had paid for my trip I starved on those days. The trip was full of hardship. Around 2:00 A.M. on June 6, 1979, the overworked engine broke down. Our boat drifted downwind, and so did my life. During this period, I left my life to chance. Early the morning of June 7, the weather changed suddenly. It was raining and the wind was blowing and, because our boat's engine was broken, the boat bobbed up and down with the waves. We were frightened because we had no control over our boat with a dead engine; we prayed to God for help in the heavy rain. Meanwhile, we

From Le Tan Si, "A Terrifying Escape," *The Far East Comes Near: Autobiographical Accounts of Southeast Asian Students in America,* ed. Lucy Nguyen Hong-Nhiem and Joel Martin Halpern. Copyright © 1989 by the University of Massachusetts Press. Used with permission.

Vietnamese boat people rescued at sea, 1979.

anchored to make the boat safer. I thought and thought about my life, parents, and friends, and I also wondered if my death was near. Our supply of food and water was gradually decreasing as our boat drifted on the sea, so we starved. We prayed for a savior who could help and rescue us from this hardship.

Around 11:00 A.M. that day, a strange boat came toward our boat. It was a Thai boat in which there were six Thai fishermen. The Thai fishermen tried to help us repair our engine, but they were not able to; however, they took our engine apart. Then they gave us lunch and some cans of water, and they told us that they would help us. By noon, the Thai fishermen towed our boat to Malaysia after they and Vinh, the boat's owner, talked over our situation.

Our boat passed into Thailand's territorial waters. Ten minutes later, the Thai "fishermen" displayed guns, knives, and hooks in order to frighten us. We understood then that the Thai fishermen were pirates. They quickly took our valuables, such as rings, earrings, chains, watches, and bracelets, because they saw another boat coming toward us. Perhaps the pirates were afraid that it might have been a Thai patrol boat, so they left right after they robbed us. However, this other boat was also a fishing boat. They passed by our boat without pity; in fact, they laughed at us, because they perceived that we had been robbed recently. I had not been robbed by the pirates, because I had hidden my gold ring in my mouth, but I was a little scared by the pirates. Almost all of us were flabbergasted at the recent occurrence. We understood that we were faced with Thai pirates and would probably die next time.

"Thai pirates" are words I will never forget for the rest of my life. I don't like to remember why. In fact, they were simple fishermen but they availed themselves of the opportunity of becoming pirates. More than one thousand Vietnamese were killed or committed suicide when confronted by such robbers. From the Vietnamese newspaper I learned that pirates captured over one hundred Vietnamese girls and women and took them to a deserted island to rape them. Some of those females killed themselves. Others contracted venereal disease. The pirates raped the Vietnamese girls and women on our boats, and killed the people who struggled with them. . . .

. . . The pirates, the same we had encountered that morning, jumped aboard. I was the first person who dove into the ocean when I heard someone call "jump," and then others followed. I was in the water a few minutes with fear, because I realized that if I stayed long in the ocean I might be a shark's prey, so my people and I swam back to our boat. Then the pirates checked everyone elaborately and robbed some more of our valuables. Next, the pirates ordered us to get in the front of our boat, where almost all the people fainted from gasoline vapors. The owner of our boat told us that someone had emptied out the gas tank because he wanted to be supported with that tank in the sea.

Those real situations made me think about death, which seemed to lessen my own energy. Besides, I thought that if I were to have an easy death I would have to pass out. Pass out . . . the phrase haunted my mind continually until I heard someone laughing. The laughter became fainter and fainter in my ears, and I lost consciousness.

The day after, I woke up and I was very happy that I had not died that night. The pirates left us an hour after they had robbed us. Then I went back to the cabin and found my ring, which I had thrown into the engine room. So I was not robbed the second time either. After that, I had my property in the corner of our boat. I felt starved again, so I thought in my starved mind that the pirates came to us, because we had some food and water.

Around 10:30 A.M. on June 9, other pirates came to rob us, and they gave us some food and water. They left us after they took a gold ring from us, but they refused to help us by towing our boat to land or to Malaysia. We despaired and could not do anything with our boat, so everyone prayed again to God to help us. A few hours later it rained so we had some rainwater by using a parachute to catch it. The rain stopped around 3:00 P.M., but we had no control over our boat. We would sail by the parachute, and our boat would drift to our country or Cambodia in one or two weeks, but we would probably die of starvation before then while our boat floated on the sea. No one had a choice. Everyone's life was left to chance. Fortunately, a Thai boat came toward us after we sailed about ten minutes. They were saviors. They let us have a night on their boat, gave us some soup and water, and tried to repair our engine. . . . On June 10, the Thai fishermen drew our boat to Malaysia. When we spotted the Malaysian islands, they left us after they gave us some food and water. Then we thanked God and our saviors from the bottom of our hearts before we joyfully sailed our boat to Malaysia.

We arrived at the shore about 5:00 P.M. on June 11, and our engine was broken again. We then stopped at the Malaysian seashore and spent a night there. During our time on the island, we exchanged gasoline for some food, packs of cigarettes, and water. Next day, June 12, a Malaysian patrol boat came toward us and towed us toward them. The captain promised us that they would take us to the Malaysian refugee camp on the next day; we were pleased with that news. . . .

About 10:00 A.M. on June 13, the patrol boat's captain refused to guide our boats to their refugee camp, because their government had stopped accepting refugees. There were about thirty thousand Vietnamese refugees in the refugee camp, so the camp was full. Then the captain ordered his patrol boat to tow our boats to Singapore. That news disappointed us and struck us with consternation. . . . However, they towed us for only about thirty hours; then they left us after they told us to navigate our boats to some islands. We again resigned ourselves to our fate. I thought about death again because our engine was broken. . . .

Finally, our boat came to the unknown islands about 9:00 P.M. on June 14. I saw that there were many Vietnamese people on those islands, and then I learned that I had arrived in Indonesia. I really had survived, because I was a legal refugee in the Indonesian refugee camp when I landed on those islands.

I had a miraculous escape, but my mind was still haunted by death. I did not lose my golden ring, which helped me buy some food in the refugee camp. In January 1980, approval was given for me to migrate to the United States. I lived in the KuKu and Galang refugee camps for fourteen months under the support of the United Nations. On August 20, 1980, I set foot in Seattle. I then really had freedom and a new life in this country.

4. An Account of Cultural and Religious Conflict Between American Doctors and Hmong Refugees in a Thai Refugee Camp, 1982

In 1982, Mao Thao, a Hmong woman from Laos who had resettled in St. Paul, Minnesota, visited Ban Vinai, the refugee camp in Thailand where she lived for a year after her escape from Laos in 1975. She was the first Hmong-American ever to return there, and when an officer of the United Nations High Commissioner for Refugees, which administered the camp, asked her to speak about life in the United States, 15,000 Hmong, more than a third of the population of Ban Vinai, assembled in a soccer field and questioned her for nearly four hours. Some of the questions they asked her were: Is it forbidden to use a *txiv neeb* to heal an illness in the United States? Why do American doctors take so much blood from their patients? After you die, why do American doctors try to open up your head and take out your brains? Do American doctors eat the livers, kidneys, and brains of Hmong patients? When Hmong people die in the United States, is it true that they are cut into pieces and put in tin cans and sold as food? . . .

. . . The limited contact the Hmong had already had with Western medicine in the camp hospitals and clinics had done little to instill confidence, especially when compared to the experiences with shamanistic healing to which they were accustomed. A *txiv neeb* might spend as much as eight hours in a sick person's home;

---

doctors forced their patients, no matter how weak they were, to come to the hospital, and then might spend only twenty minutes at their bedsides. *Txiv neebs* were polite and never needed to ask questions; doctors asked many rude and intimate questions about patients' lives, right down to their sexual and excretory habits. *Txiv neebs* could render an immediate diagnosis; doctors often demanded samples of blood (or even urine or feces, which they liked to keep in little bottles), took X rays, and waited for days for the results to come back from the laboratory—and then, after all that, sometimes they were unable to identify the cause of the problem. *Txiv neebs* never undressed their patients; doctors asked patients to take off all their clothes, and sometimes dared to put their fingers inside women's vaginas. *Txiv neebs* knew that to treat the body without treating the soul was an act of patent folly; doctors never even mentioned the soul. *Txiv neebs* could preserve unblemished reputations even if their patients didn't get well, since the blame was laid on the intransigence of the spirits rather than the competence of the negotiators, whose stock might even rise if they had had to do battle with particularly dangerous opponents; when doctors failed to heal, it was their own fault.

To add injury to insult, some of the doctors' procedures actually seemed more likely to threaten their patients' health than to restore it. Most Hmong believe that the body contains a finite amount of blood that it is unable to replenish, so repeated blood sampling, especially from small children, may be fatal. When people are unconscious, their souls are at large, so anesthesia may lead to illness or death. If the body is cut or disfigured, or if it loses any of its parts, it will remain in a condition of perpetual imbalance, and the damaged person not only will become frequently ill but may be physically incomplete during the next incarnation; so surgery is taboo. If people lose their vital organs after death, their souls cannot be reborn into new bodies and may take revenge on living relatives; so autopsies and embalming are also taboo. (Some of the questions on the Ban Vinai soccer field were obviously inspired by reports on the widespread practice of autopsy and embalming in the United States. To make the leap from hearing that doctors removed organs to believing that they ate them was probably no crazier than to assume, as did American doctors, that the Hmong ate human placentas—but it was certainly scarier.)

The only form of medical treatment that was gratefully accepted by at least some of the Hmong in the Thai camps was antibiotic therapy, either oral or by injection. Most Hmong have little fear of needles, perhaps because some of their own healers (not *txiv neebs,* who never touch their patients) attempt to release fevers and toxicity through acupuncture and other forms of dermal treatment, such as massage; pinching; scraping the skin with coins, spoons, silver jewelry, or pieces of bamboo; applying a heated cup to the skin; or burning the skin with a sheaf of grass or a wad of cotton wool. An antibiotic shot that could heal an infection almost overnight was welcomed. A shot to immunize someone against a disease he did not yet have was something else again. . . .

In 1985, the International Rescue Committee assigned Dwight Conquergood, a young ethnographer with a special interest in shamanism and performance art, to design an environmental health program for Ban Vinai. He later wrote:

> I heard horror story after horror story from the refugees about people who went to the hospital for treatment, but before being admitted had their spirit-strings cut from their wrists by a nurse because "the strings were unsanitary and carried germs." Doctors confidently cut off neckrings that held the life-souls of babies intact. Instead of working

in cooperation with the shamans, they did everything to disconfirm them and undermine their authority. . . . Is it any wonder that the Hmong community regarded the camp hospital as the last choice of available health care options? In the local hierarchy of values, consulting a shaman or herbalist, or purchasing medicine available in the Thai market just outside the entrance to the camp, was much preferred and more prestigious than going to the camp hospital. The refugees told me that only the very poorest people who had no relatives or resources whatsoever would subject themselves to the camp hospital treatment. To say that the camp hospital was underutilized would be an understatement.

Unlike the other camp volunteers, who commuted from an expatriate enclave an hour away, Conquergood insisted on living in Ban Vinai, sharing the corner of a thatched hut with seven chickens and a pig. His first day in the camp, Conquergood noticed a Hmong woman sitting on a bench, singing folk songs. Her face was decorated with little blue moons and golden suns, which he recognized as stickers the camp clinic place on medication bottles to inform illiterate patients whether the pills should be taken morning or night. The fact that Conquergood considered this a delightful example of creative costume design rather than an act of medical noncompliance suggests some of the reasons why the program he designed turned out to be the most (indeed, possibly the only) completely successful attempt at health care delivery Ban Vinai had ever seen.

Conquergood's first challenge came after an outbreak of rabies among the camp dogs prompted a mass dog-vaccination campaign by the medical staff, during which the Ban Vinai inhabitants failed to bring in a single dog to be inoculated. Conquergood was asked to come up with a new campaign. He decided on a Rabies Parade, a procession led by three important characters from Hmong folktales—a tiger, a chicken, and a *dab* [evil spirit]—dressed in homemade costumes. The cast, like its audience, was one hundred percent Hmong. As the parade snaked through the camp, the tiger danced and played the *geej,* the *dab* sang and banged a drum, and the chicken (chosen for this crucial role because of its traditional powers of augury) explained the etiology of rabies through a bullhorn. The next morning, the vaccination stations were so besieged by dogs—dogs carried in their owners' arms, dogs dragged on rope leashes, dogs rolled in on two-wheeled pushcarts—that the health workers could hardly inoculate them fast enough. Conquergood's next production, a sanitation campaign in which a parade of children led by Mother Clean (a huge, insanely grinning figure on a bamboo frame) and the Garbage Troll (dressed in ragged clothes plastered with trash) sang songs about latrine use and refuse disposal, was equally well received.

During Conquergood's five months in Ban Vinai, he himself was successfully treated with Hmong herbs for diarrhea and a gashed toe. When he contracted dengue fever (for which he also sought conventional medical treatment), a *txiv neeb* informed him that his homesick soul had wandered back to Chicago, and two chickens were sacrificed to expedite its return. Conquergood considered his relationship with the Hmong to be a form of barter, "a productive and mutually invigorating dialog, with neither side dominating or winning out." In his opinion, the physicians and nurses at Ban Vinai failed to win the cooperation of the camp inhabitants because they considered the relationship one-sided, with the Westerners holding all the knowledge. As long as they persisted in this view, Conquergood believed that what the medical establishment was offering would continue to be rejected, since the Hmong would view it not as a gift but as a form of coercion.

5. Xang Mao Xiong Tells His Daughter of the Problems Hmong Parents Face in America, 1994

A problem that we Hmong parents face today in America is disciplining our children. It is so difficult! Not only are our children not listening to us, but we parents can be thrown in jail for trying to teach them what is right. In Laos, we disciplined our children by a good beating. If a child fights with our children or with his or her brothers and sisters, or talks back to his or her parents, or steals, then he or she receives a beating. After a few such beatings, children learn their lesson and become better persons. But today, here in America, if we hit our children, if they are smart they will tell their teacher or call the police. The children of today have no respect for their elders and do not fear their parents. Americans do not understand our culture, and we do not understand theirs. Therefore, we run into problems when raising our children in the United States.

Another major problem I have experienced since arriving in the United States is speaking and understanding English. I did not even know the difference between "yes" and "no" when I first came, yet I was required to find a job to support my family. I did not have the least idea where to start looking. I had no special skills

Photograph of the Xiong family in Lompoc, 1993.

and could not read or write English. How could I fill out employment application forms? I did not know how. Luckily, there were two Hmong named Touby Lo and Ka Pao Xiong who worked in Isla Vista for a social service agency called Indochina. This agency helped find employment for the new arrivals—for Cambodians, Vietnamese, lowland Lao, and Hmong.

My very first job in America, at which I am still employed, had very, very low pay. I started at $3.15 an hour. Though the pay was low, I was tired of being on welfare. I was tired of filling out forms and making monthly reports, tired of having to get papers signed for not working. If I did not fill out those papers and get them signed each month, my family and I would be removed from the welfare rolls. I decided, therefore, to take the job. No more papers! I could buy what I wanted without having to report to the welfare department. I was not used to depending on the government for financial support. In Laos, we had grown our own crops and earned our living by the sweat of our brow.

The American language is very difficult because a lot of different words can have the same meaning. One problem I have had in learning English is that after I learned what one word means, I got all confused when I found that another word had the same meaning. For example, good, nice, beautiful, perfect have similar meanings. In Hmong, different words have different meanings. American English is very hard for us adults to learn. It is easy for our children, but not for us.

When I first arrived in the United States, the first thing I noticed were all the cars on the streets and freeways. I feared crossing the street, even at a traffic light. I was also afraid to go to the grocery store on my own for I worried about getting lost. It really frustrated me that I was not able to be independent. It took me years to get adjusted and to learn my way around town.

Besides being afraid of getting lost in a strange place, I was homesick. I missed my country. The mountains, trees, flowers, and animals here are all so different. There is nothing here to remind me of my country, and that makes me sad. The sky, the earth, and the mountains in Santa Barbara County are not the same as those in Laos. The people and the social environment are also different. I am sad not knowing whether I will ever see the flowers and bamboo groves in Laos again.

6. *Golden Venture* Refugees Wage a Hunger Strike to Protest Their Detention, 1995

At a spartan county jail on the outskirts of this farming community, a group of 22 illegal Chinese immigrants, some of them survivors of the shipwreck of the *Golden Venture* off New York, say they have gone on a hunger strike to protest their detention for more than two years and the Government's plans to deport them.

The protesting refugees are all women; most of those who did not come to the United States aboard the *Golden Venture,* a smuggling vessel that ran aground off the coast of Queens on June 6, 1993, were arrested in Southern California. All have been held in various prisons and detention centers awaiting the outcome of their

From Kenneth B. Noble, "*Golden Venture* Refugees on Hunger Strike in California to Protest Detention," *New York Times,* December 2, 1995. Copyright © 1995 New York Times Co., Inc. Used with permission.

asylum appeals. According to the Immigration and Naturalization Service and the New York City Medical Examiner's office, of the *Golden Venture*'s 286 passengers, 10 died after the grounding and 6 were never captured; 76 have been released and 47 have been deported to China. The remaining 147 are still behind bars here and at four other prisons and jails around the country.

The 10 who are here at the Kern County jail in Lerdo say they are entitled to political asylum because of China's family planning policies of forced abortions or sterilizations. But for the most part, their quest for asylum appears futile, lawyers for the women here say, and their deportations are imminent.

For one thing, current immigration law is weighed against them. A 1989 ruling by the Board of Immigration Appeals invalidated political asylum claims based solely on China's family planning practices. Immigration experts say that refugees must now show they face forced abortions and sterilizations because of their political opinions, not merely because of their Chinese citizenship. Legal challenges to that ruling have so far failed.

And after languishing in various detention centers awaiting their appeals, some of the women here say they have grown desperate. While some want to remain in the United States, other say they simply want to be released from prison—even if they must starve themselves to death to do so.

"I feel terrible now, but I won't stop because I want to be free of the jail," said Tin Chin Wang, a 25-year-old-apparel maker who was captured shortly after arriving near San Diego in a ship about two years ago. Inside the jail's interview room, she looked haggard and disoriented, and she cried at times. "There is no pain in dying, but it hurts when they keep you in jail," she said.

Another woman, Quing Cai, who was aboard the *Golden Venture* when it ran aground off New York, said she was certain she would be killed if she returned to China. "After all I've gone through here, I have no fear of death," she said through a translator. She added that prison guards had placed her in solitary confinement in an effort to force her to eat, a charge that prison officials have denied.

Paula Harris, a lawyer for the Chinese American Foundation, which has represented the women in appeals proceedings before the Immigration and Naturalization Service said, "I don't think the public has a clue that these people are still being detained, or certainly how they're being treated."

This is a final desperate act to try to get some intervention," said John M. A. Burgess, a San Francisco lawyer who is also representing the Chinese refugees. "Many of them face sterilization and imprisonment for two to three years if they're returned to China."

But Russ Bergeron, a spokesman for the immigration service in Washington, suggested that the plight of the women might be exaggerated by their advocates. "As of yesterday," Mr. Bergeron said in a telephone interview, "there were nine individuals who still claim to be on a hunger strike."

"While they are refusing the meals provided them by the detention facility, we believe they're eating food which was purchased from the canteen at the facility," Mr. Bergeron said. "We have had previous instances in other facilities involving other individuals where hunger strikes were declared after the stockpiling of food."

He added: "The condition of these individuals are monitored on a daily basis. Anyone giving indication of a medical problem is given medical attention." Thus far, Mr. Bergeron said, only one person has been treated outside the prison; she was hospitalized for three hours, given intravenous fluids and released.

Sgt. Gary Davis, a shift supervisor at the Kern County Sheriff's Department, which runs the facility, said it was his understanding that the Chinese detainees began their hunger strike on Nov. 9. He said that nine women were now refusing to eat and that they had lost an average of 10 pounds." And at this point, they continue to not accept the food that is offered to them three times a day," Sergeant Davis said.

The hunger strike marks a new chapter in the long, grim saga of the *Golden Venture,* which arrived off the Queens shore about 2 A.M. on that June day. Some *Golden Venture* passengers spent up to three years in transit to the United States, herded through Southeast Asia and Africa as their smugglers arranged safe passage. Most had already given the smugglers $5,000 as a down payment for their trip, with an additional $25,000 due on their arrival in the United States.

The passengers were crammed into a 40-foot-by-20-foot hold and had a single ladder to the deck. There were no life boats or life jackets; privacy and sanitation were almost nonexistent. Water was severely rationed.

When the ship arrived in New York after months at sea, many dived into the chilly waters in the mistaken belief that as long as they touched American soil, they would eventually be released. At least five drowned. Others suffered heart attacks or died of hypothermia. Many more, clad only in rags or underwear and clutching plastic bags of belongings, dragged themselves out of thundering, 53-degree seas.

The *Golden Venture* case opened a window on the ugly underworld of smuggling humans from China to America, helping to expose a vast and highly lucrative business. Since then, American law-enforcement officials have estimated that tens of thousands of Asian laborers, many of them from China's coastal Fujian Province, have been brought to work for little more than slave wages.

Twenty-one defendants, members of the *Gold Venture*'s crew and suspected organizers of the smuggling operation, were convicted in Federal court in 1994 and 1995. They received sentences ranging from less than a year for crew members to 10 years for Kin Sin Lee, believed to have been No. 2 in the smuggling ring. The man who is believed to have masterminded the operation, Lee Peng Fei, was recently caught in Bangkok.

7. Business Consultant George P. Koo Criticizes Harry Wu's Campaign Against the Chinese Government, 1996

The publicity attendant upon his arrest in China last summer endowed Harry Wu with far more influence than he possessed before his attempted clandestine entry. He is now appearing everywhere to disrupt and disturb American foreign policy on China and influence world opinion towards China. He has challenged the World Bank on their investment policy in China and told Boeing how they should not do business with China. He is telling Congress how it should vote on China's trade

From George P. Koo, "Is Harry Wu Telling the Truth?" *AsianWeek,* April 26, 1996. Copyright 1996 AsianWeek. Used with permission.

status and even predicting a subsequent overriding veto from the President. Just last week, Wu cancelled an appearance at Stanford University due to, according to his spokesman, a request to testify before the United Nations Human Rights Commission in Geneva.

Unfortunately, the Media tends to overlook Harry Wu's web of deceit built on grains of half truths, elaborated with exaggerations and gross misrepresentations. Normally the veracity of any one person is not worth fussing about. In Wu's case, he is capable of doing considerable damage to public interest, especially in the coming months as the national policy towards China comes to the forefront of debate.

One simple example of his propensity for deceit is his own statement in the February issue of *Playboy*. He said, "I videotaped a prisoner whose kidneys were surgically removed while he was alive, and then the prisoner was taken out the next day and shot. The organs remain fresher that way. The tape was broadcast by BBC." One has to wonder about the professional qualifications of the interviewer to record such an outrageous statement unchallenged. Organ transplants from prisoners has been one of Wu's most dramatic accusations about China and pivots on the now discredited evidence presented by the BBC broadcast.

Inconsistencies and shifting statements abound from Wu's public utterances and activities. . . . I believe Wu has sponsors and supporters with vested interests in containing China through public opinion, irrespective of truth and facts. One of Wu's more obvious sponsors is the AFL-CIO.

Shortly after Wu's arrest in China became known, an ABC Nightline program revealed that his clandestine trip into China via Kazakstan was financed by the AFL-CIO, and the attorney who accompanied Wu was on the AFL-CIO payroll. After the two were detained, she was promptly released and that was how the world first heard about Wu's arrest. In retrospect, she was an essential part of Wu's cover and protection. . . .

According to data presented to the House Ways and Means Trade Subcommittee in May 1995 by Robert Kapp, president of the Washington-based US-China Business Council, America exported $9.3 billion worth of goods to China in 1994, equivalent to the support of approximately 187,000 jobs. According to Department of Commerce data presented at the same testimony, China will be buying $90 billion worth of power generation equipment, $65 billion worth of commercial jets, $40 billion of telecommunication equipment, $18.2 billion of oil field and gas machinery and $4.3 billion of computers in the coming years. Getting a fraction of that business will create many more jobs than the low cost goods imported from China that AFL-CIO object to. These are goods America can no longer produce competitively even if imports from China are curtailed.

AFL-CIO's agenda on China and its dependence on Wu is no secret; the media simply are not seen fit to report the matter. In a testimony before the House of Representatives in July, 1995, Peggy Taylor, Director of the AFL-CIO Department of Legislation, specifically mentioned "this lucrative trade" in organ transplants from prisoners as a reason to deny Most Favored Nation (MFN) trading status to China. There is no need to speculate as to where her "data" came from.

Cut through all the hypocrisy about defending human rights, and one sees Wu performing dubious activities to support the AFL-CIO in their efforts to stop the flow of low cost goods from China. . . .

... China is no Utopia; it has many social and political problems, and the road to rule of law will be long and steep. But China is not what Harry Wu says it is. The American public and political leadership need to know the real China in order to be able to make sound and well-grounded decisions that will affect the populations of both great nations for generations to come.

8. Chinese Refugee and Human Rights Activist Harry Wu Criticizes U.S. Trade Policies Toward China, 2000

As you may know, after spending nineteen years of my life in the Laogai—China's forced labor camp system—I have dedicated myself to investigating China's forced labor system. I have also spent much time researching the Laogai's "older brother," the Soviet Gulag. Last August, I visited one of the centers of the former Siberian Gulag in the city of Magadan. Beginning in 1932, Stalin sent one million people to these Soviet labor camps. Of course the total number of people he sent to the Gulag is much larger. After Khrushchev condemned Stalin in 1956, Magadan was no longer a Gulag city. But still, the West knew that the Soviet Union was based on principles other than freedom and democracy. Here, in the seat of American government, we know that these words are not just clichés—they mean that a government is accountable to its people because it respects their dignity, and that there are mechanisms in place to ensure that accountability. These concepts do not exist in China, and they will not exist as long as the Chinese Communist Party controls the government of China. Maintaining one-party rule is the ultimate goal of this party. . . .

The Chinese Communists are building up their navy and buying Russian battleships. They are continuing to abuse human rights—the State Department human Rights report released last month says that the human rights situation in China is getting worse. But still, one of the most popular theories in politics today is that the best way to promote democracy and improve human rights in China is to build up trade and investment. Of course, this theory has only been applied to Communist China, not to any other authoritarian countries.

This argument has been repeated in the current debate over permanent NTR [Normal Trade Relations] and China's entry into the WTO [World Trade Organization]. The reasons for this "dollars to democracy" approach are the following:

1. Better and newer information and communication systems will help the flow of truth to the people.
2. China will learn to follow the rules of the international community and become more disciplined.

Please allow me to briefly address these supposed ways that increased trade will lead to greater democracy in China.

First, the education revolution and the spread of information are supposed to bring democracy to China. Of course, you cannot dismiss the achievements that have

---

From Harry Wu, "Testimony of Harry Wu," *Finance Committee of the United States Senate,* March 23, 2000; reprinted at http://finance.senate.gov/3-23wu.htm.

been made. There are some small cracks in the wall. But the Chinese government is doing everything they can to seal up those cracks as quickly as possible. The government still controls the media, just like it controls all of the economy. Censorship is used in all forms of media in China, and those seeking to work outside the confines of the state-controlled media may be subject to detention and imprisonment. And it is foreign companies and foreign technology that are helping the government keep control of information. For example, a telecommunications firm that wanted to put China on its satellite network agreed to bounce back the satellite signals to China, so that Chinese security can trace calls if they want. Rupert Murdoch, in order to get into the Chinese market, agreed to pull CNN from his cable system, and in September, one media official at the Fortune conference in Shanghai told journalists that they should not report things that will offend their host country.

The second way in which economic engagement is supposed to bring democracy is the idea that by joining the international community, China will learn international norms and become more disciplined. This is a nice ideal. But the truth is that China has done more to change international institutions than international institutions have changed China. As an example, next week I go to Geneva to attend the annual meeting of the UN Human Rights Commission. This is supposed to be an important opportunity to put international pressure on countries that violate human rights. I do believe it is important to have a strong, consistent voice at this commission. But anyone who has been to Geneva during this meeting in a year where there is a resolution against China knows that China has managed to undermine the whole process. The meeting has become more about backroom deals for building projects and favors than human rights.

Resolutions at the United Nations are not enough to encourage China to respect human rights. They are also not enough to demonstrate that the United States is serious about making human rights part of its foreign policy. This is at the center of the current debate about Permanent Normal Trade Relations Status for China. The annual NTR debate could have the potential to be a strong tool against the human rights abuses of the Chinese regime. Just because it was never used in the past, does not mean that it is useless. Normal Trade Relations status is very important leverage, and the United States should not give it up.

There is a saying that what is good for Wall Street is good for the United States. This is not necessarily true. The foreign policy of the United States should not only achieve the goals of the executives of multinational companies. . . .

I wish that foreign businesses would be honest and admit why China is good for US business. The biggest advantage is the cheap and disciplined labor force. It is very good for US business to have a strong communist party, because then they do not have to worry about giving workers benefits, or dealing with strikes.

Everyday in China, people are making demands like those made at Tiananmen Square in 1989. Listening to these people would be a way to bring about stability. It is tragic that this regime refuses to recognize the basic fact that democracy is the best way to stability. It is even more tragic that all of the human rights abuses continue without any serious consequences in the international arena.

China has learned that as long as it negotiates trade agreements, it can continue to repress its own people.

The international community must tell China clearly: we expect to see a peaceful, prosperous, free and democratic China, not a prosperous and stable communist China. Peace and prosperity are possible only when human rights, democracy and freedom are respected.

✺ E S S A Y S

The following two essays reveal the problems policymakers, refugee personnel, and social scientists have had in interpreting and assessing refugee needs and concerns. American officials initially tried to prevent Southeast Asian refugees from congregating in ethnic enclaves because they assumed dispersion would facilitate assimilation into American society. They also classified families into nuclear units without recognizing the importance of extended kinship ties for many refugees. But many Southeast Asian refugees remigrated to form ethnic communities and to reunite extended families. Vietnamese refugees, for example, established Little Saigons in places like Westminster, California, and the Hmong created vibrant communities in Fresno, California, and other areas. The first essay, by Gail Paradise Kelly, who was a professor of education at the State University of New York at Buffalo before her death, discusses how American resettlement personnel created inappropriate programs for Vietnamese refugees that were based on incorrect assumptions about Vietnamese gender roles and labor experiences. The second essay, by San Jose State University anthropologists James M. Freeman and Usha Welaratna, criticizes the way policymakers and social scientists have portrayed the "success" of Vietnamese refugees and the "failure" of Cambodian refugees based on the basis of economic criteria only. By showing the importance of religious, ethical, and cultural values in refugee views of "adjustment," Freeman and Welaratna make a compelling case for more studies that analyze refugee perspectives on life in America.

Education and Sex Role Socialization
of Vietnamese Immigrant Women

GAIL PARADISE KELLY

The distinction between women's roles among classes changed drastically as a result of twenty years of warfare and inflation in Vietnam. Peasant women continued, as before, to work as farmers, traders, or craftspeople to sustain the family. Petty trade items changed, as many began to sell Coca-Colas and other Western manufactured items siphoned from American stores. The war, especially after 1964, forced urbanization. Strategic hamlets, the establishment of free-fire zones, defoliation programs, search-and-destroy missions, and programs such as Phoenix, which assassinated countless villages thought to be Vietcong, made the countryside uninhabitable. Cities such as Saigon, Hue, and Da Nang swelled; Saigon alone tripled its population between 1962 and 1975. Changes in locale brought changes in peasant women's occupations and intensified the pressures of subsistence. Peasant women became bar

---

Edited material from chapter 12 written by Gail Paradise Kelly from *Unequal Sisters: A Multicultural Reader in U.S. Women's History,* ed. Vicki Ruiz and Ellen Dubois, 3/e. Reprinted by permission of the estate of Gail Paradise Kelly.

girls, prostitutes, laundresses, and maids and continued as petty traders in Coca-Cola, cigarettes, liquor and beer, and drugs to urban Vietnamese and the military, both American and Vietnamese. Further, as the toll in death and mutilation among men, mostly of the lower classes who could not afford to buy their way out of military service, increased, women frequently became the sole support of their families, either as heads of households or as the only persons capable of earning a living.

The war appreciably altered the role of middle-class women by bringing incredible inflation to urban areas, which obliterated the buying power of men supporting their families. The American press wrote much about how this inflation led to widespread corruption, including bribery and theft from American military warehouses. Corruption was one outgrowth of the inflation; another result was extensive moonlighting. . . . The war, in short, changed women's roles in all classes. Women became an integral part of the Vietnamese economy, often working as the sole support of the family. . . . Their roles, in reality and by self-definition, were not that of housewife, nor did those roles arise from Confucian notions of womanhood, as camp officials and many Americans working with refugees believed. Occupationally, the majority did not fit into American job categories. For the most part, as I will show in this article, it was assumed that in America they would take on the role of housewife and mother, consistent with American conceptions of sex-role behavior. This was not only assumed but enforced; educational efforts in the camps, including English-language classes, vocational courses, cultural orientation meetings, and printed materials circulated in the camps, were almost without exception directed at resocializing these women into American stereotypic roles. . . .

. . . The Survival English course, taught at three levels, had sixteen lessons that covered topics such as meeting strangers, finding a place to live, occupations, renting apartments, shopping, "John's interest," and applying for jobs. The first lesson began with greetings and sex identifications. Students were drilled on phrases such as "Hello," "Good afternoon," "My name is . . ." "I'm a man," I'm a woman," I'm a boy," "I'm a girl," "Do you speak English?" Subsequent vocabulary included locations of lavatories, days of the week, numbers, food, time, and job titles. Once vocabulary was introduced as words, lessons centered on the pattern of sentences and conversations. In all but two of the sixteen lessons, the conversations took place between "Mr. Brown" and Mr. Jones," with Mr. Brown responding to Mr. Jones' questions. For example, Mr. Jones (no doubt the refugee) inquired, in the lesson on numbers, how he might go about buying a house. In the lesson on occupations, Mr. Jones asked what kind of job he might get to support his wife and two children. Mr. Jones said he could work as a room clerk, salesman, cashier, laborer, plumber, bricklayer, cook, cleaning person, secretary, typist, seamstress, or nurse's aide. Women appeared in the dialogues in only two instances: in a lesson on budgeting and shopping, and in a lesson called "Conversation." Both are explicit in delineating male/female roles. In the conversation Miss Jones becomes part of the drill in two places—with the pattern sentence "Miss Jones missed the bus to the Miss Universe competition" and "She is an attractive girl." In the shopping sequences, all levels of English classes made it clear that women could shop only for small items. In the basic classes, teaching persons who knew no English, Mrs. Brown shopped for dresses, shoes, food, aspirin, baby needs, and cosmetics; Mr. Brown, on the other hand, shopped for shirts, houses, cars, and furniture. In the advanced classes this division of labor between the sexes was expanded. "Marie" (no doubt the advanced classes' equivalent of Mrs. Brown) compared prices on food and other commodities, thereby saving her husband *his* hard-earned money. She was wise and would buy nothing but food without consulting her husband, Tim. In the lesson she found out where the cheapest sofa and sewing machine in town could be bought, but took her husband to the stores to decide for them where they should make their purchases. . . .

English-language classes, in short, transmitted, as do many American texts used in schools, stereotypical roles. Women were noticeably absent in class materials. When they appeared, their qualities were reduced to beauty and interest in it, and their roles were that of wife and mother, particularly shopper. It is interesting to note that in the Survival English course, designed specifically for Vietnamese refugees, occupations reserved for American women (typist, seamstress, nurse's aide) were presented as jobs for Vietnamese men. Not only were the programs allocating Vietnamese men into lower-class women's occupations, but they also presented immigrant men with nonoccupational roles traditionally reserved for U.S. women—it is Mr. Jones, in the Survival English course, who finds out where stores are, gets a doctor, selects a church, locates the children's school, and so on. In the Survival English materials, women ventured out of the house only to shop. . . .

. . . Many camp officials and school personnel were gravely concerned about the stability of the immigrant family and the consequences for individuals and the social order should the Vietnamese family disintegrate. (Some veterans of the Agency for International Development working in the camps believed this had already happened under the stress of the war and was the reason the South Vietnamese government fell. They were determined to reconstruct what they thought was the traditional Vietnamese family among the immigrants, believing this to be the only way for them to survive in America.) Schoolteachers, curriculum coordinators, and administrative and resettlement personnel emphasized time after time the role of education in reinforcing the Vietnamese family and the supremacy of the father, which they assumed was characteristic of both Vietnamese and American families. It was thought that only through the reinforcement and/or reestablishment of patriarchal relations could immigrants "adjust" well to America. And, as the curriculum coordinator of the adult school pointed out to me in one of our lengthy interviews, the school's role was not just to teach English; its mission was to help its students "adjust" to America and live happily there. . . .

The major emphasis in the classroom was on occupations—teaching Vietnamese refugees how to describe their work skills to prospective employers. In class the teacher began with the phrase, "What kind of work do you do?" He then drew stick figures showing different kinds of work—ditch-digging, selling, and so on, naming them all. After introducing phrases like "I'm a ditch digger; I am a mechanic," he asked each of his thirty or more students, "What kind of work do you do?" The first student to respond was a young man, obviously a former soldier. He responded by imitating a gun with his fingers and replied, "I rat-a-tat-tat." The teacher corrected him with, "I work with my hands." Next to recite was a middle-aged woman who had lacquered teeth (indicating she came from a rural, lower-class family). She made a motion that looked like casting nets (I found out later she came from coastal Vung-Tau and fished for a living). The teacher responded with, "I am a housewife." The woman looked puzzled. The teacher then drew a stick figure on the blackboard representing a woman with a broom in her hand, inside a house. He repeated "I am a housewife," pointing to the woman. She and the women sitting with her began a lively discussion in Vietnamese and started laughing. The teacher then drilled all the women as a group repeatedly with the phrase "I am a housewife." . . .

. . . The Pennsylvania Commission for Women, believing that the school and camp authorities were inadequately preparing women for life in America, set up a series of programs called "Women in America" to rectify these deficiencies—much to the chagrin, I might add, of camp authorities and school personnel.

"Women in America": A Counter to English Classes?

"Women in America" represented to some extent an alternative to the kind of sex-role socialization evident in the English-language classes. Those who designed it firmly believed in women's rights and fluidity of sex roles, and that Vietnamese women were in a stage of bondage similar to that in nineteenth-century China. The program coordinator, an American woman in her late twenties, had lived for several years in Taiwan, Hong Kong, and Japan and saw the Vietnamese family and women's roles within it in light of her limited observations aboard. To her, it was only recently that these women had stopped having their feet bound. According to her, their role was only to produce male heirs for the family and to accede to their mother-in-law's and husband's wishes within the household where they were confined. She told me that camp authorities, through their educational programs and their practices (specifically the practice of not intervening in known cases of wife beating at Indian Town gap), reinforced Vietnamese women's traditional roles, which, she believed, were both oppressive and impractical in America. The "Women in America" programs, thus, were set up to explain to immigrant women their roles and rights in the United States. . . .

The content of the classes varied in minor ways at each meeting, depending on responses to them. At several meetings discussion centered on snow or shopping, as women, excluded from English-language classes, sought out information about America in general and took the opportunity to meet Americans and ask questions that intrigued them most. Generally, the class organizers tried to cover four topics—family life, women's rights, jobs for women, and women's organizations—each night before allowing refugees to change the subject. The four main topics were presented by four women from the Pennsylvania Commission for Women, who spoke in English with simultaneous translation into Vietnamese. The first speaker covered the family. Her presentation stressed men's participation in housework and child care and was accompanied by pictures of men bathing children, doing dishes, shopping, and so on. There were almost no pictures of women engaged in these tasks. The second presentation told women they had a right to abortion on demand and could divorce their husbands, vote, own property, and work if they chose to. It stressed women's rights to plan family size, and said that two children was the desirable number for happy families. The third presentation was on jobs. It told Vietnamese women that while some American women worked, some chose not to work. With the aid of photographs, the speaker surveyed the world of work for women, showing photos of women as bulldozer operators, nurses, teachers, librarians, salesclerks, karate teachers, engineers, corporate presidents, and so on. The person giving the presentation paused when she showed the picture of a nurse at work, and told the class that it was an excellent occupation for women. At this point, a middle-aged immigrant asked if women could be butchers. The response given was that the presenter knew of no woman butchers in America. The final talk was on women's organizations. This was primarily a detailed enumeration of groups such as the YWCA, Planned Parenthood, the National Welfare Rights Organization, and the League of Women Voters.

These classes did indeed present women's roles and work in quite a different light than did other formal education within the camps. Unlike the English-language classes, women were depicted outside the home, with the possibility of financial independence. The series, however, did not have as much an impact as the English-language classes, for no more than thirty-persons attended the meetings each night. Several of those who attended were men who, in the discussions following the presentations, made speeches claiming that men in America had no rights at all. The impact of the programs was all the more limited because there was no real incentive for refugees to attend them or take them seriously. Camp authorities and teachers openly disapproved of the meetings, and ran movies and English classes during the times they were scheduled. Further, camp authorities made it clear to refugees that only by learning English would they adjust well to America. By September, when the "Women in America" series began, area commanders, who were responsible for barrack sections of the camps, pressured adults into going to English-language classes; they did not exert any such pressure for persons to attend the other series. Apparently they resented the classes because they believed "Women in America" would disrupt the Vietnamese family, make Vietnamese men anxious about resettling in America and having to cope with aggressive women, and in the long run would make camp authorities' task more difficult. . . .

. . . Vietnamese were being resettled in an American society in an economic recession, during which there were few jobs available to Americans, let alone to immigrants who barely spoke English and possessed few skills. Jobs for which most refugees were qualified were among the lowest-paying in the society. Under American definitions of the nuclear family, the Vietnamese family averaged seven persons. Men working as day laborers and nurse's aides were not likely to earn enough to sustain an entire family, so that women would be forced to work, either to supplement family income or as the sole source of family income. A year after the camps closed, 73 percent of the immigrants who had once been professionals, technicians, managers, and businessmen found themselves blue-collar workers; another 17 percent became clerical and sales personnel. Only 10 percent went into jobs equivalent to those they had held in Vietnam. Most worked in jobs paying minimum wages; many of these jobs were temporary. Yearly incomes were so low that close to 50 percent of all Vietnamese families in the United States received some form of welfare.

While the camp educational programs were a point of entry for Vietnamese into the society and culture of Americans, they did not serve this purpose equally for men and women. Rather, they prepared only Vietnamese men for integration into the U.S. workforce and society. Vietnamese women were not the focus of integrational efforts. "Women in America" alone tried to prepare the women for entry into the U.S. workforce. However, like the other educational efforts, this program impinged upon Vietnamese culture and set U.S. terms for Vietnamese adjustment to the society. The educational programs also fostered the lowering of Vietnamese expectations by preparing men for occupations usually reserved for women in U.S. society. While preparing men for women's roles, they also positioned Vietnamese men to usurp women's roles within the family. The schools taught Vietnamese men to take care of schooling, medical care, shopping, and the like.

English-language programs, *Dat Lanh,* and even the "Women in America" programs, regardless of their points of disagreement, were all directed toward getting Vietnamese to enter the society and culture of Americans regardless of their desires. Most Vietnamese were ambivalent about becoming integrated into American society; they opposed the U.S. resettlement policy, openly expressing their desire to remain Vietnamese within the United States. Of this, Americans were well aware. Article after article in *Dat Lanh* derided Vietnamese unwillingness to leave the "Little Vietnams" of the camps and become Americans. After the camps closed, Vietnamese opposition to U.S. resocialization policies became overt, as they abandoned their original places of resettlement and left the diaspora designed for them, to form their own Vietnamese communities.

Vietnamese and Cambodian Views of "Successful" Adjustment in America

JAMES M. FREEMAN AND USHA WELARATNA

Overview

Since 1975, over 950,000 Indochinese refugees and immigrants from Vietnam, Laos, and Cambodia have sought and been granted refuge in or admission to the United States. Numerous books, documentary films, and TV programs have publicized the sufferings and plight of these people as well as their attempts to adjust to their new cultural and social environment. Despite nearly two decades of indirect or direct involvement in the Indochina war, and another 15 years of admitting Indochinese refugees and immigrants into the United States, most Americans neither understand nor appreciate their lifestyles, values, and traditions. Most of the expressed concern about refugees continues to focus on whether they can adapt to and fit themselves into American culture. Most studies about them and most federally funded projects that pupport to assist them perpetuate, whether intentionally or not, an assimilationist outlook in which the primary concern is the degree by and the speed at which refugees achieve economic self-sufficiency. Based on this view, Vietnamese refugees and immigrants typically are described as successful in adjusting to the United States, while Cambodians are often cited as less successful. Overlooked in this view are the social and cultural needs of refugees from *their* points of view; in other words, how Vietnamese and Cambodians themselves view their own adjustments. That is the subject of our paper.

Official American Views of Adjustment

There are many views of "success" and "successful refugee adjustment" in America. But the official views presented to refugees, and used to manipulate them to behave in certain ways, are the ones outlined in the Refugee Act of 1980. According to this act, the primary goal of the federal resettlement program is "the achieve-ment of self-sufficiency as quickly as possible" for refugees admitted to the United States. Many but not all Americans subscribe to these views. Since passage of this act, the vast majority of refugees who have come here are from Vietnam, Cambodia, and Laos. Ruben Rumbaut and Kenji Ima, two sociologists from San Diego State University who have conducted comparative studies of the adaptations of Southeast Asian refugees, observe that in order to achieve the "self-sufficiency" goal of the act, the focus of the refugee resettlement program has been on the placement of adult refugees in regular employment.

Since refugee resettlement programs are meant for all refugees, each group receives similar assistance. However, Rumbaut and Ima have found that while the Vietnamese have been successful in establishing economic "self-sufficiency," the Khmer (Cambodians) have yet to match the same level of self-sufficiency. They claim the reason is that the Vietnamese have been here longer and are more educated. Their views on Vietnamese and Khmer refugee adjustments are reiterated by an offi-cial of a refugee resettlement agency in Santa Clara County, California. In an inter-view with Usha Welaratna this official said, "When compared with other refugee groups both from Southeast Asia and from countries such as Iran and Ethiopia, many Cambodians have not mainstreamed successfully. They have not found jobs, not be-come citizens, and not learned English." She noted in particular that when compared with Vietnamese, the Khmer are unsuccessful. In her view, the reason is that peasants and tribal groups listen to their leaders, and Cambodians, who are mainly peasants, want to stay with their group, in contrast to the Vietnamese who are much more indi-vidualistic and westernized. This official believes that while some Cambodians are good workers who are liked by their employers, others are unemployed because they have acquired a "welfare mentality" and use ailments such as headaches as reasons for not finding employment. While acknowledging that depression is a reality for these survivors of the Cambodian holocaust, she also asserts that depression could be overcome simply by finding work and learning English. In her view, the problem is that Cambodians do not try hard enough. This view is echoed by an English as a Second Language (ESL) teacher who in an interview said to Welaratna that Khmer refugees probably attend class simply to socialize with friends.

The views above project American values into the interpretation of observable Cambodian behaviors and judge Cambodian ways of life from an American per-spective without considering how Cambodians view their condition.

There are a few voices that contrast with the mainstream views mentioned above. Elena Yu and William Liu, who have addressed the American perception of successful refugee adjustment, point out that the Indochinese refugees have had no control over the studies dealing with their own community. They state, "The choice of research topic itself is defined by those who wish to take some actions on the refugees who have no power to defend themselves." Gisele Bousquet, a foreign-born research associate at the University of California, Berkeley, takes this argument a step further and suggests that:

> Social scientists are imposing their own American values. They are proposing a research
> model in order to satisfy government and funding agencies rather than the Indochinese
> refugees. The economic integration as the theoretical orientation taken in these studies
> on the Indochinese refugees, inevitably determines the power relations created between
> the observer and the observed. The social scientists writing and publishing papers on

refugees, generated sets of questions and problems in which "scientific knowledge" is intended to contribute to policy-making regarding the refugees. The emphasis of these studies on Indochinese economic self-sufficiency reflects government concerns, and assumes a world view that may bear no relation to that of refugees.

Vietnamese Views of Adjustment

In *Hearts of Sorrow: Vietnamese-American Lives* (1989), James Freeman documents the life histories of Vietnamese refugees and immigrants in their homeland and the connections between their childhood environments, their responses to traumatic events, and their ways of adjustment during their first decade in the United States. The book conveys aspects of the refugee and adjustment experience through the eyes of refugees. Particularly striking is the finding that for many Vietnamese, beneath the outer appearance of economic success lies the heartache of family separation, conflict, unanticipated change, loneliness, and the feeling of being ill-at-ease in the United States. While Americans extolled their rapid economic successes and gains (or criticized them as dangerous economic competitors), they viewed themselves as having failed because members of their families had grown apart. As one patriarchal elder in an economically successful professional family announced sadly, "Here in America, my wife and I will die a lonely death, abandoned by our children." An elderly grandmother, lonely and feeling neglected in her daughter's house, moved out, preferring to live with women her own age.

A young woman expressed sorrow in another way. As she handed Freeman the final assignment that completed her undergraduate education, he asked the young Vietnamese woman if she planned to attend her graduation ceremony. Tears came to her eyes and she replied softly, "No, my parents are no longer alive; they die in Vietnam. My education meant so much to them. I cannot go when they are not there to celebrate." Freeman observes, "Never can she celebrate without triggering memories and sadness."

Refugees from other communities also experience the predicament that, beneath the surface of success in America, lies sorrow. But what is distinctive about the Vietnamese version is its particular cultural expression. One young man said, "On the outside I am like an American. I drive to work in my car. I eat hamburgers at lunch. But on the inside, I am Vietnamese; I cannot forget my mother, hungry in Vietnam, while I have it easy here." Others say, "Life is not at ease here." But there is no homeland to which they can return. Communist Vietnam is not Vietnam as they knew it. They realize that they represent the end of an era, a way of life that will never again be seen. The tragedy of their lives is highlighted for many in the opening verses of the *Tale of Kieu,* Vietnam's most famous literary work, by Nguyen Du, Vietnam's greatest poet:

> Those vicissitudes we have experienced
> Cause our hearts to break.

In this long narrative poem written in the early 19th century, the heroine Thuy-Kieu retains her chaste outlook and purity over many years while being betrayed, dishonored, and subjected to terrible ordeals and suffering. In literal translation the passage reads: "To experience the events of the mulberry-covered sea, while watching over these events, causes sorrows of the heart." The "mulberry-covered sea" refers to the time it takes for the sea to transform itself into a mulberry field and back again into the sea, a poetic expression for momentous upheavals that occur in nature or in the lives of a people, to the fate of a nation, and to a mourning for the sufferings endured by the Vietnamese over the centuries. *Hearts of Sorrow,* the title of Freeman's book, is inspired by Nguyen Du's immortal words; it is the theme that connects the life stories.

Consider also the words and poetry of a Vietnamese youth, a boat person who at the age of 16 arrived in America as an unaccompanied minor, without parents or close relatives. Placed in a high school grade because of his age even though he had not completed elementary school in Vietnam, he encounters great difficulty getting anything out of school. His dominant memory of the high school is that of being attacked by four Mexican-American youths who stabbed him and told him to go back to his own country. But what is most devastating is his loneliness in America. He comments, "I am lonely, I live in a strange land, and I have no direction like I did in Vietnam. I have no friends, no family, no lover. I am alone with my dreams. When I think of how lonely I am in America, I wonder why I am here, what I have to live for. And my poems speak of my unhappiness." Here is one such poem:

Why Am I in This World

Some cans of beer scattered on the table
Slowly I nibbled some pieces of dried meat,
And nipped some bitter liquid.
It was already dawn, but in my stupor,
I though it was still dark.

"Why am I in this world?" I wondered.
"Why should I continue to live,
When I have neither a country nor a home
And when I had only "liquid" and "smoke" as friend?
Why am I in this world at all?" I wondered.

The young poet ended his narrative by saying, "I remember crying twice in my life. The first time was when my father hit me. The second time was when I left my country."

Cambodian Views of Adjustment

Rumbaut and Ima assert that the Khmer have not achieved economically as quickly as the Vietnamese because they do not look for technologically advanced "high status" jobs. They say that even refugee children educated in America tend to choose "low status" jobs entailing human services such as nursing, catering, and electrical repair work. They speculate that the reason may be Buddhist teachings promoting non-aggression, passivity, and the belief in doing good deeds to earn better future lives.

While Rumbaut and Ima are partly correct, their discussion blurs the important distinction between Cambodian and American points of view. For Cambodians, service jobs are not low status. In Cambodia, the significance of good deeds applies not only to future lives but to the present. An individual's *good conduct* rather than his wealth brings recognition. Furthermore, Buddhist teachings advocate not only non-aggression, but also mutual cooperation. Therefore, what American researchers perceive as *low status* jobs entailing human services are *high status* from the Khmer perspective. For example, one 16-year-old refugee said, "I think it is important to help people. My religion says do good things, kind things to people."

Rumbaut and Ima state that the Khmer family and community seem "loose" on the surface due to the absence of obvious "vertical and family oriented patterns seen in the Vietnamese structure," which the authors say is a primary reason for the more immediate success of the Vietnamese in achieving self-sufficiency. In contrast, Welaratna found that even those with an opportunity to meet the American model of success often do not choose to make use of it. Examples were a 22-year-old woman who held a well-paying job and a 16-year-old who started her first job a few months earlier. Both were survivors of the "Killing Fields" holocaust of Pol Pot, in which between one and three million Cambodians were killed or died due to starvation or sickness. Both gave their money to their mothers and did not believe that their economic independence gave them the right to assert individual independence. The 22-year-old said, "To me, money is no big deal. Of course it is something you need to live, but it's not the main thing. I am not like Americans. I don't take what I have for granted. There's more to life, more to families than money and stuff. . . . To me, to have a pretty close family is more important." This is also an example of how the Pol Pot experience pulls people back to their ultimate values.

Khmer social values, reinforced by Theravada Buddhist values (the branch of Buddhism followed in Cambodia, Burma, Thailand, Laos, and Sri Lanka), and now the Pol Pot tragedy, impart to Cambodian refugees a deep moral obligation to do their duty to their people. The detailed life histories collected by Welaratna also show that it is an obligation which is not externally institutionalized by a patrilineal hierarchy, but taught internally by a way of life with deep roots not immediately obvious to an outside observer. Refugees and immigrants make many kinds of adjustments to America; it is important to distinguish between economic and other types. The "official" American criterion for evaluation of refugees emphasizes whether or not they are an economic liability. But from a Cambodian point of view, economic success, while important, is not enough; holding the highest paying job is not the primary consideration. If a person holds a job but that person's family is falling apart and the people are disturbed, then by Cambodian standards that cannot be called "successful adjustment." Many people in the Cambodian community are not making a lot of money, but are self-sufficient and are living a life they find fulfilling. A refugee from a peasant background said she would like to grow vegetables for a living. When told this activity involved hard work, she replied, "Growing vegetables is hard work, but I feel happy. So it is not hard work." The 22-year-old woman commented, "Money comes and goes. To me, the main thing is happiness. . . . It is what is within you that really counts."

Cambodian and American criteria for what constitutes a good life thus usually differ. Cambodians prefer a cooperative, harmonious, non-aggressive environment in family and society to a more remunerative, aggressive competitive lifestyle that is valued in much of America. Cambodians themselves are quite clear and articulate about this distinction, especially as seen in American speech and behavior. A Cambodian refugee comments, "one of my [Cambodian] girl friend[s], if you see her you would think that she was probably born here, she is so Americanized. The way she talks, the way she eats, the way she acts, what she wouldn't do. She is a year older than me, but she acts like a kid. When we get together, she is always fighting with my friends. I don't recall getting into an argument with any friends."

Most Cambodian refugees in America have survived the Pol Pot holocaust. Despite this and the difficulties they have encountered in America, many are, from their view, making good adjustments in America. They may not make a lot of money, but they are gainfully employed in jobs that satisfy them, and they are keeping their families intact. From the Cambodian perspective, this constitutes successful adjustment.

Conclusion

Issues of adjustment involve more than the development of economic self-sufficiency—the American view. Economic or job success does not signify success for many Vietnamese and Cambodian refugees if it comes at the expense of disruption of family, often the only institution that provides any meaningful long-term economic and emotional support for refugees. They do not live for houses, cars, and gadgets alone, though they may value these along with economic self-sufficiency. Their concept of the person involves their participation in family and their following of social values that are rewarding and symbolically significant.

This paper indicates why it is important to pay serious attention to the needs and concerns of people from *their* points of view. The life histories collected by Freeman and by Welaratna provide such views.

Finally, there are practical and policy implications that follow from considering *refugee* views of themselves and their adjustments in America. For example, as part of her field research, Welaratna taught English to Cambodian refugees in their homes. She found that in the economically and socially depressed neighborhoods in which they live, Cambodian refugees daily face difficulties vastly different from the artificially constructed problems presented in ESL lessons. In class, refugees are expected to become familiar with and solve problems irrelevant to them, such as how to write checks and deposit money in banks, or how to borrow books from the public library. Yet many of the new refugees in ESL classes receive public assistance and do not have savings at the end of the month. Even those refugees who are employed and have savings are not used to depositing money in banks; in Cambodia they kept savings at home or with relatives. While in the future these refugees will need to know how to use banks, what they need *now* is survival English to enable them to cope with the *actual* crises they face daily. Because so many men were killed during the Pol Pot holocaust, Cambodian refugee households in America typically are headed by women; they are largely illiterate or minimally literate in their own language. Door-to-door salespeople and church people harass and exploit them; ESL lessons do not teach the refugees how to deal with these people, who often push themselves into refugee homes.

In great measure, the failure of many Cambodians to learn English is not due to lack of ability or interest, but rather because the lessons themselves are unsuitable, with no meaning or application to the lives of these refugees.

Without English, Cambodian refugees are unable to find jobs enabling them to become economically self-sufficient. Although many Cambodians in Santa Clara County work on assembly lines, these jobs do not enable them to use or quickly acquire English, nor do they given them the satisfaction they would derive from human services jobs.

In conclusion, refugee assistance and policy are determined by the economic and political needs of federal and state governments, not by the needs of refugees themselves, and this discrepancy accounts for the failure of many refugee programs.

☙ F U R T H E R   R E A D I N G

Criddle, Joan D., and Teeda Butt Mam. *To Destroy You Is No Loss: The Odyssey of a Cambodian Family* (1987).

Donnelly, Nancy. *Changing Lives of Refugee Hmong Women* (1997).

Du, Phuoc Long, and Laura Richard. *The Dream Shattered: Vietnamese Gangs in America* (1996).

Espiritu, Yen Le. "Beyond the 'Boat People': Ethnicization of American Life," *Amerasia Journal* 15, no. 2 (1989): 49–67.

Fadiman, Anne. *The Spirit Catches You and You Fall Down* (1997).

Freeman, James M. *Hearts of Sorrow: Vietnamese-American Lives* (1989).

Gold, Steven J. *Refugee Communities: A Comparative Field Study* (1992).

Haines, David W., ed. *Refugees as Immigrants: Cambodians, Laotians, and Vietnamese in America* (1989).

Hayslip, Le Ly, with Jay Wurts. *When Heaven and Earth Changed Places: A Vietnamese Woman's Journey from War to Peace* (1990).

Hendricks, Glenn L., Bruce T. Downing, and Amos S. Deinard, eds. *The Hmong in Transition* (1986).

Him, Chanrith. *When Broken Glass Floats: Growing Up Under the Khmer Rouge* (2000).

Howard Katsuyo K., ed. *Passages: An Anthology of the Southeast Asian Refugee Experience* (1990).

Kelly, Gail Paradise. *From Vietnam to America: A Chronicle of the Vietnamese Immigration to the United States* (1977).

Kibria, Nazli. *Family Tightrope: The Changing Lives of Vietnamese Americans* (1993).

Luu, Van. "The Hardships of Escape for Vietnamese Women," in *Making Waves: An Anthology of Writings by and About Asian American Women,* ed. Asian Women United of California (1989), 60–72.

Ngor, Haing S., and Roger Warner. *Surviving the Killing Fields: The Cambodian Odyssey of Haing S. Ngor* (1988).

Pran, Dith, ed. *Children of Cambodia's Killing Fields* (1997).

Rutledge, Paul. *The Role of Religion in Ethnic Self-Identity: A Vietnamese Community* (1985).

Scott, Joanna C. *Indochina's Refugees: Oral Histories from Laos, Cambodia and Vietnam* (1989).

Smith-Hefner, Nancy J. *Khmer American: Identity and Moral Education in a Diasporic Community* (1998).

Tenhula, John. *Voices from Southeast Asia: The Refugee Experience in the United States* (1991).

Vo, Linda Trinh. "The Vietnamese American Experience: From Dispersion to the Development of Post-Refugee Communities," in *Asian American Studies: A Reader,* ed. Jean Yu-wen Shen Wu and Min Song (2000), 290–305.

Wu, Harry, and George Vecsey. *Troublemaker: One Man's Crusade Against China's Cruelty* (1996).

Wu, Harry, and Carolyn Wakeman. *Bitter Winds: A Memoir of My Years in China's Gulag* (1994).

Ying, Yu-Wen, and Chua Chiem Chao. "International Relationship in Iu Mien American Families," *Amerasia Journal* 22, no. 3 (1996): 47–64.

Zhou, Min, and Carl L. Bankston III. *Growing Up American: How Vietnamese Children Adapt to Life in the United States* (1998).

CHAPTER
13

Panethnicity, Asian American Activism, and Identity 1965–2000

During the turmoil of the 1960s, politicians and the mainstream media began to portray Chinese Americans and Japanese Americans as "model minorities" that were able to overcome a history of racism and discrimination through hard work, love of education, and patriotism. These presentations often contrasted satisfied and "successful" Asian Americans with angry and militant African Americans. The message of these depictions was clear: while other minorities complained about racism, Asian Americans had pulled themselves up by their own bootstraps.

    Some of the Asian Americans who entered college in the 1960s and were exposed to campus activism began to challenge these accounts. Most of these activists were young, urban, and middle class. Although there were Filipino American and Korean American activists, most activist leaders were either first- or second-generation Chinese Americans or third-generation Japanese Americans. Inspired by the civil rights, antiwar, and ethnic pride movements, these activists tried to transcend ethnic differences among Asian Americans by emphasizing a common bond of struggle against white racism. They often emulated "black power" activists who championed grassroots mobilization, political protest, self-determination, and cultural pride. Some advocated reform, and others supported socialist revolution, but all encouraged Asian Americans to resist racial oppression. Activists tried to cultivate pride in Asian and Asian American culture by organizing artistic, musical, and theatrical programs; they developed Asian American journals and magazines and joined radical political groups that attacked the Vietnam War and U.S. government policies. The Asian American Political Alliance, for example, denounced the Vietnam War as a racist war that massacred civilians and celebrated the goals and struggle of Vietnamese Communists. Another antiwar group, Asian Americans for Action, mobilized to fight imperialism abroad and the "internal colonialism" in America that caused Asian Americans to feel inferior to white Americans. Other examples of the diverse activism of the 1960s and 1970s include student strikes for the development of Asian American studies programs; demonstrations against urban renewal programs that

would have evicted poor and elderly Asian Americans; the creation of health, voca-
tional, and childcare programs within ethnic enclaves; and the successful campaign
to repeal Title II of the Internal Security Act, which allowed for the recreation of
internment camps.

☙ D O C U M E N T S

The first two documents show how young Asian American activists in the 1970s tried
to counter mainstream media accounts of Asian Americans as uncomplaining "model
minorities" with depictions of angry protesters. In Document 1, excerpted from an
Asian American movement article published in 1969, Amy Uyematsu defines a "yellow
power" consciousness that emulated articulations of "black power" and demanded militant demonstrations against racism. Uyematsu's article and Document 2, a photograph
of activists protesting the Vietnam War in the late 1960s, demonstrate the commitment of
many activists to antiimperialism and revolutionary politics.

But different views of political ideology, class conflict, and sexism also divided
Asian American activists. Document 3, from a 1971 skit written and performed by
women activists to expose Asian American male sexism, is a humorous depiction of a
problem that led some women to leave the movement and caused others to form separate
women's organizations. Document 4 provides excerpts from the 1973 song "We Are the
Children" by A Grain of Sand. This group, consisting of Charlie Chin, Joanne Miyamoto,
and Chris Iijima, believed music could be a site of political activism and could help
forge panethnic unity between the descendants of migrant laborers, railroad workers,
concentration camp survivors, and other victims of oppression in America.

Documents 5–7 discuss examples of Asian American activism in the 1980s and
1990s. Document 5 provides excerpts from a 1992 government report on the history
of anti-Asian violence. The report describes how Asian American activists successfully
lobbied the Justice Department to bring federal civil rights charges against the individuals who killed Vincent Chin in Detroit, Michigan, in 1982 and Jim Loo in Raleigh,
North Carolina, in 1989. Although recent activists agree that the Asian American community needs to band together to protest hate crimes, they often disagree about how
to define the "Asian American" community. In Document 6, Professor Dana Takagi
urges scholars in Asian American studies to explore the links between sexual and racial
identities. Noting the tendency of many researchers to emphasize ethnic-based experiences, Takagi argues that including an analysis of homosexuality can shed light on more
complex and intertwining constructions of "Asian American" identity. Document 7 contains selections from a 2000 essay by Haunani-Kay Trask, a native Hawaiian nationalist
and a professor of Hawaiian studies at the University of Hawai'i. Trask criticizes Asian
American scholars and activists for framing the struggle for Hawaiian sovereignty as a
domestic civil rights issue rather that as an international human rights issue. Denouncing
"Asian settler" scholarship for assuming the authority to speak for and about native
Hawaiians, Trask calls for an acknowledgment of the role of Asian Americans in the
oppression of native Hawaiians.

The final set of documents reflect concerns raised by the government's prosecution
of Wen Ho Lee, a Los Alamos scientist who was born in Taiwan and became a naturalized U.S. citizen. Charged in 1999 with fifty-nine counts of mishandling classified
information and violating the Atomic Energy Act, Lee was held in solitary confinement
for nine months on suspicion of passing on nuclear weapons design information to China.
Never charged with espionage, however, he was freed in September 2000 after pleading
guilty to a single felony count of mishandling security information by downloading

secret computer files. As the media publicized claims that Chinese Americans were more prone to espionage because of "ethnic" ties, Chinese Americans began to declare that Wen Ho Lee was a victim of ethnic profiling. In Document 8, Air Force Captain Ted W. Lieu movingly describes his personal battle against assumptions that he must be a "foreigner" even when he wears his U.S. uniform and medals. In Document 9, Angela Oh, a lawyer and the only Asian American to serve on the advisory board to President Clinton's Initiative on Race, declares that the Lee case illustrates how China is being cast as the "great 21st century threat" to America. Oh describes how the case has also caused many Asian Americans to join together for the first time in a pan-Asian coalition to fight racial profiling and such selective prosecutions. In Document 10, Wen Ho Lee relates the horrible conditions he endured in solitary confinement. Finally, in Document 11, Judge James A. Parker apologizes to Wen Ho Lee and condemns the Executive Branch for embarrassing the entire nation by subjecting Lee to such miserable conditions.

1. Activist Amy Uyematsu Proclaims the Emergence of "Yellow Power," 1969

Within the past two years, the "yellow power" movement has developed as a direct outgrowth of the "black power" movement. The "black power" movement caused many Asian Americans to question themselves. "Yellow power" is just now at the stage of "an articulated mood rather than a program—disillusionment and alienation from white America and independence, race pride, and self-respect." Yellow consciousness is the immediate goal of concerned Asian Americans.

In the process of Americanization, Asians have tried to transform themselves into white men—both mentally and physically. Mentally, they have adjusted to the white man's culture by giving up their own languages, customs, histories, and cultural values. They have adopted the "American way of life" only to discover that this is not enough.

Next, they have rejected their physical heritages, resulting in extreme self-hatred. Yellow people share with the blacks the desire to look white. Just as blacks wish to be light-complected with thin lips and unkinky hair, "yellows" want to be tall with long legs and large eyes. The self-hatred is also evident in the yellow male's obsession with unobtainable white women, and in the yellow female's attempt to gain male approval by aping white beauty standards. Yellow females have their own "conking" techniques—they use "peroxide, foam rubber, and scotch tape to give them light hair, large breasts, and double-lidded eyes."

The "Black is Beautiful" cry among black Americans has instilled a new awareness in Asian Americans to be proud of their physical and cultural heritages. Yellow power advocates self-acceptance as the first step toward strengthening personalities of Asian Americans.

Since the yellow power movement is thus far made up of students and young adults, it is working for Asian-American ethnic studies centers on college campuses such as Cal and U.C.L.A. The re-establishment of ethnic identity through education is being pursued in classes like U.C.L.A.'s "Orientals in America." As one student in the course relates:

> I want to take this course for a 20-20 realization, and not a passive glance in the ill-reflecting mirror; the image I see is W.A.S.P., but the yellow skin is not lily white . . . I want to find out what my voluntarily or subconsciously suppressed Oriental self is like; also what the thousands of other (suppressed?) Oriental selves are like in a much larger mind and body—America . . . I want to establish my ethnic identity not merely for the sake of such roots, but for the inherent value that such a background merits.

The problem of self-identity in Asian Americans also requires the removal of stereotypes. The yellow people in America seem to be silent citizens. They are stereotyped as being passive, accommodating, and unemotional. Unfortunately, this description is fairly accurate, for Asian Americans have accepted these stereotypes and are becoming true to them.

The "silent" Asian Americans have rationalized their behavior in terms of cultural values which they have maintained from the old country. For example, the Japanese use the term "enryo" to denote hesitation in action or expression. A young Buddhist minister, Reverend Mas Kodani of the Los Angeles Senshin Buddhist Temple, has illustrated the difference between Japanese "enryo" and Japanese-American "enryo": in Japan, if a teacher or lecturer asks, "Are there any questions?" several members of the class or audience respond; but in the United States, the same question is followed by a deathly silence. . . .

Today the Asian Americans are still scared. Their passive behavior serves to keep national attention on the black people. By being as inconspicuous as possible, they keep pressure off of themselves at the expense of the blacks. Asian Americans have formed an uneasy alliance with white Americans to keep the blacks down. They close their eyes to the latent white racism toward them which has never changed.

Frightened "yellows" allow the white public to use the "silent Oriental" stereotype against the black protest. The presence of twenty million blacks in America poses an actual physical threat to the white system. Fearful whites tell militant blacks that the acceptable criterion for behavior is exemplified in the quiet, passive Asian American.

The yellow power movement envisages a new role for Asian Americans:

> It is a rejection of the passive Oriental stereotype and symbolizes the birth of a new Asian—one who will recognize and deal with injustices. The shout of Yellow Power, symbolic of our new direction, is reverberating in the quiet corridors of the Asian community.

As expressed in the black power writings, yellow power also says that "When we begin to define our own image, the stereotypes—that is, lies—that our oppressor has developed will begin in the white community and end there."

Another obstacle to the creation of yellow consciousness is the well-incorporated white racist attitudes which are present in Asian Americans. They take much false pride in their own economic progress and feel that blacks could succeed similarly if they only followed the Protestant ethic of hard work and education. Many Asians support S. I. Hayakawa, the so-called spokesman of yellow people, when he advises the black man to imitate the Nisei: "Go to school and get high grades, save one dollar out of every ten you earn to capitalize your business." But the fact is that the white power structure allowed Asian Americans to succeed through their own efforts while the same institutions persist in denying these opportunities to black Americans.

Certain basic changes in American society made it possible for many Asian Americans to improve their economic condition after the war. In the first place, black people became the target group of West Coast discrimination. During and after World War II, a huge influx of blacks migrated into the West, taking racist agitation away from the yellows and onto the blacks. From 1940 to 1950, there was a gain of 85.2 percent in the black population of the West and North; from 1950 to 1960, a gain of 71.6 percent; and from 1960 to 1966, a gain of 80.4 percent.

The other basic change in society was the shifting economic picture. In a largely agricultural and rural West, Asian Americans were able to find employment. First- and second-generation Japanese and Filipinos were hired as farm laborers and gardeners, while Chinese were employed in laundries and restaurants. In marked contrast is the highly technological and urban society which today faces unemployed black people. "The Negro migrant, unlike the immigrant, found little opportunity in the city; he had arrived too late, and the unskilled labor he had to offer was no longer needed." Moreover, blacks today are kept out of a shrinking labor market, which is also closing opportunities for white job-seekers.

Asian Americans are perpetuating white racism in the United States as they allow white America to hold up the "successful" Oriental image before other minority groups as the model to emulate. White America justifies the blacks' position by showing that other non-whites—yellow people—have been able to "adapt" to the system. The truth underlying both the yellows' history and that of the blacks has been distorted. In addition, the claim that black citizens must "prove their rights to equality" is fundamentally racist.

Unfortunately, the yellow power movement is fighting a well-developed racism in Asian Americans who project their own frustrated attempts to gain white acceptance onto the black people. They nurse their own feelings of inferiority and insecurity by holding themselves as superior to the blacks. . . .

The Relevance of Power for Asians in America

The emerging movement among Asian Americans can be described as "yellow power" because it is seeking freedom from racial oppression through the power of a consolidated yellow people. As derived from the black power ideology, yellow power implies that Asian Americans must control the decision-making processes affecting their lives.

One basic premise of both black power and yellow power is that ethnic political power must be used to improve the economic and social conditions of blacks and yellows. In considering the relevance of power for Asian Americans, two common assumptions will be challenged: first, that the Asian Americans are completely powerless in the United States: and second, the assumption that Asian Americans have already obtained "economic" equality.

While the black power movement can conceivably bargain from a position of strength, yellow power has no such potential to draw from. A united black people would comprise over ten percent of the total American electorate; this is a significant enough proportion of the voting population to make it possible for blacks to be a controlling force in the power structure. In contrast, the political power of yellows would have little effect on state and national contests. The combined populations of Chinese, Japanese and Filipinos in the United States in 1960 was only 887, 834—not even one-half percent of the total population.

However, Asian Americans are not completely weaponless, in the local political arena. For instance, in California, the combined strength of Chinese, Japanese, and Filipinos in 1960 was two percent of the state population. Their possible political significance lies in the fact that there are heavy concentrations of these groups in San Francisco and Los Angeles. . . . In city and country government, a solid yellow voting bloc could make a difference. . . .

Even under the assumption that yellow political power could be significant, how will it improve the present economic situation of Asian Americans? Most yellow people have attained middle-class incomes and feel that they have no legitimate complaint against the existing capitalist structure. . . .

Although it is true that some Asian minorities lead all other colored groups in America in terms of economic progress, it is a fallacy that Asian Americans enjoy full economic opportunity. If the Protestant ethic is truly a formula for economic success, why don't Japanese and Chinese who work harder and have more education than whites earn just as much? . . .

The myth of Asian American success is most obvious in the economic and social position of Filipino Americans. In 1960, the 65,459 Filipino residents of California earned a median annual income of $2,925, as compared to $3,553 for blacks and $5,109 for whites. Over half of the total Filipino male working force was employed in farm labor and service work; over half of all Filipino males received less than 8.7 years of school education. Indeed, Filipinos are a forgotten minority in America. Like blacks, they have many legitimate complaints against American society.

A further example of the false economic and social picture of Asian Americans exists in the ghetto communities of Little Tokyo in Los Angeles and Chinatown in San Francisco. In the former, elderly Japanese live in run-down hotels in social and cultural isolation. And in the latter, Chinese families suffer the poor living conditions of a community that has the second highest tuberculosis rate in the nation.

Thus, the use of yellow political power is valid, for Asian Americans do have definite economic and social problems which must be improved. By organizing around these needs, Asian Americans can make the yellow power movement a viable political force in their lives.

2. Asian Americans Protest Against the Vietnam War in Los Angeles, late 1960s

Asian Americans protest against the Vietnam War.

3. A Skit on Sexism Within the Asian American Movement, 1971

In the Movement Office

Sister: (walking in) What do you think of women's liberation?

Brother 2: Well, Chairman Mao says "Unite and take part in production and political activity to improve the economic and political status of women."

Brother 1: Far out. Hey man, we better start getting the conference together. (all sit)

Brother 2: Yeah, I been thinking about that. Hey, did you dig on the article brother Alan put out? It turns down some heavy shit!

Brother 1: Right on! Let's put it on a stencil and run it off for the conference. Here, sister, can you type it up (hands it to her without waiting for her to answer) . . . and do this one on illegal search and seizure, too.

Sister: Here's an article that Yuki wrote on women. It's really heav . . .

Photographic Collections, Visual Communications/Courtesy of Photographic Collections, Visual Communications.

From Miya Iwataki, "The Asian Women's Movement—A Retrospective," *East Wind* 2, no. 1 (Spring/ Summer 1983): 37.

Brother 1: Yeah, that illegal search and seizure is important because the students need to get their shit together as far as legal matters are concerned. Hey, before you start typing, can you get me some coffee?

Brother 2: Me too. I take two sugars. (she gets up without saying anything, goes to get the coffee. Brothers look her up and down)

Brother 2: When do you think we should have it? During Christmas vacation?

Brother 1: Yeah, right on. Let's try the first weekend. Maybe we can get the Center. Hey sister, can you call the Center right now and get a confirmation?

Sister: (bringing back the coffee) We can't use the Center anymore. Remember what happened last . . .

Brother 2: Oh, shit! We can't use the Center. Last year someone left cigarette burns in the furniture and those s.o.b.'s aren't letting anyone use it on weekends.

Sister: The first weekend of Christmas vacation might be rough for the students because of papers and . . .

Brother 1: Fuck that shit! If they place their priorities on a bullshit paper, fuck'em.

Brother 2: Right on! Hey, I got a meeting now. Can you get some press releases out and start contacting people for a general meeting? Thanks baby, you're a righteous sister.

Brother 1: Yeah, I got to split now, too. I have to go out in the field and do some people's work. I'll try to help you if I get back in time. But I know you can take care of business, baby. (both split)

Sister: (alone and pissed off) What's going on! I got a goddamn meeting too! The people's work . . . What the hell do they think this is!!

4. A Song of Struggle and Solidarity by A Grain of Sand, 1973

We Are the Children
words and music: Iijima-Miyamoto

This is another of the first songs we wrote. It only touched on our people's plight and experiences in this country. We've heard that sisters and brothers in Hawaii and other places have added verses to it. We say right on—it is your song.

> We are the children of the migrant worker
> We are the offspring of the concentration camp.
> Sons and daughters of the railroad builder
> Who leave their stamp on Amerika.
>
> (chorus)
> Sing a song for ourselves.
> What have we got to lose?
> Sing a song for ourselves.
> We got the right to choose.   (3x)

From *A Grain of Sand: Music of the Struggle by Asians in America,* Chris Kando Iijima et al., © 1973 Paredon Records.

We are the children of the Chinese waiter,
Born and raised in the laundry room.
We are the offspring of the Japanese gardner,
Who leave their stamp on Amerika.
(chorus)

Foster children of the Pepsi Generation,
Cowboys and Indians—ride, red-man, ride!
Watching war movies with the nextdoor neighbor,
Secretly rooting for the other side.
(chorus)

We are the cousins of the freedom fighter,
Brothers and sisters all around the world.
We are a part of the Third World people
Who will leave their stamp on Amerika.
Who will leave our stamp on Amerika.
(chorus)   (3x)

5. A Government Report on the Murders of Vincent Chin and Jim Loo, 1992

Vincent Chin—The racially motivated murder of Vincent Chin and the inability of the American judicial system to bring his murderers to justice became a vivid symbol and source of outrage during the mid-1980s. The facts of the case are as follows.

On the evening of June 19, 1982, Vincent Chin, a 27-year-old Chinese American, met with some friends in a Detroit bar to celebrate his upcoming wedding. He was accosted by Ronald Ebens and Michael Nitz, two white automobile factory workers, who reportedly called him a "Jap" and blamed him for the loss of jobs in the automobile industry. Ebens and Nitz chased Chin out of the bar, and, when they caught up with him, Nitz held Chin while Ebens beat him "numerous times in the knee, the chest, and the head" with a baseball bat. Chin died of his injuries 4 days later.

Ebens and Nitz were initially charged with second-degree murder but subsequently allowed to plead guilty to manslaughter. In March 1983 the defendants were each sentenced to 3 years' probation and fined $3,780 by Wayne Circuit County Judge Charles Kaufman, who reasoned that the defendants had no previous history of violence and were unlikely to violate probation.

The U.S. Department of Justice brought Federal civil rights charges against Ebens and Nitz to a Federal grand jury, which indicted them on November 2, 1982. On June 18, 1984, Ebens was found guilty of interfering with Chin's civil rights, and on September 18, 1984, he was sentenced to 25 years in prison. However, Nitz was acquitted of the Federal civil rights charges.

From United States Commission on Civil Rights, *Civil Rights Issues Facing Asian Americans in the 1990s: A Report of the United States Commission on Civil Rights, February 1992* (Washington, D.C.: U.S. Government Printing Office, 1992), 25–28.

Ebens' conviction was overturned by the Sixth Circuit Court of Appeals in September 1986 for technical reasons, including issues pertaining to the admissibility of audio tapes and prosecutorial misconduct (overzealousness) in preparing witnesses. When Ebens came up for retrial in the Eastern District of Michigan, the defense moved for a change of venue on the grounds that Ebens could not get a fair trial in Detroit. The defense motion was granted, and the trial was moved to Cincinnati. The case was retried during the month of April 1987, and this time Ebens was acquitted.

The acquittal of Ebens in the second Federal trial means that neither Ebens nor Nitz ever went to prison for Vincent Chin's killing. Some have speculated that the main reason that the Cincinnati jury acquitted Ebens is that the jury could not comprehend the reality of anti-Asian bias as it existed in Detroit in the early 1980s. Whereas Detroit in the early 1980s was the scene of a massive media campaign against foreign imports, especially those from Japan, a campaign that inflamed anti-Asian sentiments in that city, there had not been the same type of campaign in Cincinnati. Also, there were very few Asians in Cincinnati, and anti-Asian sentiments were not widespread.

Others contend that the Cincinnati jury's acquittal of Ebens reflects a fundamental problem with current Federal civil rights laws. Ebens was charged under Federal criminal civil rights law section 245(b), which prohibits (among other things) the racially motivated interference by force or threat of force with a person's use of public facilities, such as restaurants and bars. Some experts argue that the jury may have been confused about what had to be shown for there to be a civil rights violation under section 245(b): even though the jury may have felt that the attack was indeed racially motivated, it might not have thought that Ebens specifically intended to interfere with Chin's use of a public facility (the bar).

Jim (Ming Hai) Loo—Seven years after Vincent Chin's killing, another Chinese American was killed in Raleigh, North Carolina under similar circumstances.

Jim (Ming Hai) Loo, 24, had immigrated to the United States from China 13 years before, was working in a Chinese restaurant, and was saving money so that he could attend college. On the evening of Saturday, July 29, 1989, during an altercation that began in a nearby pool hall, Loo was hit on the back of the head by a handgun held by Robert Piche. He fell onto a broken beer bottle, which pierced his eye and caused a bone fragment to enter his brain, resulting in his death on July 31.

Loo and several Vietnamese friends had been playing pool in the pool hall, when Robert Piche, 35, and his brother, Lloyd Piche, 29, began calling them "gooks" and "chinks" and blaming them for American deaths in Vietnam. Lloyd Piche said, "I don't like you because you're Vietnamese. Our brothers went over to Vietnam, and they never came back," and "I'm gonna finish you tonight." Although the manager forced the Piche brothers to leave the pool hall, they waited outside for Loo and his friends, and attacked them as they left the pool hall. Robert Piche and his brother first attacked one of Loo's friends, Lahn Tang, with a shotgun, but when Tang escaped, Robert swung a pistol at another of Loo's friends, Jim Ta. He missed his intended victim and hit Loo on the head instead.

Although Lloyd Piche made most of the racial remarks, he did not strike the fatal blow. He was sentenced to 6 months in prison for disorderly conduct and simple assault (on Tang), both of which are misdemeanors. In March 1990, Robert Piche was found guilty of second-degree murder and assault with a deadly weapon and sentenced to a total of 37 years in prison. He will be eligible for parole after serving 4½ years. Although Judge Howard E. Manning Jr. gave Piche a stiff lecture, the sentence was less than he could have meted out: under North Carolina law, Piche could have been given life in prison.

Many Asian American community leaders, struck by the similarities between Loo's murder and Chin's, pressed the U.S. Department of Justice to bring Federal civil rights charges against Robert and Lloyd Piche. They were particularly anxious to see a prosecution of Lloyd Piche, who received a minimal sentence despite being the chief instigator of the incident. After a lengthy investigation, the Justice Department announced on March 29, 1991, that it had indicted Lloyd Piche on Federal civil rights charges, but it did not indict Robert Piche. In making the announcement, Attorney General Thornburgh said:

> This is a heinous crime committed against innocent patrons of a public facility. Such egregious behavior, especially with death resulting, cannot go unpunished.
>
> This country was built on the freedom to enjoy life, liberty and the pursuit of happiness. When innocent patrons of a public facility are harassed and ultimately killed simply because of their race, religion or national origin, the government has a moral and legal obligation to step in and prosecute.

Lloyd Piche was indicted on eight counts of violating Federal civil rights laws. On July 15, 1991, in a Federal district court in Wilmington, North Carolina, Lloyd Piche was found guilty on all eight counts. On October 15, 1991, Lloyd Piche was sentenced to 4 years in prison and ordered to pay over $28,000 in restitution to the Loo family. Although the Justice Department had sought the maximum sentence under Federal sentencing guidelines, Piche's sentence was less than the minimum sentence (6 to 7½ years) under the Federal guidelines.

There are many similarities between the Loo and the Chin murders. In each case, the victim was a young man spending an evening relaxing with friends in a public facility (a bar in Chin's case, a pool hall in Loo's). In each case, an altercation began inside the public facility, and violence leading to murder erupted outside of the facility. In each case, the victim was killed after being mistaken for or associated with Asians of other nationalities. In Chin's case, his killers were venting hostility against foreign Japanese, and in Loo's case, his murderers apparently mistook him for a Vietnamese. Thus, both Chin and Loo became victims simply because they were of Asian descent.

Together, the Chin and Loo murders underscore the harsh reality of racially motivated violence against Asians. They also signal in differing ways the general public's lack of awareness of and to some extent indifference towards anti-Asian discrimination. The 3-year probation and almost nominal fines imposed by Judge Kaufman on Chin's murderers are suggestive of very little value being placed on an Asian American life. The ultimate failure of the American justice system to convict Ebens of civil rights charges, perhaps partly because of the Cincinnati jury's difficulty in believing in the existence of anti-Asian hatred, also implies that many Americans view racial hatred purely as a black-white problem and are unaware that Asian Americans are also frequently targets of hate crimes. Finally, neither murder was given much national prominence. Chin's killing did receive some national attention, but Loo's killing (in stark contrast to the murder of a young black man in Bensonhurst that occurred at roughly the same time) was hardly covered by the national media and raised no national sense of outrage.

Unlike the Vincent Chin case, Loo's murder resulted in a successful Federal prosecution—the first ever successful Federal civil rights prosecution where the victim was Asian American. If given sufficient attention, the Federal civil rights trial of Lloyd Piche could do much to highlight the racial aspect of Loo's killing and will send a message that anti-Asian racism will not be tolerated by the United States Government.

6. Professor Dana Takagi Notes How Sexuality Complicates Definitions of "Asian America," 1999

Our attempts to locate gay Asian experiences in Asian American history render us "uninformed" in an ironic double sense. On the one hand, the field of Asian American Studies is mostly ignorant about the multiple ways that gay identities are often hidden or invisible within Asian American communities. But the irony is that the more we know, the less we know about the ways of knowing. On the other hand, just at the moment that we attempt to rectify our ignorance by adding say, the lesbian, to Asian American history, we arrive at a stumbling block, an ignorance of how to add her. Surely the quickest and simplest way to add her is to think of lesbianism as a kind of ad hoc subject-position, a minority within a minority. But efforts to think of sexuality in the same terms that we think of race, yet simultaneously different from race in certain ways, and therefore, the inevitable "revelation" that gays/lesbians/ bisexuals are like minorities but also different too, is often inconclusive, frequently ending in "counting" practice. While many minority women speak of "triple jeopardy" oppression—as if class, race, and gender could be disentangled into discrete additive parts—some Asian American lesbians could rightfully claim quadruple jeopardy oppression—class, race gender, and sexuality. Enough counting. Marginalization is not as much about the *quantities* of experiences as it is about *qualities* of experience. And, as many writers, most notably feminists, have argued, identities whether sources from sexual desire, racial origins, languages of gender, or class roots, are simply not additive.

Not Counting

A discussion of sexualities is fraught with all sorts of definition conundrums. What exactly does it mean, sexualities? The plurality of the term may be unsettling to some who recognize three (or two, or one) forms of sexual identity: gay, straight, bisexual. But there are those who identify as straight, but regularly indulge in homoeroticism, and, of course, there are those who claim the identity gay/lesbian, but engage in heterosexual sex. In addition, some people identify themselves sexually

From Dana Takagi, "Maiden Voyage: Excursion into Sexuality and Identity Politics in Asian America," *Amerasia Journal 20,* no. 1 (winter 1999): 2–7, 14–15. Copyright © 1999 Regents of the University of California. Used with permission.

but do not actually have sex, and, there are those who claim celibacy as a sexual practice. For those who profess a form of sexual identity that is, at some point, at odds with their sexual practice or sexual desire, the idea of a single, permanent, or even stable sexual identity is confining and inaccurate. Therefore, in an effort to capture the widest possible range of human sexual practices, I use the term sexualities to refer to the variety of practices and identities that range from homoerotic to heterosexual desire. In this essay, I am concerned mainly with homosexual desire and the question of what happens when we try to locate homosexual identities in Asian American history.

Writing, speaking, acting queer. Against a backdrop of lotus leaves, sliding *shoji* panels, and the mountains of Guilin. Amid the bustling enclaves of Little Saigon, Koreatown, Chinatown, and Little Tokyo. Sexual identity, like racial identity, is one of many types of recognized "difference." If marginalization is a qualitative state of being and not simply a quantitative one, then what is it about being "gay" that is different from "Asian American?"

The terms "lesbian" and "gay," like "Third World," "woman," and "Asian American," are political categories that serve as rallying calls and personal affirmations. In concatenating these identities we create and locate ourselves in phrases that seem a familiar fit: black gay man, third world woman, working class Chicana lesbian, Asian American bisexual, etc. But is it possible to write these identities—like Asian American gay—without writing oneself into the corners that are either gay and only gay, or, Asian American and only Asian American? Or, as Trinh T. Minh-ha put it, "How do you inscribe difference without bursting into a series of euphoric narcissistic accounts of yourself and your own kind?"

It is vogue these days to celebrate difference. But underlying much contemporary talk about difference is the assumption that differences are comparable things. For example, many new social movements activists, including those in the gay and lesbian movement, think of themselves as patterned on the "ethnic model." And for many ethnic minorities, the belief that "gays are oppressed too" is a reminder of a sameness, a common political project in moving margin to center, that unites race-based movements with gays, feminists, and greens. The notion that our differences are "separate but equal" can be used to call attention to the specificity of experiences or to rally the troops under a collective banner. Thus, the concept of difference espoused in identity politics may be articulated in moments of what Spivak refers to as "strategic essentialism" or in what Hall coins "positionalities." But in the heat of local political struggles and coalition building, it turns out that not all differences are created equally. For example, Ellsworth recounts how differences of race, nationality, and gender, unfolded in the context of a relatively safe environment, the university classroom:

> Women found it difficult to prioritize expressions of racial privilege and oppression when such prioritizing threatened to perpetuate their gender oppression. Among international students, both those who were of color and those who were White found it difficult to join their voices with those of U.S. students of color when it meant a subordination of their oppressions as people living under U.S. imperialist policies and as students for whom English was a second language. Asian American women found it difficult to join their voices with other students of color when it meant subordinating their specific oppressions as Asian Americans. I found it difficult to speak as a White woman about

gender oppression when I occupied positions of institutional power relative to all students in the class, men and women, but positions of gender oppression relative to students who were White men, and in different terms, relative to students who were men of color.

The above example demonstrates the tensions between sameness and difference that haunt identity politics. Referring to race and sexuality, Cohen suggests that the "sameness" that underlies difference may be more fiction than fact:

> . . . the implied isomorphism between the "arbitrariness of racial categorizations" and the "sexual order" elides the complex processes of social differentiation that assign, legitimate, and enforce qualitative distinctions between different types of individuals. Here the explicit parallel drawn between "race" and "sexuality," familiar to so many polemical affirmations of (non-racial) identity politics, is meant to evoke an underlying and apparently indisputable common sense that naturalizes this particular choice of political strategy almost as if the "naturalness" of racial "identity" could confer a corollary stability on the less "visible" dynamics of sexuality.

There are numerous ways that being "gay" is not like being "Asian." Two broad distinctions are worth noting. The first, mentioned by Cohen above, is the relative invisibility of sexual identity compared with racial identity. While both can be said to be socially constructed, the former are performed, acted out, and produced, often in individual routines, whereas the latter tends to be more obviously "written" on the body and negotiated by political groups. Put another way, there is a quality of voluntarism in being gay/lesbian that is usually not possible as an Asian American. One has the option to present oneself as "gay" or "lesbian," or alternatively, to attempt to "pass," or, to stay in "the closet," that is, to hide one's sexual preference. However, these same options are not available to most racial minorities in face-to-face interactions with others.

As Asian Americans, we do not think in advance about whether or not to present ourselves as "Asian American," rather, that is an identification that is worn by us, whether we like it or not, and which is easily read off of us by others.

A second major reason that the category "gay" ought to be distinguished from the category "Asian American" is for the very different histories of each group. Studying the politics of being "gay" entails on the one hand, an analysis of discursive fields, ideologies, and rhetoric about sexual identity, and on the other hand, knowledge of the history of gays/lesbians as subordinated minorities relative to heterosexuals. . . . Similarly, studying "Asian America" requires analysis of semantic and rhetorical discourse in its variegated forms, racist, apologist, and paternalist, and requires in addition, an understanding of the specific histories of the peoples who recognize themselves as Asian or Asian American. But the specific discourses and histories in each case are quite different. Even though we make the same intellectual moves to approach each form of identity, that is, a two-tracked study of ideology on the one hand, and history on the other, the particular ideologies and histories of each are very different.

In other words, many of us experience the worlds of Asian America and gay America as separate places—emotionally, physically, intellectually. We sustain the separation of these worlds with our folk knowledge about the family-centeredness and supra-homophobic beliefs of ethnic communities. Moreover, it is not just that these communities know so little of one another, but, we frequently take great care to keep those worlds distant from each other. What could be more different than the scene at gay bars like "The End Up" in San Francisco, or "Faces" in Hollywood, and, on the other hand, the annual Buddhist church bazaars in the Japanese American community or Filipino revivalist meetings? These disparate worlds occasionally collide through individuals who manage to move, for the most part, stealthily, between these spaces. But it is the act of deliberately bringing these worlds closer together that seems unthinkable. Imagining your parents, clutching bento box lunches, thrust into the smoky haze of a South of Market leather bar in San Francisco is no less strange a vision than the idea of Lowie taking Ishi, the last of his tribe, for a cruise on Lucas' Star Tours at Disneyland. "Cultural strain," the anthropologists would say. Or, as Wynn Young, laughing at the prospect of mixing his family with his boyfriend, said, "Somehow I just can't picture this conversation at the dinner table, over my mother's homemade barbecued pork: 'Hey, Ma. I'm sleeping with a sixty-year-old white guy who's got three kids, and would you please pass the soy sauce?'"

Thus, "not counting" is a warning about the ways to think about the relationship of lesbian/gay identities to Asian American history. While it may seem politically efficacious to toss the lesbian onto the diversity pile, adding one more form of subordination to the heap of inequalities, such a strategy glosses over the particular or distinctive ways sexuality is troped in Asian America. Before examining the possibilities for theorizing "gay" and "Asian American" as non-mutually exclusive identities, I turn first to a fuller description of the chasm of silence that separates them.

Silences

The concept of silence is a doggedly familiar one in Asian American history. For example, Hosokawa characterized the Nisei as "Quiet Americans" and popular media discussions of the "model minority" typically describe Asian American students as "quiet" along with "hard working" and "successful." In the popular dressing of Asian American identity, silence has functioned as a metaphor for the assimilative and positive imagery of the "good" minorities. More recently, analysis of popular imagery of the "model minority" suggest that silence ought to be understood as an adaptive mechanism to a racially discriminatory society rather than as an intrinsic part of Asian American culture.

If silence has been a powerful metaphor in Asian American history, it is also a crucial element of discussions of gay/lesbian identity, albeit in a somewhat different way. In both cases, silence may be viewed as the oppressive cost of a racially biased or heterosexist society. For gays and lesbians, the act of coming out takes on symbolic importance, not just as a personal affirmation of "this is who I am," but additionally as a critique of expected norms in society, "we are everywhere." While "breaking the silence" about Asian Americans refers to crashing popular stereotypes about them, and shares with the gay act of "coming out" the desire to define oneself rather than be defined by others, there remains an important difference between the two.

The relative invisibility of homosexuality compared with Asian American identity means that silence and its corollary space, the closet, are more ephemeral, appear less fixed as boundaries of social identities, less likely to be taken-for-granted than markers of race, and consequently, more likely to be problematized and theorized in discussions that have as yet barely begun on racial identity. Put another way, homosexuality is more clearly seen as *constructed* than racial identity. Theoretically speaking, homosexual identity does not enjoy the same privileged stability as racial identity. The borders that separate gay from straight, and, "in" from "out," are so fluid that in the final moment we can only be sure that sexual identities are as Dianna Fuss notes, "in Foucaldian terms, less a matter of final discovery than a matter of perpetual invention." . . .

Rethinking Identity Politics

. . . This gist of this essay has been to insist that our valuation of heterogeneity not be ad-hoc and that we seize the opportunity to recognize non-ethnic based differences—like homosexuality—as an occasion to critique the tendency toward essentialist currents in ethnic-based narratives and disciplines. In short, the practice of including gayness in Asian America rebounds into a reconsideration of the theoretical status of the concept of "Asian American" identity. The interior of the category "Asian American" ought not be viewed as a hierarchy of identities led by ethnic-based narratives, but rather, the complicated interplay and collision of different identities. . . .

. . . Moreover, our search for authenticity of voice—whether in gay/lesbian Asian American writing or in some other identity string—will be tempered by the realization that in spite of our impulse to clearly (de)limit them, there is perpetual uncertainty and flux governing the construction and expression of identities.

7. Hawaiian Sovereignty Leader Haunani-Kay Trask Criticizes Asian "Settler" Privilege and Collaboration with Colonialism, 2000

After nearly two thousand years of self-governance, we were colonized by Euro-American capitalists and missionaries in the eighteenth and nineteenth centuries. In 1893, the United States invaded our nation, overthrew our government, and secured an all-white planter oligarchy in place of our reigning *ali'i,* Queen Lili'uokalani. By resolution of the American Congress and against great Native opposition, Hawai'i was annexed in 1898. Dispossession of our government, our territory, and our legal citizenship made of us a colonized Native people.

Today, modern Hawai'i, like its colonial parent the United States, is a settler society. Our Native people and territories have been overrun by non-Natives, including Asians. Calling themselves "local," the children of Asian settlers greatly outnumber us. They claim Hawai'i as their own, denying indigenous history, their long collaboration in our continued dispossession, and the benefits therefrom.

Part of this denial is the substitution of the term "local" for "immigrant," which is, itself, a particularly celebrated American gloss for "settler." As on the continent, so in our island home. Settlers and their children recast the American tale of nationhood: Hawai'i, like the continent, is naturalized as but another telling illustration of the uniqueness of America's "nation of immigrants." The ideology weaves a story of success: poor Japanese, Chinese, and Filipino settlers supplied the labor for wealthy, white sugar planters during the long period of the Territory (1900–1959). Exploitative plantation conditions thus underpin a master narrative of hard work and the endlessly celebrated triumph over anti-Asian racism. Settler children, ever industrious and deserving, obtain technical and liberal educations, thereby learning the political system through which they agitate for full voting rights as American citizens. Politically, the vehicle for Asian ascendancy is statehood. As a majority of voters at mid-century, the Japanese and other Asians moved into the middle class and eventually into seats of power in the legislature and the governor's house.

For our Native people, Asian success proves to be but the latest elaboration of foreign hegemony. The history of our colonization becomes a twice-told tale, first of discovery and settlement by European and American businessmen and missionaries, then of the plantation Japanese, Chinese, and eventually Filipino rise to dominance in the islands. Some Hawaiians, the best educated and articulate, benefit from the triumph of the Democratic Party over the *haole* Republican Party. But as a people, Hawaiians remain a politically subordinated group suffering all the legacies of conquest: landlessness, disastrous health, diaspora, institutionalization in the military and prisons, poor educational attainment, and confinement to the service sector of employment.

While Asians, particularly the Japanese, come to dominate post-Statehood, Democratic Party politics, new racial tensions arise. The attainment of full American citizenship actually heightens prejudice against Natives. Because the ideology of the United States as a mosaic of races is reproduced in Hawai'i through the celebration of the fact that no single "immigrant group" constitutes a numerical majority, the post-statehood euphoria stigmatizes Hawaiians as a failed indigenous people whose conditions, including out-migration, actually worsen after statehood. Hawaiians are characterized as strangely unsuited, whether because of culture or genetics, to the game of assimilation. . . .

Against this kind of disparaging colonial ideology, Hawaiians have been asserting their claims as indigenous people to land, economic power and political sovereignty for at least the last twenty years. Hawaiian communities are seriously engaged in all manner of historical, cultural, and political education. *Hālau hula* (dance academies), language classes, and varied resistance organizations link cultural practice to the struggle for self-determination. In this way, cultural groups have become conduits for reconnection to the *lāhui,* or nation. Political education occurs as the groups participate in sovereignty marches, rallies, and political lobbying. The substance of the "nation" is made obvious when thousands of Hawaiians gather to protest the theft of their sovereignty. The power of such public rituals to de-colonize the mind can be seen in the rise of a new national identification among Hawaiians. After the 1993 sovereignty protests at the Palace of our chiefs, Hawaiians, especially the youth, began to discard national identity as Americans and reclaim indigenous identification as Natives. . . .

Ka Lahui Hawai'i leads a commemorative march to protest the 1893 overthrow of the Hawaiian government by U.S. Marines and white sugar planters, 1993.

On the international stage, the vehicle which has represented Hawaiians most effectively is Ka Lāhui Hawai'i. . . . [T]he goals of Ka Lāhui Hawai'i are simple: final resolution of the historic claims of the Hawaiian people relating to the overthrow, State and Federal misuse of Native trust lands (totaling some two million acres) and resources, and violations of human and civil rights. Resolution of claims will be followed by self-determination for Hawaiians; Federal recognition of Ka Lāhui Hawai'i as the Hawaiian Nation; restoration of traditional lands, natural resources, and energy resources to the Ka Lāhui National Land Trust. . . .

Asians and *haole* have been thrown into a cauldron of defensive actions by our nationalist struggle. Either they must justify their continued benefit from Hawaiian subjugation, thus serving as support for that subjugation, or they must repudiate American hegemony and work with the Hawaiian nationalist movement. In plain language, serious and thoughtful individuals, whether *haole* or Asian, must choose to support a form of Hawaiian self-determination created by Hawaiians. . . .

. . . For non-Natives, the question that needs to be answered every day is simply the one posed in the old union song, "which side are you on?"

Photograph by Bruce Asato, *Honolulu Advertiser,* reprinted in *Amerasia Journal* 26, no. 2 (2000): 1.

8. Captain Ted W. Lieu Is Asked If He Is in the Chinese Air Force, 1999

"Are you in the Chinese Air Force?" the elegantly dressed lady sitting next to me asked. For a moment I was left speechless. We were at an awards dinner, and I was wearing my blue U.S. Air Force uniform, complete with captain's bars, military insignia and medals. Her question jarred me and made me realize that even Air Force blue was not enough to reverse her initial presumption that people with yellow skin and Asian features are somehow not Americans.

Unfortunately, this was not just an isolated incident. And now in the wake of the rising tensions between the United States and China, we must be even more vigilant to ensure that Asian Americans are not caught in the cross-fire. I have had strangers come up to me and attempt to mimic the Chinese language in a derogatory manner. I have been told countless times that I speak "good" English. I have been asked why someone like me would be interested in watching NFL football. On any given day, if I walk around with a camera, I will be mistaken for a tourist from Asia.

Most of the discrimination I have encountered centered on the view that I am not a part of this great nation, even though I grew up in Ohio, graduated from law school in Washington, D.C., and received my commission in the U.S. Air Force in 1991.

Sometimes the discrimination is subtler than a blatant headline or a hate crime, but it still can be insidious. After the bombing of the Chinese Embassy, a news station sent a reporter to get "the Chinese American response." It was clear the reporter was attempting to elicit some sort of anti-American sentiment. The erroneous presumption, however, is that Chinese Americans are somehow linked to the government or nation of China. This subtle linkage, when carried to an extreme, is the same insidious rationale that justified the interning of thousands of Japanese Americans during World War II. And when Asian Americans are improperly linked to a foreign country, that linkage fundamentally calls into question our loyalty.

I fear this burden of having to prove our loyalty will only increase in the wake of the Cox committee's report. I do not know whether Wen Ho Lee, the Chinese American scientist who was fired from Los Alamos National Laboratory, is guilty of espionage. But I do know that the more than 300,000 Asian American scientists, and the more than 10 million Asian Americans in this country, are not guilty of anything more than having an Asian surname.

A recent news article reported that an Asian American lab employee was asked if he had "dual loyalties"; that snickering broke out when an Asian American was introduced to lead a session on computer security; and that many Asian American scientists now express fear that they will face discrimination on the job.

America is a nation founded by immigrants and built on the ideal that anyone can be an American if he or she believes in the principles and values of the Constitution. Indeed, the Vietnamese American immigrant who does not yet speak "good" English but is starting a small business and believes in freedom and democracy is much more American than a fifth-generation white separatist who blew up a federal building because he had a problem with federalism.

Let us also never forget the Japanese American soldiers of the 442nd infantry battalion, the most highly decorated combat unit in World War II, who gave their blood to this country while their families were kept in American internment camps.

It is time to reverse the irrational and insidious presumption that Asian Americans are foreigners, have dual loyalties or are somehow linked to the government of a foreign country.

As an officer in the U.S. Air Force, one day I may be called to give my life for my country. It would be a shame if some people still question what I mean when I say "my country."

9. Lawyer Angela E. Oh Describes the Significance of the Government Prosecution of Los Alamos Scientist Wen Ho Lee, 2000

Compared to the thousands of other criminal cases filed by the federal government each year, nothing is unique about Dr. Lee's dilemma except its political, social, and media aspects. As news of the case continues to be reported, we Asian Americans are feeling a familiar uneasiness about the events unfolding. The fact that this case has emerged in the midst of a Presidential campaign in which many Chinese Americans have "opted out" because of the fund-raising experiences of 1996 has added complexity to the political landscape for Asian Americans.

Unfortunately, the case may have reinforced the feelings of antipathy and alienation toward politicians and politics when it should inspire greater involvement in the political process, particularly since it so clearly demonstrates that America's foreign relations policies have a direct impact on Asian American citizens. Whether Wen Ho Lee is innocent or not is a question to be answered by a judge or jury. Whether Wen Ho Lee's case will mark a significant loss of political ground for Asian Americans, however, is a question that must be answered by Asian Americans.

For many of us following the case, the political symbolism of this prosecution is enormous. At a time when China should be viewed as a major potential partner in formulating new foreign policy initiatives, in establishing innovative new business opportunities, and in introducing expansive cultural and intellectual exchange programs. America has begun to set its sights on China as its next candidate for national enmity. China is being cast as "the great 21st century threat" against America, and many foresee turmoil for Asian Americans. The Los Alamos investigation raises reasonable anxiety about the peace and security of our nation. However, without diminishing the importance of national security concerns, Asian Americans know too well the consequences of silence in the face of mounting fears and questioned loyalty.

The case of Wen Ho Lee and a current climate of China-bashing have also had a major impact on Asian American society, and they are deservedly receiving our political attention. In terms of community organizing, the inter-generational and cross-ethnic support for Dr. Lee has been impressive. Dr. Lee is, like tens of thousands of others, a naturalized citizen, and his ethnic heritage has played a significant role in decisions to investigate, interrogate, and incarcerate. Not only has his case spurred interest among Chinese Americans, but it has created pan-Asian coalitions among individuals and organizations with no prior history of mutual support to monitor the case. The results have been extraordinary. Defense committees and new alliances have formed in all parts of the nation. Detailed analysis of the information gathered has brought attention to problems such as racial profiling, employment discrimination, abuse of authority, and selective prosecution. Moreover, this case has helped to clarify for many lay persons the role of anti-discrimination agencies such as the U.S. Commission on Civil Rights, and the operation of the American criminal justice system. . . .

. . . Now, members of the scientific community are seeking new alliances with broader Asian American political, civic, and legal organizations that understand the political and social landscape that has emerged.

The Wen Ho Lee case is already a significant story in Asian American history.

10. Accused Spy Wen Ho Lee Describes His First Month of Imprisonment, 2000

I think my spirits were at their lowest point during this time. For my first month in detention, I wasn't allowed out of my cell except once a day, Monday through Friday, to walk 15 feet down the hall from my cell to take a shower. On weekends, I couldn't even do that. I had no idea whether it was night or day; I didn't see the sun or moon for more than a month, except for those few days in December for my detention hearings. A light stayed on in my cell at all times, even when I tried to sleep. One hour per week, I could see my family during their visiting hour—with two FBI agents standing right by us, listening to every word. Once, when Alberta [my daughter] was telling me about something new in her job, the FBI agents made her stop, just because she was talking about computers. I also was allowed out of my cell when my lawyers visited, once or twice a week, to meet with them. Otherwise I stayed in my cell for 24 hours, as there was no outdoor exercise time for me during that first month. No books, no newspapers, no television, no radio, no paper, no pens, no hot water, no contact with anyone except under very restrictive conditions. . . .

. . . [W]ith the full knowledge and personal approval of Attorney General Janet Reno, prosecutor Robert Gorence, who became the acting U.S. attorney after Kelly resigned, mandated the following jail conditions:

Solitary confinement, no contact with anyone else except as defined, so that I would be unable to communicate any classified information;

No written or recorded communications with anyone;

No attorney phone calls allowed to be patched through to a third party;

Only attorneys permitted to visit;

From *My Country Versus Me,* Wen Ho Lee with Helen Zia, © 2001 Hyperion, pp. 243–246. Reprinted by permission.

Severe restrictions on the use of translators;

Correspondence to me requiring translation could only be done by a court-approved translator;

If any of the monitored phone calls violate these stringent rules, all family phone calls would be terminated;

All mail correspondence to and from me would first be screened, analyzed, and photocopied by the government.

. . . I thought I was being treated like every prisoner—shackled and chained, with a 24-hour personal watch guard jotting down my every move, whether I was awake or asleep, when I showered, when I used the toilet. The guards, at least, got a break from the routine; they changed shifts every eight hours. For me, there was no letup in this degrading treatment. . . . Nancy Hollander made many requests on my behalf—to allow my family to speak Chinese to one another; to get my family's visiting time changed to Saturday so it would be easier for my children to travel to see me; to get more fruit for me; to allow me to have a radio; to arrange for exercise time. Each request was a struggle in itself. Nancy's persistence made it possible for me to survive in jail. It also helped that many people wrote letters to Janet Reno and other government officials about my jail conditions. Nancy told a reporter that she was shocked by my conditions: "I've had murder clients, drug clients, clients accused of taking millions of dollars from the federal government, you name it, but I've never had a client treated like Wen Ho Lee."

Not knowing my rights as an American to be free from "cruel or unusual" punishment, I accepted my treatment without question. I didn't know to complain that I was constantly cold, shivering most of the time because all I had was the red jumpsuit, undershorts, and two thin blankets.

11. Judge James A. Parker Apologizes to Wen Ho Lee for the Way He Was Treated by the Executive Branch, 2000

I find it most perplexing, although appropriate, that the Executive Branch today has suddenly agreed to your release without any significant conditions or restrictions whatsoever on your activities. . . .

From the beginning, the focus of this case was on your motive or intent in taking the information from the secure computers and eventually downloading it on to tapes. There was never really any dispute about your having done that, only about why you did it.

What I believe remains unanswered is the question: What was the government's motive in insisting on your being jailed pretrial under extraordinarily onerous conditions of confinement until today, when the Executive Branch agrees that you may be set free essentially unrestricted? This makes no sense to me.

From court transcript, U.S. District Court for the District of New Mexico, *USA* v. *Wen Ho Lee,* No. 99-1417-JC, Transcript of Proceeding 9-13-2000,: reprinted at www.quarterly-report.com/human_interest/parker_opinion.htm.

A corollary question I guess is: Why were you charged with the many Atomic Energy Act counts for which the penalty is life imprisonment, all of which the Executive Branch has now moved to dismiss and which I just dismissed? . . .

. . . I feel that the 278 days of confinement for your offense is not unjust; however, I believe you were terribly wronged by being held in custody pretrial in the Santa Fe County Detention Center under demeaning, unnecessarily punitive conditions. I am truly sorry that I was led by our Executive Branch of government to order your detention last December. . . .

I am sad for you and your family because of the way in which you were kept in custody while you were presumed under the law to be innocent of the charges the Executive Branch brought against you.

I am sad that I was induced in December to order your detention, since by the terms of the plea agreement that frees you today without conditions, it becomes clear that the Executive Branch now concedes, or should concede, that it was not necessary to confine you last December or at any time before your trial.

I am sad because the resolution of this case [dragged] on unnecessarily long. Before the Executive Branch obtained your indictment on the 59 charges last December, your attorney, Mr. Holscher, made a written offer to the Office of the United States Attorney to have you explain the missing tapes under polygraph examination. . . .

At the inception of the December hearing, I asked the parties to pursue that offer made by Mr. Holscher on behalf of Dr. Lee, but that was to no avail. . . .

It is only the top decision makers in the Executive Branch, especially the Department of Justice and the Department of Energy and locally, during December, who have caused embarrassment by the way this case began and was handled. They did not embarrass me alone. They have embarrassed our entire nation and each of us who is a citizen of it.

I might say that I am also sad and troubled because I do not know the real reasons why the Executive Branch has done all of this. We will not learn why because the plea agreement shields the Executive Branch from disclosing a lot of information that it was under order to produce that might have supplied the answer.

Although, as I indicated, I have no authority to speak on behalf of the Executive Branch, the President, the Vice-president, the Attorney General, or the Secretary of the Department of Energy, as a member of the Third Branch of the United States Government, the Judiciary, the United States Courts, I sincerely apologize to you, Dr. Lee, for the unfair manner you were held in custody by the Executive Branch.

Court will be in recess.

✎ *E S S A Y S*

The following two essays analyze how activists in the 1960s and 1990s promoted different interpretations of the history of racial discrimination against Asian Americans and other people of color to support their campaigns. The first essay, by Yen Le Espiritu, a sociologist in the Ethnic Studies Department at the University of California at San Diego, describes expressions of panethnicity in the Asian American movement of the 1960s and 1970s. Espiritu recounts how pan-Asian alliances helped create new organizations, media, and Asian American studies programs. She also, however, notes that Asian American solidarity was weakened by accusations of ethnic chauvinism among Chinese

American and Japanese American leaders, debates about Marxist ideology, and problems in establishing relationships between middle-class student activists and the working-class residents of ethnic enclaves. The second essay is by L. Ling-chi Wang, chair of the Ethnic Studies Department and director of Asian American studies at the University of California at Berkeley. Wang's essay critically evaluates depictions of Asian Americans in recent debates about affirmative action. Charging that both advocates and opponents of affirmative action have been guilty of marginalizing and distorting the experiences of Asian Americans, Wang exhorts Asian Americans to take control of these representations and to develop multiracial coalitions.

Panethnicity and Asian American Activism

YEN LE ESPIRITU

The Construction of Pan-Asian Ethnicity

Although broader social struggles and internal demographic changes provided the impetus for the Asian American movement, it was the group's politics—confrontational and explicitly pan-Asian—that shaped the movement's content. Influenced by the internal colonial model, which stresses the commonalities among "colonized groups," college students of Asian ancestry declared solidarity with fellow Asian Americans—and with other Third World minorities. Rejecting the label "Oriental," they proclaimed themselves "Asian American." Through pan-Asian organizations, publications, and Asian American studies programs, Asian American activists built pan-Asian solidarity by pointing out their common fate in American society. The pan-Asian concept enabled diverse Asian American groups to understand their "unequal circumstances and histories as being related."

From "Yellow" to "Asian American"

Following the example of the Black Power movement, Asian American activists spearheaded their own Yellow Power movement to seek "freedom from racial oppression through the power of a consolidated yellow people." In the summer of 1968, more than one hundred students of diverse Asian backgrounds attended an "Are You Yellow?" conference at UCLA to discuss issues of Yellow Power, identity, and the war in Vietnam. In 1970, a new pan-Asian organization in northern California called itself the "Yellow Seed" because "Yellow [is] the common bond between Asian-Americans and Seed symboliz[es] growth as an individual and as an alliance." This "yellow" reference was dropped when Filipino Americans rejected the term, claiming that they were brown, not yellow. At the first Asian American national conference in 1972, Filipino Americans "made it clear to the conferees that we were 'Brown Asians'" by forming a Brown Asian Caucus. It is important to note, however, that Filipino American activists did not reject the term "yellow" because they objected to the pan-Asian framework. Quite the contrary, they rejected it because it allegedly excluded them from that grouping.

Other community organizers used the term "Oriental" to define their organizations and service centers. In Southern California, the Council of Oriental Organizations (COO) became the political base for the diverse Asian American communities. In 1968, COO lobbied for federal funding to establish the Oriental Service Center in Los Angeles County, serving Chinese, Japanese, Filipinos, and Koreans. But Asian American activists also rejected *Oriental* because the term conjures up images of "the sexy Susie Wong, the wily Charlie Chan, and the evil Fu Manchu." It is also a term that smacks of European colonialism and imperialism: *Oriental* means "East"; Asia is "east" only in relationship to Europe, which was taken as the point of reference. To define their own image and to claim an *American* identity, college students of Asian ancestry coined the term *Asian American* to "stand for all of us Americans of Asian descent." While *Oriental* suggests passivity and acquiescence, *Asian Americans* connotes political activism because an Asian American "gives a damn about his life, his work, his beliefs, and is willing to do almost anything to help Orientals become Asian Americans."

The account above suggests that the creation of a new name is a significant symbolic move in constructing an ethnic identity. In their attempt to forge a pan-Asian identity, Asian American activists first had to coin a composite term that would unify and encompass the constituent groups. Filipino Americans' rejection of the term "yellow" and the activists' objection to the cliché-ridden *Oriental* forced the group to change its name to Asian American. . . .

Pan-Asian Organizations

Influenced by the political tempo of the 1960s, young Asian Americans began to join such organizations as the Free Speech Movement at the University of California at Berkeley, Students for a Democratic Society, and the Progressive Labor Party. However, these young activists "had no organization or coalition to draw attention to themselves as a distinct group." Instead, they participated as individuals—often at the invitation of their white or black friends. While Asian American activists subscribed to the integrationist ideology of the 1960s and 1970s social movements, they also felt impotent and alienated. There was no structure to uphold their own identity. As an example, when the Peace and Freedom Party was formed on the basis of black and white coalitions, Asian American activists felt excluded because they were neither black nor white.

In the late 1960s, linking their political views with the growth of racial pride among their ranks, Asian Americans already active in various political movements came together to form their own organizations. Most of the early pan-Asian organizations were college based. In 1968, activists at the University of California, Berkeley founded one of the first pan-Asian political organizations: the Asian American Political Alliance (AAPA). According to a co-founder of the organization, its establishment marked the first time that the term "Asian American" was used nationally to mobilize people of Asian descent. AAPA was formed to increase the political visibility and effectiveness of Asian American activists:

> There were so many Asians out there in the political demonstrations but we had no effectiveness. Everyone was lost in the larger rally. We figured that if we rallied behind our own banner, behind an Asian American banner, we would have an effect on the larger public. We could extend the influence beyond ourselves, to other Asian Americans.

AAPA differed from the traditional Asian cultural groups on most college campuses in two primary ways: its political activism and its pan-Asian emphasis. Reflecting the various political movements from which its members had come, AAPA took progressive stands against the war in Vietnam and in support of other Third World movements. Espousing a pan-Asian framework, AAPA brought together young Chinese, Japanese, and Filipino American activists. Shortly after AAPA was formed at the University of California at Berkeley, a sister organization was established at San Francisco State College (now University). Like its Berkeley counterpart, San Francisco State AAPA "was a vehicle for students to share political concerns in a pan-Asian organization." AAPA's influence also spread to Southern California as Asian American students formed similar organizations on the UCLA and California State University, Long Beach campuses.

Pan-Asian organizations also mushroomed in other parts of the country. In 1969, through the initiative of West Coast students, Asian American organizations began to form on East Coast campuses. For example, in New York, young Asian Americans organized Asian Americans for Action, or Triple A. At Columbia University, Asian Americans involved in white radical politics came together to found their own Asian American Political Alliance. Students at Yale prepared and taught a course on "Asians in America." Similarly, in the Midwest, the civil rights, antiwar, and United Farm Workers movements drew Asian Americans together. Out of these political gatherings emerged a group of Asian American activists who subsequently formed Madison's Asian Union, Illinois' Asian American Alliance, and Minneapolis' Asian American Political Alliance.

Not only did pan-Asian organizations reinforce the cohesiveness of already existing networks, but they also expanded these networks. By the mid-1970s, *Asian American* had become a familiar term. Although first coined by college activists, the pan-Asian concept began to be used extensively by professional and community spokespersons to lobby for the health and welfare of Americans of Asian decent. . . .

Asian American Studies

On college and university campuses, the most important legacy of the Asian American movement was the institutionalization of Asian American studies. Beginning in 1968, under the slogan of self-determination, Asian American and other U.S. Third World students fought for an education more relevant and accessible to their communities. Reflecting the larger national struggle over cultural hegemony, these students demanded the right to control their educational agenda, to design their own programs, and to evaluate their instructors. In 1968, after the most prolonged and violent campus struggles in this country's history, Asian American studies programs were established at San Francisco State College (now University) and at the University of California at Berkeley. These campus struggles emboldened students at other colleges to fight for ethnic studies courses, programs, and departments and forced college administrations to heed such demands. In succeeding years, Asian American Studies programs were established on major campuses throughout the country. Since 1968, the field has progressed from experimental courses to degree programs. For example, UC Berkeley and UCLA now offer B.A. and M.A. degree programs in Asian American Studies respectively.

Although varied in their curriculum development and course offerings, Asian American Studies programs built, and continue to build, an Asian American heritage, putting courses and reading selections together and expounding similarities—as well as differences—in the experiences of Asian peoples in the United States. Indeed, the curriculum was designed to help students "know who they are as Asian Americans." Clearly part of the heritage being created hinges on Asian Americans' shared history of racial discrimination. Many courses stress an Asian American identity and experience, yielding highly emotional discussions on subjects dealing with discrimination, alienation, and racism. Such an emphasis is evident in the following statement of curriculum philosophy for Asian American Studies:

> Throughout much of America's history, Asians in this country have been the victims of contempt and exploitation. Often they were singled out as scapegoats in periods of severe economic depression, such as the nation-wide anti-Chinese agitations and riots in the 1870's and 1880's, and Asian Americans were regarded as enemies during times of international conflicts, particularly the Second World War and the Korean War.

This statement links together the experiences of Chinese, Japanese, and Korean Americans; in so doing, it calls attention to their collective identity.

Also, Asian American scholars began to reinterpret Asian history in the United States to bring out what is common to all Asian Americans. These histories highlight a record of violence against Asians, who were denied the rights of citizenship, forbidden to own land, interned in relocation camps, and forced to live in poverty-stricken enclaves. For example, in discussing discriminatory laws and informal acts perpetrated against Chinese, Korean, Filipino, and Japanese immigrants, Lowell Chun-Hoon concluded that "what is significant [about this exploitation] is that all of these varied Asian groups, each representing a separate country and unique culture, encountered a similar or identical pattern of racial oppression and economic exploitation." Also, Asian Americans were treated increasingly as a single unit of analysis in academic studies. A survey of studies on Asian groups in the United States indicates that works dealing with "Asians" increased dramatically during the 1970s and 1980s. Articles published in these decades represent 37 percent of such articles published in this country, " almost three times as many works" as might have been expected. . . .

In sum, Asian American Studies provides an institutional means to reach more Asian American students and to create "an Asian American awareness expressing a unity of all Asians, Chinese, Japanese, Filipino, Korean, Samoan, and Hawaiian." Its by-products—the Association for Asian American Studies, national conferences, research centers, and publications—further stimulate pan-Asian solidarity because they provide a forum for Asian Americans to discuss common problems and experiences. In these settings," the experiences of different Asian groups were compared and recognized as historically intertwined." . . .

Asian American News Media

Pan-Asian periodicals came out of the Asian American movement, the efforts of Asian American student organizations on university campuses across the country. In fact, "these newspapers, pamphlets, and magazines were the lifeblood of the movement." While the traditional ethnic press continued to be important, its neglect and disdain of such political issues as civil rights, the Vietnam war, and ethnic studies prompted young dissidents to launch their own publication. Much of their journalism was committed to the empowerment of the Asian American people.

Although not always successful, some publications attempted to formulate a pan-Asian perspective rather than any singular ethnic outlook. In 1969, five UCLA students put up $100 each to launch the monthly publication *Gidra*, the first and most widely circulated pan-Asian publication. In all, during its five years of publication, about two hundred individuals participated in producing *Gidra* . . .

Besides functioning as a source of news for young Asian American activists, these media efforts also forged pan-Asian consciousness. Through articles, poetry, and photographs in a variety of publications, and by meeting together, these young Asian Americans across the country began to communicate with one another and to share their frustrations and their dreams. From these efforts, they began "to formulate their own values, establish their own identities and sense of pride, and create a new 'culture' which they can truly call Asian American." . . .

Antiwar Movement

The antiwar movement united Asian Americans along racial lines. For many Asian American activists, the American invasion of Vietnam involved more than the issues of national sovereignty or imperialism; it also raised questions of racism directed against Asian people. Watching the images of war on the evening television news, "an increasing number of Asian American college and high school students realized with a shock that the 'enemy' whom American soldiers were maiming and killing had faces like their own." Seeing unarmed, unresisting civilians napalmed in Vietnam angered young Asian Americans and stirred them to protest the prevailing assumption that Asian lives were cheap. To emphasize the racist nature of the war, Asian American protesters discarded the popular slogans "Give peace a chance" and "Bring the GIs home," and touted their own "Stop killing our Asian brothers and sisters" and "We don't want your racist war." According to Asian American antiwar activists, the slogan "Bring our boys home" clearly proclaimed that the primary concern was to avoid American, not Vietnamese, casualties.

As Asian people fighting in an Asian country, Asian American G.I.s were particularly repulsed by the atrocities committed against the Vietnamese people:

> For some G.I.'s in Vietnam, there are no Vietnamese people. To them the land is not populated by people but by "Gooks," considered inferior, unhuman animals by the racist-educated G.I. Relieved in his mind of human responsibility by this grotesque stereotype, numerous barbarities have been committed against these Asian peoples, since "they're only 'Gooks.'". . .

Because of their racial similarity to the "enemy," Asian American G.I.s also endured anti-Asian racism. Many Asian Americans complained that their superior officers and fellow G.I.s lumped them together with other Asian groups: regardless of their ethnic background, Asian American soldiers were indiscriminately called Gook, Jap, Chink, or Ho Chi Minh. An Asian American G.I. related that, upon entering basic training, he was called a "Gook" and was made to stand in front of his platoon as an example of "what the enemy looked like." The "Gook" stereotype "portrays Koreans, Vietnamese, Cambodians, Laotioans, and other Asians as subhuman beings who do not value individual human life and who all look like the treacherous Chinese Communist enemy." . . . The stereotype angered and ethnicized Asian American G.I.s. As a former American G.I. of Japanese ancestry related, "I became ethnicized when I was in Vietnam. I saw how whites were treating the Vietnamese, calling them Gooks, running them over with their trucks. I figured I am a Gook also."

At times, the race question alienated Asian Americans from the majority of the antiwar protesters. . . . In 1971, the Asian American contingent refused to join the main antiwar march in Washington, D.C. because the coordinating committee failed to adopt the contingent's antiracist statement for the march. On other occasions, the contingent's appeals "were met with hostility and rejection." When Asian Americans did take part in the white-dominated marches, they passed out their own leaflets, which denounced racism and imperialism. . . .

In sum, Asian American emphasis on race and racism differentiates their antiwar protest from that of whites. In characterizing the Vietnam war as a racist act against Asians, Asian American activists proclaimed racial solidarity not only with each other but also with the Vietnamese people, their "Asian brothers and sisters." In the process, pan-Asian political consciousness became transnationalized, encompassing the political struggles not only in America but also in Asia. As an Asian American activist stated, "As long as there are U.S. troops in Asia, as long as the U.S. government and the military wage wars of aggression against Asian people, racism against Asians will serve the interest of this country. Racism against them is often racism against us.

New Left Movement

In the late 1960s and early 1970s, a significant number of Asian Americans also became active in New Left activities and organizations such as the Free Speech Movement (FSM), Students for a Democratic Society (SDS), the Weathermen and the Progressive Labor Party. Asian American Marxist organizations grew out of these New Left activities. Diverging from the Old Left emphasis on the working class as the leading revolutionary stratum, the New Left sought to organize people across class lines. The New Left also looked away from the Soviet Union and to the Vietnamese National Liberation Front and the People's Republic of China as new models of socialism. It was the New Left's version of socialism and the movement's growing admiration for Asian countries that influenced the thinking of Asian American Marxists.

As in the antiwar movement, the Asian American New Left separated itself from the dominant New Left movement over the issues of racism and national oppression. It was over these questions that Asian American working people acquainted themselves with Marxism—a Marxism that emphasized race as well as class. Influenced by the call for national liberation by the Black Power movement and Asian socialist countries, Asian American Marxists added racial self-determination to their revolutionary agenda. . . .

Varied in their understanding and application of Marxism, Asian American Marxist organizations struggled over the relative importance of nation building and party building. . . .

In 1972, in an attempt to apply Marxism to the national question, the Marxist-oriented organization East Wind adopted the "Asian nation" line. Echoing the separatist call in the black community, East Wind declared that as a racially oppressed minority, Asian Americans were entitled to form their own nation. Although East Wind dropped the Asian nation line in 1975, it continued to stress the importance of national liberation. On the other hand, organizations such as the New York–based Asian Study Group advocated party building and criticized other Asian American revolutionary groups for their preoccupation with "band-aid" social service programs. Many of these differences remained unresolved, eventually dissolving friendships as well as organizations. . . .

Women's Movement

Although Asian American women had been involved in each stage of the Asian American movement, they were often restricted to such subordinate tasks as taking minutes, typing, making coffee, and answering phones. The small number of Asian American women who achieved leadership positions in the movement found themselves called "bossy" and "unfeminine." Asian American feminists who challenged Asian American sexism were often cast as betraying Asian American nationalism—as assimilationists.

Sexist oppression prevailed even in the most revolutionary Asian American organizations. For example, the San Francisco—based Red Guards initially claimed that women's worth was only in staying at home and in producing children. Along the same lines, the Marxist-oriented I Wor Kuen championed forsaking monogamy to liberate relations between men and women and to build collective solidarity. In actuality, this sexual liberation was "a cover for degeneracy and the most blatant forms of male supremacy and the oppression of women." . . .

Frustrated with male chauvinism, Asian American women began meeting separately from men to discuss feminist concerns. Their collective anger was nurtured by the progressive ideology of the women's movement of the late 1960s. Although they borrowed heavily from the general women's movement, Asian American women seldom joined these middle-class, white-dominated organizations. Like black, Chicana, and Native American women, Asian American women felt alienated and at times exploited by these women's organizations.

In its early development, the women's movement was in fact insensitive to the issues of minority and lower-class women. In contrast, Asian American and other Third World feminists emphasized the "triple oppression" concept: their gender was inextricably linked to their race and class. . . .

. . . Distancing themselves from the general feminist movement, Asian American women organized their own movement. For Asian American women activists, the ideology of feminism had to be incorporated into the larger identity of being Asian American. According to Susie Ling, "The Asian Women's Movement's umbilical cord was still very much attached to the larger Asian American Movement." Asian American women chose two major paths of activism: they worked within the Asian American community or within Marxist-Leninist groups. In 1971, Asian American women in Los Angeles organized Asian Sisters to address the drug problems of young Asian American women. It was one of the first social service projects for Asian American women by Asian American women. In 1972, they established Little Friends Playground to provide childcare for the community. The Marxist-Leninist groups that Asian American women were involved in remain Asian American–oriented today. Asian American women were also concerned with the social conditions of their Asian sisters in China and Vietnam. For example, in 1971, the Los Angeles Asian women's movement sent delegates to the Vancouver Indochinese Women's Conference to express their solidarity with these women.

The Limits of Pan-Asianism

Although pan-Asian consolidation certainly has occurred, it has been by no means universal. For those who wanted a broader political agenda, the pan-Asian scope was too narrow and its racial orientation too segregative. For others who wanted to preserve ethnic particularism, the pan-Asian agenda threatened to remove second- and third-generation Asians "from their conceptual ties to their community." These competing levels of organization mitigated the impact of pan-Asianism.

Moreover, pan-Asianism has been primarily the ideology of native-born, American educated, and middle-class Asians. Embraced by students, artists, professionals, and political activists, pan-Asian consciousness thrived on college campuses and in urban settings. However, it barely touched the Asian ethnic enclaves. When the middle-class student activists carried the enlarged and politicized Asian American consciousness to the ethnic communities, they encountered apprehension, if not outright hostility. Conscious of their national origins and overburdened with their day-to-day struggles for survival, most community residents ignored or spurned the movement's political agenda. . . .

Even among those who were involved in the Asian American movement, divisions arose from conflicting sets of interests as sub groups decided what and whose interests would be addressed. Often times, conflicts over material interests took on ethnic coloration, with participants from smaller subgroups charging that "Asian American" primarily meant Chinese and Japanese American, the two largest and most acculturated Asian American groups at the time. For example, most Asian American Studies programs did not include courses on other Asian groups, but only on Chinese and Japanese. Similarly, the Asian American women's movement often subsumed the needs of their Korean and Filipino members under those of Chinese and Japanese women. Chinese and Japanese Americans also were the instructors of Asian American ethnic studies, directors and staff members of many Asian American projects, and advisory and panel members in many governmental agencies.

The ethnic and class inequality within the pan-Asian structure has continued to be a source of friction and mistrust, with participants from the less dominant groups feeling shortchanged and excluded. . . .

. . . By the late 1960s, pan-Asianism was possible because of the more amicable relationships among the Asian countries, the declining residential segregation among diverse Asian groups in America, and the large number of native-born, American-educated political actors. Disillusioned with the larger society and estranged from their traditional communities, third- and fourth-generation Asian Americans turned to the alternative strategy of pan-Asian unification. Through pan-Asian organizations, media, and Asian American Studies programs, these political activists assumed the role of "cultural entrepreneurs" consciously creating a community of culture out of diverse Asian peoples. This process of pan-Asian consolidation did not proceed smoothly nor did it encompass all Asian Americans. Ethnic chauvinism, competition for scarce resources, and class cleavages continued to divide the subgroups. However, once established, the pan-Asian structure not only reinforced the cohesiveness of already existing networks but also expanded these networks.

Asian Americans and Debates About Affirmative Action

L. LING-CHI WANG

In the past two years, both proponents and opponents have written extensively on the topic of affirmative action. But a national dialogue has yet to take place because both sides are locked in intractable positions, unwilling and unable to listen to and understand each other. Since the beginning of 1995, the national debate has become increasingly acrimonious and polarized. The July 20, 1995 decision of the Regents of the University of California to abolish its long standing affirmative action policy on admissions, faculty and staff hiring, and contracts, as well as the anti-affirmative action California initiative, known as the California Civil Rights Initiative (CCRI), to be placed on the November 1996 ballot, have contributed to the polarization of the national debate. The recent Republican victory in the 1994 elections and several U.S. Supreme Court decisions have greatly strengthened the forces opposed to affirmative action. Despite clear demographic and political shifts in the past three decades, there is a conspicuous absence of any critical, yet constructive, appraisal of the policy.

As one who has supported and worked on issues related to affirmative action during the past 28 years in the Asian American community, I would like to share my understanding and appraisal of the policy and the position I think Asian Americans should take in the national debate. While Asian Americans have slowly become more visible in the political debate, both proponents and opponents of affirmative action have largely misrepresented and marginalized the perspectives and positions of Asian Americans. I shall begin by briefly placing affirmative action in historical and political perspectives, at the risk of being redundant, since misinformation and confusion over both the intents and objectives of affirmative action policy still exist. I shall then outline where Asian Americans are situated in the unfolding national debate. Finally, I shall conclude with a critique of affirmative action as it has been practiced in the past thirty years and what Asian Americans can do to help reconfigure affirmative action within the context of a re-envisioned multiracial America. Asian Americans are central to this debate and play a vital role in shaping its outcome.

Affirmative Action in Perspective

The issue of fairness and justice in the distribution of scarce resources in our race- and class-conscious society lies at the heart of the current debate over affirmative action. Scarcity invariably creates competition and conflict. In this competition, political and economic elites have the power to define universalistic and meritocratic criteria for distributing scarce resources. For example, access to a University of California (UC) education is considered a scarce resource—in 1993, only 20,413 out of 272,800 high school graduates, which is less than ten percent, were admitted into the nine-campus system. The criteria established by the Regents of the

University—grade point average (GPA) and standardized test scores—are assumed to be both fair and reliable and, therefore, universal.

The Johnson administration introduced affirmative action policies, pursuant to Executive Order 11246 in 1965, to help dismantle entrenched segregation and discrimination based on race and gender and to promote racial equality and integration. Opponents of affirmative action argue that it is unfair because it subverts meritocracy, condones mediocrity, promotes group rights, racial quotas, reverse discrimination, and above all, invites big government intrusion. Following the logic of the US Supreme Court decision in *Bakke v. the University of California* (1978), they argue that affirmative action in college admissions is morally wrong and un-American, despite its good intentions, because it grants *group rights* based on race and gender at the expense of *individual rights and merits.*

The July 20, 1995, decision by the UC Regents illustrates the argument against affirmative action policies in college admissions. Writing in defense of his anti-affirmative action resolution, UC Regent Ward Connerly declared,

> We have not "killed" or "scrapped" affirmative action. We have not adopted an academic meritocracy. Instead, the regents have eliminated what amounts to a racial Monopoly board in which students are allowed to proceed with their college educations on the basis of their color or the origin of their ancestors. . . . The University of California still has the "welcome mat" out for students of all races. We cherish our diversity and want more of it; we just want to achieve it *naturally* rather than *artificially.*

Likewise, explaining his anti-affirmative action position, UC Regent Stephen Nakashima wrote,

> The Regents' decision to terminate the discriminatory preference accorded to "minority" persons in hiring and contracting resulted from an increasing awareness that discrimination should not beget discrimination. The history books are full of tragedies born of what someone sincerely thought was justified to correct some prior wrong or to enhance the position of some *groups.* . . . In the popular *vernacular,* "the playing field has been leveled" after years of requiring only Asians and white males to bear the burden of a tilted field.

The arguments of Connerly and Nakashima are based on the following major assumptions: (1) the US is and should be a *naturally* color-blind society; (2) granting group rights or privileges based on race or gender in the distribution of scarce resource(s) is *artificial* and discriminatory to Asian Americans and whites and, therefore, illegal and wrong; (3) affirmative action policies condone mediocrity and sacrifice merit and excellence; and (4) the sole criteria for the distribution of scarce resources are those based on individual merits and rights.

All four assumptions are flawed. The US has never existed *naturally* as a color-blind society. From the framing of its Constitution to its past and present policies for women and communities of color, the US has created *artificial* social barriers and relied on institutionalized segregation based on race and gender. For example, Harvard University denied admissions to qualified women and minorities for the first 328 years of its 358 year history, artificially protecting and perpetuating the group rights and privileges of white male gentiles. Its policy of excluding women and minorities can be characterized as affirmative action for white males or a policy that condoned mediocrity. Harvard invoked the concept of individual merit only when its protected privileged status for the white male group was challenged in the 1960s. Thus, throughout US history, artificial group rights or privileges have been used to favor white males at the expense of minorities and women.

Under intense pressure from the civil rights movement, universities reluctantly adopted affirmative action policies for minorities and women in the late 1960s as a token concession. Thus, affirmative action was introduced as a device to lend Harvard and other universities an appearance of fairness and integration. Harvard redefined "merit" by adding an "ethnic docket" to its list of other dockets, including wealthy alumni, athletes, and graduates of preparatory schools, in the admission process. This policy was never intended to promote substantive equality or integration; rather, it was designed to allow a small number of token minorities and women into white male dominated universities and work places.

Consequently, under the guise of affirmative action, elite universities like Harvard and the University of California admit more children of well-connected alumni than underrepresented minorities under "affirmative action." It seems that benefactors of "affirmative action" include *all* students admitted by non-competitive criteria, such as legacy, leadership qualities, athletic ability, disability, and historical racial or gender discrimination.

After 30 years of affirmative action, the racial divide in the US remains as wide and deep as that identified by President Johnson's Commission on Civil Disorder in the wake of urban riots in 1967. The Commission concluded in 1968,

> What white Americans have never fully understood—but what the Negro can never forget—is that white society is deeply implicated in the ghetto. White institutions created it, white institutions maintain it, and white society condones it.

That was in 1968. Today, "white Americans" still do not understand the racial divide. Despite federal measures to abolish racial discrimination, such as the 1954 *Brown v. Board of Education* decision and the Civil Rights Act of 1964, the US has not succeeded in eliminating racial fissures. Yet many continue to believe that the US is a color-blind society. The opponents of affirmative action rest their case on this presumption of color-blindness and demand that public policies be carried out without distinction of race, gender, color, or national origin.

Asian Americans in the Affirmative Action Discourse

I will now discuss how opposing sides view and treat Asian Americans and then offer a more inclusive and multiracial vision of the US. Asian Americans have become a major focus of the national debate as both sides of the affirmative action issue use Asian Americans to advance their respective arguments. These arguments point to the complexity of race relations in the US and the need to rethink race and race relations. Among the examples of unfairness cited most frequently by opponents of affirmative action is the policy's adverse impact on Asian Americans. For example, in the 1980s, the opponents of affirmative action seized Asian American complaints of discriminatory admission policies in several top research universities as a means to dismantle affirmative action. More recently, the opponents of affirmative action have cited the lawsuit against San Francisco Unified School District action, the *Brian Ho* case, as an example of injustice engendered by affirmative action. Opponents exploit the "model minority" myth, in which Asian Americans are portrayed as highly motivated and hardworking people, by depicting them as victims of an unfair policy that favors group rights over individual merits.

Anti-affirmative action arguments rely on three major flawed assumptions. First, they assume that Asian Americans are a homogeneous group, ignoring the diverse composition of the group—which ranges from recent refugees from Southeast Asia to descendants of California's Chinese pioneers. Secondly, they assume that a legacy of historical and institutional racism against Asian Americans does not exist. They assume that Asian Americans are intergrated into the mainstream and do not face discrimination nor experience anti-Asian sentiment. Lastly, they assume that Asian Americans no longer need affirmative action programs to overcome past injustice and racial discrimination. Thus, they assume that Asian Americans, in departure from the past, no longer constitute a racial minority and are fully integrated into the white majority.

Defenders of affirmative action also view Asian Americans as a model minority; two perspectives have emerged from them. Some claim that Asian Americans no longer need or deserve to be included in affirmative action programs. With good intention, supporters use the "success of Asian Americans" as an argument for reserving affirmative action for other minorities. They argue that, while Asian Americans once experienced discrimination, they now compete on a level-playing field because of affirmative action and, therefore, no longer need affirmative action programs. In other words, affirmative action has become a sound, temporary public policy which can outlive its usefulness once those who have experienced discrimination in the past have achieved success.

Other proponents of affirmative action presume that all Asian Americans oppose affirmative action since they are already a "model minority." They see the Asian American presence in the debate as a monkey wrench in their "black-versus-white" paradigm of racial discourse. In their view, there is no room for an Asian American presence in both their theories and public policy formulations. In short, they want to exclude Asian Americans from racial discourse, even in times of backlash against affirmative action. They marginalize, if not exclude, those Asian Americans who strongly support affirmative action in public forums and protest rallies. In my opinion, their exclusionary posture aids and abets opponents of affirmative action.

Thus, while opponents of affirmative action divide the Asian American communities by national origin and class and pit Asian Americans against other minorities, a tactic which is both divisive and racist, supporters of affirmative action also deliberately exclude and marginalize Asian Americans in a fashion just as divisive and racist. Both sides incorrectly view Asian Americans as a model minority and erroneously assume their homogeneity and uniform success. While about half of the Asian American population is successful according to educational, occupational, and income measures, the other half—many of whom are non-English-speaking recent immigrants and refugees—is not and needs public assistance and affirmative action. Nonetheless, both halves need affirmative action—they are equally susceptible to racism and discrimination which pose a constant threat to their lives, human dignity, and basic rights.

Asian Americans should not allow themselves to be used or marginalized in intellectual discourses, policy formulations, and political debates over affirmative action. They need to speak out against these misrepresentations promoted by both sides of the debate and articulate their positions forcefully. Their presence is essential for understanding the complexity of current race relations in the US and to re-thinking race and race relations in the 21st century.

Re-envisioning Multiracial America

The nation is at a critical juncture in its history. After five hundred years of racial oppression and exclusion, fundamental questions remain. What kind of society should historically oppressed communities seek for themselves and their children? What should be the vision for the US as a whole in the 21st century?

The social progress made through integration and affirmative action, including the creation of a sizable black middle class, has fallen far short of the substantive changes necessary to create a truly equal society which is free of racism and sexism. As much as one-half to two-thirds of African Americans still live in near or dire poverty. For millions of Americans of all races, the dream of racial equality and economic justice remains unfulfilled.

The integrationist paradigm and strategy used in the past three decades failed for five important reasons. First, affirmative action, in the final analysis, is a token concession which was granted under tremendous political pressure during the height of the civil rights movement. It promotes integration for some and alienation for most, including poor whites. It is a temporary and discretionary policy of political expediency which can be taken back at any time. Second by adopting the terms and conditions of integration, affirmative action is judged as fair and universal when it ensures advantages to white males. Furthermore, beneficiaries of affirmative action are deemed less qualified and undeserving, even if they are fully qualified. For these reasons, affirmative action, in its current form, is denounced as a program that unfairly privileges minorities and women at the expense of white males. Third, by adopting the terms and conditions of integration, affirmative action also requires women and minority groups to fight for their own shares of the token concession. Built into these terms is a self-defeating, divide-and-conquer strategy based largely on identity politics in which minorities and women are pitted against each other in a contest to determine which group faces greater discrimination and victimization. While identity politics and victimology are necessary and empowering, they pose limits and present pitfalls. Fourth, the dominant race relations paradigm assumes a black versus white dichotomy which marginalizes other racial minorities. Under this bipolar paradigm, civil rights is a black issue, relegating the civil rights issues of Asian Americans, Chicanos/Latinos, Native Americans, and women to the fringe. This paradigm prevents a multiracial vision of America from emerging, promotes inter- and intra-minority conflict, and, above all, undermines solidarity among racial minorities, women, and poor whites in their efforts to combat racism, sexism, and economic injustice. Last but not least, the race-based policy obscures the significance of class within each racial group, especially within the Asian American communities. As a result, class interests are frequently confused with or manipulated as race-based interests and vice versa. For these five reasons, it is important to re-think race relations and civil rights. It is time to reformulate affirmative action and to re-envision America as a multiracial democracy.

The political backlash which began during the Nixon era has now become a tsunami sweeping across the nation. The backlash has been greatly reinforced by a growing sense of vulnerability among the predominantly white population as the US loses its dominant position in the global economy and its population becomes increasingly multiracial through immigration from Asia and Latin America. This backlash is particularly evident in California, as exemplified by legislative strategies such as Proposition 187, the English-only proposition, and gerrymandering reapportionment.

There is, however, a legacy of the 1960s that has long been forgotten which deserves our attention and support. I am referring to the Third World legacy which united racial minority and white students in the fight against racial oppression and created the ethnic studies departments now found in various universities across the nation. For the first and only time in US history, racial minority groups joined hands with whites in a common cause to transform institutions of higher education. They steadfastly refused to be divided and conquered. The concept of Third World may be passé but the vision of multiracial democracy and the idea of solidarity among oppressed groups are more urgent than ever if the US is to transform itself.

Racial minorities and women in California have an opportunity and an obligation to build a new society for the US. This is especially true in multiracial cities like Los Angeles and San Francisco, where racial minorities and women are clearly in the majority. But, it is also in these cities that they are hopelessly divided and against each other, compelled by the current power structure to accept and live with political domination and economic injustice. This situation must be reversed. It must, however, also go beyond simply chipping away power and privilege from the white males and striving for group gains, and in turn, using the same power and privileges to exclude and oppress others. I hope for a new society and new government which will not repeat the same mistakes and atrocities of the past.

Toward this end, America needs a bold new vision for itself. I suggest a critical re-examination of affirmative action, especially its limits, and an attempt to learn from past mistakes. It is certainly important to build a united force of minorities, women, and white males to defeat the racially motivated backlash against affirmative action and other progressive programs. I cannot overemphasize the importance of coalition building. The backlash, however, cannot be defeated simply to return to business as usual. The nation should return to the promise of equality and justice embodied in the Declaration of Independence and mandated in our Constitution. America must re-envision itself and become a political and economic democracy that is truly multiracial, what historian Harold Cruse called "democratic ethnic pluralism." This means that the US identity is not simply conceptualized as black and white, but as multicolor, including Asian Americans, Chicanos/Latinos, Native Americans, women, and gay of all colors and classes.

The anti-affirmative action forces issue a rare challenge for Asian Americans. They occupy a unique position in meeting this challenge and can help break the deadlock between the opposing sides of the affirmative action debate. Asian Americans could not have asked for a better opportunity and vehicle to take up this challenge. To take full advantage of this opportunity, they must have the courage to critically examine their past actions as well as their successes and failures. They must avoid repeating past mistakes and be prepared to modify past policies, including affirmative action policy. To achieve a multiracial political and economic democracy, a multiracial vision and coalition is needed. Asian Americans must join with others who share this vision to defeat the forces of reaction and to re-envision, transform, and rebuild America.

☙ *F U R T H E R　　R E A D I N G*

Aguilar-San Juan, Karin, ed. *The State of Asian America: Activism and Resistance in the 1990s* (1994).

Asian Women United of California, ed. *Making Waves: An Anthology of Writings by and About Asian American Women* (1989).

Eng, David, and Alice Hom, eds. *Q & A: Queer in Asian America* (1998).

Gee, Emma, et al., eds. *Counterpoint: Perspectives on Asian America* (1976).

Ho, Fred. *Legacy to Liberation: Politics and Culture of Revolutionary Asian/Pacific America* (2000).

Hune, Shirley. "Opening the American Mind and Body: The Role of Asian American Studies," *Change* 21, no. 6 (November/December 1989): 56–63.

Kibria, Nazli. "The Racial Gap: South Asian American Racial Identity and the Asian American Movement," in *A Part Yet Apart: South Asians in Asian America,* ed. Lavina Dhingra Shankar and Rajini Srikanth (1998), 69–78.

Kondo, Dorinne. "Art, Activism, Asia, and Asian Americans," in *About Face: Performing Race in Fashion and Theater* (1997), 227–260.

Leadership Education for Asian Pacifics: Asian Pacific American Public Policy, *The State of Asian Pacific America: Policy Issues to the Year 2020* (1993).

Lee, Wen Ho, with Helen Zia, *My Country Versus Me* (2000).

Leong, Russell, ed. *Asian American Sexualities: Dimensions of the Gay and Lesbian Experience* (1996).

Lim-Hing, Shirley, ed. *The Very Inside: An Anthology of Writing by Asian and Pacific Island Lesbian and Bisexual Women* (1994).

Ling, Susie. "The Mountain Movers: Asian American Women's Movement in Los Angeles," *Amerasia Journal* 15, no. 1 (1989): 51–67.

Morales, Royal F., *Makibaka, the Pilipino American Struggle* (1974).

Nakanishi, Don. "Linkages and Boundaries: Twenty-Five Years of Asian American Studies," *Amerasia Journal* 21, no. 3 (1995/96): xvii–xxv.

National Asian Pacific American Legal Consortium, *Selected Incidents of Anti-Asian Violence in 1993* (1993).

Ong, Paul, ed. *The State of Asian Pacific America: Economic Diversity, Issues and Policies* (1994).

Root, Maria P. P., ed. *The Multiracial Experience: Racial Borders as the New Frontier* (1996).

———. *Racially Mixed People in America* (1992).

Shah, Sonia, ed *Dragon Ladies: Asian American Feminists Breath Fire* (1997).

Stober, Dan, and Ian Hoffman. *A Convenient Spy: Wen Ho Lee and the Politics of Nuclear Espionage* (2001).

Tachiki, Amy, et al., eds. *Roots: An Asian American Reader* (1971).

Takagi, Dana Y. *Retreat from Race: Asian-American Admissions Policies and Racial Politics* (1992).

Trask, Haunani-Kay. *From a Native Daughter: Colonialism and Sovereignty in Hawaii* (1993).

Umemoto, Karen. "On Strike': San Francisco State College Strike 1968–69: The Role of Asian American Students," *Amerasia Journal* 15, no. 1 (1989), 3–41.

Wei, William. *The Asian American Movement* (1993).

Yamamoto, Eric. *Interracial Justice: Conflict and Reconciliation in Post-Civil Rights America* (1999).

Zia, Helen. *American Dreams: The Emergence of an American People* (2001).

New Formations of
Asian American Culture,
1990–2001

By the 1990s, popular literature, films, and a wide variety of cultural productions by Asian American artists had proliferated and garnered commercial and critical success. Authors like Maxine Hong Kingston and Amy Tan were widely anthologized, and their writings became a mainstay of high school and college literature courses. Film audiences flocked to see action star Jackie Chan and films directed by John Woo and Ang Lee. Commentators even wrote articles in mainstream newspapers and magazines celebrating Asian and Asian American influences on American culture.

Asian Americans, however, have called for a more serious consideration of the meaning and significance of this thriving "Asian American culture." Some prominent artists have been accused of reinforcing racial, ethnic, and gender stereotypes to appeal to mainstream audiences. Their defenders have proclaimed the need for artistic freedom and charged these critics with attempting to impose political and cultural censorship. Heated debates about these issues reflect conflicting interpretations of the responsibilities of artists, standards of artistic integrity, aesthetic values, and the impact of cultural productions on sociopolitical contexts.

These controversies surrounding the roles of Asian American artists reveal fundamental disagreements about the relationship between culture and history. Do contemporary artists have a duty to challenge and debunk negative stereotypes that have been promoted throughout the history of Asian America? Should cultural productions be evaluated for the way they depict past and present Asian American communities? Does recognizing the tremendous influence of popular culture on perceptions of Asian Americans require us to monitor these productions for accuracy? Is it even possible to determine if a portrayal is "accurate"? Have critics, in their zeal to promote "positive" images, tried to turn artists into historians and denigrated artists' aesthetic power?

Responses to these questions are complicated by the recognition that there is not a single "representative" Asian American culture. In fact, the very boundaries between "Asian" and "Asian American" culture are obviously permeable in this

457

transnational age. Evidence of diasporic influences can be found everywhere. Ethnic enclaves are constantly being transformed by the arrival of new immigrants. Modern transportation and communication systems make it easy for immigrants to maintain ties with their homelands and for fifth-generation Asian Americans to learn about their ancestry. Plane travel makes it possible for people to reside in multiple locations and cultures. Individuals who cannot abide long flights, however, need only go to a nearby ethnic enclave or log on to the Internet for the most recent cultural products from Asia. Even the line between Asian and American culture becomes harder to establish when films distributed by the Hong Kong cinema and Hollywood are designed to please mainstream American, Asian American, and Asian audiences. Such conditions make it clear that simple definitions of Asian, American, and Asian American culture are problematic. Undoubtedly future studies will focus less on generalizations about culture and more on the interplay of multiple constructions of race, ethnicity, class, gender, nation, community, and identity revealed by specific cultural productions.

☙ D O C U M E N T S

The first set of documents provides different views of relationships between artists and Asian American communities. Document 1 is excerpted from a 1990 newspaper article by Edward Iwata. Iwata reviews the fiery public debate generated by the popularity of Maxine Hong Kingston's *Woman Warrior* since the memoir was first published in 1976. Condemned by critics like Frank Chin for supposedly catering to white racist assumptions and misrepresenting Asian and Asian American history, Kingston also has outspoken defenders. Kingston's supporters praise her innovative style and attention to gender constructions and accuse her critics of promoting censorship. Document 2 recounts protests against Vietnamese American author Le Ly Hayslip. These critics accuse Hayslip of misrepresenting Vietnamese history in her memoir *When Heaven and Earth Changed Places* and Oliver Stone of reinforcing these distortions in his film *Heaven and Earth*. They denounce Hayslip and Stone for depicting South Vietnamese soldiers as torturers and Vietnamese women as prostitutes. They also claim that Hayslip's East Meets West Foundation, funded in part by the proceeds of her books and Stone's film, is a tool of the Vietnamese Communist government and not a humanitarian organization devoted to providing educational and health services in Vietnam

Document 3, a 1998 magazine article, describes the growing popularity of Asian American hip-hop and rap music. Gaining attention and respect in the early 1990s, artists like Jamez and Q-Bert combine musical practices and techniques in ways that challenge notions of "black," "white," and "Asian" music. Documents 4 and 5 address the decision of the Association of Asian American Studies (AAAS) to revoke a fiction award earlier given to Lois-Ann Yamanaka for her 1997 novel *Blu's Hanging*. The novel portrayed three Japanese American children on the island of Molokai and their struggle to survive the death of their mother and poverty. Some Asian Americans admired Yamanaka's use of pidgin and her memorable characterizations. Others, however, were appalled by the book's presentation of a Filipino American sexual predator. After learning that the AAAS gave the book a fiction award, the Filipino American Studies Caucus and Anti-Racism Coalition drafted a resolution declaring that the award violated the organization's goal of promoting "better understanding and closer ties between and among various subcomponents within Asian American Studies" and should be revoked. Drawing attention to interethnic tension within academia and Hawai'i, the campaign succeeded in rescinding the award when the resolution passed by a vote of ninety-one to fifty-five.

The second set of documents illustrates both change and continuity in recent Asian American cultural productions. Document 6 describes how residents in New York once objected to the designation of a "Little India" section of the city but now celebrate parades commemorating India's independence from Britain and Indian immigrant contributions to the city. Document 7 notes little change in Hollywood depictions of certain racial stereotypes. This 2000 memo by the Media Action Network for Asian Americans, a watchdog group that monitors media portrayals, bemoans the continued presentation of Asian Americans as gangsters, sexual nerds, dragon ladies, and lotus blossoms in Hollywood films and television shows. Future Hollywood depictions, however, may contain fewer stereotypes and stilted performances or may be countered by other depictions because of the growing clout of Asian actors and directors described in Document 8.

1. A Journalist Recounts the Battle Between Writers Frank Chin and Maxine Hong Kingston over the Soul of Asian American Literature, 1990

Last spring, a small circle of writers and scholars eagerly pored over a new book by Maxine Hong Kingston, the best-selling author of "The Woman Warrior" and "China Men."

They knew Kingston had wrestled with the manuscript for years. A few even had heard she wrote the book, in part, to defend herself against her longtime literary foe, Frank Chin, a combative writer and the first Asian-American to have his plays staged in New York.

The rumors were true, according to most people who closely follow the Asian-American literary scene.

No white critics got it. But Kingston's "Tripmaster Monkey" (Knopf), a rollicking, surrealistic novel of the '60s in Berkeley, is a *roman à clef* of the Asian-American literary world. Although Kingston denies it, most close observers of the two writers believe much of the main character, Wittman Ah Sing, is modeled after Chin.

In one of the best-kept secrets in American letters, Kingston and Chin have locked pens in a literary duel that has lasted more than a decade.

Call it a clash of writing philosophies between a proud feminist and a Chinese-American Norman Mailer. A debate over how writers of color should portray the myths of their cultures. Or, as some see it, a vendetta by a male author embittered by Kingston's success.

Since the debut of "Woman Warrior" in 1976, Chin has attacked Kingston in forum after forum, in essay after essay. He charges her writing is "white, racist art" that distorts beloved Asian myths and folk tales to fit her feminist views.

Silent on the issue for years, Kingston has spoken out in recent months. In an interview at her home in Oakland last fall, she compared Chin's views to censorship in China. "I'm afraid Frank Chin is staging his own Cultural Revolution in this country."

But at the end of her novel, she ventures a peace offering to all men: the warlike Wittman evolves into a loving pacifist.

From Edward Iwata, "Word Warriors," *Los Angeles Times*, June 24, 1990, pp. E1, E9. Copyright © 1990 the Los Angeles Times, Inc. Used with permission.

In contrast, Chin mocks Kingston in his new book of short stories. "The China-man Pacific & Frisco R. R. Co." (Coffee House Press). In one tale, Chin parodies "Woman Warrior" by writing of a woman author who changes the Joan of Arc myth by turning her into a man who is castrated and burned at the stake.

Many wish for a debate between the two authors. But Chin avoids events Kingston plans to attend. Last year, he refused to join a star-studded lecture series at UCLA that featured Kingston, novelist Amy Tan ("The Joy Luck Club"), drama-tist David Henry Hwang ("M. Butterfly") and psychologist Jean Shinoda Bolen ("Goddesses in Everywoman").

The literary dispute is more than an academic parlor game. Educators from Stanford to Yale are debating the values of non-white thought. Literature reflects a culture, defines a people. In this sense, the struggle between Chin and Kingston is a literary battle for the soul of Asian America.

"Maxine and Frank are brilliant writers," said Jeanne Wakatsuki Houston, the co-author of "Farewell to Manzanar" and a close friend of Kingston. "It's sad this has all happened."

The children of immigrants, Kingston and Chin both were born 50 years ago in the Year of the Angry Dragon. Both studied literature at UC Berkeley during the Days of Rage and plunged into the politics of the era. Both envied each other's early writings.

Chin was the first to rise to literary stardom. After he founded the Asian Amer-ican Theater Company in San Francisco, his groundbreaking plays, "Chickencoop Chinaman" and "Year of the Dragon," debuted Off Broadway in the early 1970s. Critics from the New Yorker to the Village Voice praised his theater for its power, originality and humor. The playwright raged over the fragile psyches of Asian-American men and against the Charlie Chan and Dr. Fu Man Chu stereotypes. He railed against meek minorities who swallowed the racist images of Asian males as eunuchs or yellow devils.

Novelist Ishmael Reed likens Chins to Malcolm X. "Frank forces Asian-Americans to confront their devils," said Reed, a friend. "He tells the truth."

Chin, however has written little fiction since his glory days. He teaches sporadi-cally. Many speak of him today as if he's a relic of a more militant era.

Kingston soared into the big leagues in the late 1970s. Her two award-winning memoirs, "Woman Warrior" and "China Men," put her in the world's pantheon of revered authors. Her books are taught widely in literature, women's studies, history and sociology classes. Vintage has printed more than 500,000 paperback copies of "Woman Warrior."

Feminists and many Asian Americans see Kingston as a literary pioneer who triumphed over racism and sexism. Her work is "a crucible" for Asian-American issues, said Elaine Kim, a dean in the School of Letters and Sciences at UC Berkeley. "She opened a lot of doors for us," observed author Tan.

Chin and Kingston first sparred by letter. In 1976, Kingston and her editor asked Chin to endorse her soon-to-be-published book. The book was conceived as a fiction collection, but Kingston's publisher, Knopf, felt it would sell better as an autobiogra-phy. They titled it, "The Woman Warrior: Memoirs of a Girlhood Among Ghosts."

A barrage of correspondence followed, as the two authors plunged into a debate over the moral issues unique to artists of color.

Chin wrote Kingston that her prose was moving and lyrical. But he couldn't back this book that purported to be a nonfiction account of a Chinese American. He argued that autobiographies by Asian Americans were cloying bids for white acceptance. "I want your book to be an example of yellow art by a yellow artist," he wrote, "not the publisher's manipulation of another Pocahontas."

A dismayed Kingston wrote Chin that she was "experimenting" with genres, blending the novel and memoir. "Who knows whether the stories are 'real' or not?" she explained.

Soon the literary duel turned into a full-blown cultural debate. . . .

The stormy issue always arises at conferences of Asian-American educators. Many women refuse to appear on panels with the brash Chin. Many compare the dispute to the tussle between novelists Reed and Alice Walker over the portrayal of black men in "The Color Purple."

Others say Chin is guilty of censorship. "I admire Frank's work very much," said playwright Hwang. "I also admire Yeats, but I don't admire that he embraced fascism once in his life."

"A lot of people have had sleepless nights over this one," said Steve Sumida, a literature professor at the University of Michigan and a friend of both writers. "There are so many conflicting loyalties."

In recent interviews, Kingston has insisted that Asian Americans must create their own unique mythology. She believes the tales will die if they do not change for a modern audience.

"I don't claim I'm an archivist preserving myths, writing the exact, original version," she said. "I'm writing a living myth that's changing all the time."

In Kingston's mythology, she changes Fa Mu lan, a warrior girl immortalized in a popular Chinese folk ballad, into a "female avenger" who slays an evil, women-hating baron.

The swordswoman Fa Mu Lan gains strength from vows carved onto her back. In real Chinese folklore, those vows are cut into the back of a male hero, a great general named Yue Fei.

Kingston defends her version of Fa Mu Lan, having said recently: "I changed the literal tale, but no way did I change the spirit of the myth."

In his search for a mythology for Asian Americans, Chin turned to classical Chinese literature. He found a new ethic he calls the "heroic tradition," based on outlaw bands and philosophers in works such as "Romance of the Three Kingdoms" and philosopher/general Sun Tzu's "The Art of War." Another hero of Chin's: Kwan Kung, the god of literature and war.

The outlaws showed courage, loyalty and integrity, according to Chin. That heroic moral code died when the Chinese came to America. To help revive the tradition, Chin recently published two children's books based on old Chinese tales.

Feminist scholars brush aside the heroic tradition. Kim of UC Berkeley called it "just another old boy's club." UCLA literature professor King Kok Cheung said the tradition glorifies "aggression and martial valor."

In a new anthology, "Divisive Issues in Contemporary Feminism," Cheung writes that "the stage is set for a confrontation between heroism and feminism in Chinese-American letters."

Chin contends there is a spirit of equality in the ancient tales.

"The image in romantic lore is of two warriors, a man and a woman, armed against the world," he said. "Where are the bound feet? There's more misogyny in the Bible and Greek literature than in Chinese mythology." . . .

The character many believe to be Kingston's incarnation of Chin is Wittman, a jive-talking playwright in Berkeley in the '60s. Wittman roams a fantastical landscape, crashing parties and quoting Rilke. At one point, he pole-vaults across heaven with his huge penis.

Kingston and her publisher, Knopf, say the Wittman character has nothing to do with Chin. The character is a composite that came to her vividly from her dreams and paintings, Kingston says.

In an interview last fall, Kingston spoke at length for the first time about Frank Chin. She recalled the thrill of Chin's theatrical debut in New York, and the later PBS broadcast of "Year of the Dragon."

"It was a very daring breakthrough," she said. "The music of his language was beautiful. But I almost feel like Frank's in a time warp. I would really like to see him bring his art into the '90s."

Over the years, Chin's accusations appear to have haunted Kingston, even influenced her work. According to one theory, Kingston views Chin as a literary soul mate, her male alter ego. "If I am to grow at all as a writer and a person," she wrote Chin in a 1976 letter, "I have to wrestle with an understanding about men and write about them/you."

Moreover, according to friends of the two, some of Chin's warnings in his letters to Kingston came true. When "Woman Warrior" started rising on the bestseller lists, Kingston grew troubled over the patronizing tone coming from white book reviewers. They left the impression that "Woman Warrior" was a tour guide's inside look at a strange, exotic people.

"Maxine was afraid a lot of the praise she was getting was racist praise," recalled literature professor Sumida. "You can imagine how terrible this was when she wanted to promote understanding, not confirm stereotypes. In a way, Frank Chin was right." . . .

In Chin's fictional world, his male characters fight to gain that respect, that lost childhood. They search for a "true" Asian-American manhood and history amid tourist Chinatowns and mythic Wild West landscapes.

Chin's enemies scoff at his literary scholarship. They accuse him of "Maxine-bashing." His protests, they say, only mask his envy of Kingston's success.

Chin is an easy target. His temper and intellectual arrogance have driven away all but a cadre of loyalists.

One awkward episode unfolded at the East West Players Theater in Los Angeles a few years ago. Chin was giving a reading of a new play. The young playwright Hwang, recently graduated from Stanford, wanted to meet Chin, one of his literary heroes.

After the reading, the two were introduced. But when Chin learned the stranger he was greeting was Hwang, his hand grew limp. He growled and stalked away from his stunned admirer.

Friends describe Chin as a loyal, proud, generous man. He lavishes public praise on writers he admires while never mentioning his own work.

Others call Chin a private, deeply tormented person. "Most people write for the pure pleasure of finding the truth or shaping opinions," said a close friend of Chin. "That's not why Frank writes. At some point, the anger always gets triggered."

"I've gotten angrier over the years," Chin said. "Why? Almost all the literature now is a rejection of everything Asian and an acceptance of everything white. Look at Kingston's great achievements."

The "Angry Man" persona is the key to Chin's manhood and complexity. Chin thinks each bold word of his, each righteous act, will save his Asian America from the hated stereotypes, from death by assimilation—and from Maxine Hong Kingston.

Proud beyond reason, Chin seems trapped by his persona, the thinking goes. Acknowledge or befriend Kingston. That might betray his life's work, the justification for his rage.

As for Kingston, some think she is trapped by her reputation as a feminist mother beyond reproach. Students and professors fawn over her at readings. Essays on her by feminist critics are almost worshipful. A male scholar says Kingston might tarnish her image if she publicly admitted Chin helped shape her writing. But Kingston's myths are daring, open, compassionate. She evolves as her art evolves, most literary experts agree. "I'm the modern-day incarnation of Fa Mu Lan," she said.

Nearly all agree that Chin's true myth is still in the making. Until he confronts the hatred that obscures his vision, he is still an Asian Eldridge Cleaver, whose literary cause is a violent crusade.

2. Vietnamese Americans Condemn Depictions of South Vietnam by Le Ly Hayslip and Oliver Stone, 1994

They can never forgive or forget. Nor do they want to. For a small group of expatriate Vietnamese who live in Orange County, to forgive the Communist government that chased them from their homes—leaving family, friends and neighbors dead—is to trample the memory of what once was their nation, the Republic of Vietnam.

The expatriates, who vented their anger at author Le Ly Hayslip in a surprisingly hostile demonstration Jan. 9, said that even after nearly 20 years they must speak out against anyone who supported or worked for the Vietnamese Communists, the Cong San.

"Until the Communists change their philosophy—no, until they leave our country—we can never work with them," said Chuyen Nguyen, editor and publisher

---

From Lily Dizon, "Expatriates Vent Anger at Author, Movie Portrayals," *Los Angeles Times,* January 16, 1994. Copyright © 1994 the Los Angeles Times, Inc. Used with permission.

of *Tieng Chuong* ("Sound of the Bell"), a conservative newspaper in Little Saigon. "And people who say they support normalization are traitors."

The protesters, many of whom were officers in the South Vietnamese army or former political detainees, object to the fact that Hayslip's personal saga—which includes aiding the Viet Cong—is the subject of Oliver Stone's latest movie, "Heaven and Earth."

The protesters, who belong to a variety of Vietnamese American political groups, also say they are bitter that Hayslip and Stone advocate normalization with Hanoi, a position the nationalists adamantly oppose as long as the current regime is in power.

For the last few years, they have been bucking efforts to normalize relations between the United States and Vietnam once the POW-MIA issue is resolved. So far, they said, the battle has been futile. "Politically, we have no power in our hands. At the national level, we, the Vietnamese community, have no voice," said Nguyen, whose newspaper recently printed a scathing attack on Hayslip and the movie.

"Oliver Stone and Le Ly Hayslip, they have a loud voice called filmmaking— and what did they do with that voice? They exploited us. They portrayed honorable Republican soldiers who fought for democracy as evil people," Nguyen said.

"As a movie maker, Oliver Stone used us," said Nguyen, 44. "As a Vietnamese woman, Le Ly betrayed us." The movie has, however, received at least one favorable review in the Vietnamese press and regularly plays—with a dubbed Vietnamese soundtrack—to packed houses at the Thu Do Theater on Westminster Avenue.

In the past, some ardent nationalists have protested and even threatened people who publicly support normalization. Last year, Dr. Co Pham, president of the Vietnamese Chamber of Commerce, who hosted a Vietnamese diplomat at his home, received threatening letters and phone calls.

While demonstrations outside Pham's office did not result in violence, Pham said he feared for his life. He hired a bodyguard and began wearing a bulletproof vest. The Jan. 9 demonstration against Hayslip was hostile enough that the frightened author canceled her appearance in what she said was an effort to protect her visiting mother and two sisters.

That protest, leaders said, was called because "Heaven and Earth" shamed nationalist soldiers. "I was an officer in the Army of the Republic of Vietnam," said Hau Nguyen, president of the Vietnam Political Detainees Mutual Assn., a Southern California support group which sponsors former war prisoners who want to emigrate to the United States. "I spent four years of my life in jail because I fought for what I believed in. We fought for freedom from the communists."

"And in the movie, that woman tells the world that we are bad men, that we plundered villages and killed the peasants, that we tortured innocent women," Nguyen said, his voice strained with anger and pain.

Of the dozens of people who protested Hayslip's appearance, a handful were women who said they objected to what they believe is the reinforcement of the stereotype of Asian women as prostitutes. "Even as (Hayslip) says that the movie tells of her personal story and she is not speaking for all Vietnamese women in her movie, she and Oliver Stone have promoted it as a movie 'about the Vietnamese through the eyes of a Vietnamese woman,'" said Ngoc Anh, 44, a staff writer for *Tieng Chuong*.

"What else are people watching their movie going to think?" Kim Ha, a Garden Grove author whose own published memoir detailed her escape from Vietnam, said she holds no grudge against Hayslip. "After watching the movie, I feel so sad for her because she has lost so much," said Ha, 43. "I praised her for her bravery and her honesty and her determination to overcome the obstacles in her life.

"But what makes me angry," said Ha, who is currently trying to get her auto-biography published in English, "is the fact that she was raised a Communist; her family supported communism. And her books and her movie left a bad impression about the Vietnamese woman."

Stone erred in his judgment, Ha and others said, when he used Hayslip's life story and proclaimed it a representation of Vietnamese women who suffered. "She was pro-Communist; most of us fought against them," Ha said. "She was a prostitute; most of us were not." "There were women who lost their sons, their husbands and those who nursed the wounded through the war without any recognition," Ha said. "We have all these honorable women. And who is perceived as a symbol of the beautiful Vietnamese woman but an illiterate country woman who spied for the Viet Cong and prostituted herself with the American soldiers?"

The expatriates are enraged that instead of repudiating her political past, Hayslip, with Stone's support, advocates normalization with the current government in Viet-nam. The protesters said they believe that Hayslip's East Meets West Foundation is a front organization that attempts to aid the Vietnamese government economically. They claimed Hayslip is using the nonprofit organization to make money for herself.

Because of the divergent views on the normalization debate, the nationalists said they will never let up on their fight against Hayslip, Stone, or anyone who advocates a relationship with the current regime in Vietnam.

"There are things in life that could change," said Chuyen Nguyen. "On this issue, there is no compromise. . . ." Hau Nguyen added: "I will never trust anyone who has been in touch with the Communists."

3. Asian American Hip-Hop and Rap Artists Gain Recognition (1990s), 1998

It's been a long time coming, but Asian American hip-hop is finally breaking across the horizon. Asian American youths have long been a vital part of the hip-hop culture, a youthful style and music that defies easy categorization—as fans (hip-hoppers), breakdancers (B-boys), DJs (turntablists), writers (graffiti artists) and MCs (rappers). But their contributions have long gone unrecognized by many who perceived the music and culture in monochrome black and white.

Asian American performers began emerging in the early 1990s, especially at college and community events. Politically-charged Asian American rap groups like the Asiatic Apostles (Davis, Calif.), Yellow Peril (New Jersey), and the Seoul Brothers (Seattle) started making small waves; while in the Bay Area and Los Angeles, squads of mostly Filipino American DJs and dancers were gaining notoriety. . . .

From Oliver Wang, "Asian Americans and Hip-Hop," *Asianweek*, November 12–18, 1998. Copyright © 1998 AsianWeek. Used by permission.

An L.A.-transplant who now calls home the heavily Asian American neighborhood of Flushing, Queens, Jamez (James Chang) reflects the growing international identity of hip-hop evident in his recently-released full-length album Z-Bonics, which showcases his unique fusion of Korean music with hip-hop aesthetics.

Dubbing his efforts as part of an "Azian/Pacific Renaissance," Jamez rhymes from a conscious perspective, seeing hip-hop as a fundamental means of communicating across generations and cultures. Not unlike the nascent Asian American rappers of the early '90s, Jamez wields hip-hop as a tool for social and political empowerment, embedding his songs with social commentary rarely found in today's parties-and-pistols monotony. Songs like "Day in the Life" and "7-Train" root themselves in the realities of class and race that arise in daily urban life.

Jamez's most unique contribution is his fusion of traditional Korean musical practices, like Poongmul drumming, with beats to create a style of hip-hop that he hopes will educate Korean American youths about their heritage. "So many of us are influenced by Western standards of beauty, speech and music. I want to expose Asian Americans to their rich legacy of music. Our beat of life," Jamez says.

In recognizing hip-hop as a growing universal language among American youths of all cultures, Jamez uses his music as a way of creating new identities for young Asian Americans.

Q-Bert (Robert Quitevis) is perhaps the most recognized and respected Asian American rap artist to date. But he's not a rapper—the only speaking he does is with his hands as a pioneer in the DJ-derived art form known as turntablism, a method of scratching vinyl that produces a completely new sound. Taking "skratching" to a new artistic level, DJ Q-Bert, and scores of other Filipino American DJs up and down the West Coast have revolutionized turntablism and are among the newly emerging aesthetic's main shapers.

Turntablism involves a range of practices—from unbelievable sound manipulation through hand-play alone, to extensive hunting for quirky samples to scratch and cut up, to amazing feats of team performance that reaches orchestral magnitude.

After a long wait, DJ Q-Bert has finally released his solo debut CD, Wave Twisters—the title is a play on how DJs twist soundwaves with precision wrist-action. Despite the relatively primitive equipment—turntables and mixers that haven't changed basic technological principles in more than 20 years—DJs like Q-Bert are on the cutting edge of future music.

Wave Twisters might sound chaotic at the first listen, especially for untrained ears, but as each layer of sonic fabric is gradually peeled away, musical compositions of intricate complexity and inspired creativity emerge. The album is a manifestation of Q-Bert's own designs on the future of music. "Instead of just playing guitars and horns, there's more into it, because there's more sounds you can use with turntables. There's a whole universe that's yet to be discovered with turntables."

An often unspoken question centers on race and ethnicity. Traditionally, hip-hop culture has seen strictly through the black-white lens of American race relations—the presumption being that blacks innovate and whites imitate. The inclusion of Latino performers, and now Asian American artists in that community serves to complicate matters.

Yet it also points to the amazing multicultural and international appeal of hip-hop to youths of various ethnic groups. Most Asian American artists are quick to acknowledge that hip-hop stems from an African American tradition. At the same time, they also believe that they are contributing to hip-hop's expansion and evolution in ways that don't exploit or betray the heritage or spirit of the movement.

The relation these artists have to the larger Asian American community is also complicated. Q-Bert, for example, headlined at the 1997 San Francisco Asian American Jazz Festival, but he rarely talks about his ethnicity—or its relation to his artistry—in interviews. In some ways, calling his crew the Invisibl Skratch Piklz has some unintended irony since the fact that most of the Piklzes are Filipino American is rarely mentioned at all—either by themselves or press coverage.

Especially as so-called "electronica" expands into the mainstream pop world, turntablists are ensuring that their contributions remain heard. While Asian American rappers still face an uphill battle among skeptical label execs and audiences, Asian American DJs have made their mark and are now accepted as unquestioned pioneers who are sure to be a continuing force as turntablism evolves.

On the other side of the spectrum, Jamez's work comes out of a desire to incorporate a Korean American identity into hip-hop aesthetics. While he doesn't want to limit his audience to just Korean American youths, his concepts of an Azian/Pacific Renaissance and "Azian" hip-hop are explicit reflections of his artistic and political perspectives. Perhaps unintentionally, Jamez continues a tradition of music "made for, by and about" Asian Americans that pioneering folk-jazz groups like A Grain of Sand and Hiroshima began more than 20 years ago.

4. The Association of Asian American Studies Rescinds a Fiction Award to Lois-Ann Yamanaka Because of Her Portrayals of Filipino Americans in Hawai'i, 1998

Fiction writer Lois-Ann Yamanaka, known for her raw depictions of life in working-class Hawaii, now finds herself the main character in a real-life saga: the story of how her latest novel touched off an uprising that ended up upending the nation's premier group of Asian American professors.

It begins with the debut of Yamanaka's third novel, *Blu's Hanging,* a brutally frank portrayal of three Japanese American children on the island of Molokai as they struggle with their mother's death. Soon after hitting the shelves, the book and its author were enveloped in a verbal fusillade of caustic e-mail and bitter editorials. Critics called Yamanaka, a 36-year-old Japanese American, a racist and her book a divisive diatribe that reinforced stereotypes of Filipino Americans as sexual deviants. Her supporters defended her right to free expression and pointed out that other ethnicities, particularly Japanese Americans, didn't look good in the book, either.

This summer, the controversy reached a climax at the Association of Asian American Studies' annual convention in Hawaii. One day after the group gave its fiction award to Yamanaka, a member revolt forced it to rescind the honor. All but one of the board members then quit, leaving the organization in limbo and re-examining its own tenets.

Here's what the author herself had to say about the bitter saga and its impact on her own life:

How has the recent controversy around the award affected you personally?

I felt like the rug was being pulled out from under me every day. I understand the nature of what I do as a writer and that it involves criticism—literary criticism is part of the game. I understand that. Instead, what made me upset was when it started getting personal and people were directly calling me a racist. I tried not to get upset about it, but at some point I was like "Whoa!" I just wanted to go home to Hilo and be around my family and friends. . . . It's been a real rough time. . . .

When you were writing Blu's Hanging *and creating the characters, such as Uncle Paulo, did you predict that they would generate this kind of controversy?*

Nooooo. But trying to understand where all this is coming from, I've really searched myself, asked myself "What am I doing? How am I doing it?" But I know my heart's intention and I know that I didn't write anything with the intent to hurt or harm; I was intent on telling the story the way it wanted to be told . . . and there's no real way that I can convince someone who's so set that I did this to hurt people that it's not the way it was.

This whole controversy seems to have called into question the responsibility of a writer, especially an ethnic writer, to his or her community. How do you feel about this?

These critics want me to be the spokesperson for everybody, to speak for all ethnic groups and to do it fairly. I don't think that's my job. I don't think that I was born or called upon to do that. Maybe there's a young writer out there that's been called to do what they're asking me to do. I just hope that whoever this writer is has not been scared into fear because of what happened to me, you know? Because if this happened when I first started writing, I would have been scared shitless.

A lot of teachers and professors have spoken about Filipino students who have read your book and have been very upset. What would you say to these students?

I would tell them that they were reacting, which is perfectly fine because literature should provoke a reaction. . . . Now they've got to act on [that reaction]. It's one thing to protest an award . . . but there's another thing that requires a lot more courage, and that is to go into your room and tell your grandfather's story or your mother's story or your own story. That's where the power is. It's not in group-think.

5. Silent Protest Against a Fiction Award Presented to Lois-Ann Yamanaka by the Association for Asian American Studies, 1998

Members of the Filipino American Studies Caucus and the Anti-Racism Coalition protest the presentation of the Fiction Award to Lois-Ann Yamanaka's novel *Blu's Hanging* at the 1998 Association for Asian American Studies Conference.

6. A New York City Parade Celebrates India's Independence, 2000

H. R. Shah, the president of the Federation of Indian Organizations (FIO), and his teammates are to be proudly parading down Madison Avenue on Aug. 20 to celebrate India's independence from British rule on Aug. 15, 1947, and to showcase our cultural heritage and our contributions to the adopted land.

They are to be surrounded by an elite collection of local elected officials, aspiring politicians and Indian movie stars. They are expected to be cheered by the tens of thousands of screaming compatriots, a far cry from the space assemplage on the first parade in 1981, organized by Suresh Singh and other FIA (sic) officials when our community here was still in infancy.

A predecessor to the parade was an annual India Festival in Central Park, organized by Prof. Paramatama Saran, his brother Dharmatama Saran, Ashoke Varma and others. The honored guest at the first festival on May 19, 1974 was the New York

Photograph by Mary Uyematsu Kao; reprinted in *Amerasia Journal* 26, no. 2 (2000): 158. © 1998, Mary Uyematsu Kao.

From Mohan Jethwani, "City's India Day Parade Tradition," *India in New York* 4, no. 7 (August 18, 2000). Excerpted with permission from India Abroad Publications.

Philharmonic conductor, Zubin Mehta. I had the privilege of representing the mayor and delivering his speech, which ended with *"Hamara Shahar up aap ka bhi shahar hai/Aayeeye iska jhunda hum subh fakhar say bulund karen."* (This city of ours is also your city now, let's together unfurl its flag with pride).

The first India Day to be proclaimed by the mayor on the steps of City Hall, followed by a reception in the Blue Room, was held on Aug. 14, 1974. The mayoral proclamation read:

> The City of New York in recognition of the great cultural contributions of Indian-Americans dedicates this day in their honor. Our city's ever-growing Indian-American community participates fully in every aspect of New York life. Our own mingled ethnic heritage has been significantly enriched by the influence of Indian traditions in music, art, literature and cuisine.
>
> Throughout our city, New Yorkers delight in the multitude of Indian-inspired establishments which reflect our great respect for the Indian nation and Indian people who have come here to live. Now, therefore, I, Abraham D. Became, Mayor of the City of New York, do hereby proclaim Aug. 14, 1974, as "India Independence Day" in New York City, and call upon all New Yorkers to join in celebrating this significant occasion.

In 1979, during Mayor Edward Koch's administration, we tried for the "Little India" designation for the area bounded by 27th and 30th Stress from Lexington to Fifth Avenues in Manhattan. Vijay Bhatt, the original owner of the Shalimar restaurant on East 29th Street, organized the Little India Merchants Association. Koch's staff members, especially his senior aide Herb Rickman (and the council majority leader, the late Thomas Cuite) were receptive, but some members of the local community were against it.

In her letter to the mayor, Gertrude Huston, president of the Rose Hill Neighborhood Association, wrote, "We object to this area being proclaimed or designated 'Little India' for may reasons. We do not want be a part of a newly created ghetto."

Although we did not get the permanent designation, Manhattan Community Board No. 5, then chaired by Daniel Biederman, agreed that a "special recognition of this community was in order." In November 1979, the board passed a resolution, by a vote of 35 to 1, for an annual "Little India Day" or "Little India Day Week" mayoral proclamation. But soon thereafter Jackson Heights, resembling more a bustling Bombay Bazaar than a small enclave in Manhattan, began to ascertain its claim to the Little India designation. . . .

The parade not only celebrates our heritage and accomplishments, but also honors all our past endeavors and sacrifices.

7. The Media Action Network for Asian Americans Condemns Hollywood Stereotypes, 2000

Asian cultures as inherently predatory.   For decades, Americans have viewed Asian immigrants as "taking" from this country without giving anything back. This perception was reinforced by early laws making it difficult for Asians to immigrate and impossible for them to become naturalized citizens. Although these laws have

---

From Media Action Network for Asian Americans, "A Memo from MANAA to Hollywood: Asian Stereotypes," April 3, 2000; reprinted at http://janet.org/~manaa/a_stereotypes.html.

since been repealed, the image of the Asian as alien predator still infuses popular media. In the movie "Falling Down," for example, the white main character accuses a Korean grocer of draining American resources without bothering to fit into American society. This accusation "justifies" the lead character's destruction of the Korean's grocery store. Similarly, the movie "Rising Sun" portrays Japanese businessmen taking over American industry by murder and deceit. And countless movies and TV episodes have portrayed Chinatowns as breeding grounds of crime.

Stereotype-Buster: **Asians as positive contributors to American society.**

Asian Americans restricted to clichéd occupations.   Asians and Asian Americans make their living in a wide array of professions, but too often, Asian American professionals are depicted in a limited and predictable range of jobs: restaurant workers, Korean grocers, Japanese businessmen, Indian cab drivers, TV anchorwomen, martial artists, gangsters, faith healers, laundry workers, and prostitutes. This misrepresents the diversity of the Asian American work force.

Stereotype-Buster: **Asian Americans in diverse, mainstream occupations: doctors, lawyers, therapists, educators, U.S. soldiers, etc.**

Asian racial features, names, accents, or mannerisms as inherently comic or sinister.   Because distinctive Asian characteristics are less common in the United States, movies and TV shows often fall back on them for quick and easy gags or gasps. For example, the thick accent of the goofy Chinese exchange student in "Sixteen Candles"—who is given the sophomoric name "Long Duk Dong"—is used for cheap laughs, while the numerous Fu Manchu movies have presented the Asian character's culturally distinctive speech and appearance as emblems of unfathomable evil.

Stereotype-Buster: **Asian names or racial features as no more "unusual" than those of white.**

Asians relegated to supporting roles in projects with Asian or Asian American content.   Usually, when a project features Asian subject matter, the main character will still be white. "The Killing Fields" and "Seven Years in Tibet" are only two efforts that follow this "rule." But the most infamous example is the internment-camp movie "Come See the Paradise" (a box-office flop), which misleadingly focused on a white protagonist and pushed its more interesting Japanese American characters into the background of their own history. However, the success of "Gandhi," "The Last Emperor," and "The Joy Luck Club" proves that mainstream audiences will pay to see Asian and Asian American lead characters. Using Asian American protagonists can even create more interesting and uncommon story ideas.

Stereotype-Buster: **More Asian and Asian American lead roles.**

Asian male sexuality as negative or non-existent.   Although Asian women are frequently portrayed as positive romantic partners for white men ("Sayonara," "The World of Suzie Wong," ad infinitum), Asian men are almost never positively paired with women of *any* race. Western society still seems to view Asian male sexuality as a problem. Consequently, Asian men are usually presented either as threatening corrupters of white women or as eunuchs lacking any romantic feelings. For example, in the action movie "Showdown in Little Tokyo," the Asian villain forces himself upon a white woman and murders her before threatening the Asian female love interest. Predictably, the white hero kills the Asian villain and "wins" the Asian woman—while the hero's Amerasian sidekick is given no love life at all.

Stereotype-Buster: **More Asian men as positive romantic leads.**

Unmotivated white-Asian romance.   In "Daughter of the Dragon," the daughter of Fu Manchu lays her eyes on a British detective and instantly falls in love with him. "The Bounty" and "Come See the Paradise" also contain scenes where an Asian woman falls in love with a white man at first sight. The repetition of this conceit sends the signal that Asian women are romantically attracted to white men *because they are white.* It insinuates that whiteness is inherently more important than any other romantic quality and inherently more appealing than any other skin color.

Stereotype-Buster: **Interracial romances should be as well-motivated and well-developed as same-race romances.**

Asian women as "China dolls."   Asian women are often portrayed as ex-otic, subservient, compliant, industrious, eager to please. While nicknamed the "China doll," "geisha girl," or "lotus blossom," this sexually loaded stereotype isn't restricted to Chinese or Japanese women. This portrayal is epitomized by the self-effacing title character of the opera "Madame Butterfly," but it can also be seen in works like "Teahouse of the August Moon" and "Tai-Pan."

Stereotype-Buster: **Asian women as self-confident and self-respecting, pleasing themselves as well as their loved ones.**

Asian women as "dragon ladies."   Another major female stereotype views Asian women as inherently scheming, untrustworthy, and back-stabbing. This por-trayal is nicknamed the "dragon lady," after the Asian villainess in the vintage comic strip "Terry and the Pirates." Other examples of the stereotype are the daughter of Fu Manchu (in numerous books and movies) and the gangsters' molls in "The Year of the Dragon."

Stereotype-Buster: **Whenever villains are Asian, it's important that their villainy not be attributed to their ethnicity.**

8. Hollywood Recruits Asian Stars from the Hong Kong Cinema Industry, 2001

Is Hollywood actually capable of saying sorry? It seems unlikely, but saying sorry to the Chinese for the sorry treatment of Oriental actors over the years would seem to be a good idea right now.

Following the unprecedented success of *Crouching Tiger, Hidden Dragon,* American producers have signed up a host of Asian stars aiming to introduce them to multiplexes around the world. There's *Rush Hour 2,* a couple of big-budget Jet Li movies and a number of intriguing Chow Yun-Fat projects. Meanwhile, Columbia Pictures Film Production Asia, the people who made *Crouching Tiger,* are working on four Chinese-set US-backed movies, with Donald Sutherland in Beijing shooting the comedy, *Big Shot's Funeral,* directed by Feng Xiaogang, with Hong Kong star Tony Leung (*In the Mood for Love*) playing a Taiwanese detective in the thriller, *Double Vision.* The Chinese (whether Hong Kong, Taiwanese, mainland or home-grown) presence in the US movie industry has never been more substantial.

Which is why it might be wise for Hollywood to repent about how Charlie Chan was played by men with names like Sidney Toler and Warner Oland, apologise for the old yellow-peril movies and most of all, the day David Carradine was chosen over Bruce Lee to star in the TV series *Kung Fu.* The time has come to say sorry that Nancy Kwan, who became a star in the 1960's *The World of Suzie Wong,* ran out of decent parts so quickly.

And Hollywood could find a word or two of regret about the attitudes that made silent star Anna May Wong leave town in 1928, announcing: "I was tired of the parts I had to play. Why is it that on the screen the Chinese are nearly always the villain of the piece, and so cruel a villain—murderous, treacherous, a snake in the grass? We are not like that. How could we be, with a civilization so many times older than that of the West? We have our rigid code of behaviour, of honour. Why do they never show those on the screen?"

The movie industry is not going to apologise for the sake of its conscience, of course. It is just that, as with the Latin American craze in recent years, it is clear there is money to be made from the domestic Asian-American market, and much more from the huge south-east Asian market.

Making movies that play on both sides of the Pacific is the purpose behind Columbia Pictures Film Production Asia. But *Crouching Tiger, Hidden Dragon* was the climax to a long, slow struggle, mainly by veterans of the Hong Kong movie industry. Thirty years ago, San Francisco-born, University of Washington–educated Bruce Lee had to leave LA and go to Hong Kong to become a film star. Only now is the reverse trip becoming more frequent. The youngest member of the *Crouching Tiger* cast, Zhang Ziyi, has been snapped up to play a villain in *Rush Hour 2.* And because her English isn't up to much, her part will be subtitled. Times have changed.

The advance, though, has been glacier-like at times. It is only since 1998's *Rush Hour* that Jackie Chan, who, for two decades, had been a megastar not only across south-east Asia, but in India, and much of the rest of the world, finally cracked the big time in the US. Li, the other leading martial-arts star, has moved faster, having gone from villain in his first US movie (*Lethal Weapon 4*) to romantic lead in his second (*Romeo Must Die*).

"Jet Li got a deal with Warner Bros because women in test audiences loved him in Lethal Weapon 4," according to producer Chris Lee. "You'll definitely be seeing more of the Asian male as romantic hero, instead of just gun-wielding villain or sexless geek." . . .

When Hong Kong's most famous director, John Woo, arrived in Hollywood, he didn't bring his stars with him, choosing instead to establish himself by working with John Travolta and Tom Cruise. Those who have made it to the US have found that working habits are different too. Until recently, many Hong Kong films were shot silently, so that both Mandarin and Cantonese dialogue could be dubbed on afterwards. The films are made quickly there; stars can make up to 12 a year. And despite the century and a half of British colonial rule, many Hong Kong stars, including Chan, when he first arrived in the US, don't speak much English. Add up those factors and you can see why some suggest the chief beneficiaries of the Asian awakening will be US-born actors like Lucy Liu. . . .

It might not last, but right now, the *Crouching Tiger* effect is very strong. "For me, it was a long time coming and it was just so thrilling every time they announced a Chinese name and pronounced it right," said *ER*'s Ming-Na on Oscar night.

Even when the frenzy subsides, there will will be no going back to the days of the Warner Bros memo re *Kung Fu,* which read: "The American public won't sit for a Chinaman appearing in their living-rooms every week."

✪ E S S A Y S

The following three essays provide a variety of perspectives on possible links between Asian American cultural productions, histories, communities, and identities. The first essay, by Candace Fujikane, professor of English at the University of Hawai'i, examines arguments about race and censorship advanced during debates about Lois-Ann Yamanaka's novel *Blu's Hanging,* interethnic relations in Hawai'i, and the role of the Association of Asian American Studies. In the second essay, Sandhya Shukla, an anthropologist at Columbia University, analyzes the origins and impact of the creation of "entrepreneurial communities" and diasporic newspapers by Indian immigrants in New York. The third essay, by Peter Feng, professor of English and women's studies at the University of Delaware, poses provocative questions about the prospects for defining "Asian American cinema" given the diversity of cultures within Asia and identities in America.

Racism, Censorship, and Lois-Ann Yamanaka's *Blu's Hanging*

CANDACE FUJIKANE

The 1998 controversy over the selection of Lois-Ann Yamanaka's novel *Blu's Hanging* for the Association for Asian American Studies (AAAS) Fiction Award . . . took on phenomenal proportions in large part due to already existing local Filipino community concerns in Hawai'i over Yamanaka's representation of Filipino men as sexual predators in her 1993 collection of poetic novellas, *Saturday Night at the Pahala Theatre.* For over ninety years, Filipino communities in Hawai'i have faced discrimination and racial profiling based on stereotypes of Filipino sexual violence, and the persistence of these stereotypes attests to continuing local Filipino subordination within a system of local Japanese and white structural power. Despite letters of protest that poured in to the AAAS Board by Filipinos and their supporters in Hawai'i and across the continent, the three Chinese American members of the

From Candace Fujikane, "Sweeping Racism Under the Rug of 'Censorship': The Controversy over Lois-Ann Yamanaka's *Blu's Hanging,*" *Amerasia Journal* 26, no. 2 (2000). Copyright © 2000 Regents of the University of California. Used with permission.

Fiction Award Committee presented the award to Yamanaka for her novel *Blu's Hanging* at the 1998 AAAS national conference in Honolulu. After much discussion and debate, the membership voted to rescind the award presented by the Award Committee.

The revocation of the award was immediately seized by the local and national media and renarrated as a story of "censorship." The cover story of censorship, in fact, enabled another story, the story of local Japanese racism and political dominance in Hawai'i, to "slink out of sight." This racism disappeared in discussions of the controversy through the abstraction of the censorship argument away from material conditions and structures of domination. Public outcry against censorship has historically been a much more popular national headline in the United States than protests against racism have ever been in a "liberal democracy" that denies the presence of racism: the censorship story offers the possibility of an imaginary resolution to material inequalities through the language of rights and equality for all under the First Amendment, while an examination of racism exposes the very inequalities that the rhetoric of egalitarianism covers over. Although local Filipino and Filipino American protests against the AAAS Fiction Award did not involve the state's regulation of artistic expression or the banning, boycotting or burning of books, those who used the censorship arguments immediately collapsed the irreducible structural differences between state-enforced censorship and the anti-racism protests of a subordinated minority group. In this way, the irony of the "censorship" argument is that it was used in turn to silence a minority group exercising its First Amendment rights by speaking out about racism.

If the media's focus on the story of "censorship" rather than on the issue of racism is consistent with the state's denial of racial inequalities, the censorship argument was also used by Asian Americans who denied structural inequalities among Asian American ethnic groups on the continent. Those who used the censorship arguments often compared the controversy over *Blu's Hanging* to literary debates over questions of representation in Maxine Hong Kingston's *The Woman Warrior* and Jessica Hagedorn's *Dogeaters*. Such comparisons tell us much about a fundamental problem that occurs when "Asian American" is homogenized as a category of identity. Criticisms of Kingston's and Hagedorn's representations of their own ethnic communities arose within those communities; at issue in the *Blu's Hanging* controversy are local Filipino protests against a local Japanese writer's history and pattern of representing local Filipino sexual violence in the context of local Japanese structural power. Many Asian Americans not only conflated conflicts within an ethnic group and conflicts between ethnic groups, but their assumption that the constituency at stake was a homogenous "Asian American" one presented a pretext of a unitary "Asian American" community joined in shared struggle while obscuring the text of local Filipino protests against local Japanese racism and protecting the text of local Japanese structural dominance in Hawai'i. . . .

The erasure of systemic local Japanese racism in the *Blu's Hanging* controversy was performed through a language of rights and freedoms that attempted to foreclose a discussion of racism. Such arguments protecting "artistic freedom" assert that fiction is free from and unfettered by any connections to the material conditions of our lives, thereby rendering the realm of fiction exempt from any charges of racism. It is precisely, however, *Blu's Hanging*'s status as fiction that allows it to perform the work of ideology. As Asian American writers and critics have shown, fictional representations of Charlie Chan, Fu Manchu, and Madama Butterfly/Miss Saigon do have discriminatory effects on Asian Americans. In their critiques of the ideological and discursive nature of fiction, these writers and critics illustrate that fictional representations circulate through and beyond any attempts to cordon literature off from our everyday lives. . . .

Critics of *Blu's Hanging* do not argue that the novel represents all Filipino Americans, but, like other critics of popular, stereotypical images of Asian Americans, we raise questions about systems of power that enable and endorse particular articulations of racism. . . .

In their own accounts, local Filipino students describe both the phantasmatic effects that literature has on our social and political imaginations and the ways that literature can exacerbate discriminatory conditions that Filipinos in Hawai'i face. Christine Takahashi Quemuel, a teaching assistant in the UH (University of Hawai'i) Ethnic Studies Department, explains,

> I've talked to local Filipino male students in my class, and they say that this book makes them feel like every time they walk down the street, there are people who shrink away from them because they're thinking, "Oh, there goes another Filipino, going home to rape his nieces." That's how this book makes them feel. They already feel disempowered, and the book disempowers them even more. They are afraid to say what they feel because they are not literature majors, and they feel even further disempowered.

This is not the oversimplified situation the media have described whereby local Filipinos are mistaking fiction for reality. Although many readers will not automatically assume local Filipino men to be rapists, many others find that the novel affirms historically entrenched ideologies that criminalize Filipinos. These local Filipino students' fears were confirmed by students and others in Hawai'i who argued during the controversy that "Filipinos really are like that." Readers have even cited Hawai'i rape statistics to prove the "truth" of Yamanaka's portrayal of Uncle Paulo despite the fact that rape and incest occur in *all* ethnic communities. These assertions point to the structural racism that renders some "truths" more visible than others as a matter of power, a problem of visibility to which I will return.

Uncle Paulo's character is not a free-floating product of Yamanaka's imagination. His character emerged out of a context of long-standing and deeply-rooted racist fears of Filipino sexual violence, much like racist stereotypes on the continent of African American sexual violence. Linda Revilla, a fiction writer and a developmental psychologist who teaches courses in the UH Ethnic Studies Department, explains that "This is how it has been for 90 years for Filipinos in Hawai'i. . . . What Yamanaka is doing is nothing new." Revilla quotes a UH student who writes:

> Throughout my days at elementary school . . . Filipinos were labeled as being stupid, backwards, and capable of only the most menial jobs available. . . . In my own experiences I knew that these generalizations were false, but still I feared association with them. These images and stereotypes persisted in the consciousness of the student body for so long that I began to look at being Filipino as a curse. It embarrassed me that I should be a part of a race so disregarded and dehumanized by society.

Revilla further explains that these conditions span two generations for this student, who describes how her experiences mirror those of her own father decades earlier.

Revilla writes, "every semester that I teach a course on Filipinos in Hawai'i, the majority of student essays that I read say the same thing: 'I denied being Filipino.' 'I grew up ashamed of being Filipino.'"

Darlene Rodrigues, a third-generation local Filipina poet, summarizes the problems regarding the novel's reification of essentialist categories of ethnicity and race:

> [Yamanaka] shows us that poverty-stricken local Japanese have strength and courage, that they are full of humanity and resilience. Filipino characters in her works, however, are not allowed the full spectrum of humanity found in the likes of her Japanese characters, Ivah, Blu, and Maisie. There is a difference between a writer showing us how an adolescent narrator can only perceive Filipinos from her own narrow point of view, and a writer creating Filipino characters whose actions confirm the stereotypes. A community such as the Filipino one in Hawai'i is diverse in history, people, and even its languages. . . . The community that I know and am a part of, however, is nowhere to be found in *Blu's Hanging*. This is not just a case of "gone missing"; it's one of complete erasure of the diversity and richness of Filipino communities.

We can ask what is seen and not seen in the telling of these events, how the glossing over of particularities enables some stories to be visible so that others may disappear, how dominant groups benefit from the visibility of some stories and the invisibility of others. The disappearance of contextual specificities and the glossing over of textual problems in *Blu's Hanging* can be traced in a form letter originally written by a Japanese American writer supporting Yamanaka that was later sent to the AAAS Board by eighty-two writers. The form letter states:

> 1) I wish to protest the AAAS Board's decision in 1997 to ignore the choice of its 1997 literary awards committee to give a book award to Lois-Ann Yamanka [sic] for *Wild Meat and the Bully Burgers*. I also urge the Board to recognize the decision of its literary awards committee to give a book award to Yamanaka's *Blu's Hanging* in 1998.
>
> 2) I am concerned too with a reading of Yamanaka's work which ignores or misreads the way a fictional character or narrator functions in a literary work.
>
> 3) I also wish to reaffirm that writers often must, by the nature of their enterprise, upset and question prevailing views, evoke extreme and visceral reactions, and write in ways where ambiguity and complexity take precedence over "political correctness" or safe and comforting portraits of the world, our community, or the individuals who reside there.
>
> 4) I am also concerned with the way the AAAS has sometimes seemed to organize "witch hunts" against various writers. This is not to say that writers should be immune from criticism. Indeed, criticism is a necessary part of the creation of a literary culture. Perhaps, though, it might be helpful for people to look into the mechanism and psychological reasons why those within a community wish to tear someone from the community apart once they have become successful. Rather than encouraging literary variety and creativity and recognizing the difficulty of the tasks which writers and other artists perform, the AAAS seems at times to have been attempting to invoke comformity [sic] and silence.

The first literary argument raised in the form letter centers on the unreliability of the narrator. . . .

Uncle Paulo's sexual violence, however, consists of irreducible acts that anchor the text. Ivah tells us what she sees of Uncle Paulo's actions, not what she imagines, and other characters corroborate her narrative account. . . . The entire Ogata family is traumatized when Uncle Paulo rapes Blu, and that scene serves as a pivotal moment in the novel that reaffirms Ivah's decision to leave home with the conviction that she is providing a way out of their oppressive situation for Blu and Maisie. Leonard Andaya, a professor of history at the University of Hawai'i, comments on the problems posed by such fictional representations: "Growing up on a sugar plantation camp in Spreckelsville, Maui, I absorbed the stereotype of Filipinos as sexually depraved, but my feeling was that those were not the actual things that happened in the camps. *Blu's Hanging,* however, carries out those stereotypical perceptions into 'reality' by having characters perform stereotypical acts." . . .

Criticisms of racist representations in *Blu's Hanging* go beyond a desire for "positive role models" by demanding that we ask hard questions about the persistence of some representations and the absence of others. . . . The elusive text is indeed one of local Japanese ascendancy to political power after the 1954 Democratic Party "Revolution." Such political power enabled local Japanese to exert greater control over the narration of history, and the stereotypes of sexually predatory Filipino men, like stereotypes of African American men, persist and have been compulsively repeated historically to secure systems of power based on racialized differences. The stereotypes originated on the plantations where Filipino bachelors were regarded as sexual threats, but the cover story of the stereotype depends upon the disappearance of other stories. The stereotypes redirect attention away from other ethnic communities' anxieties over women's agency and conditions of exploitation: women from Japanese, Chinese, and other ethnic camps married Filipino men while other women were prostituted by men from their own communities in Filipino bachelor camps. That accounts of actual Filipino wife-stealing have been popularized more widely than corresponding accounts of Japanese wife-stealing testifies to the ways that history is renarrated to sustain the interests of dominant groups. . . .

. . . Readers have argued that the value of *Blu's Hanging* lies in its provocation of a critical discussion of racism in Hawai'i, but as I have argued, the novel actually reinscribes existing conditions of racism: the discussion of racism was a result of the *critical intervention* of local Filipinos and Filipino Americans who challenged the novel's racist representations. Bennette Evangelista's article in the local Filipino newspaper, *The Fil-Am Courier,* raised community concerns that were later discussed in the local Japanese newspaper *The Hawaii Herald,* as well as in the free alternative paper, the *Honolulu Weekly.* As Evangelista laid the groundwork in Hawai'i for community discussions of Yamanaka's work, local Filipino and Filipino American students, university professors and writers worked within the AAAS to open up a space for a discussion of the novel. Jonathan Okamura, a member of the Anti-Racism Coalition, explains that "The reason the resolution to revoke the award was approved was primarily due to the initiative and commitment of the Filipino American graduate students. They organized and led our planning meetings prior to the vote on the resolution, drafted the resolution itself, spoke courageously at the open forums on the issue, and recruited student and faculty supporters from other Asian American groups. . . .

. . . August Espiritu argues . . . that the censorship arguments were made by misrepresenting the history of anti-racism critiques directed at Yamanaka's work:

> The framing of the issue on the basis of freedom of speech or censorship is based on a deliberate obfuscating of the meaning of censorship and a misrepresentation of the goals of the protest . . . no one among the Filipino American Studies Caucus or Anti-Racism

Coalition ever called for the "suppression" or "deletion" of the book or any of its parts. Nor did we ever call for the banning of the book, advocate any boycott, or prevent anyone from reading or purchasing the book. Thus, to use the word censorship against the protesters is not only inaccurate but irresponsible and is a conscious misrepresentation of the goals of the protest. In fact, over and over again, in letters, one-to-one discussions, as well as in public pronouncements, members of the protest enjoined everyone to read the book, buy it, or check it out from the library, and discuss it.

The term "censorship," like the term "political correctness," was used to foreclose a meaningful discussion of racism and literature. Unlike censorship, which is used by the state to arrest production of a work of art and to hide it from view, a minority community critical of *Blu's Hanging* upheld the principles of freedom of speech by calling for readers to read the novel and to participate in an informed discussion of it. . . .

. . . Since the anti-racism protests against the AAAS Award presented to *Blu's Hanging* was not about state-enforced censorship, it was precisely the absence of the state that led to a series of uneasy substitutions orchestrated to evoke the *specter* of the state. . . . By portraying the AAAS and its members as a dominant power and yet simultaneously framing the organization by its marginality, these articles reinforce the threat of Asian American Studies while at the same time dismissing its importance." The media's ambivalence toward Asian American Studies stems from the way many wanted to see it as emblematic of the "repressive" state at the same time that it cannot help but evoke a history of racial inequalities that, as I have argued, has never been a popular national headline.

Through sleights of writing and rhetoric, the anti-racism nature of the protests had to be contained and made to "disappear" in order to make the "liberal" state the champion of freedom of speech while evoking the shadow of the "repressive" state as the agent of censorship. The compulsion to represent the controversy in the light of state-enforced censorship became even clearer when Yamanaka was compared to writers persecuted during the Cultural Revolution, to Salman Rushdie, and to the victims of Mc-Carthyite witch hunts. Local Filipino and Filipino American activists were displaced by groups who represent institutional power within Asian American Studies: the AAAS or "politically correct academics" at universities or those from dominant ethnic groups in the AAAS, namely local Japanese and Japanese Americans. It then became easier to compare these groups—however marginalized they continue to be on the continent in relation to the state—to conservative representatives of a repressive state: the Red Guard, the Ayatollah, McCarthy, Dan Quayle and Newt Gingrich. . . .

. . . Letters of protest against the AAAS Award sent to the AAAS Board and reprinted in Hawai'i in *The Fil-Am Courier* raise questions for Asian Americans on the continent about the dominance of East Asian American scholarship in Asian American Studies. Elizabeth Pisares, then an English graduate student at UC Berkeley, writes, "In short, the Fiction Award Committee's decision is symptomatic of a larger crisis: the ethnic stratification of the Asian American studies disciplinary coalition, which is not unique to the local politics and culture of Hawai'i, but was always and remains a problem for mainland Asian America." August Espiritu also argues that "As Asian Americans, we cannot be satisfied with challenging white racism alone. We have to challenge racism everywhere, including amongst ourselves." Asian Americans must engage in self-critical examination, or we will continue to reproduce the very systems of domination that we seek to change.

During the controversy, many local Asians and Asian Americans argued that an examination of conflicts within our communities serves the interests of the state by "playing the plantation game" and submitting to institutional strategies of "divide and conquer" by which the state pits minority groups against each other. The problem with this formulation, however, is that we no longer live on the plantations. As we continue to struggle against anti-Asian racism and violence, we must also face the fact that Asian American ethnic groups like local Japanese in Hawai'i now exercise considerable institutional and state power. It is precisely the denial of structural inequalities among local Asians and Asian Americans that preserves the very inequalities upon which the state and its ideologies of egalitarianism in fact depend. And in a place like Hawai'i where local Japanese dominate state institutions, the denial of local Japanese racism clearly benefits local Japanese, who substantially *comprise* the state.

As local Asians and Asian Americans, we are settlers, and we cannot hide behind the cover story of our own oppression. Those of us who have spoken about racism in local Japanese communities have been "disciplined" by being characterized as "anti-Japanese." Such a characterization preserves local Japanese structural power by realigning our critical position with anti-Japanese white racism. What remains, however, what cannot be assimilated into this equation, is the substantive issue at stake: how we as local Japanese oppress other groups.

To speak out against local Japanese racism and colonialism is not to malign local Japanese communities but rather to hold ourselves accountable to a broader vision of justice.

Transnational Community, Culture, and Little India

SANDHYA SHUKLA

In April of 1999, for the negligible sum of one thousand dollars, India began to issue the "Persons of Indian Origin Card" to enable Indians in the diaspora to visit India sans visa, own property, buy government bonds and apply to universities in India, for a period of twenty years. A link between the more cultural yearnings for homeland and the economic agenda of the state might be seen in public officials' divergent justifications for the program: Home Minister L. K. Advani, from the Bharatiya Janata Party, noted: "I have seen the hunger of Indians abroad to have their children linked to their country of origin," while chief commissioner for Investments and Non-Resident Indians at the Indian Investment Center of the government, A. R. Nanda, pronounced: "I hope the new card will encourage more investment." Such statements and the very initiation of a program to give "national" rights to "non-nationals" offer a crystallization of academic arguments about the changing nature of the nation-state, the mutability and mobility of culture, and most of all, the transformed circumstances of migrants in the world, in what some have called the era of "globalization." Group longings for a place and a culture far away give rise to a

From Sandhya Shukla, "New Immigrants, New Forms of Transnational Community: Post-1965 Indian Migrations," *American Journal* 25, no. 3 (1999/2000). Copyright © 1999 Regents of the University of California. Used with permission.

collective imaginary that is "India," and the flexible accumulation of late capitalism produces both an international economic class of Indians and also a particular trajectory of externally directed development for the emergent nation-state of India. . . .

Conceptualizing cultural moments of the Indian diaspora, however, requires some shift in the consideration of the very idea of "community." Scholars and popular observers alike are accustomed to think of community as comprising a set of peoples with shared interests around work, residence, culture or generation; indeed a group of such factors is commonly cited as integral to "community formation." Geography often plays a central role in how community is understood; many studies of ethnic communities, in particular, have been shaped by an attention to specific parts of urban spaces in which immigrants have located themselves and, eventually, become American, through negotiations between nostalgia for homeland cultures and the demands of work and urban life in the United States. Ideas of ethnic community formation, in their emphasis on U.S.-based localities, have thus been associated with the eventual process of national assimilation that immigrants from northern, southern and eastern Europe were able to accomplish, if not be completely defined by. . . .

. . . This stage of building and defining community across time and space accommodates the specific business and residential concentrations of Indian immigrants in the United States that establish geography as a primary referent for "community," as well as the more generalized constellations of "Indianness," both imaginative and institutionalized, that make for a diasporic social formation, of what might also be called a set of communities. Stories of the past, of colonialism, of independence, of difficulties in immigrating, and of limited economic opportunity all sustain relationships between the different modes of people coming together and self-identifying as a group—claiming an ethnic identity (of being "Indian") within the rubric of multicultural societies like the United States—and of developing a sense of shared political and economic interests—the stuff of "community." Perhaps most of all, there is the nation-state of India, independent for less than twenty years when immigration began to proceed to the United States in full force, developing in the cognizance of many of its peoples desiring a connection to the homeland. . . .

. . . The effort to create the category of the Non-Resident Indian, of NRI, illustrates some of the successes of this bridging of the local interests of Indian migrants in the diaspora and broader needs of the nation-state, what in effect is an instance of "Indian community." . . .

. . . Indian immigrants had already begun to build cultural and political associations like the Association of Indians in America and the Federation of Indian Associations and create newspapers, among others, *India Abroad,* to address (and possibly, construct) a diasporic community. And, beginning in the 1970s, investment in India, in manufacturing concerns and technological ventures, had become a major interest for middle-class Indians in the United States.

A number of important cultural productions linked together local social life (and its attendant push for ethnic identity) and new transnational economic practices. The development of the newspaper *India Abroad* reveals the multiple cultural and economic considerations at work in the formation of an NRI community. It was in the late 1960s, at the early stage of the influx of immigrants into the United States, that Gopal Raju, an immigrant from south India living in New York, looked around him and saw the development of significant populations of Indians. He sensed the need for a publication to provide news to these diverse peoples and started *India Abroad* in 1970, first as a monthly, then as a fortnightly and finally as a weekly paper. Addressing the inception of a coherent and self-conscious Indian immigrant community, Raju's choice of a name for the paper reflected the broadly diasporic address necessary to travel through all types of difference: religious, regional and linguistic. The discursive gesture of a nation being constructed outside of its state ("India, abroad") also lent the community formation it mirrored a degree of domestic and international mobility; it created and supported the transnational in ways that are central to how "ethnicity" would be developed. . . .

. . . *India Abroad* initially sought a broader audience; editor Gopal Raju noted his original intention to "cover all Indians outside India, including the United States, Canada and Britain." But the explosion of populations of Indians all over North America and Britain (not to mention other places) made such an endeavor too difficult to organize, and the U.S. edition of the newspaper, with its local reading population, became central to the production of "India, abroad." . . .

Political and cultural orientations to India were reflected in the subject matter of *India Abroad.* Early editions of the paper read very much like newspapers from India, with the special inclusion of columns that described cultural events of immigrants residing in the New York area, for dance and music programs especially. The material interests of Indian capitalism were well represented; in article after article of early editions of *India Abroad,* one can see alongside the economic stirrings of immigrants for individual betterment, the clearly articulated needs of the Indian nation-state. Investment in India was the *raison d'être* for many *India Abroad–* sponsored activities.

Throughout the 1970s, articles touted the stability of developing Indian enterprises, with advice about how to invest in India. In 1974, the Indian embassy and the Council of Scientific and Industrial Research of India sponsored a series of seminars in the United States that were devoted, as *India Abroad* opined, to "help India meet her needs." . . .

This close relationship, between a business organization in India and a major organ for immigrant news, is one representation among many of the nurturing of Indian American (NRI) interests around material objectives in India. It also reflects a primary mode of affiliation for a developing Indian diasporic community: economic and political transnationalism. Even at an early stage of development of immigrant populations, an intense concern with the state of the Indian economy and politics back home accompanied the more widely observed cultural connection to things Indian. . . .

That the reference point for being Indian in the United States, from the 1970s until the present, has been a sustained interest in India shows how ethnic identity (here), the process of becoming Indian American, has been shaped by that intense national(ist) focus on another place. It is distinct from the homeland nostalgia of earlier immigrant groups precisely because of the specific historical and political conditions of post-1965 immigrant experience, in which the nation-state of India embarks on a number of new international projects. This form of diasporic community, with political, financial and cultural interests that traverse not only local geographic lines (like the neighborhood) but also national boundaries, is also grounded in the process of class formation. The members of the first large-scale Indian migration to the United States came in the 1960s to greet an economy that was in a period of expansion. The occupational experiences of mostly middle-class and credentialed Indians during this period seemed to match the ideals and actualities of growth and opportunity. Technological transformations meant new jobs in medicine, the sciences (natural and applied), business and education, for which this group of Indians was exceptionally qualified. It was this early group of economically successful migrants that economic (and cultural) appeals from India spoke to. And it was this developing Indian American middle-class that assumed a central role in producing a sense of community in the diaspora: through financial remittances, through the leadership of groups like the Association of Indians in America, and through the production of cultural performances. . . .

. . . What was in effect a diasporic imaginary, of the nation of India, captured different groups of people, sub-communities, even, but in its totality, also produced a community itself. That invocation of "Indian community," however fictive it might seem for such a diverse group of elements, nonetheless remained present in the lives of many middle-class Indian immigrants.

While the NRI as a diasporic formation embodies some of the shifts in what it means to think of community outside the neighborhood, with Indianness in the transnational, not the local site, more territorial renderings of "Indian community" also yield similar insights. Since the 1970s, with the increasing growth and concentration of Indian populations in a number of U.S. cities, particularly the New York metropolitan area, Chicago and Los Angeles, new centers of Indian American business arose to serve the needs and desires of immigrant consumers. Colloquially and in some cases, formally, known as "Little Indias," these geographical spaces represent possibilities for Indian community formation of a different kind from the NRI-diaspora, but remain in some important ways linked to it.

Jackson Heights, New York, is perhaps the most prominent signifier for an Indian space in the diaspora. Its concentration of electronic stores, sari shops and eateries, in the city of New York where Indian immigrants are most populous, constitute for many an important site for consuming and realizing a sense of being Indian. . . .

By 1980, the majority of the 74th Street block between Roosevelt Avenue and 37th Avenue housed South Asian shops. Because the goods—food, clothing, and electronics—had relevance for the cultures more widely of people from Pakistan and Bangladesh as well as from India, non-Indian South Asian merchants also occupied stores in Jackson Heights, and almost all of the businesses began to market themselves to "Indo-Pak-Bangla" constituencies. The area eventually comprised over a hundred stores in the area (on the block itself and a few surrounding blocks) that were South Asian-owned, and/or had almost exclusively South Asian clientele.

While some Indians have lived in the immediate Jackson Heights area, they did not make up a residential majority or even a significant minority in the extremely diverse area, which to this day continues to have significant numbers of Jewish, Greek, Italian, Columbian, Korean and Japanese peoples. Most of the shop-owners live on Long Island or in more well-to-do areas of Queens, and the workers in the stores, when not related to the owners, come from various parts of Queens. Though the resident Indian population in the area certainly frequents the shops, it is hardly central to the production of 74th Street as an ethnic space; merchants rely on a broader, dispersed, constituency for their goods.

The crowds of South Asians in the 74th Street area, that succeed in making this place appear to others to be an "Indian space," exist on shopping days. The "Indian community" represented here is both transitional and transient, and defined not by residence but by consumption. While territory does play a role in defining this community—it is in and through Jackson Heights that consumption is realized—it is articulated to an audience beyond whom it literally contains. Shared interests here include the distribution and sale of consumer goods like saris and appliances and services, like those in an Indian beauty salon. The ethnic consumer market, almost completely South Asian and in large part Indian, is not specific to the Queens Indian population that can most readily access the area, but more dispersed, extending outward to reach Indian populations throughout New York, New Jersey and Connecticut. . . .

. . . This ethnic place has stood in for a whole set of historical experiences that span the globe. The representation of 74th Street, even to the locals, vacillates between a broad, diasporic meaning and more localized understandings of community. Popular renderings of such an "Indian community" occurred with reference to both the shopping area and to the shoppers that existed there every day and most especially on weekends, but also assume a xenophobic or exoticist cast, with an air of being foreign—the very term "Little India" can certainly be read in a variety of ways. Many Indian and American shoppers alike are surprised to hear that Indians do not make up the residential majority in the area.

The production and consumption of ethnic goods in Jackson Heights shuts off at six or seven o' clock. The "community" there is akin to a kind of performance, with a beginning and an end, and regulated by the customs of United States consumer capitalism. Ethnic production and consumption are based only secondarily in local investments, in the city blocks and the residential neighborhood, and assume more meaning in symbolic and material renderings of India, for the most part, and of Pakistan and Bangladesh additionally. International references shape the consumer experiences in Jackson Heights and construct ethnicity for all parties involved. The temporary, almost fleeting nature of that consumption and production of Indianness in Jackson Heights has made for a very different type of ethnic community than those in Italian or Irish neighborhoods in Brooklyn and Queens, for example.

Jackson Heights is but one example of an entrepreneurial concentration that has responded to the consumer needs of an increasing population of immigrants, and that has produced a relationship between the more materially observable place and the imaginative (re)creation of Indianness. . . .

. . . Merchants and, to some extent, consumers, actualize a production of "India" through consolations and investments in a local space that, in strategic fashion, can absorb the breadth of a variety of other Indian communities, regional/ethnic, religious, class-specific, and social. Emerging from a certain success of middle-class Indian Americans, "Little Indias" have effects that radiate outward to encompass working-class south Asians who desire products, like foodstuffs and clothing, to recreate their cultures in a foreign place.

The NRI and the "Little India" illustrate new types of diasporic community formation. Shared interests exist in renderings of the nation, of India, in material, cultural and political terms, for immigrants all over the United States (and the world). In these communities, transnationality, an ability to economically, physically and imaginatively cross borders, shapes the lived experience of their members and participants. In establishing a sense of what Indianness is, on a large scale, these communities may be seen to play down the process of Americanization; this occurs in spite of the fact that evocations of the American dream operate in and through immigrants' ideas about themselves. . . .

. . . The "Persons of Indian Origin Card" program that opened this essay is only the latest chapter in a broader set of developments. One can hardly help but notice the ironies of the nation of India in this contemporary moment claiming as a type of citizen the Indian migrant abroad who has benefited from the developmentalist policies of the Indian state, such as scientific and technical education, but who nonetheless acts as a "foreign" investor. How we understand this scenario, of nationality and migration, has a great deal to do with the degree of flexibility we can accord to ideas of community, nation and culture.

Defining Asian American Cinema

PETER FENG

The term "Asian American Cinema," which includes works in video and film, implies first of all that there is such a thing as Asian American Culture. But is there such a thing as a unified Asian American Culture? Of course, the term culture is itself a slippery one—is there such a thing as American Culture, for example? Europeans might say yes; many Americans, especially people of color, would say no.

The first thing we must recognize is the diversity of the cultures of Asia. A survey of the many languages spoken in Asia should make that point manifestly obvious. Even within the country of China, there are several distinct ethnicities and hundreds of different dialects; Chinese in Taiwan, Hong Kong, and Singapore all live in very different cultures from each other. Furthermore, political conflicts and historical enmities further divide the various Asian nations; for example, the legacy of Japanese imperialism continues to anger many Koreans. Put simply, the label "Asian" is not used is Asia—it is only used in the West.

Even in the West, the term means different things to different people. In England, Asian means Pakistani and/or Indian—what Americans call "South Asians." By contrast, in the U.S. Asian often means "East Asian"—Chinese, Japanese, Korean— and "Southeast Asian"—Vietnamese, Laotian, Cambodian, Thai—as well as referring to the Philippines and the Indonesian archipelago. "Asian" does not refer to Australia, or to the "eastern" republics of the former Soviet Union. For most people, "Asian" is simply a nicer term than the derogatory "Oriental."

When people from these disparate cultures arrived in the U.S., they did not automatically bond with each other. Indeed, plantation owners in Hawaii took advantage of the linguistic differences and historical enmities between Chinese, Japanese, Koreans, and Filipinos, playing the groups against each other, confident that they would not organize collectively. It took a generation or two of children born in the U.S. who shared the English language and recognized that racism treated them all as "Orientals" despite their differences, to come together as Asian Americans, and even then this odd coalition was unsure whether to define itself racially or culturally. Ideally, the "Asian American" banner connotes solidarity while denoting diversity.

In that sense, "Asian American" is not a cultural term at all, nor even an ethnic label, but rather the name of a coalition of Americans who have come to realize that their political situation—determined in part by how Asians are seen by outsiders—requires them to act together. Thus, when the men who killed Vincent Chin in 1982 were let off with a fine and probation but no jail time, Chinese Americans were joined in protest and action by other Asian Americans, who realized that the lenient sentence threatened not just Chinese Americans but all Asians.

Not only is the term "Asian American Culture" oxymoronic, ethnically—specific terms like Korean American are not necessarily more valid, at least not if we focus on cultural traditions established since arriving in the U.S. Have Korean Americans who have arrived since the Seventies found a place in American culture akin to that of the Korean immigrants who worked the sugar cane fields in the early part of this century? As Judi Nihei, the Artistic Director for the Seattle-based Northwest Asian American Theatre, notes, it might have been possible once to talk about Japanese American Culture, "because the period of immigration is basically limited. The generations are well defined, and they stopped. I mean, from World War II until the Japanese corporations started moving to America in the Seventies, there was no additional Japanese immigration. So Japanese American culture is probably pretty specific, it hasn't been confused with any new immigrant cultures. On the other hand, I'd say there are maybe three or four Chinese American cultures [since Chinese immigration is more difficult to label in terms of historical patterns]."

Attempting to label Asian American movies ethnically thus opens a door which becomes impossible to close: if we draw a distinction between Japanese American and Chinese American Cinema, don't we also have to make distinctions between New York and San Francisco Chinese Americans, between pre- and post-Communist China immigrants, between Mandarin and Cantonese speakers? And while an informed audience might seek out, for example, movies about urban Japanese Americans while ignoring movies about Japanese American farm workers, what are the chances of defining Japanese American Cinema in such specific terms? After all, in the media marketplace, such a film is more likely to be described as "Asian American," since that term describes a larger target audience. The confusion between films of particular interest to the Asian American market and Asian American films is profound, politically, in mass media.

So in an important sense this discussion is moot. Perhaps it does not matter whether "Asian American Cinema" makes any political or esthetic sense—after all, the term has currency in the cinematic marketplace, as evidenced by the National Asian American Telecommunications Association, the Seattle Asian American Film Festival, the Los Angeles Asia Pacific Film & Video Festival, and New York's Asian American International Film Festival.

Although the appellation of "Asian American Cinema" may be a fait accompli, many Asian American filmmakers are not happy with the ways that some of these festivals organize their screenings. Of the New York Festival, Curtis Choy complains,

"Asian American International? What's that? It just means Asian movies get lumped in with the Asian American stuff." Mainstream media critics also lump Asian American media with the product from Asia: Time magazine's Richard Corliss, in an article entitled "Pacific Overtures," conflated Chen Kaige's *Farewell My Concubine,* Oliver Stone's *Heaven and Earth,* the videos for Madonna's *Rain* and Janet Jackson's *If,* and Ang Lee's *The Wedding Banquet* as examples of "Asian chic." "That's not a valid expression of our media-making heritage or society," says Abe Ferrer, a filmmaker and festival programmer.

Notes Spencer Nadasako (*Life is Cheap . . . but Toilet Paper Is Expensive*), "Anything Asian, anything that comes from Asia, is considered Asian American film: critics say it's a boon for Asian American filmmakers. You've got the Zhang Yimous and the Chen Kaiges and John Woo's *Hard Target* [written of] as Asian American Cinema. It just takes one Asian actor or director, and it gets classed as Asian American Cinema. You don't see films out of Africa called African American, you don't see Luis Buñuel called a Mexican American filmmaker."

Even when the label is "correctly" applied to films made by Asian Americans, that label often becomes all that a media critic can see. Filmmaker Hyun Mi Oh notes, "The discussion of Ang Lee's *The Wedding Banquet* focused purely upon the content of the work. Whereas the way Quentin Tarantino's films have been analyzed always stresses his individuality and his style, the way he uses generic conventions, his own specific signature." Similarly, Roddy Bogawa (*Some Divine Wind*) has noted that no one commented on the strong Warhol influence in his work—at least, not until he made *If Andy Warhol's Super-8 Camera Could Talk?* in 1994.

Finally, however, it cannot be denied that the market for Asian American Cinema—limited though it is—does enable some films to be made. Hyun Mi Oh notes, "For makers, one of the most valuable things about the term Asian American Cinema is it gives you the tools—the actual apparatus—so you can actually make things, and it wouldn't be possible otherwise. I am glad that there are Asian American forums to exhibit in, grants slated for Asian Americans, it's of practical use to me. If those institutions didn't exist I couldn't fund some of my projects, I couldn't show some of my projects—but it's still imposed from the outside, it doesn't arise naturally from the material itself."

So in a sense there is a market for Asian American Cinema—the problem is, it's a market that looks for Asian faces and looks no further. A more precise definition of Asian American Cinema will not take hold until a significant and vocal number of film critics, festival programmers, filmmakers, and audience members agree that there are some movies which are Asian American—and some movies which are not. As Choy and Nakasako point out, a logical place to start would be to exclude movies made in Asia, especially movies which do not deal at all with life in America.

In 1992 a collection of essays entitled *Reading the Literatures of Asian America* was published. Editors Shirley Geok-lin Lim and Amy Ling included essays about Canadian authors, thus suggesting that "Asian America" included Canada. In this article, I have included a group of Toronto-based filmmakers in the discussion, and I therefore run the risk of effacing whatever it is that makes their films Canadian. Including the work of Helen Lee, Richard Fung, Midi Onodera, and others in this discussion raises the question, "What is America, anyway?"

The relationship between Asian American and Asian Canadian aesthetic practices animates much of Helen Lee's work as a critic, curator, and filmmaker. Lee lists both Canada and the U.S. as countries of origin for *My Niagara,* the film was shot primarily in Toronto, but postproduction took place in New York as well, when Lee worked for Women Make Movies and attended New York University. *My Niagara* does not set out to define how Asian Canadians are different from Asian Americans; nor does it argue for conflation (while some spectators will surely recognize some Toronto landmarks, Lee's film leaves open the possibility that her protagonist might be read as either Asian American or Asian Canadian). Similarly, Lee's earlier film, *Sally's Beauty Spot,* highlights the fluidity of representation within the Asian diaspora, juxtaposing Korean Canadian Sally (Lee's sister) with "Eurasian" (Chinese-English—actually Scottish) Nancy Kwan's famous portrayal of Suzie Wong, the Hong Kong hooker-with-heart. What are we to make of a film which draws on icons of Asian femininity which cross ethnic and national boundaries—is it an example of how all English-speaking Asians are somehow "American"? Does the cultural dominance of the U.S. completely efface cultural borders, media and otherwise? Lee herself suggests that the situation is either "an embodiment of Asian diasporic aesthetics," or "an exercise in dominant cultural politics—if you can ever call 'Asian American' dominant."

This careful attention to the ethnic and national identity of video and film-makers suggests that "identity politics" and auteur-based film criticism have joined forces. But where is it written that Asian Americans can make films only about Asian Americans—after all filmmaker Wayne Wang made the film *Slamdance,* and James Wong Howe directed *Go, Man, Go!,* a 1954 movie about the Harlem Glob-trotters. And yet, the filmmakers and critics that I spoke with returned to the nebulous concept of "Asian American issues" to define Asian American Cinema with astonishing regularity, even while expressing their uncertainty about such definitions. This problem was so familiar to everyone concerned that I used shorthand to refer to it—I called it "The Gregg Araki question"—and everyone knew that I was asking, "If an Asian American filmmaker makes a movie which doesn't engage with Asian American issues, would you include it in your definition of Asian American Cinema?"

The responses were revealing. Abe Ferrer noted that filmmakers like Araki (probably best known for *The Living End*) and Roddy Bogawa "expand the definition of what our community is all about by incorporating the notion that we're not exclusively about cultural recovery, we're not exclusively preoccupied with depicting our heritage through the recurrent themes of immigration, the Internment, [the murder of] Vincent Chin [and the ensuing court cases]; they demonstrate that many of us have other influences that we've grown up with, and examining those influences is a valid addition to the kind of language or subject matter that we're embracing." A strict, content-based definition of Asian American Cinema thus runs the risk of defining the cultural experiences of Asian Americans so narrowly as to promote one "correct" Asian American Experience.

"Even when Araki, or Bogawa, or [Jon] Moritsugu (*My Degeneration*) aren't dealing with traditional Asian American themes, there's something about their films, their screenplays—something—it doesn't feel like white independent filmmaking," claims Spencer Nakasako. "It's not a question of some 'x-factor' which makes it

Asian American, but, for example, you can sense from the characters, from the way people talk to each other—there's some guilt going on, some kind of uniquely sansei [third-generation Japanese American] anger." But while "sansei attitude" might define a corpus of films made by Asian Americans, "attitude" in itself does not constitute a "Cinema." Many mainstream media critics have labeled films as varied as *Reality Bites, Slacker,* and *Go Fish* as "Generation X" or "twentysomething" movies—often to the consternation of the filmmakers and their audiences—but that does not mean there is such a thing as "Generation X Cinema."

Rather than using the market-based approach to define Asian American Cinema, it might make more sense to refer to modes of production, and, indeed, many filmmakers agree that there was a coherence to Asian American media production in the Seventies that is absent today. Around 1970 a group of Asian Americans in the Los Angeles area raised the banner of "Visual Communications"—VC for short—and began producing films cooperatively. VC has undergone many transformations, but it maintains a palpable commitment to cultural intervention which shows that the lessons of the Sixties are still with us today. Talk to Abe Ferrer, who's been with VC since 1984, and phrases like "self-determination," "community definition," and "cultural reclamation" reverberate. A sense of "community" pervades much Asian American media from the same period: the same names recur constantly in film credits in different capacities as filmmakers lent their support to each other's projects. Curtis Choy (*The Fall of the I-Hotel*) asserts, "We did feel a certain unity, we did support each other verbally and with our hearts. In the early Seventies, what I wanted to do, my dream, was to produce something, anything, it didn't have to be a feature—something that was written, produced, teched, completely controlled by Asians."

Many of the Asian American filmmakers who started out in the Seventies speak of Asian American Cinema in the past tense. There is a difference between Asian American Cinema and the "Asian American Cinema Movement," a term which I use to describe the community orientation and the palpable sense of discovery which pervades the Seventies films. For what it's worth, many of the up-and-coming Asian American filmmakers also sense a Great Divide between the Seventies and the Eighties. "For me Asian American Cinema describes a period of film-making rather than an ongoing cultural presence," says Hyun Mi Oh. "The term describes mostly films of a documentary tradition of the Sixties and Seventies—I don't know what I would call what is happening now, to me it doesn't make sense to call it Asian American Cinema."

"If there is such a thing as Asian American Cinema, then it's based on content and theme." Oh's words suggest that definitions of Asian American Cinema inevitably return to larger questions of definition for the Asian American community. Cultural traditions, language differences, and different experiences in the U.S. separate Asian Americans, while a shared sense of political purpose strains to hold Asian Americans together. But given the ethnic diversity of Asian Americans; given the divide between content-based and authorship-based definitions of Asian American Cinema; and given the shifts in modes of production from the Sixties to the Nineties, is it at all possible to speak of a coherent Asian American Cinema?

That of course depends on how you define coherence. The difference between a political movement and a political coalition is in a sense simply a question of contingency, of defining issues which will sustain political solidarity as opposed to issues which promote short-term consensus. Perhaps the Asian American Cinema Movement describes a very specific historical moment, and left us with a mantle which later video and filmmakers have slipped into (some comfortably, some less so). Can we coin a term which links together many divergent forms of cinematic expression while acknowledging their diversity—the plural "Asian American Cinemas" perhaps? The problem is that this plural term, while acknowledging heterogeneity, still insists on unity even while it allows for dissension—Gregg Araki's films are still considered to be exceptions to the general rule.

Judi Nihei proposes a distinction between Asian American filmmakers—a category based on cultural labels and authorship—and a more specific definition of Asian American Cinema: "Asian American stories through the eyes of Asian American filmmakers. So that there are Asian American filmmakers who are making stories about things besides Asian America, and I don't know that you would classify their work specifically as Asian American Cinema. And there are non-Asian filmmakers making stories about Asian Americans, and I think that you would exclude their films as well. That's a very specific, probably very limited at this point, area of film." If we employ Nihei's framework, then it is the responsibility of festival programmers (for example) to make it known whether they are providing a forum for Asian American media artists, regardless of subject matter, or if they are programming movies about Asian American experiences. It is significant that Nihei insists on a definition which does not oppose authorship and subject matter, but one which assumes that an Asian American perspective ("through the eyes of Asian Americans," as she puts it) should be operative.

Ultimately, those of us who are interested in Asian American Cinema are interested in Asian American perspectives, whether the subject matter is ourselves, American culture more generally, or the whole world of cinematic possibility. As long as Asian Americans continue to question who we are—and when we stop questioning we'll be figuratively and literally dead—there will be no easy answers. And that is how it should be.

FURTHER READING

Bonus, Rick. *Locating Filipino Americans: Ethnicity and the Cultural Politics of Space* (2000).

Cheung, King-Kok. "The Woman Warrior Versus the Chinaman Pacific: Must a Chinese American Critic Choose Between Feminism and Heroism?" in *Conflicts in Feminism,* ed. Marianne Hirsch and Evelyn Fox Keller (1992), 234–251.

Chin, Frank. "Come All Ye Asian American Writers of the Real and the Fake." in *The Big Aiiieeeee! An Anthology of Chinese American and Japanese American Literature,* ed. Jeffrey Paul Chan et. al. (1991), 1–52.

Chow, Karen Har-Yen. "Imagining Asian Americans: From Mono-ethnic to Transnational Community Identity in Asian American Literature and Film," Ph.D. dissertation, U.C. Santa Barbara (1998).

Eng, David L. *Racial Castration: Managing Masculinity in Asian America* (2000).

Feng, Peter X. *Screening Asian Americans* (2002).

Hamamoto, Darrell Y. *Monitored Peril: Asian Americans and the Politics of TV Representation* (1994).

Hamamoto, Darrell Y., and Sandra Liu. *Countervisions: Asian American Film Criticism* (2000).

Hing, Bill Ong. *To Be an American: Cultural Pluralism and the Rhetoric of Assimilation* (1997).

Kingston, Maxine Hong. *The Woman Warrior: Memoirs of a Childhood Among Ghosts* (1976).

Lee, Rachel C. *The Americas of Asian American Literature: Gendered Fictions of Nation and Transnation* (1999).

Lee, Robert G. *Orientals: Asian Americans in Popular Culture* (1999).

Lesinger, Johanna. *From the Ganges to the Hudson: Indian Immigrants in New York City* (1995).

Li, David Leiwei. *Imagining the Nation: Asian American Literature and Cultural Consent* (1998).

Lim, Shirley Geok-lin, and Amy Ling, eds. *Reading the Literatures of Asian America* (1992).

Ling, Jinqi. *Narrating Nationalism: Ideology and Form in Asian American Literature* (1998).

Ma, Sheng-mei. *The Deathly Embrace: Orientalism and Asian American Identity* (2000).

———. *Immigrant Subjectivities in Asian American and Asian Diaspora Literatures* (1998).

Marchetti, Gina. *Romance and the "Yellow Peril": Race, Sex, and Discursive Strategies in Hollywood Fiction* (1993).

Mimura, Glen M. "New Ethnicities on the Edge of Time," Ph.D. dissertation, U.C. Santa Cruz (2000).

Miyoshi, Masao. "A Borderless World: From Colonialism to Transnationalism and the Decline of the Nation-State," *Critical Inquiry* 19 (1993): 726–751.

Mura, David. *Where the Body Meets Memory: An Odyssey of Race, Sexuality, and Identity* (1996).

Ng, Franklin, ed. *Asians in America: The Peoples of East, Southeast, and South Asia in American Life and Culture* (1998).

Okihiro, Gary Y. *Margins and Mainstreams: Asians in American History and Culture* (1994).

San Juan, E. *From Exile to Diaspora: Veterans of the Filipino Experience in the United States* (1998).

Sumida, Stephen H. *And the View from the Shore: Literary Traditions of Hawaii* (1991).

Tan, Amy. *The Joy Luck Club* (1989).

Tuan, Mia. *Forever Foreign or Honorary White? The Asian Ethnic Experience Today* (1999).

Wat, Eric C. "Preserving the Paradox: Stories from a Gay-Loh," *Amerasia Journal* 20, no. 2 (1994): 149–160.

Wong, Eugene Franklin. *On Visual Media Racism: Asians in the American Motion Pictures* (1978).

Wong, Sau-ling. "Autobiography as Guided Chinatwon Tour? Maxine Hong Kingston's *The Woman Warrior* and the Chinese American Autobiographical Controversy," in *Multicultural Autobiography: American Lives*, ed. James Robert Payne (1992), 248–279.

Xing, Jun. *Asian America Through the Lens: History, Representations and Identity* (1998).

Yamanaka, Lois-Ann. *Blu's Hanging* (1998).

CHAPTER
15

Erasing Borders and Boundaries: Asian Americans in the Twenty-First Century

As we begin the twenty-first century, the constant movement of capital, trade, technology, and people across countries and continents challenges any fixed notions of national, regional, racial, ethnic, and communal identities. Although scholars continue to study the growth of the "Asian American" population in the United States, they recognize that this label bears little relation to the term as used to describe individuals living a century ago.

The results of the 2000 U.S. census confirmed the tremendous expansion and diversification of the Asian American population. The number of individuals identifying an Asian ancestry on the census grew from 6.9 million in 1990 to 11.9 million in 2000. This increase of 72 percent gave Asian Americans the fastest growth rate of any racial population in America in the 1990s. Although still much smaller than the country's African American or Hispanic populations, the Asian American share of the total U.S. population rose from 2.9 percent to 4.4 percent and established a prominent presence in many states and metropolitan areas.

Some commentators expressed little surprise at this overall growth because the Asian American population has doubled every ten years since the government began lifting immigration barriers in 1965. The 2000 census, however, also provided new data on the remarkable variety of racial identifications and residential locations of Asian Americans. In 1990, individuals were limited to choosing one of five racial categories—white, black, Asian–Pacific Islander, American Indian–Alaska Native, or "other"—when completing the census. The 2000 census split Asian and Pacific Islander into separate categories and allowed participants to mark one or more of sixty-three racial classifications. Approximately 874,000 individuals identified themselves as "Native Hawaiian" or "Other Pacific Islander." Individuals also could identify themselves as Asian Indian, Chinese, Filipino, Japanese, Korean, Vietnamese, or write in an "Other Asian" category.

In the year 2000, Chinese Americans were still the largest single national-origin group within the Asian American community. Reaching 2.7 million, they comprised almost a quarter of the Asian American total. Filipinos maintained a 20 percent share of the total and numbered 2.4 million. The fifth largest group in 1990, Asian Indians became the fastest growing group in 2000. More than doubling over the decade, the Asian Indian population grew to 1.9 million. Three other groups counted more than a million members, and each represented about a tenth of the total Asian American population. Japanese Americans have the longest history in the country but experienced little new immigration. The number of Korean Americans increased by half, and the population of Vietnamese Americans doubled since 1990.

The census numbers also illustrated how Asian Americans have changed the demography of the United States in the last three decades. In 1970, there were only 1.5 million Asian Americans in the entire country. The 2000 census revealed that the New York City, Los Angeles, and San Francisco areas each had over 1.5 million residents of Asian ancestry. Asian Americans have both reinvigorated traditional ethnic enclaves—the Chinatowns, Little Tokyos, Manilatowns, Koreatowns, and Little Saigons—and spread to former white suburbs and rural areas. Still prominent in Hawai'i, California, Washington, and New York, they're also becoming highly visible in other states. For example, the Asian American population in New Jersey rose by 94 percent to reach 524,356. Few people anticipated that Fort Lee, New Jersey, a suburb of New York City, would become 30 percent Asian American in 2000. The numbers in Pennsylvania rose to 248,601, a jump of 83 percent, while the population in Indiana almost doubled. Individuals also migrated in significant numbers to states that have had few Asian Americans in the past. The 25,401 Asian Americans in Arkansas represented a 105 percent increase, while the 6,009 in South Dakota reflected a 105 percent increase in 2000.

Although increasing numbers of individuals claim an "Asian" racial ancestry, the very meaning of this label has become much more complex. Denying the very existence of racial distinctions because of genetic research, some scientists insist there is only a single "human race." Other scholars recognize that despite the genetic evidence, individuals, groups, and nations continue to perceive "racial" differences. Old distinctions between races, however, are increasingly being questioned. By allowing people to mark more than one racial category, the 2000 census provided new data on 6.8 million individuals who identified a mixed-race background. In Virginia, for example, 14 percent or 43,534 of the 304,559 who identified themselves as Asian also marked at least one other race. In South Dakota, 27 percent of the "Asian" population also checked off another race on their census forms.

Some of these individuals still associate more with a single traditional "racial" or "ethnic" community. Others embrace a variety of ancestral heritages as part of their identity. Tiger Woods, for example, proclaimed himself a "Cablinasian" to celebrate the Caucasian, Black, American Indian, and Asian components of his heritage. Still others, however, see themselves as part of a new, cross-cultural, multiracial, and multiethnic community. They view themselves as separate and distinct from other ethnic groups and communities of color. Some have become activists to convince the government to add a stand-alone "multiracial" category to the census. Others have opposed this campaign because they fear that such an addition would reduce the representation of traditional racial groups and decrease their political clout and funding for educational programs, healthcare facilities, and block grants for community development. Scholars in the future undoubtedly will spend considerable time studying the growth of the mixed-race population, the diverse views and experiences of mixed-race individuals, and the impact of these individuals on Asian American culture, community, and politics.

Future research also will analyze the tremendous diversity among Asian Americans. Scholars will reexamine relationships between immigrants and later generations from China, Japan, Okinawa, Korea, the Philippines, the Pacific Islands, Vietnam, Laos, Cambodia, Thailand, India, Pakistan, Indonesia, Bangladesh, Burma, Sri Lanka, and Malaysia. The remarkable ethnic diversity within the population has been matched by differentiation within ethnic groups based on generation, class, gender, sexual orientation, educational backgrounds, language skills, political views, and a multitude of other factors. Even generational statuses, once a useful category to distinguish the experiences of immigrants and their American-born children, now belie simple generalizations. For example, Chinese immigrants now include politically conservative presidents of multinational corporations, radical gay activists with Ph.D.s, and struggling day laborers. Indian immigrants own successful high-tech companies, work as low-paid computer assemblers, and produce leading feminist scholarship.

Finally, ongoing relationships between Asian countries and Asian Americans will receive much greater attention. Scholars will continue to document the role of Asian Americans on "homeland politics," anticolonial struggles, and third-world liberation movements. The impact of globalization, however, will inspire many new studies. Recent research has shed light on the interaction between migration patterns, worldwide economic conditions, and political trends. Scholars have noted that highly mobile individuals continuously traverse geographical, political, and cultural borders. Scholars have called such people "transnationals," "global tribes," and "diasporic groups." Anthropologist Aihwa Ong has studied "Hong Kong astronauts" who "orbit" throughout the Pacific Rim as they monitor their global investments. Hong Kong and Singapore, long-established sites for the creation of transnational commercial and financial networks, have been joined by new diasporic nodes in places like Vancouver, Canada. Preliminary studies have examined the "deterritorialized" identity and "flexible citizenship" of transnationals who often have stronger relationships with coethnics than with nation states. Future studies should help illuminate the impact of transnational economic transactions, social relationships, and cultural encounters on diasporic groups, the United States, Asia, and the Pacific Rim.

D O C U M E N T S

The first three documents reflect the impact of globalization and changing constructions of race and ethnicity on Asian Americans. Document 1 is written by Mallika Dutt, a lawyer and human rights advocate. Dutt founded Sa Khi for South Asian Women, an organization that helps battered women and domestic workers. She also served as an associate director of the Center for Women's Global Leadership and recently founded Breakthrough, an organization that uses popular culture, media, and the Internet to raise consciousness about social justice issues, economic exploitation, racism, and women's rights. In Document 1, Dutt calls on migrant women throughout the G-7 countries—the United Kingdom, the United States, Canada, Germany, France, Italy, and Japan—to recognize their common oppression by global economies and to mobilize a community of migrant women of different races and ethnicities to develop effective strategies to improve their work and living conditions.

Whereas Document 1 calls for the building of coalitions across nations, Document 2 demonstrates the impact of cross-racial and cross-ethnic alliances within a single local community. In Document 2, Roger Sanjek, an urban anthropologist at City University of New York Queens College, describes how residents of New Elmhurst, New York, overcame language and cultural differences to protect and improve the lives of their families. As the document notes, women like Lucy Schilero played a critical role in establishing the interpersonal networks that helped the community organize to promote safer streets, educational programs, and political empowerment.

In Document 3, Maria P. P. Root announces a bill of rights for people of mixed-race heritage. Root, a clinical psychologist and president of the Washington State Psychological Association, is of Filipino, Spanish, Chinese, Portuguese, German, and Irish heritage. A leading scholar on interracial families and mixed-race identity, Root condemns attempts to impose a singular label on mixed-race individuals. In Document 3, Root proclaims that she and all mixed-race individuals have the right to identify themselves however they see fit.

Whereas Root celebrates diverse racial heritages, the last document reflects Asian American fears of racial profiling in times of crisis in America. Americans, regardless of race or ethnicity, were horrified and shocked by the terrorist attacks on the World Trade Center and Pentagon on September 11, 2001. The following day, John Tateishi, the National Executive Director of the Japanese American Citizens League, issued a press release announcing that his organization was participating in blood donor drives to help the victims of the "9-11" attack and intervening to assist Arab Americans and Muslims who were "being collectively blamed or specifically pursued as scapegoats through unsubstantiated accusations or biased treatment by investigative agencies or the public." Many Asian Americans praised President George W. Bush for publicly defending Muslims during a visit to the Islamic Center of Washington. Others, however, worried about the heated political rhetoric against terrorists, talk-radio calls for mass internment, and the secrecy surrounding the government detention of suspected terrorists.

Americans of South Asian ancestry as well as Arab Americans, became targets of hate crimes and civil rights violations. A Sikh man in Phoenix, Arizona, was shot dead at his gas station and his family believed he was killed because he wore a turban. A Pakistani convenience store owner was killed in Dallas. Other South Asians who committed minor immigration violations, such as overstaying a visa, found themselves arrested and detained for interrogation. Pakistani and Indian immigrants were among the 1,100 people detained after the attack and held in secret. One illegal Pakistani immigrant, Mohammed Rafiq Butt, died of heart failure while in custody. Mike Mcphate, a graduate student in journalism and Asian Studies at the University of California at Berkeley, describes in Document 4 how the campaign against unwarranted detentions and hate crimes has helped heal rifts within the South Asian community in America.

1. Activist Mallika Dutt Organizes Migrant Women in Seven Countries (1995), 1997

Migrant women play a specific, critical role in the global economy, as revealed by current economic transformations. Technological changes, the directions of capital flows and the increasing presence of transnational corporations all rely heavily on cheap female migrant labor to maintain their profit bases. For example, there has been a large shift from full-time jobs with benefits to contingent and temporary jobs. Exploitative working conditions with little or no benefits abound and migrant women provide the linchpin in the maintenance of these new structures.

Working conditions of a temporary and exploitative nature are not a new phenomenon for migrant women. What is particularly interesting to explore at this moment in history is the fact that what has been the reality for migrant women is

"Migrant Women and the Global Economy." This material was adapted from the publication entitled *Migrant Women's Human Rights in G-7 Countries,* produced by the Family Violence Prevention Fund and the Center for Women's Global Leadership. Edited by Mallika Dutt, Leni Marin, and Helen Zia, 1997, pp. 1–4.

now becoming the model of work for increasing numbers of women around the world. Governments experiencing economic restructuring, structural adjustment programs and the burdens of debt which are now affecting more and more women have always relied on migrant women to balance their payments. For example, women from the Philippines who have been working overseas as domestic workers, nurses, prostitutes and garment workers have provided a critical source of foreign exchange for their government.

The increase in the number of migrant women performing different kinds of work has been accompanied by an increase in anti-immigrant sentiment. Countries are increasing penalties for undocumented entry, tightening borders and indulging in racist, anti-immigrant rhetoric. It is no accident that at the moment economies are becoming globalized and the free market is being celebrated as the only model of economic development, that racism and xenophobia are on the rise. The global economy demands unfettered mobility for capital flows and access to markets. However, profit maximization can only be realized if workers are not able to cross borders as easily and their condition is kept vulnerable enough to keep their wages low.

Unfortunately, for migrant women in G-7 countries, the common experience has been that the mainstream women's movement has not incorporated our issues into their agenda. While migrant women have created dynamic and important organizations to demand their human rights, their voices remain at the margins of public debate. The challenge we face is how to move the human rights of migrant women from margin to center. Many of us feel that we must not only organize separately and autonomously, but also have an impact on the mainstream, however one constructs it. Moving from margin to center is also about redefining the categories "center" and "margin." Without such a redefinition we risk becoming a part of a social/political/economic construct that has created the human rights violations in the first place.

We can talk about margin and center at two levels. At one level, we need to explore how to make what we call the women's movement more inclusive and representative of the realities of all kinds of women. In that context, redefining the center would mean an identity of womanhood or a definition of woman that does not immediately have the connotation of referring only to a certain class or a certain race or particular category of "woman." We could begin to use the term "woman" in a way that represents the realities of many different kinds of women so that we do not constantly have to keep qualifying the word "woman" by adding such words as "migrant" or "Asian" because we do not feel represented. No one qualifier can encompass the whole personhood of a woman because even a migrant woman can have many identities. Redefining the center in this context would bring the voices of migrant women into the definition of womanhood.

At the second level of moving from margin to center, we need to realize that our objective of changing the women's movement to address our concerns is really a step towards another goal: to change the conditions that have led to the oppression of migrant women in the first place. The redefinition of that center means taking on the question of what a national and international economy should look like. This redefinition is an enterprise that requires not just the voices of migrant women but the voices of many different communities of people. In order to make this redefinition process effective, one must begin by conceptualizing one's self as already being at the center.

This mainstreaming of migrant women's concerns can be assisted by using the human rights framework. Human rights concepts are an important tool in organizing around migrant women's rights, particularly in light of the increased use of migrant labor combined with the growing intensity [of] immigrant bashing, ethnocentrism and xenophobia. In mainstream society, when you voice a human rights concern, there is a resonance to what that claim means in the international arena. Human rights claims are based on the assumption that all of us—as human beings—are entitled to certain minimal standards of living that we as a society agree to abide by. By stating that the rights of migrant women are fundamental human rights in a world which subjects them to the worst jobs, the worst wages and the worst working conditions, one places migrant women into the definition of humanity.

If the lives of migrant women are viewed through this human rights framework, then the interconnectedness of different human experiences also become apparent. One can better understand the connections among women of color, women from the South, women from Eastern Europe and women from different parts of the world who move from economies that are more devastated to economies that are less devastated to do the work that others won't perform.

One must be careful in using the human rights framework, however. One cannot argue that women's rights are human rights unless all women are included in that analysis—otherwise we are simply replicating the same process that led to women being excluded from the human rights paradigm in the first place. Power differences and inequality exist among women and must be acknowledged. It is when women are viewed as a monolith that the concerns of communities like migrant women become marginalized.

The human rights movement and the migrant women's movement have not been completely separate efforts; however, they are not well integrated either. If migrant women do not speak and do not organize to advocate their rights, then they will remain marginalized or their concerns will be represented by voices that do not include them.

Migrant women in different parts of the world have come together fairly recently. For example, in the case of the US and Mexico or the Philippines and Singapore, there are obvious geographic reasons for coming together to organize. However, this attempt to create a community of migrant women from G-7 countries is a relatively new effort. It is a historic effort because all of us who have been doing this work in our own countries have become more aware of the similarities of our experiences. Many of us have also used the human rights framework because it provides a tool and a useful way to organize.

We began this as a G-7 country effort because we saw that there is a certain relationship that exists among the receiving countries and the sending countries. The focus on G-7 countries had to do with the fact that the politics and the economies of these countries drive much of what is happening in the rest of the world. For example, the policies of the World Bank, the International Monetary Fund and the World Trade Organization are very much driven by the interests of G-7 countries, so that if we could take on those entities it would affect patterns in other parts of the world. However, other women have pointed out that what happens in the G-7 context can be applied to other parts of the world as well where similar socio-economic and political differences might exist. For example, movements of women do not only take place on a North-South basis but include Filipino women going to Kuwait, or Nepali women being trafficked to India. Perhaps we need to think in a more international context than simply the G-7 context. However, as an organizing strategy, the idea was to try to come together prior to the next G-7 meeting.

Our goal is to explore and share the strategies that we have individually and collectively developed and used to address our conditions, because we believe that those strategies are not just for the marginalized, for the exploited, for the vulnerable, but are in fact valuable lessons and models of organizing that women can share across the board.

As we look at our communities, which are facing increasing economic devastation and racism, as we look at the increase in the number of women who are migrants and refugees, we see that our role as women and the strategies that we are exploring are critical to move our issues beyond the margin, as examples of where we can move towards in the next millennium.

2. Residents of New Elmhurst, New York, Develop Multiracial and Multiethnic Coalitions to Improve Their Neighborhood (1992), 1998

The 110th Precinct house is located on 43rd Avenue, an Elmhurst street of one-and two-family homes. With scores of cars belonging to police officers filling up the block, parking was a severe problem for residents. In 1984 Joe Bellacicco, a 43rd Avenue resident, and Carmela George began a petition for a police parking garage. (Bellacicco and George had known each other since childhood, their fathers having emigrated from Italy on the same ship.) Bellacicco called an outdoor meeting of his block's residents to discuss the problem.

Among those attending was Lucy Schilero, a beautician who had grown up on 43rd Avenue in the 1950s and 1960s. She had moved to Jackson Heights when she married in the 1970s and had worked in Queens, in Manhattan (where her customers included Raquel Welch and Jacqueline Onassis), and on Long Island. In 1977 she and her Italian American husband moved back to 43rd Avenue to her grandmother's house. Her Italian immigrant parents lived on the same street.

Thirty-five people came to the 1984 block meeting, but Joe Bellacicco "didn't want an organization," Schilero recalled, "only a meeting for parking. But the people wanted it. We had a second meeting . . . at the 110th Precinct. I sat in the back then. Complaints came out. The old-time Americans felt there was no point, but we the ethnics—my father had an Italian accent—wanted to keep it. The attendance dropped. In the summer of 1985 there were about ten people. Then things started to mushroom in 1986 after we heard the 110th might move."

In 1985 Rose Rothchild, then CB4 [Community Board 4] chair, proposed converting the existing precinct house into a school and relocating the 110th to Corona. Northside Democratic Club and Corona Taxpayers leaders supported this plan. The Newtown Civic Association favored the school but wanted the precinct

Reprinted from Roger Sanjek, *The Future of Us All: Race and Neighborhood Politics in New York City.* Copyright © 1998 by Cornell University. Used by permission of the publisher, Cornell University Press, pp. 286–289.

moved elsewhere in Elmhurst. In the end, the 110th remained in place, but during 1985–1986 Schilero and her neighbors worried that they might lose the protection the precinct house provided: "We bought homes with . . . a police station there."

After a 110th officer told her, "Talk to Rose [Rothchild]," Schilero began attending CB4 meetings in 1986. There she met Richard Bearak, the City Planning Department liaison for CD4 [Community District 4] and began to learn from him about zoning and land-use matters. She reported back to her neighbors, and soon at 43rd Avenue Block Association meetings "we were getting people all the way from [the St. Bart's vicinity in Elmhurst], Jackson Heights, and around PS19 [Public School 19] [in Corona], all concerned about the 110th moving." Carmela George and her block association members also began to attend 43rd Avenue association meetings.

Also in 1986 Lucy Schilero circulated a petition to keep the 110th Precinct where it was. She collected 4,000 signatures, mostly in her own Baxter-Roosevelt section of Elmhurst. "I went door to door on the petition. I hit churches, trains [at IRT stations], and stores first, then the houses. St. Bart's helped. Some Newtown Civic Association people were angry about that, but I got 1,500 names in one day in August 1986. I got 150 names from the Elmhurst Baptist Church. All the people on our block helped, fifty people. We had everything in Spanish, Greek, Italian, Chinese, Korean, French. I met Iranians, Turkish [people], to help translate."

She also met tenant association leaders from several Elmhurst apartment buildings. Their groups had formed to fight illegal rent increases and evictions, and to wage rent strikes and court suits against deteriorating services. Some were involved in protracted battles with absentee investors who had purchased blocks of occupied units when buildings were converted to co-ops. "I met the Wallington Tenants Association, the Elmhurst Avenue Tenants Association, the Whitney Tenants Association, and they introduced me to other buildings, including a Cuban tenants association in one building. Now I felt less lonely after [the] Newton [Civic Association] and Corona [Taxpayers] said no [to keeping the 110th where it was]."

Lucy Schilero's personal network also began to change. She still kept in touch with "Irish, Polish" friends from high school and work, but "my old friends have spread out from Elmhurst. Most moved to Long Island and have homes there, for the schools." But as a result of her organizing,

> now, I have new ethnic friends: Hindu, Spanish (a lot), Chinese. My Ecuadorian neighbor Lucy Galindo is a good friend and in touch with Spanish residents. She translates. Achilles Selearis [a Greek immigrant] went with me door to door. He helped a lot, especially with Muslims, who would not talk to a woman by herself. There are immigrants from France who are my neighbors. . . . [White] friends in Maspeth and Middle Village say to me, "How can you live here? It's like Manhattan." I tell them we have to live with one another or we won't survive. A [white] neighbor said to me, "Lucy, the blacks are moving in." I said, "There's black trash and white trash. Nobody's backyard is clean." . . . I told a Hindu boy who was called "black" that I was called "black guinea" when we moved [here]. [The Irish and Germans] said we would make homemade wine. . . . The Hindus and Shiites are the hardest to relate with. The man at the Geeta Temple, he's been great, but he won't come to meetings. I want to get Haitians, I want to bring one with me on my rounds. Jamaicans are moving in now; I see the Rasta hairdos. . . . I like the diversity of the area. The world is at your doorstep. I haven't tried all the food—I enjoy the ethnic foods. I like the stores. . . . The newcomers are people we want to keep here. They are hard-working people, like the old immigrants. They [all] have to interrelate; they are now neighbors.

Schilero had volunteered in a literacy program when she lived in Jackson Heights, but her organizing skills were self-taught. "One time I said to a Chinese neighbor, 'The sewer is backing up into my house and into your house.' And he said, 'Oh yeah, bad, bad, bad.' And that's how it started with some of them, that was the beginning of the break. The others saw it and they said, 'How about us?' And we had a whole block."

In 1986 Lucy Schilero formed the Coalition of United Residents for a Safer Community, comprising the 43rd Avenue Block Association and the tenant associations she met through petitioning. She had maintained contact with leaders of all these groups and shared information on quality-of-life issues that mattered to them, particularly drug selling along Roosevelt Avenue, sanitation, police response, and illegal occupancy. Through this coalition network she was able to circulate petitions rapidly, including one to keep open the Elmhurst Hospital pharmacy and walk-in clinics threatened by Dinkins administration cuts in 1991.

In 1987 the 43rd Avenue Block Association meetings officially became coalition meetings. There Schilero reported on what she learned at public hearings and at CB4, which she joined in 1990, and on her contacts with other civic groups and elected officials. And she stressed voter registration. Coalition meetings, held three times year, also featured speakers from the 110th Precinct and various government agencies. At first elected officials were unwilling to come, but soon they were eager to address audiences numbering up to one hundred and more diverse than anywhere else in CD4.

A Puerto Rican CUNY [City University of New York] professor living on her street provided Spanish translations of petitions and meeting flyers. Two weeks before each meeting Schilero called leaders of the coalition groups, and several active members expanded this telephone tree along Chinese, Spanish, and Greek branches. During meetings, people at the back of the room translated for non-English speakers. By 1990, Korean, Bengali, Urdu, and Vietnamese were also in use within the coalition's communication network. By this time Lucy Schilero was herself a more effective speaker and meeting organizer: the "ums" and "you knows" of the mid-1980s were gone; printed agendas were more detailed and informative; and audience responses were smoothly integrated into meeting business.

In 1990 the coalition held an awards dinner at the Knights of Columbus Hall in Elmhurst. The audience of 150 was a mix of older whites, many Latin Americans of all ages, Greek and Italian immigrants, and East and South Asians. Joe Bellacicco, the 43rd Avenue Block Association president, introduced Schilero, who in turn introduced CB4 district manager Rose Rothschild, representatives from the Mayor's Community Assistance Unit and the borough president's office (both of whom remarked on the impressive Friday night turnout), the 110th's commanding officer, and the Queens borough police commander, Francis X. Smith, who proclaimed he was "an Elmhurst boy."

Schilero reviewed accomplishments since 1985 and congratulated the audience for supporting the coalition. Then engraved plaques were presented: to two former 110th Precinct commanders and several C-POP [Community Patrol Office Program] and community relations officers; to Rothschild and the borough president's CD4 liaison, Ivonne Garcia; to the head of each coalition organization and to the Vietnamese, Chinese, Bangladeshi, and Latin American members who did translations;

and to two Chinese and Greek boys for their help. Throughout the evening Lucy Schilero's mother took photographs.

Many of the same coalition members were present in 1992 when Lucy Schilero organized a nine-block National Night Out march from PS19 to the 110th Precinct house. Before the march began, she explained the precise route to the crowd and used signs to cue groups of children for the television cameras sent by three TV stations to cover the 250 marchers as they set off.

Led by two police vans and four scooters and carrying signs protesting drugs and crime, the throng included older whites, PS19 summer program teachers, and a majority of Latin American and East and South Asian parents and children. One black Latin American man had long dreadlocks, and a few South Asian woman wore Punjabi *salwar-kamiz* pants and blouses. African American CB4 member Priscilla Carrow, who arrived from Sherwood Village to join the marchers, was surprised by the diversity. Twenty 110th officers—white, black, Latin American, and Asian—also marched. Neighborhood residents were added along the route, and Sergeant Pete Petrone counted almost nine hundred as they neared the precinct house. There everyone was invited inside for cookies and soda in the same meeting room where Lucy Schilero had attended her first block association meetings eight years earlier.

3. Psychologist Maria P. P. Root Proclaims a Bill of Rights for Racially Mixed People, 1996

BILL OF RIGHTS FOR RACIALLY MIXED PEOPLE

I have the right
  not to justify my existence in this world
  not to keep the races separate within me
  not to be responsible for people's discomfort with my physical ambiguity
  not to justify my ethnic legitimacy

I have the right
  to identify myself differently than strangers expect me to identify
  to identify myself differently than how my parents identify me
  to identify myself differently than my brothers and sisters
  to identify myself differently in different situations

I have the right
  to create a vocabulary to communicate about being multiracial
  to change my identity over my lifetime—and more than once
  to have loyalties and identify with more than one group of people
  to freely choose whom I befriend and love

---

4. South Asians Unite Against Bigotry Following the 9-11 Attack on the World Trade Center, 2001

Binay Bhutani, the Indian-born leader of a conservative Hindu association in the San Francisco Bay Area, has never made a habit of checking in with other religious leaders in his community. But the Saturday, after the terrorist attacks in New York and Washington, D.C., Bhutani was horrified by reports of hate crimes targeted at Sikhs across the country. He couldn't sit still. He walked three blocks from his home in Fremont to a Sikh temple and introduced himself.

"I just told them, 'If you need anything, call us,'" Bhutani said. "They were really happy to hear that."

The relations between India's Hindus, Sikhs and Muslims have historically been rocky. Many people still remember the communal bloodbath that engulfed the region in 1947, when modern India and Pakistan came into existence. India accuses Islamic militants trained in Pakistan of terrorizing the Hindu population in the state of Kashmir. In 1992, right-wing Hindus razed an ancient mosque in the northern Indian city of Ayodhya, sparking Hindu-Muslim riots all over the subcontinent. In 1984, when two of her Sikh bodyguards assassinated Indian Prime Minister Indira Gandhi to protest her government's violent suppression of Sikh separatists, thousands of Sikhs were slaughtered all over northern India.

Many of the Bay Area's 150,000 Indians, most of whom flooded into Silicon Valley for high-tech work over the last decade, carried with them a hangover from the region's religious and political disunity.

But for most, the New York tragedy has, for the time being, eclipsed past grievances. Religious and cultural groups of every kind, from Muslims to Hindus, from Afghans to Bengalis, have met in parks, religious halls, and on the street.

Muslim leader Ifthekar Hai said, "I've never seen anything like this before." Haj helped found the United Muslims of America. His calendar is crammed with multi-faith engagements; in the next few weeks he will speak at a church, a cathedral, a monastery, and a synagogue.

On a warm Sunday in San Jose, two weeks after the terrorist attacks, over a thousand members of Indian religious, cultural and professional groups assembled in Cesar Chavez Park under a dusk-red sky to wave plastic American flags, preach about unity and pray for the victims of the tragedy.

Biren Chowdhary, President of the Federation of Indo-American Associations of the Bay Area, said American patriotism has brought the community together. "We have been fragmented," he said. "But our cause is America. Everything else follows."

But while Muslims constitute about 15 percent of the Indian population, out of over 60 groups invited to the park, only one, the Indian Muslim Relief Committee, was Islamic. Deepka Lalwani, president of the Milpitas Chamber of Commerce, which helped organize the event, hoped Muslim groups would volunteer to come on their own. "It would be a time-consuming task to go out and find them," she said.

South Asian leaders in the Bay Area unequivocally promote the need for unity, but for many Muslims and Hindus, especially those from the older generations, the mistrust runs deep. Bhutani leads the Fremont chapter of the conservative Hindu Swayamsevak Sangh. While "ordinary" Muslims and Hindus get along fine, he said, Muslims fanatics keep the communities apart. His organization has never had relations with Islamic groups, and the terrorist attacks will not change that.

Younger South Asians, though, said India and Pakistan's historical wounds are less pertinent for them. "There is a definite barrier between Hindus and Muslims," said Nina Merchant, a leader of INDUS, an umbrella organization for all South Asian groups at University of California at Berkeley. "But our generation doesn't identify with that so much."

In an unusual display of unity, a spontaneous alliance of several South Asian student groups recently took part in a sit-in to protest a cartoon in the campus newspaper that depicted two of the dead hijackers in Hell waiting for Allah to reward them with virgin women. About 50 protestors from a variety of South Asian persuasions camped out with sleeping bags until sunrise waiting for an apology that never came, said organizer Abdul-Rahman Zahzah.

Zahzah, leader of the Arab Americans and Muslims United, said South Asians groups have been forced to unite in the face of acts of bigotry in recent weeks. The Council of Islamic-American Relations has recorded over 700 anti-Muslim, anti-Arab incidents since the attacks. Since the tragedy, Zahzah's organization has organized workshops with other South Asian groups to educate the public about who they are, emphasizing that they are American.

Wajahat Ali, a leader of the Muslim Student Union, which held an open prayer meeting after the attacks, said U.C. Berkeley South Asians had good relations before. But "never on this scale," he said. "We can't afford to be separate right now," Ali said. "We need to come together for our own safety and survival."

E S S A Y S

The following two essays challenge conventional definitions of "Asian" and "Asian American" identity. In the first essay, K. Connie Kang, a journalist and author of *Home Was the Land of Morning Calm: A Saga of a Korean-American Family,* notes how rising numbers have brought both greater influence and greater problems for California's Asian Americans. Kang's article, published by the *Los Angeles Times* in 1998, describes the diverse ethnic, class, political, and cultural backgrounds that often make it difficult for California's fastest-growing racial group to develop cross-ethnic and cross-racial coalitions. The second essay is by Cynthia L. Nakashima, a doctoral candidate in ethnic studies at the University of California at Berkeley and co-editor with Teresa Williams-Leon of *The Sum of Our Parts: Mixed-Heritage Asian Americans.* Nakashima's essay discusses the proliferation of mixed-race community organizations, magazines, academic research, artistic work, and political activism in the 1990s. She analyzes and compares three approaches to multiraciality—calls for inclusion and legitimacy within traditional racial/ethnic communities, calls for shaping a new multiracial community, and calls to dismantle dominant group boundaries and create connections across communities. Nakashima argues that all three approaches and perspectives can peacefully coexist and be viewed as dimensions rather than divisions of the multiracial experience.

At a Crossroads: California's Diverse and Changing Asian American Population

K. CONNIE KANG

A century and a half after first landing on these shores as cheap labor, people of Asian ancestry have become California's best-educated and fastest-growing racial group.

Driven by a wave of immigration, the Asian American population has almost tripled since 1980. The community of 3.8 million—12% of the state's population—is having an impact beyond its numbers, and is approaching a critical mass that promises to alter the way Californians work and play, shop and do business.

For a group that until several decades ago could not own land, testify in court, become naturalized citizens or marry freely, the record is striking. Asian Americans' affluence and achievements have challenged the notion that to be a minority is to be disadvantaged.

They are the largest student group on top UC campuses and have the highest rate of obtaining advanced college degrees. They have started hundreds of high-tech firms, and own some of the biggest banks in the Los Angeles area. Their contributions to everyday life range from Play-Doh and Prozac to daisy-wheel printers and Bing cherries, from the music of Yo-Yo Ma to the novels of Amy Tan.

But greater numbers also have brought greater problems: Asian Americans have the fastest-rising welfare population and persistent gang activity. An undercurrent of racial tensions, friction between Asian newcomers and natives, intergenerational conflicts and a nagging identity crisis afflict the community.

And Asian Americans say that they do not feel fully vested in America's social, corporate and political life. They often are made to feel like foreigners, no matter how long their families have been here.

"On one hand, we have been successful in high tech, in education, science and several other fields," said historian L. Ling-chi Wang of UC Berkeley. "But on the other hand, we remain a minority in the eyes of the majority, and America continues to view Asian Americans not as an integral part of its identity, society and culture. "That's where the uniqueness of Asian Americans really is."

The government projects that by 2000 there will be nearly 5 million Asian Americans in the state, the most in the nation. And, experts say, millions of Californians will have Asian American employers and landlords, and Asian tongues will be languages of commerce as ties to the Pacific Rim grow stronger.

The concept of an "Asian American" is a recent invention, widely used by demographers to make sense of ethnic changes and by community leaders to help instill a sense of pride and unity. The term was coined by UCLA historian Yuji Ichioka in the late 1960s. Many question now whether it adequately describes a diverse people whose family origins extend from East Asia and Southeast Asia to the Indian subcontinent, as well as the Philippines and Indonesia.

The label embraces more than 30 ethnicities—some with historical animosities—and scores of languages. They range from fourth- and fifth-generation Japanese and Chinese Americans to Southeast Asian refugees and transnational "astronauts," who commute between California and Asia.

Increasingly, the traditional lines of nationality and culture are blurred by the constant interchange with Asia in what futurologist John Naisbitt calls the "new global configuration." "Asian Americans, as well as Asians who are educated and have worked in America, will be a bridge between the East and the West," he wrote in his 1996 book, "Megatrends Asia." "Having lived in both worlds, they will act as mediators and interpreters for business and political communities that are so interrelated that national and regional boundaries are irrelevant."

They also are turning upside-down conventional concepts of what it means to be a minority in America. Many Asian Americans have been able to compete in the marketplace because of their high educational attainment, professional skills and business acumen. "The old-fashioned scenario [is], 'Here come all those Asian immigrants, and now they are going to spend the next generation adjusting to America,'" said state librarian Kevin Starr, an authority on California history. "Forget it. They get off the plane at Los Angeles International Airport [and] two days later, they're creating jobs and wealth for people."

Asian Americans also are struggling over issues that will help shape California in the 21st century, when no single racial group will be a majority.

Their rising numbers, and even their successes in the classroom and the business community, have at times engendered envy and resentment among other groups.

So many have blended into the middle class that some fear that the cultural identity of Asian Americans is in danger of vanishing. The concern is particularly acute for people of Japanese descent, who have the highest rate of intermarriage with other ethnic groups. Marriage between Asians and non-Asians has been rising steadily in the past three decades, resulting in a proliferation of racially mixed Asian Americans.

"Asian Americans have become a crucial barometer of the contemporary racial climate," said UC Berkeley sociologist Michael Omi.

Approaching Critical Mass

Asian Americans are making a tremendous impact in California's landscape—both social and economic.

—FORMER UC BERKELEY CHANCELLOR CHANG-LIN TIEN

In ways subtle and striking, Asian Americans are influencing everything in California from food to commerce to entertainment. Flip through the central Los Angeles telephone directory, and you'll see six pages of Kims, compared with four of Smiths and 5½ of Lopezes. Trips along Atlantic Boulevard in the San Gabriel Valley, Bolsa Avenue in Westminster's Little Saigon, or Olympic Boulevard in Koreatown evoke the sights and smells of Taipei, Hanoi or Seoul.

Many major Southland supermarkets stock Japanese sushi, Korean kimchi (pickled cabbage), Chinese greens and Indian spices. Non-Asian youngsters from the suburbs frequent amusement arcades in Little Tokyo and read Asian comic books.

An Eastern approach to management—involving values such as seeking consensus and nonverbal communication—increasingly is being embraced by companies that do business with Pacific Rim firms.

Asian Americans who can move easily in several cultures and languages have become valuable bridges to Asian economies. For instance, George Koo, past chairman of the 700-member Asian American Manufacturers Assn., has a thriving Silicon Valley consulting business helping U.S. companies in Asia.

In some areas, real estate agents allow for a feng shui expert to ensure a site and building are in harmony with nature before a deal is closed with people of Chinese ancestry. Developers who cater to wealthy Asians sometimes design homes with this in mind. "It's a two-way street," said Edward T. Chang, professor of ethnic studies at UC Riverside. "People tend to view assimilation as a one-way street of immigrants adapting to the dominant society, but they don't recognize the other spectrum—of natives being changed [by immigrants]."

Hundreds of Asian American congregations have taken over or share quarters with traditional Christian churches in Southern California. Groups such as Asian Promise Keepers and Campus Crusade for Christ are attracting young Asians by the thousands. And an Asian theology has emerged that interprets the Bible in the context of Asian history and experience, according to Syngman Rhee, a professor at Union Theological Seminary in Richmond, Va. "Asian American Christian presence and participation are very important, both in tangible and intangible ways," said Rhee, president in 1992 and 1993 of the National Council of Churches. He was the first Asian American to lead the organization representing 34 major denominations and 50 million people.

At elite universities, where they once benefited from affirmative action but now are overrepresented, Asian Americans have had an impact on student life and the curriculum. Chinese and Japanese are among the six most popular foreign languages courses in college. The SAT IIs, which are used in admissions, include achievement tests for those who studied Japanese, Chinese and Korean.

In banking, five of the 10 biggest banks in Los Angeles County are Asian- or Asian American-owned, according to industry sources. "We bridge a gap between California and Asian countries, in providing financial services and lending services," said Li-Pei Wu, chief executive officer of General Bank in Los Angeles.

In the health and science fields, Asian Americans have pursued cutting-edge research. Professors Chih-Ming Ho of UCLA and Yu-Chong Tai of Caltech are refining technology with uses ranging from disease diagnosis to reduction of drag on airline wings. The emerging importance of Asian Americans is most evident in California's high-technology industry, the wellspring of much of the state's economic revival. A third of the Silicon Valley work force is Asian American.

Although Asian Americans generally have stalled in the middle management ranks of major U.S. corporations, many have become executives in high-tech companies.

John S. Chen, 42, is president and chief executive of Sybase Inc. of Emeryville, a $1-billion-a-year software company with 6,000 employees. Ko Nishimura, 59, is chairman, president and CEO of Solectron Corp., a Milpitas-based electronics firm with 18,000 employees and $3.7 billion in revenues last year.

Times are changing, said Chuck K. Chan, 47, founding partner of Alpine Technology Ventures, a venture capital firm based in Cupertino. The prevailing stereotype, he said, was that "Asians are quiet. Their language is bad and they cannot write English properly."

"Our generation is crossing the language, cultural and perception barriers of being pigeonholed [and is gaining] wide acceptance."

New Immigrants Lead the Way

Being an American can mean different things to different people, but . . . each experience contributes to the national story and each achievement leads the nation forward.
                    —BILL ONG HING, AUTHOR OF "TO BE AN AMERICAN:
                    CULTURAL PLURALISM AND THE RHETORIC OF ASSIMILATION"

Chang-Lin Tien, the first Asian American to head a major university, had been a popular UC chancellor for a year when a supporter congratulated him on a job well done. Then he broached the subject of Tien's Chinese accent. He offered to pay for "linguistic surgery" to eliminate Tien's accent through speech lessons.

"It presented a real dilemma for me," Tien recalled. "I didn't want to make that person feel uncomfortable, yet I wanted to convince him that I liked my accent, It's part of my identity."

Eventually, the chancellor's accent became as much of a hallmark as his ebullient personality.

Tien, who was born in China and emigrated from Taiwan, is not alone. Two-thirds of Asian Americans are foreign-born, and many speak with an accent.

Most came after passage of the 1965 amendments to the Immigration and Nationality Act, which allowed more Asians to enter the country. The law permitted families to reunite and heralded an influx of doctors, scientists and other professionals.

The immigrants diversified the predominantly American-born population and helped create significant new Asian American middle and upper classes.

In June, when the Committee of 100, an exclusive group of Chinese Americans, held its national convention in the Silicon Valley, it honored four entrepreneurs and executives who all happen to be immigrants: Chen of Sybase; Pauline Lo Alker, president and CEO of Network Peripherals; Jerry Yang, founder of Yahoo!; and Albert Yu, senior vice president of Intel Corp.

Many immigrants brought 2,500-year-old Confucian values of respect for learning, family and authority.

Along with "study, study, study," they admonish their children not to bring "shame" to the family and their race. They also want their children to be bicultural and bilingual, well-positioned for what some predict will be the Pacific Century.

Instead of watching cartoons on Saturday mornings, tens of thousands of youngsters attend language schools, where they learn their ancestral culture.

Angie Chang, who will be a sixth-grader at Wilson Elementary School in San Gabriel, has been attending Korean school every Saturday since first grade. Her fluency enables her to talk to her grandmother and enjoy Korean TV shows.

Her favorite video, "Six Siblings," is a drama about a widow raising six children in poverty-stricken Korea in the 1960s. It has given her an appreciation for her life in America. "It tells you how poor Korea was and how much people suffered and how lucky we are," she said.

Before the Asian American population boom, young Asians often avoided speaking their parents' language outside the home because they were ashamed or were concerned that they would not be accepted as Americans.

"There was this kind of enforced Americanization that was held up as an ideal," said UCLA's Ichioka. "You were supposed to get rid of your parents' language, dump your old culture and traits, and make yourself in the image of Anglo-Saxon, New England Americans."

Now, some students on UC campuses combine other majors with Asian American studies. Many take time off to study and live in Asia.

"They are Americans but there is something that doesn't satisfy them," said Henry Der, deputy state schools chief and former head of Chinese for Affirmative Action. "Why do they feel like they have to go through Asian routes? What compels Asian groups to form on campuses?"

Seeking Power in Politics

They used to think politics was dirty. You'd never see an [Asian] engineer or a computer scientist on a weekday night, sitting in a political meeting. Now you do.
—DAVID E. LEE, EXECUTIVE DIRECTOR OF THE
CHINESE AMERICAN VOTERS EDUCATION COMMITTEE

Asian Americans scripted the 1996 elections as the political coming out for a group that had long felt marginalized. They registered more than 75,000 new voters, bringing the total to 1.3 million nationwide—split almost evenly among the two major parties and independents.

They gave more money than ever to both Democrats and Republicans. And they hoped for at least one Cabinet post. There were no Cabinet appointments, but a dozen figures of Asian descent were caught up in the Democratic fund-raising scandal. Instead of driving Asian Americans away, the painful episode appears to have politically energized the community.

More Asian Americans than ever sought federal, state and local offices in California's June primary, including congressional seats. And a similar increase was evident elsewhere in the country.

Of the 24 candidates in California, 14 won nomination, prompting Harold Fong, chair of the Asian Pacific American caucus of the state Democratic Party, to say the showing "speaks volumes of the growing political strength and maturity" of the community.

For the first time, Asian Americans, now 6% of the state's voters, felt they could affect a statewide race. Taking advantage of California's first blanket primary, many crossed party lines to vote for Treasurer Matt Fong, who won the GOP's U.S. Senate nomination.

"Though many Asian Americans lost, we all won as they hit the campaign trail, trampling the stereotype of us as a passive, quiet, apolitical people who do not take democracy seriously," said commentator Phil Tajitsu Nash in AsianWeek.

Asian Americans, who have the largest percentage of independent voters of any ethnic group, are conducting much of their political activity outside the major parties. And much of their new vigor comes from immigrants, often small-business people who vote their pocketbook and interests.

"Immigrants are not intimidated by the dominant culture," said Lee. "They are doing the stuff that [the] American-born have never done."

There are not many locales where Asian Americans can swing an election, because their population tends to be scattered, from cities to suburbs.

San Francisco, where Chinese settled during the Gold Rush era, is an exception. The influx of Asian immigrants has spawned new Chinatowns along Clement and Irving streets in the once-white western reaches of the city.

Asian Americans represent a third of the population and 18% of registered voters. They hold three spots on the Board of Supervisors, own 25% of the real estate, and make up more than half of the school population.

The new arrivals are challenging the city's liberal Democratic power structure, including Asians who are part of it.

Last year, two Chinese American immigrants—Rose Tsai and Julie Lee—led the November ballot drive to rebuild the quake-damaged Central Freeway.

Despite opposition from major political players, including the Chinese American Democratic Club and the Chinese Chamber of Commerce, the self-described housewives got Proposition H passed.

The vote represented a significant moment in Chinese American political history, wrote columnist William Wong in the San Francisco Examiner. "The political temblor was generated by a ragtag army of Chinese American immigrants who had the audacity to defy City Hall, Mayor [Willie] Brown, downtown business interest, gay-lesbian groups, environmentalists and assorted liberals."

The city's activists have an advantage. Unlike Los Angeles—where Chinese, Filipinos, Japanese and Koreans form sizable groups—San Francisco is dominated by ethnic Chinese. This makes it easier to organize and to communicate.

"If we can't make it in San Francisco, we can't make it anywhere," Tsai said.

After the fund-raising scandal erupted, community leaders across the nation moved to start a counterpart to the National Assn. for the Advancement of Colored People.

This "pan-Asian movement" could unite the various communities, leaders said, and help translate Asian Americans' economic clout and high degree of education into political might.

"Asians, more than any other immigrant group of its size, are poised to mature politically," said Lee of the voter education project.

"We see professionals who had never voted before, highly educated people from Taiwan and engineers in the Silicon Valley joining clubs and organizing their neighborhoods."

Fearing Loss of Identity

*We need to be more accepting of the differences within our own ethnic group. . . .
Some Japanese Americans don't look Japanese American at all.*
—BILL WATANABE, EXECUTIVE DIRECTOR OF
LITTLE TOKYO SERVICE CENTER

After five generations in the United States, with only a trickle of immigration to help replenish its population, the Japanese American community is at a crossroads.

The first-generation issei mostly are deceased. The second-generation nisei mostly are retired. The third-generation sansei are in charge. They are heavily assimilated. Half of those who are married have non-Japanese spouses, and they maintain relatively few ties to cultural and religious institutions that helped hold the community together for nearly 120 years.

They have not been California's largest Asian group since 1970. By 1990, they had dropped to third, behind Filipinos and Chinese. Now, a decade after World War II internees won reparations, many fear Japanese Americans will lose their cultural identity entirely. Attention is turning to preserving the community's history. Work has started on a $45-million expansion of the Japanese American National Museum in Little Tokyo.

Community groups also are organizing national conferences on ways to tap the ties that bind this geographically dispersed group. "We have no choice but to be more inclusive—to include Japanese Americans of mixed ancestry, postwar immigrants, and others who make up the diversity of our community," said Al Muratsuchi, a former official of the Japanese American Citizens League.

With Japanese Americans intermarrying at the rate of 50% in cities and 70% in rural areas, Japanese Americans often look white, Latino or black. For almost two decades, studies show, families with one Japanese parent have exceeded the number of families with two Japanese parents.

While some contend that intermarriage is hastening the community's demise, others say the trend is a part of the American passage. "Instead of looking at interracial marriage as an end of the Japanese American community, we should extend the definition," suggested Rebecca Chiyoko King, a San Francisco sociologist, who is half Japanese and half white.

She was awakened to her ethnic heritage as a first-grader at a friend's home in a Chicago suburb.

Young Rebecca was shocked when her friend's mother served hot dogs with "yellow and red" stuff on top.

"When you grow up with shoyu [soy sauce] hot dogs, you don't think of other peoples' hot dogs," said King.

For Curtiss Takada Rooks, whose father is African American and whose mother is an issei, lessons of dual heritage also came early. "You had to look Dad in the eyes when he talked, but with Mom, you didn't," he said, explaining different norms of civility.

"As a hapa [half], I claim Japanese American-ness," said Rooks, who teaches American culture at Loyola Marymount University. In the 21st century, a typical Japanese American will be of mixed race, predicts Greg Mayeda, president of the Hapa Issues Forum, a Bay Area-based organization of racially mixed Asians. "They can have freckles and light brown hair and nontraditional Japanese names, but they will still be considered full-fledged members of the Japanese American community."

Others lament intermarriage because it dilutes their culture and could result in the loss of traditional values such as enryo, or self-restraint.

The Japanese American community faces an important choice, said Chris Komai, whose grandfather was the publisher of Los Angeles-based Rafu Shimpo, the oldest Japanese American newspaper in the continental U.S.

"Do you want to remain attached to each other? If we do, how?"

The Rich and the Invisible Poor

Poor Asians, like poor Jews, seem like a contradiction. Yet, it's the reality.
—Don T. Nakanishi, director of the
UCLA Asian American Studies Center

No racial group in California offers such stark contrasts of affluence and poverty, education and illiteracy.

The 1990 census shows that Asian Americans had the highest percentage of households with annual incomes of $75,000 or more—slightly ahead of whites. People of Asian Indian heritage, whose English proficiency and education level are high, led the way.

People of Asian ancestry had a median household income of $42,960 by 1997—higher than any racial group except whites. But Asian Americans are also the fastest-growing segment on welfare. The rate of households on welfare has climbed from 9.7% to 12% since 1980.

A sizable segment of the community, particularly Southeast Asian refugees, lives in dire poverty. And, although about 40% of Asian Americans have college or postgraduate education, one in seven lacks a high school diploma.

They are part of the invisible poor who shatter the "model minority" label so often attached to Asian Americans.

"On one hand, we have people who are really moving up on the economic ladder, and on the other, we have some groups that are really stuck," said Stewart Kwoh, president of the Asian Pacific American Legal Center.

Although Asians on welfare come from all the ethnic subgroups, about one in three Southeast Asians receives public aid. More than two-thirds of Cambodians and Laotians are on the rolls.

Many Southeast Asian refugees were uprooted from villages, ill-prepared for urban life in the West. In America, their family foundations are shaken, especially when male heads of household are emasculated by inability to find work and other problems. "Back home in Laos, the husband has the authority in the family," said Leo Pandac, who runs a drug and alcohol treatment program near downtown. "With Americanization of children and the wife, the husband doesn't wield the same influence."

For example, Pandac said that when domestic violence erupts, the wife often calls the police and the husband gets arrested, undermining his authority.

More than 1 million Southeast Asian refugees arrived in the United States between 1975 and 1991, starting with the Vietnamese after the fall of Saigon.

Many don't have much in common with other Asian Americans. For example, there is little to connect a Cambodian refugee in Long Beach's Little Phnom Penh and a Monterey Park doctor from Taiwan.

Asian Americans from many walks of life, from grocery store owners to high-tech executives, are coming to realize their community needs to be concerned not only about impoverished Asians, but also about the rest of California's multiethnic society. "Our emphasis on education, hard work and the family has brought us far, despite racism," said retired appellate Judge Harry W. Low, the former president of the century-old Chinese American Citizens Alliance.

But Low and others maintain that Asian Americans need to foster community involvement to become part of the nation's civic culture. "When you contrast the

Jewish and Asian ethos, we have a glaring absence of public sense of charity to others, which comes from the Judeo-Christian heritage," said K. W. Lee, former editor of the *Korea Times* English edition. "Call it community conscience, social conscience or civic conscience, we need that. That's the final rite of passage in the long journey of Asians in America."

Improving relations with other races remains perhaps the most daunting challenge in California, where anti-Asian discrimination dates to the violent backlash last century against Chinese laborers who were scapegoated over depressed wages and unemployment. More recently, Asian business owners, particularly those of Korean descent, suffered some of the heaviest losses in the 1992 Los Angeles riots. And Asian Americans continue to be one of the groups targeted for hate crimes.

"Asian Americans cannot shape the future of California without significantly relating with Latinos and blacks," said Berkeley historian Wang. "Our future lies in our ability to work jointly to create a new America where we can create a new identity."

Approaches to Multiraciality

CYNTHIA L. NAKASHIMA

A Pattern of Voices: Three Approaches Within "the Movement"

Certain themes and issues seem to be central to the experiences of multiraciality, across racial/ethnic mix, geographical location, and time period; for example, locating one's racial/ethnic identity in various contexts and at different life stages, being pressured to "choose" a monoracial identification by external forces, and questions and issues of group belongingness and loyalty. Perhaps these can be considered parts of a "core" of the mixed-race experience, or perhaps simply a mixed-race version of the core of the human experience. But although there are important commonalities to being racially mixed in America, how individuals approach their multiraciality can vary dramatically—from person to person, and within a single person over time and place.

Within today's dialogue on mixed race, three dominant voices inform us on how to approach multiraciality. On the one hand, there is considerable overlap between the voices, to the point that many of us (myself included) subscribe to all three simultaneously. On the other hand, certain ideological incongruities exist, at least on the surface, that require sorting out. In order to begin this task, I want first to establish what the ideologies are.

The Struggle for Inclusion and Legitimacy
in the Traditional Racial/Ethnic Communities
The struggle by mixed-race people for inclusion and legitimacy in the traditional racial/ethnic communities can take many different shapes; from people who want all of their racial/ethnic communities to accept mixed-race people as full members

---

From Cynthia L. Nakashima, "Voices from the Movement: Approaches to Multiraciality," in *The Multiracial Experience: Racial Borders as the New Frontier,* ed. Maria P. P. Root, 81–97. Copyright © 1996 Sage Publications. Reprinted by permission of the publisher.

without erasing the differences of a multiracial experience, to people who want a specific racial/ethnic community to accept them as full members, without making issue of their multiracial background. Perhaps the most extreme form of the latter position would be to avoid the multiracial dialogue by "passing" as monoracial. But many people of mixed race, at least those whose parents are racially different from each other, are not willing or able to actively hide their heritage, and so they will very likely be forced to participate in the dialogue at some level—even if to say, "Well yes, my father is Irish, but I really identify as a Chicana."

The struggle for inclusion and legitimacy in the traditional racial/ethnic communities can be expressed explicitly; this has occurred in many Asian American communities, where mixed-race people have recently become active in demanding recognition and legitimacy. But more often the desire is expressed less explicitly, by exhibiting on the individual level one's ability to "fit in" to a community, thus "proving" that one's multiraciality does not preclude racial/ethnic authenticity.

One of the ways that racially mixed people might attempt to persuade others to believe in their authenticity is by the "badges" that they wear, such as clothing, hairstyle, speech patterns, mannerisms, name, and so on. Phil Tajitsu Nash, a man of Japanese/European American heritage, legally changed his middle name to his mother's Japanese maiden name when he was writing for Asian American newspapers. Valur Edvardsson, who is Icelandic and African American, felt that he had to alter his speech and his behavior in order to prove his legitimacy among other African Americans. Norma Elena Soto, a woman of Chinese, Mexican, Spanish, and French heritage, wondered which of her badges she might need on a given day in her poem, "Woman of Color":

> But, should someone
> see my white skin and
> question my credentials,
> how would I prove any qualifications?
> I could smile
> to slant my eyes,
> speak Spanish and disclose
> my Hispanic name . . .
> maybe pick up an accent
> and start bowing a lot.

We also "prove" our racial/ethnic legitimacy through our associations with people—friends, lovers, and even family members. Many of the multiracial people interviewed by Lise Funderburg discussed their awareness that their choice of friends, especially in their school years, made an enormous impact on how legitimate African Americans perceived them to be. Funderburg herself, who is European and African American, has discussed how people will automatically "dismiss" her because she looks "white" and is married to a European American man. Several years ago, when I won a scholarship from a Japanese American organization, I was happy and relieved when my Grandma Nakashima volunteered to accompany me to meet the sponsoring family at their home, because I knew that her presence would testify to my "Japaneseness."

Similarly, the desire for inclusion in a racial/ethnic community can be expressed by which badges and which associations we choose not to call attention to; so that a mixed-race male college student might hesitate to hug a white female friend in the company of an African American female friend, or a mixed-race actress, trying out for an "Asian" role, might wear a wig to hide her very curly hair. Some multiracial people are critical of this process of proving their authenticity, even as they participate in it. Kip Fulbeck, a Chinese/European American artist, wrote in "anger and frustration" of how mixed-race Asian Americans "come in bright-eyed and hopeful to a place that could be home and find we have to change our names or adopt Asian ones to pass on paper.

Another way for mixed-race people to struggle for inclusion and legitimacy in the traditional racial/ethnic communities is by proving their knowledge of and attachment to the culture, history, and/or political interests of that group. Velina Hasu Houston has argued that Amerasians like herself, who have a parent who is directly from Asia, are "more richly grounded in Asian culture and custom" than many of the "pure-blooded" Asian Americans who define themselves as "real" Asians whereas mixed-race people are not. As Larene LaSonde, who is African American, Russian, Jewish, Scot-Irish and Cherokee, said, among other African Americans, "My politics had to be better than anybody else's, [and] my ethics had to be in place because I was never trusted. I had to be surer of my facts than anybody else." The mixed-race writer Lisa Jones recently took this method one step further in the African American magazine *Essence,* presenting her European American Jewish mother's knowledge and commitment to African American historical, cultural, and political issues.

The ways that mixed-race people struggle for inclusion and legitimacy vary, both by what kind of inclusion and legitimacy each individual wants from a community and by what each racial/ethnic communities requires of the individual. In many Asian American communities, physical appearance plays a very important role in the level of acceptance a mixed-race person experiences. Also, having an Asian surname, which suggests patrilineal Asian heredity, seems to be an advantage. In many Latino communities, where racial phenotype varies greatly, language is considered an important indicator of legitimacy. In the African American community, which also claims a wide range of physical types, a person's lifestyle and cultural behavior are given considerable weight. Each of these communities' criteria for belonging have arisen out of specific historical, cultural, and political contexts and continue to change as conditions change.

I have purposefully avoided, until now, the situation of mixed-race people struggling for inclusion and legitimacy in the European American "community" because of the complexity of comparing the dominant society with nondominant racial/ethnic groups. The desire for inclusion and legitimacy in the dominant society is wrapped up in issues of power, access to resources, standards of beauty, and so on—something that monoracial people of color experience similarly to mixed-race people. There is probably an important distinction between the kind of legitimacy sought by a mixed-race person with European American family ties, compared to a person of color without those connections, but I have not explored this issue enough to consider it here.

In the case of mixed-race people who are struggling for legitimacy in a specific European American ethnic group (e.g., the Italian American community), issues of belonging are more like those of the racial/ethnic groups that we have been looking at—for example, language, cultural behavior, name, and certainly physical appearance. Physical appearance is perhaps the most important badge of whiteness in contemporary society, although heredity (i.e., the one-drop rule) is still significant.

The Shaping of a Shared Identity and Common Agenda
Among Racially Mixed People into a New Multiracial Community

The developing of a mixed-race community is what people generally envision when they talk about "the multiracial movement." The theory underlying this approach is that the experience of being racially/ethnically mixed has enough common themes to make people of mixed-race a meaningful reference group.

There are two "sites" where mixed racial/ethnic community building generally takes place:

1. Within a specific racial/ethnic community or communities (e.g., organizations that have been geared to specific racial/ethnic "mixtures," such as African/European American or Asian/non-Asian American, and their specific set of issues)
2. Across racial/ethnic communities with the goal of pan-multiracialism (e.g. organizations, such as the Association for Multiethnic Americans [AMEA], which unite around the more general issues of racially mixed people).

It could be argued that the first kind of mixed-race community building, which takes place within a specific racial/ethnic community, is ideologically and strategically located somewhere between the first and second voices because of the importance that it puts on the traditional racial/ethnic communities.

One of the more obvious expressions of mixed-race community building is, as I mentioned above, the many organizations that have formed across the country for interracial families and racially mixed individuals. Most of these groups function primarily as social and support groups, publishing newsletters that provide resources and information for mixed-race families (e.g. lists of children's books with positive multiracial characters). But some of the multiracial organizations have been formed with the goal of mobilizing around a common political need or issue, such as racial classification or Amerasian immigration and resettlement.

Another overt example of community building is the existence of magazines—namely, *Interrace, New People,* and *Biracial Child*—that feature articles by and about interracial couples, mixed-race children, families with transracially adopted children, and multiracial adults. *Interrace* presents articles that speak to a mixed-race "community" on issues such as "Best and Worst Cities for Interracial Couples, Families and Multiracial People to Live," and "Popular Myths About Interracial Couples." The magazine regularly features celebrities who are either involved in an interracial relationship or who are racially mixed themselves, in very much the same way that the traditional racial/ethnic communities feature their "own" celebrities.

A very recent phenomenon that reflects the growth of the idea of a multiracial community is the existence of books and films on the mixed-race experience, published and produced for a popular audience. There have been at least two anthologies of writings by people of mixed heritage in the past few years. In each of these books, the introduction talks about the common themes, experiences, and yearnings of the writers, who, while culturally diverse, share a status as mixed. There has also been a deluge of nonfictional storytelling by people who are multiracial. These personal histories, although perhaps not explicitly asserting a desire to build a mixed-race community, are certainly written and published in the context of the growing dialogue on multiraciality, and thus they reflect the idea that the mixed-race experience is both common enough and special enough to warrant published accounts. . . .

In academia, there has also been a recent explosion in interest on multiraciality. Although scholarly research has historically treated people of mixed race as a population for the purpose of study, there tends to be a much greater level of sophistication in more recent research, extending the idea of a mixed-race population beyond the simple facts of heredity to encompass the common themes of the multiracial experience. This is reflected in Root's edited volume, *Racially Mixed People in America,* and in Zack's edited volume *American Mixed Race: The Culture of Microdiversity.* It is also the basis for many contemporary university courses on multiraciality. For example, in a course on people of mixed race, literature that is normally looked at in the context of a traditional racial/ethnic group's literature might be viewed alongside other works by people of mixed-race—such as, Nella Larsen's *Passing* and *Quicksand* with Leslie Marmon Silko's *Ceremony* and Diana Chang's *Frontiers of Love.*

The Struggle to Dismantle Dominant Racial Ideology and Group Boundaries and to Create Connections Across Communities into a Community of Humanity

The third approach to multiraciality is perhaps the most difficult to define because it comes in the greatest variety of forms. The central ideology is that binary thinking and the boundaries that it facilitates must be destroyed in order to destroy oppressions based on race/ethnicity, gender, sexuality, class, and so on. Mixed-race people, who do not completely "fit in" to any of the racial/ethnic groups but who frequently have ties to more than one, should use their neither/both positionality to resist and destroy the dominant racial/ethnic structure—to be, as Weisman calls it, "supraracial."

This ideology is clearly articulated in Zack's concept of *deracination,* which is aimed at mixed-race people but can hypothetically be adopted by anyone. Deracination refers to an "antirace" racial identity, similar to having no religious affiliation. As Zack put it,

> The concept of race is an oppressive cultural invention and convention, and I refuse to have anything to do with it. . . . Therefore I have no racial affiliation and will accept no racial designations. If more people joined me in refusing to play the unfair game of race, fewer injustices based on the concept of race would be perpetrated.

Although deracination might seem exotic, it is essentially the same as the philosophies on race that are expressed in certain religious theologies, such as that of the Baha'i; and in the frequent testimonies of mixed-race people whose parents told them to write in "human race" rather than to check any of the race/ethnicity boxes.

The other dimension to resisting racial ideology is the proactive building of connections and communication across racial/ethnic groups. Seeing mixed-race people as a "bridge" between cultures has been a common theme, both in recent discussions of people of mixed race and in creative expression by people of mixed race. In an essay entitled, "Leaves from the Mental Portfolio of an Eurasian," published in 1909, writer Sui Sin Far discussed, among other things, her role as a "defender" of the Chinese in America. Her essay concluded, "I give my right hand to the Occidentals and my left to the Orientals, hoping that between them they will not utterly destroy the insignificant 'connecting link.' And that's all." European/Native American writers Louise Erdrich and Michael Dorris made a similar statement about what they refer to as "the lost tribe of mixed bloods": "As the hooks and eyes that connect one core to the other we have our roles to play. 'Caught between two worlds,' is the way we're often characterized, but I'd put it differently. We are the *catch."* At Stanford University, a group largely composed of people of mixed race formed a group called Cross Cultures that "focuses on uniting students of different cultures in a comfortable, nonthreatening atmosphere."

Since the late 1960s, American society has toyed with the idea of people of mixed race as the "children of the future." In the past decade, multiculturalism, which places a high value on a society's diversity, has made the valuing of a mixed-race person's "microdiversity" all the more obvious. At the same time, the ideas of *multiple positionalities* and *transgressing boundaries,* which have come out of postmodern and deconstructionist dialogues on culture, have functioned to shift the emphasis away from the disadvantaged and "marginal" aspects of being neither/both to the advantaged and liminal aspects. Mixed-race people are viewed as a form of the "citizen of the world" model, along with others who are transnational, multilingual, multicultural, transgendered, and so on; they move back and forth across the various borders, existing above the limitations of having only one culture or language or government or gender. The titles of two recent conferences at the University of California, Berkeley—"Displacing Borders" and "Boundaries in Question"— give an idea of how multiracial people are being resituated by the contemporary intellectual community. . . .

Exposing the fallacy of race and group boundaries is something that multiracial people frequently engage in, perhaps especially those who have positive relationships with family members who are racially different from each other. At a panel discussion on the future of the African American community, one mixed-race panelist surprised the audience by shifting the discussion away from issues such as media images of African Americans and the development of black-owned businesses to a consideration of the experiences that we, as humans, share across race, ethnicity, gender, class, and sexuality—experiences such as birth, death, love, hate, fear, sex, illness, family. The panelist made the point that although the categories we "belong to" shape our lives in important ways, we also belong to the human experience, and what is essential about the human experience is also important.

Different Approaches, Different Perspectives: Dissent in the Movement?

. . . The mixed-race movement, as well as mixed-race individuals, is sometimes accused of sending out mixed messages about race and ethnicity. For example, do mixed-race people think that they are "like" people in the traditional racial/ethnic groups, or that they are different from them? Do they think that race is important, or that it is not important? These are questions that are asked of multiracial people not only by monoracial people, but by other multiracial people, and by themselves. I will now discuss some of the points of contention that can and do occur between the three dominant voices in the dialogue on multiraciality.

Many mixed-race people who assert a monoracial identity are suspicious of the motivations behind asserting a multiracial identity and worry about the potential damage that the movement might have on a specific racial/ethnic community. Some feel threatened by the idea of a mixed-race identity and community, because an emphasis on what is common among mixed people might be interpreted as an emphasis on what is different between themselves and those who are "full-blooded." As one of Funderburg's interviewees said about the mixed-race movement:

> Somebody said "mixed" once, as in a race separate from Blacks and Whites. I was just like, "Excuse me? We have enough races as it is. . . . I have no desire to be put on a little pedestal . . . I don't need any more separation in my life.

Also, mixed-race people who identify with one of their racial/ethnic communities to the exclusion of other communities have said that the mixed-race movement holds a bias toward identifying as multiracial and pathologizes those who do not identify this way. Chuan referred to "interracial populism" and criticized *Interrace* magazine as "clearly not designed to encourage either dialogue or self-determination—on the contrary, it is trying to tell interracials what they can and can't be." Similarly, Jones critiques those who she calls the "interracial/biracial nationalists," and asks "Is there now to be a biracial party line to tow and a biracial lifestyle to upkeep?"

On the other hand, people involved in the building of a sense of community among racially mixed people have criticized those who struggle for acceptance in a traditional group for being "beggars," for being disloyal to family members, and for being dishonest about their heredity. Jamoo, a writer who has contributed regularly to *Interrace,* posed the question of whether or not mixed-race celebrities who "pass" as monoracial should be publicly "outed" so that they can serve as role models for the multiracial community. He concluded that they should not be outed, but:

> It saddens me that the "closet" mixed-race people in Hollywood and elsewhere feel a need to pass as white to be accepted or that Pebbles has to pretend to be a black girl so she can sell more records. I guess they made their choices just as I made mine, the only difference is that I know I made the right one.

In this way, those who "deny" their multiraciality are held in suspicion very much as those who assert their multiraciality have always been.

Coming from the perspective that racial ideology is inherently oppressive and should be rejected in its entirety, the idea of mixed race is seen as a perpetuation and reification of something completely lacking in value. The use of *race* as a word and a concept is offensive in and of itself, and the desire for a multiracial community and identity is a dangerous step toward creating another racial and ethnic category, similar to the "Coloureds" of South Africa. In terms of postmodern thought, there is a concern with what is called the "elevation of hybridity"; in the context of race and ethnicity, that multiracials as a group are currently being culturally constructed and that they will not only join the other "groups" with their own set of boundaries and limitations, but that they might become the new ideal against which others will be degraded and oppressed. This concern was reflected in a keynote lecture given by a professor at a recent conference on cultural studies. The professor highlighted her point that scholarly fields such as women's and ethnic studies are problematic in their essentialism by disclosing that there has even been mention of creating a new field of multiracial studies.

If those who emphasize the destruction of racial categories find fault with the idea of a multiracial community, they also worry about those people of mixed race who struggle for inclusion in a traditional group. To them, this struggle is nothing more than an attempt to participate in a system that will inevitably oppress and degrade them. The only worthwhile struggle is against race itself—as Rainier Spencer said, both the attempt to create a mixed-race classification and the adherence to hypodescent function to validate the "racial fantasy" and the "racial fallacy" that imprisons this society.

The response to these claims, both by those who emphasize a monoracial identity and by those who employ a multiracial identity, is that although dismantling the racial schema is, indeed, a nice idea, racial ideology is a central feature of our society and that exalting the struggle to dismantle it is impractical, utopian, and, as one of Funderburg's interviewees stated it, "cheesey." Association of Multiracial Americans (AMEA) has said, "It might be argued that racial and ethnic classifications should be done away with entirely. But such a view is utopian and also distorts the reality of continuing communal divisions based on race and ethnicity." In addition, critics of the "citizen of the world" approach point out that there is considerable real value to the ties that people have to their communit(ies), so the danger of destroying group boundaries is that we will destroy what is inside these boundaries, too.

Finally, many multiracial people feel that the assertion that mixed-race people are models of multiculturalism or bridges between groups is an unrealistic and unfair expectation and that it threatens to erase the significance of race and racial oppression in this society. It also contributes to a resentment toward multiracial people and the mixed-race movement by drawing attention away from persisting inequality and focusing instead on the feel-good idea of a raceless or color-blind future.

Perhaps the most concrete expression of the ideological differences that exist between the three voices of multiraciality involves the struggle to reform racial classification (i.e., the U.S. Census). The various racial classification models that have been proposed and the debates surrounding these models are both symptomatic and symbolic of the ideological and strategic differences that we have considered. Whether mixed-race people should continue to check "just one" racial category, should demand the right to identify multiracially, or should refuse to participate in racial classification at all is a debate that has come to dominate the mixed-race movement.

Common Ground: Possibilities for an Integrated Voice

Now that I have established the dominant three approaches to multiraciality and the ideological and practical conflicts that can and do grow out of differences between the approaches, I will argue that, as with the various races, there is nothing immutable that separates the voices from each other. In fact, each of the approaches is central to the experience of multiraciality, and many racially mixed people subscribe to all three simultaneously. Rather than viewing the three voices as ideological divisions in the mixed-race movement, they should be viewed as ideological dimensions of the movement.

The task, then, is to work on the construction of an integrated voice. This is not to say that diverse perspectives, on multiraciality or any other topic, is a thing to be overcome. Rather, the process of looking for a perspective that leaves room for diversity within is an exercise in *cognitive flexibility* and general tolerance. Also, in looking for a multiracial identity that allows for a variety of approaches, I believe that we might come across what lies at the heart of the multiracial movement.

The following is my attempt to construct a multiracial voice that integrates the three approaches discussed in this chapter: The ties that we have to our racial/ethnic communities matter to us, and we have the right to claim them and to have full access to them. But, we have other ties too, and the fact that we have multiple ties creates experiences that connect us to others who have multiple ties, contemporarily and historically, in the United States and abroad. This experience of having multiple ties simultaneously leads us to question group boundaries and to reject these boundaries as oppressive and false.

In viewing the voices as dimensions of a unified perspective, I want to consider the possibility that there is an element of process to the dimensions. *Perhaps people of mixed race shift their emphasis from one approach to another, in response to changes in their environment* (which can be related to age and development), and as they either find that certain of their needs have been met or have remained unmet by a specific approach. For example, a person who is biracial Japanese/European American might first explore his or her multiraciality in terms of his or her membership in the Japanese American community. Then, upon feeling secure in this identification, he or she may begin to recognize and explore the commonalities between people of all racial/ethnic mixtures. Through this exploration, he or she might learn that the concept of race is entirely dishonest and oppressive. At this point, he or she might begin to emphasize the task of "transgressing boundaries."

Although I believe that the processual movement through the voices would often occur in the order given in the example above—the emphasis first on the traditional communities, next on the multiracial community, and finally on a community of humanity—I can easily imagine the process operating in other orders. The process of movement through the dimensions is unlikely to be linear or with an ending point. But the dimensions are fluid to the extent that changing life circumstances can shift an individual's emphasis from one to another without signifying any core ideological change.

Implications of an Integrated Voice

Besides being an exercise in cognitive flexibility and tolerance, the integration of the three dominant voices in the dialogue on multiraciality has the potential to affect our work in multiple ways. Keeping in mind that each of the voices is valid and "normal" and that people of mixed race can identify with all three simultaneously can affect:

1. our research on and analysis of racially mixed people;
2. our agendas as activists in the multiracial movement; and
3. our understanding of ourselves and our needs as people of multiple communities and cultures.

A recognition of the centrality of all three voices might also serve as a system of checks and balances in order to avoid the potential "nightmares" of the multiracial movement. By listening to the questions and the critiques that we pose to each other—Isn't the concept of mixed race an acceptance of the concept of race? Isn't a monoracial identification an internalization of the "one drop rule"? Do mixed race people have enough in common, experientially and culturally, to make "multiracial" a meaningful identity? Can a person of color survive in America without a racial identity? What are the effects of multiracial identification on communities of color?—we can remain vigilant in steering the dialogue and the movement in the direction of destroying racial oppression. . . .

In my opinion, we need to take "multiracial" in the direction of *supraracial,* without jeopardizing our communities of color and without giving up the connections that add value to our lives. Our best chance of achieving this is to enlist a variety of perspectives on what it is to be racially mixed in America. For many, being racially mixed means building connections between ourselves and our traditional communities. For many, it means building connections between people who are multiracial. For many, it means building connections with others on the basis of shared humanity. And for many, it means all of these things. Whether we are constructing a model of multiracial identity or a model of racial classification, we should recognize and reflect the diversity of voices that make up the multiracial movement.

FURTHER READING

Chow, Rey. *Writing Diaspora: Tactics of Intervention in Contemporary Cultural Studies* (1993).

Dirlik, Arif. "Asians on the Rim: Transnational Capital and Local Community in the Making of Contemporary Asian America," *Amerasia Journal* 22, no. 3 (1996): 1–24.

———, ed. *What Is in a Rim? Critical Perspectives on the Pacific Region Idea* (1993).

Douw, Leo, Cen Huang, and Micahel Godley, eds. *Qiaoxiang Ties: Interdisciplinary Approaches to Cultural Capitalism in South China* (1999).

Fallows, James. *Looking at the Sun: The Rise of the New East Asian Economic and Political System* (1994).

Hamilton, Gary, ed. *Business Networks and Economic Development in East and Southeast Asia* (1991).

Hu-DeHart, Evelyn. *Across the Pacific: Asian Americans and Globalization* (1999).

Kotkin, Joel. *Tribes: How Race, Religion, and Identity Determine Success in the New Global Economy* (1992).

Lever-Tracy, Constance, David Ip, and Noel Tracy. *The Chinese Diaspora and Mainland China: An Emerging Economic Synergy* (1996).

Lowe, Lisa. "Heterogeneity, Hybridity, Multiplicity: Marking Asian American Differences," *Diaspora* 1, no. 1 (1991): 24–44.

———. *Immigrant Acts: On Asian Cultural Practices* (1996).

Ong, Aihwa. *Flexible Citizenship: The Cultural Logics of Transnationality* (1999).

———. "On the Edge of Empires: Flexible Citizenship Among Chinese in Diaspora," *Positions* 1, no. 3 (1993): 745–778.

Ong, Aihwa, and Donald Nonini, eds. *Undergrounded Empires: The Cultural Politics of Modern Chinese Transnationalism* (1997).

Ong, Paul, Edna Bonacich, and Lucie Cheng, eds. *The New Asian Immigration in Los Angeles and Global Restructuring* (1994).

Rafael, Vincent, ed. *Discrepant Histories: Translocal Essays on Filipino Cultures* (1995).

Reid, Anthony, ed. *Sojourners and Settlers: Histories of Southeast Asia and the Chinese* (1996).

Root, P. P., ed. *The Multiracial Experience: Racial Borders as the New Frontier* (1996).

———. *Racially Mixed People in America* (1992).

San Juan, E. *From Exile to Diaspora: Veterans of the Filipino Experience in the United States* (1998).

Sawada, Mitziko. *Tokyo Life, New York Dreams: Urban Japanese Visions of America* (1996).

Sinn, Elizabeth, ed. *The Last Half Century of Chinese Overseas* (1998).

Spickard, Paul. *Mixed Blood: Intermarriage and Ethnic Identity in Twentieth-Century America* (1989).

Suleri, Sara. "Women Skin Deep: Feminism and the Postcoloniality of the Artifice of History: Who Speaks for 'Indian' Pasts?" *Representations* 37 (1992): 1–26.

Tadiar, Neferti. "Domestic Bodies of the Philippines," *Sojourn* 12, no. 2 (1997): 153–191.

Van der Veer, Peter. *Nation and Migration: The Politics of Space in South Asian Diaspora* (1995).

Wang, Gungwu, ed. *China and the Overseas Chinese* (1991).

Wang, Ling-Chi L. "The Structure of Dual Domination: Toward a Paradigm for the Study of the Chinese Diaspora in the United States, *Amerasia Journal* 21, no. 1–2 (1995): 149–169.

Wilson, Rob, and Arif Dirlik, eds. *Asia/Pacific as Space of Cultural Production* (1995).

Wilson, Rob, and Wimal Dissanayake, eds. *Global/Local: Cultural Production in the Transnational Imaginary* (1996).

Wolf, Diane L. "Family Secrets: Transnational Struggles Among Children of Filipino Immigrants," *Sociological Perspectives* 40, no. 3 (1997): 457–482.

Women of the South Asian Descent Collective. *Our Feet Walk the Sky: Women of the South Asian Diaspora* (1993).

Wong, Sau-ling Cynthia. "Denationalization Reconsidered: Asian American Cultural Criticism at a Theoretical Crossroads," *Amerasia Journal* 21, no. 1–2 (1995): 1–27.

Zack, Naomi, ed. *American Mixed Race: The Culture of Microdiversity* (1995).